College Writing Skills with Readings

First Canadian Edition

John Langan
Atlantic Community College

Sharon Winstanley
Seneca College

2003-59

McGraw-Hill Ryerson Limited
Toronto New York Auckland Bogotá Caracas
Lisbon London Madrid Mexico Milan New Delhi
San Juan Singapore Sydney Tokyo

COLLEGE WRITING SKILLS WITH READINGS
First Canadian Edition

CAN©OPY

ISBN: 0-07-552631-X

1 2 3 4 5 6 7 8 9 10   BBM   5 4 3 2 1 0 9 8 7 6

Printed and bound in Canada

Care has been taken to trace ownership of copyright material contained in this text. The publisher will gladly take any information that will enable them to rectify any reference or credit in subsequent editions.

Sponsoring Editor: Dave Ward
Supervising Editor: Margaret Henderson
Production Editor: Kate Forster
Developmental Editor: Laurie Graham
Production Co-ordinator: Nicla Dattolico
Designer: Rafael Hernandez
Cover Design: Dianna Little
Typesetter: Bookman Typesetting Company
Typeface: Times Roman
Printer: Best Book Manufacturers

Canadian Cataloguing in Publication Data
Langan, John, 1942–
    College writing skills with readings

1st Canadian ed.
Includes index.
ISBN 0-07-552631-X

1. English language - Rhetoric.   2. College readers.
I. Winstanley, Sharon.   II. Title

PE1408.L3178 1996   808'.0427   C95-933244-8

CONTENTS

PART TWO
TYPES OF ESSAY DEVELOPMENT

PART THREE
SPECIAL SKILLS

PART FOUR
HANDBOOK OF SENTENCE SKILLS

PART FIVE
READINGS FOR WRITING

READINGS LISTED BY RHETORICAL MODE

Note: Some selections are cross-linked because they illustrate more than one rhetorical method of development.

ARGUMENTATION AND PERSUASION

TO THE INSTRUCTOR

College Writing Skills with Readings, First Canadian Edition is a writing text and rhetoric for Canadian college students. As with previous editions, the aim of this text is to impart to students the skills, knowledge, and practices needed for the effective creation of the traditional five-paragraph essay and the longer research essay. Most of the new reading selections included in this edition are by Canadian authors, and most were published recently. Selections from the previous edition have been retained as excellent readings and rhetorical exemplars. The first Canadian edition of *College Writing Skills with Readings* is, like previous editions, a practical book with special features to aid instructors and their students.

SPECIAL FEATURES

- **Four principles are presented as keys to effective writing.** These four principles—unity, support, coherence, and sentence skills—are highlighted on page 123 and the inside front cover and reinforced throughout the book. Part One focuses on the first three principles; Part Four serves as a concise handbook of sentence skills. In Part Two, students learn how to apply the four principles within different patterns of essay development, or rhetorical modes. Part Three introduces the student to the application of the four basic principles to specialized writing situations such as essay-style examination answers and the research essay. Finally, the reading selections in Part Five stimulate discussion, demonstrate various relevant rhetorical types, and generate writing assignments wherein the student demonstrates application of the four principles in a variety of carefully developed essays.

- **Activities, questions, and assignments are numerous and varied.** In the first two chapters, there are more than twenty activities of varying levels of difficulty to help students learn to develop, state, and support a thesis. There are more than one hundred activities in the entire book. Such activities serve as essential bridges between the text's explanation of a skill or piece of knowledge and the student's engagement with various stages of the writing process.

A variety of writing assignments follow each of the types of essay development in Part Two. Some topics are highly structured, for students needing such support; others present more of a challenge to the student. Instructors thus have the option of selecting those assignments best suited to the individual needs of their students.

■ ***Clear thinking is stressed throughout the text.*** This first Canadian edition retains *College Writing Skills'* focus on the importance of clarity of concept to clarity of expression. The focus on logic begins in the prefatory section "To the Student" on page xvii. Early in the text, students encounter the two principles fundamental to clear thinking and expression: *making one clear point* and *providing sound support to back up that point.* The primacy of focus on these principles continues throughout the book: a section on outlining in Part One offers practice in distinguishing between main and supporting ideas, and writing assignments in Part Two give direction in planning essays which support and develop a central point. Numerous other diverse activities in the book require students to develop and apply basic thinking skills, and a planning form to help students prepare outlines for well-thought-out essays appears on the inside back cover. Students learn that clear writing is inseparable from clear thinking.

■ ***The traditional essay is emphasized.*** Students are asked to write formal essays with an introduction, three supporting paragraphs, and a conclusion. A solidly reasoned essay always requires work for any writer. That work involves mental discipline and close attention to a set of rules. The result is nearly always the clear expression and explanation of a well-considered and well-supported idea. Writing an essay wherein there is a succinct yet complete thesis statement and wherein each of the three supporting paragraphs begins with a topic sentence is more challenging than writing a free-form or expressive essay. Longer research essays and reports are subject to the same structural and conceptual demands, so that skill in writing the five-paragraph essay forms an invaluable base for more complex college and professional writing requirements. The demands of the traditional essay are significant, but the rewards are great.

Such a rigorous approach only seems limiting. Students are already aware that rules can be modified, if not broken. Indeed, in the general media to which students are exposed daily, they can see those rules being broken constantly (usually to the detriment of clear communication and sound thinking). The English language itself often seems to be mutating into curious new forms, and relative values seem to be replacing accepted standards for expression. Given such a linguistic and intellectual environment, first-year college students do not need practice in breaking or going beyond the rules; they need practice in thoroughly learning the rules. Freedom to move effectively beyond the rules is possible only when students know what the rules are. Power and versatility of expression become real possibilities only after acceptance and successful application of the basic rules.

- **Writing is treated as a process.** The second chapter, "Important Factors in Writing," discusses prewriting, rewriting, and editing. In addition, many writing assignments are accompanied by "Suggestions on How to Proceed" that give step-by-step directions in the process of writing a paper.

- **Lively models are provided.** One (though by no means the only) way that students learn is by imitation. The Canadian edition of *College Writing Skills with Readings* therefore provides student and model essays with each assignment. Students read and evaluate these essays in terms of the four standards: unity, support, coherence, and sentence skills. Most of the essays follow the 1-3-1 format and average about five hundred words, so that students have clear and appropriate models for the essays they will be asked to write. The book assumes that students are especially interested in and challenged by the writing of their peers. Samples of the power of good student writing can only encourage attention to honesty, detail, and directness.

- **The text is versatile.** The five parts of this text each deal with a distinct area of writing, so that instructors may easily select the skills or subjects they wish to present, and a sequence they find suitable. Information within the book's five parts is clearly set out for ease of access.

- **Prose readings are included in Part Five.** The readings deal with contemporary and universal human concerns and will stimulate lively class discussions and response writing as well as individual thought. They are a rich source of material for a wide range of writing assignments.

    Part Five contains two special features. The first is the emphasis placed on helping students to become stronger readers. Brief introductory sections offer tips on good reading, and ten questions after each selection help students practise effective comprehension skills. The second special feature is the detailed background information provided with most of the writing assignments. Students are guided towards thinking about an assignment, and often given specific ideas about how to proceed.

- **Response writing assignments on specific rhetorical models are included.** At the end of each chapter in Part Two, an additional writing assignment is included, titled "Writing about a Reading Selection"; this assignment asks students to respond to one of the professional essays in Part Five by writing an essay using the mode of development under consideration.

NEW FEATURES OF THE CANADIAN EDITION

■ Because of the obvious and increasing importance of computers in education and business, generic instructions for their use in most stages of the writing process have been added to this book. Word processing cannot eliminate the hard work of thinking and writing, but it can facilitate both the prewriting and editing stages of essay creation. This addition of tips for students writing at the computer is intended to help students make intelligent use of available technological assistance. Such information is additional, not intrusive to the thrust or rhythm of the text's content, so that if word processing is not required, or not applicable to a teaching environment, the added material may simply be passed over.

■ New information about Canadian reference sources and updated library resource technology appears in the chapters "Using the Library" and "Writing a Research Essay." Again, while the fundamental requirements and skills needed for research have not changed, the quantity, variety, and accessibility of information available increases daily. The Canadian edition of the book offers the student an introduction to the types of technological help college libraries may now offer.

■ Two-thirds of the reading selections in the Canadian edition of *College Writing Skills with Readings* are by Canadian authors. The authors represented range from Maritime regional writers through Toronto urbanites to West Coast and Northern voices. Canada's geographical presence and immensity are important, as is the diversity of its population, and it is hoped that these two aspects of our national identity are apparent in the essays in this edition.

■ Without harming the integrity of previous editions of this book, several changes have been made to orthography, cultural references, and minor points in textual content. Spelling is based on the Oxford dictionaries, but adheres to usages which are generally accepted as Canadian rather than strictly British. Hyphenation of words follows Oxford as well. Changes to pedagogical content, reference sources, and sample essays have been made to reflect Canadian culture and media.

■ One point of grammatical evolution is apparent in the text. The pronoun referents "they" and "their" have been used with the singular of "student," rather than continual use of "his or her," or other variants. This reflects the Canadian editor's personal preference, and individual teachers may wish their students to use more traditional forms.

ACKNOWLEDGMENTS

Reviewers to whom I am grateful for their acuity, care, and intelligent comments include Margo Bath, Durham College; Janice Burk, Sault College; Lynn Courtney, Mohawk College; James Howard, Selkirk College; Fred Joblin, Georgian College; George McNabb, Centennial College; Aileen Ouvrard, Champlain Regional College; Carolyn Speakman, Lethbridge Community College.

I wish especially to thank Laurie Graham, Developmental Editor in the College Division of McGraw-Hill Ryerson, for her patience, tact, and consideration in assisting me with this text, and David Ward, Editor-in-Chief of the College Division of McGraw-Hill Ryerson, for initiating and pursuing this project.

As well, I must acknowledge what I have learned from three groups of people who have endured my opinions, helped me to clarify my own thinking, and, in many ways, helped me to make my contribution to this book: my students, my family, and members of the faculty of the School of English at Seneca College.

Finally, I owe a great debt of gratitude to John Langan for having provided me with a text excellent in both content and design, from which I taught with pleasure and learned with ease.

SHARON WINSTANLEY

TO THE STUDENT

The experience I had writing my first college essay has helped shape this book. I received a C– for the essay. Scrawled beside the grade was the comment, "Not badly written, but ill-conceived." I remember going to the instructor after class, asking about his comment as well as the word "Log" that he had added in the margin at various spots. "What are all these logs you put in my paper?" I asked, trying to make a joke of it. He looked at me a little wonderingly. "Logic, Mr. Langan," he answered, "logic." He went on to explain that I had not thought out my paper clearly. There were actually two ideas rather than one in my thesis, one supporting paragraph had nothing to do with either idea, another paragraph lacked a topic sentence, and so on. I've never forgotten his last words. "If you don't think clearly," he said, "you won't write clearly."

I was speechless, and I felt confused and angry. I didn't like someone telling me that I didn't know how to think. I went back to my room and read over my paper several times. Eventually, I decided that my teacher was right. "No more logs," I said to myself. "I'm going to get these logs out of my papers."

My instructor's advice was invaluable. I learned that if you plan and think through an essay first, you'll have completed a major stage of the work. *College Writing Skills with Readings* develops this idea by breaking down the writing process into a series of easily followed steps.

Part One of the book presents the four basic steps or principles you'll need to write strong essays:

1 Begin with a clearly stated point or thesis.
2 Provide logical, detailed support for your thesis.
3 Organize your supporting material effectively.
4 Revise and edit carefully so that the material is presented in clear, error-free sentences.

Part Two describes a number of different ways you can organize and develop essays. Each chapter opens with a brief introduction followed by several essays written by students. Then comes a series of questions so that you can evaluate the essays in terms of the basic principles explained in Part One. Finally, a number of writing topics are presented, along with prewriting hints to help you plan and write an effective paper.

Part Three helps with the many types of writing you will do in college: exam essays, summaries, reports, reviews, and the research paper. You will see that all these kinds of writing are variations of the essay form you have already learned.

Part Four offers review and practice in the skills needed to write sentences that are clear, error-free, and varied. Included is a series of selections to sharpen your proofreading and editing ability.

Finally, Part Five consists of a series of high-interest reading selections that will give you many ideas for writing. A special feature of Part Five is an introductory guide to effective reading. Each selection is then accompanied by comprehension questions that will give you practice in key reading skills. In addition, there are discussion questions and writing assignments that will help direct your thinking about each selection.

For your convenience, the book contains the following:

■ On page 123 and the inside front cover, there is a checklist of the four basic steps in effective writing.

■ On the inside back cover, there is an essay outline form to use when planning an essay. On page 10, there is an essay outline diagram.

■ On the last page, there is a list of correction symbols.

Get into the habit of referring to these guides on a regular basis; they can help ensure that you will produce clearly thought out, well-written essays.

In summary, *College Writing Skills with Readings* will help you learn, practice, and apply the thinking and writing skills you need to communicate effectively. But your starting point must be a determination to do the work needed to become a strong writer. Remember that the ability to express yourself clearly and logically can open doors for you, both in school and in your career. If you decide—and only you can decide—that you want this kind of power, this book will help you reach that goal.

JOHN LANGAN

PART ONE

BASIC PRINCIPLES OF ESSAY WRITING

INTRODUCTION
TO THE
ESSAY FORM

This chapter will explain:

- **The importance of supporting a point in writing**
- **The difference between a paragraph and an essay**
- **The general structure of an essay**

AN IMPORTANT DIFFERENCE
BETWEEN WRITING AND TALKING

In your everyday conversation, you make all kinds of points or assertions. You say, for example, "It's not safe to walk in our neighbourhood after dark"; "My boss is a hard person to work for"; or "Poor study habits keep getting me into trouble." The points that you make concern personal matters as well as, at times, outside issues: "That trade will be a disaster for the team"; "Lots of TV commercials are degrading to women"; "Students should have to work for a year before attending college."

The people you are talking with do not always challenge you to give reasons for your statements. They may know why you feel as you do, or they may already agree with you, or they simply may not want to put you on the spot; and so they do not always ask, "Why?" The people who read what you write, however, may not know you, agree with you, or feel in any way obliged to you. So if you want to communicate effectively with them, you must provide solid evidence for any point you make. An important difference, then, between writing and talking is this: *In writing, any idea that you advance must be supported with specific reasons or details.*

Think of your readers as reasonable persons. They will not take your views on faith, but they are willing to accept what you say as long as you support it. So remember to support with specific evidence any statement that you make.

THE PARAGRAPH: POINT AND SUPPORT

In conversation you might say to a friend who has suggested a movie, "No thanks. Going to the movies is just too much of a hassle. Parking, people, everything." From shared past experiences, your friend may know what you are talking about, so that you will not have to explain your statement. But in writing, your point would have to be backed up with specific reasons and details.

Below is a paragraph on why movie-going is a nuisance. A *paragraph* is a unit of writing of around 150 words which treats one opening point, or idea. It usually consists of an opening point called a *topic sentence* followed by a series of sentences which support that point.

The Hazards of Movie-Going

Although I love movies, going to see them drives me slightly crazy. First of all, getting to the movie can take a lot of time. I have a thirty-five-minute drive down a congested highway. Then, with a popular film, I usually have to wait in a long line at the ticket window. Another problem is that the theatre itself is seldom a pleasant place to be. A musty smell suggests that there has been no fresh air in the theatre since it was built. Half the seats seem to be falling apart. And the floor often has a sticky coating that gets on your shoes. The worst problem of all is some of the other movie-goers. Kids run up and down the aisle. Teenagers laugh and shout at the screen. People of all ages loudly drop paper cups and popcorn tubs, cough and burp, and elbow you out of the armrest on either side of your seat. All in all, I would rather stay home and wait for the latest movie hits to appear on TV in the safety and comfort of my own living room.

Notice what the supporting evidence has done here. It has provided you, the reader, with a basis for understanding *why* the writer makes the point that is made. Through this specific evidence, the writer has explained and successfully communicated the idea that movie-going can be a nuisance.

The evidence that supports the point in a paper often consists of a series of reasons followed by examples and details that support the reasons. That is true of the paragraph above: three reasons are provided, with examples and details that back up those reasons. Supporting evidence in a paper can also consist of anecdotes, personal experiences, facts, statistics, and the opinions of experts.

Activity

The paragraph on movie-going, like almost any piece of effective writing, has two essential parts: (1) a point is advanced, and (2) that point is then supported. Taking a minute to outline the paragraph will help you understand these basic parts clearly. Write in the following space the point that has been advanced in the paragraph. Then add the words needed to complete the outline of the paragraph.

Point _____

_____

Support 1. _Time getting there_____

      a. _Long drive_____

      b. _____

    2. _____

      a. _____

      b. _____

      c. _____

    3. _Other movie-goers_____

      a. _____

      b. _____

      c. _People of all ages_____

         (1) _____

         (2) _Cough and burp_____

         (3) _____

POINT AND SUPPORT IN AN ESSAY

Much of your college writing will be in the form of five-hundred-word essays— papers of several paragraphs that support a single point. An *essay* typically consists of an introductory paragraph, three supporting paragraphs, and a concluding paragraph. The central idea, or point, developed in an essay is called a *thesis statement* rather than, as in a paragraph, a topic sentence. A thesis appears in the introductory paragraph, and the specific support for the thesis appears in the paragraphs that follow. The supporting paragraphs allow for a fuller treatment of the evidence that backs up the central point than would be possible in a single-paragraph paper.

Longer essays and research papers will also be part of your college writing career. While there will be more than three internal paragraphs in such essays, the structuring requirements and support of ideas remain the same as for the five-paragraph essay.

Why Write Essays?

Mastering the essay form will help, first of all, on a practical level. For other courses, you will write specific forms of essays, such as the report and research paper. Many of your written tests will be in the form of essay exams. In addition, the basic structure of an essay will help in career-related writing, from a job application letter to the memos and reports that may become part of your work.

On a more abstract level, essay writing serves other valuable purposes. It will make you a better reader. You will become more aware of other writers' ideas and the evidence they provide (or fail to provide) to support those ideas. Most important, essay writing will make you a better thinker. Writing an essay forces you to sort out and organize your ideas and think them through clearly. You will learn to identify just what your ideas are and what support exists to back them up. Essay writing, in short, will give you practice in the process of clear and logical reasoning. Your ability to recognize ideas and to measure their validity will help you make sound decisions not just in school and career but in all phases of your everyday life.

A Model Essay

The following model should help you understand clearly the form of an essay. The writer of the paragraph on movie-going later decided to develop her subject more fully. Here is the essay that resulted.

The Hazards of Movie-Going

Introductory paragraph

    I am a movie fanatic. When friends want to know what picture won the Oscar in 1980 or who played the police chief in *Jaws*, they ask me. My friends, though, have stopped asking me if I want to go out to the movies. The problems in getting to the theatre, the theatre itself, and the behaviour of some patrons are all reasons why I often wait for a movie to show up on TV.

First supporting paragraph

    First of all, just getting to the theatre presents difficulties. Leaving a home equipped with a TV and a video recorder isn't an attractive idea on a humid, cold, or rainy night. Even if the weather co-operates, there is still a thirty-minute drive to the theatre down a congested highway, followed by the hassle of looking for a parking space. And then there are the lines. After hooking yourself to the end of a human chain, you worry about whether there will be enough tickets, whether you will get seats together, and whether many people will sneak into the line ahead of you.

Second supporting paragraph

    Once you have made it to the box office and got your tickets, you are confronted with the problems of the theatre itself. If you are in one of the run-down older theatres, you must adjust to the musty smell of seldom-cleaned carpets. Escaped springs lurk in the faded plush or cracked leather seats, and half the seats you sit in seem loose or tilted so that you sit at a strange angle. The newer multiplex theatres offer their own problems.

Sitting in an area only one-quarter the size of a regular theatre, movie-goers often have to put up with the sound of the movie next door. This is especially jarring when the other movie involves racing cars or a karate war and you are trying to enjoy a quiet love story. And whether the theatre is old or new, it will have floors that seem to be coated with rubber cement. By the end of a movie, shoes almost have to be pried off the floor because they have become sealed to a deadly compound of spilled pop, hardening bubble gum, and crushed Ju-Jubes.

Third supporting paragraph

Some of the patrons are even more of a problem than the theatre itself. Little kids race up and down the aisles, usually in giggling packs. Teenagers try to impress their friends by talking back to the screen, whistling, and making what they consider to be hilarious noises. Adults act as if they were at home in their own living rooms and comment loudly on the ages of the stars or why movies aren't as good anymore. And people of all ages crinkle candy wrappers, stick gum on their seats, and drop popcorn tubs or cups of crushed ice and pop on the floor. They also cough and burp, squirm endlessly in their seats, file out for repeated trips to the washrooms or refreshment stand, and elbow you out of the armrest on either side of your seat.

Concluding paragraph

After arriving home from the movies one night, I decided that I was not going to be a movie-goer anymore. I was tired of the problems involved in getting to the movies and dealing with the theatre itself and some of the patrons. The next day I arranged to have cable TV service installed in my home. I may now see movies a bit later than other people, but I'll be more relaxed watching box office hits in the comfort of my own living room.

GENERAL STRUCTURE OF AN ESSAY

The essay just presented—"The Hazards of Movie-Going"—is a good example of the standard short essay you will write in college English. It is a composition of slightly over five hundred words that consists of a one-paragraph introduction, a three-paragraph body, and a one-paragraph conclusion. The roles of these paragraphs are described and illustrated below.

Introductory Paragraph and Thesis of an Essay

The introductory paragraph of an essay should start with several sentences that attract the reader's interest. It should then advance the *central idea* or *thesis* that will be developed in the essay. *The thesis often includes a plan of development— a "preview" of the major points that will support the thesis.* These supporting points should be listed in the order in which they will appear in the essay. In some cases, the plan of development is presented in a sentence separate from the thesis; in other cases, it is omitted.

Activity

1. In "The Hazards of Movie-Going," which sentences are used to attract the reader's interest?
   a. First sentence
   b. First two sentences
   c. First three sentences
2. The thesis in "The Hazards of Movie-Going" is presented in which sentence?
   a. Third sentence
   b. Fourth sentence
3. The thesis contains a plan of development.
   a. Yes
   b. No
4. Write down the words in the thesis that announce the three major supporting points in the essay:
   a. _____
   b. _____
   c. _____

Supporting Paragraphs, or "Body," of an Essay

Most essays have three supporting points or main ideas, developed at length over three separate paragraphs. (Some essays will have two supporting points, others four or more. For the purposes of this book, your goal will be three supporting points for most essays.) Each of the supporting paragraphs should begin with a *topic sentence* that states the point to be detailed in that paragraph. Just as the thesis provides a focus for the entire essay, the topic sentences provide a focus for each supporting paragraph. Within each paragraph, a sufficient number of supporting details clarify, describe, and support the main supporting point or idea of that paragraph.

Activity

1. What is the topic sentence for the first supporting paragraph of the essay?

   _____

   _____

2. The first topic sentence is then supported by details about (*fill in the missing words*):

   a. _____

   b. _____

   c. <u>Long ticket line</u>_____

3. What is the topic sentence for the second supporting paragraph of the essay?

   _____

   _____

4. The second topic sentence is then supported by details about (*fill in the missing words*):

   a. <u>Problems of old theatres (mustiness and _____)</u>

   b. <u>Problems of new theatres (_____ and sound of adjoining movie)</u>

   c. <u>Problem of old and new theatres (_____)</u>

5. What is the topic sentence for the third supporting paragraph of the essay?

   _____

   _____

6. The third topic sentence is then supported by details about (*fill in the missing words*):

   a. <u>Patrons (kids, _____ , and _____)</u>

   b. <u>Distractions caused by people of all ages</u>

- For further information on paragraph structure and choice of supporting details, see Chapter 3, pages 39–45.

Concluding Paragraph of an Essay

The concluding paragraph often summarizes the essay by restating briefly the thesis and, at times, the main supporting points of the essay. In addition, the writer often presents a concluding thought about the subject of the paper.

Activity

1. Which two sentences in the concluding paragraph restate the thesis and supporting points of the essay?

   a. First and second

   b. Second and third

   c. Third and fourth

2. Which sentence contains the concluding thought of the essay?
   a. First
   b. Second
   c. Third
   d. Fourth

Diagram of an Essay

The following diagram shows you at a glance the different parts of a standard college essay.

Title of the Essay

Introduction

Opening remarks to catch reader's interest
Thesis
Plan of development (optional)

Topic sentence (main idea 1 and supporting point 1)
Specific evidence—supporting details

*Body
(supporting
paragraphs)*

Topic sentence (main idea 2 and supporting point 2)
Specific evidence—supporting details

Topic sentence (main idea 3 and supporting point 3)
Specific evidence—supporting details

Conclusion

Summary (optional)
General closing remarks

This diagram, along with the essay outline form that appears on the inside back cover of the book, will serve as a helpful guide when you are writing or evaluating essays.

IMPORTANT FACTORS IN WRITING

This chapter will discuss the importance of:

- **Your attitude about writing**
- **Knowing or discovering your subject**
- **Keeping a journal**
- **Prewriting**
- **Outlining**
- **Revising, editing, and proofreading**

The previous chapter introduced you to the essay form, and the chapters that follow will explain the basic steps in writing an essay and the basic standards for evaluating it. The purpose of this chapter is to describe a number of important general factors that will help you create good papers. These factors include (1) having the right attitude about writing, (2) knowing or discovering your subject, (3) keeping a journal, (4) prewriting, or having ways of getting started in writing, (5) outlining, and (6) revising, editing, and proofreading.

Your Attitude about Writing

One way to wreck your chances of learning how to write competently is to believe that writing is a "natural gift." People with this attitude think that they are the only ones for whom writing is an unbearably difficult activity. They feel that everyone else finds writing easy or at least tolerable. Such people typically say "I'm not any good at writing" or "English was not one of my good subjects." They imply that they simply do not have a talent for writing, while others do. The result of this attitude is that people do not do their best when they write—or, even worse, that they hardly ever try to write. Their attitude becomes a self-fulfilling prophecy: their writing fails chiefly because they have brainwashed themselves into thinking that they don't have the "natural talent" needed to write. Unless their attitude changes, they probably will not learn how to write effectively.

A realistic attitude about writing—to replace the mistaken notion of writing as a "natural gift"—should build on the following two ideas.

1   *Writing is hard work for almost everyone.* It is difficult to do the intense and active thinking that clear writing demands. (Perhaps television has made us all so passive that the active thinking necessary in both writing and reading now seems harder than ever.) It is frightening to sit down before a blank sheet of paper and know that an hour later, nothing on it may be worth keeping. It is frustrating to discover how much of a challenge it is to transfer thoughts and feelings from one's head onto a sheet of paper. It is upsetting to find that an apparently simple writing subject often turns out to be complicated. But writing is not an automatic process: we will not get something for nothing—and we should not expect to. Competent writing results only from plain hard work—from determination, sweat, and head-on battle.

2   *Writing is a skill.* Writing is a skill like driving, typing, or preparing a good meal. Like any skill, it can be learned—if you decide that you are going to learn and then really work at it. This book will give you the extensive practice needed to develop your writing skills.

Activity

Answering these questions will help you evaluate your attitude about writing.

1. How much practice were you given writing essays in high school?

    _____ Much   _____ Some   _____ Little

2. How much feedback (positive or negative comments) from teachers were you given on your essays?

    _____ Much   _____ Some   _____ Little

3. How did your teachers seem to regard your writing?

    _____ Good   _____ Fair   _____ Poor

4. Do you feel that some people have a gift for writing and others do not?

    _____ Yes   _____ Sometimes   _____ No

5. When do you start writing a paper?

_____ Several days before it is due

_____ About a day before it is due

_____ At the last possible minute

Many people who answer *Little* to questions 1 and 2 also answer *Poor*, *Yes*, and *At the last possible minute* to the other questions. On the other hand, people who answer *Much* or *Some* to questions 1 and 2 tend to have more favourable responses to the other questions. People with little *experience* in writing often have understandably negative feelings about their writing *ability*. But they should realize that writing is a skill they can learn with practice.

Knowing or Discovering Your Subject

Knowing Your Subject

Whenever possible, try to write on a subject which interests you. You will then find it easier to put the necessary time into your work. Even more important, try to write on a subject that you already know something about. If you do not have direct experience with a subject, you should at least have indirect experience— knowledge gained through thinking, prewriting (to be explained on pages 17–26), reading, or talking about the subject.

If you are asked to write on a topic about which you have no experience or knowledge, you should do whatever research is required to gain the information you need. The chapter "Using the Library" on pages 257–274 will show you how to use the library to look up relevant information. Without direct or indirect experience, or information gained through research, you will not be able to provide the specific evidence needed to develop the point you are trying to make. Your writing will be starved for specifics.

Discovering Your Subject

At times you will not know your subject when you begin to write. Instead, you will discover it in the *process* of writing. For example, when the author of the paper on movie-going in the previous chapter first sat down to write her paper, her topic was going to be the drawbacks of old movie houses. As she began to accumulate details, she quickly realized that her topic was really the drawbacks of movie-going in general. In other words, she only *thought* she knew her paper's focus when she began to write. In fact, *she discovered her subject in the course of writing*.

Another writer, without at first knowing his exact point, knew he wanted to write about a time when he had belonged to a gang and cruelly mugged some-one. He began by getting down the grim details of the actual mugging. As he developed the details, he realized gradually what point he wanted to make. The paper that resulted, "A Night of Violence," appears on page 209.

A third student author started with the idea that using computers in the class-room can be a real challenge. As she began getting details onto paper, her point became clearer, and she realized that she wanted to argue that computers in the classroom are a bad idea. Her paper, "A Vote against Computers," is on page 218.

The moral of these examples is that sometimes you must write a bit in order to find out just what you want to write. Writing can help you think about and explore your topic and decide on the final direction of your paper. The techniques presented in the section on "Prewriting" starting on page 17 will suggest specific ways to discover and develop a subject.

One related feature of the writing process bears mention. Do not feel that you must proceed in a linear fashion when you write. That is, do not assume that the writing process must be a railroad track on which you go straight from your cen-tral point to "supporting detail one" to "supporting detail two" to "supporting detail three" to your concluding paragraph. Instead, proceed in whatever way seems most comfortable as you draft the paper. You may want to start by writing the closing section of your paper or by developing your third supporting detail.

Do whatever is easiest—and as you get material down on the page or see your words on the processor screen, it will make what you have left to do a bit easier. Sometimes, of course, as you work on one section, it may happen that another focal point for your paper will emerge. That's fine: if your writing tells you that it wants to be something else, then revise or start over as needed to take advan-tage of that discovery. Your goal is to wind up with a paper that makes a point and supports it solidly. Be ready to change direction and to make whatever adjust-ments are needed to reach your goal.

Activity 1

Answer the following questions.

1. What are three ways to get the knowledge you need to write on a subject?

   a. _____

   b. _____

   c. _____

2. A student begins to write a paper about the best job he ever had. After writing for about half an hour, he realizes that his details are all about what a wonderful person his boss was. What has happened in the process of writing?

_____

3. Suppose you want to write a paper about problems that come with a holiday season. You think you can discuss family, personal, and financial problems. You feel you have the most details about financial problems. Should you start with that area, or with one of the other two areas?

_____

Activity 2

Write for five minutes about the house, residence, or apartment where you live. Simply write down whatever details come to you. Don't worry about being neat; just pile up as many details as you can.

Afterwards, go through the material. Try to find a potential focus within all those details. Do the details suggest a simple point that you could make about the place where you live? If so, you've seen a small example of how writing about a topic can be an excellent way of discovering a point about that topic.

Keeping a Journal

Because writing is a skill, the more you practise it, the better you will become at it. One excellent way to get writing practice is to keep a daily (or "almost daily") journal.

At some point during the day—perhaps during a study period after your last class of the day, or right before dinner, or right before going to bed—spend fifteen minutes or so writing in your journal. Keep in mind that you do not have to plan what to write about or be in the mood or worry about making mistakes as you write; just write down whatever words come out. You should write at least one page in each session.

You may want to use a notebook that you can easily carry with you for on-the-spot writing. Or you may decide to write on loose-leaf paper that can be transferred later to a journal folder on your desk. No matter how you proceed, be sure to date all entries.

The content of your journal should be some of the specific happenings, thoughts, and feelings of the day. Your starting point may be a comment by a teacher, a classmate, or a family member; a gesture or action that has amused, angered, confused, or depressed you; something you have read or seen on television—anything, really, that has caught your attention and that you decide to explore a bit in writing. These are your "writing prompts," your "hooks." Some journal entries may focus on a single subject; others may wander from one topic to another.

Your instructor may ask you to make journal entries a specific number of times a week, for a specific number of weeks. He or she may require that you turn in your journal every so often for review and feedback. If you are keeping the journal on your own, try to make entries three to five times a week every week of the semester.

Keeping a journal will help you develop the habit of thinking on paper, and it can help you make writing a familiar part of your life. Your journal can also serve as a source of ideas for possible papers.

Following is an excerpt from one student's journal. As you read, look for a general point and supporting material that could be the basis for an interesting paper.

September 6

My first sociology class was tonight. The parking lot was jammed when I got there. I thought I was going to be late for class. A guard had us park on a field next to the regular lot. When I got to the room, it had the usual painted-cinder-block construction. Every school I have ever been in since first grade seems to be made of cinder block. Everybody sat there without saying anything, waiting for the teacher to arrive. I think they were all a bit nervous like me. I hoped there wasn't going to be a ton of work in the course. I think I was also afraid of looking foolish somehow. This goes back to elementary school, when I wasn't a very good student and teachers sometimes embarrassed me in class. I didn't like elementary school, and I hated high school. Now here I am six years later in college of all places. Who would have thought that I would end up here? The teacher appeared—a woman who I think was a bit nervous herself. I think I like her. Her name is Barbara Hanlin. She says we should call her Barbara. We got right into it, but it was interesting stuff. I like the fact that she asks questions, but then she lets you volunteer. I always hated it when teachers would call on you whether you wanted to answer or not. I also like the fact that she answers the questions and doesn't just leave you hanging. She takes the time to write important ideas on the board. I also like the way she laughs. This class may be OK.

Activity

1. If the writer of the journal entry above was looking for ideas for an essay, he or she could probably find several in this single entry. For example, the stu-

dent might write a narrative about the roundabout way he or she apparently wound up in college. See if you can find in the entry an idea that might be the basis for an interesting essay, and write your point in the space below.

_____

2. Take fifteen minutes right now to write a journal entry on this day in your life. On a separate sheet of paper, just start writing about anything that you have seen, said, heard, thought, or felt today, and let your thoughts take you where they may.

Prewriting

If you are like many people, you may sometimes have trouble getting started with your writing. A mental block may develop when you sit down before a blank sheet of paper. You may not be able to think of a topic or an interesting slant on a topic. Or you may have trouble coming up with interesting and relevant details that you can use to support your topic. Even after starting a paper, you may hit snags or moments of wondering, "Where to go next?"

The following pages describe five techniques that will help you think about and develop a topic and get words down on paper. These techniques, which are often called *prewriting techniques*, are a central part of the writing process. They are

1 Brainstorming
2 Freewriting
3 Diagramming
4 Making a list
5 Preparing a scratch outline

With these prewriting techniques, except for diagramming, writing even early drafts directly on the computer can be a liberating experience. Try various approaches to writing. You can delete, add, and move words, phrases, and paragraphs on-screen easily, which lessens both the physical work of writing and the frustration of staring at pile-ups of crossed-out words and unreadable messes. Moreover, you lose the fear of writing something "permanently stupid"; anything on the screen can be altered easily. You will find that ease in blocking and moving sentences, phrases, and whole paragraphs in later drafts will facilitate the creation of essays which flow smoothly and logically. If you print out double-spaced drafts of your essays, you will find it easy to work with hard copy, as well as with the on-screen copy.

TECHNIQUE 1: BRAINSTORMING

In *brainstorming*, you generate ideas and details by asking as many questions as you can think of about your subject. Such questions include *What? When? Why? How? Where?* and *Who?*

Following is an example of how one person, Brent, used brainstorming to generate material for a paper. Brent felt he could write about a depressing coffee shop he had visited, but he was having trouble getting started. So he asked himself a series of questions about the experience and, as a result, accumulated a series of details that provided the basis for the paper he finally wrote.

Here are the questions Brent asked and the answers he wrote:

<u>Why</u> did I stop at the coffee shop?	I was on the way home after driving all day, and I was tired. I decided to get a cup of coffee at the next coffee shop.
<u>How</u> do I feel about coffee shops?	I've always liked coffee shops. I was looking forward to a friendly server and talk with the customers at the counter.
<u>What</u> was the coffee shop like?	It was lonely. There were only a few people, and it was very quiet. Only one server was on duty. Even the parking lot looked lonely—garbage was blowing around, and it was raining.
<u>Who</u> was in the coffee shop?	Two workers were sitting at the counter. There was also a young man sitting by himself at the far end of the counter. He looked depressed. There was a middle-aged couple in a booth. They weren't talking to each other—one was doodling, the other staring.
<u>What</u> happened at the coffee shop?	I got out of there as fast as possible. I just wanted to get away from that lonely place and reach my home.

After brainstorming, Brent's next step was to prepare a scratch outline. He then prepared several drafts of the paper. The effective essay that eventually resulted from Brent's prewriting techniques appears on page 199.

Activity

To get a sense of the brainstorming process, use a sheet of paper to ask yourself a series of questions about a *pleasant* coffee shop or restaurant you have visited. See how many details you can accumulate about that restaurant in ten minutes.

TECHNIQUE 2: FREEWRITING

When you do not know what to write about a subject, or when you start to write but then become blocked, freewriting sometimes helps. In *freewriting*, you write without stopping for ten minutes or so. You do not worry about checking your spelling or punctuation, erasing mistakes, or finding exact words. If you get stuck, you write, "I am looking for something to say," or repeat words until you get an idea. There is no need to feel inhibited, since mistakes do not count and you do not have to hand in your paper.

Freewriting will limber up your writing muscles and make you familiar with the act of writing. It is a way to break through mental blocks about writing and the fear of making errors. As you do not have to worry about making mistakes, you can concentrate on discovering what you want to say about a subject. Your initial ideas and impressions will often become clearer after you have gotten them down on paper. Through continued practice in freewriting, you will develop the habit of thinking as you write. And you will learn a technique that is a helpful way to get started on almost any paper.

Here is the freewriting that one student did to accumulate details for a paper on why she had decided to put her mother in a nursing home.

> I'm still upset about the whole thing, but seeing everything going downhill really forced the decision. Mom just needed so much help with all the pills and dressing and bathing. She needed more help than Daddy could handle by himself. Prescription drug bills in this country can be outrageous, and provincial medical insurance doesn't pay. Mom needed someone to work out her special diet because it was so complicated. The wheelchair rental was expensive. The hardest thing was the fact that she was breaking down emotionally, saying things like, "You don't care about me." We cared, but we worried about Dad. What an enormous strain he was under in all this. Mom really acted emotionally disturbed at times. She would call for an ambulance and tell them she was dying. Dad started to lose weight. The bills coming in started to fill an entire shopping bag. Some people think we were cruel, but we didn't have any other choice. My father doesn't drive, so he was walking all over town to get medicine and food.

The writer's next step was to use the freewriting as the basis for a scratch outline. The effective paper that eventually resulted from the author's freewriting, a scratch outline (see "Technique 5" on page 22), and a good deal of rewriting appears on page 147.

Activity

To get a sense of the freewriting process, use a sheet of paper to freewrite about some of your own everyday worries. See how many ideas and details you can accumulate in ten minutes.

TECHNIQUE 3: DIAGRAMMING

Diagramming, also known as *mapping* or *clustering*, is another prewriting activity that can help you generate ideas and details about a topic. In diagramming, you use lines, boxes, arrows, and circles to show relationships between the ideas and details that come to you.

Diagramming is especially helpful to people who like to do their thinking in a very visual way. Whether you use a diagram, and just how you proceed with it, is up to you.

Here is the diagram that one student, Todd, prepared for a paper on differences between McDonald's and a fancy restaurant. This diagram, with its clear picture of relationships, was especially helpful for the comparison-contrast paper that Todd was doing. His final essay appears on page 159.

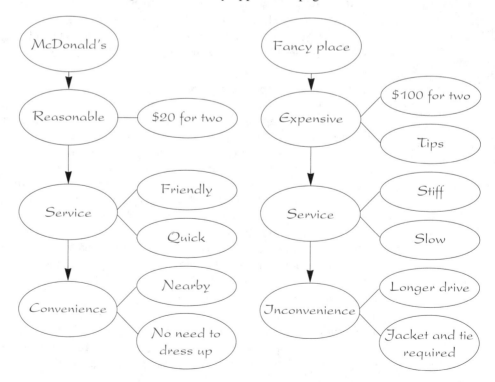

Activity

To get a sense of diagramming, use a sheet of paper to make a diagram of differences between two teachers or two jobs. See how many ideas and details you can accumulate in ten minutes.

TECHNIQUE 4: MAKING A LIST

Another prewriting technique is *making a list*. To get started on a paper, list as many different items as you can think of concerning your topic. Do not worry about repeating yourself, about sorting out major points from minor details, or about spelling or punctuating correctly. Simply make a list of everything about your subject that occurs to you. Your aim is to generate details and to accumulate as much raw material for writing as possible.

Following is a list prepared by one student, Jan, who was gathering details for an essay called "Benefits of Television." Her first step was simply to jot down thoughts and details that occurred to her.

Entertainment
Movies and sports events
Video games
Educational (important—save for last)
Relaxing after work
Covers major world events
Can be used with computers
Reduce stress (used for high-blood-pressure patients)
Rent videocassettes
Shows for children (Bookmice, Sesame Street)
Special cable services (sports, concerts)
College courses on TV

Notice that partway down her list Jan put in parentheses a note to herself that one thought (about the educational benefits of television) seems most important and should be saved for last. Very often, as you make a list, ideas about how to develop and organize a paper will occur to you. Jot them down, or simply type them in at the side of your list.

Making a list is an excellent way to get started. Often, you then go on to make a scratch outline and write the first draft of your paper. (A scratch outline for Jan's list appears in the next section.)

Activity

To get a sense of making a list, use a sheet of paper to list specific problems you will face this semester. See how many ideas and details you can accumulate in ten minutes.

TECHNIQUE 5: PREPARING A SCRATCH OUTLINE

A scratch outline can often be the *single most helpful technique* for writing a good paper. It is an excellent complement to the prewriting techniques already mentioned. In a *scratch outline*, you think carefully about the exact point you are making, about the exact details you will use to support it, and about the exact order in which you will arrange them. The scratch outline is a plan or blueprint to help you achieve a unified, supported, and organized composition.

When you are planning an essay consisting of an introduction, three supporting paragraphs, and a conclusion (this is known as a *one-three-one* essay), a scratch outline is especially important. It may be only a few words, but it will be the bedrock upon which your whole essay will rest.

Here is the scratch outline Jan prepared for her general list on television:

```
Television can have real benefits.
1.  Relaxation
2.  Entertainment
3.  Education
```

This brief outline made it clear to Jan that she could develop her essay on the basis of three distinct supporting points. While the outline appears simple, it represents a good deal of thinking on Jan's part. In the essays that you write, you should always try to develop such a basic outline.

With this outline, Jan knew she had a solid plan and a workable paper. As the next step in her writing process, she then felt comfortable about developing her scratch outline further by detailing the items that fit under each benefit:

```
1.  Relaxation
    a.  After work
    b.  Reduce stress
2.  Entertainment
    a.  Network programming
    b.  Cable programming
    c.  Videocassettes and videodiscs
    d.  Video game
```

3. Education
   a. Children's shows
   b. College courses
   c. World events
   d. Computer capability

These scratch outlines enabled Jan to decide what to put into the paper, and in what order. Without having to write actual sentences, she took a giant step toward a paper that is unified (she left out items that are not related), supported (she added items that develop her point), and organized (she arranged the items in a logical way). These criteria for an effective essay are discussed on pages 89–113; and the essay that resulted from Jan's list and outlines is on pages 97 and 98.

Activity

To get a sense of preparing a scratch outline, develop such an outline on reasons why you did or did not do well in high school. See how many ideas and details you can accumulate in ten minutes.

COMBINED USE OF THE FIVE PREWRITING TECHNIQUES

Very often a scratch outline follows brainstorming, freewriting, diagramming, and making a list. At other times, however, the scratch outline may substitute for the other four techniques. Also, you may use several techniques almost simultaneously when writing a paper. You may, for example, ask questions while making a list; you may diagram and outline a list as you write it; you may ask yourself questions and then freewrite answers to them. The five techniques are all ways to help you go about the process of writing a paper.

Activity 1

Answer the following questions.

1. Which of the prewriting techniques do you already practise?

   _____ Brainstorming

   _____ Freewriting

   _____ Diagramming

   _____ Making a list

   _____ Preparing a scratch outline

2. Which prewriting technique involves asking questions about your topic?

   _____

3. Which prewriting technique shows in a very visual way the relationship between ideas and details?

   _____

4. Which prewriting technique involves writing quickly about your topic without being concerned about grammar or spelling?

   _____

5. Which prewriting technique is almost always part of writing an essay?

   _____

6. Which prewriting techniques do you think will work best for you?

   _____

Activity 2

Below are examples of how the five prewriting techniques could be used to develop the topic "Problems of Combining Work and College." Identify each technique by writing *B* (for brainstorming), *F* (for freewriting), *D* (for the diagram), *L* (for the list), or *SO* (for the scratch outline) in the answer space.

_____

```
Never enough time
Miss campus parties
Had to study (only two free hours a night)
Give up activities with friends
No time to rewrite papers
Can't stay at school to play video games or talk to friends
Friends don't call me to go out anymore
Sunday no longer relaxed day—have to study
Missing sleep I should be getting
Marks aren't as good as they could be
Can't watch favourite TV shows
Really need the extra money
Tired when I sit down to study at nine o'clock
```

_____

What are some of the problems of combining work and school?

Schoolwork suffers because I don't have time to study or rewrite papers. I've had to give up things I enjoy, like sleep and touch football. I can't get into the social life at college, because I have to work right after class.

How have these problems changed my life?

My marks aren't as good as they were when I didn't work. Some of my friends have stopped calling me. My relationship with a girl I liked fell apart because I couldn't spend much time with her. I miss TV.

What do I do in a typical day?

I get up at 7 to make an 8 a.m. class. I have classes till 1:30 p.m., and then I drive to the supermarket where I work. I work till 7 p.m., and then I drive home and eat dinner. After I take a shower and relax for a half hour, it's about 9 p.m. This gives me only a couple of hours to study—read textbooks, do math exercises, write essays. My eyes start to close well before I go to bed at 11 p.m.

Why do I keep up this schedule?

I can't afford to go to school without working, and I need a degree to get the accounting job I want. If I invest my time now, I'll have a better future.

_____

Juggling a job and college has created major difficulties in my life.
1. Little time for studying
   a. Not reading textbooks
   b. Not rewriting papers
   c. Little studying for tests
2. Little time for enjoying social side of college
   a. During school
   b. After school
3. No time for personal pleasures
   a. Favourite TV shows
   b. Sunday football games
   c. Sleeping late

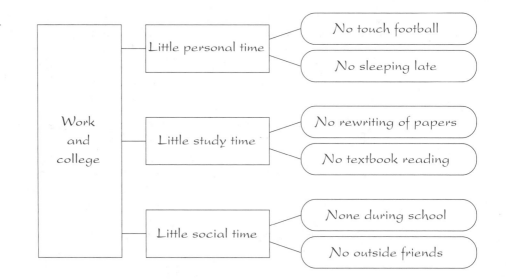

It's hard working and going to school at the same time. I never realized how much I'd have to give up. I won't be quitting my job because I need the money and the people are friendly at the place where I work. I've had to give up a lot more than I thought. We used to play touch football games every Sunday. They were fun and we'd go out for drinks afterwards. Sundays now are for catch-up work with my courses. I have to catch up because I don't get home every day until 7 p.m., and I have to eat dinner first before studying. Sometimes I'm so hungry I just eat cookies or chips. Anyway, by the time I take a shower it's 9 p.m. or later and I'm already feeling tired. I've been up since 7 a.m. Sometimes I write an English paper in twenty minutes and don't even read it over. I feel that I'm missing out on a lot in college. The other day some people I like were sitting in the cafeteria listening to music and talking. I would have given anything to stay and not have to go to work. I almost called in sick. I used to get invited to parties but I don't much anymore. My friends know I'm not going to be able to make it, so they don't bother. I can't sleep late on weekends or watch TV during the week.

Outlining

As already mentioned, outlining is central to writing a good paper. An outline lets you see, and work on, the bare bones of a paper, without the distraction of a clutter of words and sentences. It develops your ability to think in a clear and logical manner. Outlining provides a quick check on whether your paper will be *unified*. It suggests right at the start whether your paper will be adequately *supported*. And it shows you how to plan a paper that is *well organized*.

The following series of exercises will help you develop the outlining skills so important to planning and writing a solid essay.

Activity 1

One key to effective outlining is the ability to distinguish between major ideas and details that fit under those ideas. The exercise below will develop your ability to generalize from a list of details and to determine a major thought.

Examples

Writing instruments

Pencil
Ball-point pen
Crayon
Felt-tip marker

Outer garments

Coat
Shawl
Jacket
Cape

1. _____

Spiderman
Superman
Wonder Woman
Batman

2. _____

Gas
Electricity
Water
Phone

3. _____

Calgary Sun
Winnipeg Free Press
Le Devoir
Toronto Star

4. _____

Tinsel
Mistletoe
Lights
Wreaths

5. _____

Chicken
Turkey
Cornish game hen
Duck

6. _____

Dictionary
Almanac
Encyclopedia
Atlas

7. _____

Chain
Handlebars
Gearshift
Wheel spokes

8. _____

Loans
Chequing accounts
Savings accounts
Cheque cashing

9. _____   10. _____
    Wrinkles   Crutch
    Hearing loss   Cane
    Brittle bones   Metal walker
    Thinning hair   Artificial leg

Activity 2

Major and minor ideas are mixed together in the two lists below. Put the ideas into logical order by filling in the outlines that follow.

1. Thesis: My high school had three problem areas.

Involved with drugs	a. _____
Leaky ceilings	(1) _____
Students	(2) _____
Unwilling to help after class	b. _____
Formed cliques	(1) _____
Teachers	(2) _____
Buildings	
Ill-equipped gym	c. _____
Much too strict	(1) _____
	(2) _____

2. Thesis: Working as a dishwasher in a restaurant was my worst job.

Ten-hour shifts	a. _____
Heat in kitchen	(1) _____
Working conditions	(2) _____
Minimum wage	b. _____
Hours changed every week	(1) _____
No bonus for overtime	(2) _____
Hours	
Pay	c. _____
Noisy work area	(1) _____
	(2) _____

Activity 3

Again, major and minor ideas are mixed together. In addition, in each outline one of the three major ideas is missing and must be added. Put the ideas into a logical order by filling in the outlines that follow and adding a third major idea.

1. Thesis: Joining an aerobics class has many benefits.

Make new friends
Reduce mental stress
Social benefits
Strengthens heart
Improves self-image
Mental benefits
Tones muscles
Meet interesting instructors

a. _____

(1) _____

(2) _____

b. _____

(1) _____

(2) _____

c. _____

(1) _____

(2) _____

2. Thesis: My favourite times in school were the days before holiday vacations.

Lighter workload
Teachers more relaxed
Sports events
Less work in class
Friendlier atmosphere
Less homework
Holiday concerts
Students happy about vacation

a. _____

(1) _____

(2) _____

b. _____

(1) _____

(2) _____

c. _____

(1) _____

(2) _____

Activity 4: Making an "Essay Skeleton"

Read the following model essay and outline it in the spaces provided. This activity will give you practice at *analyzing*, or breaking down, your own essay drafts into "skeletons." By making an "X-ray" or "skeleton" of your essay draft, you will see your main ideas and the quality of your supporting details more clearly. Write out the central point and topic sentences and summarize in a few words the supporting material that fits under each topic sentence. One item is summarized for you as an example.

Losing Touch

Steve, a typical Canadian, stays home on workdays. He plugs into his personal computer terminal in order to hook up with the office. After work, he puts on his stereo headphones, watches a movie on his home video recorder, or challenges himself to a CD-ROM version of electronic baseball. On many days, Steve doesn't talk to any other human beings, and he doesn't see any people except those on television. Steve is imaginary, but his lifestyle is very possible. The inventions of modern technology seem to be cutting us off from contact with our fellow human beings.

Thesis: _____

_____

The world of business is one area in which technology is isolating us. Many people now work alone at home. With access to a large central computer, employees such as secretaries, insurance agents, and accountants do their jobs at display terminals in their own homes. They no longer actually have to see the people they're dealing with. In addition, employees are often paid in an impersonal way. Workers' salaries are automatically credited to their bank accounts, eliminating the need for paycheques. Fewer people stand in line with their co-workers to receive their pay or cash their cheques. Finally, personal banking is becoming a detached process. Customers interact with machines rather than people to deposit or withdraw money from their accounts. Even some bank loans are approved or rejected, not in an interview with a loan officer, but through a display on a computer screen.

First topic sentence: _____

_____

Support: 1. *Many people now work alone at home.*

2. _____

3. _____

    a. _____

    b. _____

Another area that technology is changing is entertainment. Music, for instance, was once a group experience. People listened to music at concert halls or in small social gatherings. For many people now, however, music is a solitary experience. Walking along the street or sitting in their living rooms, they wear headphones to build a wall of music around them. Movie entertainment is changing, too. Movies used to be social events. Now, fewer people are going out to see a movie. Many more are choosing to rent movies, or wait for a film to appear on cable television. Instead of being involved with the laughter, applause, or hisses of the audience, viewers watch movies in the isolation of their own living rooms.

Second topic sentence: _____

_____

Support: 1. _____

2. _____

Education is a third important area in which technology is separating us from others. From elementary schools to colleges, students spend more and more time sitting by themselves in front of computers. The computers give them feedback, while teachers spend more time tending the computers and less time interacting with their classes. A similar problem occurs in homes. As more families buy computers, increasing numbers of students practise their math and reading skills with software programmes instead of with their friends, brothers and sisters, and parents. Last, alienation is occurring as a result of two other high-tech inventions, videotapes and CD-ROMs. People are buying videotapes and discs on subjects such as cooking, real estate investment, speaking, and speed-reading. They then practise their skills at home rather than by taking group classes in which a rich human interaction can occur.

Third topic sentence: _____

_____

Support: 1. _____

2. _____

3. _____

Technology, then, seems to be driving human beings apart. Soon, we may no longer need to communicate with other human beings in order to do our work, entertain ourselves, or play the games we enjoy. Machines will be the co-workers and companions of the future.

Revising, Editing, and Proofreading

An effective paper is almost never written all at once. Rather, it is written in a step-by-step process in which you take it through a series of stages—from prewriting to final draft.

In the first stage, described above, you *prewrite*, getting your initial ideas and impressions about the subject down on paper. You accumulate raw material through brainstorming, freewriting, diagramming, and making lists and scratch outlines.

In the second stage, you *write and revise several drafts* of your paper. You fill out and shape your paper, adding and subtracting as needed to move it as close as you can to its final form. You work to make clear the single point of your paper, to develop fully the specific evidence needed to support that point, and to organize and connect the specific evidence. In the second draft, use your word-processing programme's options to block, move, insert, and delete words, phrases, and sentences so that you may concentrate on adding details that will further support the central point of your paper. At the same time, you may also eliminate details that, you now realize, do not truly back up your thesis. In the third draft, you may work on reorganizing details, checking for logical order of details, and adding connections between supporting paragraphs so that your material will hold together more tightly.

Ideally, you should now set your paper aside for a while, so that you can move into the editing and proofreading stage with a fresh, rested mind. In this last stage, you first *edit* the next-to-final draft; that is, you check it carefully for sentence skills—for correct grammar, mechanics, punctuation, and usage. Then you *proofread* the final copy of the paper using your computer's spell-checker and your dictionary to check for any typing mistakes. Editing and proofreading are important steps that some people avoid, often because they have worked too hard (or too little) on the previous stages.

Remember that correcting mistakes in the next-to-final and final versions can turn an average paper into a better one and a good paper into an excellent one. A later section of this book will give you practice in editing and proofreading in the form of a series of editing tests (pages 471–480).

Activity 1

Answering the questions below will help you evaluate your attitude about revising, editing, and proofreading.

1. When do you typically start work on a paper?

   _____ Several nights before it's due

   _____ Night before it's due

   _____ Day it's due

2. How many drafts do you typically write when doing a paper?

   _____ One   _____ Two   _____ Three   _____ Four or more

3. How would you describe your editing (checking the next-to-final draft for errors in grammar, punctuation, mechanics, and usage)?

   _____ Do little or no editing

   _____ Look quickly for and correct obvious errors

   _____ Use the spell-checker, then consult a grammar handbook and a dictionary about all possible errors

4. How would you describe your proofreading (checking the final draft for typing or handwriting errors)?

   _____ Do not look at the paper again after the last word is written

   _____ May glance quickly through the paper

   _____ Read the paper over carefully to find mistakes

5. Do you ever get back papers marked for obvious errors?

   _____ Frequently _____ Sometimes _____ Almost never _____ Never

Activity 2

Following is a supporting paragraph from a student essay called "Problems of Combining School and Work." The paragraph is shown in four different stages of development: (1) First full draft, (2) second draft, (3) next-to-final draft, (4) final draft. The four stages appear in scrambled order. Write the number *1* in the answer blank for the first full draft and number the remaining stages in sequence.

_____

   I have also given up some special personal pleasures in my life. On Sundays, for example, I used to play street hockey or football, now I use the entire day to study. Another pleasure Ive had to give up is good old-fashioned sleep. I never get as much as I like because their just isnt time. Finally I miss having the chance to just sit in front of the TV, on weeknights. In order to watch the whole line-up of movies and sports that I used to watch regularly. These sound like small pleasures, but you realize how important they are when you have to give them up.

—————— I've had to give up special personal pleasures in my life. I use to spend Sundays playing pick-up games, now I have to study. Im the sort of person who needs alot of sleep, but I dont have the time for that either. Sleeping nine or ten hours a night woul'dnt be unusual. Psychologists have shown that each individual need a different amount of sleep, some people as little as five hours, some as much as nine or ten. so I'm not unusual in that. But I've given up that pleasure too. The third thing is that I can't watch the TV shows I use to enjoy. This is another personal pleasure I've had to give up trying to balence work and school. These sound like small pleasures, but you realize how important they are when you have to give them up.

—————— Besides missing the social side of college life, I've also had to give up some of my special personal pleasures. I used to spend Sunday afternoons, for example, playing street hockey or touch football, depending on the season. Now, I use Sunday as a catch-up day for my studies. Another pleasure I've lost is sleeping late on days off and weekends. I once loved mornings when I could check the clock, bury my head in the pillow, and drift off for another hour. These days I'm forced to crawl out of bed the minute the alarm lets out its piercing ring. Finally, I no longer have the chance to just sit, for three or four hours at a time, watching the movies and sports programmes I enjoy. A leisurely night of Hockey Night in Canada or a network premiere of a Clint Eastwood movie is a pleasure of the past for me now.

—————— Besides missing the social side of college life, I've also had to give up some of my special personal pleasures. I used to spend Sunday afternoons, for example, playing street hockey or touch football, depending on the season. Now I use Sunday as a day for my studies. Another pleasure I've had to give up is sleeping late on days off and weekends. I once loved mornings when I could check the clock, bury my head in the pillow, and drifting off for another hour. These days I'm forced to get out of bed the minute the alarm lets out it's piercing ring. Finally, I no longer have the chance to just sit watching the movies and sports programmes I enjoy. A liesurely night of Hockey Night in Canada or a network premere of a Clint Eastwood movie is a pleasure of the past for me now.

■ Which sample paragraph conveys its meaning most clearly?

_____

Why?

_____

■ Which errors are most distracting to the reader?

_____

_____

THE FIRST AND SECOND STEPS IN ESSAY WRITING

This chapter will show you how to:

- **Start an essay with a point or thesis**
- **Support that point or thesis with specific evidence**

Now that you have a sense of the general structure of an essay—and of important general factors in writing—it is time to consider the basic steps involved in writing an essay. The four steps are as follows:

1. Begin with a point or thesis.
2. Support the thesis with specific evidence.
3. Organize and connect the specific evidence.
4. Write clear, error-free sentences.

This chapter will describe the first two steps, and the chapter that follows (see page 63) will present the last two.

Step 1:
Begin with a Point or Thesis

Your first step in writing is to decide what point you want to make and to write out that point in a single sentence. Formulating your point or *thesis* right at the start will help in two ways. First, you will find out at once whether you have a clear and workable thesis. Second, you will be able to use the thesis as a guide while writing your essay. If you frequently ask yourself, "Does this support my thesis?" you will know what material to include. With the thesis as a guide, your chances of drifting away from the point of the essay are greatly reduced.

WRITING A GOOD THESIS

To write a good thesis, you must begin with a subject that is neither too broad nor too narrow. Suppose a teacher asks you to write a paper on some aspect of marriage. Such a topic is obviously too broad to cover in a five-hundred-word essay. You would have to write a book to support adequately any point you might make about the general subject of marriage. What you need to do, then, is to limit your subject. Narrow it down until you have a thesis that you can deal with specifically in four hundred to five hundred words. In the box that follows are examples of narrowed subjects.

General Subject	Limited Subject	Thesis
Marriage	Honeymoon	A honeymoon is perhaps the worst way to begin a marriage.
Family	Older sister	My older sister helped me overcome my shyness.
Television	TV preachers	TV evangelists use sales techniques to promote their messages.
Children	Disciplining of children	My husband and I have several effective ways of disciplining our children.
Sports	Players' salaries	High players' salaries are bad for the game, for the fans, and for the values our children are developing.

Activity

Sometimes a subject must go through several stages of limiting before it is narrow enough to write about. Below are four lists reflecting several stages that writers went through in moving from a general subject to a narrow thesis statement.

Number the stages in each list from *1* to *5*, with *1* marking the broadest stage and *5* marking the thesis.

List 1

_____ Teachers

_____ Education

_____ Math teacher

_____ My high school math teacher was incompetent.

_____ High school math teacher

List 2

_____ Bicycles

_____ Dangers of bike riding

_____ Recreation

_____ Recreational vehicles

_____ Bike riding in the city is a dangerous activity.

List 3

_____ Financial institutions

_____ Bank

_____ Dealing with customers

_____ Working in a bank

_____ I've learned how to handle unpleasant bank customers.

List 4

_____ Camping

_____ First camping trip

_____ Summer vacation

_____ My first camping trip was a disastrous experience.

_____ Vacations

Later in this chapter, you will get more practice in narrowing general subjects to thesis statements.

COMMON ERRORS IN WRITING A THESIS

When writing thesis statements, people often make one of several mistakes that undermine their chances of producing an effective essay. One mistake is to substitute an announcement of the subject for a true thesis idea. Other mistakes include writing theses that are too broad or too narrow, or theses that have more than one idea. Following are examples of all four errors.

1 Announcements

The subject of this paper will be my parents.
I want to talk about unemployment in our country.
"Generation X" is the concern of this essay.

2   Statements That Are Too Broad

My parents have been the most influential people in my life.

Unemployment is a major concern of everyone in our country.

"Generation X" is changing views of employment and the economy.

3   Statements That Are Too Narrow

My parents had only one child.

In the last year there has been a real increase in unemployment in our town.

The members of "Generation X" make up a large socio-economic group in North America.

4   Statements That Contain More Than One Idea

My parents helped me grow in important ways, although in other respects I was limited.

The problem of Canada's increasing unemployment rates must be solved, and measures must be taken to re-educate those out of work.

"Generation X" has had many advantages, but it also faces many problems.

In the first group above, the sentences are not thesis statements but simple announcements of a topic idea. For instance, "The subject of this paper will be my parents" does not make a point but merely tells, in a rather weak and unimaginative way, the writer's general subject. A thesis statement must advance a point about a limited subject.

In the second group above, all the statements are too broad to be supported adequately. For example, "My parents have been the most influential people in my life" could not be supported with specific details in five hundred words or less. There are many autobiographies in which authors have devoted entire chapters to detailing the influence of their mothers or fathers on their lives.

In the third group above, there is no room in any of the three statements for support to be given. For instance, "My parents had only one child" is too narrow to be expanded into a paper. It is a simple fact that does not lend itself to much discussion. Such a statement is sometimes called a *dead-end statement*; there is no place to go with it. On the other hand, "My parents helped me grow in three important ways" is a point that you could go on to write about in an essay.

In the last group, each of the statements contains more than one idea. For instance, "My parents helped me grow in important ways, although in other respects I was limited" appears to have two separate ideas ("parents helped me grow" *and* "in other respects I was limited"). Thus the reader does not know what the real focus will be.

Activity

Part A: Write *TN* in the space next to each statement that is too narrow to be developed in an essay. Write *TB* beside each statement that is too broad to be covered in an essay.

_____ 1. The way our society treats its elderly people is unbelievable.

_____ 2. The first car that I owned was a Ford.

_____ 3. Computers have changed our society.

_____ 4. People who eat a lot of red meat are almost three times more likely to get colon cancer than people who eat mostly fish and chicken.

_____ 5. Action must be taken against drugs.

Part B: Write *A* beside each sentence that is an announcement rather than a thesis statement. Write *2* beside each statement that contains more than one idea.

_____ 6. My last car was dependable, but many North American cars are poorly made.

_____ 7. The subject of this essay is daily prayer in elementary schools.

_____ 8. Soap operas show many stereotyped characters, although they also portray real problems in North American life.

_____ 9. I am going to write on my ideas concerning "F" grades.

_____ 10. The hardest teacher I ever had taught me a lesson I will never forget.

Step 2:
Support the Thesis
with Specific Evidence

The first essential step in writing a successful essay is to formulate a clearly stated thesis. The second basic step is to support the thesis with specific reasons or details.

To ensure that your essay will have adequate support, you may find an informal outline very helpful. Write down a brief version of your thesis idea and then work out and jot down the three points that will support that thesis.

Here is the informal outline that was prepared by the author of the essay on movie-going:

Movie-going is a problem.
1. Getting there
2. Theatre itself
3. Patrons

An informal outline like this one looks simple, but achieving it often requires a great deal of careful thinking. The time spent, though, on developing a logical outline is invaluable. Once you have planned out the steps that logically support your thesis, you will be in an excellent position to go on to write an effective essay.

Activities in this chapter will give you practice in the crucial skill of clearly planning an essay.

Activity

Complete any five of the six informal outlines that follow, by adding a third logical supporting point (*c*) that will parallel the two already provided (*a* and *b*).

1. The first day on a new job can be nerve-wracking.
    a. Meeting new people
    b. Finding your way around a new place

    c. _____

2. My stepmother has three qualities I admire.
    a. Patience
    b. Thoughtfulness

    c. _____

3. At our school, the library is the worst place to study.
    a. Uncomfortable chairs and tables
    b. Little privacy

    c. _____

4. College students should live at home.
   a. Stay in touch with family
   b. Avoid distractions of residence or apartment life

   c. _____

5. _____ is the worst job I've ever had.
   a. Difficult boss
   b. Poor pay

   c. _____

6. College is a stressful situation for many people.
   a. Worry about grades
   b. Worry about being accepted

   c. _____

THE IMPORTANCE OF SPECIFIC DETAILS

Just as a thesis must be developed with three supporting points, those supporting points must be developed with specific details. Specific details have two key values. First of all, details excite the reader's interest. They make writing a pleasure to read, for we all enjoy learning particulars about people, places, and things. Second, details serve to explain a writer's points. They give the evidence needed for us to see and understand general ideas.

All too often, the body paragraphs in essays contain vague generalities rather than the specific supporting details that are needed to engage and convince a reader. Here is what one of the paragraphs in "The Hazards of Movie-Going" would have looked like if the writer had not vividly detailed the supporting evidence.

> Some of the other patrons are even more of a problem than the theatre itself. Many people in the theatre often show themselves to be inconsiderate. They make noises and create disturbances at their seats. Included are people in every age group, from the young to the old. Some act as if they were at home in their own living rooms watching the TV set. And people are often messy, so that you're constantly aware of all the food they're eating. People are also always moving around near you, creating a disturbance and interrupting your enjoyment of the movie.

The box below contrasts the vague support in the preceding paragraph with the specific support in the essay.

Vague Support	*Specific Support*
1. Many people in the theatre show themselves to be inconsiderate. They make noises and create disturbances at their seats. Included are people in every age group, from the young to the old. Some act as if they were at home in their own living rooms watching the TV set.	1. Little kids race up and down the aisles, usually in giggling packs. Teenagers try to impress their friends by talking back to the screen, whistling, and making what they consider to be hilarious noises. Adults act as if they were at home in their own living rooms and comment loudly on the ages of the stars or why movies aren't as good anymore.
2. And people are often messy, so that you're constantly aware of all the food they're eating.	2. And people of all ages crinkle candy wrappers, stick gum on their seats, and drop popcorn tubs or cups of crushed ice and pop on the floor.
3. People are also always moving around nearby, creating a disturbance and interrupting enjoyment of the movie.	3. They also cough and burp, squirm endlessly in their seats, file out for repeated trips to the washrooms or refreshment stand, and elbow you out of the armrest on either side of your seat.

The effective paragraph from the essay provides details that make vividly clear the statement that the patrons are a problem in the theatre. The writer specifies the exact age groups (little kids, teenagers, and adults) and the offenses of each (giggling, talking and whistling, and loud comments). She specifies the various food excesses (crinkled wrappers, gum on seats, dropped popcorn and pop containers). Finally, she provides concrete details that enable us to see and hear other disturbances (coughs and burps, squirming, constant trips to the bathroom, jostling for elbow room). The ineffective paragraph asks us to guess about these details; in the effective paragraph, we vividly see and hear them.

In the strong paragraph, then, the sharp details capture our interest and enable us to share in the writer's experiences. They provide pictures that make each of us feel, "I am there." The particulars also enable us to understand clearly the writer's point that patrons are a problem. You should aim to make your own writing equally convincing by providing detailed support in your papers.

Activity

Write *S* in front of the two selections below that provide specific evidence to support their opening points. Write *X* in front of the two selections that follow their opening points with vague, general, and wordy sentences.

1. Building a wooden deck can be an enjoyable project only if you take certain precautions.

   Get a building permit before you start. If you don't have one, you may have to tear down everything you've built when the town's building inspector learns of your project. Also, purchase pressure-treated lumber for any posts that will be set into the ground. Ordinary wood, not treated with preservatives, will eventually rot from contact with soil and moisture.

2. My mother was a harsh disciplinarian.

   When I did something wrong, no matter how small, she would inflict serious punishment. She had expectations that I was to live up to, and she never changed her attitude. When I did not behave as I should, I was dealt with severely. There were no exceptions as far as my mother was concerned.

3. Some things are worse when they're "improved."

   A good cheesecake, for one thing, is perfect. It doesn't need pineapple, cherries, blueberries, or whipped cream smeared all over it. Plain old blue jeans, the ones with five pockets and copper rivets, are perfect too. Manufacturers only made them worse when they added baggy or too-narrow legs, took away the pockets, tightened the fit, and plastered white logos and designers' names all over them.

4. Pets can be more trouble than children.

   My dog, unlike my children, has never been completely house-broken. When he's excited or nervous, he still has an occasional problem. My dog, unlike my children, has never learned how to take care of himself when we're away, despite the fact that we've given him plenty of time to do so. We don't have to worry about our grown children anymore. However, we still have to hire a dog-sitter for him.

THE IMPORTANCE OF ADEQUATE DETAILS

One of the most common and serious problems in student writing is inadequate development. You must provide *enough* specific details to support fully the point in a body paragraph of an essay. You could not, for example, include a paragraph about a friend's unreliability and provide only a short example. You would have to add several other examples or provide an extended example showing your friend as an unreliable person. Without such additional support, your paragraph would be underdeveloped.

Students may try to disguise unsupported paragraphs through repetition and generalities. Do not to fall into this "wordiness trap." Be prepared to do the plain hard work needed to ensure that each paragraph has solid support.

Activity 1

Both of the following body paragraphs were written on the same topic, and both have clear opening points. Which one is adequately developed? Which one, on the other hand, has only several particulars and uses mostly vague, general, wordy sentences to conceal the fact that it is starved for specific details?

Eternal Youth?--No Thanks

I wouldn't want to be a teenager again, first of all, because I wouldn't want to worry about talking to girls. I still remember how scary it was to call up a girl and ask her out. My heart would race, my pulse would pound, and perspiration would trickle down my face, adding to my acne by the second. I never knew whether my voice would come out deep and masculine, like Leslie Nielsen's, or squeaky, like Pee Wee Herman's. Then there were the questions: Would she be at home? If she were, would she want to talk to me? And if she did, what would I say? The one time I did get up the nerve to take a girl in my homeroom to a movie, I was so tongue-tied that I stared silently at the box of popcorn in my lap until the feature finally started. Needless to say, I wasn't very interesting company.

Terrors of My Teenage Years

I wouldn't want to be a teenager again, first of all, because I wouldn't want to worry about talking to girls. Calling up a girl to ask her out was something that I completely dreaded. I didn't know what words to express or how to express them. I would have all the symptoms of nervousness when I got on the phone. I worried a great deal about how I would sound, and I had a lot of doubts about the girl's reaction. Once, I managed to call up a girl to go out, but the evening turned out to be a disaster. I was too unsure of myself to act in a confident way. I couldn't think of anything to say and just kept quiet. Now that I look back on it, I really made a fool of myself. Agonizing over my attempts at relationships with the opposite sex made adolescence a very uncomfortable time.

The first paragraph offers a series of well-detailed examples of the author's nerve-wracking experiences, as a teenager, with girls. The second paragraph, on the other hand, is underdeveloped. It speaks only of the "torture" of calling up a girl, whereas the first paragraph supplies such particulars as "My heart would race, my pulse would pound, and perspiration would trickle down my face." The second paragraph describes in a general way being "worried about my voice," whereas in the first paragraph, the author wonders if his voice will "come out deep and masculine, like Leslie Nielsen's, or squeaky, like Pee Wee Herman's." And there is no specific description in the second paragraph of the evening that turned into a disaster. In summary, the second paragraph lacks the full detailed support needed to develop its opening point convincingly.

Activity 2

Take a few minutes to write a paragraph supporting the point that "My room is a mess." Afterwards, you and your classmates (or the other students in the small group you may be working within) should all read your paragraphs aloud. The most well-received paragraphs will be those with plenty of specific details.

Practice in Advancing and Supporting a Thesis

You now know the two most important steps in competent essay writing: (1) advancing a point or thesis and (2) supporting that thesis. The purpose of this section is to expand and strengthen your understanding of these two basic steps. You will first work through a series of activities on *developing* a thesis:

1 Identifying the different parts of an essay
2 Evaluating thesis statements
3 Completing thesis statements
4 Writing a thesis statement
5 Limiting a topic and writing a thesis

You will then sharpen your understanding of how to *support* a thesis effectively by working through the following activities:

6 Making words and phrases specific

7 Making sentences specific

8 Providing specific evidence

9 Identifying adequate supporting evidence

10 Adding details to complete an essay

1 IDENTIFYING THE DIFFERENT PARTS OF AN ESSAY

Activity

This activity will sharpen your sense of the different parts of an essay. A student essay titled "Coping with Old Age" appears below with no indentations between paragraphs. Read the essay carefully, and then double-underline the thesis and single-underline the topic sentence for each of the three supporting paragraphs and the first sentence of the conclusion. Then write the numbers of those sentences in the spaces provided at the end.

Coping with Old Age

¹I recently read about an area of Russia where many people live to be well over a hundred years old. ²Being 115 or even 125 isn't considered unusual there, and these old people continue to do productive work right up until they die. ³Canada, however, isn't such a healthy place for older people. ⁴Since I retired from my job, I've had to cope with the physical, mental, and emotional stresses of being "old." ⁵For one thing, I've had to adjust to physical changes. ⁶Now that I'm over sixty, the trusty body that carried me around for years has turned traitor. ⁷Aside from the deepening wrinkles on my face and neck, and the wiry grey hairs that have replaced my brown hair, I face more frightening changes. ⁸I don't have the energy I used to. ⁹My eyes get tired. ¹⁰Once in a while, I miss something that's said to me. ¹¹My once-faithful feet seem to have lost their comfortable soles, and I sometimes feel I'm walking on marbles. ¹²In order to fight against this slow decay, I exercise whenever I can. ¹³I walk, I stretch, and I climb stairs. ¹⁴I battle constantly to keep as fit as possible. ¹⁵I'm also trying to cope with mental changes. ¹⁶My mind was once as quick and sure as a champion gymnast. ¹⁷I never found it difficult to memorize answers in school or to remember the names of people I met. ¹⁸Now, I occasionally have to search my mind for the name of a close neighbour or favourite television show.

[19]Because my mind needs exercise, too, I challenge it as much as I can. [20]Taking a college course like this English class, for example, forces me to concentrate. [21]The mental gymnast may be a little slow and out of shape, but he can still do a backflip or turn a somersault when he has to. [22]Finally, I must deal with the emotional impact of being old. [23]Our society typecasts old people. [24]We're supposed to be unattractive, senile, useless leftovers. [25]We're supposed to be the crazy drivers and the cranky customers. [26]At first, I was angry and frustrated that I was considered old at all. [27]And I knew that people were wrong to stereotype me. [28]Then I got depressed. [29]I even started to think that maybe I was a cast-off, one of those old animals that slow down the rest of the herd. [30]But I have now decided to rebel against these negative feelings. [31]I try to have friends of all ages and to keep up with what's going on in the world. [32]I try to remember that I'm still the same person who sat at a first-grade desk, who fell in love, who comforted a child, who got a raise at work. [33]I'm not "just" an old person. [34]Coping with the changes of old age has become my latest full-time job. [35]Even though it's a job I never applied for, and one for which I had no experience, I'm trying to do the best I can.

Thesis statement: _____

Topic sentence of first supporting paragraph: _____

Topic sentence of second supporting paragraph: _____

Topic sentence of third supporting paragraph: _____

First sentence of the conclusion: _____

2 EVALUATING THESIS STATEMENTS

As was explained on pages 37–38, some writers substitute announcements of a subject for a true thesis idea. Others write statements that are too narrow to need support or development. Contrasting with such dead-end statements are ones that are wide open—too broad to be adequately supported in the limited space of a five-hundred-word essay. Finally, some thesis statements are vague, often containing more than one idea. They suggest that a writer has not thought out his or her main point sufficiently.

Activity 1

Write *A* beside the sentences that are announcements rather than thesis statements. Write *OK* beside the statement in each pair that is a clear, limited point that could be developed in an essay.

1. _____ a. This essay will discuss the people you meet in exercise class.

   _____ b. The kinds of workout clothes worn in my aerobics class identify the "jocks," "strugglers," and "clotheshorses."

2. _____ a. I made several mistakes in the process of trying to win the respect and affection of my teenage stepson.

   _____ b. My thesis in this paper is relationships between step-parents and stepchildren.

3. _____ a. A period of loneliness can teach you to use your creativity, sort out your values, and feel empathy for others.

   _____ b. Loneliness is the subject of this paper.

4. _____ a. This paper will be about sharing housework.

   _____ b. Deciding who will perform certain unpleasant household chores can be the crisis that makes or breaks a marriage.

5. _____ a. My concern here is to discuss the "near-death" experiences reported by some patients.

   _____ b. There are several possible explanations for the similar "near-death" experiences reported by some patients.

Activity 2

Write *TN* beside statements that are too narrow to be developed in an essay. Write *OK* beside the statement in each pair that is a clear, limited point.

1. _____ a. I had squash, tomatoes, and corn in my garden last summer.

   _____ b. Vegetable gardening can be a frustrating hobby.

2. _____ a. The main road into our town is lined with billboards.

   _____ b. For several reasons, billboards should be abolished.

3. _____ a. There are more single-parent households in our country than ever.

   _____ b. Organization is the key to being a successful single parent.

4. _____ a. In my first job, I learned that I had several bad work habits.

   _____ b. Because I was late for work yesterday, I lost an hour's pay and was called in to see the boss.

5. _____ a. Some Canadians abuse alcohol because liquor has become such an important part of our personal and public celebrations.

   _____ b. Consumption of wine, beer, and hard liquor actually does not increase in Canada every year.

Activity 3

Write *TB* beside statements that are too broad to be developed in an essay. Write *OK* beside the statement in each pair that is a clear, limited point.

1. _____ a. In many ways, sports are an important part of Canadian life.

   _____ b. Legalized gambling in some Canadian cities has changed people's daily lives for the worse.

2. _____ a. Modern life makes people suspicious and unfriendly.

   _____ b. A succession of frightening news stories has made me lose my trust in strangers.

3. _____ a. Toy ads on television teach children to be greedy, competitive, and snobbish.

   _____ b. Advertising has a bad influence on the values that children develop in life.

4. _____ a. Learning new skills can be difficult and frustrating.

   _____ b. Learning a skill like writing takes work, patience, and a sense of humour.

5. _____ a. I didn't get along with my family, so I did many foolish things.

   _____ b. Running away from home taught me that my parents weren't as terrible as I thought.

Activity 4

For each pair of statements, write *2* beside the one that contains more than one idea. Write *OK* beside the one in each pair that is a clear, limited point.

1. _____ a. Working with old people changed my stereotyped ideas about the elderly.

   _____ b. My life has moved in new directions since the rewarding job I had working with older people last summer.

2. _____ a. The new architecture on this campus is very unpleasant, although the expansion was desperately needed.

   _____ b. Our new college library building is ugly, intimidating, and inefficient.

3. _____ a. Among the most entertaining ads on TV today are those for mail-order products.

   _____ b. Although ads on TV for mail-order products are often misleading, they can still be very entertaining.

4. _____   a. My room-mate and I are compatible in most ways, but we still have conflicts at times.

_____   b. My room-mate has his own unique systems for studying, writing term papers, and cleaning his room.

5. _____   a. Although some good movies have come out lately, I prefer to watch old movies because they're more interesting.

_____   b. Movies of the thirties and forties had better plots, sets, and performers than the ones made today.

3   COMPLETING THESIS STATEMENTS

Activity

Complete the following thesis statements by adding a third supporting point that will parallel the two already provided. You might want to check first the section on parallelism (pages 363–366) to make sure you understand parallel form.

1. Because I never took college preparatory courses in high school, I entered college deficient in mathematics, study skills, and _____.

2. A good salesperson needs to like people, to be aggressive, and _____
_____.

3. Rather than blame myself for failing the course, I blamed the professor, my adviser, and even _____.

4. Anyone who buys an old house planning to fix it up should be prepared to put in a lot of time, hard work, and _____.

5. Our old car eats gas, makes funny noises, and _____.

6. My mother, my boss, and my _____ are three people who are very important in my life right now.

7. Getting married too young was a mistake because we hadn't finished our education, we weren't ready for children, and _____
_____
_____.

8. Some restaurant patrons seem to leave their honesty, their cleanliness, and their _____ at home.

9. During my first semester at college, I had to learn how to manage my time, how to manage my diet, and _____.

10. Three experiences I wish I could forget are the time I fell off a ladder, the time I tried to fix my parents' lawn mower, and _____

_____

_____.

4   WRITING A THESIS STATEMENT

Activity

This activity will give you practice in writing an effective thesis—one that is neither too broad nor too narrow for the supporting points in an essay. An added value of the activity is that sometimes you will construct your thesis after you have decided what your supporting points will be. You will need to know, then, how to write a thesis that will match exactly the points that you have developed.

1. Thesis: _____
   a. My first car was a rebellious-looking one which matched the way I felt and acted as a teenager.
   b. My next car reflected my more mature and practical adult self.
   c. My latest car seems to tell me that I'm aging; it shows my growing concern with comfort and safety.

2. Thesis: _____
   a. Attending a college offers the chance to prepare for a career or further educational demands.
   b. If the college is nearby, there are no room and board costs.
   c. The course credits that are accumulated can be transferred to some universities.

3. Thesis: _____
   a. First, I tried simply avoiding the snacks aisle of the supermarket.
   b. Then I started limiting myself to only five units of any given snack.
   c. Finally, in desperation, I began keeping the cellophane bags of snacks in a padlocked cupboard.

4. Thesis: _____
   a. The holiday can be frightening for little children and can encourage vandalism in older ones.

    b. Children can be struck by cars while wearing vision-obstructing masks and dark costumes.

    c. More and more incidents of deadly treats filled with razor blades or contaminated with poisons are occurring.

5. Thesis: _____

    a. First of all, I was a typical "type A" personality: anxious, impatient, and hard-driving.

    b. I also had a family history of relatives with heart trouble.

    c. My unhealthy lifestyle, though, was probably the major factor.

5 LIMITING A TOPIC AND WRITING A THESIS

The following two activities will give you practice in distinguishing general from limited subjects and in writing a thesis.

Activity 1

Look carefully at the ten general and limited subjects below. Then see if you can write a thesis for any five of the limited subjects.

Hint: To create a thesis for a limited subject, ask yourself, "What point do I want to make about _____ (*my limited subject*)?"

General Subject	*Limited Subject*
1. Apartment	1. Sharing an apartment with a roommate
2. Self-improvement	2. Behaviour toward others
3. Family	3. My mother
4. Eating out	4. Fast-food restaurants
5. Automobiles	5. Bad driving habits
6. Health	6. Regular exercise
7. Owning a house	7. Do-it-yourself repairs around the house
8. Hockey	8. NHL expansion
9. Parenthood	9. Being a single parent
10. Pollution	10. Noise pollution

Thesis statements for five of the limited subjects:

_____

_____

_____

_____

_____

_____

_____

_____

Activity 2

Here is a list of ten general subjects. Limit five of the subjects. Then write theses about those five limited subjects.

General Subject	*Limited Subject*
1. Pets	_____
2. Teenagers	_____
3. Television	_____
4. Work	_____
5. College	_____
6. Doctors	_____
7. Holidays	_____
8. Cooking	_____
9. Money	_____
10. Shopping	_____

Thesis statements for five of the limited subjects:

_____

_____

_____

_____

_____

_____

_____

_____

_____

_____

6 MAKING WORDS AND PHRASES SPECIFIC

To be an effective writer, you must use specific rather than general words. Specific words create pictures in the reader's mind. They help capture interest and make your meaning clear.

Activity

This activity will give you practice at changing vague, indefinite words into sharp, specific ones. Add three or more specific words to replace the general word or words italicized in each sentence. Make changes in the wording of a sentence as necessary.

>*Several of our appliances* broke down at the same time.
>
>_Our washer, refrigerator, and television broke down at the_
>_same time._

1. *Salty snacks* are my diet downfall.

_____

_____

_____

2. *Several sections* of the newspaper were missing.

_____

_____

_____

3. *Various gifts for men* were displayed in the department-store window.

_____

_____

_____

4. *Several items in my purse* had been crushed.

_____

_____

_____

5. I swept aside the *things* on my desk in order to spread out the road map.

_____

_____

_____

6. The waitress told us we could have *several types of potatoes*.

_____

_____

_____

7. The doctor examined *various parts of my body* before diagnosing my illness as bronchitis.

_____

_____

_____

8. The *food choices* in the cafeteria were unappetizing.

_____

_____

_____

9. Ali threw all the *junk* from the bottom of his closet into a large cardboard carton.

_____

_____

_____

10. Our neighbour's family room has *a lot of electronic equipment.*

_____

_____

_____

7 MAKING SENTENCES SPECIFIC

Again, you will practise changing vague, indefinite writing into lively, image-filled writing that helps capture your reader's interest and makes your meaning clear.
Compare the following sentences:

General	*Specific*
She walked down the street.	Crystal wandered slowly along Rogers Lane.
Animals came into the space.	Hungry lions padded silently into the sawdust-covered arena.
The man signed the paper.	The biology teacher hastily scribbled his name on the course withdrawal slip.

The specific sentences create clear pictures in our minds. The details *show* us exactly what has happened. Here are four ways to make your sentences specific.

1 Use exact names.
He sold his *camper.*   *Vince* sold his *Winnebago.*

2 Use lively verbs.
The flag *moved* in the breeze.   The flag *fluttered* in the breeze.

3 Use descriptive words (modifiers) before nouns.
A man strained to lift the crate.
A *heavyset, perspiring* man strained to lift the *heavy wooden* crate.

4 Use words that relate to the senses—sight, hearing, taste, smell, touch.

That man jogs five miles a day.

That *fragile-looking, grey-haired* man jogs five miles a day. *(sight)*

A noise told the crowd that there were two minutes left to play.

A *piercing whistle* told the *cheering* crowd that there were two minutes left to play. *(hearing)*

When he returned, all he found in the refrigerator was bread and milk.

When he returned, all he found in the refrigerator was *stale* bread and *sour* milk. *(taste)*

Neil stroked the kitten's fur until he felt its tiny claws on his hand.

Neil stroked the kitten's *velvety* fur until he felt its tiny, *needle-sharp* claws on his hand. *(touch)*

Tammy placed a sachet in her dresser drawer.

Tammy placed a *lilac-scented* sachet in her dresser drawer. *(smell)*

Activity

With the help of the methods described above, add specific details to any ten of the twelve sentences that follow. Use separate paper.

Examples   The person got off the bus.

The teenage boy bounded down the steps of the shiny

yellow school bus.

She worked hard all summer.

All summer, Sherry sorted peaches and blueberries in the

hot, noisy canning factory.

1. The car would not start.
2. The test was difficult.
3. The boy was tired.
4. My room needs cleaning.
5. The student was bored.
6. The game was exciting.

7. A fire started.
8. A vehicle blocked traffic.
9. A large rock fell.
10. The salesperson was obnoxious.
11. The child started to cry.
12. The lounge area was busy.

8   PROVIDING SPECIFIC EVIDENCE

Activity

Provide three details that logically support each of the following points. Your details can be drawn from your direct experience or they can be invented. In each case, the details should show in a specific way what the point expresses in only a general way. State your details briefly in several words rather than in complete sentences.

Example   We quickly spruced up the apartment before our guest arrived.

1.   Hide toys and newspapers in spare closet

2.   Vacuum pet hairs off sofa

3.   Spray air freshener around living room

1.   The dinner was a disaster.

_____

_____

_____

2.   My seven-year-old nephew has some disgusting habits.

_____

_____

_____

3.   There are several reasons why I put off studying.

_____

_____

_____

4.   My parents never allowed me to think for myself.

_____

_____

_____

5.   I have several ways in which I can earn extra cash.

_____

_____

_____

6. My car needs repairs.

_____

_____

_____

7. Friday evening, I didn't sit still for a minute.

_____

_____

_____

8. Mr. or Ms. _____ was the worst teacher I ever had.

_____

_____

_____

9 IDENTIFYING ADEQUATE SUPPORTING EVIDENCE

Activity

The following body paragraphs were taken from student essays. Two of the paragraphs provide sufficient details to support their topic sentences convincingly. Write *AD* for *adequate development* beside those paragraphs. Three paragraphs use vague, wordy, general, or irrelevant sentences as an excuse for real supporting details. Write *U* for *underdeveloped* beside those paragraphs.

_____ 1.　　Another consideration in adopting a dog is the cost. Initial fees for shots and a licence might add up to $100. Annual visits to the vet for heartworm pills, rabies or distemper shots, and general checkups could cost $150 or more. Then, there is the cost of food. A ten-kilo bag of dry food (the cheapest kind) costs around $20. A large dog can eat that much in a couple of weeks.

_____ 2.　　People can be cruel to pets simply by being thoughtless. They don't think about a pet's needs or simply ignore the needs. It never occurs to them that their pet can be experiencing a great deal of discomfort as a result of their failure to be sensitive. The cruelty is a result of the basic lack of attention and concern--qualities that should be there, but aren't.

_____ 3.　　If I were in charge of the night-time programming on a TV network, I would make changes. I would completely eliminate some shows. In fact, all of the shows that proved of little interest would be cancelled. Commercials would also change, so that it would be possible to watch them without wanting to turn off the TV set. I would expand the good shows so that people would come away with an even better experience. My ideal network would be a great improvement over the average line-up we see today on any of the major networks.

_____ 4.　　A friend's rudeness is much more damaging than a stranger's. When a friend says sharply, "I don't have time to talk to you just now," you feel hurt instead of angry. When a friend shows up late for lunch or a shopping trip, with no good reason, you feel that you're being taken for granted. Worst, though, is a friend who pretends to be listening to you but whose wandering eyes reveal a lack of attention. Then you feel betrayed. Friends, after all, are supposed to make up for the thoughtless cruelties of strangers.

_____ 5.　　Giving my first shampoo and cut to a real person, after weeks of practising on wigs, was a nerve-wracking experience. The customer was a woman who was very set in her ways. She tried to describe what she wanted, and I tried without much success to understand what she had in mind. Every time I did something, she seemed to be indicating in one way or another that it was not what she wanted. I got more and more nervous as I worked on her hair, and the nervousness showed. The worst part of the ordeal happened at the very end, when I added the final touches. Nothing, to this woman, had turned out right.

10　ADDING DETAILS TO COMPLETE AN ESSAY

Activity

The following essay needs specific details to back up the ideas in its supporting paragraphs. In the spaces provided, add a sentence or two of clear, convincing details for each idea. This activity will give you practice at supplying specific details and an initial feel for writing an essay.

Life without Television

Introduction　　When my family's only television set went to the repair shop the other day, my parents, my sister, and I thought we would have a terrible week. How could we get through the long evenings in such a quiet house? What would it be like without all the shows to keep us company? We soon realized, though, that living without television for a while was a stroke of good fortune. It became easy for each of us to enjoy some activities alone, to complete some postponed chores, and to spend rewarding time with each other and friends.

*First
supporting
paragraph*

First of all, with no television to compete for our time, we found plenty of hours for personal interests. We all read more that week than we had read during the six months before. _____

_____

_____

_____

We each also enjoyed some hobbies we had ignored for ages. _____

_____

_____

_____

In addition, my sister and I both stopped procrastinating with our homework. _____

_____

_____

_____

*Second
supporting
paragraph*

Second, we did chores that had been hanging over our heads for too long. There were many jobs around the house that had needed attention for some time. _____

_____

_____

We also had a chance to do some long-postponed shopping. _____

_____

_____

_____

And each of us also did some letter writing or other paperwork that was long overdue. _____

_____

_____

*Third
supporting
paragraph*

Finally, and probably most important, we spent time with each other. Instead of being in the same room together while we stared at a screen, we actually talked for many pleasant hours. _____

_____

_____

Moreover, for the first time in years my family played some games together. _____

_____

_____

And because we didn't have to worry about missing this or that show, we had some family friends over on a couple of evenings and spent an enjoyable time with them. _____

_____

_____

Conclusion

Once our television set returned, we were not prepared to put it in the attic. But we had a sense of how it can take over our lives if we are not careful. We are now more selective. We turn on the set for our favourite shows, certain sports events, and the news, but we don't leave it running all night. As a result, we find we can enjoy television and still have time left over for other activities and interests.

THE THIRD
AND FOURTH
STEPS
IN ESSAY
WRITING

This chapter will show you how to:

- **Organize and connect the specific evidence in the body paragraphs of an essay**
- **Begin and end the essay with effective introductory and concluding paragraphs**
- **Write clear, error-free sentences**

You know from the previous chapter that the first two steps in writing an effective essay are advancing a thesis and supporting it with specific evidence. The third step is to organize and connect the specific evidence, which appears in the supporting paragraphs of the essay. Most of this chapter will deal with the chief ways to organize and connect this supporting information in a paper. The chapter will also discuss how to start the essay smoothly with a suitable introductory paragraph and how to finish it effectively with a well-rounded concluding paragraph. Finally, the chapter will look briefly at the sentence skills that make up the fourth and final step in writing a successful paper.

Step 3:
Organize and Connect
the Specific Evidence

At the same time that you are generating the specific details needed to support a thesis, you should be thinking about ways to organize and connect those details. All the details in your essay must cohere, or stick together; in this way, your reader will be able to move smoothly and clearly from one bit of supporting information to the next. This section will discuss the following ways to organize and connect supporting details: (1) common methods of organization, (2) transitions, and (3) other connecting words.

COMMON METHODS OF ORGANIZATION

Time order and emphatic order are common methods used to organize the supporting material in an essay. (You will learn more specific methods of development in Part Two of this book.)

Time, or *chronological, order* simply means that details are listed as they occur in time. *First* this is done; *next* this; *then* this; *after* that, this; and so on. Here is an outline of an essay in this book in which time order is used.

Thesis: However, for success in exercise, you should follow a simple plan consisting of arranging the time, making preparations, and following the sequence with care.

   1. To begin with, set aside a regular hour for exercise.
   2. Next, prepare for your exercise session.
   3. If this is your first attempt at exercising, start slowly.

Fill in the missing word: The topic sentences in the essay use the words <u>To begin with</u> and _____ to help show time order.

Here is one supporting paragraph from the essay:

Next, prepare for your exercise session. You do this, first, by not eating or drinking anything for an hour before the session. Why risk an upset stomach? Then, dress comfortably in something that allows you to move freely. Since you'll be in your own home, there's no need to invest in a high-fashion dance costume. A loose T-shirt and shorts are good. A bathing suit is great in summer, and in winter a set of long underwear is warm and comfortable. If your hair tends to flop in your eyes, pin it back or wear a headband or scarf. After dressing, prepare the exercise area. Turn off the phone and lock the door to prevent interruptions. Shove the coffee table out of the way so you won't bruise yourself on it. Finally, get out the simple materials you'll need to exercise on.

Fill in the missing words: The paragraph uses the following words to help show time order: _____ Next _____, _____, _____, _____, and _____.

Emphatic order is sometimes described as "save-the-best-till-last" order. It means that the most interesting or important detail is placed in the last part of a paragraph or in the final supporting paragraph of an essay. (In cases where all the details seem equal in importance, the writer should impose a personal order that seems logical or appropriate to the details in question.) The last position in a paper is the most emphatic position because the reader is most likely to remember the last thing read. *Finally, last of all,* and *most important* are typical words showing emphasis. Here is an outline of an essay in the book that uses emphatic order:

Thesis: Celebrities lead very stressful lives; for, no matter how glamorous or powerful they are, they have too little privacy, too much pressure, and no safety.

1. For one thing, celebrities don't have the privacy an ordinary person does.
2. In addition, celebrities are under constant pressure.
3. Most important, celebrities must deal with the stress of being in constant danger.

Fill in the missing words: The topic sentences in the essay use the words _____ For one thing _____, _____, and _____ to help show emphatic order.

Here is the third supporting paragraph from the essay:

Most important, celebrities must deal with the stress of being in constant danger. The friendly grabs, hugs, and kisses of enthusiastic fans can quickly turn into uncontrolled assaults on a celebrity's hair, clothes, and car. Also, celebrities often get strange letters from people who become fixated on their idols or from people who threaten to harm them. Worst of all, threats can turn into deeds. One fan's obsessive pursuit of Anne Murray and the murder of John Lennon came about because two unbalanced people tried to transfer the celebrity's fame to themselves. Famous people must live with the fact that they are always fair game--and never out of season.

Fill in the missing words: The words _____ are used to mark the most emphatic detail in the paragraph.

Some essays use a combination of time order and emphatic order. For example, the essay on movie-going in the first chapter includes a time order: The writer first talks of getting to the theatre, then of the theatre itself, and finally of the behaviour of patrons during the movie. At the same time, the writer uses an emphatic order, ending with the most important reason for her dislike of movie-going: "Some of the other patrons are even more of a problem than the theatre itself."

Activity

Part A: Read the essays referred to below and identify their method of organizing details—through time order, emphatic order, or a combination of both.

1.   "My First Professional Performance" (page 206)

   _____

2.   "A Vote for McDonald's" (page 159)

   _____

3.   "Everyday Cruelty" (page 124)

   _____

Part B: See if you can now complete the explanations that follow.

The essay titled "My First Professional Performance" uses *(add the missing word)* _____ order. The writer begins with the problems she experienced when she arrived at the carnival grounds, moves on to problems during the performance, and ends with the concert's rather abrupt finish. "A Vote for McDonald's" uses *(add the missing word)* _____ order. The writer presents three advantages of eating at McDonald's and ends with the most important one: reasonable prices. "Everyday Cruelty" uses a combination of *(add the missing words)* _____ order and _____ order. It moves from the beginning to the end of a particular workday. It also ends with the "worst incident of mean-spiritedness" that the writer witnessed that day.

TRANSITIONS

Transitions are signals that help readers follow the direction of the writer's thought. They are like signposts on the road that guide travellers. In the box that follows are some common transitional words and phrases, grouped according to the kind of signal they give to readers. Note that certain words provide more than one kind of signal.

Addition signals: one, first of all, second, the third reason, also, next, another, and, in addition, moreover, furthermore, finally, last of all

Time signals: first, then, next, after, as, before, while, meanwhile, soon, now, during, finally

Space signals: next to, across, on the opposite side, to the left, to the right, above, below, nearby

Change-of-direction signals: but, however, yet, in contrast, although, otherwise, still, on the contrary, on the other hand

Illustration signals: for example, for instance, specifically, as an illustration, once, such as

Conclusion signals: therefore, consequently, thus, then, as a result, in summary, to conclude, last of all, finally

---

Activity

1. Underline the four *addition* signals in the following selection:

> The simplest way of coping with stress is to modify or remove its source--for example, by leaving a stressful job. Obviously this is often impossible, which is why learning to manage stress is so important. There are important things you can do to manage the daily stress in your life. One step is to become involved in any type of full-body exercise. Because stress prepares the body for action, its effects can be broken up by using the body. A second way you can relieve stress is by meditation. Meditation is an ideal stress-reliever for several reasons. It quiets the body and promotes relaxation. Moreover, it's easy to learn--taking an expensive commercial course is unnecessary. Another benefit of meditation is that it takes many forms, so it can satisfy many people with many different interests.

2. Underline the three *time* signals in the following selection:

Once you've snagged the job of TV sports reporter, you have to begin working on the details of your image. First, invest in two or three truly loud sports jackets. Look for broad stripes and gigantic plaid patterns in odd colour combinations like purple and green or orange and blue. These should become familiar enough to viewers so that they will associate that crazy jacket with that dynamic sportscaster. Next, try to cultivate a distinctive voice that will be just annoying enough to be memorable. A nasal whine or a gravelly growl will do it. Be sure to speak only in tough, punchy sentences that seem to be punctuated with imaginary exclamation points. Finally, you must share lots of pompous, obnoxious opinions with your viewers. Your tone of voice must convey the hidden message, "I dare anyone to disagree with me." When the home teams lose, call them bums. When players strike, talk sarcastically about the good old days. When a sports franchise leaves town, say, "Good riddance."

3. Underline the three *space* signals in the following selection:

The vegetable bin of my refrigerator contained an assortment of weird-looking items. Next to a shrivelled, white-coated lemon was a pair of oranges covered with blue fuzz. To the right of the oranges was a bunch of carrots that had begun to sprout points, spikes, knobs, and tendrils. The carrots drooped into U-shapes as I picked them up with the tips of my fingers. Near the carrots was a net bag of onions; each onion had sent curling shoots through the net until the whole thing resembled a mass of green spaghetti. The most horrible item, though, was a head of lettuce that had turned into a pool of brown goo. It had seeped out of its bag and coated the bottom of the bin with a sticky, evil-smelling liquid.

4. Underline the two *change-of-direction* signals in the following selection:

Taking small children on vacation, for instance, sounds like a wonderful experience for the entire family. But vacations can be scary or emotionally overwhelming times for children. When children are taken away from their usual routine and brought to an unfamiliar place, they can become very frightened. That strange bed in the motel room or the unusual noises in Grandma's spare bedroom may cause nightmares. On vacations, too, children usually clamour to do as many things in one day as they can and to stay up past their usual bedtime. And, since it is vacation time, parents may decide to give in to the children's demands. A parental attitude like this, however, can lead to problems. After a sixteen-hour day of touring the amusement park, eating in a restaurant, and seeing a movie, children can experience sensory and emotional overload. They become cranky, unhappy, or even rebellious and angry.

5. Underline the two *illustration* signals in the following selection:

> Supermarkets also use psychology to encourage you to buy. For example, in most supermarkets, the milk and the bread are either at opposite ends of the store or located far away from the first aisle. Even if you've stopped at the market only for staples like these, you must pass hundreds of items in order to reach them. The odds are that instead of leaving with a litre of milk, you'll leave with additional purchases as well. Special displays, such as a pyramid of canned green beans in an aisle or a large end display of cartons of paper towels, also increase sales. Because you assume that these items are a good buy, you may pick them up. However, they may not even be on sale! Store managers know that customers are automatically attracted to these displays, and they will use them to move an overstocked product.

6. Underline the two *conclusion* signals in the following selection:

> Finally, my grandmother was extremely thrifty. She was one of those people who hoard pieces of used aluminum foil after carefully scraping off the cake icing or beef gravy. She had a drawer full of old eyeglasses that dated back at least thirty years. The lens prescriptions were no longer accurate, but Gran couldn't bear to throw away "a good pair of glasses." She kept them "just in case," but we could never figure out what situation would involve a desperate need for a dozen pairs of old eyeglasses. We never realized the true extent of Gran's thriftiness, though, until after she died. Her house was to be sold, and therefore we cleaned out its dusty attic. In one corner was a cardboard box filled with five- and ten-centimetre pieces of string. The box was labelled, in Gran's spidery hand, "String too short to be saved."

TRANSITIONAL SENTENCES

Transitions occur not only *within* the supporting paragraphs in an essay but also *between* the paragraphs. *Transitional*, or *linking*, *sentences* are used to help tie together the supporting paragraphs in an essay. They enable the reader to move smoothly and clearly from one idea and paragraph in an essay to the next idea and paragraph. Here are the two linking sentences in the essay on movie-going:

> Once you have made it to the box office and got your tickets, you're confronted with the problems of the theatre itself.

The words *made it to the box office* remind us of the point of the first supporting paragraph, while *confronted with the problems of the theatre itself* presents the point to be developed in the second supporting paragraph.

Some of the other patrons are even more of a problem than the theatre itself.

The words *the theatre itself* echo the point of the second supporting paragraph, while *some of the other patrons* announces the topic of the third supporting paragraph.

Activity

Given below is a brief sentence outline of an essay. In the outline, the second and third topic sentences serve as transitional or linking sentences. They both remind us of the point in the preceding paragraph and announce the point to be developed in the present paragraph. In the space provided, add the words needed to complete the second and third topic sentences.

Thesis

The most important values I learned from my parents are the importance of family support, of hard work, and of a good education.

First supporting paragraph

First, my parents taught me that family members should stick together, especially in times of trouble. ...

Second supporting paragraph

In addition to teaching me about the importance of _____

_____

my parents taught me the value of _____

_____....

Third supporting paragraph

Along with the value of _____

my parents emphasized the benefits of _____

_____....

OTHER CONNECTING WORDS

In addition to transitions, there are three other kinds of connecting words that help tie together the specific evidence in a paper: repeated words, pronouns, and synonyms. Each will be discussed in turn.

Repeated Words

Many of us have been taught by English teachers—correctly so—not to repeat ourselves in our writing. On the other hand, repeating *key* words can help tie together the flow of thought in a paper. Below is a selection that uses repeated words effectively to remind readers of the key idea on which the discussion is centred:

> One reason for studying psychology is to help you deal with your children. Perhaps your young daughter refuses to go to bed when you want her to and bursts into tears at the least mention of "lights out." A little knowledge of psychology comes in handy. Offer her a choice of staying up until 7:30 with you or going upstairs and playing until 8:00. Since she gets to make the choice, she does not feel so powerless and will not resist. Psychology is also useful in rewarding a child for a job well done. Instead of telling your ten-year-old son what a good boy he is when he makes his own bed, tell him how neat it looks, how happy you are to see it, and how proud of him you are for doing it by himself. The psychology books will tell you that being a good boy is much harder to live up to than doing one job well.

Pronouns

Pronouns (*he, she, it, you, they, this, that*, and others) are another way to connect ideas as you develop a paper. Using pronouns to take the place of other words or ideas can help you avoid needless repetition in a paper. (Note, however, that although pronouns are helpful, they should be used with care in order to avoid the unclear or inconsistent pronoun references described in this book on pages 367–379.) Here is a selection that makes use of pronouns:

> Another way for people to economize at an amusement park is to bring their own food. If they pack a nourishing, well-balanced lunch of cold chicken, carrot sticks, and fruit, they will avoid having to pay high prices for hamburgers and hot dogs. They will also save on calories. Also, instead of filling up on soft drinks, they should bring a thermos of iced tea. It is more refreshing than pop, and it is a great deal cheaper. Every dollar that is not spent at a refreshment stand is one that can be spent on another ride.

Synonyms

Using synonyms (that is, words that are alike in meaning) also can help move the reader clearly from one step in the thought of a paper to the next. In addition, the use of synonyms increases variety and interest by avoiding needless repetition of the same words.

Note the synonyms for *method* in the following selection:

There are several methods of fund-raising that work well with small organizations. One technique is to hold an auction, with everyone either contributing an item from home or obtaining a donation from a sympathetic local merchant. Because all the merchandise, including the services of the auctioneer, has been donated, the entire proceeds can be placed in the organization's treasury. A second fund-raising procedure is a car wash. Club members and their children get together on a Saturday and wash all the cars in the neighbourhood for a few dollars apiece. A final, time-tested way to raise money is to give a bake sale, with each family contributing home-made cookies, brownies, layer cakes, or cupcakes. Sold by the piece or by the box, these baked goods will satisfyingly fill both the stomach and the cashbox.

Activity

Read the selection below and then answer the questions about it that follow:

¹When I think about my childhood in the 1930s, today's energy crisis and lowered thermostats don't seem so bad. ²In our house, we had only a wood-burning cookstove in the kitchen to keep us warm. ³In the morning, my father would get up in the icy cold, go downstairs, and light a fire in the black iron range. ⁴When he called us, I would put off leaving my warm bed until the last possible minute and then quickly grab my school clothes. ⁵The water pitcher and washing basin in my room would be layered with ice, and my breath would come out as white puffs as I ran downstairs. ⁶My sisters and I would all dress--as quickly as possible--in the chilly but bearable air of the kitchen. ⁷Our schoolroom, once we had arrived, didn't provide much relief from the cold. ⁸Students wore woollen mitts which left their fingers free but covered their palms and wrists. ⁹Even with these, we occasionally suffered chilblains. ¹⁰The throbbing patches on our hands made writing a painful process. ¹¹When we returned home in the afternoon, we spent all our indoor hours in the warm kitchen. ¹²We hated to leave it at bedtime in order to make the return trip to those cold bedrooms and frigid sheets. ¹³My mother made up hot-water bottles and gave us hot bricks to tuck under the covers, but nothing could eliminate the agony of that penetrating cold when we first slid under the covers.

1. How many times is the key word *cold* repeated? _____

2. Write here the pronoun that is used for *father* (sentence 4): _____;

   mitts (sentence 9): _____; *kitchen* (sentence 12): _____.

3. Write here the words that are used as a synonym for *cookstove* in sentence 3: _____; write in the words that are used as a synonym for *chilblains* in sentence 10: _____; write in the word that is used as a synonym for *cold* in sentence 12: _____.

INTRODUCTIONS, CONCLUSIONS, AND TITLES

So far, this chapter has been concerned with ways to organize the supporting paragraphs of an essay. A well-organized essay, however, should also have a strong introductory paragraph, an effective concluding paragraph, and a good title.

Introductory Paragraph

A well-written introductory paragraph will perform several important roles:

1 It will attract the reader's interest, encouraging him or her to go on and actually read the essay. Using one of the methods of introduction described below can help draw the reader into your paper.

2 It will supply any background information needed to understand the essay. Such information is sometimes needed so that the reader has a context in which to understand the ideas presented in the essay.

3 It will present a thesis statement. This clear, direct statement of the main idea to be developed in the paper usually occurs near the end of the introductory paragraph.

4 It will indicate a plan of development. In this "preview," the major points that will support the thesis are listed in the order in which they will be presented in the essay. In some cases, the thesis and plan of development may appear in the same sentence. In some cases, also, the plan of development may be omitted.

Common Methods of Introduction: Here are some common methods of introduction. Use any one method, or combination of methods, to introduce your subject in an interesting way to the reader.

1 ***Begin with a broad, general statement of your topic and narrow it down to your thesis statement.*** Broad, general statements ease the reader into your thesis statement by providing a background for it. In the example below, the writer talks generally about diets and then narrows down to comments on a specific diet.

Bookstore shelves today are crammed with dozens of different diet books. The Canadian public seems willing to try any sort of diet, especially those that promise instant, miraculous results. And authors are more than willing to invent new fad diets to cash in on this craze. Unfortunately, some of these fad diets are ineffective or even unsafe. One of the worst is the "10-Day diet." It is impractical, doesn't achieve the results it claims, and is a sure route to poor nutrition.

2 *Start with an idea or situation that is the opposite of the one you will develop.* This approach works because your readers will be surprised, and then intrigued, by the contrast between the opening idea and the thesis that follows it.

When I decided to return to school at age thirty-five, I wasn't at all worried about my ability to do the work. After all, I was a grown woman who had raised a family, not a confused teenager fresh out of high school. But when I started classes, I realized that those "confused teenagers" sitting around me were in much better shape for college than I was. They still had all their class-room skills in bright, shiny condition, while mine had grown rusty from disuse. I had totally forgotten how to locate information in a library, how to write a report, and even how to speak up in class discussions.

3 *Explain the importance of your topic to the reader.* If you can convince your readers that the subject in some way applies to them, or is something they should know more about, they will want to keep reading.

Diseases like scarlet fever and whooping cough used to kill more young children than any other cause. Today, however, child mortality due to disease has been almost completely eliminated by medical science. Instead, car accidents are the number one killer of our children. And most of the children fatally injured in car accidents were not protected by child-safety seats, belts, or restraints of any kind. Several steps must be taken to remedy this serious problem.

4 *Use an incident or brief story.* Stories are naturally interesting. They appeal to a reader's curiosity. In your introduction, an anecdote will grab the reader's attention right away. The story should be brief and should be related to your main idea. The incident in the story can be something that happened to you, something you have heard about, or something you have read about in a newspaper or magazine.

Early Sunday morning the young mother dressed her little girl warmly and gave her a candy bar, a picture book, and a well-worn stuffed rabbit. Together, they drove downtown to a United church. There the mother told the little girl to wait on the stone steps until children began arriving for Sunday school. Then the young mother drove off, abandoning her five-year-old because she couldn't cope with being a parent anymore. This incident is one of thousands of cases of child neglect and abuse that occur annually. Perhaps the automatic right to become a parent should no longer exist. Would-be parents, instead, should be forced to apply for licences granting them the privilege of raising children.

5 *Ask one or more questions.* But remember that questions need answers. You may simply want the reader to think about possible answers, or you may plan to answer the questions yourself later in the paper.

What is love? How do we know that we are really in love? When we meet that special person, how can we tell that our feelings are genuine and not merely infatuation? And, if they are genuine, will these feelings last? Love, as we all know, is difficult to define. But most people agree that true and lasting love involves far more than mere physical attraction. It involves mutual respect, the desire to give rather than take, and the feeling of being wholly at ease.

6 *Use a quotation.* A quotation can be something you have read in a book or article. It can also be something that you have heard: a popular saying or proverb ("Never give advice to a friend"); a current or recent advertising slogan ("Reach out and touch someone"); a favourite expression used by friends or family ("My father always says … "). Using a quotation in your introductory paragraph lets you add someone else's voice to your own.

"None but a mule deserves his family," says a Moroccan proverb. Last summer, when my sister and her family came to spend their two-week vacation with us, I became convinced that the proverb was right. After only three days, I was thoroughly sick of my brother-in-law's corny jokes, my sister's endless complaints about her boss, and their children's constant invasions of our privacy.

Activity

The box below summarizes the six kinds of introduction. Read the introductions that follow and, in the space provided, write the number of the kind of introduction used in each case.

1. General to narrow	4. Incident or story
2. Starting with an opposite	5. Questions
3. Stating importance of topic	6. Quotation

_____ The ad, in full colour on a glossy magazine page, shows a beautiful kitchen with gleaming counters. In the foreground, on one of the counters, stands a shiny new food processor. Usually, a feminine hand is touching it lovingly. Around the main picture are other, smaller shots. They show mounds of perfectly sliced onion rings, thin rounds of juicy tomatoes, heaps of matchstick-sized potatoes, and piles of golden, evenly grated cheese. The ad copy tells you how wonderful, how easy, food preparation will be with a processor. Don't believe it. My processor turned out to be expensive, difficult to operate, and very limited in its use.

_____ People say, "You can't tell a book by its cover." Actually, you can. When you're browsing in the drugstore or supermarket and you see a paperback featuring an attractive young woman in a low-cut dress fleeing from a handsome dark figure in a shadowy castle, you know exactly what you're getting. Every romance novel has the same elements: an innocent heroine, an exotic setting, and a cruel but fascinating hero.

_____ Canadians have become incredibly lazy. Instead of cooking a simple, nourishing meal, we pop frozen sandwiches into the microwave oven. Instead of studying a daily newspaper, we are contented with the capsule summaries on the TV news. Worst of all, instead of walking even a few blocks to the local convenience store, we jump into our cars. This dependence on the automobile, even for short trips, has robbed us of a valuable experience--walking. If we drove less and walked more, we would save money, become healthier, and discover fascinating things about our surroundings.

Concluding Paragraph

A concluding paragraph is your chance to remind the reader of your thesis idea. Also, the conclusion brings the paper to a natural and graceful end, sometimes leaving the reader with a final thought on the subject.

Common Methods of Conclusion: Any one of the methods below, or a combination of methods, may be used to round off your paper.

1 *End with a summary and final thought.* When armed forces instructors train new recruits, each of their lessons follows a three-step formula:

a Tell them what you're going to tell them.
b Tell them.
c Tell them what you've told them.

An essay that ends with a summary is not very different. After you have stated your thesis ("Tell them what you're going to tell them") and supported it ("Tell them"), you restate the thesis and supporting points ("Tell them what you've told them"). Don't, however, use the exact wording you used before. Here is a summary conclusion:

> Catalogue shopping at home, then, has several advantages. Such shopping is convenient, saves you money, and saves you time. It is not surprising that growing numbers of devoted catalogue shoppers are welcoming those full-colour mail brochures that offer everything from turnip seeds to televisions.

Note that the summary is accompanied by a final comment that "rounds off" the paper and brings the discussion to a close. This combination of a summary and a final thought is the most common method of concluding an essay.

2 *Include a thought-provoking question or short series of questions.* A question grabs the reader's attention. It is a direct appeal to your reader to think further about what you have written. A question should follow logically from the points you have already made in the paper. A question must deal with one of these areas:

a Why the subject of your essay is important
b What might happen in the future
c What should be done about this subject
d Which choice should be made

You may provide an answer to your question in the conclusion. Be sure, though, that your question is closely related to your thesis. Here is an example:

> What, then, will happen in the twenty-first century when most of the population will be over sixty years old? Retirement policies could change dramatically, with the age-sixty-five testimonial dinner and gold watch postponed for five or ten years. Even television changes as the Depends generation replaces the Pepsi generation. Glamorous grey-haired models could sell everything from toilet paper to televisions. Ads for pre-paid

funerals air already during prime viewing time. New soap operas and situation comedies reveal the secrets of the "sunset years." It is becoming a different world indeed as the young gradually find themselves outnumbered.

3 ***End with a prediction or recommendation.*** Like questions, predictions and recommendations also involve your readers. A prediction states what will or may happen in the future:

> If people stopped to think before acquiring pets, there would be fewer instances of cruelty to animals. Many times, it is the people who adopt pets without considering the expense and responsibility involved who mistreat and neglect their animals. Pets are living creatures. They do not deserve to be acquired as carelessly as one would acquire a stuffed toy.

A recommendation suggests what should be done about a situation or problem:

> Stereotypes such as the flustered female, harried executive, and dotty grandparent are insulting enough to begin with. Placed in magazine ads or television commercials, they become even more insulting. Now these unfortunate characters are not just being laughed at; they are being turned into hucksters to sell products to an unsuspecting public. Consumers should boycott companies whose advertising continues to use such stereotypes.

Activity

In the space provided, note whether each concluding paragraph ends with a summary and final thought (write *S* in the space), ends with a prediction or recommendation (write *P/R*), or ends with a question (write *Q*).

_____   1.   Disappointments are unwelcome, but regular, visitors to everyone's life. We can feel depressed about them, or we can try to escape from them. The best thing, though, is to accept a disappointment and then try to use it somehow: step over the unwelcome visitor and then get on with life.

_____   2.   Holidays, it is clear, are often not the fulfilling experiences they are supposed to be. They can, in fact, be nerve-wracking. How can one deal with the problem? Most experts agree that a person should schedule plenty of activities: more time with family, volunteer work, even overtime on the job. Staying active is preferable to the depressing time one might spend at home with only the hollow and flickering images on the TV for company.

_____   3.   Some people dream of starring roles, their names in lights, and their pictures on the cover of <u>People</u> magazine. I'm not one of them, though. A famous person gives up private life, feels pressured all the time, and is never completely safe. So let someone else have that cover story. I'd rather lead an ordinary, but calm, life than a stress-filled one.

Titles

A title is usually a very brief summary of what your paper is about, a sign-post to lead your reader into your essay. It is often no more than several words. You may find it easy to write the title *after* you have completed your paper.

Following are the introductory paragraphs for two of the essays in this text, along with the titles of the essays.

Introductory Paragraph

I'm not just a consumer--I'm a victim. If I order a product, it is sure to arrive in the wrong colour, size, or quantity. If I hire people to do repairs, they never arrive on the day scheduled. If I owe a bill, the computer is bound to overcharge me. Therefore, in self-defence, I have developed the following consumer's guide to complaining effectively.

Title: How to Complain

Introductory Paragraph

Schools divide people up into categories. From first grade on up, students are labelled "advanced" or "deprived" or "remedial" or "antisocial." Students pigeon-hole their fellow students, too. We've all known the "brain," the "jock," the "dummy," and the "teacher's pet." In most cases, these narrow labels are misleading and inaccurate. But there is one label for a certain type of college student that says it all. That is, of course, "zombie."

Title: Student Zombies

Note that you should not underline the title. Nor should you put quotation marks around it. On the other hand, you should capitalize all but small connecting words in the title. Also, when processing your essay, you should allow two double lines of spacing between your title and the first line of text. If you are handwriting a draft, leave two lines between the title and your first line. (See "Manuscript Form," page 299.)

Activity

Write an appropriate title for each of the introductory paragraphs that follow.

_____ 1.   For my birthday this month, my wife has offered to treat me to dinner at the restaurant of my choice. I think she expects me to ask for a meal at La Maison, the classiest, most expensive restaurant in town. However, I'm going to eat my birthday dinner at McDonald's. When I compare the two restaurants, the advantages of eating at McDonald's are clear.

Title: _____

_____ 2.   I've been in lots of coffee shops, and they've always seemed to be warm, busy, friendly, happy places. That's why, on a recent Monday night, I stopped in a coffee shop for a cup of coffee. I was returning home after an all-day car trip and needed something to help me make the last ninety kilometres. A coffee shop at midnight, however, was not the place I had expected. It was different--and lonely.

Title: _____

_____ 3.   If you see rock-concert audiences only on television or in newspaper photos, the people at these events may all seem to be excited teenagers. However, if you attended a few rock shows, you would see that several kinds of people make up the crowd. At any concert, you would find the typical fan, the out-of-place person, and the troublemaker.

Title: _____

Step 4:
Write Clear, Error-Free Sentences

The fourth step in writing an effective paper is to follow the agreed-upon rules or conventions of written English. These conventions—or, as they are called in this book, *sentence skills*—must be followed if your sentences are to be clear and error-free.
Here are the most common of these conventions.

1   Write complete sentences rather than fragments.

2   Do not write run-on sentences.

3   Use verb forms correctly.

4   Make sure that subject, verbs, and pronouns agree.

5   Eliminate faulty parallelism and faulty modifiers.

6   Use pronoun forms correctly.

7   Use capital letters where needed.

8 Use correctly the following marks of punctuation: apostrophe, quotation marks, comma, semi-colon, colon, hyphen, dash, parentheses.

9 Use correct paper format.

10 Eliminate wordiness.

11 Choose words carefully.

12 Check for possible spelling errors.

13 Eliminate careless errors.

14 Vary your sentences.

Space will not be taken here to explain and offer activities in all the sentence skills. Rather, they will be treated in detail in Part Four of this book, where they can be referred to easily as needed. Note that both the list of sentence skills on page 123 and the inside front cover (item 4) and the correction symbols on the last page of the book contain page references, so that you can turn quickly to those skills which give you problems.

Practice in Organizing and Connecting Specific Evidence

You now know the third step in effective writing: organizing the specific evidence used to support the thesis of a paper. You also know that the fourth step—writing clear, error-free sentences—will be treated in detail in Part Four. This closing section will expand and strengthen your understanding of the third step in writing. You will work through the following series of activities:

1 Organizing through time or emphatic order
2 Providing transitions
3 Identifying transitions and other connecting words
4 Completing transitional sentences
5 Identifying introductions and conclusions

1 ORGANIZING THROUGH TIME OR EMPHATIC ORDER

Activity 1

Use time order to organize the scrambled lists of supporting ideas below. Put *1* beside the supporting idea that should come first in time, *2* in front of the idea that logically follows, and *3* in front of the idea that comes last in time.

1. Thesis: When I was a child, Disney movies frightened me more than any other kind.

   _____ As a five-year-old, I found the story of *Pinocchio*, a boy transformed into a puppet, terrifying.

   _____ Although I saw *Bambi* when I was old enough to begin poking fun at "baby movies," the scene during which Bambi's mother is killed has stayed with me to this day.

   _____ About a year after *Pinocchio*, I gripped my seat in fear as the witches and goblins of *Fantasia* flew across the screen.

2. Thesis: Beware of these pitfalls if you want to make the perfect cheesecake.

   _____ There's only one way to remove the cake cleanly and easily from its pan.

   _____ Plan in advance to have your equipment ready and the ingredients at room temperature.

   _____ Remember to time the baking process and regulate the oven temperature while the cake is baking.

3. Thesis: Applying for unemployment benefits was a confusing, frustrating experience.

   _____ It was difficult to find both the office and a place to park.

   _____ When I finally reached the head of the line after four hours of waiting, the clerk had problems processing my claim.

   _____ There was no one to direct or help me when I entered the large office, which was packed with people.

Activity 2

Use emphatic order (order of importance) to arrange the following scrambled lists of supporting ideas. For each thesis, write *1* in the blank next to the point that is perhaps less important or interesting than the other two, *2* beside the point that appears more important or interesting, and *3* beside the point that should be most emphasized.

1. Thesis: My after-school job has been an invaluable part of my life this year.

   _____ Better yet, it has taught me how to get along with many kinds of people.

_____ Since it's in the morning, it usually keeps me from staying up too late.

_____ Without it, I would have had to drop out of school.

2. Thesis: We received some odd gifts for our wedding.

_____ The winner in the odd-gift category was a large wooden box with no apparent purpose or function.

_____ Someone gave us a gift certificate for a massage.

_____ Even stranger, my uncle gave me his favourite bowling ball.

3. Thesis: Donna is my most loyal friend.

_____ She has even taken time off from work to do special favours for me.

_____ She's always there in real emergencies or emotional crises.

_____ She once lent me her favourite necklace to wear on a date.

2 PROVIDING TRANSITIONS

Activity

In the spaces provided, add appropriate transitions to tie together the sentences and ideas in the following essay. Draw from the words given in the boxes above the paragraphs. Use each word only once.

Annoying People

Some people keep "enemies lists" of all the people they don't especially   1
like. I'm ashamed to confess it, but I, too, have an enemies list--a mental
one. On this list are all the people I would gladly live without, the ones who
cause my blood pressure to rise to the boiling point. The top three places on
the list go to people with annoying nervous habits, people who talk in movie
theatres, and people who smoke in restaurants.

| For example | First of all | Another | However |

_____, there are the people with nervous habits.   2

_____, there are the ones who make faces. When in deep
thought, they twitch, squint, and frown, and they can be a real distraction

when I'm trying to concentrate during an exam. _____ type of nervous character makes useless designs. These people bend paper-clips into abstract sculptures as they talk or string the clips into necklaces.

_____, neither of these groups is as bad as the people who make noises. These individuals, when they are feeling uncomfortable, bite their fingernails or crack their knuckles. If they have a pencil in their hands, they tap it rhythmically against whatever surface is handy--a desk, a book, a head. Lacking a pencil to play with, they jingle the loose change or keys in their pockets. These people make me wish I were hard of hearing.

On the contrary   Then   As a result   After   second

A _____ category of people I would gladly do away with   3
is the ones who talk in movie theatres. These people are not content to sit

back, relax, and enjoy the film they have paid to see. _____
they feel compelled to comment loudly on everything from the hero's hair-

style to the appropriateness of the background music. _____,

no one hears a word of any dialogue except theirs. _____
they have been in the theatre for a while, their interest in the movie may

fade. _____ they will start discussing other things, and the people around them will be treated to an instant replay of the last family scandal or soap opera episode. These stories may be entertaining, but they don't belong in a movie theatre.

Otherwise   But   Last of all

_____, there are the restaurant smokers. If I have   4
ordered an expensive dinner, I don't appreciate having another diner's smelly cigar smoke compete with the aroma of my sirloin steak. Even the appetizing smell of Swiss Chalet chicken or a Harvey's burger can be spoiled by the sharp fumes sent out by a nearby cigarette smoker. Often, I have to lean over to the next table and ask the offender to stop smoking.

_____, it is impossible for me to taste my food.

So long as murder remains illegal, the nervous twitchers, movie talkers,   5
and restaurant smokers of the world are safe from me. _____
if ever I am granted the power of life or death, these people had better think twice about annoying me. They might not have long to live.

3 IDENTIFYING TRANSITIONS AND OTHER CONNECTING WORDS

Activity

The following selections use connecting words to help tie ideas together. The connecting words you are to identify are set off in italics. In the space, write *T* for *transition*, *RW* for *repeated word*, *S* for *synonym*, or *P* for *pronoun*.

_____ 1. Kate wears a puffy, quilted, down-filled jacket. In this *garment*, she resembles a stack of inflated inner tubes.

_____ 2. Plants like poinsettias and mistletoe are pretty. *They* are also poisonous.

_____ 3. A strip of strong cloth can be used as an emergency fan-belt replacement. *In addition*, a roll of duct tape can be used to patch a leaky hose temporarily.

_____ 4. Newspapers may soon be brought to your home, not by paper carriers, but by computers. Subscribers will simply punch in a code, and the *machines* will display the desired pages.

_____ 5   I'm always losing my soft contact lenses, which resemble little circles of thick plastic wrap. One day I dropped both of *them* into a cup of hot tea.

_____ 6. The moulded plastic chairs in the class-rooms are hard and uncomfortable. When I sit in one of these *chairs*, I feel as if I were sitting in a bucket.

_____ 7. One way to tell if your skin is aging is to pinch a fold of skin on the back of your hand. If *it* doesn't smooth out quickly, your skin is losing its youthful tone.

_____ 8. I never eat sloppy joes. *They* look as if they've already been eaten.

_____ 9. Clothing intended just for children seems to have vanished. *Instead*, children wear scaled-down versions of everything adults wear.

_____ 10. Some successful salespeople use voice tones and hand gestures that are almost hypnotic. Customers are not conscious of this *hypnotic* effect but merely feel the urge to buy.

_____ 11. The giant mosquitoes in Northern Ontario are the subject of local legends. A visitor, according to one tale, saw one of the *insects*, thought it was a dive bomber, and tried to run from it.

_____ 12. Some thieves scour garbage cans for credit-card receipts. *Then*, they use the owner's name and card number to order merchandise by phone.

_____ 13. When the phone rang, I dropped the garden hose. *It* whipped around crazily and squirted water through the kitchen screen door.

_____   14. There are many phobias other than the ones described in psychology textbooks. I have *phobias*, for instance, about toasters and lawn mowers.

_____   15. My mother believes that food is love. *Therefore*, when she offers home-made cookies or cupcakes, I hate to hurt her feelings by refusing them.

4   COMPLETING TRANSITIONAL SENTENCES

Activity

Following are brief sentence outlines from two essays. In each outline, the second and third topic sentences serve as transitional, or linking, sentences. They both remind us of the point in the preceding paragraph and announce the point to be developed in the present paragraph. In the space provided, add the words needed to complete the second and third topic sentences.

Thesis 1

Cheaper cost, greater comfort, and superior electronic technology make watching football at home more enjoyable than attending a game at the stadium.

First supporting paragraph

For one thing, watching the game on TV eliminates the cost of attending the game. . . .

Second supporting paragraph

In addition to saving me money, watching the game at home is more _____ than sitting in a stadium. . . .

Third supporting paragraph

Even more important than _____ and _____, though, is the _____ which makes a televised game better than the "real thing." . . .

Thesis 2

In order to set up a day-care centre in your home, you must make sure your house will conform to provincial and municipal regulations, obtain the necessary legal permits, and advertise your service in the right places.

First
supporting
paragraph

> First of all, as a potential operator of a home day-care centre, you must make sure your house will conform to provincial and municipal regulations. . . .

Second
supporting
paragraph

> After making certain that _____
>
> _____ ,
>
> you must obtain _____ . . . .

Third
supporting
paragraph

> Finally, once you have the necessary _____
>
> you can begin to _____ .

5   IDENTIFYING INTRODUCTIONS AND CONCLUSIONS

Activity

The box below lists six common kinds of introductions and three common kinds of conclusions. Read the three sets of introductory and concluding paragraphs that follow. Then, in the space provided, write the number of the kind of introduction or conclusion used in each case.

Introductions	**Conclusions**
1. General to narrow	1. Summary and final thought
2. Starting with an opposite	2. Question(s)
3. Stating importance of topic	3. Prediction or recommendation
4. Incident or story	
5. Question(s)	
6. Quotation	

_____

Shortly before Easter, our local elementary school sponsored a fund-raising event at which class-room pets and their babies--hamsters, guinea pigs, and baby chicks--were available for adoption. Afterward, as I was driving home, I saw a hand drop a baby hamster out of the car ahead of me. I couldn't avoid running over the tiny creature. One of the parents had taken the pet, regretted the decision, and decided to get rid of it. Such people have never stopped to consider the real obligations involved in owning an animal. . . .

_____ A pet cannot be thrown onto a garbage heap when it is no longer wanted or tossed into a closet if it begins to bore its owner. A pet, like us, is a living thing that needs physical care, affection, and respect. Would-be owners, therefore, should think seriously about their responsibilities before they acquire a pet.

_____ What would life be like if we could read each other's minds? Would communications be instantaneous and perfectly clear? These questions will never be answered unless mental telepathy becomes a fact of life. Until then, we will have to make do with less-perfect means of communication, such as letters, telephone calls, and face-to-face conversations. Each of these has its drawbacks. . . .

_____ Neither letters, phone calls, nor conversations guarantee perfect communication. With all our sophisticated skills, we human beings often communicate less effectively than howling wolves or chattering monkeys. Even if we <u>were</u> able to read each other's minds, we'd probably still find some way to foul up the message.

_____ "Few things are harder to put up with," said Mark Twain, "than the annoyance of a good example." Twain obviously knew the problems faced by siblings cursed with older brothers or sisters who are models of perfection. All our lives, my older sister Shelley and I have been compared. Unfortunately, my looks, talents, and accomplishments always ended up on the losing side. . . .

_____ Although our looks, talents, and accomplishments were constantly compared, Shelley and I have somehow managed not to turn into deadly enemies. Feeling like the ugly duckling of the family, in fact, helped me to develop a drive to succeed and a sense of humour. In our sibling rivalry, we both managed to win.

THE FOUR BASES FOR EVALUATING ESSAY WRITING

This chapter will show you how to evaluate an essay for four goals in essay writing:

- **Unity**
- **Support**
- **Coherence**
- **Sentence skills**

In the preceding chapters, you learned the four essential steps in writing an effective essay. The box below shows how the steps lead to four standards, or bases, you can use in evaluating an essay.

Four Steps ⟶	*Four Bases* ⟶	*Four Goals Defined*
1 If you advance a single point and stick to that point,	you will have *unity* in your paper.	**Unity:** a single main idea pursued and supported by the points and details of the essay
2 If you support the point with specific evidence,	you will have *support* in your paper.	**Support:** for each supporting point, specific and definite details
3 If you organize and connect the specific evidence,	you will have *coherence* in your paper.	**Coherence:** supporting points and details organized and connected clearly
4 If you write clear, error-free sentences,	you will have effective *sentence skills* in your paper.	**Sentence Skills:** sentence structure, grammar, spelling, and punctuation free of errors

This chapter will discuss the four bases of unity, support, coherence, and sentence skills and will show how these four bases can be used to evaluate a paper.

Base 1: Unity

Activity

The following student essays are on the topic "Problems or Pleasures of My Teenage Years." Which one makes its point more clearly and effectively, and why?

Teenage Pranks

Looking back at some of the things I did as a teenager makes me break out in a sweat. The purpose of each adventure was fun, but occasionally things got out of hand. In my search for good times, I was involved in three notable pranks, ranging from fairly harmless to fairly serious.   1

The first prank proved that good, clean fun does not have to be dull. As a high school student, I was credited with making the world's largest dessert. With several friends, I spent an entire year collecting boxes of jelly powder. Entering our school's indoor pool one night, we turned the water temperature up as high as it would go and poured in box after box of the strawberry powder. The next morning, school officials arrived to find the pool filled with twenty thousand litres of the quivering, rubbery stuff. No one was hurt by the prank, but we did suffer through three days of a massive clean-up.   2

Not all my pranks were harmless, and one involved risking my life. As soon as I got my driver's licence, I wanted to join the "Fliers' Club." Membership in this club was limited to those who could make their cars fly a distance of at least three metres. The qualifying site was an old quarry field where friends and I had built a ramp made of dirt. I drove my battered Ford Pinto up this ramp as fast as it would go. The Pinto flew three metres, but one of the tires exploded when I landed. The car rolled on its side, and I luckily escaped with only a bruised arm.   3

Risking my own life was bad enough, but there was another prank where other people could have been hurt, too. On this occasion, I accidentally set a valley on fire. Two of my friends and I were sitting on a hill sharing a few beers. It was a warm summer night, and there was absolutely nothing to do. The idea came like a thunderclap. We collected a supply of large plastic garbage bags, emergency highway flares, and the half tank of helium left over from a science-fair experiment. Then we began to construct a fleet of UFOs. Filling the bags with helium, we tied them closed with wire and suspended several burning flares below each bag. Our UFOs leaped into the air like an army of invading Martians. Rising and   4 darting in the blackness, they convinced even us. Our fun turned into horror, though, as we watched the balloons begin to drop onto the wooded valley of expensive homes below. Soon, a brush fire started and, quickly sobered, we hurried off to call the fire department anonymously.

Every so often, I think back on the things that I did as a teenager. I   5
chuckle at the innocent pranks and feel lucky that I didn't harm myself or others with the not-so-innocent ones. Those years were filled with wild times. Today I'm older, wiser--and maybe just a little more boring.

Problems of My Adolescence

In the unreal world of television situation comedies, teenagers are   1
carefree, smart, funny, wisecracking, secure kids. In fact, most of them are more "together" than the adults on the shows. This, however, isn't how I recall my teenage years at all. As a teen, I suffered. Every day, I battled the terrible physical, family, and social troubles of adolescence.

For one thing, I had to deal with a demoralizing physical problem--   2
acne. Some days, I would wake up in the morning with a red bump the size of a tail-light on my nose. Since I worried constantly about my appearance anyway, acne outbreaks could turn me into a crying, screaming maniac. Plastering on a layer of orange-coloured Clearasil, which didn't fool anybody, I would slink into school, hoping that the boy I had a crush on would be absent that day. Within the last few years, however, treatments for acne have improved. Now, skin doctors prescribe special drugs that clear up pimples almost immediately. An acne attack could shatter whatever small amount of self-esteem I had managed to build up.

In addition to fighting acne, I felt compelled to fight my family. As a   3
teenager, I needed to be independent. At that time, the most important thing in life was to be close to my friends and to try out new, more adult experiences. Unfortunately, my family seemed to get in the way. My little brother, for instance, turned into my enemy. We're close now, though. In fact, Eddie recently painted my new apartment for me. Eddie used to barge into my room, listen to my phone conversations, and read my secret letters. I would threaten to tie him up and leave him in a garbage dumpster. He would scream, my mother would yell, and all hell would break loose. My parents, too, were enemies. They wouldn't let me stay out late, wear the clothes I wanted to wear, or hang around with the friends I liked. So I tried to get revenge on them by being miserable, sulky, and sarcastic at home.

Worst of all, I had to face the social traumas of being a teenager. Things   4
that were supposed to be fun, like dates and dances, were actually horrible. On the few occasions when I had a real date, I agonized over everything-- my hair, my weight, my pimples. After a date, I would come home, raid the kitchen, and drown my insecurities in a sea of junk food. Dances were also stressful events. My friends and I would sneak a couple of beers just to get up the nerve to walk into the school gym. Now I realize that teenage

drinking is dangerous. I read recently that the number one killer of teenagers is drunk driving. At dances, I never relaxed. It was too important to look exactly right, to act really cool, and to pretend I was having fun.

I'm glad I'm not a teenager anymore. I wouldn't ever want to feel so   5
unattractive, so confused, and so insecure again. I'll gladly accept the crow's-feet and stomach bulge of adulthood in exchange for a little peace of mind.

The _____ essay makes its point more clearly and effectively because

_____

_____

_____

UNDERSTANDING UNITY

The first essay is more effective because it is unified. All the details in the essay are on target; they support and develop each of the essay's three topic sentences ("The first prank proved that good, clean fun does not have to be dull"; "Not all my pranks were harmless, and one involved risking my life"; and, "Risking my own life was bad enough, but there was another prank where other people could have been hurt, too").

On the other hand, the second essay contains some details irrelevant to the essay's topic sentences. In the first supporting paragraph (paragraph 2), the sentences, "Within the last few years, however, treatments for acne have improved. Now, skin doctors prescribe special drugs that clear up pimples almost immediately," do not support the writer's topic statement that she had to deal with the physical problem of acne. Such details should be left out in the interest of unity. Go back to the second essay and cross out the two sentences in the second supporting paragraph (paragraph 3) and the two sentences in the third supporting paragraph (paragraph 4) that are off target and do not help support their topic sentences.

You should have crossed out the following two sentences: "We're close now … apartment for me" and "Now I realize … drunk driving."

The difference between the first two essays leads us to the first base or standard of effective writing: *unity*. To achieve unity is to have all the details in your paper related to your thesis and three supporting topic sentences. Each time you think of something to put into your paper, ask yourself whether it relates to your thesis and supporting points. If it does not, leave it out. For example, if you were writing a paper about the problems of being unemployed and then spent a couple of sentences talking about the pleasures of having a lot of free time, you would be missing the first and most essential base of good writing. The pages ahead will consider the other three bases that you must touch in order to succeed in your writing.

Base 2: Support

Activity

The following model essays were written on the topic "Dealing with Disappointment." Both are unified, but one communicates more clearly and effectively. Which one, and why?

Dealing with Disappointment

One way to look at life is as a series of disappointments. Life can certainly appear that way because disappointment crops up in the life of everyone more often, it seems, than satisfaction. How disappointments are handled can have a great bearing on how life is viewed. People can react negatively by sulking or by blaming others, or they can try to understand the reasons behind the disappointment. 1

Sulking is one way to deal with disappointment. This "Why does everything always happen to me?" attitude is common because it is an easy attitude to adopt, but it is not very productive. Everyone has had the experience of meeting people who specialize in feeling sorry for themselves. A sulky manner will often discourage others from wanting to lend support, and it prevents the sulker from making positive moves toward self-help. It becomes easier just to sit back and sulk. Unfortunately, feeling sorry for oneself does nothing to lessen the pain of disappointment. It may, in fact, increase the pain. It certainly does not make future disappointments easier to bear. 2

Blaming others is another negative and non-productive way to cope with disappointment. This all-too-common response of pointing the finger at someone else doesn't help one's situation. This posture will lead only to anger, resentment, and, therefore, further unhappiness. Disappointment in another's performance does not necessarily indicate that the performer is at fault. Perhaps expectations were too high, or there could have been a misunderstanding as to what the performer actually intended to accomplish. 3

A positive way to handle disappointment is to try to understand the reasons behind the disappointment. An analysis of the causes for disappointment can have an excellent chance of producing desirable results. Often understanding alone can help alleviate the pain of disappointment and can help prevent future disappointments. Also, it is wise to try to remember that what would be ideal is not necessarily what is reasonable to expect in any given situation. The ability to look disappointment squarely in the face and then go on from there is the first step on the road back.

Continuous handling of disappointment in a negative manner can lead to a negative view of life itself. Chances for personal happiness in such a state of being are understandably slim. Learning not to expect perfection in 4 an imperfect world and keeping in mind those times when expectations were actually surpassed are positive steps toward allowing the joys of life to prevail.

Reactions to Disappointment

Gertrude Stein said that we have "to learn to do everything, even to die." In our lives, we may face and master many unavoidable adversities; one misery everyone experiences is disappointment. No one gets through life without experiencing many disappointments. Strangely, though, most people seem unprepared for disappointment and react to it in negative ways. They feel depressed or try to escape their troubles instead of using disappointment as an opportunity for growth.   1

One negative reaction to disappointment is depression. A woman trying to win a promotion, for example, works hard for over a year in her department. Helen is so sure she will get the promotion, in fact, that she has already picked out the car she will buy when her salary increase comes through. However, the boss names one of Helen's co-workers to the spot. The fact that all the other department employees tell Helen that she is the one who really deserved the promotion doesn't help her deal with the crushing disappointment. Deeply depressed, Helen decides that all her goals are doomed to defeat. She loses her enthusiasm for her job and can barely force herself to show up every day. Helen tells herself that she is a failure and that doing a good job just isn't worth the work.   2

Another negative reaction to disappointment, and one that often follows depression, is the desire to escape. Kevin fails to get into the college his brother is attending, the college that was the focus of all his dreams, and decides to escape his disappointment. Why worry about college at all? Instead, he covers up his real feelings by giving up on his schoolwork and getting completely involved with friends, parties, and "good times." Or Linda doesn't make the varsity basketball team--something she wanted very badly--and so refuses to play sports at all. She decides to hang around with a new set of friends who get high every day; then she won't have to confront her disappointment and learn to live with it.   3

The positive way to react to disappointment is to use it as a chance for growth. This isn't easy, but it's the only useful way to deal with an inevitable part of life. Helen, the woman who wasn't promoted, could have handled her disappointment by looking at other options. If her boss doesn't recognize talent and hard work, perhaps she could transfer to another department. Or she could ask the boss how to improve her performance so that she would be a certain choice for the next promotion. Kevin, the boy who didn't get into the college of his choice, should look into other schools. Going to another college may encourage him to be his own person, step out of his brother's shadow, and realize that being turned down by one college   4 isn't a final judgement on his abilities or potential. Rather than escape into drugs, Linda could improve her basketball skills for a year or pick up another sport--like swimming or tennis--that would probably turn out to be more useful to her as an adult.

Disappointments are unwelcome, but regular, visitors to everyone's life. We can feel depressed about them or we can try to escape from them. The best thing, though, is to accept a disappointment and then try to use it somehow: step over the unwelcome visitor on the doorstep and get on with life.

5

The _____ essay makes its point more clearly and effectively because

_____

_____

_____

UNDERSTANDING SUPPORT

The second essay is more effective, for it offers specific examples of the ways people deal with disappointment. We see for ourselves the kinds of reactions people have to disappointment.

The first essay, on the other hand, gives us no specific evidence. The writer tells us repeatedly that sulking, blaming others, and trying to understand the reasons behind the disappointment are the reactions people have to a let-down. However, the writer never *shows* us any of these responses in action. Exactly what kinds of disappointments is the writer talking about? And how, for instance, does someone analyse the causes of disappointment? Would a person make up a list of causes on a piece of paper, or review the causes with a concerned friend, or speak to a professional therapist? In an essay like this, we would want to see *examples* of how sulking and blaming others are negative ways of dealing with disappointment.

Consideration of the two essays leads us to the second base of effective writing: *support*. After realizing the importance of specific supporting details, one student writer revised a paper she had done on being lost in the woods as the worst experience of her childhood. In the revised paper, instead of talking about "the terror of being separated from my parents," she referred to such specifics as "tears streamed down my cheeks as I pictured the faces I would never see again" and "I clutched the locket my parents had given me as if it were a lucky charm that could help me find my way back to the campsite." All your papers should include such vivid details!

Base 3: Coherence

Activity

The following two essays were written on the topic "Positive or Negative Effects of Television." Both are unified, and both are supported. However, one communicates more clearly and effectively. Which one, and why?

Harmful Effects of Watching Television

In a recent cartoon, one character said to another, "When you think   1
of the awesome power of television to educate, aren't you glad it doesn't?"
It's true that television has the power to educate and to entertain, but
unfortunately, these benefits are outweighed by the harm it does to
dedicated viewers. Television is harmful because it creates passivity,
discourages communication, and presents a false picture of reality.

Television makes viewers passive. Children who have an electronic   2
baby-sitter spend most of their waking hours in a semi-conscious state.
Older viewers watch tennis matches and basketball games with none of the
excitement of being in the stands. Even if children are watching Bookmice
or Sharon, Lois & Bram, they are being educated passively. The child actors
are going on nature walks, building crafts projects, playing with animals,
and participating in games, but the little viewers are simply watching. Older
viewers watch a studio audience discuss issues with Dini Petty, but no one
will turn to the home viewers to ask their opinion.

Worst of all, TV presents a false picture of reality that leaves viewers   3
frustrated because they don't have the beauty or wealth of characters on
television. Viewers absorb the idea that everyone else in North America
owns a lavish apartment, suburban house, sleek car, and expensive
wardrobe. Every detective, police officer, oil baron, and lawyer, male or
female, is suitable for a pin-up poster. The material possessions on TV
shows and commercials contribute to the false image of reality. News
anchors and reporters, with their perfect hair and make-up, must fit
television's standard of beauty. From their modest homes or cramped
apartments, many viewers tune in daily to the upper-middle-class world
that TV glorifies.

Television discourages communication. Families watching television do   4
very little talking except for brief exchanges during commercials. If Uncle
Bernie or the next-door neighbours drop in for a visit, the most comfortable
activity for everyone may be not conversation but watching Hockey Night
in Canada. The family may not even be watching the same set; instead, in
some households, all the family members head for their own rooms to
watch their own sets. At dinner, plates are plopped on the coffee table in
front of the set, and the meal is wolfed down during the CBC Newshour.

During commercials, the only communication a family has all night may consist of questions like "Do we have any popcorn?" and "Where's the television page?"

Television, like cigarettes or saccharine, is harmful to our health. We 5 are becoming isolated, passive, and frustrated. And, most frightening, the average viewer spends more time watching television than ever.

The Benefits of Television

We hear a lot about the negative effects of television on the viewer. 1 Obviously, television can be harmful if it is watched constantly to the exclusion of other activities. It would be just as harmful to listen to CDs or to eat constantly. However, when television is watched in moderation, it is extremely valuable, as it provides relaxation, entertainment, and education.

First of all, watching TV has the value of sheer relaxation. Watching 2 television can be soothing and restful after an eight-hour day of pressure, challenges, or concentration. After working hard all day, people look forward to a new episode of a favourite show or yet another showing of Casablanca or Red River. This period of relaxation leaves viewers refreshed and ready to take on the world again. Watching TV also seems to reduce stress in some people. This benefit of television is just beginning to be recognized. One doctor, for example, advises his patients with high blood pressure to relax in the evening with a few hours of television.

In addition to being relaxing, television is entertaining. Along with the 3 standard comedies, dramas, and game shows that provide enjoyment to viewers, television offers a variety of movies and sports events. Moreover, in most areas, viewers can pay a monthly fee and receive special cable programming, or purchase satellite dishes. With these services, viewers can watch first-run movies, rock and classical music concerts, and specialized sports events, like European soccer and Grand Prix racing. Viewers can also buy or rent movies to show on their television sets through VCRs or videodisc players. Still another growing area of TV entertainment is video games. Cartridges are available for everything from electronic baseball to Mortal Kombat, allowing the owner to have a video game arcade in the living room.

Most important, television is educational. Preschoolers learn colours, 4 numbers, and letters from public television programs, like Bookmice, that use animation and puppets to make learning fun. Science shows for older children, like The Nature of Things, go on location to analyse everything from volcanoes to salmon spawning. Adults, too, can get an education (college credits included) from courses given on television. Also, television widens our knowledge by covering important events and current news. Viewers can see and hear politicians' speeches, sensational trials, natural disasters, and election results as they are happening. Finally, a television set hooked up to a home computer can help its owner learn how to manage the household budget, invest in the stock market, or master a foreign language.

Perhaps because television is such a powerful force, we like to criticize   5
it and search for its flaws. However, the benefits of television should not be
ignored. We can use television to relax, to have fun, and to make ourselves
smarter. This electronic wonder, then, is a servant, not a master.

The _____ essay makes its point more clearly and effectively because

_____

_____

_____

_____

UNDERSTANDING COHERENCE

The second essay is more effective because the material is organized clearly and logically. Using emphatic order, the writer develops three positive uses of television, ending with the most important use: television as an educational tool. The writer also includes transitional words that act as signposts, making movement from one idea to the next easy to follow. The major transitions include *First of all, In addition,* and *Most important;* transitions within paragraphs include such words as *Moreover, Still another, too, Also,* and *Finally.* And the writer of the second essay uses a linking sentence ("In addition to being relaxing, television is entertaining") to tie the first and second supporting paragraphs together clearly.

Although the first essay is unified and supported, the writer does not have any clear and consistent way of organizing the material. The most important idea to be developed (signalled by the phrase *Worst of all*) is discussed in the second supporting paragraph instead of being saved for last. None of the supporting paragraphs organizes its details in a logical fashion. The first supporting paragraph, for example, discusses older viewers, then younger viewers, then jumps back to older people again. The third supporting paragraph, like the first, leaps from an opening idea (families talking only during commercials), to several intervening ideas, back to the original idea (talking during commercials). In addition, this essay uses practically no transitional devices to guide the reader.

These two essays lead us to the third base of effective writing: *coherence.* All the supporting ideas and sentences in a paper must be organized so that they cohere, or "stick together." As has already been mentioned, key techniques for tying together the material in a paper include a clear method of organization (such as time order or emphatic order), transitions, and other connecting words.

Base 4: Sentence Skills

Activity

Following are two versions of a student's essay. Both are unified, supported, and organized, but one version communicates more clearly and effectively. Which one, and why?

"revenge"

[1]Revenge is one of those things that everyone enjoy. [2]People don't like to talk about it, though. [3]Just the same, there is nothing more tempting, more satisfying, or more rewarding than revenge. [4]The purpose is not to harm your victims. [5]But to let them know that I am upset about something they are doing. [6]Careful plotting can provide you with relief from bothersom co-workers, gossiping friends, or nagging family members.

1

[7]Co-workers who make comments about the fact that you are always fifteen minutes late for work can be taken care of very simply. [8]All you have to do is get up extra early one day. [9]Before the sun comes up, drive to each co-worker's house, reach under the hood of his car, and disconnected the centre wire that leads to the distrib. cap. [10]The car will be unharmed, but it will not start, and your friends at work will all be late for work on the same day. [11]If youre lucky, your boss might notice that you are the only one there and will give you a raise. [12]Later if you feel guilty about your actions you can call each person anonymously and tell them how to get the car running.

2

[13]Gossiping friends at school are also perfect targets for a simple act of revenge. [14]A way to trap either male or female friends are to leave phony messages on their lockers. [15]If the friend that you want to get is male, leave a message that a certain girl would like him to stop by her house later that day. [16]With any luck, her boyfriend will be there. [17]The girl won't know what's going on, and the victim will be so embarrassed that he probably won't leave his home for a month. [18]The plan works just as well for female friends, too.

3

[19]When Mom and Dad and your sisters and brothers really begin to annoy you, harmless revenge may be just the way to make them quite down for a while. [20]The dinner table, where most of the nagging probably happens, is a likely place. [21]Just before the meal begins, throw a handful of raisins into the food. [22]Wait about 5 minutes and, after everyone has began to eat, clamp your hand over your mouth and begin to make odd noises. [23]When they ask you what the matter is, point to a raisin and yell, Bugs. [24]Dumping the food in the disposal, the car will make a bee-line for mcdonald's. [25]That night, you'll have your first quiet, peaceful meal in a long time.

4

[26]A well-planned revenge does not have to hurt anyone. [27]The object is simply to let other people know that they are beginning to bother you. [28]You

5

should remember, though, to stay on your guard after completing your revenge. [29]The reason for this is simple, co-workers, friends, and family can also plan revenge on you.

Revenge

Revenge is one of those things that everyone enjoys. People don't like   1
to talk about it, though. Just the same, there is nothing more tempting, more satisfying, or more rewarding than revenge. The purpose is not to harm your victims but to let them know that you are upset about something that they are doing to you. Careful plotting can provide you with relief from bothersome co-workers, gossiping friends, or nagging family members.

Co-workers who make comments about the fact that you are always   2
fifteen minutes late for work can be taken care of very simply. All you have to do is get up extra early one day. Before the sun comes up, drive to each co-worker's house. Reach under the hood of your co-worker's car and disconnect the centre wire that leads to the distributor cap. The car will be unharmed, but it will not start, and your friends at work will all be late for work on the same day. If you're lucky, your boss might notice that you are the only one there and will give you a raise. Later, if you feel guilty about your actions, you can call your co-workers anonymously and tell them how to get their cars running again.

Gossiping friends at school are also perfect targets for a simple act of   3
revenge. A way to trap either male or female friends is to leave phony messages on their lockers. If the friend that you want to get is male, leave a message that a certain girl would like him to stop by her house later that day. With any luck, her boyfriend will be there. The girl won't know what's going on, and the victim will be so embarrassed that he probably won't leave his home for a month. The plan works just as well for female friends, too.

When Mom and Dad and your sisters and brothers really begin to   4
annoy you, harmless revenge may be just the way to make them quiet down for a while. The dinner table, where most of the nagging probably happens, is a likely place. Just before the meal begins, throw a handful of raisins into the food. Wait about five minutes and, after everyone has begun to eat, clamp your hand over your mouth and begin to make odd noises. When they ask you what the matter is, point to a raisin and yell, "Bugs!" They'll all dump their food in the disposal, jump into the car, and head for McDonald's. That night, you'll have your first quiet, peaceful meal in a long time.

A well-planned revenge does not have to hurt anyone. The object is   5
simply to let other people know that they are beginning to bother you. You should remember, though, to stay on your guard after completing your revenge. The reason for this is simple. Co-workers, friends, and family can also plan revenge on you.

The _____ essay makes its point more clearly and effectively because

_____

_____

_____

UNDERSTANDING SENTENCE SKILLS

The second essay is more effective because it uses *sentence skills*, the fourth base of competent writing. See if you can find and explain briefly the twenty sentence-skills mistakes made in the first essay. Use the space provided. The first mistake is described for you as an example. Note that comparing the first essay with the corrected essay will help you locate the mistakes.

1. The title should not be set off with quotation marks. _____
2. _____
3. _____
4. _____
5. _____
6. _____
7. _____
8. _____
9. _____
10. _____
11. _____
12. _____
13. _____
14. _____
15. _____
16. _____
17. _____
18. _____
19. _____
20. _____

Practice in Using the Four Bases

You are now familiar with the four standards, or bases, of effective writing: unity. support, coherence, and sentence skills. In this section you will expand and strengthen your understanding of the four bases as you:

1 Evaluate essays for unity

2 Evaluate essays for support

3 Evaluate essays for coherence

4 Evaluate essays for all four bases: unity, support, coherence, sentence skills

1 EVALUATING ESSAYS FOR UNITY

Activity

Both of the essays below contain irrelevant sentences that do not relate to the thesis of the essay or support the topic sentence of the paragraph in which they appear. Cross out the irrelevant sentences and put the numbers of those sentences in the spaces provided.

Playing on the Browns

[1] For the past three summers, I have played first base on a softball team known as the Browns. [2] We play a long schedule, including play-offs, and everybody takes the games pretty seriously. [3] In that respect, we're no different from any other of the hundred or so teams in our City. [4] But in one respect, we <u>are</u> different. [5] In an all-male league, we have a woman on the team--me. [6] Thus I've had a chance to observe something about human nature by seeing how the men have treated me. [7] Some have been disbelieving; some have been patronizing; and fortunately, some have simply accepted me.

[8] One new team in the league was particularly flabbergasted to see me start the game at first base. [9] Nobody on the Comets had commented one way or the other when they saw me warming up, but playing in the actual game was another story. [10] The Comet first-base coach leaned over to me with a disbelieving grin and said, "You mean, you're starting, and those three guys are on the bench?" [11] I nodded and he shrugged, still amazed. [12] He probably thought I was the manager's wife. [13] When I came up to bat, the Comet pitcher smiled and called to his outfielders to move way in on me. [14] Now, I don't have a lot of power, but I'm not exactly feeble. [15] I used to work out on the exercise machines at a local health club until it closed, and now I lift weights at home a couple of times a week. [16] I wiped the smirks off their faces with a line drive double over the left fielder's head.

The number of the irrelevant sentence: _____

[17]The next game, we played another new team, and this time their attitude was a patronizing one. [18]The Argyles had seen me take batting practice, so they didn't do anything so rash as to draw their outfield way in. [19]They had respect for my ability as a player. [20]However, they tried to annoy me with phony concern. [21]For example, a redheaded Argyle got on base in the first inning and said to me, "You'd better be careful, Hon. [22]When you have your foot on the bag somebody might step on it. [23]You can get hurt in this game." [24]I was mad, but I have worked out several mental techniques to control my anger because it interferes with my playing ability. [25]Well, this delicate little girl survived the season without injury, which is more than I can say for some of the "he-men" on the Argyles.

3

The number of the irrelevant sentence: _____

[26]Happily, most of the teams in the league have accepted me, just as the Browns did. [27]The men on the Browns coached and criticized me (and occasionally cursed me) just like anyone else. [28]Because I'm a religious person, I don't approve of cursing, but I don't say anything about it to my team-mates. [29]They are not amazed when I get a hit or stretch for a wide throw. [30]My average this year was higher than the averages of several of my team-mates, yet none of them acted resentful or threatened. [31]On several occasions I was taken out late in a game for a pinch runner, but other slow players on the team were also lifted at times for pinch runners. [32]Every woman should have a team like the Browns!

4

The number of the irrelevant sentence: _____

[33]Because I really had problems only with the new teams, I've concluded that it's when people are faced with an unfamiliar situation that they react defensively. [34]Once a rival team has got used to seeing me on the field, I'm no big deal. [35]Still, I suspect that the Browns secretly feel we're a little special. [36]After all, we won the championship with a woman on the team.

5

How to Con a Teacher

[1]Enter college, and you'll soon be reminded of an old saying: "The pen is mightier than the sword." [2]That person behind the teacher's desk holds your future in his or her ink-stained hands. [3]So your first important assignment in college has nothing to do with required readings, examinations, or even the hazards of registration. [4]It is, instead, how to con a teacher.

1

[5]The first step in conning a teacher is to use body language. [6]You may be able to convince your instructor you are special without even saying a word. [7]When you enter the class-room, be sure to sit in the front row. [8]That way, the instructor can't possibly miss you. [9]Then, as your teacher lectures, take notes frantically. [10]The teacher will be flattered that you think so much of his or her words that you want to write them all down. [11]Using a felt-tip

2

pen is superior to a pen or pencil; it will help you write faster and prevent aching wrists. [12]While you are writing, be sure to smile at the teacher's jokes and nod violently in agreement with every major point. [13]Most important of all, as class continues, sit with your body pitched forward and your eyes wide open, fixed firmly, as if hypnotized, on your teacher's face. [14]Make your whole body suggest that you are watching a star.

The number of the irrelevant sentence: _____

[15]Once you have mastered body language, it is time to move on to the second phase of teacher conning: class participation. [16]Everyone knows that the student who is most eager to learn is the one who responds to the questions that are asked and even comes up with a few more. [17]Therefore, be sure to be responsive. [18]Questions such as "How does this affect the future of Canada?" or "Don't you think that someday all of this will be done by computer?" can be used in any class without prior knowledge of the subject matter. [19]Many students, especially in large classes, get lost in the crowd and never do anything to make themselves stand out. [20]Another good participation technique is to wait until the instructor has said something that sounds profound and then ask him or her to repeat it slowly so you can get it down word for word in your notes. [21]No teacher can resist this kind of flattery.   3

The number of the irrelevant sentence: _____

[22]However, the most advanced form of teacher conning happens after class is over. [23]Don't be like the others who slap their notebooks closed, pick up their books, and rush out the door before the class has formally ended. [24]Did you ever notice how students begin to get restless about five minutes before class ends, even if there's no clock on the wall? [25]Instead, be reluctant to leave. [26]Approach the instructor's desk hesitantly, almost reverently. [27]Say that you want to find out more about the topic. [28]Is there any extra reading you can do? [29]Even better, inquire if the instructor has written anything on the topic--and whether you could borrow it. [30]Finally, compliment your teacher by saying that this is the most interesting course you've ever taken. [31]Nothing beats the personal approach for making a teacher think you care.   4

The number of the irrelevant sentence: _____

[32]Body language, questions, after-class discussions--these are the secrets of teacher conning every college student should know. [33]These kinds of things go on in high school, too, and they're just as effective on that level. [34]Once you master these methods, you won't have to worry about a thing-- until the final exam.   5

The number of the irrelevant sentence: _____

2   EVALUATING ESSAYS FOR SUPPORT

Activity

Both of the student essays below lack supporting details at certain key points. Identify the spots where details are needed in each essay.

Formula for Happiness

[1]Everyone has his or her own formula for happiness. [2]As we go through life, we discover the activities that make us feel best. [3]I've already discovered three keys for my happiness. [4]I depend on karate, music, and self-hypnosis.

[5]An activity which helps me to feel good physically is karate. [6]Before taking karate lessons, I was tired most of the time, my muscles felt like foam rubber, and I was also about twenty pounds overweight. [7]After about three months of these lessons, I began to notice an improvement in my physical condition. [8]I have also noticed that my endurance has increased. [9]At the end of my workday, I used to drag myself home to eat and watch television all night. [10]Now, I still have enough energy to play with my children, go shopping, or see a movie. [11]Karate has made me feel healthy, strong, and happy.

The spot where supporting details are needed occurs after sentence _____.

[12]Singing with a choral group has helped me to achieve emotional well-being through the expression of my feelings. [13]In common situations where other people would reveal their feelings, I would remain quiet. [14]Since joining the chorus, however, I have had an outlet for my joy, anger, or sadness. [15]When I sing, I pour my emotions into the music and don't have to feel shy about expressing myself. [16]For this reason, I enjoy singing certain kinds of music the most, since they demand real depth of feeling.

The first spot where supporting details are needed occurs after sentence _____.

The second spot occurs after sentence _____.

[17]A very important activity which gives me peace of mind is self-hypnosis. [18]This is a total relaxation technique which I learned from a hypnotist several years ago. [19]Essentially I breathe deeply and concentrate on relaxing all the muscles of my body. [20]I then repeat a key suggestion to myself. [21]Because I practise self-hypnosis, I have gained control over several bad habits that have long been haunting me. [22]I have also learned to reduce the stress that goes along with my secretarial job. [23]Now I can handle the boss's demands or unexpected work without feeling tense.

The first spot where supporting details are needed occurs after sentence _____.

The second spot occurs after sentence _____.

[24]In short, my physical, emotional, and mental well-being have been   5
greatly increased through karate, music, and self-hypnosis. [25]These
activities have become important elements in my formula for happiness.

Problems of a Foreign Student

[1]About ten months ago I decided to leave my native country and come to   1
Canada to study. [2]When I got here, I suddenly turned into someone labelled
"foreign student." [3]A foreign student, I discovered, has problems. [4]Whether
from Japan, like me, or from some other country, a foreign student has to
work twice as hard as Canadian students do to succeed in college.

[5]First of all, there is the language problem. [6]Canadian students have   2
the advantage of comprehending English without working at it. [7]But even
they complain that some professors talk too fast, mumble, or use big
words. [8]As a result, they can't take notes fast enough to keep up, or they
misunderstand what was said. [9]Now consider my situation. [10]I'm trying to
cope with a language that is probably one of the hardest in the world
to learn. [11]Dozens of English slang phrases--"mess around," "hassle,"
"get into"--were totally new to me. [12]Other language problems gave me
trouble, too.

The spot where supporting details are needed occurs after sentence _____.

[13]Another problem I face has to do with being a stranger to North   3
American culture. [14]For instance, the academic world is much different in
Japan. [15]In Canada, professors seem to treat students as equals. [16]Many
classes are informal, and the relationship between teacher and student is
friendly; in fact, students call some teachers by their first names. [17]In
Japan, however, the teacher-student relationship is different. [18]Lectures,
too, are more formal, and students show respect by listening quietly and
paying attention at all times. [19]This more casual atmosphere occasionally
makes me feel uncomfortable in class.

The spot where supporting details are needed occurs after sentence _____.

[20]Perhaps the most difficult problem I face is a social one. [21]Canadian   4
students may have some trouble making new friends or may feel lonely at
times. [22]However, they usually manage to find other people with the same
backgrounds, interests, or goals. [23]It is twice as hard to make friends,
though, if a person has trouble making the small talk that can lead to a
relationship. [24]I find it difficult to become friends with other students
because I don't understand some aspects of Canadian life. [25]Students
would rather talk to someone who is familiar with these things.

The spot where supporting details are needed occurs after sentence _____.

[26]Despite all the handicaps that I, as a foreign student, have to   5
overcome, I wouldn't give up this chance to go to school in Canada. [27]Each
day, the problems seem a little bit less overwhelming. [28]Like a little child
who is finally learning to read, write, and make sense of things, I am
starting to enjoy my experience of discovering a brand-new world.

3 EVALUATING ESSAYS FOR COHERENCE

Activity

Both of the essays that follow could be revised to improve their coherence.
Answer the questions about coherence that come after each essay.

Noise Pollution

[1]Natural sounds--waves, wind, bird songs--are so soothing that   1
companies sell tapes of them to anxious people seeking a relaxing
atmosphere in their homes or cars. [2]One reason why "environmental
sounds" are big business is the fact that ordinary citizens--especially city
dwellers--are bombarded by noise pollution. [3]On the way to work, on the
job, and on the way home, the typical urban resident must cope with a
continuing barrage of unpleasant sounds.

[4]The noise level in an office can be unbearable. [5]From nine o'clock to   2
five, phones ring, printers and keyboards clack and clatter, intercoms buzz,
and Xerox machines thump back and forth. [6]Every time the receptionists
can't find people, they resort to a nerve-shattering public address system.
[7]And because the managers worry about the employees' morale, they
graciously provide the endless droning of canned music. [8]This effectively
eliminates any possibility of a moment of blessed silence.

[9]Travelling home from work provides no relief from the noisiness of the   3
office. [10]The ordinary sounds of blaring taxi horns and rumbling buses are
occasionally punctuated by the ear-piercing screech of car brakes. [11]Taking
a shortcut through the park will bring the weary worker face to face with
chanting religious cults, free-lance musicians, screaming children, and
barking dogs. [12]None of these sounds can compare with the large radios
many park visitors carry. [13]Each radio blasts out something different, from
heavy-metal rock to baseball, at decibel levels so strong that they make ear-
drums throb in pain. [14]If there are birds singing or wind in the trees, the
harried commuter will never hear them.

[15]Even a trip to work at 6 or 7 a.m. isn't quiet. [16]No matter which route   4
a worker takes, there is bound to be a noisy construction site somewhere
along the way. [17]Workers will shout from third-storey windows to warn
their co-workers below before heaving debris out and sending it crashing to
earth. [18]Huge front-end loaders will crunch into these piles of rubble and

back up, their warning signals letting out loud, jarring beeps. [19]Jackhammers begin an ear-splitting chorus of rat-a-tat-tat sounds guaranteed to shatter sanity as well as concrete. [20]Before reaching the office, the worker is already completely frazzled.

[21]Noise pollution is as dangerous as any other kind of pollution. [22]The endless pressure of noise probably triggers countless nervous breakdowns, vicious arguments, and bouts of depression. [23]And imagine the world problems we could solve, if only the noise stopped long enough to let us think.

5

1. In "Noise Pollution," what is the number of the sentence to which the transition word *Also* could be added in paragraph 2? _____

2. In the last sentence of paragraph 2, to what does the pronoun *This* refer?

_____

3. What is the number of the sentence to which the transition word *But* could be added in paragraph 3? _____

4. What is the number of the sentence to which the transition word *Then* could be added in paragraph 4? _____

5. What is the number of the sentence to which the transition word *Meanwhile* could be added in paragraph 4? _____

6. What word is used as a synonym for *debris* in paragraph 4?

_____

7. How many times is the key word *sounds* repeated in the essay? _____

8. The time order of the three supporting paragraphs is confused. Which supporting paragraph should come first? _____ Second? _____ Third? _____

Computer Cowardice

[1]A first-semester English essay assignment turned into a major crisis for me, just three weeks after I started college. [2]I had done pretty well in high school, and I registered in college after four years of working full-time: what terrors could school hold for me? [3]A phobia I'd tried to hide even from myself surfaced in the class I was enjoying the most. [4]I left the class without speaking to the instructor about my problem. [5]My hands were sweating, and I couldn't figure out how to disguise my dilemma. [6]Suddenly I realized I had to stop avoiding computers. [7]Within an hour, I had enrolled in a beginners' course at my college's computer facility, I had been given an easy-to-understand pamphlet on basic computer procedures, and I was ready to confront my computer cowardice. [8]Learning the first steps in a

1

basic word-processing programme helped me to polish up my typing skills, took the terror out of computers, and opened up a whole new area of interest for me.

[9]I had never been good at typing, or what I now call keyboarding. [10]When I took typing in junior high, like other male students I didn't think it was that important as a subject. [11]I found the typing exercises boring and repetitive, and they all seemed designed to tie my fingers in knots. [12]My friends and I decided typing wasn't something we were going to need in our high-powered careers as executives and racing drivers. [13]We figured typing was a necessity for secretaries, but not for us. [14]I braved the embarrassment of achieving a mark of fifty-one in the subject, and rarely gave typing another thought. [15]Embarrassment and shame returned in full force during my first word-processing class. [16]Almost everyone could type at what seemed incredible speeds, while I pecked out tiny sentences one finger at a time. [17]To my surprise, after a month of daily practice, keyboarding felt faster than handwriting.

[18]More important, my fears of computers shrank as I confronted the once-hated machines. Instead of avoiding conversations with friends about the wonders of their new computers, I began to join in hesitantly. [19]Only a month or so ago, I hadn't understood any of the computer terms I heard and read; now I knew what a "hard drive" was. [20]The terrors of those screens, clicking keyboards, and humming printers subsided as I learned how to use each item. [21]I began to look forward to the challenges of entering "the information age." After three weeks of training, I managed to hand in my painstakingly processed and spell-checked first essay for that English class. [22]Once I'd avoided tasks at work where I would have needed computer training, and hoped to continue to somehow avoid contact with the dreaded PC in a career as a library assistant. [23]Now I began to realize how much help the computer offered in something as basic as drafting an essay.

[24]The best reward for confronting my "computer phobia," though, was the way it altered my career goals. [25]Classes in Library Technology at my college made extensive use of various computerized information systems, and research projects required me to use the CD-ROM and microfiche catalogues. [26]Now that I was able to move beyond basic word-processing and make use of these facilities, I began to find computers fascinating, not intimidating. [27]I stopped wasting energy on avoiding new areas of learning, and began to take extra courses in Information Management and Retrieval. [28]To my surprise, new career opportunities would now be available to me in managing library resources for businesses and law firms. [29]I could combine some of my work experience with my new skills. [30]A whole new future was before me.

[31]Happily, facing a long-time fear early in my college career proved to be a turning point in both learning about myself and discovering new job opportunities. [32]Being terrified about processing a two-page English essay led to overcoming resistance to a basic skill like keyboarding, and to

overcoming my much larger "computer cowardice." [33]Confronting a seemingly small fear can sometimes lead to great discoveries.

1. In "Computer Cowardice," what is the number of the sentence to which the transition words *For one thing* could be added in paragraph 2? _____

2. What is the number of the sentence to which the transition word *Also* could be added in paragraph 2? _____

3. What is the number of the sentence to which the transition word *But* could be added in paragraph 2? _____

4. In sentence 11, to what does the pronoun *they* refer? _____

5. What is the number of the sentence to which the transition word *However* could be added in paragraph 3? _____

6. What word is used as a synonym for *fears* in paragraph 3?

   _____

7. How many synonyms for the word *fear* appear in the essay? _____

8. Which type of ordering principle for ideas is used in this essay: chronological or emphatic? _____

4   EVALUATING ESSAYS FOR ALL FOUR BASES: UNITY, SUPPORT, COHERENCE, AND SENTENCE SKILLS

Activity

In this activity, you will evaluate two essays in terms of the four bases of unity, support, coherence, and sentence skills. Comments follow each supporting paragraph. Circle the letter of the *one* statement that applies in each case.

Chiggers

I had lived my whole life not knowing what chiggers are. I thought   1
they were probably a type of insect Humphrey Bogart encountered in
The African Queen. I never had any reason to really care, until one day
on a winter vacation in Florida. Within twenty-four hours, I had vividly
experienced what chigger bites are, learned how to treat them, and learned
how to prevent them.

First of all, I learned that chiggers are the larvae of tiny mites found in   2
the palmetto scrub and twitch grass of Florida beaches and that their bites

are always multiple and cause intense itching. A beautiful February day seemed perfect for a walk along an empty stretch of beach. I am definitely not a city person, and I couldn't stand to be surrounded by people, parties, and hotels. As I walked through the beach grass, palmetto, and pines, I noticed what appeared to be a dusting of reddish seeds or pollen on my legs. Looking more closely, I realized that each speck was a tiny insect. I casually brushed off a few and gave them no further thought. I woke up the next morning feeling like an inflamed pincushion. Most of my body was speckled with measle-like bumps that at the slightest touch burned and itched like a mosquito bite raised to the twentieth power. When antiseptics and calamine lotion failed to help, I raced to a walk-in clinic for emergency aid.

a. Paragraph 2 contains an irrelevant sentence.

b. Paragraph 2 lacks supporting details at one key spot.

c. Time order in Paragraph 2 is confused.

d. Paragraph 2 contains two run-on sentences.

Healing the bites of chiggers, as the doctor diagnosed them to be, is not   3
a simple procedure. It seems there is really no wonder drug or commercial product to help the cure. The victim must rely on a harsh and primitive home remedy and mostly wait out the course of the painful bites. First, the doctor explained, the skin must be bathed carefully in alcohol. An antihistamine spray applied several hours later will soothe the intense itching and help prevent infection. Before using the spray, I had to saturate each bite with gasoline or nail polish to kill any remaining chiggers. A few days after the treatment, the bites finally healed. Although I was still in pain, and desperate for relief, I followed the doctor's instructions. I carefully applied gasoline to the bites and walked around for an hour smelling like a gas station.

a. Paragraph 3 contains an irrelevant sentence.

b. Paragraph 3 lacks supporting details at one key spot.

c. Time order in paragraph 3 is confused.

d. Paragraph 3 contains one sentence fragment.

Most important of all, I learned what to do to prevent getting chigger   4
bites on future tropical adventures. Mainly, of course, stay out of pine woods and out of beach scrub-growth on hot days. But if the temptation is too great on an especially beautiful day, I'll be sure to wear the right type of clothing, like a long-sleeved shirt, long pants, knee socks, and closed shoes. In addition, I'll cover myself with clouds of super-strength insect repellent. I will then shower thoroughly as soon as I get home, I also will probably burn all my clothes if I notice even one suspicious red speck.

a. Paragraph 4 contains an irrelevant sentence.
b. Paragraph 4 lacks supporting details at one key spot.
c. Paragraph 4 lacks transitional words.
d. Paragraph 4 contains a run-on and a fragment.

> I will never forget my lessons on the cause, cure, and prevention of   5
> chigger bites. I would gladly accept the challenge of rattlesnakes and bears
> in the wilds of Western Canada but will never again confront a siege of
> chiggers on a deserted Florida beach.

The Hazards of Being an Only Child

> Many people who have grown up in multi-child families think that being   1
> an only child is the best of all possible worlds. They point to such benefits
> as the only child's annual new wardrobe and lack of competition for parental
> love. But single-child status isn't as good as people say it is. Instead of
> having everything they want, only children are sometimes denied certain
> basic human needs.

> Only children lack companionship. An only child can have trouble   2
> making friends, since he or she isn't used to being around other children.
> Often, the only child comes home to an empty house; both parents are
> working, and there are no brothers or sisters to play with or to talk to
> about the day. At dinner, the single child can't tell jokes, giggle, or throw
> food while the adults discuss boring adult subjects. An only child always
> has his or her own room but never has anyone to whisper to half the night
> when sleep doesn't come. Some only children thrive on this isolation and
> channel their energies into creative activities like writing or drawing. Owing
> to this lack of companionship, an only child sometimes lacks the social ease
> and self-confidence that come from being part of a closely knit group of
> contemporaries.

a. Paragraph 2 contains an irrelevant sentence.
b. Paragraph 2 lacks supporting details at one key spot.
c. Paragraph 2 lacks transitional words.
d. Paragraph 2 contains one fragment and one run-on.

> Second, only children lack privacy. An only child is automatically the   3
> centre of parental concern. There's never any doubt about which child tried
> to sneak in after midnight on a week-day. And who will get the lecture the
> next morning. Also, whenever an only child gives in to a bad mood, runs
> into his or her room, and slams the door, the door will open thirty seconds
> later, revealing an anxious parent. Parents of only children sometimes don't
> even understand the child's <u>need</u> for privacy. For example, they may not

understand why a teenager wants a lock on the door or a personal telephone. After all, the parents think, there are only the three of us, there's no need for secrets.

a. Paragraph 3 contains an irrelevant sentence.
b. Paragraph 3 lacks supporting details at one key spot.
c. Paragraph 3 lacks transitional words.
d. Paragraph 3 contains one fragment and one run-on.

Most important, only children lack power. They get all the love; but if something goes wrong, they also get all the punishment. When a bottle of perfume is knocked to the floor or the television is left on all night, there's no little sister or brother to blame it on. Moreover, an only child has no recourse when asking for a privilege of some kind, such as permission to stay out to a late hour or to take an overnight trip with friends. There are no older siblings to point to and say, "You let them do it. Why won't you let me?" With no allies their own age, only children are always outnumbered, two to one. An only child hasn't a chance of influencing any major family decisions, either.

4

a. Paragraph 4 contains an irrelevant sentence.
b. Paragraph 4 lacks supporting details at one key spot.
c. Paragraph 4 lacks transitional words.
d. Paragraph 4 contains one fragment and one run-on.

Being an only child isn't as special as some people think. It's no fun being without friends, without privacy, and without power in one's own home. But the child who can triumph over these hardships grows up self-reliant and strong. Perhaps for this reason alone, the hazards are worth it.

5

PART TWO

TYPES
OF
ESSAY
DEVELOPMENT

INTRODUCTION TO ESSAY DEVELOPMENT

This chapter will discuss:

- **Nine patterns of essay development**
- **Point of view**
- **Writing for a specific purpose and audience**
- **Peer review of your papers**
- **The order of each chapter**
- **A personal checklist for your papers**

NINE PATTERNS OF ESSAY DEVELOPMENT

Traditionally, all writing has been divided into the following forms:

- Exposition

Examples	Comparison and contrast
Process	Definition
Cause and effect	Division and classification

- Description
- Narration
- Argumentation and persuasion

In *exposition*, the writer provides information about and explains a particular subject. The patterns of development in exposition include (1) giving examples, (2) detailing the process of doing or making something, (3) analyzing causes or effects, (4) comparing or contrasting, (5) defining a term or concept, (6) dividing something into parts or grouping it into categories. In this part of the book, each of the six patterns of exposition is presented in a separate chapter.

There are also individual chapters devoted to (7) description, (8) narration, and (9) argument. A *description* is a verbal picture of a person, place, or thing. In a *narration*, a writer tells the story of something that happened. *Argumentation* or *persuasion* is an attempt to prove a point or defend an opinion.

You will have a chance, then, to learn how nine different patterns can help organize material in your papers. Each of the nine patterns has its own internal logic and provides its own special strategies for imposing order on your ideas.

As you practise each pattern, you should keep two points in mind:

- While each essay that you write will involve one predominant pattern, very often one or more additional patterns may be involved as well. For example, consider the three model essays in the next chapter ("Examples"). The first essay, "Everyday Cruelty," is developed through a series of examples. But there is also an element of narration, as the writer presents examples that occur as he proceeds through his day. In the second essay, "Altered States," the use of examples is again the predominant pattern, but in a lesser way the author is also explaining the causes of altered states of mind. The third essay, "Childhood Fears," also presents a series of examples but to a lesser degree also relies on narration and cause-and-effect.

- More important, an essay you write in almost any pattern will probably involve some form of argumentation. You will advance a point and then go on to support your point. To convince the reader that your thesis is valid, you may use a series of examples, or narration, or a description, or some other pattern of organization. In "Everyday Cruelty," for instance, the author uses examples to support his point that people inflict little cruelties on each other. In an essay that appears later in Part Two, a writer supports the point that a certain coffee shop is depressing by providing a number of descriptive details (see page 199). Another writer describes a certain experience in her life as embarrassing and then uses a narrative to persuade us of the truth of this statement (see pages 206–207). And another writer advances the opinion that a fast-food restaurant can be preferable to a fancy one and then supplies comparative information about both to support his claim (see page 159). Much of your writing, in short, will have the purpose of persuading your reader that the idea you have advanced is valid.

POINT OF VIEW IN WRITING

When you write, you can take any of three approaches, or points of view: first-person, second-person, or third-person.

First-Person Approach

In the first-person approach—a strongly individualized point of view—you draw on your own experience, and speak to your audience in your own voice, using pronouns like *I*, *me*, *mine*, *we*, *our*, and *us*.

The first-person approach is most common in narrative essays based on personal experience. It also suits other essays where most of the evidence presented consists of personal observation.

Here is a first-person supporting paragraph from an essay on camping:

> First of all, I like comfort when I'm camping. My motor home, with its completely equipped kitchen, shower stall, toilet, double bed, and colour television, resembles a mobile motel room. I can sleep on a real mattress, clean sheets, and fluffy pillows. Next to my bed are devices that make me feel at home: a radio, an alarm clock, and a TV remote-control unit. Unlike the poor campers huddled in tents, I don't have to worry about cold, rain, heat, or annoying insects. After a hot shower, I can slide into my best nightgown, sit comfortably on my down-filled quilt, and read the latest best-seller while a thunderstorm booms outside.

Second-Person Approach

In the second-person approach, the writer speaks directly to the reader, using the pronoun *you*. The second-person approach is considered appropriate for giving direct instructions and explanations to the reader. That is why *you* is used throughout this book.

You should expect to use the second-person approach only when writing a process essay. Otherwise, as a general rule, *never* use the word *you* in writing. (If doing so has been a common mistake in your writing, you should review the rule about pronoun point of view on page 371.)

Third-Person Approach

The third-person approach is by far the most common point of view in academic writing. In the third person, the writer includes no direct references to the reader (*you*) or the self (*I, me*). Third person gets its name from the stance it suggests—that of an outsider or "third person," observing and reporting on matters of public rather than private importance. In this approach, you draw on information that you have gotten through observation, thinking, or reading.

Here is the paragraph on camping, recast in the third person. Note the third-person pronouns *their*, *them*, and *they*, which all refer to *campers* in the first sentence.

> First of all, modern campers bring complete bedrooms with them. Winnebagoes, various makes of motor homes, and Airstream trailers lumber into Canada's campgrounds every summer like mobile motel rooms. All the comforts of home are provided inside. Campers sleep on real mattresses with

clean sheets and fluffy pillows. Next to their beds are the same gadgets that litter their night tables at home--radios, alarm clocks, and TV remote-control units. It's not necessary for them to worry about annoyances like cold, heat, rain, or buzzing insects, either. They can sit comfortably in bed and read the latest best-sellers while a thunderstorm booms outside.

WRITING FOR A SPECIFIC PURPOSE AND AUDIENCE

The three most common purposes of writing are to *inform*, to *entertain*, and to *persuade*. As already said, most of the writing you will do in this book will involve some form of persuasion. You will advance a point or thesis and then support it in a variety of ways. To some extent, also, you will write papers that provide readers with information about a particular subject.

Your audience will be primarily your instructor, and sometimes other students as well. Your instructor is really a symbol of the larger audience you should see yourself as writing for—an educated, adult audience that expects you to present your ideas in a clear, direct, organized way. If you can learn to persuade or inform such an audience through your writing, you will have accomplished a great deal.

However, it will also be helpful for you to write some papers for a more specific audience. By so doing, you will develop an ability to choose words and adopt a tone of voice that is right for a given purpose and a given group of people.

In this part of the book, then, there is an assignment at or near the end of each chapter that asks you to write with a very specific purpose in mind and for a very specific audience. You will be asked, for example, to imagine yourself as a second-year college student making a presentation to incoming students about how to prepare for college life, as a client of a video introduction service presenting himself or herself to potential dates, as a reader of a local newspaper writing a letter responding to a recent editorial, and as an author of a campus newspaper column giving advice on romance. Through these and other assignments, you will learn how to adjust your style and tone of voice to a given writing situation.

HOW TO PROCEED

Using Part Two: The Progression in Each Chapter

After each type of essay development is explained, in the following chapters, student papers illustrating that type are presented, and then there are questions about the papers. The questions relate to unity, support, and coherence—the principles of effective writing explained earlier.

You are then asked to write your own essay. In most cases, the first assignment is fairly structured and provides a good deal of guidance for the writing process. The other assignments offer a wide and interesting choice of writing topics. In each case, the last or next-to-last assignment involves writing an essay with a specific purpose and for a specific audience. And in three instances (examples, cause-and-effect, and comparison or contrast), the final assignments require outside reading of literary works; a student model is provided for each of these assignments.

Using Peer Review

In addition to having your instructor as an audience for your writing, you will benefit by having another student in your class as an audience. On the day a paper is due, or on a day when you are writing papers in class, your teacher may ask you to pair up with another student. That student will read your paper, and you will read his or her paper.

Ideally, read the other paper aloud while your peer listens. If that is not practical, read it in a whisper while your peer looks on. As you read, both you and your peer should look and listen for spots where the paper does not read smoothly and clearly. Check or circle the trouble spots where your reading snags. Your peer should then read your paper, marking possible trouble spots.

Then, each of you should do three things.

1   Identification: On a separate sheet of paper, write at the top the title and author of the paper you have read. Under it, write your own name as the reader of the paper.

2   Outline: "X-ray" the paper for its inner logic by making up a scratch outline. The scratch outline need be no more than twenty words or so, but it should show clearly the logical foundation on which the essay is built. It should identify and summarize the overall point of the paper and the three areas of support for the point. Your outline can look as follows:

Point: _____

Support:

(1) _____

(2) _____

(3) _____

For example, here is a scratch outline of the essay on movie-going on pages 6–7:

Point: *Going out to the movies presents too many problems.*

Support: *(1) Getting to the theatre*

(2) Dealing with theatre itself

(3) Putting up with other patrons

3 Comments: Under the outline, write the heading "Comments." Then make some useful comments.

Here is what you should comment on:

■ Look at the spots where your reading of the paper snagged. Are words missing or misspelled? Is parallel structure lacking? Are there mistakes with punctuation? Is the meaning of a sentence confused? Try to figure out what the problems are and suggest ways of fixing them.

■ Are there spots in the paper where you see problems with *unity*, *support*, or *organization*? If so, offer comments. For example, you might say, "More details are needed in the first supporting paragraph," or "Some of the details in the last supporting paragraph don't really back up your point."

■ Finally, note something you really liked about the paper. You might, for instance, mention good use of transitions or a specific detail that is especially realistic or vivid.

After you have completed your evaluation of the paper, give it to your classmate. Your teacher may provide you with the option of rewriting a paper in light of the "peer feedback." Whether or not you rewrite, be sure to hand in the "peer evaluation form" with your paper.

Using a Personal Checklist

After you have completed a paper, there are three ways you should check it yourself. You should *always* do the first two checks, which take only a few minutes. Ideally, you should then take the time to do the detailed third check as well.

1 Read the paper *out loud*. If it does not sound right—if it does not read smoothly and clearly—then make the changes needed to ensure that it will be smooth and clear.

2 Make sure you can answer two basic questions clearly and concisely: "What is the point of my essay? What are the three distinct bits of support for my point?"

3 Last, evaluate your paper in terms of the detailed checklist that appears on the opposite page. (This checklist is repeated on the inside front cover of the book.) The numbers in parentheses refer to the pages of this book that discuss each skill.

Checklist of the Four Steps in Writing an Effective Essay

1 Unity

- Clearly stated thesis in the introductory paragraph of your paper (pages 7; 35–39; 45–54)
- All the supporting paragraphs on target in backing up your thesis (90–92; 102–104)

2 Support

- Three separate supporting points for the thesis (8–9; 22–23; 26–31; 39–41)
- *Specific* evidence for each of the three supporting points (39–43; 54–59; 93–95)
- *Plenty of* specific evidence for each supporting point (44–45; 59–62; 105–107)

3 Coherence

- Clear method of organization (64–66; 81–82; 96–98; 107–110)
- Transitions and other connecting words (67–73; 83–87)
- Effective introduction, conclusion, and title (7–9; 73–80)

4 Sentence Skills

- Fragments eliminated (306–319)
- Run-ons eliminated (319–331)
- Correct verb forms (332–340; 347–354)
- Subject and verb agreement (341–346)
- Faulty parallelism and faulty modifiers eliminated (355–366)
- Faulty pronouns eliminated (367–379)
- Adjectives and adverbs used correctly (380–385)
- Capital letters used correctly (386–393)
- Punctuation marks where needed:
  - **a** Apostrophe (394–399)
  - **b** Quotation marks (400–406)
  - **c** Comma (407–416)
  - **d** Colon; Semi-colon (417; 418)
  - **e** Dash; Hyphen (418; 420)
  - **f** Parentheses (419)
- Correct paper format (299–300)
- Needless words eliminated (455–457)
- Correct word choices (450–455)
- Possible spelling errors checked (430–434)
- Careless errors eliminated through proofreading (32–34; 470–480)
- Sentences varied (460–469)

EXAMPLES

In our daily conversations, we often provide *examples*—that is, details, particulars, specific instances—to explain statements that we make. Here are several statements and supporting examples:

The first day of school was frustrating.	My sociology course was cancelled. Then, I couldn't find the computer lab. And the lines at the bookstore were so long that I went home without buying my textbooks.
That washing machine is unreliable.	The water temperature can't be predicted; it stops in mid-cycle; and it sometimes shreds my clothing.
My grandfather is a thrifty person.	He washes and reuses aluminum foil. He wraps gifts in newspaper. And he's worn the same Sunday suit for twenty years.

In each case, the examples help us see for ourselves the truth of the statement that has been made. In essays, too, explanatory examples help your audience fully understand your point. Lively, specific examples also add interest to your paper.

In this section, you will be asked to provide a series of examples to support your thesis. First read the essays ahead; they all use examples to develop their points. Then answer the questions that follow.

ESSAYS TO CONSIDER

Everyday Cruelty

Last week, I found myself worrying less about problems of world politics and urban crime and more about smaller evils. I came home one day with a bad taste in my mouth, the kind I get whenever I witness the

1

little cruelties that people inflict on each other. On this particular day, I had seen three especially mean-spirited things happen,

I first thought about mean-spirited people as I walked from the bus stop to the office where I work. I make this walk every day, and it's my first step away from the comforts of home and into the tensions of the city. For me, a landmark on the route is a tiny patch of ground that was once strewn with rubbish and broken glass. The city is trying to make a "mini-park" out of it by planting trees and flowers. Every day this spring, I watched the skinny saplings put out tiny leaves. When I walked past, I always noted how big the tulips were getting and made bets with myself on when they would bloom. But last Wednesday, as I reached the park, I felt sick. Someone had knocked the trees to the ground and trampled the budding tulips into the dirt. Someone had destroyed a bit of beauty for no reason.

At lunchtime on Wednesday, I witnessed more meanness. Along with dozens of other hungry, hurried people, I was waiting in line at Harvey's. Also in line was a young mother with two tired, impatient children clinging to her legs. The mother was trying to calm the children, but it was obvious that their whining was about to give way to full-fledged tantrums. The lines barely moved, and the lunch-time tension was building. Then, one of the children began to cry and scream. The little boy's blood-curdling yells resounded through the restaurant, and people stared angrily at the helpless mother. Finally, one man turned to her and said, "Lady, you shouldn't bring your kids to a public place if you can't control them." The woman was exhausted and hungry. Someone in line could have helped her with her problem. Instead, even though many of the customers in the restaurant were parents themselves, they treated her like a criminal.

The worst incident of mean-spiritedness that I saw that day happened after I left work. As I walked to the bus stop, I approached an old woman huddled in a doorway. She was wrapped in a dirty blanket and clutched a plastic bag packed with her belongings. She was one of the "street people" our society leaves to fend for themselves. Canada, one of the wealthiest countries on earth, should not allow such suffering. Some of these victims even live in cardboard boxes during the coldest winters. Approaching the woman from the opposite direction were three teenagers who were laughing and talking in loud voices. When they saw the old woman, they began to shout crude remarks at her. One of them grabbed her shopping bag and pretended to throw it out into the street. The woman stared helplessly at them, like a wounded animal surrounded by hunters. Then, having had their fun, the teenagers went on their way.

I had seen enough of the world's coldness that day and wanted to leave it behind. At home, I huddled in the warmth of my family. I wondered why we all contribute to the supply of petty cruelty. There's enough of it already.

Altered States

Most Canadians are not alcoholics. Most of us do not smoke marijuana to get high. LSD, for the most part, went out of style along with the flower children of the sixties. Nevertheless, many Canadians are walking and driving around with their minds slightly out of kilter. In its attempt to cope with modern life, the human mind seems to have evolved some defence strategies. Confronted with inventions like the automobile, the television, and the shopping mall, for example, the mind will slip--all by itself--into an altered state. 1

First of all, the mind must now cope with the automobile. In the past, no human being ever sat for hours at a time, in the same position, staring at endless white lines and matched pairs of small red tail-lights. In order to deal with this unnatural situation, the mind goes on automatic pilot. A primitive, less-developed region of the brain takes over the actual driving. It tells the foot when to apply pressure to the brake and gas pedal and directs the eyes to stay open. Meanwhile, the rest of the brain continues on with higher functions. It devises excuses for being late for work. It replays, better than any video system, yesterday's Oilers game. Or, it creates a pleasant imaginary world where its owner wins all arguments, tells hilarious jokes, and attracts the opposite sex like a magnet. By splitting into two halves, the mind deals with the boredom of driving. 2

The mind has defences not only against the car but also against television. Since too much staring at flickering images of police officers, detectives, and talk-show hosts can be dangerous to human sanity, the mind automatically goes into a TV hypnosis state. The eyes see the sitcom or the dog food commercial, but the mind goes into a holding pattern. None of the televised images or sounds actually enters the brain. This is why, when questioned, people cannot remember commercials they have seen five seconds before or why the TV cops are chasing a certain suspect. In this hypnotic, trance-like state, the mind resembles an armoured armadillo. It rolls up in self-defence, letting the stream of televised information pass by harmlessly. 3

Perhaps the most dangerous threat to the mind, however, is the shopping mall. In the modern mall, dozens of stores, restaurants, and movie theatres compete for the mind's attention. There are hundreds of questions to be answered. Should I start with the upper or lower mall level? Which stores should I look in? Should I bother with the sweater sale at the Bay? Should I eat fried chicken or a burger for lunch? Where is my car parked? To combat this mental overload, the mind goes into a state resembling the white-out experienced by mountain climbers trapped in a blinding snowstorm. Suddenly, everything looks the same. The shopper is unsure where to go next and cannot remember what he or she came for in the first place. The mind enters this state deliberately, so that the shopper has no choice but to leave. 4

Therefore, the next time you see drivers, TV viewers, or shoppers with eyes as glazed and empty as polished doorknobs, you'll know these people are in a protective altered state. Be gentle with them. They are merely trying to cope with the mind-numbing inventions of modern life. 5

Childhood Fears

I remember my childhood as being generally happy and can recall   1
experiencing some of the most carefree times of my life. But I can also
remember, even more vividly, moments of being deeply frightened. As a
child, I was truly terrified of the dark and of getting lost; these fears were
very real and caused me some extremely uncomfortable moments.

Maybe it was the strange way things looked and sounded in my familiar   2
room at night that scared me so much. There was never total darkness, but
a street-light or passing car lights made clothes hung over a chair take on
the shape of an unknown beast. Out of the corner of my eye, I saw curtains
seem to move when there was no breeze. A tiny creak in the floor would
sound a hundred times louder than in the daylight, and my imagination
would take over, creating burglars and monsters on the prowl. Darkness
always made me feel so helpless, too. My heart would pound, and I would
lie very still so that the "enemy" wouldn't discover me.

Another of my childhood fears was that I would get lost, especially on   3
the way home from school. Every morning I got on the school bus right
near my home--that was no problem. After school, though, when all the
buses were lined up along the curb, I was terrified that I'd get on the wrong
one and be taken to some unfamiliar neighbourhood. I would scan the bus
for the faces of my friends, make sure the bus driver was the same one
that had been there in the morning, and even then ask the others over and
over again to be sure I was on the right bus. On school or family trips to an
amusement park or a museum, I wouldn't let the leaders out of my sight.
And of course, I was never very adventurous when it came to taking walks
or hikes, because I would go only where I was sure I could never get lost.

Perhaps one of the worst fears of all I had as a child was that of not   4
being liked or accepted by others. First of all, I was quite shy. Second, I
worried constantly about my looks, thinking people wouldn't like me
because I was too fat or wore braces. I tried to wear the "right" clothes
and even had intense arguments with my mother over the importance of
wearing "sneakers" instead of saddle shoes to school. I'm sorry now that
we had these arguments, especially since my mother is quite sickly and
has spent the last year in and out of the hospital. Being popular was so
important to me then, and the fear of not being liked was a powerful one.

One of the processes of evolving from a child to an adult is being able   5
to recognize and overcome or outgrow our fears. I've learned that darkness
does not have to take on a life of its own, that others can help me when I'm
lost, and that friendliness and sincerity will encourage people to like me.
Understanding the things that scared us as children helps us to cope with
our lives as adults.

■ Questions

About Unity

1. Which sentence in paragraph 4 of "Childhood Fears" should be omitted in the interest of paragraph unity? (*Fill in the first two or three words.*)

   _____

2. Which two sentences in paragraph 4 of "Everyday Cruelty" should be omitted in the interest of paragraph unity?

   _____   _____

3. Which thesis statement fails to mention all three of its supporting points in its plan of development? _____

About Support

4. After which sentence in paragraph 4 of "Childhood Fears" are more supporting details needed? _____

5. Which essay uses a single extended example in each of its supporting paragraphs? _____

About Coherence

6. Which words in paragraph 4 of "Altered States" signal that the most important idea was saved for last? _____

7. What are the two transition words in paragraph 4 of "Childhood Fears"?

   _____   _____

8. Which topic sentence in "Altered States" functions as a linking sentence between paragraphs? _____

About the Introduction and Conclusion

9. Circle below the kind of introduction used in "Childhood Fears."
   a. Broad, general statement narrowing to thesis
   b. Idea that is the opposite of the one to be developed
   c. Quotation
   d. Anecdote
   e. Questions

10. Which transition word signals the conclusion of "Altered States"?

    _____

WRITING THE ESSAY

■ Writing Assignment 1

For this assignment, you will complete an unfinished essay by adding appropriate supporting examples. Here is the incomplete essay:

Problems with My Apartment

> When I was younger, I fantasized about how wonderful life would be when I moved into my own apartment. Now I'm a bit older and wiser, and my fantasies have turned into nightmares. My apartment has given me nothing but headaches. From the day I signed the lease, I've had to deal with an unco-operative building owner, an incompetent caretaker, and inconsiderate neighbours.

> First of all, the owner of the building has been unco-operative.

> I've had a problem not only with the owner but also with an incompetent caretaker.

> Perhaps the worst problem has been with the inconsiderate neighbours who live in the apartment above me. ...

> Sometimes, my apartment seems like a small, friendly oasis surrounded by hostile enemies. I never know what side trouble is going to come from next: the owner, the caretaker, or the neighbours. Home may be where the heart is, but my sanity is thinking about moving out.

Note: If you do not have experience with an apartment, write instead on problems of living in a student residence, or problems of living at home. Revise the introduction and conclusion so that they fit your topic. Problems in living in a college residence might include:

Restrictive residence regulations

Inconsiderate students on your floor

A difficult room-mate

Problems in living at home might include:

Lack of space

Inconsiderate brothers and sisters

Conflict with your parent or parents

How to Proceed

a Brainstorm the assignment by making up answers to the following questions. Use separate paper.

How has the owner been unco-operative?

In what ways have you been inconvenienced?

Has he or she been unco-operative more than once?

What has been your reaction?

What has been the owner's reaction?

What kinds of things have you said to each other?

Who is the caretaker?

What has he or she tried to fix in the apartment?

In what ways has he or she been incompetent?

How has the caretaker inconvenienced you?

Has the caretaker's incompetence cost you money?

What is the worst example of the caretaker's incompetence?

Who are the neighbours?

How long have they lived upstairs?

What kinds of hassles have you had?

Have these incidents happened several times?

If you have spoken to the neighbours, what did they say?

What is the worst problem with these neighbours?

The answers to these questions should serve as an excellent source of details for the essay.

b Keep in mind that you may use one extended example in each paragraph (as in the essay "Everyday Cruelty") or two or three short examples (as in "Childhood Fears").

c As you are writing drafts of your three supporting paragraphs, ask yourself repeatedly:

Do my examples truly show the apartment owner as *unco-operative?*
Do my examples truly show the caretaker as *incompetent?*
Do my examples truly show my neighbours as *inconsiderate?*

Your aims in this assignment are twofold: (1) to provide *adequate* specific details for the three qualities in question and (2) to provide *enough* specific details so that you solidly support each quality.

d When you are satisfied that you have provided effective examples, proofread your paragraphs carefully for the sentence skills listed on page 123 and the inside front cover. Then write out the full essay on separate paper and submit it to your instructor.

■ **Writing Assignment 2**

Write an essay on the good or bad qualities (or habits) of a person you know well. The person might be a member of your family, a friend, a room-mate, a boss or supervisor, a neighbour, a teacher, or someone else. Listed below are some descriptive words that can be applied to people. They are only suggestions; you can write about other qualities as well.

Honest	Persistent	Irresponsible	Spineless
Bad-tempered	Shy	Stingy	Good-humoured
Ambitious	Sloppy	Trustworthy	Co-operative
Bigoted	Hard-working	Aggressive	Disciplined
Considerate	Supportive	Courageous	Sentimental
Argumentative	Suspicious	Compulsive	Defensive
Soft-hearted	Open-minded	Jealous	Dishonest
Energetic	Lazy	Modest	Insensitive
Patient	Independent	Sarcastic	Unpretentious
Reliable	Stubborn	Self-centred	Neat
Generous	Flirtatious		

You may want to write about three related qualities of one person (for example, "My brother is stubborn, bad-tempered, and suspicious") or about one quality that is apparent in different aspects of a person's life (for example, "My wife's sensitivity is apparent in her relationships with her friends at work, my parents, and our teenage son").

■ Writing Assignment 3

Write an essay that uses examples to develop one of the following statements or a related statement of your own.

> If you look hard enough, you can see complete strangers being kind to one another.
>
> The tabloids sold at supermarket check-outs use several techniques to lure consumers into buying them.
>
> The Stanley Cup is scarcely Canadian nowadays.
>
> The best things in life are definitely not free.
>
> Living with a room-mate can help you learn honesty, tolerance, and consideration.
>
> There's more joy in simple pleasures than in life's great events.
>
> Looking for a job can be a stressful process.
>
> Pets in Canada are treated like surrogate children.
>
> Our lives would be improved without the automobile.
>
> Canadian culture is infatuated with violence.

Be sure to choose examples that actually support your thesis. They should be relevant facts, statistics, personal experiences, or incidents you have heard or read about.

Organize each paragraph by grouping several examples that support a particular point. Or use one extended example—an incident or story that may take up a full paragraph.

Save the paragraph containing the most vivid, convincing, or important examples for last.

■ Writing Assignment 4

In this essay, you will write with a specific purpose and for a specific audience. Imagine that you have completed a year of college and have agreed to take part in your college's summer orientation program for incoming students. You will be meeting with a small group of new students to help them get ready for college life.

Prepare a brief presentation to the new students in which you make the point that they must be ready to take on more responsibility than they may have had to do in high school. Make vividly clear—using several hypothetical students as examples—just what the consequences of inappropriate behaviour can be. To organize your presentation, you might want to focus on three of the following areas: teachers, class attendance, time control, class note-taking, textbook study, establishing regular times and places for study, and getting help when needed. Each area could be developed with detailed examples in a separate supporting paragraph.

■ Writing Assignment 5

Write an essay based on an outside reading. It might be a selection in one of the following books (most should be available in your college library) or another selection recommended by your instructor.

Diane Ackerman, *A Natural History of Love**
Dave Barry, *Greatest Hits**
Pierre Berton, *Just Add Water and Stir**
Douglas Coupland, *Generation X, Shampoo Planet*
Robertson Davies, *A Voice in the Attic**
Ken Dryden, *The Game*
Northrop Frye, *The Educated Imagination**
William Gibson, *Johnny Mnemonic, Neuromancer*
Peter Goddard, *Shakin' All Over: The Rock n' Roll Years in Canada*
Ray Guy, *That Far Greater Bay**
Joy Kogawa, *Obasan*
Anne Morrow Lindbergh, *Gift from the Sea*
William Least Heat Moon, *Blue Highways*
Farley Mowat, *Canada North**
Richard Needham, *The Hypodermic Needham**
George Orwell, *Shooting an Elephant and Other Essays*
Paul Quarrington, *Whale Music*
Daniel Richler, *Kicking Tomorrow*
Mordecai Richler, *Hunting Tigers Under Glass**
Erika Ritter, *Urban Scrawl*
Margaret Visser, *Much Depends on Dinner**

Base your essay on some idea in the selection you have chosen and provide a series of examples to back up your idea. A student model is given on the following page.

*Or any other collection of essays by the same author.

In "A Hanging," George Orwell describes the execution of a condemned   1
man in a Burmese prison. The prisoner, a Hindu, is marched from his cell,
led onto a gallows, and killed when the drop opens and the noose tightens.
The entire procedure takes eight minutes. As he depicts this brief incident,
Orwell uses a series of details that make us sharply aware of the enormity
of killing another human being.

The moments leading up to the hanging are filled with tension. Six tall   2
guards, two of them armed with rifles, surround the prisoner, "a puny wisp
of a man." To prevent his escape, the guards not only handcuff the man but
also chain his handcuffs to their belts and lash his arms to his sides. The
guards, nervous about fulfilling their duty, treat the Hindu like "a fish
which is still alive and may jump back into the water." Meanwhile, the jail
superintendent prods the head jailer to get on with the execution. The
superintendent's irritability is a mask for his discomfort. Then, the
procession toward the gallows is interrupted by the appearance of a
friendly dog, "wagging its whole body, wild with glee at finding so many
human beings together." This does not ease the tension but increases it. The
contrast of the lively dog licking the doomed man's face momentarily stuns
the guards and arouses in the superintendent a sense of angry urgency.

Next, in the gallows scene, Orwell uses vivid details that emphasize the   3
life within the man who is about to die. The condemned prisoner, who has
been walking steadily up to this point, moves "clumsily" up the ladder. And
until now, he has been utterly silent. But, after the noose is placed around
his neck, he begins "crying out to his god." The repeated cry of "Ram! Ram!
Ram!" is "like the tolling of a bell," a death knell. The dog begins to whine
at the sound, and the guards go "grey," their bayonets trembling. It is as if
the hooded, faceless man on the wooden platform has suddenly become a
human being, a soul seeking aid and comfort. The superintendent, who has
been hiding his emotions behind a stern face, gives the execution order
"fiercely." The living man of moments ago simply ceases to be.

After the hanging, Orwell underscores the relief people feel when the   4
momentous event is over. The jail superintendent checks to be sure that the
prisoner is dead and then blows out "a deep breath" and loses his "moody
look." "One felt an impulse," Orwell says, "to sing, to break into a run, to
snigger." Suddenly, people are talking and chattering, even laughing. The
head jailer's story about a condemned prisoner who clung to the bars of his
cell so tightly that it took six men to move him sets off a gale of laughter.
On the road outside the prison, everyone who participated in the execution
has a whisky. The men, having been so close to death, need to reassure
themselves of the fact that they are alive. They must laugh and drink, not
because they are insensitive, but because they are shaken. They must try to
forget that the dead man is only thirty metres away.

"A Hanging" sets out to create a picture of death in the midst of life.   5
Orwell tries to make us see, through the details he chooses, that killing a
person results in "one mind less, one world less." Such an act--"cutting a
life short when it is in full tide"--violates the laws of life and nature.

■ **Writing Assignment 6:**
Writing about a Reading Selection

Read the selection titled "In Praise of the F Word" on pages 643–644. Then write an essay with a thesis that rejects Mary Sherry's idea that failing marks in schools are vital to educational and personal development. Your thesis could be similar to this one: "Using failure as a weapon will only intimidate students, not improve their performance." In your introduction, refer to Sherry's essay and state that you disagree with her ideas. Here is a model introduction you might use:

> In the essay "In Praise of the F Word," Mary Sherry argues that "no-fail" educational systems have led to fraudulent educations, puzzled students, and dissatisfied employers. She states that schools have become dishonest in their evaluation of students. But Sherry's views are old-fashioned and limited in their accuracy. Using failure as weapon will only intimidate students, not improve their performance.

You might organize the essay by discussing, in separate paragraphs, any three of the following:

Failing marks, delivered to an unprepared student, can only lower self-esteem.

Failing marks may not take into account individual or cultural problems.

Failing marks may indicate inaccurate initial placement of a student.

Failing students is a return to a "punishment-oriented" educational system.

Support each of your topic sentences with specific examples. A student writing about failing marks as a return to "punishment-oriented" education might use examples based on the following ideas to flesh out the topic sentence, "Schools have developed in a healthy direction away from offering only the 'carrot or stick' approach to marking and motivation."

1. Students are more motivated by positive goals than by negative consequences.

2. The threat of failure is a source of intimidation for uncertain or insecure students.

3. Careful attention to student performance produces more successful students than does punishment.

Your examples should be as specific and definite as you can make them in order to be convincing.

Write an outline for your essay by listing the ideas you plan to include and the examples you will use in the order that seems best to you.

In your conclusion, you might state that schools and colleges do their best to educate in a positive and supportive way without resorting to threats and punishment.

Note: As an alternative assignment, you may wish to write an essay supporting Sherry's contention that failure in school is a valid and appropriate option for teachers and students.

PROCESS

Every day we perform many activities that are *processes*, that is, series of steps carried out in a definite order. Many of these processes are familiar and automatic: for example, loading film in a camera, diapering a baby, or making an omelette. We are thus seldom aware of the sequence of steps that makes up each activity. In our jobs, we are asked to follow, or to give instructions. We then become increasingly aware of the importance of both sequence and completeness for each step in a process. In other cases, such as when a person asks us for directions to a particular place or when we try to read and follow the directions for a new table game that someone has given us, we may be painfully conscious of the whole series of steps involved in the process.

In this section, you will be asked to write a *process essay*—one that explains clearly how to do or make something. To prepare for this assignment, you should first read the student process papers that are presented and then respond to the questions that follow them.

ESSAYS TO CONSIDER

Successful Exercise

Regular exercise is something like the weather--we all talk about it, but 1
we tend not to do anything about it! Television exercise classes, records and
tapes, and new videocassettes and discs, as well as the instructions in
books, magazines, and pamphlets, now make it easy to have a personal,
low-cost exercise programme without leaving home. However, for success in
exercise, you should follow a simple plan consisting of arranging the time,
making preparations, and following the sequence with care.

To begin with, set aside a regular time for exercise. If you have a heavy 2
schedule at work or school, this may be difficult, since you're rushed in the
morning and exhausted at night, and you have no time in between.
However, one solution is simply to get up half an hour earlier in the
morning. Look at it this way: if you're already getting up too early, what's
an extra half hour? Of course, that time could be cut to fifteen minutes
earlier if you could lay out your clothes, set the breakfast table, fill the
coffee maker, and gather your books and materials for the next day before
you go to bed.

Next, prepare for your exercise session. To begin with, get yourself 3
ready by not eating or drinking anything before exercising. Why risk an
upset stomach? Then, dress comfortably in something that allows you to
move freely. Since you'll be in your own home, there's no need to invest in
a high-fashion dance costume. A loose T-shirt and shorts are good. A
bathing suit is great in summer, and in winter a set of long underwear is
warm and comfortable. If your hair tends to flop in your eyes, pin it back
or wear a headband or scarf. Prepare the exercise area, too. Turn off the
phone and lock the door to prevent interruptions. Shove the coffee table out
of the way so you won't bruise yourself on it or other furniture. Finally, get
out the simple materials you'll need to exercise on.

If this is your first attempt at exercising, start slowly. You do not need 4
to do each movement the full number of times at first, but you should <u>try</u>
each one. After five or six sessions, you should be able to do each one the
full number of times. Try to move in a smooth, rhythmic way; doing so will
help prevent injuries and pulled muscles. Pretend you're a dancer and make
each move graceful, even if it's just climbing up off the floor. After the last
exercise, give yourself five minutes to relax and cool off--you have earned
it. Finally, put those sore muscles under a hot shower and get ready for a
great day.

Establishing an exercise programme isn't difficult, but it can't be 5
achieved by reading about it, talking about it, or watching models exercise
on television. To begin with, you're going to have to get up off that couch
and do something about it. Otherwise, as my doctor likes to say, "If you
don't use it, you'll lose it."

How to Complain

I'm not just a consumer--I'm a victim. If I order a product, it is sure to   1
arrive in the wrong colour, size, or quantity. If I hire people to do repairs,
they never arrive on the day scheduled. If I owe a bill, the computer is
bound to overcharge me. Therefore, in self-defence, I have developed the
following consumer's guide to complaining effectively.

The first step is getting organized. I save all sales slips and original   2
boxes. Also, I keep a special file for warranty cards and appliance
guarantees. This file does not prevent a product from falling apart the
day after the guarantee runs out. One of the problems today is the shoddy
manufacturing that goes into many products. However, these facts give
me the ammunition I need to make a complaint. I know the date of the
purchase, the correct price (or service charge), where the item was
purchased, and an exact description of the product, including model and
serial numbers. When I compose my letter of complaint, I find it is not
necessary to exaggerate. I just stick to the facts.

The next step is to send the complaint to the person who will get   3
results quickly. My experience has shown that the president of a company
is the best person to contact. I call the company to find out the president's
name and make sure I note the proper spelling. Then I write directly to
that person, and I usually get prompt action. For example, the head of CCM
arranged to replace my son's ten-speed "lemon" when it fell apart piece
by piece in less than a year. Another time, the president of a Calgary
department store finally had a twenty-dollar overcharge on my bill
corrected after three months of arguing with the computer had brought
no results.

If I get no response to a written complaint within ten days, I follow   4
through with a personal telephone call. When I had a new bathtub installed
a few years ago, the plumber left a gritty black substance on the bottom of
the tub. No amount of scrubbing could remove it. I tried every cleanser on
the supermarket shelf, but I still had a dirty tub. The plumber shrugged off
my complaints and said to try Fantastik. The manufacturer never answered
my letter. Finally, I made a personal phone call to the president of the firm.
Within days a well-dressed executive showed up at my door. In a business
suit, white shirt, striped tie, and rubber gloves, he cleaned the tub. Before
he left, he scolded in an angry voice, "You didn't have to call the president."
The point is, I did have to call the president. No one else cared enough to
solve the problem.

Therefore, my advice to consumers is to keep accurate records, and   5
when you have to complain, go right to the top. It has always worked
for me.

How to Pick the Perfect Class Schedule

As you look at the computer printout that lists your courses for next 1
semester, do you experience a terrible sinking feeling in the pit of your
stomach? Have you gotten stuck with unwanted courses or a depressing
time schedule that cannot be changed? If so, you obviously don't know how
to select the perfect schedule. But by following a few simple procedures, you
can begin any semester with the right courses at the most convenient times.

First, you must find the right courses. These are the ones that combine 2
the least amount of work with the fewest tests and the most lenient
professors. Ask your friends and acquaintances about courses in which they
received A's after attending only 25 per cent of the classes. Ask around,
too, to see which professors have given the same tests for the last fifteen
years. Photocopies of these tests are usually cheap and widely available.
Then, pick up a copy of the master schedule and study it carefully. Find the
tell-tale course titles that signal an easy glide through a painless subject.
Look for titles like "History of the Animated Cartoon," "WordPerfect for
Beginners," and "Rock Music of the 1950s."

Next, when you have accumulated lists of easy instructors and subjects, 3
you can begin to block out time periods. The ideal schedule will vary
according to your individual needs. If you stay up late in order to watch old
movies or work the graveyard shift, you may want a daily schedule that
begins no sooner than noon. You should schedule only afternoon courses,
too, if you're one of those people who would rather be tortured than forced
to leave a warm, cosy bed in the morning. On the other hand, if you are a
"lark" who bounds out of bed at dawn, you may want to get your classes
out of the way as early as possible. That way you have the rest of the day
free. Morning classes are also necessary if you are a soap opera fanatic
who can't miss one day's events in Pine Valley or Port Charles.

Finally, you must outsmart the registration process. You want your 4
ideal schedule to pass through official channels untouched. The main way to
do this is to register early. Ignore things like registration by first letter of
last name or by diploma name. Desperate stories about dying relatives or
heartless employers will get you quickly through a registration line. If a
course does happen to be closed because you simply couldn't register at
7:00 a.m., you may still be able to get in. Talk to the professor and
convince him or her that a serious, ambitious, hard-working student like
yourself would be a shining asset to the class. Be sure to carry a list of
back-up courses to registration, though, just in case one of your chosen
classes switches professors or changes time periods. Be ready to fill in
vacant slots with courses that meet your strict requirements.

By following these suggestions, any student can pick the perfect class 5
schedule. College can thus become a non-irritating, almost pleasant activity
that disrupts your real life as little as possible. And you never know--you
might even learn something in "Creative TV Watching."

■ **Questions**

About Unity

1. Which supporting paragraph in "Successful Exercise" lacks a topic sentence? (*Write the paragraph number.*) _____

2. Which sentence in paragraph 2 of "How to Complain" should be omitted in the interest of paragraph unity? (*Fill in the first two or three words.*)

   _____

About Support

3. After which sentence in paragraph 3 in "Successful Exercise" are more specific details needed? _____

4. Which paragraph in "How to Complain" uses a single extended example to support its topic sentence? _____

5. What are the three key stages in the process of "How to Complain"?

   a. _____

   b. _____

   c. _____

6. What are the three key stages in the process of "Picking the Perfect Class Schedule"?

   a. _____

   b. _____

   c. _____

About Coherence

7. What are the four main transition words in paragraph 3 of "Successful Exercise"? _____   _____   _____   _____

8. Which topic sentence in "How to Pick the Perfect Class Schedule" functions as a linking sentence between paragraphs? _____

About the Introduction and Conclusion

9. Which method of introduction is used in "How to Pick the Perfect Class Schedule"?

   _____

10. Which essay ends with a recommendation?

WRITING THE ESSAY

■ Writing Assignment 1

Choose one of the ten topics below that you think you can write about in a process paper.

How to do grocery shopping in a minimum of time
How to select a car (new or used), apartment, or home
How to do household cleaning efficiently
How to drive defensively
How to protect a home from burglars
How to gain or lose weight
How to relax
How to study for an important exam
How to play a position (third base, guard, goalie, etc.) in a team sport skilfully
How to plan an event (party, wedding, garage sale, etc.)

How to Proceed

a Now freewrite for ten minutes on the topic you have tentatively chosen. Do not worry about spelling, grammar, organization, or other matters of correct form. Just write whatever comes into your head regarding the topic. Keep writing for more than ten minutes if any additional details about the topic occur to you.

  This freewriting will give you a base of raw material that you can draw on in the next phase of your work on the essay. After freewriting for ten minutes, you should have a sense of whether there is enough material available for you to write a process essay about the topic. If so, continue as explained below. If not, choose another topic and freewrite about this new topic for ten minutes.

b State your thesis in a single clear sentence. In your thesis, you can (1) say it is important that your audience know about this process ("Knowing how to register a complaint can save time and frustration") or (2) state your opinion of this process ("Growing your own tomatoes is easier than you might think").

c Make a list of all the steps that you are describing. Here, for example, is the list prepared by the author of "How to Complain":

Save sales slips and original boxes
Engrave items with ID number in case of burglary
Write letter of complaint
Make photocopy of letter
Create file of warranties and guarantees
Send complaint letter directly to president
Call company for president's name
Follow through with telephone call if no response
Make thank-you call after action is taken

d Number your items in time order; strike out items that do not fit in the list; add others you can think of. Thus:

1 Save sales slips and original boxes
~~Engrave items with ID number in case of burglary~~
4 Write letter of complaint
~~Make photocopy of letter~~
2 Create file of warranties and guarantees
5 Send complaint letter directly to president
3 Call company for president's name
6 Follow through with telephone call if no response
~~Make thank-you call after action is taken~~

e After making the list, decide how the items can be grouped into a minimum of three steps. For example, with "How to Complain," you might divide the process into (1) getting organized, (2) sending the complaint to the president, and (3) following up with further action. Or, with a topic like "How to Grow Tomatoes," you might divide the process into (1) soil preparation, (2) planting, and (3) care.

f Use your list as a guide to write the first rough draft of your paper. As you write, try to think of additional details that will develop your opening sentence. Do not expect to finish your paper in one draft. You should, in fact, be ready to write a series of lists and drafts as you work towards the goals of unity, support, and coherence.

g Be sure to use transitions such as *first*, *next*, *also*, *then*, *after*, *now*, *during*, and *finally* so that your paper moves smoothly and clearly from one step in the process to the next.

h While working on your paper, refer to the checklist on page 123 and the inside front cover to make sure you can answer *Yes* to the questions about unity, support, and coherence. Also, refer to the checklist when you proofread the next-to-final draft for sentence-skills mistakes, including spelling.

■ **Writing Assignment 2**

Any one of the topics below can be written as a process paper. Follow the steps suggested for the first essay.

How to break a bad habit
How to live with a two-year-old, a teenager, or a parent
How to make someone like you
How to make excuses
How to fall out of love
How to improve reading skills
How to do well at a job interview
How to care for an aging relative
How to stay young
How to improve a school or a place of work

■ **Writing Assignment 3**

Everyone is an expert at something. Write a process essay on some skill that you can perform very well. Write from the point of view that "This is how _____ *should* be done." (Remember that a skill can be anything from "starting a fire" to "setting up a new stereo system" to "dealing with unpleasant customers" to "using a personal computer.")

■ **Writing Assignment 4**

In this essay, you will write with a specific purpose and for a specific audience. Imagine that you are "Val Valentine," the author of a column in the campus newspaper that gives advice on romance. Someone has written to you asking how he can get to know a woman he has admired from afar (or how *she* can get to know a man she has admired from afar).

In your reply, suggest a process to the writer by which someone can meet and get to know another person on campus. You may describe a realistic process or a humorous one, in which you exaggerate the steps involved.

■ **Writing Assignment 5**

Write an essay in which you summarize, in your own words, the steps involved in doing a research paper or in preparing for and taking an essay exam. Both of these processes are explained in Part Three of this book. Before starting this paper, you should read "Preparing a Summary" on pages 241–250.

■ Writing Assignment 6: Writing about a Reading Selection

Do *either* of the following.

Option 1:   Read the selection titled "Coffee" on pages 606–607. This essay *undoes*, or reverses, the steps in the process of making a cup of coffee. Write a *prescriptive*, or "how to" process essay about the steps you follow in some task or activity you perform often: for example, getting to college, cooking a specific dish, or ringing up a customer's purchase at work. Check with your instructor to make sure that the process you will describe will be appropriate for a brief essay.

Start by imagining how you would teach someone else to perform this task; break the activity down into a series of clear steps. Then follow steps *d* through *h* under "How to Proceed" on pages 142–143.

Think of the audience for your instructions as someone who is going to learn from you how to do this activity. Make your essay detailed enough so that it could serve as a brief training guide for that person.

Option 2:   Read the selection titled "How to Make It in College, Now That You're Here" on pages 634–639. Then write a process essay with the thesis, "Here are the tips that will help a student succeed in _____" (name a course in which you are now enrolled or one that you have taken in the past). To get started, think of the advice you would like to have had *before* you took that particular course: What would you have wanted to know about the professor? The assignments? The exams? Policies about attendance, lateness, and so on? Pick three tips that you believe would be most helpful to another student about to enrol in the class, and discuss each one in a separate supporting paragraph. Model your introduction after the one in "How to Make It in College" by telling your readers that, on the basis of your own experience, you are going to pass on the secrets for succeeding in this course.

Below are three sample topic sentences for an essay on "How to Succeed in Communications 101."

First topic sentence: First of all, a student who wants a good grade in Communications 101 should be prepared at every class meeting for a surprise quiz.

Second topic sentence: In addition, students should speak up during class discussion, for Professor Knox adds "participation" into final grades.

Third topic sentence: Most important, students should start early on term essays and turn them in on time.

CAUSE
AND
EFFECT

Why did Stacey decide to move out of her parents' house? What made you quit a well-paying job? Why are horror movies so popular? Why has Ben acted so depressed lately? Why did our team fail to make the league play-offs?

Every day we ask questions similar to those above and look for answers. We realize that many actions do not occur without causes, and we realize also that a given action can have a series of effects—for good or bad. By examining the causes or effects of an action, we seek to understand and explain things that happen in our lives.

You will be asked in this section to do some detective work by examining the cause of something or the effects of something. First read the three essays that follow and answer the questions about them. All three essays support their thesis statements by explaining a series of causes or a series of effects.

ESSAYS TO CONSIDER

A Necessary Decision

Have you ever seen a supermarket bag crammed full of medical bills for 1 just one person? Well, I have. I had known that my mother was sick as a result of a failing kidney, but I had not realized how much trouble my parents were having in dealing with that sickness. Only when I had saved enough money to visit them in Alberta did I discover just how critical the situation had become. The problems were so serious, in fact, that I had to make the decision to put my mother in a nursing home.

First, there were countless bills. Many were for drugs, since Mother 2 was taking about twenty-four pills a day along with receiving insulin injections. Then there were bills for specialized home medical equipment, and for the bathtub rails and house modifications needed. Next, there were the Wheel-Transport bus bills for my mother's trips three times a week to the dialysis clinic. And finally, there were clinic bills for each of the special therapists and dieticians she had visited. Unable to contend with the insurance paperwork needed to pay the bills, my father had stuffed all incoming bills into a Safeway shopping bag in the closet.

She was confined to a wheelchair and needed help moving around. She 3 had to have assistance in getting dressed and undressed, going to the bathroom, and getting into and out of bed. She also needed a very specialized diet involving a combination of foods for renal, diabetic, and gallbladder patients. In addition, she required emotional support. Sometimes she was so depressed, she wouldn't eat unless she was urged to. "I'm going to die; just let me die in peace," she would say, or "You don't love me anymore now that I'm sick." These constant needs, I concluded, would benefit from professional care.

Finally, I was concerned not only with my mother's needs but also with 4 my father's welfare. He assumed total responsibility for my mother. Since he doesn't drive, he walked everywhere, including to the grocery store, drugstore, laundromat, hospital, and clinic. Also, he did all the housework; he fed, dressed, bathed, and medicated my mother; and he prepared her special meals and snacks. In addition, her behaviour was a strain on him. She would wait until he was in the kitchen, and then she would call the police or ambulance to say she was dying. Or she would wait until 3 a.m. and telephone each of her children to say good-bye. Never robust, my father dropped from 125 pounds to 98 pounds under the strain, caught a bad cold, and finally telephoned me for help.

I conferred with a social worker, found a nursing home, and signed my 5 mother in. My father is able to get a bus that takes him, within twenty minutes, right to the nursing home door. He has gained weight and has gotten back in control of things to the point where he can handle the paperwork again. Even my mother has recovered to the extent that she is making my daughter a quilt. My decision was not easy, but it has turned out to be the best one for both my parents.

The Joys of an Old Car

Some of my friends can't believe my car still runs. Others laugh when they see it parked outside the house and ask if it's an antique. But they aren't being fair to my fourteen-year-old Toyota. In fact, my "antique" has opened my eyes to the rewards of owning an old car. 1

One obvious reward is economy. Fourteen years ago, when my husband and I were newly married and nearly broke, we bought the car--a shiny, red, year-old leftover--for a mere $1,800. Today it would cost five times as much. We save money on insurance, since it's no longer worthwhile for us to have collision coverage. Old age has even been kind to the Toyota's engine, which required only three major repairs in the last several years. And it still delivers twenty kilometres per litre in the city and thirty on the highway--not bad for a senior citizen. 2

The second benefit is dependability. If a Toyota passes the fifty-thousand-kilometre mark with no major problems, it will probably go on forever. Our car breezed past that mark many years ago and has run almost perfectly ever since. Even on the coldest, snowiest mornings, I can count on my car to sputter to life and roll sure-footedly down the driveway. The only time it didn't start, unfortunately, was the day I had a final exam. The Toyota may have the body of an old car, but beneath its elderly hood hums the engine of a teenager. 3

Last of all, there is the advantage of familiarity. When I open the door and slide into the driver's seat, the soft vinyl envelops me like a well-worn glove. I know to the millimetre exactly how much room I have when I turn a corner or back into a parking space. When my gas gauge is on empty, I know that five litres are still in reserve and I can plan accordingly. The front wheels invariably begin to shake when I go more than eighty kilometres an hour, reminding me that I am exceeding the speed limit. With the Toyota, the only surprises I face are the ones from other drivers. 4

I prize my fourteen-year-old car's economy and dependability, and most of all, its familiarity. It is faded, predictable, and comfortable, like a well-worn pair of jeans. And, like a well-worn pair of jeans, it will be difficult to throw away. 5

Stresses of Being a Celebrity

Last week, a woman signing herself "Want the Truth in Westport" wrote 1
to Ann Landers with a question she just had to have answered. "Please find
out for sure," she begged the columnist, "whether or not Oprah Winfrey has
had a face-lift." Fortunately for Ms. Winfrey's privacy, Ann Landers refused
to answer the question. But the incident disturbed me. How awful it would
be to be a celebrity, I thought, and always be in the public eye. Celebrities
lead very stressful lives, for no matter how glamorous or powerful they
are, they have too little privacy, too much pressure, and no safety.

For one thing, celebrities don't have the privacy an ordinary person 2
has. The most personal details of their lives are splashed all over the front
pages of the National Enquirer and other tabloids so that bored
supermarket shoppers can read about "k.d. lang and Her New Love" or
"John Candy's Last Moments." Even a celebrity's family is hauled into the
spotlight. A teenage son's arrest for pot possession or a wife's drinking
problem becomes the subject of glaring headlines. Photographers hound
celebrities at their homes, in restaurants, and on the street, hoping to get a
picture of an O.J. Simpson entering court or a Mickey Rourke in a fistfight.
When celebrities try to do the things that normal people do, like eat out or
attend a football game, they run the risk of being interrupted by
thoughtless autograph hounds or mobbed by aggressive fans.

In addition, celebrities are under constant pressure. Their physical 3
appearance is always under observation. Famous women, especially,
suffer from the "she really looks old" or the "boy, has she put on weight"
spotlight. Unflattering pictures of celebrities are photographers' prizes to be
sold to the highest bidder; this increases the pressure on celebrities to look
good at all times. Famous people are also under pressure to act calm and
collected under any circumstances. There's no freedom to blow off steam or
to do something just a little crazy. Therefore, people who forget this must
suffer the consequences.

Most important, celebrities must deal with the stress of being in 4
constant danger. The friendly grabs, hugs, and kisses of enthusiastic fans
can quickly turn into uncontrolled assaults on a celebrity's hair, clothes,
and car. Celebrities often get strange letters from people who become
fixated on their idols or from people who threaten to harm them. One fan's
obsessive pursuit of Anne Murray and the murder of John Lennon came
about because two unbalanced people tried to transfer the celebrity's fame
to themselves. Famous people must live with the fact that they are always
fair game--and never out of season.

Some people dream of starring roles, their names in lights, and their 5
pictures on the cover of People magazine. I'm not one of them, though. A
famous person gives up private life, feels pressured all the time, and is
never completely safe. So let someone else have that cover story. I'd rather
lead an ordinary, but calm, life than a stress-filled public one.

■ **Questions**

About Unity

1. Which supporting paragraph in "A Necessary Decision" lacks a topic sentence? (*Write the paragraph number.*) _____

2. Which sentence in paragraph 3 of "The Joys of an Old Car" should be omitted in the interest of paragraph unity? (*Write the first two or three words.*)

    _____

3. Rewrite the thesis statement of "The Joys of an Old Car" to include a plan of development.

    _____

    _____

About Support

4. How many effects are given to develop the thesis in "Stresses of Being a Celebrity"? (*Check the right answer.*)

    _____ 1   _____ 2   _____ 3   _____ 4

    How many are given in "The Joys of an Old Car"?

    _____ 1   _____ 2   _____ 3   _____ 4

5. After which sentence in paragraph 3 of "Stresses of Being a Celebrity" are more specific details needed? _____

6. How many examples are given to support the topic sentence "One obvious reward is economy" in "The Joys of an Old Car"?

    _____

About Coherence

7. Which topic sentence in "A Necessary Decision" functions as a linking sentence between paragraphs? _____

8. What are the three main transition words in paragraph 3 of "Stresses of Being a Celebrity"?

    _____   _____   _____

9. What are the three transition words in "The Joys of an Old Car" that signal the three major points of support for the thesis?

    _____   _____   _____

About the Introduction

10. Select from below the two methods of introduction that combine to form the first paragraph of "Stresses of Being a Celebrity."

   a. Broad, general statement narrowing to thesis

   b. Idea that is the opposite of the one to be developed

   c. Quotation

   d. Anecdote

   e. Questions

Activity 1

Complete the following outline of the essay titled "A Necessary Decision." The effect is the author's decision to put her mother in a nursing home; the causes of that decision are what make up each supporting paragraph. Summarize each cause in a few words. The first cause and one detail are given for you as an example.

Thesis: The problems were so serious, in fact, that I had to make the decision to put my mother in a nursing home.

1. _Countless bills_

   a. _Bills for drugs_

   b. _____

   c. _____

   d. _____

2. _____

   a. _____

   b. _____

   c. _____

3. _____

   a. _____

   b. _____

   c. _____

Activity 2

In scratch-outline form on separate paper, provide brief causes or effects for at least four of the ten statements below. Note the example. Make sure that you have three *separate* and *distinct* items for each statement. Also, indicate whether you have listed three causes or three effects.

Example   Many youngsters are terrified of school.

1. _Afraid of not being liked by other students_ ⎫
2. _Fearful of failing tests_   ⎬ _Causes_
3. _Intimidated by teachers_   ⎭

1. The availability of fast-food outlets has changed the eating habits of many Canadians.

2. I would recommend (*or* not recommend) _____ (*name a certain course*) to other students.

3. The women's movement has had an enormous impact on women's lives.

4. There are several steps provincial governments should take to make automobile driving a safer matter.

5. Exercise has changed my life.

6. Students often have trouble adjusting to college for several reasons.

7. Videocassette recorders have changed the way we watch television.

8. _____ is a popular sport for several reasons.

9. Computers have begun to affect the lives of many families.

10. There are several advantages (*or* drawbacks) to living at home while going to school.

WRITING THE ESSAY

■ Writing Assignment 1

Decide, perhaps through discussion with your instructor or classmates, which of the outlines prepared above would be most promising to develop into an essay. Make sure that your supporting reasons are logical ones that actually back up your thesis statement. Ask yourself in each case, "Does this reason truly support my thesis idea?" See "How to Proceed" on the following page.

How to Proceed

a   On separate paper, make a list of details that might go under each of the supporting points. Provide more details than you can possibly use. Here, for example, are the details generated by the writer of "The Joys of an Old Car" when she was working on her third supporting paragraph:

Car's familiarity:

Know how much space I have to park
Front wheels shake at eighty kilometres per hour
Know what's in glove compartment
Worn seat--comfortable
Know tire inflation (kilograms of pressure)
Can turn corners expertly (space)
Gas tank has reserve
Radio push buttons are set for favourite stations
Know how hard to step on brake
Know that reverse gear is over, <u>then</u> down

b   Decide which details you will use to develop each of your supporting paragraphs. Also, number the details in the order in which you will present them. Here is how the writer of "The Joys of an Old Car" made decisions about the details in her final supporting paragraph:

2   Know how much space I have to park
4   Front wheels shake at eighty kilometres per hour
    ~~Know what's in glove compartment~~
1   Worn seat—comfortable
    ~~Know tire inflation (kilograms of pressure)~~
2   Can turn corners expertly (space)
3   Gas tank has reserve
    ~~Radio push buttons are set for favourite stations~~
    ~~Know how hard to step on brake~~
    ~~Know that reverse gear is over, then down~~

c   As you are working on the drafts of your paper, refer to the checklist on page 123 and the inside front cover. Make sure that you can answer *Yes* to the questions about unity, support, and coherence.

d   You may also want to refer to pages 73–78 for suggestions on writing an effective introduction and conclusion to your essay.

e   Finally, use the checklist on page 123 and the inside front cover when you are proofreading the next-to-final draft of your paper for sentence-skills mistakes, including spelling.

■ Writing Assignment 2

Below are six thesis statements for a "cause" paper and six for an "effect" paper. In scratch-outline form, provide brief supporting points for four of the twelve.

List the Causes

1. Canadians tend to get married later in life than they used to.
2. Childhood is the unhappiest time of life.
3. Being young is better than being old. (*Or vice versa.*)
4. _____ is the most difficult course I have ever taken.
5. My relationship with _____ (name a relative, employer, or friend) is better than ever.
6. It is easy to fall into an unhealthy diet in our society.

List the Effects

7. Punishment for certain crimes should take the form of community service.
8. Growing up in the family I have has influenced my life in important ways.
9. The average work-week should be no more than thirty hours long.
10. A bad (*or* good) teacher can affect students in significant ways.
11. The drinking age should be raised to twenty-one in every province.
12. The fact that both parents often work has led to a number of changes in the typical family household.

■ Writing Assignment 3

If friendly aliens from a highly developed civilization decided to visit our planet, they would encounter a contradictory race of beings—us. We human beings would have reasons to feel both proud and ashamed of the kind of society the aliens would encounter. Write an essay explaining whether you would be proud or ashamed of the state of the human race today. Give reasons for your feeling.

■ Writing Assignment 4

In this essay, you will write with a specific purpose and for a specific audience. Imagine that a friend of yours is having a hard time learning anything in a class taught by Professor X. You volunteer to attend the class and see for yourself. You also get information from your friend about the course requirements.

Afterwards, you write a letter to Professor X, calling attention to what you see as causes of the learning problems that students are having in the class. To organize your essay, you might develop each of these causes in a separate supporting paragraph. In the second part of each supporting paragraph, you might suggest changes that Professor X could make to deal with each problem.

■ Writing Assignment 5

Write an essay in which you advance an idea about a poem, story, play, literary essay, or novel. The work you choose may be assigned by your instructor or require your instructor's approval. Use a series of two or more reasons and specific supporting evidence for each reason to develop your idea. A student model follows.

Paul's Suicide

Paul, the main character in Willa Cather's short story "Paul's Case," is a 1 young man on a collision course with death. As Cather reveals Paul's story, we learn about elements of Paul's personality that inevitably come together and cause his suicide. Paul takes his own life as a result of his inability to conform to his society, his passive nature, and his emotional isolation.

First of all, Paul cannot conform to the standards of his own society. 2 At school, Paul advertises his desire to be part of another, more glamorous world by wearing fancy clothes that set him apart from the other students. At home on Cordelia Street, Paul despises everything about his middle-class neighbourhood. He hates the houses "permeated by kitchen odours," the "ugliness and commonness of his own home," and the respectable neighbours sitting on their front porches every Sunday, "their stomachs comfortably protruding." Paul's father hopes that Paul will settle down and become like the young man next door, a near-sighted clerk who works for a corporate steel magnate. Paul, however, is repelled by the young man and all he represents. It seems inevitable, then, that Paul will not be able to cope with the office job his father obtains for him at the firm of Denny & Carson; and this inability to conform will, in turn, lead to Paul's theft of a thousand dollars.

Paul's suicide is also due, in part, to his passive nature. Throughout his 3 life, Paul has been an observer and an onlooker. Paul's only escape from the prison of his daily life comes from his job as an usher at Pittsburgh's Carnegie Hall; he lives for the moments when he can watch the actors, singers, and musicians. However, Paul has no desire to be an actor or musician. As Cather says, "What he wanted was to see, to be in the atmosphere, float on the wave of it, to be carried out ... away from everything." Although Paul steals the money and flees to New York, these uncharacteristic actions underscore the desperation he feels. Once at the Waldorf in New York, Paul is again content to observe the glamorous world he has craved for so long: "He had no especial desire to meet or to know any of these people; all he demanded was the right to look on and conjecture, to watch the pageant." During his brief stay in the city, Paul enjoys simply sitting in his luxurious rooms, glimpsing the show of city life through a magical curtain of snow. At the end, when the forces of ordinary life begin to close in again, Paul kills himself. But it is typical that he does not use the gun he has bought. Rather, more in keeping with his passive nature, Paul lets himself fall under the wheels of a train.

Finally, Paul ends his life because he is emotionally isolated. Throughout 4 the story, not one person makes any real contact with Paul. His teachers do not understand him and merely resent the attitude of false bravado that he uses as a defence. Paul's mother is dead; he cannot even remember her. Paul is completely alienated from his father, who obviously cares for him but who cannot feel close to his withdrawn, unhappy son. To Paul, his father is only the man waiting at the top of the stairs, "his hairy legs sticking out of his nightshirt," who will greet him with "inquiries and reproaches." When Paul meets a college boy in New York, they share a night on the town. But the "champagne friendship" ends with a "singularly cool" parting. Paul is not the kind of person who can let himself go or confide in one of his peers. For the most part, Paul's isolation is self-imposed. He has drifted so far into his fantasy life that people in the "real" world are treated like invaders. As he allows no one to enter his dream, there is no one Paul can turn to for understanding.

The combination of these personality factors--inability to conform, 5 passivity, and emotional isolation--makes Paul's tragic suicide inevitable. Before he jumps in front of the train, Paul scoops a hole in the snow and buries the carnation that he has been wearing in his buttonhole. Like a hothouse flower in the winter, Paul has a fragile nature that cannot survive its hostile environment.

■ Writing Assignment 6: Writing about a Reading Selection

Read the essay titled "Mind Over Myth" by Beppi Crosariol on pages 595–597. Write an essay that develops *either* of the following statements.

- There are three good reasons why people are still so baffled by computers.
- There are three good reasons why people should no longer be fooled by "computer myths."

Use specific examples to support each reason you give—either examples based on your own experience with, and knowledge of, computers, or hypothetical examples based on situations you can imagine or have observed.

To get started, you may find it helpful to freewrite for a few minutes on the topic of "people and computers": how useful computers can be, how confusing they can be at first, what computer advertisements promise, and so on.

COMPARISON
AND
CONTRAST

Comparison and contrast are two thought processes we constantly perform in everyday life. When we *compare* two things, we show how they are similar; when we *contrast* two things, we show how they are different. We may compare or contrast two brand-name products (for example, Heinz versus Hunts ketchup), or two television shows, or two cars, or two teachers, or two jobs, or two friends, or two courses of action we can take within a given situation. The purpose of comparing or contrasting is to understand each of the two things more clearly and, at times, to make judgements about them.

You will be asked in this section to write a paper of comparison or contrast. To help you prepare for this assignment, first read the three essays ahead. Then answer the questions and do the activities that follow the essays.

ESSAYS TO CONSIDER

Second Marriage

Married people live "happily ever after" in fairy tales, but they do so less and less often in real life. I, like many of my friends, got married, divorced, and remarried. I suppose, to some people, I'm a failure. After all, I broke my first solemn promise to "love and cherish until death us do part." But I feel that I'm finally a success. I learned from the mistakes I made in my first marriage. This time around, the ways my husband and I share our free time, make decisions, and deal with problems are very different. 1

I learned, first of all, not to be a clinging vine. In my first marriage, I felt that every moment we spent apart was wasted. If Ray wanted to go out to a bar with his friends to watch a football game, I felt rejected and talked him into staying home. I wouldn't accept an offer to go to a movie or join an exercise class if it meant that Ray would be home alone. I realize now that we were often on edge or angry with each other just because we spent too much time together. In contrast, my second husband and I spend some of our free time apart and try to have interests of our own. I have started playing racquetball at a health club, and David sometimes takes off to go to the local auto races with his friends. When we are together, we aren't bored with each other; our separate interests make us more interesting people. 2

I learned not only to be apart sometimes but also to work together when it's time to make decisions. When Ray and I were married, I left all the important decisions to him. He decided how we would spend money, whether we should sell the car or fix it, and where to take a vacation. I know now that I went along with this so that I wouldn't have to take the responsibility when things went wrong. I could always end an argument by saying, "It was your fault!" With my second marriage, I am trying to be a full partner. We ask each other's opinions on major decisions and try to compromise if we disagree. If we make the wrong choice, we're equally guilty. When we rented an apartment, for example, we both had to take the blame for not noticing the drafty windows and the "no pets" clause in our lease. 3

Maybe the most important thing I've learned is to be a grown-up about facing problems. David and I have made a vow to face our troubles like adults. If we're mad at each other or worried and upset, we say how we feel. Rather than hide behind our own misery, we talk about the problem until we discover how to fix it. Everybody argues or has to deal with the occasional crisis, but Ray and I always reacted like children to these stormy times. I would lock myself in the spare bedroom and pout. Ray would stalk out of the house, slam the door, and race off in the car. Then I would cry and worry till he returned. 4

I wish that my first marriage hadn't been the place where I learned how to make a relationship work, but at least I did learn. I feel better now about being an independent person, about making decisions, and about facing problems. My second marriage isn't perfect, but it doesn't have the deep flaws that made the first one fall apart. 5

A Vote for McDonald's

For my birthday this month, my wife has offered to treat me to dinner   1
at the restaurant of my choice. I think she expects me to ask for a meal at
La Maison, the classiest, most expensive restaurant in town. However, I'm
going to eat my birthday dinner at McDonald's. When I compare the two
restaurants, the advantages of eating at McDonald's are clear.

For one thing, going to La Maison is more difficult than going to   2
McDonald's. La Maison has a jacket-and-tie rule, which means I have to dig
a sport coat and tie out of the back of my closet, make sure they're semi-
clean, and try to steam out the wrinkles somehow. La Maison also requires
advance reservations. Since it is downtown, I have to leave an hour early to
give myself time to find a parking space within six blocks of the restaurant.
La Maison cancels reservations if a party is more than ten minutes late.
Going to McDonald's, on the other hand, is easy. I can feel comfortable
wearing jeans or a warm-up suit. I don't have to do any advance planning. I
can leave my house whenever I'm ready and pull into a parking space near
the door within fifteen minutes.

La Maison is a dimly lit, formal place. While I'm struggling to see   3
what's on my plate, I worry that I'll knock one of the fragile glass vases off
the table. The waiters at La Maison can be uncomfortably formal, too. As I
awkwardly pronounce the French words on the menu, I get the feeling that
I don't quite live up to their standards. Even though the food at La Maison
is gourmet, I prefer simpler meals. I don't like unfamiliar food swimming in
dead-white sauce or covered with pie pastry. Eating at La Maison is, to me,
less enjoyable than eating at McDonald's. McDonald's is a pleasant place
where I feel at ease. It is well lighted, and the bright-coloured decor is
informal. The employees serve with a smile, and the food is easy to
pronounce and identify. I know what I'm going to get when I order a certain
type of sandwich.

The most important difference between La Maison and McDonald's,   4
though, is the price difference. Dinner for two at La Maison, even one
without appetizers or desserts, would easily cost $70. And the $70 doesn't
include the cost of parking the car and tipping the waiter, which can come
to an additional $30. Once, I forgot to bring enough money. At McDonald's,
a filling meal for two will cost around $20. With the extra $80, my wife and
I can eat at McDonald's four more times, or go to the movies five times, or
buy play-off tickets to a football game.

So, for my birthday dinner celebration, or any other time, I prefer to   5
eat at McDonald's. It is convenient, friendly, and cheap. And with the money
my wife saves by taking me to McDonald's, she can buy me what I really
want for my birthday--a new Stanley power saw.

Studying: Then and Now

One June day, I staggered into a high school classroom to take my final   1
OAC exam in Canadian History. Bleary-eyed from an all-night study session,
I checked my "cheat sheets," which were taped inside the cuffs of my long-
sleeved shirt. I had made my usual desperate effort to cram the night
before, with the usual dismal results--I had made it only to page seventy-
five of a four-hundred-page textbook. My high school study habits,
obviously, were a mess. But, in college, I've made an attempt to reform my
note-taking, studying, and test-taking skills.

Taking notes is one thing I've learned to do better since high school   2
days. I used to lose interest in what I was doing and begin doodling,
drawing Martians, or seeing what my signature would look like if I became
a major executive. Now, however, I try not to let my mind wander, and I pull
my thoughts back into focus when they begin to go fuzzy. In high school, my
notes often looked like something written in Arabic. In college, I've learned
to use a semi-print writing style that makes my notes understandable.
When I would look over my high school notes, I couldn't understand them.
There would be a word like "Confederation," then a big blank, then the word
"important." Weeks later, I had no idea what Confederation was or why it
was important. I've since learned to write down connecting ideas, even if I
have to take the time to do it after class.

Ordinary during-the-term studying is another area where I've made   3
changes. In high school, I let reading assignments go. I told myself that I'd
have no trouble catching up on two hundred pages during a fifteen-minute
bus ride to school. College courses have taught me to keep pace with the
work. Otherwise, I feel as though I'm sinking into a quicksand of unread
material. When I finally read the high school assignment, my eyes would
run over the words but my brain would be plotting how to get the car for
Saturday night. Now, I use several techniques that force me to really
concentrate on my reading.

In addition to learning how to cope with daily work, I've also learned to   4
handle study sessions for big tests. My all-night study sessions in high school
were experiments in self-torture. Around 2:00 a.m., my mind, like a soaked
sponge, simply stopped absorbing things. Now, I space out exam study sessions
over several days. That way, the night before can be devoted to an overall
review rather than raw memorizing. Most important, though, I've changed my
attitude towards tests. In high school, I thought tests were mysterious things
with completely unpredictable questions. Now, I ask teachers about the kinds
of questions that will be on the exam, and I try to "psych out" which areas or
facts teachers are likely to ask about. These practices really work, and for me
they've taken much of the fear and mystery out of tests.

Since I've reformed, note-taking and studying are not as tough as they   5
once were. And there's been one benefit that makes the work worthwhile:
my college transcripts look much different from the report cards of high
school days.

■ Questions

About Unity

1. In which supporting paragraph of "A Vote for McDonald's" is the topic sentence in the middle rather than, more appropriately, at the beginning?
   (*Write the paragraph number.*) _____

2. Which sentence in paragraph 4 of "A Vote for McDonald's" should be omitted in the interest of paragraph unity? (*Write the first two or three words.*)

   _____

About Support

3. After which sentence in paragraph 3 of "Studying: Then and Now" are more supporting details needed? _____

4. In which sentence in paragraph 3 of "A Vote for McDonald's" are more supporting details needed? _____

About Coherence

5. What transition signal is used in "Second Marriage" to indicate emphatic order? _____

6. What are the transition signals used in paragraph 2 of "Second Marriage"?

   _____

7. What are the three points of contrast in paragraph 2 ("taking notes") of "Studying: Then and Now"?

   a. _____   b. _____

   c. _____

8. Which supporting paragraph in "Second Marriage" fails to follow the pattern of organization set by the other two? _____

About the Introduction and Conclusion

9. Circle the method of introduction used in "Studying: Then and Now."
   a. Broad, general statement narrowing to thesis
   b. Idea that is the opposite of the one to be developed
   c. Quotation
   d. Anecdote
   e. Questions

10. Circle the conclusion technique used in "Second Marriage."
    a. Summary   b. Prediction or recommendation   c. Question

METHODS OF DEVELOPMENT

There are two methods of development possible in a comparison or contrast essay. Details can be presented in a *one-side-at-a-time* format or in a *point-by-point* format. Each format is illustrated below.

One Side at a Time

Look at the following supporting paragraph from "A Vote for McDonald's":

> For one thing, going to La Maison is more difficult than going to McDonald's. La Maison has a jacket-and-tie rule, which means that I have to dig a sport coat and tie out of the back of my closet, make sure they're semi-clean, and try to steam out the wrinkles somehow. La Maison also requires advance reservations. Since it is downtown, I have to leave an hour early to give myself time to find a parking space within six blocks of the restaurant. La Maison cancels reservations if a party is more than ten minutes late. Going to McDonald's, on the other hand, is easy. I can feel comfortable wearing jeans or a warm-up suit. I don't have to do any advance planning. I can leave my house whenever I'm ready and pull into a parking space near the door within fifteen minutes.

The first half of the paragraph explains fully one side of the contrast; the second half of the paragraph deals entirely with the other side. When you use this method, be sure to follow the same order of points of contrast (or comparison) for each side. An outline of the paragraph shows how the points for each side are developed in a consistent sequence.

Outline (One Side at a Time)

Going to La Maison is more difficult than going to McDonald's.

1. La Maison
   a. Dress code
   b. Advance reservations
   c. Leave an hour early
   d. Find parking space

2. McDonald's
   a. Casual dress
   b. No reservations
   c. Leave only fifteen minutes ahead of time
   d. Plenty of free parking

Point by Point

Now look at the supporting paragraph below, which is from "Studying: Then and Now":

> Taking notes is one thing I've learned to do better since high school days. I used to lose interest in what I was doing and begin doodling, drawing Martians, or seeing what my signature would look like if I became a major executive. Now, however, I try not to let my mind wander, and I pull my thoughts back into focus when they begin to go fuzzy. In high school, my notes often looked like something written in Arabic. In college, I've learned to use a semi-print writing style that makes my notes understandable. When I would look over my high school notes, I couldn't understand them. There would be a word like "Confederation," then a big blank, then the word "important." Weeks later, I had no idea what Confederation was or why it was important. I've since learned to write down connecting ideas, even if I have to take the time to do it after class.

The paragraph contrasts the two methods of note-taking point by point. The outline below illustrates the method.

Outline (Point by Point)

Taking notes is one thing I've learned to do better since high school days.

1. Level of attention in class
   a. High school
   b. College
2. Handwriting
   a. High school
   b. College
3. Completeness of notes
   a. High school
   b. College

When you begin a comparison or contrast paper, you should decide right away whether you are going to use the one-side-at-a-time format or the point-by-point format. An outline is an essential step in writing and planning a clearly organized paper.

Activity 1

Complete the partial outlines given for the supporting paragraphs that follow.

Paragraph A

The most important difference between La Maison and McDonald's, though, is the price difference. Dinner for two at La Maison, even one without appetizers or desserts, would easily cost $70. And the $70 doesn't include the cost of parking the car and tipping the waiter, which can come to an additional $30. At McDonald's a filling meal for two will cost around $20. With the extra $80, my wife and I can eat at McDonald's four more times, or go to the movies five times, or buy play-off tickets to a football game.

The most important difference between La Maison and McDonald's is the price difference.

1. La Maison

   a. _____

   b. Additional costs of parking and tipping

2. _____

   a. $20 for dinner for two

   b. _____

Complete the following statement: Paragraph A uses a _____

_____ method of development.

Paragraph B

In addition to learning how to cope with daily work, I've also learned to handle study sessions for big tests. My all-night study sessions in high school were experiments in self-torture. Around 2:00 a.m., my mind, like a soaked sponge, simply stopped absorbing things. Now, I space out exam study sessions over several days. That way, the night before can be devoted to an overall review rather than raw memorizing. Most important, though, I've changed my attitude towards tests. In high school, I thought tests were mysterious things with completely unpredictable questions. Now, I ask teachers about the kinds of questions that will be on the exam, and I try to "psych out" which areas or facts teachers are likely to ask about. These practices really work, and for me they've taken much of the fear and mystery out of tests.

In addition to learning how to cope with daily work, I've also learned to handle study sessions for big tests.

1. Planning study time

    a. _____ (all-night study sessions)

    b. College (spread out over several days)

2. _____

    a. High school (tests were mysterious)

    b. _____ (_____)

Complete the following statement: Paragraph B uses a _____

_____ method of development.

Paragraph C

    I learned not only to be apart sometimes but also to work together when it's time to make decisions. When Ray and I were married, I left all the important decisions to him. He decided how we would spend money, whether we should sell the car or fix it, and where to take a vacation. I know now that I went along with this so that I wouldn't have to take the responsibility when things went wrong. I could always end an argument by saying, "It was your fault!" With my second marriage, I am really trying to be a full partner. We ask each other's opinions on major decisions and try to compromise if we disagree. If we make the wrong choice, we're equally guilty. When we recently rented an apartment, for example, we both had to take the blame for not noticing the drafty windows and the "no pets" clause in our lease.

I learned not only to be apart sometimes but also to work together when it's time to make decisions.

1. First marriage
    a. Husband made decisions.
    b. Husband took responsibility and blame.

2. _____

    a. _____

    b. Share responsibility and blame.

Complete the following statement: Paragraph C uses a _____

_____ method of development.

Activity 2

Following is a contrast essay about two sisters. The sentences in each supporting paragraph of the essay are scrambled. For each supporting paragraph, put a number *1* beside the point that all the other scrambled sentences support. Then number the rest of the sentences in a logical order. To do this, you will have to decide whether the sentences should be arranged according to the order of one side at a time or the order of point by point.

Introduction

When my sister and I were growing up, we shared the same bedroom. It wasn't hard to tell which half of the room was mine and which was Kathy's. My side was always as tidy as if a Holiday Inn housekeeper had just left. Kathy's side always looked like the aftermath of an all-night party. Back then, we argued a lot. Kathy said that I was a neatness nut, and I called her a slob. Today we get along just fine, since we have our own homes and don't have to share a room anymore. But Kathy's approach to housekeeping is still much different from mine.

First supporting paragraph

_____ Kathy, on the other hand, believes that a kitchen should look lived-in and not like a hospital operating room.

_____ I treat my kitchen as if a health inspector were waiting to close it down at the least sign of dirt.

_____ I wipe counters with spray cleaner while I wait for bread to toast.

_____ She scrambles eggs and leaves the dirty pan on the stove until the nightly clean-up.

_____ She forgets to put the bread away.

_____ When I leave the kitchen, it's usually cleaner than it was before I started to cook.

_____ The kitchen is one room that points up the contrasts between us.

_____ I wrap leftovers in neat packages of aluminum foil or seal them tightly in plastic containers.

_____ Kathy doesn't mind leaving a messy kitchen behind if she has more interesting things to do.

_____ Leftovers go naked into the refrigerator, without covers or foil.

_____ Even as I'm scrambling a couple of eggs, I begin to wash the bowl I used to mix them.

Second supporting paragraph

_____ The clothes in my closet are carefully arranged.

_____ My bedroom is a place of rest, and I can rest only when everything is in order.

_____ A peek into Kathy's bedroom in midmorning might reveal last night's cheese and crackers growing stale on the night table and several magazines hiding under the rumpled bedcovers.

_____ Some clothes are hung haphazardly in the closet, but many more are under the bed, behind the drapes, or on the deck.

_____ When I leave my bedroom in the morning, the bed is made and there are no clothes lying on the floor or over the chairs.

_____ Plastic bags cover out-of-season items, and shoes are lined up on racks.

_____ We still treat our bedrooms differently.

_____ In contrast, Kathy feels that her bedroom is a private place where she can do as she pleases.

Third supporting paragraph

_____ After I brush my hair, I check the sink for stray hairs.

_____ The spot that shows our differences the most, though, is the bathroom.

_____ My bathroom must be sanitized and germ-free.

_____ She cleans her mirror only when she gets tired of the polka-dot effect of hardened toothpaste.

_____ I clean the tub with cleanser before and after taking a bath.

_____ Needless to say, her make-up and toiletries litter every available surface.

_____ Once in a while, she points her hair dryer at the sink to blow away the accumulation of hairs in it.

_____ She cleans the tub, but only after a clearly defined brown ring has formed around it.

_____ I wipe off any spots of toothpaste or soap from the mirror and put all my cosmetics and cleaners in their proper places.

_____ Kathy, however, thinks that North Americans worry too much about germs.

Conclusion

> As adults, Kathy and I can joke about the habits that caused us so much trouble as adolescents. We can, at times, even see the other's point of view when it comes to housecleaning. But I'm afraid the patterns are pretty much set. It's too late for this "odd couple" to change.

Complete the following statement: The sentences in each supporting paragraph can be organized using a _____

_____ method of development.

WRITING THE ESSAY

■ Writing Assignment 1

Write an essay of comparison or contrast on one of the topics below:

Two courses	Two singers
Two teachers	Two dates
Two jobs	Two popular magazines
Two bosses	Two games
Two family members	Two vacations
Two friends	Two hobbies
Two pets	Two leisure activities
Two vacations	Two stores
Two sports	Two public figures

How to Proceed

a You must begin by making two decisions: (1) what your topic will be and (2) whether you are going to do a comparison or a contrast. Many times, students choose to do essays centred on the differences between two things. For example, you might write about how a math teacher you have in college differs from one you had in high school. You might discuss important differences between your mother and your father, or between two of your friends. You might contrast a factory job you had packing vegetables with a white-collar job you had as a salesperson in a shoe store.

b After you choose a tentative topic, write a simple thesis statement expressing that topic. Then see what kind of support you can generate for that topic. For instance, if you plan to contrast two restaurants, see if you can think of and jot down three distinct ways they differ. *In other words, prepare a brief outline.* An outline is an excellent prewriting technique to use when doing any essay; it is almost indispensable when planning a comparison or contrast essay. Here is a brief outline prepared by the author of the essay titled "A Vote for McDonald's":

Thesis: The advantages of McDonald's over La Maison are clear.
1. Going to the restaurants
2. Eating at the restaurants
3. Prices at the restaurants

Keep in mind that this planning stage is probably the most important single phase of work you will do on your paper. Without clear planning, you are not likely to write an effective essay.

c After you have decided on a topic and the main lines of support, you must decide whether to use a one-side-at-a-time or a point-by-point method of development. Both methods are explained and illustrated in this chapter.

d Now, freewrite for ten minutes on the topic you have chosen. Do not worry about punctuation, spelling, or other matters relating to correct form. Just get as many details as you can onto the page. You want a base of raw material that you can add to and select from as you now work on the first draft of your paper.

After you do a first draft, try to put it aside for a day or at least several hours. You will then be ready to return with a fresh perspective on the material and build upon what you have already done.

e As you work on a second draft, be sure that each of your supporting paragraphs has a clear topic sentence.

f Use transition words like *first, in addition, also, in contrast, another difference, on the other hand, but, however,* and *most important* to link together points in your paper.

g As you continue working on your paper, refer to the checklist on page 123 and the inside front cover. Make sure that you can answer *Yes* to the questions about unity, support, and coherence.

h Finally, use the checklist on page 123 and the inside front cover to proofread the next-to-final draft of your paper for sentence-skills mistakes, including spelling.

■ Writing Assignment 2

Write a comparison or contrast essay on college versus high school life. Narrow the focus of your paper to a particular aspect of school—teachers, classes, sports, social life, or students' attitudes, for example. *Or*, you may write a paper on apartment life versus living at home.

■ Writing Assignment 3

Write an essay that contrasts two attitudes on a controversial subject. The subject might be abortion, marijuana, capital punishment, homosexuality, euthanasia, prostitution, televised trials, censorship, school prayer, nuclear power plants, the unemployment insurance system, or some other matter on which there are conflicting feelings and opinions. You may want to contrast your views with someone else's or to contrast the way you felt at some point in the past with the way you feel now.

■ Writing Assignment 4

In this essay, you will write with a specific purpose and for a specific audience.

Option 1:   Your boyfriend or girlfriend wants to get married this year, but you think you'd rather just live together for a while. To help both of you think through the issue, write him or her a letter in which you compare and contrast the advantages and disadvantages of each approach. Use a one-side-at-a-time method in making your analysis.

Option 2:   Write a letter to your boss in which you compare your abilities with those of the ideal candidate for a position to which you'd like to be promoted. Use a point-by-point method in which you discuss each ideal requirement and then describe how well you measure up to it. Use the requirements of a job you're relatively familiar with, perhaps even a job you would really like to apply for one day.

■ Writing Assignment 5

Write an essay that contrasts two characters or two points of view in one or more poems, stories, plays, or novels. The work you choose may be assigned by your instructor, or it may require your instructor's approval. For this assignment, your essay may have two supporting paragraphs, with each paragraph representing one side of the contrast. A student model is given on the following page.

Warren and Mary

In "Death of the Hired Man," Robert Frost uses a brief incident--the 1
return of Silas, an aging farmhand--to dramatize the differences between a
husband and wife. As Warren and Mary talk about Silas and reveal his
story, the reader learns their story, too. By the end of the poem, Warren
and Mary emerge as contrasting personalities; one is wary and reserved,
while the other is open and giving.

Warren is a kindly man but one whose basic decency is tempered by a 2
sense of practicality and emotional reserve. Warren is upset with Mary for
sheltering Silas, who is barely useful and sometimes unreliable: "What use
he is there's no depending on." Warren feels that he has already done his
duty toward Silas by hiring him the previous summer and that he is under
no obligation to care for him now. "Home," says Warren, "is the place where,
when you have to go there/They have to take you in." Warren's home is not
Silas' home, so Warren does not have a legal or moral duty to keep the
shiftless old man. Warren's temperament, in turn, influences his attitude
toward Silas' arrival. Warren hints to Mary--through a condescending smile--
that Silas is somehow playing on her emotions or faking his illness. Warren
considers Silas' supposed purpose in coming to the farm--to ditch the
meadow--nothing but a flimsy excuse for a free meal. The best that Warren
can find to say about Silas is that he does have one practical skill: the ability
to build a good load of hay.

Mary, in contrast, is distinguished by her giving nature and her 3
concentration on the workings of human emotion. In caring for Silas, Mary
sees not his lack of ability or his laziness but the fact that he is "worn out"
and needs help. To Mary, home represents not obligation ("They have to take
you in") but unconditional love: "I should have called it/Something you
somehow haven't to deserve." Mary is observant, not only of outer
appearance but also of the inner person; this is why she thinks not that Silas
is trying to trick them but that he is a desperate man trying to salvage a
little self-respect. She realizes, too, that he will never ditch the meadow, and
she knows that Silas' insecurity prompted his arguments with the college boy
who helped with the haying. Mary is also perceptive enough to see that Silas
could never humble himself before his estranged brother. Mary's attitude is
more sympathetic than Warren's; whereas Warren wonders why Silas and his
brother don't get along, Mary thinks about how Silas "hurt my heart the way
he lay/And rolled his old head on that sharp-edged chairback."

In describing Silas, Warren and Mary describe themselves. We see a 4
basically good man, one whose spirit has been toughened by a hard life,
Warren, we learn, would have liked to pay Silas a fixed wage but simply
couldn't afford to. Life has taught Warren to be practical and to rein in his
emotions. In contrast, we see a nurturing woman, alert to human feelings,
who could never refuse to care for a lonely, dying man. Warren and Mary
are both decent people. This is the reason why, as Mary instinctively feels,
Silas chooses their home for his final refuge.

■ **Writing Assignment 6:**
Writing about a Reading Selection

Read the selection titled "Smash Thy Neighbor" on pages 506–510. Pay special attention to how the author compares and contrasts football and war in paragraphs 5–8 and compares football and the rest of society in paragraph 14. Notice how he makes the comparisons and contrasts in order to describe football more fully. Then write an essay in which you use a comparison to describe more fully three aspects of an activity, place, or person. You may use serious or humorous supporting details.

Following are some suggestions that you might consider for a thesis for this assignment.

Thesis: In a few significant ways,

■ going to college is like working at a career.
■ the high-school hallways between classes are like a three-ring circus.
■ getting divorced is like getting married.
■ caring for a pet is like caring for a child.
■ meditation is like exercise.
■ shopping for Christmas gifts is like playing professional football.
■ teachers should be like parents.
■ hate is like love.
■ raising a family is like caring for a garden.

These are only suggestions; feel free to use any other thesis that makes a comparison in order to fill out a description of an activity, person, or place. (Note that a comparison that points out similarities between things that are otherwise quite different is called an *analogy*.)

In your introduction, you might state your general thesis as well as the three points of comparison. Here, for example, is a possible introduction for an essay on meditation:

> On the surface, meditation may seem to be very different from exercise. A person who meditates is usually very still, while someone who exercises is very active. Yet the two activities are more alike than they might seem. Both require discipline, both bestow physical and mental benefits, and both can be habit-forming.

At the same time as you develop your introduction, you should prepare a general outline for your essay. The outline for the essay started by the introduction above would be as follows:

<u>Thesis</u>: Meditation is like exercise in three ways.

A. Both require discipline.
   1. Exercise
   2. Meditation
B. Both have physical and mental rewards.
   1. Exercise
   2. Meditation
C. Both can be habit-forming.
   1. Exercise
   2. Meditation

(Note that this outline uses the point-by-point method of development. Other topics might, of course, be more suited to the one-side-at-a-time method.)

As you work on your supporting paragraphs, *be sure to outline them first.* Such planning is very helpful in organizing and maintaining control over a comparison or contrast essay. Here, for example, is a sample scratch outline for a paragraph in a point-by-point essay comparing raising children to gardening.

<u>Topic sentence</u>: Just as a garden benefits from both sun and rain, so do children.

A. Benefits of sun and rain to a garden
   1. Both sun and rain required for life
   2. Increase growth
B. Benefits of sunny and rainy times to children
   1. Ups and downs natural over a life
   2. Personal growth

Each of your supporting paragraphs should be outlined in this way.

In your conclusion, you might round off the essay by summarizing the three areas of comparison and leaving your readers with a final thought. Do not, however, make the mistake of introducing a completely *new* idea ("Every couple should have children," for example) in your conclusion.

DEFINITION

In talking with other people, we at times offer informal definitions to explain just what we mean by a particular term. Suppose, for example, we say to a friend, "Bob is really an inconsiderate person." We might then explain what we mean by "inconsiderate" by saying, "He borrowed my accounting book 'overnight,' but didn't return it for a week. And when I got it back, it was covered with coffee stains." In a written definition, we make clear in a more complete and formal way our own personal understanding of a term. Such a definition typically starts with one meaning of a term. The meaning is then illustrated with a series of details.

You will be asked in this section to write an essay in which you define a term. The three student essays below are all examples of definition essays. Read them and then answer the questions that follow.

ESSAYS TO CONSIDER

Definition of a Baseball Fan

What is a baseball fan? The word <u>fan</u> is an abbreviation of <u>fanatic</u>,   1
meaning "insane." In the case of baseball fans, the term is appropriate. They
behave insanely, they are insane about trivia, and they are insanely loyal.

Baseball fans wear their official team T-shirts and warm-up jackets to the   2
mall, the supermarket, the classroom, and even--if they can get away with it--
to work. Then, whenever the team offers a give-away item, the fans rush to
the stadium to get the bumper sticker or tote bag that is being offered that
day. Baseball fans behave insanely, especially between April and October. In
addition, baseball fans cover the walls with items of every kind. When they
go to a game, which they do as often as possible, the true baseball fans put
on their team colours, grab their ball caps, pin on their team buttons, and
even bring along hand-lettered bedsheet signs proudly proclaiming "Okay
Blue Jays" or "Expos Are Number One." At the game, these fans form a
rooting section, constantly encouraging their favourite players and obediently
echoing every cheer flashed on the electronic scoreboard.

Baseball fans, in addition to behaving insanely, are also insanely   3
fascinated by trivia. Every day, they turn to the sports page and study last
night's statistics. They simply have to see who has extended his hitting
streak and how many strike-outs the winning pitcher recorded. Their
bookshelves are crammed with record books, team yearbooks, and baseball
almanacs. They delight in remembering such significant facts as who was
the last left-handed third baseman to hit into an inning-ending double play
in the fifth game of the play-offs. And if you do not show equal interest or
enthusiasm, they look at you as if they were doubting your sanity.

Last of all, baseball fans are insanely loyal to the team of their choice.   4
Should the home team lose eight in a row, their fans may begin to call them
"bums." They may even suggest, vocally, that the slumping clean-up hitter
be sent to the minors or the manager be fired. But these reactions only hide
their broken hearts. They still check the sports pages and tune in to get the
score. Furthermore, this intense loyalty makes fans dangerous, for anyone
who dares to say to a loyal fan that some other team has sharper fielding
or a better attitude could be risking permanent physical damage. Incidents
of violence on the baseball field have increased in recent years and are a
matter of growing concern.

From mid-October through March, baseball fans are like any other   5
human beings. They pay their taxes, take out the garbage, and complain
about the high cost of living or the latest home repair. But when April
comes, the colours and TVs go on, the record books come off the shelves,
and the devotion returns. For the true baseball fan, another season of
insanity has begun.

Stupidity

Although <u>stupidity</u> is commonly defined as "lack of normal intelligence," 1
stupid behaviour is not the behaviour of a person lacking intelligence but
the behaviour of a person not using *good judgement or sense.* In fact,
<u>stupidity</u> comes from a Latin word that means "senseless." Therefore,
<u>stupidity</u> can be defined as the behaviour of a person of normal intelligence
who is acting in a particular situation as if he or she weren't very bright.
Stupidity exists on three levels of seriousness.

First is the simple, relatively harmless level. Behaviour on this level is 2
often amusing. It is humorous when someone places the food from a fast-
food restaurant on the roof of the car while unlocking the door and then
drives away with the food still on the roof. We call this absent-minded. The
person's good sense or intelligence was temporarily absent. On this level,
other than passing inconvenience or embarrassment, no one is injured by
the stupid behaviour.

More dangerous than simple stupidity is the next type--potentially 3
serious stupidity. Practical jokes such as putting sugar in the restaurant
salt shakers are on this level. The intent is humorous, but there is a
potential for harm. Irresponsible advice given to others is also serious
stupidity. An example is the person who plays psychiatrist on the basis of
an introductory psychology course or a TV programme on psychiatry. The
intent may be to help, but if the victims really need psychiatric help, an
amateur telling them that they "have no ego" or characterizing them as
"neurotic" will only worsen the situation.

Even worse is the third kind of stupidity, which is always harmful. 4
Otherwise kind persons, who would never directly injure another living
thing, stupidly dump off a box of six-week-old kittens along a country road.
Lacking the heart to have "the poor things put to sleep," they sentence
them to almost certain death from parasites, upper respiratory infections,
exposure, other animals, or the wheels of a passing vehicle. Yet they are
able to tell themselves that "they will find nice homes" or "animals can get
along in the wild." Another example of this kind of stupidity is the perhaps
dated or sexist specimen of the successful local businessman who tries to
have as many office affairs as he can get away with. He risks the loss of
his job, his home, his wife and children, and the goodwill of his parents and
friends. He fails to see, though, that there is anything wrong with what he
is doing. His is the true moral stupidity of a person not willing to think
about the results of his actions or to take responsibility for them.

The common defence of the person guilty of stupidity is, "But I didn't 5
think. . . ." This, however, is an inadequate excuse, especially when serious
or harmful stupidity is involved. We are all liable when we do not think
about the consequences of our actions.

Student Zombies

Schools divide people up into categories. From first grade on up, students 1 are labelled "advanced" or "deprived" or "remedial" or "antisocial." Students pigeon-hole their fellow students, too. We've all known the "brain," the "jock," the "dummy," and the "teacher's pet." In most cases, these narrow labels are misleading and inaccurate. But there is one label for a certain type of college student that says it all. That is, of course, "zombie."

Most of us haven't known many real zombies personally, but we do 2 know how they act. Horror movies have given us portraits of zombies, the living dead, for years. They stalk around graveyards, their eyes glued open by Hollywood makeup artists, bumping like cheap toy robots into living people. The special effects in horror movies are much better now. Zombie students in college do just about the same thing. They stalk around campus, eyes glazed, staring off into space. They wander into classrooms, sit down mechanically, and contemplate the ceiling. Zombie students rarely eat, play sports, or toss Frisbees on college lawns. Instead, they mysteriously disappear when classes are over and return only when they next feel the urge to drift into a classroom. The urge may not return, however, for weeks.

Where student zombies come from is as weird as the origin of the 3 original zombies of the voodoo cults. According to voodoo legend, zombies are corpses that have come alive again. They have been reanimated by supernatural spells. Student zombies, too, are directed by a strange power. They continue to attend school although they have no apparent motivation to do so. They are completely uninterested in college-related activities like tests, marks, papers, and projects. They seem to be propelled by some inner force that compels them to wander forever through the halls of higher education.

All zombies, unfortunately, have a similar fate. In the movies, they are 4 usually shot, stabbed, or electrocuted, all to no avail. Then the hero or heroine finally realizes that a counter-spell is needed. Once the counter-spell is cast, with the appropriate props of chicken legs, human hair, and bats' eyeballs, the zombie-corpse can return peacefully to its coffin. Student zombies, if they are to change at all, must undergo a similar traumatic experience. Sometimes the evil spell can be broken by a grade transcript decorated with "F" marks. Sometimes a professor will hold a private, intensive exorcism session. Sometimes, though, the zombies blunder around for years until they are gently persuaded by the college administration to head for another institution that accepts zombies. Then, they enrol in a new college or get a job in the family business.

Every college student knows that it's not necessary to see Night of the 5 Living Dead or Voodoo Island in order to see zombies in action. Forget the campus movie theatre or the late late show. Just sit in a classroom and wait for the students who walk in without books or papers of any kind and sit in the farthest seats in the rear. Day of the Living Dead is showing every day at a college near you.

■ Questions

About Unity

1. Which essay places the topic sentence for its first supporting paragraph within the paragraph rather than, more appropriately, at the beginning?

   _____

2. Which sentence in paragraph 2 of "Student Zombies" should be omitted in the interest of paragraph unity? (*Write the first two or three words.*)

   _____

3. Which sentence in paragraph 4 of "Definition of a Baseball Fan" should be omitted in the interest of unity? _____

About Support

4. Which supporting paragraph in the essay on stupidity needs more supporting details? (*Write the paragraph number.*) _____

5. Which essay develops its definition through a series of comparisons?

   _____

6. Which sentence in paragraph 2 of the essay on baseball needs supporting details? _____

About Coherence

7. Which essay uses emphatic order, saving its most important idea for last?

   _____

8. Which two essays use linking sentences between their first and second supporting paragraphs?

   _____   _____

9. What are five major transition words that appear in the three supporting paragraphs of "Definition of a Baseball Fan"?

   a. _____   b. _____   c. _____

   d. _____   e. _____

About the Introduction

10. Circle below the kind of introduction used for "Student Zombies."
    a. Broad, general statement narrowing to thesis

    b. Idea that is the opposite of the one to be developed

    c. Quotation

    d. Anecdote

    e. Questions

WRITING THE ESSAY

■ Writing Assignment 1

Shown below are an introduction, a thesis, and supporting points for an essay that defines the word *maturity*. Using separate paper, plan out and write the supporting paragraphs and a conclusion for the essay. Refer to the suggestions on "How to Proceed" that follow.

The Meaning of Maturity

Being a mature student does not mean being an old-timer. Maturity is not measured by the number of years a person has lived. Instead, the yardstick of maturity is marked by the qualities of self-denial, determination, and dependability.

Self-denial is an important quality in the mature student. . . .

Determination is another characteristic of a mature student. . . .

Although self-denial and determination are both vital, probably the most important measure of maturity is dependability. . . .

How to Proceed

a Prepare examples for each of the three qualities of maturity. For each quality, you should have one extended example that takes up an entire paragraph or two or three shorter examples that together form enough material for a paragraph.

b To generate these details, ask yourself the following questions:

What could I do, or have I done, that would be an example of self-denial?

What has someone I know ever done that could be described as self-denial?

What kind of behaviour on the part of a student could be considered self-denial?

Write down quickly whatever answers occur to you for the questions. Don't worry about writing correct sentences; just concentrate on getting down as many details relating to self-denial as you can think of. Then repeat the questioning and writing process with the qualities of determination and dependability as well.

c Draw from and add to this material as you work on the drafts of your essay. Also, refer to the checklist on page 123 and the inside front cover to make sure you can answer *Yes* to the questions about unity, support, and coherence.

d Write a conclusion for the essay by adding a summarizing sentence or two and a final thought about the subject. See page 77 for an example.

e Finally, use the checklist on page 123 and the inside front cover to proofread the next-to-final draft for sentence-skills mistakes, including spelling.

■ Writing Assignment 2

Write an essay that defines one of the terms below. Each term refers to a certain kind of person.

Snob	Optimist	Slob
Cheapskate	Pessimist	Tease
Loser	Team player	Practical joker
Good neighbour	Scapegoat	Black sheep of a family
Busybody	Bully	Procrastinator
Complainer	Religious person	Loner
Con artist	Hypocrite	Straight arrow

Refer to "How to Proceed" on the following page.

How to Proceed

a If you start with a dictionary definition, be sure to choose just one meaning of a term. (A dictionary often provides several different meanings associated with a word.) Also, don't begin your paper with the overused line, "According to Oxford, . . ."

b Remember that the thesis of a definition essay is actually some version of "What _____ means to me." The thesis presents what *you* think the term actually means.

c You may want to organize the body of your paper around three different parts or qualities of your term. Here are the three-part divisions of the four essays considered in this chapter:

Maturity "is marked by qualities of self-denial, determination, and dependability."

"Stupidity exists on three levels of seriousness."

Baseball fans are fanatics in terms of "their behaviour, their fascination with trivia, and their loyalty."

Student zombies usually have the same kind of behaviour, origin, and fate.

Each division in a three-part breakdown should be supported by either a series of examples or a single extended example.

d Be sure to outline the essay before you begin to write. As a guide, put your thesis and three supporting points in the spaces below.

Thesis: _____

_____

_____

Support: 1. _____

2. _____

3. _____

e While writing your paper, use as a guide the checklist of the four bases on page 123 and the inside front cover. Make sure you can answer *Yes* to the questions about unity, support, coherence, and sentence skills.

■ Writing Assignment 3

Write an essay that defines one of the terms below.

Persistence	Responsibility	Fear
Rebellion	Insecurity	Arrogance
Sense of humour	Assertiveness	Conscience
Escape	Jealousy	Class
Laziness	Practicality	Innocence
Danger	Nostalgia	Freedom
Curiosity	Gentleness	Violence
Common sense	Depression	Shyness
Soul	Obsession	Idealism
Family	Self-control	Religious faith

As a guide in writing your paper, use the suggestions in "How to Proceed."

■ Writing Assignment 4

In this essay, you will write with a specific purpose and for a specific audience.

Option 1: You work in a doctor's office and have been asked to write a brochure that will be placed in the patients' waiting room. The brochure is intended to tell patients what a healthy life-style is. Write a definition of a *healthy life-style* for your readers, using examples wherever appropriate. Your definition might focus on both mental and physical health and might include eating, sleeping, exercise, and recreational habits.

Alternatively, you might decide to take a playful point of view and write a brochure defining an *unhealthy life-style*.

Option 2: Your French class will be hosts to some students from Quebec. The class is preparing a mini-dictionary of slang for the visitors. Your job is to write a paragraph in which you define the phrase *to gross out*. In your paper, include a general definition as well as several examples showing how the phrase is used and the circumstances in which it would be appropriate. By way of providing background, you may also want to include the non-slang meaning of *gross* which led to the slang usage. To find the information, consult a dictionary.

Alternatively, you may write about any other slang term. If necessary, first get the approval of your instructor.

■ Writing Assignment 5: Writing about a Reading Selection

Read the selection titled "Shame" on pages 488–491. Then write an essay in which you define a term, as Dick Gregory does in "Shame," through narration. You can use one of the terms listed in Writing Assignment 3 or think up one of your own. In your introduction, fill in a brief background for your readers—when and where the experience happened. Your thesis should express the idea that because of this experience, you (or the person or people you are writing about) learned the meaning of the word _____ (fill in the term you have chosen). Break the narrative at logical points to create three supporting paragraphs. You might first want to look at the examples of narrative essays given on pages 206–209.

Alternatively, you might develop your definition with three experiences that seem to embody the word you have chosen. These could be experiences of your own, ones you know about, or ones you have read about. Develop each in a separate supporting paragraph.

DIVISION
AND
CLASSIFICATION

When you return home from your weekly trip to the supermarket with five bags packed with your purchases, how do you sort them out? You might separate the food items from the non-food items (like toothpaste, paper towels, and detergent). Or you might divide and classify the items into groups intended for the freezer compartment, the refrigerator, and the kitchen cupboards. You might even put the items into groups like "to be used tonight," "to be used soon," and "to be used last." Sorting supermarket items in such ways is just one small example of how we spend a great deal of our time organizing our environment in one manner or another.

In this section, you will be asked to write an essay in which you divide or classify a subject according to a single principle. To prepare for this assignment, first read the division and classification essays below and then work through the questions and the activity that follow.

ESSAYS TO CONSIDER

Mall People

Having fun can exhaust one's bank account. By the time a person 1
drives to the city and pays the tired-looking parking attendant the hourly
fee to park, there is little money left to buy movie tickets, let alone popcorn
and soft drinks to snack on. As a result, people have turned from wining,
dining, and movie-going to the nearby free-parking, free-admission shopping
malls. Teenagers, couples on dates, and the nuclear family can all be
observed having a good time at this alternative recreation spot.

Teenagers are the largest group of mall-goers. The guys saunter by in 2
sneakers, T-shirts, and blue jeans, complete with a package of cigarettes
sticking out of their pockets. The girls stumble along in high-heeled shoes
and daring tank tops, with hairbrushes tucked snugly in the rear pockets of
their tight-fitting jeans. Travelling in a gang that resembles a wolf pack, the
teenagers make the shopping mall their hunting ground. Their raised voices,
loud laughter, and occasional shouted obscenities can be heard from as far
as half a mall away. They come to "pick up chicks," to "meet guys," and
basically just to "hang out."

Couples are now spending their dates at shopping malls. The young 3
lovers are easy to spot because they walk hand in hand, stopping to sneak
a quick kiss after every few steps. They first pause at jewellery store
windows so they can gaze at diamond engagement rings and gold wedding
bands. Then, they wander into furniture departments in the large mall
stores. Whispering happily to each other, they imagine how that five-piece
living room set or brass headboard would look in their future home. Finally,
they drift away, their arms wrapped around each other's waists.

Mom, Dad, little Jenny, and Fred, Jr., visit the mall on Friday and 4
Saturday evenings. Jenny wants to see some of the special mall exhibits
geared towards little children. Fred, Jr., wants to head for the places that
young boys find appealing. Mom walks around looking at various things
until she discovers that Jenny is no longer attached to her hand. She finally
finds her in a favourite hiding place. Meanwhile, Dad has arrived at a large
store and is admiring the products he would love to buy. Indeed, the mall
provides something special for every member of the family.

The teenagers, the couples on dates, and the nuclear family make up 5
the vast majority of mall-goers. These folks need not purchase anything to
find pleasure at the mall. They are shopping for inexpensive recreation, and
the mall provides it.

Movie Monsters

Dracula rises from the grave--again. Mutant insects, the product of 1
underground nuclear testing, grow to the size of boxcars and attack our
cities. Weird-looking aliens from beyond the stars decide to invade our
planet. None of these events, if they ever happened, would surprise horror-
movie fans. For years, such movie-goers have enjoyed being frightened by
every type of monster Hollywood has managed to dream up, whether it be
natural, artificial, or extraterrestrial.

One kind of movie monster is a product of nature. These monsters may 2
be exaggerated versions of real creatures, like the single-minded shark in
Jaws or the skyscraper-climbing gorilla in King Kong. They may be extinct
animals, like the dinosaurs that terrorize cave-dwellers and explorers in
movies. Actually, cave-dwellers and dinosaurs would never have met, for
some unexplained event caused the dinosaurs to become extinct before the
cave-dwellers existed. "Natural" monsters sometimes combine human and
animal features. Cat people, werewolves, and vampires fit into this
category; so do Bigfoot and the Abominable Snowman. All these monsters
seem to frighten us because they represent nature at its most threatening.
We may have come a long way since the Stone Age, but we're still scared of
what's out there beyond the camp-fire.

The second type of movie monster is a product of humans. Every giant 3
lobster or house-sized spider that attacks Tokyo or Cleveland is the result
of a mad scientist's meddling or a dose of radiation. In these cases, humans
interfere with nature, and the results are deadly. Frankenstein's monster,
for example, is put together out of spare parts stolen from graveyards. His
creator, an insane scientist in love with his own power, uses a jolt of
electricity to bring the monster to life. The scientist, along with lots of
innocent villagers, dies as a result of his pride. In dozens of other monster
movies, creatures grow to enormous proportions after wandering too close
to atomic bomb sites. Our real fears about the terrors of technology are
given the shape of giant scorpions and cockroaches that devour people.

The third type of movie monster comes from outer space. Since the movies 4
began, odd things have been crawling or sliding down the ramps of spaceships.
To modern movie fans, the early space monsters look suspiciously like actors
dressed in rubber suits and metal antennas. Now, thanks to special effects,
these creatures can horrify the bravest movie-goer. The monster in Alien, for
example, invades a spaceship piloted by humans. The monster, which resembles
a ten-pound raw clam with arms, clamps onto a crew member's face. Later, it
grows into a slimy six-footer with a double jaw and long, toothed tongue.
Movies like Alien reflect our fear of the unfamiliar and the unknown. We don't
know what's out there in space, and we're afraid it might not be very nice.

Movie monsters, no matter what kind they are, sneak around the edges 5
of our imaginations long after the movies are over. They probably play on
fears that were there already. The movies merely give us the monsters that
embody those fears.

Selling Beer

The other night, my six-year-old son turned to me and asked for a light beer. My husband and I sat there for a moment, stunned, and then explained to him that beer was only for grown-ups. I suddenly realized how many, and how often, beer ads appear on television. To my little boy, it must seem that Canadians drink beer after work, or after playing ball, or while watching a football game. Beer makers have pounded audiences with all kinds of campaigns to sell beer. Each type of ad, however, seems to be targeted towards a different economic level of the TV viewing audience.

1

The first type of ad appeals to working-class people. There is the "there's nothin' halfway about it" approach, which shows the "boys" headed down to the neighbourhood tavern after a tough day on the job at the auto plant or the construction site. The Export jingle congratulates them on a job well done and encourages them to reward themselves--with a beer. Molson's Canadian uses a slightly different approach to appeal to workers. Men are shown completing a tough and unusual job and then relaxing. Beer ad jobs might be called fantasy blue-collar jobs. Some Molson's men, apparently, fly helicopters to round up cattle or manage to cap blazing oil well fires.

2

The second kind of ad aims not at working-class people but at an upper-middle-class audience. The actors in these ads are shown in glamorous or adventurous settings. Some ads show a group of friends in their thirties and forties getting together to play a fancy sport, like tennis or rugby. Upper Canada Breweries' ads, aimed at those rich enough to have a costly cottage, could feature a group of compatible couples at a barbecue.

3

The third type of ad appeals to people with a weight problem. These are the ads for the light beers, and they use sports celebrities and indirect language to make their points. For example, they never use the phrase "diet beer." Instead, they use phrases like "tastes great, and is less filling." In the macho world of beer commercials, men don't admit that they're dieting--that's too sissy. But if former football coaches and baseball greats can order a Lite without being laughed out of the bar, why can't the ordinary guy?

4

To a little boy, it may well seem that beer is necessary to every adult's life. After all, we need it to recover from a hard day at work, to celebrate our pleasurable moments, and to get rid of the beer bellies we got by drinking it in the first place. At least, that's what advertisers tell him--and us.

5

■ Questions

About Unity

1. Which paragraph in "Mall People" lacks a topic sentence? _____
Write a topic sentence for the paragraph:

_____

2. Which sentence in paragraph 2 of "Movie Monsters" should be omitted in the interest of paragraph unity? _____

3. Which paragraph in "Selling Beer" does not logically support the thesis statement? _____

About Support

4. Which supporting paragraph in "Movie Monsters" uses a single extended example? _____

5. After which sentence in paragraph 3 of "Selling Beer" are more supporting details needed? _____

6. Which paragraph in "Mall People" lacks specific details? _____

About Coherence

7. What are the transition words used in the second supporting paragraph of "Mall People"?

   a. _____   b. _____   c. _____

8. Which topic sentence in "Selling Beer" functions as a linking sentence between paragraphs? _____

About the Introduction and Conclusion

9. Circle the kind of introduction used in "Selling Beer."
   a. Broad, general statement narrowing to thesis
   b. Idea that is the opposite of the one to be developed
   c. Quotation
   d. Anecdote
   e. Questions

10. Which two essays have conclusions that include brief summaries of the essay's supporting points?
    a. "Movie Monsters"
    b. "Mall People"
    c. "Selling Beer"

Activity

This activity will sharpen your sense of the classifying process. In each of the following groups, cross out the one item that has not been classified on the same basis as the other four. Also, indicate in the space provided the single principle of classification used for the four items. Note the examples.

Examples   Shirts
    a. Flannel
    b. Cotton
    c. ~~Tuxedo~~
    d. Denim
    e. Silk

(Unifying principle: <u>material</u>)

Sports
    a. Swimming
    b. Sailing
    c. ~~Basketball~~
    d. Water polo
    e. Scuba diving

(Unifying principle: <u>water sports</u>)

1. School subjects
    a. Algebra
    b. History
    c. Geometry
    d. Trigonometry
    e. Calculus

(Unifying principle: _____)

2. Movies
    a. *The Sound of Music*
    b. *My Fair Lady*
    c. *Dracula*
    d. *Cabaret*
    e. *The Wizard of Oz*

(Unifying principle: _____)

3. Clothing
    a. Sweat shirt
    b. Shorts
    c. T-shirt
    d. Evening gown
    e. Sweat pants

(Unifying principle: _____)

4. Fasteners
    a. Staples
    b. Buttons
    c. Zippers
    d. Snaps
    e. Velcro

(Unifying principle: _____)

5. Sources of information

    a. *Maclean's*

    b. *The Globe and Mail*

    c. *Canadian Geographic*

    d. *Harrowsmith*

    e. *Saturday Night*

(Unifying principle: _____)

6. Fibres

    a. Wool

    b. Acrylic

    c. Cotton

    d. Silk

    e. Linen

(Unifying principle: _____)

7. Tapes

    a. Cellophane

    b. Recording

    c. Masking

    d. Duct

    e. Electrical

(Unifying principle: _____)

8. Fairy-tale characters

    a. Witch

    b. King

    c. Fairy godmother

    d. Wicked queen

    e. Princess

(Unifying principle: _____)

9. Immigrants

    a. Haitian

    b. Irish

    c. Mexican

    d. Illegal

    e. German

(Unifying principle: _____)

10. Famous buildings

    a. CN Tower

    b. Expo Stadium

    c. Calgary Saddledome

    d. Montreal Forum

    e. Skydome

(Unifying principle: _____)

11. Emotions

    a. Depression

    b. Anger

    c. Jealousy

    d. Despair

    e. Affection

(Unifying principle: _____)

12. Crimes

    a. Rape

    b. Murder

    c. Robbery

    d. Prostitution

    e. Mugging

(Unifying principle: _____)

WRITING THE ESSAY

■ Writing Assignment 1

Shown below are an introduction, a thesis, and supporting points for a classification essay on college stress. Using separate paper, plan out and write the supporting paragraphs and a conclusion for the essay. Refer to the suggestions on "How to Proceed" that follow.

College Stress

Jack's heart pounds as he casts panicked looks around the classroom. He doesn't recognize the professor, he doesn't know any of the students, and he can't even figure out what the subject is. In front of him is a test. At the last minute his room-mate awakens him. It's only another anxiety dream. The very fact that dreams like Jack's are common suggests that college is a stressful situation for young people. The causes of this stress can be academic, financial, and personal.

Academic stress is common. . . .

In addition to academic stress, the student often feels financial pressure. . . .

Along with academic and financial worries, the student faces personal pressures. . . .

How to Proceed

a To develop some ideas for the essay, freewrite for five minutes apiece on (1) *academic*, (2) *financial*, and (3) *personal* problems of college students.

b Add to the material you have written by asking yourself these questions:

What are some examples of academic problems that are stressful for students?

What are some examples of financial problems that students must contend with?

What are some examples of personal problems that create stress in students?

Write down quickly whatever answers occur to you for the questions. As with the freewriting, do not worry at this stage about writing correct sentences. Instead, concentrate on getting down as much information as you can think of that supports each of the three points.

c Now go through all the material you have accumulated. Perhaps some of the details you have written down may help you think of even better details that would fit. If so, write them down. Then make decisions about the exact information that you will use in each supporting paragraph. List the details (1, 2, 3, and so on) in the order in which you will present them.

d As you work on the drafts of your paper, refer to the checklist on page 123 and the inside front cover to make sure you can answer *Yes* to the questions about unity, support, and coherence.

e Write a conclusion for the essay by adding a summarizing sentence or two and a final thought about the subject. See page 77 for an example.

f Finally, use the checklist on page 123 and the inside front cover to proofread the next-to-final draft of your paper for sentence-skills mistakes, including spelling.

■ Writing Assignment 2

Write a division and classification essay on one of the following subjects:

Crimes	Advertisements	Clothes
Dates	Churchgoers	Attitudes towards life
Teachers	Junk food	Eating places
Bosses	Jobs	Marriages
Friends	Shoppers	TV watchers
Sports fans	Soap operas	College courses
Parties	Bars	

How to Proceed

a The first step in writing a division and classification essay is to divide your tentative topic into three reasonably complete parts. *Always use a single principle of division when you form your three parts.* For example, if your topic was "Automobile Drivers" and you divided them into slow, moderate, and fast drivers, your single basis for division would be "rate of speed." It would be illogical, then, to have as a fourth type "teenage drivers" (the basis of such a division would be "age") or "female drivers" (the basis of such a division would be "sex"). You probably could classify automobile drivers on the basis of age or sex or another division, for almost any subject can be analyzed in more than one way. What is important, however, is that in any single paper, you choose only one basis for division and stick to it. Be consistent.

In "Movie Monsters," the single basis for dividing monsters into natural, artificial, and extraterrestrial is *origin*. It would have been illogical, then, to have a fourth category dealing with vampires. In "Selling Beer," the intended basis for the types of beer ads was *economic level*. The writer's first group was working-class people; his second group was upper-middle-class people. To be consistent, the third group should have been, perhaps, lower-middle-class people. Instead, the writer confusingly shifted to ads that appeal to people with a weight problem.

b To avoid such confusion in your own essay, fill in the outline below before starting your paper and make sure you can answer *Yes* to the questions that follow. You should expect to do a fair amount of thinking before coming up with a logical plan for your paper.

Topic: _____

Three-part division of the topic:

1. _____

2. _____

3. _____

Is there a single basis of division for the three parts? _____

Is the division reasonably complete? _____

c Refer to the checklist of the four bases on page 123 and the inside front cover while writing the drafts of your paper. Make sure you can answer *Yes* to the questions about unity, support, organization, and sentence skills. Also, use the checklist when you proofread the next-to-final draft of your paper for sentence-skills mistakes, including spelling.

■ **Writing Assignment 3**

In this essay, you will write with a specific purpose and for a specific audience.

Option 1:   Your younger sister or brother has moved to another city and is about to choose a room-mate. Write her or him a letter about what to expect from different types of room-mates. Label each type of room-mate in your letter ("The Messy Type," "Mr. or Ms. Clean," "The Loud-Music Lover," etc.) and explain what it would be like to live with each.

Option 2:   Unsure about your career direction, you have gone to a vocational counselling service. To help you select the type of work you are best suited for, a counsellor has asked you to write a detailed description of your "ideal job." You will present this description to three other people who are also seeking to make a career choice.

To describe your ideal job, divide work life into three or more elements, such as:

Activities done on the job

Skills used on the job

Physical environment

People you work with and under

How the job affects society

In your paper, explain your ideals for each element. Use specific examples where possible to illustrate your points.

■ **Writing Assignment 4:**
Writing about a Reading Selection

Read the selection titled "Five Parenting Styles" on pages 565–568. Then write an essay in which you divide and classify a group of people. The group you classify should be *one* of the following:

- ■ Teachers
- ■ Friends
- ■ Co-workers

On the following page are suggestions about how to write your essay.

To begin, you must think of a way—a principle of division—to divide the group you have chosen. If you were considering "co-workers," for example, you could probably imagine several principles of division, such as these:

Ways they treat the boss

Efficiency at work

Punctuality at work

Level of neatness (desks, lockers, work turned in)

Once you have a useful principle of division, you will find that you can easily divide the people you are writing about into groups. If you decided, for instance, to use "ways they treat the boss" as your principle of division, you might write about these three groups:

1. Co-workers who "butter up" the boss
2. Co-workers who get along with the boss
3. Co-workers who dislike the boss

Here are some suggested principles of division for "teachers" and "friends." You should feel free, of course, to come up with your own approach.

Teachers

Teaching methods

Methods of classroom control

Clothing styles

Testing methods

Level of dedication to the job

Friends

Level of loyalty

Where or how you first met them

Length of time you've been friends

Level of emotional closeness

Attitudes towards something (money, college, drugs, and so on)

To complete the essay, follow the suggestions on "How to Proceed" on page 192.

DESCRIPTION

When you describe someone or something, you give a picture in words to your readers. To make the word picture as vivid and real as possible, you must observe and record specific details that appeal to your readers' senses (sight, hearing, taste, smell, and touch). More than any other type of essay, a descriptive paper needs sharp, colourful details.

Here is a sentence in which almost none of the senses is used: "In the window was a fan." In contrast, here is a description rich in sense impressions: "The blades of the rusty window fan clattered and whirled as they blew out a stream of warm, soggy air." Sense impressions here include sight (*rusty window fan*, *whirled*), hearing (*clattered*), and touch (*warm, soggy air*). The vividness and sharpness provided by the sensory details give us a clear picture of the fan and enable us to share in the writer's experience.

In this section, you will be asked to describe sharply a person, place, or thing for the readers through the use of words rich in sensory details. To help you prepare for the assignment, first read the three essays ahead and then answer the questions that follow.

ESSAYS TO CONSIDER

Family Portrait

My mother, who is seventy years old, recently sent me a photograph of   1
herself that I had never seen before. While cleaning out the attic of her
Florida winter home, she came across a studio portrait she had had taken

about a year before she married my father. This picture of my mother as a twenty-year-old girl has fascinated me from the moment I began to study it closely.

The young woman in the picture has a face that resembles my own in many ways. Her face is a bit more oval than mine, but the softly waving brown hair around it is identical. The small, straight nose is the same model I was born with. My mother's mouth is closed, yet there is just the slightest hint of a smile on her full lips. I know that if she had smiled, she would have shown the same wide grin and downcurving "smile lines" that appear in my own snapshots. The most haunting features in the photo, however, are my mother's eyes. They are exact duplicates of my own large, dark brown ones. Her brows are plucked into thin lines, which are like two pencil strokes added to highlight those fine, luminous eyes. 2

I've also carefully studied the clothing and jewellery in the photograph. My mother is wearing a blouse and skirt that, although the photo was taken fifty years ago, could easily be worn today. The blouse is made of heavy eggshell-coloured satin and reflects the light in its folds and hollows. It has a turned-down cowl collar and smocking on the shoulders and below the collar. The smocking (tiny rows of gathered material) looks hand-done. The skirt, which covers my mother's calves, is straight and made of light wool or flannel. My mother is wearing silver drop ear-rings. They are about two inches long and roughly shield-shaped. On her left wrist is a matching bracelet. My mother can't find this bracelet now, despite the fact that we spent hours searching through the attic for it. On the third finger of her left hand is a ring with a large, square-cut stone. 3

The story behind the picture is as interesting to me as the young woman it captures. Mom, who was earning twenty-five dollars a week as a file clerk, decided to give her boyfriend (my father) a picture of herself. She spent almost two weeks' salary on the skirt and blouse, which she bought at a fancy department store downtown. She borrowed the ear-rings and bracelet from her older sister, my aunt Dorothy. The ring she wore was a present from another young man she was dating at the time. Mom spent another chunk of her salary to pay the portrait photographer for the hand-tinted print in old-fashioned tones of brown and tan. Just before giving the picture to my father, she scrawled at the lower left, "Sincerely, Beatrice." 4

When I study this picture, I react in many ways. I think about the trouble that Mom went to in order to impress the young man who was to be my father. I laugh when I look at the ring that was probably worn to make my father jealous. I smile at the serious, formal inscription my mother used in this stage of the budding relationship. Sometimes, I am filled with a mixture of pleasure and sadness when I look at this frozen long-ago moment. It is a moment of beauty, of love, and--in a way--of my own past. 5

My Fantasy Room

Recently, a popular comic strip had a story about a girl's going to camp   1
for two weeks. At Camp Beanbag, she tells her mother, there are no chores
or required activity. All the campers do is lie in a room in beanbag chairs
and eat junk food. This idea appealed to me, and I began to think. If I could
spend two weeks in just one place, what would that place be like? I began to
imagine the room of my dreams.

First of all, my fantasy room would be decorated in a way that would   2
make me feel totally at ease. The walls would be painted a tasteful shade of
pale green, the colour supposed to be the most soothing. Psychologists have
conducted studies proving that colour can affect a person's mood. Also, a
deep plush carpet in an intense blue would cover the floor from wall to
wall--the perfect foundation for padding silently around the room. In the
entryway, huge closets with sliding doors would contain my wardrobe of
size-eight designer originals. The closets I have now are always messy and
crowded, stuffed with old shoes and other kinds of junk. Lastly, on the
walls, silver frames would hold my memories: pictures of me with my
sports star and musician friends, news clippings reporting on my social life,
a poster advertising the movie version of my most recent best-selling novel.
Everything would be quiet and tasteful, of course.

I'd have a king-sized bed with a headboard full of buttons that would   3
allow me to turn on lights, start music playing, or run hot water for my
whirlpool bath without getting up. Tall bookcases with enough shelf space
for all the souvenirs from my world travels would line an entire wall.
Against the opposite wall would be a chrome and glass desk topped with
lined pads and a rainbow of felt-tipped pens. They would await the moment
when I became inspired enough to begin writing my next best-seller. And
for my pure-bred Persian cat, there would be a lavender satin pillow.

Finally, my fantasy room would have the latest technological advances.   4
The air-conditioning or heating, depending on the season, would function at
a whisper. A telephone, operated by a push button from my bed, would put
me in touch with the world. Or, if I were feeling antisocial, I could flick on
my quadraphonic stereo system and fill the room with music. I could select
a movie from my library of laser discs to play on my giant-screen projection
TV. Or I could throw a switch, and the satellite dish on my roof would bring
me my choice of television programmes from all over the world.

It's probably a good idea that my fantasy room exists only in my mind.   5
If it were a real place, I don't think two weeks would be long enough. I
might stay in it forever.

The Coffee Shop at Midnight

I've been in lots of coffee shops, and they've always seemed to be   1
warm, busy, friendly, happy places. That's why, on a recent Monday night, I
stopped in a coffee shop for a cup of coffee. I was returning home after an
all-day car trip and needed something to help me make the last ninety
kilometres. A coffee shop at midnight, however, was not the place I had
expected. It was different--and lonely.

My Toyota pulled to a halt in front of the dreary grey aluminum   2
building that looked like an old railroad car. A half-lit neon sign sputtered
the message "Fresh baked goods daily" on the surface of the rain-slick
parking lot. Only a half dozen cars and a battered pick-up were scattered
around the lot. An empty paper coffee cup made a hollow scraping sound as
it rolled in small circles on one cement step close to the entrance. I pulled
hard at the balky glass door, and it banged shut behind me.

The coffee shop was quiet when I entered. As there was no one on duty,   3
only the faint odour of stale grease and the dull hum of an empty refrigerated
pastry case greeted me. I looked around for a place to sit. The outside walls
were lined with empty booths which squatted back to back in their orange
vinyl upholstery. On each speckled beige-and-gold table were the usual
accessories. The kitchen hid mysteriously behind two swinging metal doors
with round windows. I glanced through these windows but could see only a
part of the large, apparently deserted cooking area. Facing the kitchen
doors was the counter. I approached the length of Formica and slid onto one
of the cracked vinyl seats bolted in soldier-like straight lines in front of it.

The people in the coffee shop seemed as lonely as the place itself. Two   4
men in rumpled work shirts sat at the counter, on stools several feet apart,
staring wearily into cups of coffee and smoking cigarettes. Their faces
sprouted what looked like day-long stubbles of beard. I figured they were
probably shift workers who, for some reason, didn't want to go home. Three
stools down from the workers, I spotted a thin young man with a mop of
black, curly hair. He was dressed in brown corduroy jeans with a checked
western-style shirt unbuttoned at the neck. He wore a blank expression as
he picked at a plate of limp french fries. I wondered if he had just returned
from a disappointing date. At the one occupied booth was a middle-aged
couple. They hadn't gotten any food yet. He was staring off into space, idly
tapping his spoon against the table, while she drew aimless parallel lines on
her paper napkin with a bent dinner fork. Neither said a word to the other.

Finally, a tired-looking server approached me with a thick order pad. I   5
ordered the coffee, but I wanted to drink it fast and get out of there. My
car, and the solitary distance ahead of me, would be lonely. But they
wouldn't be as lonely as that coffee shop at midnight.

■ Questions

About Unity

1. Which supporting paragraph in "My Fantasy Room" lacks a topic sentence?
   _____

2. Which two sentences in paragraph 2 of "My Fantasy Room" should be omitted in the interest of paragraph unity?

   _____ _____

3. Which sentence in paragraph 3 of "Family Portrait" should be omitted in the interest of paragraph unity? _____

About Support

4. How many examples support the topic sentence, "The people in the coffee shop seemed as lonely as the place itself," in "The Coffee Shop at Midnight"?

   a. One   b. Two   c. Three

5. Label as *sight*, *touch*, *hearing*, or *smell* all the sensory details in the following sentences taken from the three essays. The first one is done for you as an example.

   a. "As there was no one on duty, only the faint odour of stale grease and the dull hum of an empty refrigerated pastry case greeted me."

   b. "He was staring off into space, idly tapping his spoon against the table, while she drew aimless parallel lines on her paper napkin with a bent dinner fork."

   c. "Also, a deep plush carpet in an intense blue would cover the floor from wall to wall—the perfect foundation for padding silently around the room."

   d. "The blouse is made of heavy eggshell-coloured satin and reflects the light in its folds and hollows."

6. After which sentence in paragraph 3 of "The Coffee Shop at Midnight" are more details needed? _____

About Coherence

7. Which method of organization (time order or emphatic order) does paragraph 2 of "Family Portrait" use?

_____

8. Which sentence in this paragraph indicates the method of organization?

_____

9. Which of the following topic sentences in "The Coffee Shop at Midnight" is a linking sentence?

   a. "My Toyota pulled to a halt in front of the dreary grey aluminum building that looked like an old railroad car."

   b. "The coffee shop was quiet when I entered."

   c. "The people in the coffee shop seemed as lonely as the place itself."

10. In paragraph 2 of "My Fantasy Room," what are the major transition words?

   a. _____   b. _____   c. _____

WRITING THE ESSAY

■ Writing Assignment 1

Write an essay about a particular place that you can observe carefully or that you already know well. The place might be one of the following or some other place:

Pet shop
Exam room
Laundromat
Bar or nightclub
Video arcade
Corner store
Library study area
Basement or garage
Hotel or motel lobby
Your bedroom or the bedroom of someone you know
Waiting room at a train station or bus terminal
Winning or losing locker room after an important game
Antique shop or other small shop

How to Proceed

a Remember that, like all essays, a descriptive paper must have a thesis. Your thesis should state a dominant impression about the place you are describing. State the place you want to describe and the dominant impression you want to make in a short single sentence. The sentence can be refined later. For now, you just want to find and express a workable topic. You might write, for example, a sentence like one of the following:

The study area was noisy.

The exam room was tense.

The pet shop was crowded.

The bar was cosy.

The video arcade was confusing.

The bus terminal was frightening.

The corner store was cheerful.

The antique shop was lonely.

The bedroom was very organized.

The motel lobby was restful.

The winners' locker room was chaotic.

b Now make a list of as many details as you can that support the general impression. For example, the writer of "The Coffee Shop at Midnight" made this list:

Tired workers at counter

Rainy parking lot

Empty booths

Quiet

Few cars in lot

Dreary grey building

Lonely young man

Silent middle-aged couple

Out-of-order neon sign

No one on duty

Couldn't see anyone in kitchen

Tired-looking server

c Organize your paper according to one or a combination of the following:

Physical order—move from left to right, or far to near, or in some other consistent order

Size—begin with large features or objects and work down to smaller ones

A *special order*—use an order that is appropriate to the subject

For instance, the writer of "The Coffee Shop at Midnight" builds his essay around the dominant impression of loneliness. The paper is organized in terms of physical order (from the parking lot to the entrance to the interior); a secondary method of organization is size (large parking lot to smaller diner to still smaller people).

d Use as many senses as possible in describing a scene. Chiefly you will use sight, but to an extent you may be able to use touch, hearing, smell, and perhaps even taste as well. Remember that it is through the richness of your sense impressions that the reader will gain a picture of the scene.

e As you are working on the drafts of your paper, refer to the checklist on page 123 and the inside front cover. Make sure you can answer *Yes* to the questions about unity, support, and coherence.

■ Writing Assignment 2

Write an essay about a family photograph. You may want to use an order similar to the one in "A Family Portrait," where the first supporting paragraph deals with the subject's face, the second with clothing and jewellery, and the third with the story behind the picture. Another possible order might be (1) the people in the photo (and how they look), (2) the relationships among the people (and what they are doing in the picture), and (3) the story behind the picture (time, place, occasion, relationships, or feelings). Use whatever order seems appropriate.

■ Writing Assignment 3

Write an essay describing a person. First, decide on a dominant impression you have about the person, and then use only those details which will add to it. Here are some examples of interesting types of people you might want to write about:

College character	Enemy	TV or movie personality
Dentist	Clergyman	Street person
Bus driver	Teacher	Older person
Close friend	Child	Employer
Rival	Drunk	

■ Writing Assignment 4

In this essay, you will write with a specific purpose, for a specific audience.

Option 1: You have just attended a richly satisfying event, such as a concert, a sports contest, a stage show, or even a family gathering. Now you want to share your experience with a good friend who lives in another city. Write a letter in which you enthusiastically describe the event. Include vivid details so that your friend will be able to see, hear, and feel the event as if he or she had been there in person.

Option 2: You have subscribed to a video dating service. Clients of the service are asked to make a five-minute presentation which will be recorded on videotape. Prepare such a presentation in which you describe yourself in terms of your attitudes and beliefs, your interests, and your personal habits. Your purpose is to give interested members of the dating service a good sense of what you are like.

■ Writing Assignment 5: Writing about a Reading Selection

Do *either* of the following.

Option 1: Read the selection titled "Of Lemons and Lemonade" on pages 532–534. Then write an essay describing a location you know well. You might consider writing about one of the following:

> Your house or apartment
> Cafeteria or restaurant
> Office or store where you work
> Your block on your street
> Park or schoolyard
> Waiting room
> Area where you study
> Inside of a bus, a subway, a train, or your own car

In your introductory paragraph, you will explain where the place is and why you are familiar with it. Explain what aspects of your location are most interesting or significant to you, and why. Be sure that you state in the thesis what the dominant impression is that you have of the place.

Use any order that you feel is appropriate (left to right, near to far, top to bottom, or other) to organize your supporting paragraphs. Use vivid images, as the author of "Of Lemons and Lemonade" does, to capture your place and its meaning to you on paper.

Option 2: Read the selection titled "The Firewood Gatherers" on pages 571–573. Then write an essay describing a distinctive person you have encountered more than once. You might choose to describe a family member, an acquaintance, a friend, or simply someone you have observed closely. Consider the feelings that the most significant details about this person have aroused in you and try to capture those details vividly.

Use any order that you feel is appropriate to organize your supporting paragraphs. Include plenty of specific details that will give your reader a mental photograph of the person you are describing.

NARRATION

At times we make a statement clear by relating in detail something that has happened to us. In the story we tell, we present the details in the order in which they happened. A person might say, for example, "I was really embarrassed the day I took my driver's test," and then go on to develop that statement with an account of the experience. If the story is sharply detailed, we will be able to see and understand just why the speaker felt that way.

In this section, you'll be asked to tell a story that illustrates some point. The student essays ahead all present narrative experiences that support a thesis. Read them and then answer the questions that follow.

ESSAYS TO CONSIDER

My First Professional Performance

I was nineteen, and the invitation to play my guitar and sing at the   1
Norfolk County Carnival seemed the "big break" aspiring performers dream
about. I would be sharing the programme with well-known professionals. My
spirits were not even dampened by the discovery that I would not be paid. I

had no reason to suspect then that my first professional performance was to be the scene of the most embarrassing experience of my life.

I arrived at the carnival grounds early, which proved fortunate. The manager knew that, in addition to the amplifier and speakers, I needed an extra microphone for my guitar and a high stool. However, when I checked the stage, I found the amplifier and speakers but nothing else. I also couldn't find the manager. The drunks who would hassle me later, after I had gotten started, became another problem. Since I couldn't perform without all the equipment, I was ready to call the whole thing off. Only the large potential audience milling around the carnival grounds influenced me to go through with it. One eye on my watch, I drove to the music store, told the owner my story, borrowed the needed equipment, and got back just as the Stone Gravel Rock Band, which preceded me on the programme, was finishing its set. The band plays bluegrass music in some local clubs, and the lead singer was recently offered a professional recording contract.

I had some attentive listeners for my first song, but then problems developed. A voice boomed, "Play 'Mister Bojangles.'" A group of noisy drunks, surrounded by empty beer cans, half-eaten hot dogs, and greasy paper plates, were sprawled on picnic tables to one side of the stage. "We want to hear 'Mister Bojangles,'" roared the others, laughing. "Not today," I answered pleasantly, "but if you like 'Bojangles,' you'll like this tune." I quickly slid into my next number. Unfortunately, my comment only encouraged the drunks to act in an even more outrageous manner. As they kept up the disturbance, my audience began drifting away to escape them.

I was falsely cheered by the arrival of a uniformed policeman and several older men in work clothes. "Fans," I thought hopefully. Then I gave a start as a large engine roared very close to me, filling the air with choking diesel fumes. Only then did I realize that my "stage" was really a huge flatbed truck and that the older men in work clothes were in the cab warming up the engine. As I played a song, the policeman approached me. "Hey, lady," he said, "you're going to have to get down from there with all that stuff. They've got to take this rig away now." "I can't do that," I said. "I'm a professional musician in the middle of a performance. Tell him to turn that engine off." (In my confusion, I left the mike open, transmitting this exchange to the entire carnival grounds.) "Sorry, lady, he has to take it now," insisted the policeman. The drunks happily entered into the spirit of the thing, yelling, "Take her away. We don't want her. Yeah, haul her away." To save a small amount of self-respect, I played one more chorus before I began packing up my gear.

Fortunately, in conversations I eventually had with other performers, I heard similar stories of experiences they had when starting out. Then I would tell them about the stage that nearly rolled away with me on it, and we would laugh. Now I see that it's all part of becoming a professional.

Adopting a Challenge

My church recently staged a "Sensitivity Sunday" to make our 1
congregation aware of the problems faced by people with physical
handicaps. We were asked to "adopt a challenge" for several hours one
Sunday morning. Some members chose to be confined to wheelchairs; others
stuffed cotton in their ears, hobbled around on crutches, or wore blindfolds.

Wheelchairs had never seemed like scary objects to me before I had to 2
sit in one. A tight knot grabbed hold in my stomach when I first took a close
look at what was to be my only means of getting around for several hours.
I was struck by the irrational thought, "Once I am in this wheelchair, the
handicap might become real, and I might never walk again." This thought,
as ridiculous as it was, frightened me so much that I needed a large dose of
courage just to sit down.

After I overcame my fear of the wheelchair, I had to learn how to cope 3
with it. I wiggled around to find a comfortable position and thought I might
even enjoy being pampered and wheeled around. I glanced over my shoulder
to see who would be pushing me. It was only then that I realized I would
have to navigate the contraption all by myself! My palms reddened and
started to sting as I tugged at the heavy metal wheels. I could not seem to
keep the chair on an even course or point the wheels in the direction I
wanted to go. I kept bumping into doors, pews, and other people. I felt as
though everyone was staring at me and commenting on my clumsiness.

When the service started, more problems cropped up to frustrate me 4
even further. Every time the congregation stood up, my view was blocked. I
could not see the minister, the choir, or the altar. Also, as the church's
aisles were narrow, I seemed to be in the way no matter where I parked
myself. For instance, the ushers had to step around me in order to pass the
collection plate. This made me feel like a nuisance. Thanks to a new building
programme, however, our church will soon have the wide aisles and well-
spaced pews that will make life easier for the physically challenged. Finally,
if people stopped to talk to me, I had to strain my neck to look up at them.
This made me feel like a little child being talked down to and added to my
sense of helplessness.

My few hours as a disabled person left a deep impression on me. Now, 5
I no longer feel resentment at large tax expenditures for ramp-equipped
buses, and I wouldn't dream of parking my car in a space marked
"Handicapped Only." Although my close encounter with a challenge was
short-lived, I can now understand the obstacles, both physical and
emotional, that wheelchair-bound people must overcome.

A Night of Violence

According to my history teacher, Adolf Hitler once said that he wanted   1
to sign up "brutal youths" to help him achieve his goals. If Hitler were still
alive, he wouldn't have any trouble recruiting the brutal youths he wanted;
he could get them right here in Canadian cities. I know, because I was one
of them. As a teenager, I ran with a gang. And it took a terrible incident to
make me see how violent I had become.

One Thursday night, I was out with my friends. I was still going to   2
school once in a while, but most of my friends weren't. We spent our days
on the streets, talking, showing off, sometimes shoplifting a little or shaking
people down for a few dollars. My friends and I were close, maybe because
life hadn't been very good to any of us. On this night, we were drinking
wine and vodka on the corner. For some reason, we all felt tense and
restless. One of us came up with the idea of robbing one of the old people
who lived in the high-rise close by. We would just knock him or her over,
grab the money, and party with it.

After about an hour, and after more wine and vodka, we spotted an   3
old man. He came out of the glass door of the building and started up the
street. Stuffing bottles in our jacket pockets, we closed in behind him. Victor,
the biggest of us, said, "We want your money, old man. Hand it over."
Suddenly, the old man whipped out a homemade wooden club from under
his coat and began swinging. The club thudded against the side of Victor's
head, making bright-red blood spurt out of his nose. When we saw this, we
went crazy. We smashed our bottles over the old man's head. Then Victor
ground the jagged edges of a broken bottle into the old man's skull. As we
ran, I kept seeing the bottom of that bottle sticking up out of the man's
head. It looked like a weird glass crown.

Later, at home, I threw up. I wasn't afraid of getting caught; in fact, we   4
never did get caught. I just knew I had gone over some kind of line. I didn't
know if I could step back, now that I had gone so far. But I knew I had to.
I had seen plenty of people in my neighbourhood turn into the kind who
hated their lives, people who didn't care about anything, people who wound
up penned in jail or ruled by drugs. I didn't want to become one of them.

That night, I realize now, I decided not to become one of Hitler's "brutal   5
youths." I'm proud of myself for that, even though life didn't get any easier
and no one came along to pin a medal on me. I just decided, quietly, to step
off the path I was on. I hope my parents and I will get along better now,
too. Maybe the old man's pain, in some terrible way, had a purpose.

■ **Questions**

About Unity

1. Which sentence in paragraph 4 of "Adopting a Challenge" should be omitted in the interest of paragraph unity? _____

2. Which sentence in paragraph 2 of "My First Professional Performance" should be omitted in the interest of paragraph unity? _____

3. Which essay lacks a thesis statement?

   _____

About Support

4. Label as *sight*, *touch*, *hearing*, or *smell* all the sensory details in the following sentences taken from the three essays.

   a. "Then I gave a start as a large engine roared very close to me, filling the air with choking diesel fumes."

   b. "The club thudded against the side of Victor's head, making bright-red blood spurt out of his nose."

   c. "My palms reddened and started to sting as I tugged at the heavy metal wheels."

   d. "A group of noisy drunks, surrounded by empty beer cans, half-eaten hot dogs, and greasy paper plates, were sprawled on picnic tables to one side of the stage."

5. In "Adopting a Challenge," how many examples support the topic sentence "When the service started, more problems cropped up to frustrate me even further"? _____

6. After which sentence in paragraph 3 of "My First Professional Performance" are more specific details needed? _____

7. Which supporting paragraphs in "My First Professional Performance" use dialogue to help recreate the event?

   _____

About Coherence

8. The first stage of the writer's experience in "Adopting a Challenge" might be called *sitting down in the wheelchair*. What are the other two stages of the experience?

    a. _____

    b. _____

9. In paragraph 2 of "My First Professional Performance," which detail is out of chronological (time) order?

    _____

About the Conclusion

10. Which sentence in the conclusion of "A Night of Violence" makes the mistake of introducing a completely new idea? _____

WRITING THE ESSAY

■ Writing Assignment 1

Write an essay telling about an experience in which a certain emotion was predominant. The emotion might be disappointment, embarrassment, happiness, frustration, or any of the following:

Fear	Anger	Silliness
Pride	Nostalgia	Disgust
Jealousy	Relief	Loss
Sadness	Greed	Sympathy
Terror	Nervousness	Violence
Regret	Hate	Bitterness
Shock	Surprise	Envy
Love	Shyness	Loneliness

The experience should be limited in time. Note that the three essays presented in this chapter all describe experiences that occurred within relatively short periods. One writer described her embarrassing musical debut; another described her frustration in acting as a handicapped person at a morning church service; the third described the terror of a minute's mugging that had lifelong consequences. See "How to Proceed" on the following page.

How to Proceed

a Think of an experience or event in your life in which you felt a certain emotion strongly. Then spend at least ten minutes freewriting about that experience. Do not worry at this point about such matters as spelling or grammar or putting things in the right order; instead, just try to get down as many details as you can think of that seem related to the experience.

b This preliminary writing will help you decide whether your topic is promising enough to continue work on. If it is not, choose another emotion. If it is, do two things:

First, write out your thesis in a single sentence, underlining the emotion you will focus on. For example, "My first day in kindergarten was one of the <u>scariest</u> days of my life."

Second, make up a list of all the details involved in the experience. Then arrange those details in chronological (time) order.

c Using the list as a guide, prepare a rough draft of your paper. Use time signals such as *first*, *then*, *next*, *after*, *while*, *during*, and *finally* to help connect details as you move from the beginning to the middle to the end of your narrative.

d See if you can divide your story into separate stages (what happened first, what happened next, what finally happened). Put each stage into a separate paragraph. In narratives, it is sometimes difficult to write a topic sentence for each supporting paragraph. You may, therefore, want to start new paragraphs at points where natural shifts or logical breaks in the story seem to occur.

e One good way to recreate an event is to include some dialogue, as does the writer of "My First Professional Performance." Repeating what you have said or what you have heard someone else say helps make the situation come alive. And, in general, try to provide as many vivid, exact details as you can to help your readers experience the event as it actually happened.

f As you work on the drafts of your paper, refer to the checklist on page 123 and the inside front cover to make sure that you can answer *Yes* to the questions about unity, support, and coherence. Also use the checklist to proofread the next-to-final draft of your paper for sentence-skills mistakes, including spelling.

■ Writing Assignment 2

Think of an experience in your life that supports one of the statements below.

■ "Before I got married I had six theories about bringing up children; now I have six children and no theories."—John Wilmot, Earl of Rochester

- "The chains of habit are too weak to be felt until they are too strong to be broken."—Samuel Johnson

- "Peter's Law—The unexpected always happens."—Laurence J. Peter

- "Canada is a collection of ten provinces with strong governments loosely connected by fear."—Dave Broadfoot

- "Good people are good because they've come to wisdom through failure." —William Saroyan

- "Lying is an indispensable part of making life tolerable."—Bergen Evans

- "The key to everything is patience. You get the chicken by hatching the egg —not by smashing it."—Arnold Glasgow

- "A good scare is worth more to a man than good advice."—Ed Howe

- "Whatever women do they must do twice as well as men to be thought half as good. Luckily, this is not difficult."—Charlotte Whitton

- "Like its politicians and its wars, society has the teenagers it deserves." —J. B. Priestley

- "It's what you learn after you know it all that counts."—John Wooden

- "Wise sayings often fall on barren ground; but a kind word is never thrown away."—Sir Arthur Helps

- "What a tangled web we weave/When first we practice to deceive."—Walter Scott

- "Love is a fever which marriage puts to bed and cures."—Richard J. Needham

- "We lie loudest when we lie to ourselves."—Eric Hoffer

- "The worst country to be poor in is America."—Arnold Toynbee

- "Criticism—a big bite out of someone's back."—Elia Kazan

- "Work is what you do so that sometime you won't have to do it anymore." —Alfred Polgar

- "Work is more fun than fun."—Noel Coward

- "A little learning is a dangerous thing."—Alexander Pope

- "Nothing is so good as it seems beforehand."—George Eliot

- "Follow your heart and you perish."—Margaret Laurence

Write a narrative essay using as a thesis one of the statements. Refer to the suggestions in "How to Proceed" on page 212. Remember that the point of your story is to *support* your thesis. Feel free to select from and even add to your experience so that your story truly supports the thesis.

■ **Writing Assignment 3**

In this essay, you will write with a specific purpose and for a specific audience.

Option 1: Imagine that you are in a town one hundred kilometres from home, that your car has broken down several kilometres from a gas station, and that you are carrying no money. You thought you were going to have a terrible time, but the friendly people who helped you turned your experience into a positive one. It was such a good day, in fact, that you don't want to forget what happened.

Write a narrative of the day's events in your diary, so that you can read it ten years from now and remember exactly what happened. Begin with the moment you realized your car had broken down and continue until you're safely back at home. Include a thesis at either the beginning or the end of your narration.

Option 2: Imagine that a friend or sister or brother has to make a difficult decision of some kind. Perhaps he or she must decide how to deal with a troubled love affair, or a problem with living at home, or a conflict with a boss or co-worker. Write a narrative from your own experience that will teach him or her something about the decision that must be made.

■ **Writing Assignment 4:**
Writing about a Reading Selection

Read the selection titled "The Image of Beauty" by Catherine Pigott on pages 526–528. Write a narrative essay about an occasion or a period in your life when your image of yourself, in terms of your appearance, was inappropriate to a situation, or was challenged by those around you. How did the situation, or the views of others, make you feel? Embarrassed? Defensive? Why, specifically? Did your own view of yourself change as a result of this experience or event? How?

Possible topics for this essay might include

■ attending a social event for which you thought you had dressed properly
■ beginning to attend a new school in a very different area
■ moving to a new country and encountering new situations and people
■ starting college or a new job where you didn't know what to expect

In your introduction, provide a few sentences of background information to prepare your readers for your narrative. State your thesis in a general way so as not to give away all your reactions, or what you learned, too soon in the essay. (Notice that Catherine Pigott reserves the specifics of her thesis until after she has "told you her story.") Use your concluding paragraph to clarify and underline the significance of your narrative from your point of view—then, now, or both. (Look at the way Pigott concludes her narrative.)

Let the nature and important details of your story help you decide how to break it up into paragraphs. Decide which events, which details, created the strongest impression on you, and focus your essay on these facts.

You will also find it helpful to look at the sample narrative essays on pages 206–209. They provide examples of how other writers introduce and conclude their essays and how they create logical breaks in the stories they tell.

ARGUMENTATION AND PERSUASION

Most of us know someone who enjoys a good argument. Such a person usually challenges any sweeping statement we might make. "Why do you say that?" he or she will ask. "Give your reasons." Our questioner then listens carefully as we state our case, waiting to see if we really do have solid evidence to support our point of view. Such a questioner may make us feel uncomfortable, but we may also feel grateful to him or her for helping us clarify our opinions.

Your ability to advance sound and compelling arguments is an important skill in everyday life. You can use persuasion to make a point in a class discussion, persuade a friend to lend you money, and talk an employer into giving you a day off from work. Learning about persuasion based on clear, logical reasoning can also help you see through the sometimes faulty arguments in advertisements, newspaper articles, political speeches, and the other persuasive appeals you see and hear every day.

In this section, you will be asked to argue a position and defend it with a series of solid reasons. You are in a general way doing the same thing—making a point and then supporting it—with all the essays in the book. The difference here is that, in a more direct and formal manner, you will advance a point about which you feel strongly and seek to persuade your readers to agree with you.

ESSAYS TO CONSIDER

Teenagers and Jobs

"The lives of adolescents and adults are not as different as they used to   1
be. Students juggle jobs and school and leisure time in much the same way
their parents juggle careers and families; they make important choices--
how often they work, what classes they take, what they spend their money

on--with almost no adult input . . . if they make unwise choices, there are no safety nets." So wrote Kate Fillion of Toronto high school students ("High School Undercover," *Toronto Life*, August 1990). Many people argue that working can be a valuable experience for the young. However, working more than about fifteen hours a week is harmful to adolescents because it reduces their involvement with school, encourages a materialistic and expensive lifestyle, and increases the chance of having problems with drugs and alcohol.

Schoolwork and the benefits of extra-curricular activities tend to go by 2 the wayside when adolescents work long hours. As more and more teens have filled the numerous part-time jobs offered by fast-food restaurants and mall stores, teachers have faced increasing difficulties. They must both keep the attention of tired pupils and give homework to students who simply don't have time to do it. In addition, educators have noticed less involvement in the extra-curricular events many consider healthy influences on young people. School bands and athletic teams are losing players to work, and sports events are poorly attended by working students. Those teenagers who try to do it all--homework, extra-curricular activities, and work--may find themselves exhausted and prone to illness. A recent newspaper story, for example, described a girl who came down with mononucleosis as a result of aiming for good grades, playing on two school athletic teams, and working thirty hours a week.

Another drawback of too much work is that it may promote materialism 3 and an unrealistic lifestyle. Some parents say that work teaches adolescents the value of a dollar. Undoubtedly, it can, and it's true that some teenagers work to help out with the family budget or save for college. However, surveys have shown that the majority of working teens use their earnings to buy luxuries--stereos, tape decks, clothing, even cars. These young people, some of whom earn $500 and more a month, don't worry about spending wisely--they can just about have it all. In many cases, experts point out, they are becoming accustomed to a lifestyle they won't be able to afford several years down the road, when they'll no longer have parents to pay for car insurance, food and lodging, and so on. At that point, they'll be hard pressed to pay for necessities as well as luxuries.

Finally, teenagers who work a lot are more likely than others to get 4 involved with alcohol and drugs. Teens who put in long hours may seek a quick release from stress, just like the adults who need to drink a couple of martinis after a hard day at work. Stress is probably greater in our society today than it has been at any time in the past. Also, teens who have money are more likely, for various obvious reasons, to get involved with drugs.

Teenagers can enjoy the benefits of work while avoiding its drawbacks 5 simply by limiting their work hours during the school year. As is often the case, a moderate approach will be the most healthy and rewarding.

A Vote against Computers

I was excited when my English composition instructor announced that   1
computers would be a major part of our writing course. "Half of the classes
will be held in the computer lab," she said, "and all required work will be
done on the computer." I was thrilled while touring the new computer lab to
see all the magical-looking machines with their glowing green screens. The
machines hummed as if they were alive. I thought to myself excitedly,
"We're living in the middle of the computer revolution, and here's my
chance to get on board." But three months later, I've had some second
thoughts. I now believe that computers are a bad idea in the writing
classroom. The computer does not help me plan a paper, it requires too
much time and trouble to use, and it has changed my instructor from a
teacher to a technician.

To begin with, the computer does not help me go about writing a paper.   2
When I start an essay, I like to use a yellow pad and scribble out my ideas. I
may write a couple of sentences, scratch them out, and then write a few
more. I may make a couple of rough outlines, and then cross out parts of
them, and then combine those leftover parts to make a third outline. I
may go back to some idea I rejected at first and write another idea in the
margin. I may circle something from one part of the page and join it with
something on another part. At any one time, I want to see everything I'm
doing in front of me. With a computer, I can't do that. If I delete something,
I can't look back at it later. If I write too much, I have to scroll back and
forth, since not everything can fit on the screen at once. There's no room in
the margin for questions. And I can't circle things on the computer screen
and connect them the way I can on a sheet of paper. I want a chance to see
and change everything at once when planning a paper, and a computer does
not let me do that.

Next, the mechanics involved in using a computer are complicated and   3
time-consuming. Before I can get down to some honest-to-goodness writing, I
have to show the computer lab technician my student ID card and sign out
the appropriate software. Then I have to find an open terminal, turn on my
computer and monitor, insert the proper disks, create or find a file, and set
the required format. When I'm finished writing, I have to make sure that
my work is properly saved, that there's paper in the printer, and that the
printer is on-line. And at any point, when I have mechanical problems or
questions about the computer, I have to wait five or ten minutes or more for
the teacher or a student technician to come to help me. Worst of all, I'm not
a good typist. I spend half of my time hunting and pecking for the proper
letters on the keyboard. If I had wanted to get a lot of typing practice, I
would have taken a typing course, but this is supposed to be a writing course.

Finally, when we meet in the computer lab, the teacher spends most of   4
the class walking around and helping students log on and off the computer,
handing out and collecting software, and trying to locate and retrieve lost

documents. I sat here the other day watching the class trying to write on computers, and my impression was that 75 per cent of what the teacher did involved computers rather than writing. I've had other writing courses, before computers, where the teacher spent a lot of time going over students' work on a one-on-one basis or in a class discussion. It was in this workshop setting that I believe my writing improved the most. Now, my professor has much less time to devote to individual help and feedback. She's too busy being a computer trouble-shooter.

In conclusion, it may be wise to take another look at the use of the computer in college writing courses. At first glance the computer offers excitement and a world of promise, but I think there's a serious question about whether it actually improves students' writing.   5

Once Over Lightly: Local TV News

Are local television newscasts a reliable source of news? Do they provide   1
in-depth coverage and analysis of important local issues? Unfortunately, all too often they do not. In their battle for high ratings, local television news shows provide more entertainment than news. News personalities are emphasized at the expense of stories; visual appeal has more priority than actual news; and stories and reports are too brief and shallow.

Local TV newscasters are as much the subject of the news as are the   2
stories they present. Nowhere is this more obvious than in weather reports. Weatherpersons spend valuable news time by joking, drawing cartoons, chatting about weather fronts as "good guys" and "bad guys," and dispensing weather trivia such as statistics about relative humidity and record highs and lows for the date. Reporters, too, draw attention to themselves. Rather than just getting the story, we are shown the reporters jumping into or getting out of helicopters to get the story. When reporters interview crime victims or the residents of poor neighbourhoods, the camera angle typically includes them and their reaction as well as their subjects. When they report on a storm, they stand outside in the storm, their styled hair blowing, so we can admire how they "brave the elements." Then there are the anchorpersons, who are chosen as much for their looks

as for their skills. They too dilute the news by putting their personalities on centre stage.

Often the selection of stories and the way they are presented is based   3
on visual impact rather than news value. If a story is not accompanied by an interesting film clip, it is unlikely to be shown on the local news. The result is an overemphasis on fires and car crashes and little attention to such important issues as the local employment situation. As much as possible, every story is presented with a reporter standing "live" in front of something. If City Hall has passed a resolution, for instance, then the reporter will be shown standing live in front of City Hall. Very often, cars are zooming by or neighbourhood kids are waving at the camera or passers-by are recognizing suddenly that they are being filmed. Most people are natural hams, and they love to discover that they are on stage. Such background happenings are so distracting that viewers may not even listen to what the reporter is saying. And even if a story is not live, the visuals that accompany a story are often distracting. A recent story on falling oil prices, for example, was accompanied by footage of a working oil well that drew away attention from the important economic information in the report.

Finally, the desire of the local stations to entertain viewers is   4
demonstrated in short news stories and shallow treatment. On the average, about half a minute is devoted to a story. Clearly, stories that take less than half a minute are superficial. Even the longest stories, which can take up several minutes, are not accompanied by meaningful analysis. Instead, the camera jumps from one location to another and the newscaster simplifies and trivializes the issues. For instance, one recent "in-depth" story about the homeless consisted of a glamorous reporter talking to a homeless person and asking him what should be done about the problem. The poor man was in no condition to respond intelligently. The story then cut to an interview with a city bureaucrat who mechanically rambled on about the need for more government funding. There were also shots of homeless people sleeping in doorways and on top of heating vents, and there were interviews with people on the street, all of whom said something should be done about the terrible problem of the homeless. There was, in all of this, no real exploration of the issue and no proposed solutions. It was also apparent that the homeless were just the issue-for-the-week. After the week's coverage was over, the topic was not mentioned again.

Because of the emphasis on newscasters' personalities and on the   5
visual impact of stories and the short time span for stories, local news shows provide little more than diversion. What viewers need instead is news that has real significance. Rather than being amused and entertained, we need to deal with complex issues and learn uncomfortable truths that will help us become more responsible consumers and citizens.

■ Questions

About Unity

1. Which sentence in paragraph 4 of "Teenagers and Jobs" should be omitted in the interest of paragraph unity? _____

2. Which supporting paragraph in "A Vote against Computers" lacks a topic sentence? _____

   Write a topic sentence for the paragraph:

   _____

   _____

About Support

3. Which paragraph in "Teenagers and Jobs" develops its point by citing and then refuting an opposing point of view? _____

4. After which sentence in paragraph 4 of "Teenagers and Jobs" are specific details needed? _____

5. After which sentence in paragraph 2 of "Once Over Lightly: Local TV News" is support needed? _____

6. Which supporting paragraph of which essay uses the longest single supporting example?

   _____

About Coherence

7. What three transition words are used to introduce the three supporting paragraphs in "A Vote against Computers"?

   a. _____

   b. _____

   c. _____

8. What are the two main transition words in paragraph 2 of "Once Over Lightly: Local TV News"?

   a. _____

   b. _____

About the Introduction and Conclusion

9. Which method of introduction is used in "Teenagers and Jobs" ____? "A Vote against Computers" ____? "Once Over Lightly: Local TV News" ____?
   a. Broad, general statement narrowing to thesis
   b. Idea that is the opposite of the one to be developed
   c. Quotation
   d. Anecdote
   e. Questions

10. Which essay has a conclusion that briefly summarizes the supporting points? _____

Activity

In scratch-outline form on separate paper, provide brief supporting reasons for at least five of the fifteen statements below. Note the example. Make sure that you have three *separate* and *distinct* reasons for each statement.

Example   Recycling of newspapers, cans, and bottles should be mandatory.
        a. Towns sell recycled items rather than pay for dumping.
        b. Natural resources are protected.
        c. Respect for the environment is encouraged.

1. Couples should be required to live together for six months before marriage.
2. Many Canadians are too materialistic.
3. High schools should distribute birth control devices and information to students.
4. All teachers should be graded by their students.
5. TV commercials are often particularly insulting to women.
6. Professional boxing should be outlawed.
7. Attendance at college classes should be optional.
8. When technology makes it possible, government should control the weather.
9. People should begin planning for retirement when they are young.
10. Cigarette companies should not be allowed to advertise.
11. Television does more harm than good.
12. Killing animals for food is wrong.
13. School does not prepare you for life.
14. Governments should not pay ransom for terrorist kidnappings.
15. All companies should be required to have day-care centres.

WRITING THE ESSAY

■ Writing Assignment 1

Decide, perhaps through discussion with your instructor or class-mates, which of the outlines prepared in the preceding activity would be the most promising to develop into an essay. Make sure that your supporting reasons are logical ones that actually back up your thesis statement. Ask yourself in each case, "Does this reason truly support my thesis idea?"

How to Proceed

a On separate paper, make a list of details that might go under each of the supporting points. Provide more details than you can possibly use. Here, for example, are the details generated by the writer of "Teenagers and Jobs" when she was working on her first supporting paragraph:

School problems:

Less time for sports and other activities
Lower attendance at games
Students leave right after school
Students sleep in class and skip homework
Teachers are angry and frustrated
More time buying things like clothing and compact discs
More stress for students and less concentration
Some students try to do it all and get sick
Students miss school to go to work
Some drop out of school

b Decide which reasons and details you will use to develop each of your supporting paragraphs. Also, number the items in the order in which you will present them. Here is how the writer of "Teenagers and Jobs" made decisions on what to develop:

School problems
2 Less time for sports and other activities
~~Lower attendance at games~~
~~Students leave right after school~~
1 Students sleep in class and skip homework
~~Teachers are angry and frustrated~~
~~More time buying things like clothing and compact discs~~
~~More stress for students and less concentration~~
3 Some students try to do it all and get sick
~~Students miss school to go to work~~
~~Some drop out of school~~

c   As you are working on the drafts of your paper, refer to the checklist on page 123 and the inside front cover. Make sure that you can answer *Yes* to the questions about unity, support, and coherence.

d   You may also want to refer to pages 73–78 for suggestions on writing an effective introduction and conclusion to your essay.

e   Finally, use the checklist on page 123 and the inside front cover when you are proofreading the next-to-final draft of your paper for sentence-skills mistakes, including spelling.

■ Writing Assignment 2

Write a paper in which you argue *for* or *against* any *one* of the three comments below (options 1–3). Support and defend your argument by drawing upon your reasoning ability and general experience. Refer to "How to Proceed" on the following pages.

Option 1

In some ways, television has proved to be one of the worst inventions of recent times. All too often, television is harmful because of the shows it broadcasts and the way it is used in the home.

Option 2

College athletes devote a lot of time and energy to teams that sometimes make a great deal of money for their schools. Often athletes stress a sport at the expense of their education. And their efforts rarely give these young men and women experiences and skills that are useful after college. It is only fair, therefore, that college athletes be paid for their work.

Option 3

Many of society's worst problems with drugs result from the fact that they are illegal. During Prohibition, North America discovered that making popular substances unlawful causes more problems than it solves. Like alcohol, drugs should be legal in this country.

How to Proceed

a   Take several minutes to think about the comments. Which one in particular are you for or against—and *why*?

b On a sheet of paper, make up a brief outline of support for *your* position on one of the comments. Preparing the outline will give you a chance to think further about your position. And the outline will show whether you have enough support for your position. (If you don't, choose another position, and prepare another outline.)

This initial thinking and outlining that you do is the key to preparing a solid essay. Your goal should be to decide on a position for which you can provide the most convincing evidence.

The writer of the model essay on computers was originally asked to take a position for or against the use of computers in the classroom. After a good deal of thinking, he came up with the following brief outline:

```
I am against the use of computers.
1.  Don't help me plan an essay.
2.  Are complicated to use.
3.  Take up teacher's time.
```

While he had not yet written his first draft, he had already done the most important work on the paper.

c Next, decide how you will develop each of your three supporting points. Make up brief outlines of the three points. Here, for example, is what the author of the computer essay did:

```
1.  Don't help me plan an essay:
    Like to scribble.
    Use margins.
    Circle details on different parts of paper.
    See whole thing at once.

2.  Are complicated to use:
    Sign out software.
    Get machine started.
    Wait for help.
    Type slowly.

3.  Take up teacher's time:
    Helps students use computers.
    Has less time for writing feedback.
```

Such preliminary work is vital; to do a good paper, you must *think and plan and prewrite*. In addition to preparing brief outlines, you may also find that other prewriting techniques are useful. You may, variously, want to freewrite, brainstorm, and make up lists—all of which are described on pages 17–23 of this book.

d Decide in what order you want to present your paragraphs. Often, emphatic order (in which you end with the most important reason) is an effective way to organize an argument, for the final reason is the one your reader is most likely to remember.

e Provide as many convincing details as possible. For example, in the computer essay, the writer includes such supportive details as the following:

"If I write too much [on the computer], I have to scroll back and forth, since not everything can fit on the screen at once."

"I spend half of my time hunting and pecking for the proper letters on the keyboard."

"I sat here the other day watching the class trying to write on computers, and my impression was that 75 per cent of what the teacher did involved computers rather than writing."

f As you write, imagine that your audience is a jury that will ultimately believe or disbelieve your argument. Have you presented a convincing case? Do you need more details? If *you* were on the jury, would you be favourably impressed with this argument?

g As you are working on the drafts of your paper, keep the four bases of unity, support, coherence, and sentence skills in mind.

h Finally, proofread the next-to-final draft of your paper for sentence-skills mistakes, including spelling.

■ Writing Assignment 3

Write a paper in which you argue *for* or *against* any *one* of the three comments that follow. Support and defend your argument by drawing upon your reasoning ability and general experience.

Option 1

While it is now well known that smoking is very unhealthy, it would be very difficult in our society to make it illegal. But that does not mean smoking should be encouraged. On the contrary, cigarette advertising should be banned.

Option 2

By the time many students reach high school, they have learned the basics in most subjects. Some still have much to gain from the education that high schools offer, but others might be better off spending the next four years in other ways. For their benefit, high school attendance should be voluntary, not compulsory.

Option 3

It is sad but true that some of the most miserable days in many people's lives are their last days. It is also true there is no way to avoid dying. But establishing centres where people can choose to end their lives in peace can eliminate the long suffering that many fatal illnesses cause. The government should take an active role in creating such centres.

Remember that the best way to get started is *to think, plan, and prewrite*. Which comment do you feel most strongly for or against? What are three solid reasons you can give to support your position? After you work out a satisfactory scratch outline, go on to follow the rest of the steps described in Writing Assignment 2.

■ Writing Assignment 4

Write a paper in which you argue *for* or *against* any *one* of the three comments below. Support and defend your argument by drawing upon your reasoning ability and general experience.

Option 1

Giving students grades does more harm than good. Schools should replace grades with evaluations, which would benefit both students and parents.

Option 2

Because our jails are overcrowded and expensive, the fewer people sentenced to jail the better. Of course, it is necessary to put violent criminals in jail in order to protect others. Society, however, would benefit if non-violent criminals received punishments other than jail sentences.

Option 3

Physical punishment is often a successful way of disciplining children. After all, no child wants to experience pain. But adults who frequently spank and hit are also teaching the lesson that violence is a good method of accomplishing a goal. Non-violent methods are a more effective way of training children.

■ Writing Assignment 5

Write a paper in which you argue *for* or *against* any *one* of the three comments below. Support and defend your argument by drawing upon your reasoning ability and general experience.

Option 1

Junk food is available in school cafeterias and school vending machines, and the cafeteria menus do not encourage the best of eating habits. But good education should include good examples as well as class work. Schools should practise what they preach about a healthy diet and stop providing junk food.

Option 2

The sale of handguns to private citizens is justly banned in Canada. The Canadian Constitution does not guarantee any right to bear arms. All weapons, including handguns, are simply too dangerous to be legal.

Option 3

Many of today's young people are mainly concerned with prestigious careers, making money, and owning things. It seems we no longer teach the benefits of spending time and money to help the community, the country, and the world. Our country can strengthen these human values and improve the world by requiring young people to spend a year working in some type of community service.

■ Writing Assignment 6

In this essay, you will write with a specific purpose, for a specific audience.

Option 1: Your town is one of the few in the province that hasn't developed a recycling program. Write a speech to give at a city council meeting in which you argue for establishing a local recycling program. Include in your speech the environmental benefits of recycling. And, since we are more likely to persuade others of something if they feel they will benefit, note also how the town will benefit economically and otherwise.

Option 2: You'd like to live in a big city, but your spouse or parent refuses to budge from the suburbs. Write him or her a letter in which you argue the advantages of city life. Since the success of your argument will depend to some degree on how well you overcome the other person's objections to city life, be sure to address those as well. Use specific, colourful examples wherever possible.

Option 3: Write a letter to the editor of your local newspaper, responding to an issue that was discussed in a recent editorial in that paper. Agree or disagree with the position taken by the paper, and provide several short paragraphs of supporting evidence for your position. Actually send your letter to the newspaper. Turn in a copy to your instructor, with the editorial you responded to.

■ Writing Assignment 7

Write a paper in which you use research findings to help support one of the statements on page 222. Research the topic in one or both of these ways:

■ Look up the topic in the subject section of your library book file or computerized index. (You may want to review pages 257–260 of "Using the Library.") Subject headings for some of the statements on page 222 include *Birth control, Materialism, Day care, Marriage contracts, Animal rights, Advertising, Smoking, Retirement,* and *Terrorism.* Select the books that seem likely to give you information about your topic. Then find the books in the library stacks.

■ Look up the topic in recent issues of the *Canadian Periodical Index* or the *Readers' Guide to Periodical Literature.* (Again, you may want to review "Using the Library" first.) Try some of the same headings noted above. Select the articles that appear most likely to provide information on your topic. Then see if you can find some of these articles in your library's magazine or periodical storage area.

Reading about your topic will help you think about it. See if you can organize your paper in the form of three reasons that support the topic. Put these reasons into a scratch outline, and use it as a guide. Here is an example:

> Prayer should not be allowed in the public schools:
> a. Children who are not religious will feel excluded.
> b. Children may still pray silently whenever they please.
> c. Not all schools and teachers will keep prayer nondenominational.

Note that statistical information, the results of studies, and the advice of experts may all help develop the supporting reasons for your thesis. Do not hesitate to cite such information in a limited way; it helps make your argument more objective and compelling.

■ Writing Assignment 8: Writing about a Reading Selection

Read the selection titled "In Praise of the F Word" on pages 643–644. Notice how the author acknowledges the pressures students face in schools today, and accepts the responsibility instructors face if educational standards are raised. She then utilizes both personal and more objective details to persuade readers of the merit of failing underprepared students.

Write an essay in which you try to persuade readers that a particular academic policy, teaching method, area of professional training, or subject is either good or bad. Present your reasons, both personal and those acquired by research, clearly and in order of increasing importance. You may wish, for instance, to argue for or against one of the following:

Final examinations

Grading policies and graduation requirements

Evaluations instead of grades

"Interactive" teaching methods

Mandatory attendance

Choose a subject for which you can find three strong reasons pro or con. Each of your reasons or points will form a topic sentence for one supporting paragraph. Following, for example, is a brief outline for an essay persuading readers of the benefits of final examinations. Each of the three reasons is a topic sentence for one supporting paragraph.

Thesis: Final exams are a necessary part of students' education.
1. They motivate students to keep up with class work.
2. They allow students to demonstrate their understanding of a full semester's course material.
3. They give the student an objective view of their own achievements.

Develop your supporting paragraphs by explaining each topic sentence, using examples to illustrate your points.

PART THREE

SPECIAL
SKILLS

TAKING ESSAY EXAMS

Essay exams are perhaps the most common type of writing you will do in school. They include one or more questions to which you must respond in detail, writing your answers in a clear, well-organized manner. Many students have trouble with essay exams because they do not realize there is a sequence to follow that will help them do well on such tests. This section describes five basic steps needed to prepare adequately for an essay test and to take the test. It is assumed, however, that you are already doing two essential things: first, attending class regularly and taking notes on what happens in class; second, reading your textbook and other assignments and taking notes on them. If you are *not* consistently going to class, reading your text, and taking notes in both cases, you are likely to have trouble with essay exams and other tests as well.

To write an effective exam essay, follow these five steps:

Step 1: Anticipate ten probable questions.

Step 2: Prepare and memorize an informal outline answer for each question.

Step 3: Look at the exam carefully and do several things.

Step 4: Prepare a brief, informal outline before writing your essay answer.

Step 5: Write a clear, well-organized essay.

The following pages explain and illustrate these steps.

STEP 1: ANTICIPATE TEN PROBABLE QUESTIONS

Because exam time is limited, the instructor can give you only several questions to answer. He or she will reasonably focus on questions dealing with the most important areas of the subject. You can probably guess most of them.

Go through your class notes with a coloured pen and mark off those areas where your instructor has spent a good deal of time. The more time spent on any one area, the better the chance you will get an essay question on it. If the instructor spent a week talking about present-day changes in the traditional family structure, or the importance of the carbon molecule, or the advantages of capitalism, or key early figures in the development of psychology as a science, you can reasonably expect that you will get a question on the emphasized area.

In both your class notes and your textbooks, pay special attention to definitions and examples and to basic lists of items (enumerations). Enumerations in particular are often the key to essay questions. For instance, if your instructor spoke at length about the causes of the Great Depression, the effects of water pollution, or the advantages of capitalism, you should probably expect a question such as "What were the causes of the Great Depression?" or "What are the effects of water pollution?" or "What are the advantages of capitalism?"

If your instructor has given you study guides, look for probable essay questions there. (Some teachers choose essay questions from those listed in a study guide.) Look for clues to essay questions on any short quizzes that you may have been given. Finally, consider very carefully any review that the instructor provides. Always write down such reviews—your instructor has often made up the test or is making it up at the time of the review and is likely to give you valuable hints about it. Take advantage of them! Note also that if the instructor does not offer to provide a review, do not hesitate to *ask* for one in a friendly way. Essay questions are likely to come from areas the instructor may mention.

An Illustration of Step 1

A psychology class was given a day to prepare for an essay exam on stress—a subject that had been covered in class and that comprised a chapter in the textbook for the course. One student, Mark, read carefully through his class notes and the textbook chapter. On the basis of the headings, major enumerations, and definitions he noted, he decided that there were five likely essay questions:

1. What are the common sources of stress?
2. What are the types of conflict?
3. What are the defence mechanisms that people use to cope with stress?
4. What effects can stress have on people?
5. What are the characteristics of the well-adjusted person?

STEP 2: PREPARE AND MEMORIZE AN INFORMAL OUTLINE ANSWER FOR EACH QUESTION

Write out each question you have made up and, under it, list the main points that need to be discussed. Put important supporting information in parentheses after each main point. You now have an informal outline that you can memorize.

Note: If you have spelling problems, make up a list of words you might have to spell in writing your answers. For example, if you are having a psychology test on the principles of learning, you might want to study such terms as *conditioning*, *reinforcement*, *Pavlov*, *reflex*, *stimulus*, and so on.

An Illustration of Step 2

After identifying the likely questions on the exam, Mark made up an outline answer for each of the questions. For example, here is the outline answer that he made up for the first question:

Common sources of stress:
1. (Pressure) (internal and external)
2. (Anxiety) (sign of internal conflict)
3. (Frustration) (can't reach desired goal)
4. (Conflict) (three types of approach-avoidance)

   P A F C (People are funny creatures.)

Activity

See whether you can complete the following explanation of what Mark has done in preparing for the essay question.

First, Mark wrote down the heading and then numbered the sources of stress under it. Also, in parentheses beside each point he added _____

_____. Then he circled the four key words, and he wrote

down the first _____ of each word underneath his outline. Mark then used the first letter in each key word to make up a catch-phrase

that he could easily remember. Finally, he _____ himself over and over until he could recall all four of the sources of stress that the first letters stood for. He also made sure that he recalled the supporting material that went with each idea.

Direction Words Found in Essay Examination Questions

Term	*Meaning*
Compare	Show similarities between things.
Contrast	Show differences between things.
Criticize	Give the positive and negative points of a subject as well as evidence for these positions.
Define	Give the formal meaning of a term.
Describe	Tell in detail about something; give detailed explanation.
Diagram	Make a drawing and label it.
Discuss	Give details and, if relevant, the positive and negative points of a subject as well as evidence for these positions.
Enumerate	List points and number them 1, 2, 3, etc.
Evaluate	Give the positive and negative points of a subject as well as your judgement about which outweighs the other and why.
Illustrate	Explain by giving examples.
Interpret	Explain the meaning of something.
Justify	Give reasons for something.
List	Give a series of points and number them 1, 2, 3, etc.
Outline	Give the main points and important secondary points. Put main points at the margin and indent secondary points under the main points. Relationships may also be described with logical symbols, as follows:

1. _____

    a. _____

    b. _____

2. _____

Prove	Show to be true by giving facts or reasons.
Relate	Show connections among things.
State	Give the main points.
Summarize	Give a condensed account of the main points.
Trace	Describe the development or history of a subject.

STEP 3: LOOK AT THE EXAM CAREFULLY AND DO SEVERAL THINGS

1 Get an overview of the exam by reading *all* the questions on the test.

2 Note the direction words (*compare*, *illustrate*, *list*, and so on) for each question. Be sure to write the kind of answer that each question requires. For example, if a question says "illustrate," do not "compare." The list on the opposite page will help clarify the distinctions among various direction words.

3 Budget your time. Write in the margin the number of minutes you should spend for each essay. For example, if you have three essays worth an equal number of marks and a one-hour time limit, figure twenty minutes for each one. Make sure you are not left with only a couple of minutes to do a high mark-value essay.

4 Start with the easiest question. Getting a good answer down on paper will help build up your confidence and momentum. Number your answers plainly so your instructor knows what question you are answering first.

An Illustration of Step 3

When Mark received the exam, the question was, "Describe the four common sources of stress in our lives." Mark circled the direction word *describe*, which meant that he should explain in detail each of the four causes of stress. He also jotted a "30" in the margin when the teacher said that students would have a half hour to write their answer.

Activity

Complete the short matching quiz below. It will help you review the meanings of some of the direction words listed on the opposite page.

1. List _____   a. Tell in detail about something.

2. Contrast _____   b. Give a series of points and number them 1, 2, 3, etc.

3. Define _____   c. Give a condensed account of the main points.

4. Summarize _____   d. Show differences between two things.

5. Describe _____   e. Give the normal meaning of a term.

STEP 4: PREPARE A BRIEF, INFORMAL OUTLINE BEFORE WRITING YOUR ESSAY ANSWER

Use the margin of the exam or a separate piece of scratch paper to jot down quickly, as they occur to you, the main points you want to discuss in each answer.

Then decide in what order you want to present these points in your response. Put *1* in front of the first item, *2* beside the second, and so on. You now have an informal outline to guide you as you answer your essay question.

If there is a question on the exam which is similar to the questions you anticipated and outlined at home, quickly write down the catch-phrase that calls back the content of the outline. Below the catch-phrase, write the key words represented by each letter in the catch-phrase. The key words, in turn, will remind you of the concepts they represent. If you have prepared properly, this step will take only a minute or so, and you will have before you the guide you need to write a focused, supported, organized answer.

An Illustration of Step 4

Mark immediately wrote down his catch-phrase, "People are funny creatures." He next jotted down the first letters in his catch-phrase and then the key words that went with each letter. He then filled in several key details and was ready to write his essay answer. Here is what his brief outline looked like:

People are funny creatures.

P   Pressure (internal and external)
A   Anxiety (internal conflict)
F   Frustration (prevented from reaching goal)
C   Conflict (approach-avoidance)

STEP 5: WRITE A CLEAR, WELL-ORGANIZED ESSAY

If you have followed the steps to this point, you have done all the preliminary work needed to write an effective essay. Be sure not to wreck your chances of getting a good mark by writing carelessly. Keep in mind the principles of good writing: unity, support, organization, and clear, error-free sentences.

First, start your essay with a sentence that clearly states what your answer will be about. Then make sure that everything in your paper relates to your opening statement.

Second, though you must obviously take time limitations into account, provide as much support as possible for each of your main points.

Third, use transitions to guide your reader through your answer. Words such as *first, next, then, however,* and *finally* make it easy to follow your thought.

Last, leave time to proofread your essay for sentence-skills mistakes you may have made while you concentrated on writing your answer. Look for words omitted, written incorrectly, or misspelled (if it is possible, bring a dictionary with you); for awkward phrasings or misplaced punctuation marks; and for whatever else may prevent the reader from understanding your thought. Cross out any mistakes and make your corrections neatly above the errors. If you want to change or add to some point, insert an asterisk at the appropriate spot, put another asterisk at the bottom of the page, and add the corrected or additional material there.

An Illustration of Step 5

Read Mark's answer, reproduced below, and then do the activity that follows.

There are four common sources of stress in our lives. The first one is pressure, which can be internal or external. Internal pressure occurs when a person tries to live up to his or her own goals and standards. This kind of pressure can help (when a person strives to be a better musician, for instance) or hurt (as when someone tries to reach impossible standards of beauty). External pressure occurs when people must compete, deal with rapid change or cope with outside demands. Another source of stress is anxiety. People who are ~~anxous~~ anxious often don't know why they feel this way. Some psychologists think anxiety comes from some internal conflict, like feeling angry and trying hard to repress this ~~angry feeling~~ anger. A third source of stress is frustration, which occurs when people are prevented from reaching goals or obtaining certain needs. For example, a woman may do poorly on an exam because she has a bad cold. She feels angry and frustrated because she could not reach her goat of an A or B grade. The most common source of stress is conflict. Conflict results when a person is faced with two incompatible ~~goals.~~ desires. The person may want both goals (a demanding career and motherhood, for instance). This is called approach/approach. Or a person may want to avoid both choices (avoidance/avoidance.) Or a person may be both attracted to and repelled by a desire (as a woman who wants to marry a gambler). This is approach/avoidance.

Activity 1

The following sentences comment on Mark's essay. Fill in the missing word or words in each case.

1. Mark begins with a sentence that clearly states what his paper _____ _____. Always begin with such a clear statement!

2. Notice the _____ that Mark made when writing and proof-reading his paper. He neatly crossed out incorrectly written or unwanted words, and he used insertion signs ($\wedge$) to add omitted words.

3. The four signal words that Mark used to guide his readers, and himself, through the main points of his answer are _____, _____, _____, and _____.

Activity 2

1. Make up five questions you might be expected to answer on an essay exam in a social or physical science course (sociology, psychology, biology, or other).

2. Then make up for each of the five questions an outline answer comparable to the one on anxiety.

3. Finally, write a full essay answer, in complete sentences, to one of the questions. Your outline will serve as your guide.

Be sure to begin your essay with a statement that makes clear the direction of your answer. An example might be, "The six major kinds of defence mechanisms are defined and illustrated below." If you are explaining in detail the different causes of, reasons for, or characteristics of something, you may want to develop each point in a separate paragraph. For example, if you were answering a question in sociology about the primary functions of the family unit, you could, after starting with a statement that "There are three primary functions of the family unit," go on to develop and describe each function in a separate paragraph.

You will turn in the essay answer to your English instructor, who will evaluate it using the standards for effective writing applied to your other written assignments.

PREPARING
A SUMMARY

At some point in a course, your instructor may ask you to write a summary of a book, essay, article, TV show, or the like. In a *summary* (also referred to as a *précis* or an *abstract*), you reduce material in an original work to its main points and key supporting details. Unlike an outline, however, a summary does not use symbols such as *I, A, 1, 2,* etc., to indicate the relations among parts of the original material.

A summary may be a word, a phrase, several sentences, or one or more paragraphs in length. The length of the summary you prepare will depend on your instructor's expectations and the length of the original work. Most often, you will be asked to write a summary of one or more paragraphs.

Writing a summary brings together a number of important reading, study, and writing skills. To condense the original matter, you must preview, read, evaluate, organize, and perhaps outline the assigned material. Summarizing, then, can be a real aid to understanding; you must "get inside" the material and realize fully what is being said before you can reduce its meaning to a few words.

HOW TO SUMMARIZE AN ARTICLE

To write a summary of an article, follow the steps described below. If the assigned material is a TV show or film, adapt the suggestions accordingly.

1   Take a few minutes to preview the work. You can preview an article in a magazine by taking a quick look at the following:

  a   *Title.*   The title often summarizes what the article is about. Think about the title for a minute and how it may condense the meaning of an article.

  b   *Subtitle.*   A subtitle, if given, is a short summary appearing under or next to the title. For example, in *Maclean's* an article could have the title "Aging, Bouncing Boomers," with the following caption: "Canadians of the post-war Baby Boom generation should be feeling their age, but they aren't. Why should they? They are the healthiest, wealthiest, and largest segment of our population." In short, the subtitle, the caption, or any other words in large print under or next to the title often provide a quick insight into the meaning of an article.

  c   *First and last several paragraphs.*   In the first several paragraphs, the author may introduce you to the subject and state the purpose of the article. In the last several paragraphs, the writer may present conclusions or a summary. These previews or summaries can give you a quick overview of what the entire article is about.

  d   *Other items.*   Note any headings or subheadings that appear in the article. They often provide clues to the article's main points and give an immediate sense of what each section is about. Look carefully at any pictures, charts, or diagrams that accompany the article. Page space in a magazine or journal is limited, and such visual aids are generally used only when they help illustrate important points in the article. Note any words or phrases set off in *italic type* or **boldface print**; such words have probably been emphasized because they deal with important points in the article.

2   Read the article for all you can understand the first time through. Do not slow down or turn back. Check or otherwise mark main points and key supporting details. Pay special attention to all the items noted in the preview. Also, look for definitions, examples, and enumerations (lists of items), as these often indicate key ideas. You can also identify important points by turning any headings into questions and reading to find the answers to the questions.

3   Go back and reread more carefully the areas you have identified as most important. Also, focus on other key points you may have missed in your first reading.

4 Take notes on the material. Concentrate on getting down the main ideas and the key supporting points.

5 Prepare the first draft of your summary, keeping these points in mind:

a Identify at the start of the summary the title and author of the work. Include in parentheses the date of publication. For example, "In 'Kids "Я" Hell' (*Saturday Night*, December 1994), Charles Foran states . . ."

b Do not write an overly detailed summary. Remember that the purpose of a summary is to reduce the original work to its main points and essential supporting details.

c Express the main points and key supporting details in your own words. Do not imitate the style of the original work.

d Quote from the material only to illustrate key points. Also, limit your quotations. A one-paragraph summary should not contain more than one or two quoted sentences.

e Preserve the balance and proportion of the original work. If the original devoted 70 per cent of its space to one idea and only 30 per cent to another, your summary should reflect that emphasis.

f Revise the first draft, paying attention to the principles of effective writing (*unity*, *support*, *coherence*, and *clear, error-free sentences*) explained in Part One.

g Write the final draft of the paper.

A MODEL SUMMARY

Here is a model summary of a magazine article.

In "Just Assassins" (<u>Saturday Night</u>, December 1994), Kenneth Whyte examines Quebec's and Canada's resurgent interest in the Front de Libération Québécois. October 1995 will mark the twenty-fifth anniversary of the kidnapping and grisly murder of Quebec labour and immigration minister Pierre Laporte. Russian terrorists in art and reality may have been able to rationalize their actions as principled resistance to tyranny, but current media views of the FLQ may not show either high-mindedness or any particular tyranny in 1970s Quebec. Pierre Falardeau's feature film <u>Octobre</u> is a bleak, if realistic, portrait of the period and the main players. The terrorists are shown at close range in mundane activities, only occasionally discussing the ironic morality of freedom fighters chaining a politician to a bed. Mainly, FLQ members appear in an unflattering light, as "inarticulate, confused, overwrought, and amateurish." Directorial pursuit of realism has not endeared Falardeau to some Quebec journalists who choke on seeing Felquistes as "third-rate bums shaking as they ate fried chicken." Either Che Guevara or Camus' Kaliayev would have been preferable role models--as political assassins, they lived without access to either Canadian political liberties or material wealth. Murder is the ugliest aspect of terrorism, and, perversely, a crime which may go unpunished in terrorist intrigues. Falardeau's desire for realism would not permit him to chance an audience's revulsion at witnessing Laporte's assassination, nor would the FLQ members he depicts debate the morality or the consequences of their act. The anniversary of Laporte's death is an occasion for the examination of a repulsive crime, not a <u>souvenir</u> of a noble response to repression.

Activity 1

Write an essay-length summary of the following article. Include a short introductory paragraph that states the thesis of the article. Then summarize in your three supporting paragraphs the three important areas in which study skills can be useful. Your conclusion might be a single sentence restating the thesis.

POWER LEARNING

Jill had not done as well in high school as she had hoped. Since college involved even more work, it was no surprise that she didn't do better there. 1

The reason for her so-so performance was not a lack of effort. She attended most of her classes and read her textbooks. And she never missed handing in any assignment, even though it often meant staying up late the night before homework was due. Still, she just got by in her classes. Before long, she came to the conclusion she simply couldn't do any better. 2

Then one day, one of her teachers said something to make her think otherwise. "You can probably build some sort of house by banging a few boards together," he said. "But if you want a sturdy home, you'll have to use the right techniques and tools. Building carefully takes work, but it gets better results. The same can be said of your education. There are no shortcuts, but there are some proven study skills that can really help. If you don't use them, you may end up with a pretty flimsy education." 3

Jill signed up for a study skills course and found out a crucial fact—that learning how to learn is the key to success in school. There are certain dependable skills that have made the difference between disappointment and success for generations of students. These techniques won't free you from work, but they will make your work far more productive. They include three important areas: time control, classroom note-taking, and textbook study. 4

TIME CONTROL

Success in college depends on time control. Time control means that you deliberately organize and plan your time, instead of letting it drift by. Planning means that you should never be faced with a night-before-the-test "cram" session or an overdue term paper. 5

There are three steps involved in time control. *First*, you should prepare a large 6 monthly calendar. Buy a calendar with a large white block around each date, or make one yourself. At the beginning of the college semester, circle important dates on this calendar. Circle the days on which tests are scheduled; circle the days papers are due. This calendar can also be used to schedule study plans. You can jot down your plans for each day at the beginning of the week. An alternative method would be to make plans for each day the night before. On Tuesday night, for example, you might write down "Read Chapter 5 in psychology" in the Wednesday block. Hang this calendar where you will see it every day—your kitchen, your bedroom, even your bathroom!

The *second step* in time control is to have a weekly study schedule for the 7 semester—a chart that covers all the days of the week and all the waking hours in each day.

Time	Mon.	Tues.	Wed.	Thurs.	Fri.	Sat.	Sun.
6:00 a.m.							
7:00	B	B	B	B	B		
8:00	Math	STUDY	Math	STUDY	Math		
9:00	STUDY	Biology	STUDY	Biology	STUDY	Job	
10:00	Psychology		Psychology	↓	Psychology		
11:00	STUDY	English		English			
12:00	L		L	↓	L	↓	

Above is part of one student's schedule. On your own schedule, mark in all the fixed hours in each day—hours for meals, classes, job (if any), and travel time. Next, mark in time blocks that you can *realistically* use for study each day. Depending on the number of courses you are taking and the demands of the courses, you may want to block off five, ten, or even twenty or more hours of study time a week. Keep in mind that you should not block off time for study that you do not truly intend to use for study. Otherwise, your schedule will be a meaningless gimmick. Also, remember that you should allow time for "rest and relaxation." You will be happiest, and able to accomplish the most, when you have time for both work and play.

The *third step* in time control is to make a daily or weekly "to do" list. This may 8 be the most valuable time control method you ever use. On this list, you write down the things you need to do for the following day or the following week. If you choose to write a weekly list, do it on Sunday night. If you choose to write a daily list, do it the night before. Here is part of one student's daily list:

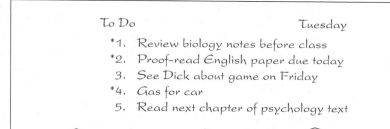

You may use a three- by five-inch notepad or a small spiral-bound notebook for this list. Carry the list around with you during the day. Always concentrate on doing first the most important items on your list. Mark high-priority items with an asterisk and give them precedence over low-priority items in order to make the best use of your time. For instance, you may find yourself wondering what to do after dinner on Thursday evening. Among the items on your list are "Clean inside of car" and "Review chapter for math quiz." It is obviously more important for you to review your notes at this point; you can clean the car some other time. As you complete items on your "to do" list, cross them out. Do not worry about unfinished items. They can be rescheduled. You will still be accomplishing a great deal and making more effective use of your time.

CLASSROOM NOTE-TAKING

One of the most important single things you can do to perform well in a college course is to take effective class notes. The following hints should help you become a better note-taker.

First, attend class faithfully. Your alternatives—reading the text or someone else's notes, or both—cannot substitute for the experience of hearing ideas in person as someone presents them to you. Also, in class lectures and discussions, your instructor typically presents and develops the main ideas and facts of the course— the ones you will be expected to know on exams.

Another valuable hint is to make use of abbreviations while taking notes. Using abbreviations saves time when you are trying to get down a great deal of information. Abbreviate terms that recur frequently in a lecture and put a key to your abbreviations at the top of your notes. For example, in sociology class, *eth* could stand for *ethnocentrism*; in a psychology class, *s-t mem* could stand for *short-term memory*. (When a lecture is over, you may want to go back and write out the terms you have abbreviated.) In addition, abbreviate words that often recur in any lecture. For instance, use *e* for example; *def* for *definition*; *info* for *information*; + for *and*, and so on. If you use the same abbreviations all the time, you will soon develop a kind of personal shorthand that makes taking notes much easier.

A third hint when taking notes is to be on the look-out for signals of importance. Write down whatever your teacher puts on the board. If he or she takes the time to put material on the board, it is probably important, and the chances are good that it will come up later on exams. Always write down definitions and enumerations. Enumerations are lists of items. They are signalled in such ways as: "The four steps in the process are ..."; "There were three reasons for ..."; "The two effects were ..."; "Five characteristics of ..."; and so on. Always number (*1, 2, 3*, etc.) such enumerations in your notes. They will help you understand relationships among ideas and organize the material of the lecture. Watch for emphasis words—words your instructor may use to indicate that something is important. Examples of such words are "This is an important reason ..."; "A point that will keep coming up later ..."; "The chief cause was ..."; "The basic idea here is ..."; and so on. Always write down the important statements announced by these and other emphasis words. Finally, if your instructor repeats a point, you can assume it is important. You might put an *R* for *repeated* in the margin, so that later you will know that your teacher has stressed it.

Next, be sure to write down the teacher's examples and mark them with an *X*. The examples help you understand abstract points. If you do not write them down, you are likely to forget them later when they are needed to help make sense of an idea. 13

Also, be sure to write down the connections between ideas. Too many students merely copy the terms the teacher puts on the board. They forget that, as time passes, the details that serve as connecting bridges between ideas quickly fade. You should, then, write down the relationships and connections in class. That way you'll have them to help tie together your notes later on. 14

Review your notes as soon as possible after class. You must make them as clear as possible while they are fresh in your mind. A day later may be too late, because forgetting sets in very quickly. Make sure that punctuation is clear, that all words are readable and correctly spelled, and that unfinished sentences are completed (or at least marked off so that you can check your notes with another student's). Add clarifying or connecting comments wherever necessary. Make sure important ideas are clearly marked. Improve the organization if necessary, so that you can see at a glance main points and relationships among them. 15

Finally, try in general to get down a written record of each class. You must do this because forgetting begins almost immediately. Studies have shown that within two weeks you are likely to have forgotten 80 per cent or more of what you have heard. And in four weeks you are lucky if 5 per cent remains! The significance of this is so crucial that it bears repeating: to guard against the relentlessness of forgetting, it is absolutely essential that you write down what you hear in class. Later on you can concentrate on working to understand fully and to remember the ideas that have been presented in class. And the more complete your notes are at this time of study, the more you are likely to learn. 16

TEXTBOOK STUDY

In many college courses, success means being able to read and study a textbook skil- fully. For many students, unfortunately, textbooks are heavy going. After an hour or two of study, the textbook material is as formless and as hard to understand as ever. But there is a way to attack even the most difficult textbook and make sense of it. Use a sequence in which you preview a chapter, mark it, take notes on it, and then study the notes. 17

Previewing

Previewing a selection is an important first step to understanding. Taking the time 18
to preview a section or chapter can give you a bird's-eye view of the way the material
is organized. You will have a sense of where you are beginning, what you will cover,
and where you will end.

There are several steps in previewing a selection. First, study the title. The title 19
is the shortest possible summary of a selection and will often tell you the limits of
the material you will cover. For example, the title "Marketing Trends in Consumer
Goods" tells you to expect a discussion of marketing developments for such items as
food and clothing. You know that you will probably not encounter any material
dealing with changes to the marketing of lumber products or heavy machinery. Next,
read over quickly the first and last paragraphs of the selection; these may contain
important introductions to, and summaries of, the main ideas. Then examine briefly
the headings and subheadings in the selection. Together, the headings and subheadings
are a mini-outline of what you are reading. Headings are often main ideas or
important concepts in capsule form; subheadings are breakdowns of ideas within main
areas. Finally, read the first sentence of some paragraphs, look for words set off in
boldface or *italics*, and look at pictures or diagrams. After you have previewed a
selection in this way, you should have a good general sense of the material to be read.

Marking

You should mark a textbook selection at the same time that you read it through 20
carefully. Use a felt-tip highlighter to shade material that seems important, or use a
ballpoint pen and put symbols in the margin next to the material: stars, checks, or
NB (*nota bene*, Latin for "note well"). What to mark is not as mysterious as some
students believe. You should try to find main ideas by looking for clues: definitions
and examples, enumerations, and emphasis words.

1 *Definitions and examples:* Definitions are often among the most important ideas 21
in a selection. They are particularly significant in introductory courses in almost
any subject area, where much of your learning involves mastering the specialized
vocabulary of that subject. In a sense, you are learning the "language" of
psychology or business or whatever the subject might be.

Most definitions are abstract, and so they usually are followed by one or 22
more examples to help clarify their meaning. Always mark off definitions and at
least one example that makes a definition clear to you. In a psychology text, for
example, we are told that "rationalization is an attempt to reduce anxiety by
deciding that you have not really been frustrated." Several examples follow,
among them: "A young man, frustrated because he was rejected when he asked
for a date, convinces himself that the girl is not very attractive or interesting."

2 *Enumerations:* Enumerations are lists of items (causes, reasons, types, and so on) 23
that are numbered *1, 2, 3, . . .* or that could easily be numbered in an outline. They
are often signalled by addition words. Many of the paragraphs in this book use
words like *First of all, Another, In addition,* and *Finally* to signal items in a series.
Textbooks use this very common and effective organizational method as well.

3 *Emphasis words:* Emphasis words tell you that an idea is important. Common 24
emphasis words include phrases such as *a major event, a key feature, the chief
factor, important to note, above all,* and *most of all.* Here is an example: "The
most significant contemporary use of marketing is its application to nonbusiness
areas, such as political parties."

Note-Taking

Next, you should take notes. Go through the chapter a second time, rereading the 25
most important parts. Try to write down the main ideas in a simple outline form. For
example, in taking notes on a psychology selection, you might write down the
heading "Kinds of Defence Mechanisms." Below the heading you would number and
describe each kind and give an example of each.

Defence Mechanisms
 a. Definition: unconscious attempts to reduce anxiety
 b. Kinds:
   (1) Rationalization: An attempt to reduce anxiety by deciding that you
       have not really been frustrated
       Example: A man turned down for a date decides that the woman
       was not worth going out with anyway
   (2) Projection: Projecting onto other people motives or thoughts of one's own
       Example: A wife who wants to have an affair accuses her husband
       of having one

Studying Notes

To study your notes, use the method of repeated self-testing. For example, look at 26
the heading "Kinds of Defence Mechanisms" and say to yourself, "What are the
kinds of defence mechanisms?" When you can recite them, then say to yourself,
"What is rationalization?" "What is an example of rationalization?" Then ask
yourself, "What is projection?" "What is an example of projection?" After you learn
each section, review it, and then go on to the next section.

Do not simply read your notes; keep looking away and seeing if you can recite 27
them to yourself. This self-testing is the key to effective learning.

Summary: Textbook Study

In summary, remember this sequence in order to deal with a textbook: previewing, 28
marking, taking notes, studying the notes. Approaching a textbook in this methodical
way will give you very positive results. You will no longer feel bogged down in a
swamp of words, unable to figure out what you are supposed to know. Instead, you
will understand exactly what you have to do, and how to go about doing it.

Take a minute now to evaluate your own study habits. Do you practise many of the 29
above skills in order to take effective classroom notes, control your time, and learn
from your textbooks? If not, perhaps you should. The skills are not magic, but they
are too valuable to ignore. Use them carefully and consistently, and they will make
academic success possible for you. Try them, and you won't need convincing.

Activity 2

Write an essay-length summary of editorial sections of the CBC television newshour *Prime Time News* or a similar show, like *W5*. In your first sentence, include the date of the show. For example, "The July 29, 1995, broadcast of CBC's *Prime Time News* dealt with three subjects most people would find of interest. The first segment of the show centred on …; the second segment examined …; the final segment discussed. …" Be sure to use parallel form in describing the three segments of the show. Then summarize each segment in the three supporting paragraphs that follow.

Activity 3

Write an essay-length summary of a cover story of interest to you in a recent issue of *Maclean's*, *The Financial Post*, *Canadian Business*, or a magazine relevant to your area of study.

HOW TO SUMMARIZE A BOOK

To write a summary of a book, first preview the book by briefly looking at:

1 *Title.* The title is often the shortest possible summary of what a book is about. Think about the title and how it may summarize the whole book.
2 *Table of contents.* The contents will tell you the number of chapters in the book and the subject of each chapter. Use the contents to get a general sense of how the book is organized. You should also note the number of pages in each chapter. If thirty pages are devoted to one episode or idea and an average of fifteen pages to other episodes or ideas, you should probably give more space to the contents of the longer chapter in your summary.
3 *Preface.* Here you will probably find out why the author wrote the book. Also, the preface may summarize the main ideas developed in the book and may describe briefly how the book is organized.
4 *First and last chapters.* In these chapters, the author may preview or review important ideas and themes developed in the book.
5 *Other items.* Note the way the author has used headings and subheadings to organize information in the book. Check the opening and closing paragraphs of each chapter to see if they contain introductions or summaries. Look quickly at charts, diagrams, and pictures in the book, since they are probably there to illustrate key points. Note any special features (index, glossary, appendixes) that may appear at the end of the book.

Next, adapt steps 2 through 5 for summarizing an article on pages 242–243.

Activity

Write an essay-length summary of a book you have read.

DOING A REPORT OR REVIEW

Each semester, you will probably be asked by at least one instructor to read a book or an article and to write a paper recording your response to the material. In these reports or reviews, your instructor will most likely expect you to do two things: *summarize the material* and *detail your reaction to it*. This type of report may be called a "book report," a "review," or an "analytic" report. An assignment of this kind will prepare you for writing business or technical reports later in your academic and professional careers. The following pages explain both parts of a report.

PART 1 OF A REPORT: A SUMMARY OF THE WORK

To develop the first part of a report or review, do the following:

1 Identify the author and title of the work and include in parentheses the publisher and publication date. An example follows on page 253. With magazines, give the date of publication.

2 Write an informative summary of the material. Condense the content of the work by highlighting its main points and key supporting points. (See pages 241–243 for a complete discussion of summarizing techniques.) Use direct quotations from the work to illustrate important ideas.

Do not discuss in great detail any single aspect of the work and neglect to mention other equally important points. Summarize the material so that the reader gets a general sense of *all* key aspects of the original work. Also, keep the summary objective and factual. Do not include in the first part of the paper your personal reaction to the work; your subjective responses will form the basis of the second part of the paper.

PART 2 OF A REPORT: YOUR RESPONSE TO THE WORK

To develop the second part of a report, do the following:

1 *Analysis.* Focus on any or all of the questions that follow. (Check with your instructors to see if they want you to emphasize specific points.)

   a How is the assigned work related to ideas and concerns discussed in the course? For example, what points made in the course textbook, class discussions, or lectures are treated more fully in the work?

   b How is the work related to problems in our present-day world?

   c How is the work related to your life, experiences, feelings, and ideas? For instance, what emotions did it arouse in you? Did it increase your understanding of an issue or change your perspective?

2 *Evaluation.* Evaluate the merit of the work: the importance of its points; its accuracy, completeness, and organization; and so on. You should also indicate here whether you would recommend the work to others, and why.

POINTS TO KEEP IN MIND WHEN WRITING A REPORT

Here are some important matters to consider as you prepare the report.

1 Apply the four basic standards of effective writing (unity, support, coherence, and clear, error-free sentences) when writing the report.

   a Make sure each major paragraph presents and then develops a single main point. For example, in the model report that follows, a paragraph summarizes the book, and the three paragraphs that follow detail three separate reactions that the student writer had to the book. The student then closes the report with a short concluding paragraph.

   b Support any general points or attitudes you express with specific reasons and details drawn from the work you are reporting on. Statements such as "I agreed with many ideas in this article" or "I found the book very interesting" are meaningless without specific evidence that shows why you feel as you do. Look at the model report to see how the main point or topic sentence of each paragraph is developed by specific supporting evidence.

   c Organize the material in the paper. Follow the basic *plan of organization* already described: an introduction, a summary of one or more paragraphs, a response of two or more paragraphs, and a conclusion. Use *transitions* to connect the parts of the paper.

   d Proofread the paper for grammar, mechanics, punctuation, and word use.

2 Document quotations from all works by placing the page number in parentheses after the quoted material (see the model report). You may use quotations in the summary and reaction parts of the paper, but do not over-rely on them. Use them only to emphasize key ideas.

A MODEL REPORT

Here is a book report written by a student in a first-year media studies course. Look at the essay closely to see how it follows the format requirements and guidelines for report or review writing described in this chapter.

Vampires of Page, Stage, and Screen: A Report on Hollywood Gothic

Introductory → Hollywood Gothic: The Tangled Web of Dracula from Novel to Stage to
paragraph Screen (New York: W.W. Norton & Co. Ltd, 1990) is David J. Skal's lively account of a figure fascinating to people everywhere: Dracula. Skal, a horror/sci-fi novelist, critic, and analyst of popular media, has also written a history of North American horror, The Monster Show (1992). Calling himself "a connoisseur of popular obsessions," the writer is an impressive authority on media psychology, copyright law, and the film industry. Hollywood Gothic shows insight and careful research into the lives of real and fictional characters. Readers meet arrogant stage directors, sinister poets, and bizarre movie-makers. Dracula creeps from surprising origins into novelist Bram Stoker's life and imagination, then into the law courts, movies, licensed goods and mass-media exploitation, pausing today for Gary Oldman, Tom Cruise, and Martin Landau as faces of the character who is "the lifeblood of dreams that never end" (199).

PART I: → Dracula lived many lives in the seventy years before he was named; he
SUMMARY emerged not from a coffin in Transylvania but from a typed and much-
Topic revised manuscript first titled The Undead. Irish journalist and theatrical
sentence for promoter Bram Stoker had unknowingly created his best work, and his only
summary "best-seller." Although Stoker was 19th-century superstar actor Henry
paragraph Irving's agent, his own limited theatrical talent resulted in a dramatic reading of Dracula so awful that Irving, along with most of the audience, left early. Surprisingly, Dracula's early life as a media figure originated not with the historic Prince Vlad the Impaler but with the English Romantic poet Lord Byron. Byron was powerful, arrogant, and charismatic: an outcast, a cynic, and an object of obsessive daily newspaper coverage in most of England and Europe. Dressed always in black, and downright perverse in some of his behaviour, Byron was the subject of an 1817 novel, The Vampyr, published the same year as Mary Shelley's Frankenstein. Both novels spawned endless sequels in print and on stage. By the 1890s Bram Stoker had seen stage-plays of The Vampyr and read popular penny-serials

and novels based on the vampire-figure. Stoker, a fundamentally ordinary man trying to make a living, transformed Byron into the five-century-old Transylvanian noble later reincarnated by Bela Lugosi. For Dracula, the media, not the blood, "was the life." Copyright and distribution rights became an international issue for the first time, and a survival issue for Stoker's widow, as her husband's novel spread to London and New York theatres and Berlin and Hollywood film studios. By day at Universal Studios in 1930, Bela Lugosi played director Tod Browning's Count, and by night a superior Spanish-language version with a no-name star was filmed on the same lot. Dracula, a household name and media commodity by mid-century, has been remade countless times as a film, revived as a play, and even performed as a ballet by Les Grands Ballets Canadiens. The vampire arises tuxedoed, neatly repackaged for any media or advertising function. Today Anne Rice, Stephen King, and even Count Numbers on Sesame Street are in debt to Byron, Bram and Florence Stoker, Tod Browning, and Bela Lugosi for keeping alive the scandal and the mystery of the vampire.

PART II: ⎯⎯⎯→ David J. Skal does not write like a "textbook" writer; instead, he is
RESPONSE witty, clear, and interesting. His humour and distinctive style make
Topic Hollywood Gothic fun, fascinating, and informative: Dracula has "patent
sentence for leather shoes and patent leather hair" (4); he is "a black hole of the
the first imagination" (7). Skal challenges our minds with interesting connections
paragraph of that stimulate me to relate today's interest in vampires to our daily media
response and environment. Mass hysteria, whether it is produced by a scandalous poet or
analysis a life-threatening disease, often seems to focus on sex and death, and our
fears connected to them. As Skal writes, "When the definitive history of the AIDS epidemic is finally written, the irrational, vampire-related undercurrents of scapegoating, blood superstition, and plague panic will no doubt be prominent considerations" (12). Next, Skal confronts the stereotype of Dracula as the "ultimate ladies' man" with a shocking possibility: could Dracula be gay? Was I as rigid in my views as Victorians, for whom "the true horror of Dracula is his polymorphous perversity"? Dracula's activities are documented as those of a "Bloodletter … who rivals his three wives in gender-bending" (34). Suddenly Anne Rice's Lestat and Nancy Kilpatrick's new Canadian vampires didn't seem so strange. I enjoy having my preconceptions challenged, as I enjoyed Skal's knowledge of minutiae like the genesis of Dracula's uniform: cash-strapped English theatrical companies always had tuxedoes and evening capes on hand, hence the vampire suit. The cape's trademark bat-like stand-up collar also arose from necessity: "Originally, the collar had a distinct theatrical function; to hide the actor's head when he stood with his back to the house, thus allowing him to slip out of the cape and down a trapdoor, effectively 'disappearing' before the audience's eyes" (73). My favourite fact concerned Dracula's accent. Once thrilling, now laughable, Bela Lugosi's accent created a myth as it crippled the actor's career. In the chapter "A Deal For the

Devil, or, Hollywood Bites," Skal reveals that Lugosi "learned English roles phonetically" (81) rather than perfect his English, and never lost the "Good Eev-en-ink" pronunciation every Dracula imitator has since used.

Topic sentence for second response paragraph —————→ I enjoy reading about personalities, and Hollywood Gothic kept me riveted with details of the lives of Bram and Florence Stoker, Tod Browning, and Bela Lugosi. Bram Stoker was less socially prominent than his wife Florence. An intimate of many artists and celebrities of her time, she had been engaged to Oscar Wilde, whom Victorians considered an "androgynous insult to proper society" (36). By contrast, Stoker was "merely competent, pinched, uncomfortable ... a stiff specimen of Victorian rectitude and restraint" (36). The mystery of such a man is how he created a character like Dracula. After a life marked by bad luck, his death left his impoverished widow forced to sell everything, including his notes for Dracula. For thirty years, the "copyright in Dracula was very nearly her only means of support" (59). She and her lawyers chased Nosferatu, the German silent movie version of Dracula, around England, Europe, and the U.S. Dracula became "her waking nightmare" (60): "reappearing at any time to taunt and to torment. Whatever her legal rights, there were certain irrational aspects of Dracula that were beyond Florence Stoker's control. Uninvited, animated by the obsessions of others, the thing had achieved a life of its own" (63). Florence's life ended in the 1930s as Dracula chose a less aristocratic victim: Tod Browning, the ex–carnival barker obsessed by freaks and the grotesque, selected by Universal to direct what would be his only hit movie, the first "talkie" Dracula. His scant movie output was bizarre and uneven, fascinating, "even if the fascination is akin to watching an auto wreck" (115) A cranky alcoholic, Browning sounded like his screen vampire when he pulled out his false teeth to tell a hotel manager, "Go bite yourself!" (117). Bela Lugosi's curse took the form of typecasting so potent that the Hungarian star wasted his career in degradingly repetitive films, ending up a self-admitted drug addict working for Z-grade director Ed Wood. Ultimately Dracula "taunted and tormented" him: ironically, his unchanging accent and manner caused "producers [to] resist offering him anything but Dracula, often on insulting terms" (187). The final bleak joke was his funeral; he was "laid out in full Dracula regalia--cape, tuxedo, and medallion" (188). Appropriately, "it was perhaps the only time in theatrical history that an actor had been so identified with a part that he took it to the grave" (190). Pathos, irony, and black humour touched the lives of all Dracula's victims.

Topic sentence for third response paragraph —————→ If Dracula's curse is only a myth from another time, I was amazed, as a student in a media course, to learn that today's realities of promotional hype, sequels, and copyright problems have existed for so long. I was impressed by the growing importance of copyright laws for new kinds of media reproductions. Movies were a novelty at the turn of this century, with few clear rules for intellectual property rights, and as we enter the twenty-first century, computerized entertainment and the "information highway" will require new types of legal protection for creators of new works. Both Florence Stoker and Bela Lugosi suffered because of rapid technical changes to the media. Florence Stoker's "nightmare" involved fighting for theatrical and film rights; Lugosi, "although there was, apparently, no kind of consumer product or novelty that could not be enhanced by his presence as a vampire" (191), never saw any profits from these items. His family's lawsuit against Universal was settled for $73,000 seventeen years after his death. Perhaps Martin Landau's portrayal in the recent film <u>Ed Wood</u> is a worthy memorial for the actor, but I wonder if Lugosi knew he had created *two* immortal monsters: Dracula, one of our "most disturbing yet irresistible dreams" (199), and a media monster, whose fame and profitability are boundless but ironically cursed.

Concluding → <u>Hollywood Gothic</u> is an excellent book; it combines entertainment
paragraph   with information in balanced proportions, mainly because of the wit and skill of David J. Skal. My early fascination with Dracula led me to read this book, but I came away better informed about the people behind the vampire legend, the media's influence on our lives, and the tragic human consequences of inadequate regulations for artistic and commercial media products. I laughed as I learned, and Skal made me want to discover more about "the creatures of the night."

Activity 1

Read a magazine article that interests you. Then write a report on the article. Include an introduction, a one-paragraph summary, a response or analysis of one or more paragraphs, and a brief conclusion. You may, if you like, quote briefly from the article. Be sure to enclose the words that you take from the article in quotation marks and put the page number in parentheses at the end of the quoted material.

Activity 2

Read a book suggested by your instructor. Then write a report on the book. Include an introduction, a one-paragraph summary, a response or analysis of one or more paragraphs, and a brief conclusion. Also, make sure that each major paragraph in your report develops a single main point. You may quote some sentences from the book, but they should be only a small part of your report. Follow the directions in Activity 1 above when you quote material.

USING THE LIBRARY

This chapter provides the basic information you need to use your college library with confidence. It also describes the basic steps you should follow in researching a topic.

Students seem to know that libraries provide study space, copying machines, and reading areas with recent copies of magazines and newspapers. But the true heart of a library consists of the following: *a main desk, book catalogues or files, book stacks, periodical or journal files, computerized database and/or CD-ROM index, and periodical storage area*. Each of these will be discussed on the pages that follow.

PARTS OF THE LIBRARY

Main Desk

The front desk or main desk is usually located near the door or in a central location. Here you will find librarians and library assistants, who are specially trained to help you to understand and make the best use of your college library's resources. There may also be racks of brochures about your library's specific sections, and the methods of finding information in these sections.

Activity

Make up a floor plan of your college library. Label the main desk, card catalogues (whether these are traditional files, on-line terminals, microfiche systems, or all three), book stacks, periodical files, CD-ROM terminals, and the periodical storage area.

Card Catalogues: Computerized or Traditional Catalogues

The card catalogue is one part of the records of all the materials available in your library. It is your starting-point for almost any research project. The catalogue may be an actual file of cards alphabetically arranged in the drawers of various cases, or it may be a set of microfiche sheets on vertical files near an illuminated projector. Increasingly, however, these files are being transferred to on-line computer terminals, which appear at various locations in the library.

Finding a Book—Author, Title, and Subject: Whether you use an actual file of cards or a computer terminal, it is important for you to know that there are three ways to look up a book: according to *author*, *title*, or *subject*. For example, suppose you wanted to see if your library had *Women in Literacy Speak*, by Betty-Ann Lloyd and other authors. You could check for the book in any of three ways:

1 You could go to the *title* section of the book file and look it up there under *W*. Note that you always look up a book under the first "significant" word in the title, excluding the words *A*, *An*, or *The*.

2 You could go to the *author* section of the book file and look it up there under *L*. An author is always listed under his or her last name. Here is the author entry in a computerized catalogue for Lloyd et al.'s book *Women in Literacy Speak*:

374.012x   1994   3 copies

WOM   **Lloyd, Betty-Ann.** Ennis, Frances. Atkinson, T. Canadian Congress
        for Learning Opportunities for Women
        Women in literacy speak / — Halifax, Nova Scotia: Fernwood
        Press, 1994. xi. 178 p: ill. 28 con
        Bibliography: p. 190–194
        ISBN/ISSN 18568377

        1. Literacy-Canada. 2. Adult Education-Canada. 3. Elementary
        Education-Canada. 4. Women's Studies-Canada/Native races.
        5. Volunteer Literacy Programmes-Canada.

        Status: In Library Locations: NH, King, Don Mills

---

3 Or, since you know the subject of the book—in this case, "literacy"—you could go to the *subject* section of the book file and look it up under L.

Generally, if you are looking for a particular book, it is easier to use the *author* or *title* section of the book file.

On the other hand, if you hope to find other books about literacy, then the *subject* section is where you should look. You will get a list of all the books in the library that deal with literacy. You'll also be given related subject headings under which you might find additional books about the subject.

■ In the catalogue card shown above, how many subject headings are listed

under which you might find books about literacy? _____

Using a Computerized/On-Line Card Catalogue: Your college's book and periodical holdings are probably listed on an on-line computerized system. There will be tables with a number of computer terminals. The instructions and codes for accessing any material by *author*, *title*, or *subject* will appear on-screen, and using any of these headings is a simple matter of a few key-strokes.

Under the *author* heading, you have seen how the screen gives you all the basic information you need to know about the book, including the call number, the book's current status, and the length and general subject-matter of the book. A useful piece of information in the entry is the fact that the book contains a bibliography, which may assist you in your research for further sources of information on your subject. The call number tells you where on the shelves of your library you will find the book, if its status is noted as "available" or "in library." The catalogue listing also gives you the number of copies of the book held by your college's library, and the other locations within the college where these copies are found. Your librarian can explain the terms of inter-library loan for copies of a book not at your own campus library.

The example of a catalogue entry under the *author* section of the holdings on the previous page could also show cross-references directing you to different books or materials written by the same author, for example:

Lloyd, Betty-Ann
Native Canadian Education Standards. pamphlet, Nova Scotia Prov. Press: 1993. [avail. Metro Ref. Lib.]

When you have examined all the information listed under the *author* classification of your book's catalogue entry, you may be directed to return to the main menu of the library's system. The on-line menu for the catalogue system will now show you codes for access to two other headings under which you can look up any given book: by *title*, or by *subject*.

Using Subject Headings to Research a Topic: Whether your library has a card catalogue, microfiche index, or computerized catalogue, it is the *subject section* which will be extremely valuable to you when you are researching a topic. If you have been given a generalized statement of a topic, and you realize that you will need to narrow your subject, the subject section will help you to find books both on the general, larger topic and on more specialized subject headings within that topic.

When you enter the access code for *subject* and the word "literacy," you may find many different book and article titles dealing with the subject of literacy for many diverse groups of people and social situations. The screen may also show you related subject headings under which you could find other publications about literacy. These related subject headings include those shown on the catalogue entry for *Women in Literacy Speak*. With the help of book titles found under subject headings, the subject headings on the catalogue entry, and the items in the book's bibliography (as well as the journal article titles and subject headings suggested in the periodical file and CD-ROM index, which will be explained later in this chapter), you can begin to formulate a limited research topic within the general subject of literacy.

There are three points to remember here: (1) Start researching a topic by using the *subject* section of the card catalogue system. (2) Look at the book titles on the catalogue entry, as well as at any cross-references listed; these sometimes suggest specific directions in which you might develop an essay. (3) Keep trying to narrow your topic. You will probably be asked to write an essay of five to fifteen pages. You do not want to choose a topic so broad that covering it would require an entire book or more. Instead, you want to find a single limited topic, perhaps of personal interest to you, that can be dealt with adequately in a relatively short research essay.

Activity

Part A: Answer the following questions about the card catalogue.

1. Is your library's book file an actual file of cards in drawers, or is the book file on computer terminals?

    _____

2. What are the three ways of looking up a book in the library?

    a. _____

    b. _____

    c. _____

3. Which section of the book file will help you research and limit a topic?

    _____

Part B: Use your library book catalogues to answer the following questions:

1. What is the title of one book by Margaret Atwood?

   _____

2. What is the title of one book by Pierre Berton?

   _____

3. Who is the author of *The Northern Magus*? (Remember to look up the title under *Northern*, not *The*.)

   _____

4. Who is the author of *Shampoo Planet*? _____

5. List two books dealing with the subject of stress reduction, and note their authors.

   a. _____

   b. _____

6. List two books dealing with the subject of René Lévesque and note their authors.

   a. _____

   b. _____

7. Look up a book titled *Cat's Eye* or *One-Eyed-Kings* or *Money* and give the following information about it:

   a. Author _____

   b. Publisher _____

   c. Date of publication _____

   d. Call number _____

   e. Subject headings, if available _____

8. Look up a book written by David Suzuki or Margaret Visser or William Gibson and give the following information about it:

   a. Title _____

   b. Publisher _____

   c. Date of publication _____

   d. Call number _____

   e. Subject headings, if available _____

Book Stacks

The book stacks are the library shelves where books are arranged according to their call numbers. The call number is your key to retrieving a book; it is as unique to your book as your Social Insurance Number or phone number is to you, and this number appears on any catalogue file for this book, as well as on the spine and on the inside of the book itself. Your library may now use electronic scanners or readers similar to those in the supermarket to locate and check out books. The call number may be included in the bar code on the inside cover of your book.

If your library has *open stacks* (which you may enter), look at the call number on your catalogue entry note, and follow these steps to find a book. If you are looking for *Women in Literacy Speak*, which has the call number 374.021x in the Dewey decimal system (libraries using the Library of Congress system have call letters made up of letters and numbers. However, you use the same basic method to locate a book), first look at the signs on the end-walls of the large bookcases which make up the stacks. Locate the number series of your book, starting with the left-hand column and working your way through your number to the final number in the right-hand column. Find the 374 classification shelves, then find 374.0 books, and 374.02 books, until you have found 374.021x, and you have your book. Don't forget to check the area around your book for other material on the same subject.

If your library has *closed stacks* (those you may not enter), you write down title, author, and call number on a slip of paper at the main desk, and give the slip to a library assistant, who will locate the book and bring it to you.

Activity

Use the book stacks to answer one of the following sets of questions. Choose the questions related to the system of classifying books (Library of Congress or Dewey Decimal) used by your library.

Option 1:
Dewey Decimal System (Numbers)

1. Books in the 200–299 area deal with
   a. language.   b. religion.   c. philosophy.   d. sports.
2. Books in the 370–372 area deal with
   a. education.   b. the military.   c. death.   d. waste disposal.
3. Books in the 613 area deal with
   a. wildflowers.   b. drugs.   c. health.   d. the solar system.
4. Books in the 916 area deal with
   a. Japan.   b. Israel.   c. China.   d. Africa

Option 2:
Library of Congress System (Letters and Numbers)

1. Books in the E92.B65 area deal with
   a. Canadian government
   b. Mackenzie King and the Liberal party
   c. Native Canadians and government
   d. Canadian immigrants and reform laws
2. Books in the HM–HN65 area deal with
   a. sociology.   b. economics.   c. history.   d. psychology.
3. Books in the M1–M220 area deal with
   a. painting.   b. music.   c. sculpture.   d. architecture.
4. Books in the PR4553–PR4595.H3 area deal with
   a. Thomas Hardy.
   b. George Eliot.
   c. Charles Dickens.
   d. Samuel Coleridge.

Periodical File

The *periodical file* is a magazine file: a collection of magazines, journals, and newspapers: any publications which are printed *periodically*, rather than in infrequent *re-editings* or *editions*, like books.

The periodical file often contains recent or very specialized information about a subject, which may not be available in a book. To ensure that your research essay is up to date in its information, as well as timely and interesting to a professor who may have read hundreds of papers on the same subject, check specialized trade, academic, or professional journals, newspapers your college may have on microfiche index, and general-interest magazines when you are doing research. Computerized systems now provide easy access to *subject* listings for periodicals.

There are two files in particular which should help you to find articles related to your topic area.

Readers' Guide to Periodical Literature: The familiar, yearly bound green volumes of the *Readers' Guide*, found in just about every library, list articles published in nearly two hundred popular (but mainly U.S.) magazines, such as *Newsweek*, *People*, *Entertainment Weekly*, and *Scientific American*. Articles are listed alphabetically under both subject and author, and are available for reading and direct reprint through a computerized version of the *Guide*.

Canadian Periodical Index: This is a good place to start research on any topic of general interest in Canada. The *CPI* lists nearly four hundred popular, specialist, and academic publications; it is published monthly and bound annually. Entries are by author and subject, with cross-references to related subjects.

Here is a typical entry from the *Canadian Periodical Index*:

Subject heading   *Title of article*   *Author of article*   *Name of periodical*

Politicians
Brains trust behind Jean Chrétien.   Peter C. Newman. *Maclean's*
   103 no 4 (Ja 22 '90): p. 29.

Volume   *Issue number*   *Date*   *Page number(s)*
number   *in volume*

Note the sequence in which information is given about the article:

1 Subject heading.

2 Title of the article. In some cases, there will be bracketed words [like these] after the title that help make clear just what the article is about.

3 Author (if it is a signed article). The author's first name is always abbreviated.

4 Whether the article has a bibliography (*bibl*) or is illustrated with pictures (*il*). Other abbreviations used are shown in the front of the *CPI*.

5 Name of the magazine. A short title like *Maclean's* is not abbreviated, but longer titles are. Refer to the list of publications in the front of the index to identify abbreviations.

6 Volume and number of the magazine, which precede the date in brackets before the colon.

7 Date when the article appeared. Dates are abbreviated: for example *Ja* stands for *January*, *F* for *February*. Other abbreviations are shown in the front of the *Canadian Periodical Index*.

8 Page numbers on which the article appears (after the colon).

Microfiche Periodical Indexes, Computerized Databases, and CD-ROM Indexes

Most college and university libraries now subscribe to *databases*, which are specialized computerized indexes of thousands of books and journal and newspaper articles, listed by author, title, and key words which describe subjects. Databases cover the arts, business, social sciences, and the humanities. These resources are fast, easy to use, and more complete than printed indexes.

If the system uses a microfiche "miniaturized page reproduction" system, then the screen in front of you will be loaded already with a microfilmed index. By pushing one of two buttons, you advance the film on-screen or move it backward. The entries can be index entries of newspaper and journal listings or photocopies of page entries in the *Readers' Guide, Canadian Periodical Index, Globe and Mail,* or *Financial Post,* or whichever databases your college has available. The most recent articles are always given first. Here is a typical printout of items from *CPI* under the heading "Politicians":

POLITICIANS
> Battling the odds: six Liberals [Sheila Copps; Donald Johnston; Clifford Lincoln; Dennis Mills; John Nunziata; Thomas Wappel] with hope . . . Paul Kaihla. il. *Maclean's* 103 no 6 (F 5 '90): p28–9
> Brains trust behind Jean Chrétien. Peter C. Newman. *Maclean's* 103 no 4 (Ja 22 '90): p29
> Hot welcome for a home-comer: barbs fly as Fisheries Minister Siddon visits the west coast. Tim Gallagher, port. *B.C. Report* 1 no 20 (Ja 22 '90): p11
> 'Little guy' to beat: Jean Chrétien returns for his second run at the Liberal leadership. Ross Laver. il port. *Maclean's* 103 no 6 (F 5 '90): cover, 22–5
> Trade, investment endeavours top priority for [minister John] Ciaccia. Richard Conrad. port. *This Week in Business* 3 no 2 (Ja 27 '90): p1,5
> *See also*
> Women in politics
> ### Quebec (Province)
> Victor again: Pierre Sévigny has conquered the anger, bitterness and private pain of political humiliation. Johan Sarrazin. port. *Montreal* 19 no 1 (Ja-F '90): p18–19
> ### United States
> Busting the mayor . . . Marion Barry is arrested on a cocaine charge. Tom Morganthau. il port. *Newsweek* 115 no 5 (Ja 29 '90): cover. 24–8
> Capital scandal: Washington's mayor [Marion Barry] faces a cocaine charge. Hilary Mackenzie. port. *Maclean's* 103 no 5 (Ja 29 '90): p30–1
> Model and the mayor: how a mystery woman brought down [Washington DC mayor Marion] Barry. Mark Miller. il. *Newsweek* 115 no 6 (F 5 '90): p21

Your college may have the computerized database facilities to allow you to obtain immediate printouts of either complete articles, abstracts (summaries), or quick descriptions of the subjects covered in a series of articles on a given topic. The more preparation and narrowing of topic you have done prior to entering and choosing your key word(s), the more precise and satisfactory will be the information you obtain in your printout. Look at the sample printout, which shows author, title, publication information, subject, and index.

```
Subjects covered
_____

Neural nets
Computer research

1 (GENERAL SCIENCE INDEX)
Bower, Bruce
Neural networks set sights on visual processing in brain
Science News 133:149 Mr 5 '88


Subjects covered
_____

Neural network computers
Brain/Localization of function

2 (GENERAL SCIENCE INDEX)
Zipser, David; Anderson, Richard A
A back-propagation programmed network that simulates
response properties of a subset of posterior parietal
neurons
Nature 331:679-84 F 25 '88


Subjects covered
_____

Neural network computers
Brain/Innervation

3 (GENERAL SCIENCE INDEX)
Anderson, Alun
Neural networks: learning from a computer cat
Nature 331:657-9 F 25 '88


Subjects covered
_____

Neural network computers
Brain/Innervation

4 (GENERAL SCIENCE INDEX)
Farnat, Nabil H.
Optical associative memories: first step toward neuro-
morphic optical data processing
Physics Today 41:S62-S63 Ja '88
```

Printouts cost a few cents per page, so take care in working out your "search words." Computers are still only as good helpers as the information with which humans supply them allows them to be.

CD-ROM (Compact Disc Read Only Memory) research indexes are the most recent development in databases. Many indexes are available on compact discs, with each disc storing up to 250 000 pages of information. Some colleges are linked to CD-ROM bases with other colleges and central libraries, which allows the student access to massive amounts of information about subjects. The trick to making use of CD-ROM terminals is getting access; the terminals are expensive, and your college may have only one copy of a given disc. You may have to reserve time for computer use, but the accuracy of the information obtained is excellent, and you can print material directly from the disc. But, as with using a database, the information the CD-ROM gives you will be only as good as your ability to focus precisely on the area of research in which you are interested: you may encounter hundreds of entries under a generalized word or phrase, and feel confused until you specify as *exactly* as possible the topic you are working on.

Activity 1

At this point in the chapter, you know the two basic steps in researching a topic in the library. What are the steps?

1. _____

2. _____

Activity 2

Use the excerpt from the *Canadian Periodical Index* on page 265 to answer the following questions.

1. Who is the author of an article titled "Hot Welcome for a Homecomer ..."?

   _____

2. What is the title of an article by Tom Morganthau?

   _____

3. Which article covers business aspects of the subject "Politicians"?

   _____

4. In which issue of *Maclean's* is there an article about an American politician?

   _____

5. On what pages of *BC Report* is the article "Hot Welcome for a Homecomer ..."?

_____

Activity 3

1. Look up a recent article on Canadian trade with Spain in the book form or computerized forms of *Reader's Guide* or *Canadian Periodical Index* and fill in the following information:

    a. Article title _____

    b. Author (if given) _____

    c. Name of magazine _____

    d. Pages _____

    e. Date _____

2. Look up a recent article on unemployment in the printed or computerized form of *Canadian Periodical Index* and fill in the following information.

    a. Article title _____

    b. Author (if given) _____

    c. Name of magazine _____

    d. Pages _____

    e. Date _____

Specialized Indexes: Once you know how to use the *Canadian Periodical Index* and the *Readers' Guide* you will find it easy to use some of the more specialized indexes in most libraries. Here are some helpful ones:

■   *Canadian News Index.* This index is published monthly and lists articles from seven major Canadian newspapers, with short summaries of some of the articles.

■   *Business Periodical Index.* The articles here are from more than three hundred publications that generally treat a subject in more detail than it would receive in the popular magazines indexed in the *Readers' Guide.* At the same time, the articles are usually not *too* technical or hard to read.

■   *Social Sciences Index.* This is an index to articles published by journals in the areas of anthropology, environmental science, psychology, and sociology. Your teachers in these areas may expect you to consult this index while doing a research project on any of these subjects.

Other specialized indexes that your library may have include the following:

Applied Science and Technology Index
Art Index
Biological Abstracts
Book Review Digest
Canadian Education Index
Canadian Essay and Literature Index
Chemical Abstracts
Computer Literature Index
Ecology Abstracts
Historical Abstracts
Humanities Index
Index to Canadian Legal Periodical Literature
Physics Abstracts
Psychological Abstracts

Some libraries have these indexes on computer, as well as the *CPI* and the *Readers' Guide*.

Activity

1. Check the periodical area in your college library. Check off each of the indexes that it includes:

   _____ *Readers' Guide Index*

   _____ *Business Periodicals Index*

   _____ *Magazine Index*

   _____ *Social Sciences Index*

   _____ *Canadian News Index*

2. Are any of these indexes available on a computer as well as in paperbound volumes? _____ If so, which ones? _____

   _____

3. What are two other indexes in this area of your library besides the five mentioned above?

_____

_____

A Note on Other Reference Materials: Every library has a reference area, often close to the place where the *Readers' Guide* is located, in which other reference materials can be found. Such general resource materials include dictionaries, encyclopedias, atlases, yearbooks, almanacs, a subject guide to books in print (this can help in locating books on a particular subject), anthologies of quotations, and other items.

You may also find in the reference area a series of filing cabinets called the *pamphlet file*. These cabinets are full of pamphlets, booklets, and newsletters on a multitude of topics. One file drawer, for example, may include all the pamphlets and the like for subjects that start with *A*. I looked in the *A* drawer of the pamphlet file in my library and found lots of small pieces about subjects like abortion, adoption, and animal rights, along with many other topics starting with *A*. On top of these filing cabinets may be a booklet titled "Pamphlet File Subject Headings"; it will quickly tell you if the file includes material on your subject of interest.

Activity

1. What is one encyclopedia that your library has?

_____

2. What unabridged dictionary does your library have?

_____

3. Where is your library's pamphlet file located?

_____

4. Is there a booklet or small file that tells you what subject headings are included in the pamphlet file? _____

Where is it? _____

Magazine Storage Area

Near your library's *Readers' Guide* or *Canadian Periodical Index*, you may notice slips of paper. Here, for instance, is a copy of the slip used in my local library:

PERIODICAL REQUEST

Name of Magazine   _____

Date of Magazine   _____

(For your reference: Title and pages of article:)

_____

As you locate each magazine and journal article that you would like to look at, fill out a slip. Take the slips to a library staff person working nearby. Don't hesitate to do this: helping you obtain the articles you want is part of his or her job.

Here's what will probably happen next:

- If a magazine that you want is a very recent one, it may be on open shelves in the library. The staff member will tell you, and you can go find it yourself.

- If the magazine you want is up to a year or so old, it may be kept in a closed area. The staff person will go find it and bring it to you.

- Sometimes you'll ask to see a magazine that the library does not carry. You'll then have to plan to use other articles, or go to a larger library. However, most college libraries or large urban libraries should have what you need.

- In many cases, especially with older issues, the magazine will be on microfilm or microfiche. (*Microfilm* is a roll of film on which articles have been reproduced in greatly reduced size; *microfiche* is the same thing but on easily handled sheets of film rather than on a roll.) The staff person will bring you the film or fiche and at your request will then show you how to load this material onto a microfiche or microfilm machine nearby.

Faced with learning how to use a new machine, many people are intimidated and nervous. What is important is that you ask for as much help as you need. Have the staff person demonstrate the machine and then watch you as you do it. While the machine may seem complex at first, in fact most of the time it turns out to be easy to use. Don't be afraid to insist that the person give you as much time as you need to learn the machine.

After you are sure you can use the machine to look up any article, check to see if the machine will make a copy of the article. Many will. Make sure you have some change to cover the copying fee, and then go back to the staff person and ask him or her to show you how to use the print option on the machine. You'll be amazed at how quickly and easily you can get a printed copy of almost any article you want.

Activity

1. Use the *Readers' Guide* or *Canadian Periodical Index* to find an article on divorce that was published in the last three months. Write the name of the magazine and the date on a slip of paper and give it to a library staff person.

   Is the article available in the actual magazine? _____ If so, is it on an open shelf or is it in a closed area where a staff person must bring it to you? _____

2. Use the *Readers' Guide* or *CPI* to find an article on divorce that was published more than one year ago. Write down the name of the magazine and the date on a slip of paper and give it to a library staff person or use the printout option with the index's database. Is the article available in the actual magazine, or is it on microfiche or microfilm?

   _____

3. Place a check if your library has:

   _____ Microfiche machine   _____ with a print option

   _____ Microfilm machine   _____ with a print option

A Summary of Library Areas

You now know the five areas of the library that will be most useful to you in doing research:

1 *Main desk.*

2 *Book catalogue or file.*   In particular, you can use the *subjects* section of the card file to get the names of books on your subject, as well as suggestions about other subject headings under which you might find books. It is by exploring your general subject in books and then in magazine articles that you will gradually be able to decide upon a subject limited enough to cover in your research paper.

3 *Book stacks.*   Here you will get the books themselves.

4 *Periodical files, indexes, and CD-ROM indexes.*   Once again, you can use the *subjects* sections of these files and key words to get the names of magazine and journal articles on your subject.

5 *Magazine storage area.*   Here you will get the articles themselves.

PRACTICE IN USING THE LIBRARY

Activity

Use your library to research a subject that interests you. Select one of the following areas, or (with your teacher's permission) one of your own choice:

Date rape

Problems of retirement

Organ donation

Housing options for the aged

Pro-choice movement

Pro-life movement

Health insurance reform

Drinking water pollution

Food poisoning (salmonella)

Cremation

Fertility drugs

Acid rain

Drug treatment programs for
adolescents

Air bags

Witchcraft in the 1990s

New treatments for AIDS

Changes in Canadian
immigration policy

Euthanasia

Hazardous substances in the home

Day-care programs that work

Capital punishment

Prenatal care

Noise control

New aid for the handicapped

New remedies for allergies

Censorship in the 1990s

Canadian prison reforms

Drug treatment programs

Sudden infant death syndrome

New treatments for insomnia

Greenhouse effect

Safe sex

Full-year attendance in schools

Self-help groups

Indoor air pollution

Gambling and youth

Non-graded schools

Earthquake forecasting

Ethical aspects of hunting

Video display terminals—
health aspects

Recent consumer frauds

Stress reduction in the
work-place

Sex in television

Everyday addictions

Toxic waste disposal

Sexual harassment in business

Telephone crimes

Heroes for the 1990s

New programs for the homeless

Marriage contracts

Research the topic first through the *subjects* section of the book catalogues and then through the *subjects* section of one or more magazine files and indexes.

On a separate sheet of paper, provide the following information:

1. Topic.

2. Three books that cover the topic directly or at least touch on the topic in some way. Include these items:

   Author
   Title
   Place of publication
   Publisher
   Date of publication

3. Three articles on the topic published in 1990 or later from the *Readers' Guide* or the *Canadian Periodical Index*. Include these items:

   Title of article
   Author (if given)
   Title of magazine
   Date
   Page(s)

4. Three articles on the topic published in 1990 or later from other indexes (such as the *New York Times Index*, *Business Periodical Index*, *Social Sciences Index*, or *Humanities Index*). Include these items:

   Title of article
   Author (if given)
   Title of magazine
   Date
   Page(s)

5. Finally, include a photocopy or printout of one of the three articles. Note whether the source of the copy was the article on paper, on microfiche, or on microfilm.

WRITING
A RESEARCH
ESSAY

The process of writing a research paper or essay can be divided into six steps:

1   Select a topic that you can readily research.

2   Limit your topic and make the purpose of your paper clear.

3   Gather information on your limited topic.

4   Plan your paper and take notes on your limited topic.

5   Write the paper.

6   Use an acceptable format and method of documentation.

This chapter explains and illustrates each of these steps and then provides a model research paper.

STEP 1: SELECT A TOPIC THAT YOU CAN READILY RESEARCH

First of all, go to the *Subjects* section of your library book file (as described on page 258) and see whether there are at least three books on your general topic. For example, if you initially choose the topic "day care," see if you can find at least three books on day care. Make sure that the books are actually available on the library shelves.

Next, go to the *Canadian Periodical Index* or *Readers' Guide* (see pages 263–264), and try to find five or more articles on your subject.

If both books and articles are at hand, pursue your topic. Otherwise, you may have to choose another topic. You cannot write a paper on a topic for which research materials are not readily available.

STEP 2: LIMIT YOUR TOPIC AND MAKE THE PURPOSE OF YOUR PAPER CLEAR

A research essay should develop a *limited* topic. It should be narrow and deep rather than broad and shallow. Therefore, as you read through books and articles on your general topic, look for ways to limit the topic.

For instance, in reading through materials on the general topic "adoption," you might decide to limit your topic to the problems that single people have in adopting a child. The general topic "drug abuse" might be narrowed to successful drug treatment programs for adolescents. After doing some reading on the worldwide problem of overpopulation, you might decide to limit your paper to the birth-control policies of the Chinese government. The broad subject "death" could be reduced to unfair pricing practices in funeral homes; "divorce" might be limited to its most damaging effects on the children of divorced parents; "stress in everyday life" could be narrowed to methods of stress reduction in the workplace.

The subject headings in the book catalogues and the periodical file will give you helpful ideas about how to limit your subject. For example, under the subject heading "Adoption" in the *book catalogue* at one library were several related headings, such as "Inter-country adoption" and "Inter-racial adoption." In addition, there was a list of eighteen books, with several of the titles suggesting limited directions for research: the tendency towards adopting older children; problems faced by the adopted child; problems faced by foster parents. Under the subject heading "Adoption" in the *periodical file* at the same library were subheadings and titles of many articles which suggested additional limited directions that a research paper might explore: corrupt practices in adoption; the increase in mixed-race adoptions; ways to find a child for adoption. The point is that *subject headings and related headings, as well as book and article titles, may be of great help to you in narrowing your topic*. Take advantage of them.

Do not expect to limit your topic and make your purpose clear all at once. You may have to do quite a bit of reading as you work out the limited focus of your paper. Note that many research papers have one of two general purposes. Your purpose might be to *make and defend a point* of some kind. (For example, your purpose in a paper might be to provide evidence that gambling should be legalized.) Or, depending on the course and the instructor, your purpose might simply be to *present information* about a particular subject. (For instance, you might be asked to do a paper that describes the latest scientific findings about what happens when we dream.)

STEP 3: GATHER INFORMATION ON YOUR LIMITED TOPIC

After you have a good sense of your limited topic, you can begin gathering information that is relevant to it.

A helpful way to proceed is to sign out the books you need from your library—or to use the copier in your library to duplicate the pages you need from those books. In addition, make copies of all the articles you need from magazines, journals, or other reference materials. Remember that, as described in "Using the Library" on page 265, you should be able to make copies of articles on microfiche or microfilm.

In other words, take the steps needed to get all your key source materials together in one place. You can then sit and work on these materials in a quiet. unhurried way in your home or some other place of study.

STEP 4: PLAN YOUR PAPER AND TAKE NOTES ON YOUR LIMITED TOPIC

Preparing a Scratch Outline

As you carefully read through the material you have gathered, think constantly about the specific content and organization of your paper. Begin making decisions about exactly what information you will present and how you will arrange it. Prepare a scratch outline of your paper that shows both its thesis and the areas of support for the thesis. It may help to try to plan at least three areas of support.

Thesis: _____

Support: (1) _____

(2) _____

(3) _____

Here, for example, is the brief outline that one student, Susan Pearle, prepared for her paper on censorship and personal responsibility:

Thesis: Parents and individuals are their own best censors.

Support: (1) Censors are often arbitrary and poorly informed.

(2) Censorship results from laziness and lack of personal involvement; people bring it on themselves.

(3) Media will control and finally censor people if they don't learn to manage information.

Note-Taking

With a tentative outline in mind, you can begin taking notes on the information that you expect to include in your paper. Write your notes on pocket-size cards or on sheets of loose-leaf paper. The notes you take should be in the form of *direct quotations*, *summaries in your own words*, or both. (At times you may also *paraphrase*—use an equal number of your own words in place of someone else's words. Since most research involves condensing information, you will summarize much more than you will paraphrase.)

A *direct quotation* must be written *exactly* as it appears in the original work. But as long as you don't change the meaning, you may omit words from a quotation if they are not relevant to our point. Show such an omission with three spaced periods known as *ellipses* in place of the deleted words:

Original passage

it is all-important to raise our children to know the reality of others as human beings with strengths and weaknesses. To communicate to our sons and daughters that to be truly human is to try to be loving and responsible, strong not because of power, but because of self-respect and respect for others.

Direct quotation with ellipses

"it is all-important to raise our children to know the reality of others as human beings. . . . To communicate to our sons and daughters that to be truly human is to try to be loving and responsible . . . because of self-respect and respect for others."

(Note that there are four dots in the first of the above examples, with the first dot indicating the period at the end of the sentence.)

In a *summary*, you condense the original material by expressing it in your own words. Summaries may be written as lists, as brief paragraphs, or both. Following is one of Susan Pearle's summary note cards:

Censorship

Laurence mistrusts censors for a good reason. One of her novels, <u>The Diviners</u>, was banned from many Canadian high schools, including the school in her home town. She suffered mentally and emotionally from the experience and found local censors to be limited and poor judges of what was good reading for high school students. Although, like many Canadians, she is offended by brutal pornography and graphic violence, she believes in the power of individual rights and rejects anyone's authority as a censor.

Laurence, 34

Keep in mind the following points about your research notes:

- Write on only one side of each card or sheet of paper.
- Write only one kind of information, from one source, on any one card or sheet. For example, the sample card above has information on only one idea (mistrust of censorship) from one source (Laurence).
- Include at the top of each card or sheet a heading that summarizes its content. This will help you organize the different kinds of information you gather.
- Identify the source and page number at the bottom.

Whether you quote or summarize, be sure to record the exact source and page from which you take each piece of information. In a research paper, you must document all information that is not common knowledge or a matter of historical record. For example, the birth and death dates of John Diefenbaker are established facts and do not need documenting. On the other hand, the number of adoptions granted to single people in 1991 is a specialized fact that should be documented. As you read several sources on a subject, you will develop a sense of what authors regard as generally shared or common information about a subject and what is more specialized information that must be documented.

If you do not document specialized information or ideas that are not your own, you will be stealing (the formal term is *plagiarizing*—using someone else's work as your own work). A good deal of the material in research writing, it can usually be assumed, will need to be documented.

STEP 5: WRITE THE PAPER

After you have finished your reading and note-taking, you should have a fairly clear idea of the plan of your paper. Make a *final outline* and use it as a guide to write your first full draft. If your instructor requires an outline as part of your paper, you should prepare either a *topic outline*, which contains your thesis plus words and phrases, or a *sentence outline*, which contains all complete sentences. A topic outline is shown in the model essay on pages 286–287. You will note that roman numerals are used for first-level headings, capital letters for second-level headings, and numbers for third-level headings.

In your *introductory paragraphs*, include a thesis statement expressing the purpose of your paper and indicate the plan of development that you will follow. The section on writing an introductory paragraph for the essay (pages 73–76) is appropriate for the introductory section of the research paper as well. Note also the opening paragraphs in the model research paper on page 288.

As you move from introduction to *main body* to *summary, conclusion,* or *both*, strive for unity, support, and coherence so that your paper will be clear and effective. Repeatedly ask, "Does each of my supporting paragraphs develop the thesis of my paper?" Use the checklist on page 123 and the inside front cover to make sure that your paper touches all four bases of effective writing. Keep in mind that a research essay will be more than five paragraphs in length. Each supporting piece of evidence, and its appropriate discussion, constitutes a separate paragraph.

STEP 6: USE AN ACCEPTABLE FORMAT AND METHOD OF DOCUMENTATION

Format

The model paper on pages 285–296 shows an acceptable format for a research paper. Comments and directions are set in small print in the margins of each page; be sure to note these.

Documentation of Sources

You must tell the reader the sources (books, articles, and so on) of the borrowed material in your paper. Whether you quote directly or summarize ideas in your own words, you must acknowledge your sources. In the past, you may have used footnotes and a bibliography to cite your sources. Now, you will learn a simplified documentation style used by the Modern Language Association. This easy-to-learn style resembles the documentation used in the social sciences and natural sciences.

Citations within a Paper:　When citing a source, you must mention the author's name and the relevant page number. The author's name may be given either in the sentence you are writing or in parentheses following the sentence. Here are two examples:

> "The whole subject is enormously complex, but I must finally come down against a censorship board, whether for the visual media or for the printed word," states Margaret Laurence (30).

> A Canadian novelist who endured censorship herself says, "The whole subject is enormously complex, but I must finally come down against a censorship board, whether for the visual media or for the printed word" (Laurence 30).

There are several points to note about citations within the paper:

- When the author's name is provided within the parentheses, only his or her last name is given.
- There is no punctuation between the author's name and the page number.

- The parenthetical citation is placed after the borrowed material but before the period at the end of the sentence.
- If you are using more than one work by the same author, include a shortened version of the title within the parenthetical citation. For example, suppose you were using several books by Margaret Laurence and you included the quotation above, which is from Laurence's essay "The Greatest Evil." Your citation within the text would be:

(Laurence, "Greatest Evil," 30)

Citations at the End of a Paper: Your paper should end with a list of "Works Cited" which includes all the sources actually used in the paper. (Don't list any other sources, no matter how many you have read.) Look at "Works Cited" in the model research paper (page 296) and note the following points:

- The list is organized alphabetically according to the authors' last names. Entries are not numbered.
- Entries without an author (such as "Painting of genitals joins masterpieces") are listed alphabetically by the first word.
- When more than one work by the same author or authors is listed, three hyphens followed by a period should be substituted for the author's or authors' names after the first entry.
- Entries are double-spaced, with no extra space between entries.
- After the first line of each entry, there is often an indentation for each additional line in the entry.

Model Entries for a List of "Works Cited": Model entries for "Works Cited" are given below. Use these entries as a guide when you prepare your own list.

Book by One Author

Baker, Nancy. The Night Inside. Toronto: Penguin Books, 1993.

Two or More Entries by the Same Author

- - -. Blood and Chrysanthemums. Toronto: Penguin Books, 1994.

Book Written by a Group

Department of the Secretary of State of Canada. The Canadian Style: A Guide to Writing and Editing. Toronto: Dundurn Press Ltd., 1991.

If you cite two or more entries by the same author (in the example above, a second book by Nancy Baker is cited), do not repeat the author's name. Instead, begin with a line made up of three hyphens followed by a period. Then give the remaining information as usual. Arrange the works by the same author alphabetically by title. Note in the examples above that the words *A*, *An*, and *The* are ignored when alphabetizing by title.

Book by Two or More Authors

Bassis, Michael A., Richard J. Gelles, and Ann Levine. <u>Sociology: An Introduction.</u> New York: Random House, 1991.

For a book with two or more authors, give all the authors' names but reverse only the first name.

Magazine Article

Callwood, June. "A Date With AIDS." <u>Saturday Night</u> Mar. 1995: 52.

Newspaper Article

Martin, Paul. "Canada's Fiscal Crunch." <u>The Globe and Mail</u> 24 Feb. 1995: B2.

Editorial

"Trade Wars Laughable." Editorial. <u>The Winnipeg Free Press</u> 15 Mar. 1995, sec. A22.

List an editorial as you would any signed or unsigned article, but indicate the nature of the piece by adding *Editorial* or *Letter* after the article's title.

Article with No Author Named

"White Tigers." <u>Owl.</u> Sept. 1994: 23.

Encyclopedia Article

Foulkes, David, and Rosalind D. Cartwright. "Sleep and Dreams." <u>Encyclopaedia Britannica.</u> 1989 ed.

Selection in an Edited Collection

McQuaig, Linda. "The New Medicine's Grave Risks." Essay Writing for
   Canadian Students. Eds. Kay L. Stewart, Chris Bullock, & Marian E.
   Allen. Scarborough, Ontario: Prentice-Hall Canada Inc., 1994.

Revised or Later Edition

Quinn, Virginia Nichols. Applying Psychology. 2d ed. New York: McGraw-
   Hill, 1990.

Note that the abbreviations *Rev. ed.*, *2d ed.*, *3d ed.*, and so on are placed right after
the title.

Chapter or Section in a Book by One Author

McGregor, Gaile. "Hat Tricks." The Wacousta Syndrome: Explorations in the
   Canadian Landscape. Toronto: University of Toronto Press, 1985.
   232–280.

Pamphlet

Your Guide to Hazardous Waste in the Home. Toronto: Metro Works
   Planning, Control and Development Division, 1995.

Television Programme

"Salmon Farming." Narr. David Suzuki. Prod. Ken Dodd. The Nature of
   Things. CBC. 21 Nov. 1993.

Film or Videotape

Not a Love Story: A Film about Pornography. Dir. Bonnie Sherr Klein.
   National Film Board, 1986.

Recording

Jordan, Sass. Rats. Aquarius Records CD 108184, 1994.

Computer Software Programme

SuperCalc3 Release 2.1. Computer Software. San Jose, Cal.: Computer
   Associates, Microproducts, 1985.

Personal Interview

Egoyan, Atom. Personal interview. 30 Mar. 1994.

Activity

On a separate sheet of paper, convert the information in each of the following references into the correct form for a list of "Works Cited." Use the appropriate model on pages 281–283 as a guide.

1. A book by Paul Rutherford called *The New Icons* and published by University of Toronto Press in 1994.

2. An article by Ann Shin titled "Radio Rethink" on pages 47–48 of the December 1994 issue of *Fuse* magazine.

3. An article by Jane Leeman titled "Alberta Youth Leaning to Reform" on page A3 of the April 15, 1994, issue of the *Calgary Herald*.

4. A book by James F. Calhoun and Joan Ross Acocella titled *Psychology of Adjustment and Human Relations* and published in a third edition by McGraw-Hill in New York in 1990.

5. An article by Katherine Griffin titled "The Unbearable Darkness of Being" on pages 62–67 of the January/February 1991 issue of *In Health*.

TRIAL BY PERSONAL RESPONSIBILITY:
THE INDIVIDUAL PARENT AS CENSOR IN THE 1990s

Susan Pearle

English 150
Section BE
Professor L. Keane

15 October 1995

OUTLINE

Thesis: Personal and parental responsibility and knowledge, not censorship, are the counterbalances to the increasing power of the media in people's lives; the history of censorship in education, arts, and entertainment is full of errors in judgement, and the greatest potential for more errors and loss of personal freedom may lie on the "information highway."

I.   Censorship is a two-sided problem to most Canadians
   A.   Disgust at media environment
   B.   Distrust and disapproval of censorship
II. Areas affected by censorship
   A.   Education
   B.   Arts
   C.   Entertainment
   D.   On-line information (not yet?)
III. Solution: Individual and parental self-education and responsibility, not external and random censors
   A.   Education: book censorship in public and high schools
      1.   Problem: censors are ill-informed, and make inept choices--children suffer
      2.   Solutions:
         a.   parents must know what their children are reading and why
         b.   parents should know who censors are and participate in children's education
   B.   Arts: works of art in all forms are judged by inadequate means
      1.   Problems:
         a.   suppression of good books leads to cultural and educational deprivation
         b.   causes for censorship are changeable and ill-understood
      2.   Solutions:
         a.   exercise of individual and parental intelligence in reading and decision-making
         b.   providing experiential examples of desirable behaviour and ethics

C. Entertainment: distinctions blur between art, consumer goods, and entertainment and what is valuable in these areas
   1. Problems:
      a. comics: good training reading or trivial, harmful time-wasters?
      b. film and visual media: educational power or potentially harmful baby-sitter?
      c. on-line information: potential risk to unsupervised children
   2. Solutions:
      a. early reading and values education
      b. supervision of viewing and consumer habits
      c. parental knowledge of, and education in, use of technology

Your last name and the page number are your header, and should appear in the upper right-hand corner of each page.

Pearle 1

Double space between lines of text. Leave a margin of 2.5 to 3 cm. all the way around the page.

Turn on the television: two sensational trials, Canadian and American. You're disgusted. Change channels: talk-shows with drug-addict pimps. Disgusted again. Try the news: "Live-Eye" coverage of a grisly accident. Turn off the TV. Read the back of NOW in Toronto: classifieds for sexual cravings tidily organized by buyer and supplier. Angry? Enter a son's room: a SPAWN comic graphic with innards and violence. Try a daughter's room: a Canadian Gothic promising blood and explicit sex. Bernardo trial Internet scraps float through the schoolyard. Beavis & Butthead and rap lyrics destroy innocence, but so does the corner store, where Cheri blazes with vibrant details. There ought to be a law . . .

There is a law; its name is censorship, and in theory, many Canadians disapprove of it. The dilemma is our bewilderment at the increasing nastiness in the media. Should there then be a "Big Brother" as judge? The answer makes most people queasy from "doublethink, the ability to hold two opposing beliefs simultaneously" (Laurence 34). Censorship implies judicious prevention of harm to those incapable of defence against vicious material. Until the mid-1950s, "the test . . . was whether a writing tended to deprave and corrupt the morals of young or immature persons" (deGrazia 12). To Oxford, "censor" is "an official with the power to suppress whole or parts of books, plays, films, letters, news, etc. on the grounds of obscenity . . . etc." (Concise Oxford Dictionary 149). Fears of potential damage to children and vulnerable minds have caused the intrusion of censorship in education, arts, and entertainment. To these, should another category be added: information relayed by computer networks? The best defence

Parenthetic citation with author and page number, but no comma.

Thesis, with plan of development.

against intrusive judges is an educated public able to make its own decisions. This argument hinges on the word <u>educated</u>. As information engulfs them, can people learn enough, manage technology well enough, so that they are their own and their children's best censors? Those not enslaved by belief, politics, or technology can only try.

In 1644 Milton wrote that such effort is difficult: "That which purifies us is trial, and trial is by what is contrary" (165). <u>Areopagitica</u>, one of the earliest texts on censorship, deals with publication rights in general, but the thrust of this quotation applies to parental responsibility regarding educational reading. Idiocies in censorship of texts are not things of the past. Nor are parental laziness and willingness to abdicate from the moral and aesthetic education of their children . . . not many parents are "purified" by the effort to guide, apparently. Presumably, outlawing <u>Huckleberry Finn</u> for its racism or immoral characters was accepted by parents for the same reasons seventy years ago as a similar ruling might be today: "The teachers [school board/trustees] must know best" or, worse yet, "Well, I haven't read it, so I don't know what to think." Both responses show lack of interest, lack of effort, and unthinking reliance on some "superior" third party by parents. The censor or judgemental committee may have no ethical or artistic values in common with a child's parents, and certainly will have no special knowledge of a given child. Parents are equipped with knowledge of their children and of their own values and "can use common sense in choosing which books to put on school curricula and which to reserve for . . . home, where parents can correct any mistaken impressions"

Pearle 3

(Landsberg 191). Even children's television and video choices receive more attention and more publicity than school reading choices, as readers' interest in a recent series of articles by Louise Brown in The Toronto Star television guide (May 1995) indicates.

Only a few years ago, thousands of Ontario parents who read local writer Robert Munsch's books to their children were probably unaware that his book The Thursday Boat was banned in public schools because of its allegedly "atheist" content. Apparently the fact that the heroine doesn't find God present on earth convinced some authority that Munsch was purveying atheism rather than the omnipresence of the Almighty, a concept some children might have found comforting, valuable, or worthy of consideration. Likewise, the message of the artist was missed when the sharp wit and ironic style of Roald Dahl displeased Canadian school authorities. "Amusement is . . . a force of liberation and pleasure for children" (Lesnik-Oberstein 76); children innately love humour and understand satire. They enjoy parodies of well-known stories, and they loathe being "talked down to." Why wouldn't they like the sneaky insinuating voice of Dahl when he confides, "I guess you think you know this story./You don't. The real one's much more gory./The phoney one, the one you know,/Was cooked up years and years ago,/And made to sound all soft and sappy/Just to keep the children happy" (Dahl 1). The fact that Cinderella is called "a dirty slut" (8) in this poem helped put Dahl on the forbidden list, even though his version of the fairy tale in fact offers a better romantic moral than the original. But how many parents read Dahl's Revolting Rhymes, either for

Ellipses, or three dots inside a quotation, show that words have been left out.

enjoyment or to find out what the fuss is about? How many went along with the ban, heedless of Michele Landsberg's warning that "those who seek to censor their child's reading will either fail or deprive their child of the riches of literature altogether" (191).

Not only public school children's books suffer from ill-advised and ill-considered censorship; Canadian high school selections, often excellent novels, have been banned without undue fuss over the years. The certainty of parents not having read such books seems to increase directly with the artistic value of such novels. An example is Margaret Laurence's The Diviners, banned in many parts of Canada until recently. Banning sometimes has the effect of making forbidden art more powerful, and Landsberg feels that this is the case with Laurence: "Books are powerful; even illiterates acknowledge the power of the printed word when they demand the banning of such fine novels as . . . The Diviners" (191). Laurence herself has written her own response to being banned in "The Greatest Evil"; she finds censorship and reliance on governing authorities as hateful as brutality and pornography in media. For Laurence personal responsibility is crucial:

> it is all-important to raise our children to know the reality of others . . . to communicate to our daughters and our sons that to be truly human is to try to be loving and responsible, strong not because of power but because of self-respect and respect for others. (57)

She feels students should "read novels in which many aspects of life are dealt with, by writers whose basic faith is in the unique and irreplaceable value of the human individual" (53).

But a local pharmacist and a minister mistook her two-sentence sketch of copulating flies for what Section 159 (8) of the Canadian Criminal Code defines as obscenity: a work where "a dominant characteristic . . . is the undue exploitation of sex." Is any work generally agreed to be art to be subjected to stupid judgements or clumsy laws? Many now-classic novels which treat both life and sex as unique and difficult gifts have been just this ineptly handled, including James Joyce's Ulysses, which The New York Times first reviewed as "a curious production, not wholly uninteresting, especially to psychopathologists" (qtd. in deGrazia 14). Ulysses was banned from the U.S. until in 1932 a Judge Woolsey defined as obscene something "which [primarily] tended to stir the sex impulse or to lead to impure and lustful thoughts" (deGrazia 31). Apparently, this was not deemed to be Ulysses' main purpose, any more than it was Margaret Laurence's.

 But art is not limited to print, and "the power of books is not the same as the direct impact of visual images" (Landsberg 191). A news item in The Toronto Star revealing a Paris museum's one-hundred-and-thirty-year hesitation before the display of a life-sized painting of naked female genitalia testifies to the force of the visual (June 15 1995 C3). Images, like music, are a universal language, and speak to everyone. A graphic/print hybrid, comic books may be a natural progression from children's picture books, but they have always been regarded with some suspicion; a critic said in 1949, "All comic books without exception are principally, if not wholly, devoted to violence" (Legman 31). The Comics Code in the early 1950s took care of part of that problem, removing from legal

The abbreviation qtd. means quoted.

Brackets mark words inserted to clarify a quotation.

distribution most crime and horror comics. But Batman returns, to both print and to film, and older readers might be shocked by the actions and words of the Caped Crusader in something like <u>Arkham Asylum</u> where Bruce Wayne's alter ego is a vampire bent on disembowelment, among other felonies. Revenue Canada is the censoring body for comics, magazines, and videos, and it stops hundreds of these every month. Comics, "code" and uncensored "non-code," have exploded in popularity. Some are decidedly grotesque in visual and textual content; others, like <u>The Invisibles</u>, which introduces teenage readers to Percy Shelley and Oscar Wilde, are quite literate and witty. The lines between entertainment and education, between art and mass-market consumer products, have begun to blur. Comics are a commodity, and as a constant diet an insufficient substitute for books--"mind stuffing," in Canadian critic Paula Fox's phrase--and a reader with inadequate early home-based values may be swept away by their potent mixture of colour, line, and limited copy.

In a society surrounded by powerful blends of images and words on pages and screens small and large, consumers and parents must take responsibility for the informative force of all these influences. Even in the 1930s, after The Hays Code had brought censorship to film, enlightened censors like Henry James Forman, author of <u>Our Movie Made Children</u>, realized that movies have "really given us another educational system, alluring, persuasive, cogent, and appealing, which involves all the . . . youth . . . as completely as our long built-up educational system itself" (qtd. in Paul 11). Substitute "TV," "videotape," or "CD-ROM disc" for the word "movies" in Forman's statement, and the reality of consumer goods' replacement of culture becomes clearer. Images are powerful teachers, but what are they teaching . . . or selling? The 1990s is part of "a culture that itself glorifies the marketplace . . . when films have become an adjunct of the advertising industry . . . the art of the marketplace is the art people choose by choosing to purchase it, not the art that guardians of the state and culture impose on them" (Paul 24). Seemingly mindless consumerism has partly replaced obscenity as yet another threat to childhood innocence and learned moral values; seven-year-olds will happily watch 90210 and any film on videotape that their friends recommend, if given the choice, but what are they learning, and what happened to childhood? Again, many parents are happy to have an "electronic baby-sitter," and are too lazy to consider the potential risk of a steady diet of the perils of Shannen Doherty, the Home Shopping Network, and Encino Man.

Nonetheless, most parents want to believe they are doing their best for their children, and computer manufacturers have convinced them that one more screen, with "brain" and keyboard attached, is a home necessity. And use of computers in schools has created many a cyber-prodigy. But what about on-line services, this new source of visual information, this new "teacher"? Is anyone policing cyberspace? A clever, unsupervised child can access, along with vast amounts of useless information, all sorts of interesting dialogues about sexual peculiarities available under various acts of freedom of information. In May 1995, the United States Senate heard a proposed "Communications Decency Act" which will impose a fine of $100,000 on anyone who "makes, transmits, or otherwise makes available any comment, proposal, or other communication which is obscene, lewd, filthy, or indecent" (Hentoff 64). But, if Canada has yet to engage in cyber-censorship, parents could learn from a U.S. public policy advocacy group which places the responsibility for on-line information firmly back in the home: "the flexibility of interactive media . . . enables parents to control what content their kids have access to" (qtd. in Hentoff 65). This control demands that parents try; that they supervise children, and, most important, that they keep up with their children technologically. Milton's voice echoes three hundred and fifty years later: "the trial" of being our own censors, which he said "purified," is "won not without dust and heat" (130).

Disgust or anger at whatever aspect of media offends is never satisfied by mere indignation. As the power of the media grows, people, especially children, are threatened by being controlled. The ultimate censor is no longer a church, a judge, or a politician; it is the all-seeing eye of Big Brother's screen as it penetrates lives with fibre-optic cable, and the only weapon is still personal responsibility. Orwell was not alone in his fears of an amoral, media-driven future; Canadian scholar and sage Marshall McLuhan also saw a frightening future in a twenty-first century populated by slaves who had abandoned responsibility for their own lives by not educating themselves to control technology. Should we abandon our own children's minds to any censor, any outside authority? Surely they and their hearts and brains are worth "the dust and heat" of "the trial."

Works Cited

Dahl, Roald. <u>Revolting Rhymes.</u> New York: Bantam Doubleday
Dell, 1983.

deGrazia, Edward. <u>Girls Lean Back Everywhere: The Law of
Obscenity and the Assault on Genius.</u> New York: Vintage
Books, 1993.

Hentoff, Nat. "Indecent Proposal." <u>Entertainment Weekly</u>
March 31 1995: 64–65.

Landsberg, Michele. <u>Michele Landsberg's Guide to Children's
Books.</u> Toronto: Penguin, 1985.

Laurence, Margaret. "The Greatest Evil." In <u>Dance on the
Earth: A Memoir.</u> Toronto: McClelland and Stewart, 1989.

Legman, Gershon. <u>Love and Death: A Study in Censorship.</u>
New York: Quick Lithographers, 1949.

Lesnik-Oberstein, Karin. <u>Children's Literature.</u> Oxford: Oxford
University Press, 1994.

Milton, John. "Areopagitica." <u>Poems and Selected Prose.</u> New
York: Bantam Books, 1966. 127–170.

"Painting of genitals joins masterpieces." <u>The Toronto Star</u> 15
June 1995: C3.

Paul, William. <u>Laughing Screaming: Modern Hollywood Horror
& Comedy.</u> New York: Columbia University Press, 1994.

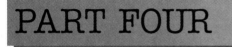

PART FOUR

HANDBOOK
OF
SENTENCE
SKILLS

MANUSCRIPT FORM

When you hand in a paper for any course, it will probably be judged first by its format. It is important, then, to make the paper look attractive, neat, and easy to read. Here is a checklist you should use when preparing a paper for an instructor:

- Is the paper full-sized, 21.5 cm x 28 cm ($8\frac{1}{2}$ by 11 inches)?
- Are there wide margins (1 to $1\frac{1}{2}$ inches) all around the paper? In particular, have you been careful not to crowd the right-hand or bottom margin?
- If the paper is word-processed, have you:

  Checked whether your instructor prefers full justification or "ragged right" line format?
  Double-spaced the text of each paragraph of your essay?
  Used any header information your instructor may require?
  Removed tear-strips from the edges of printer paper?

- If the paper is handwritten, have you:

  Used a blue or black pen?
  Been careful not to overlap letters or to make decorative loops on letters?
  Made all your letters distinct, with special attention to *a*, *e*, *i*, *o*, and *u* —five letters that people sometimes write illegibly?
  Kept all your capital letters clearly distinct from small letters?

- Have you centred the title of your paper on the first line of page 1? Have you been careful *not* to put quotation marks around the title or to underline it? Have you capitalized all the words in the title except for short connecting words like *of, for, the, and, in,* and *to*?
- If your paper is handwritten, have you skipped a line between the title and the first line of your paper?
- If your paper is word-processed, have you inserted two double lines of space between the title and the opening line of your paper?

_____   ■ Have you indented the first line of each paragraph about five spaces (1.25 cm) from the left-hand margin? If you are processing your paper, your instructor may prefer that you do not "tab" or indent a first line of a new paragraph, but leave two lines of space between each separate paragraph.

_____   ■ Have you made commas, periods, and other punctuation marks firm and clear? If typing, have you left a double space after a period?

_____   ■ If you have broken any words at the end of a line, have you been careful to break only between syllables?

_____   ■ Have you put your name, the date, and other information at the end of the paper, on the title page, or wherever your instructor has specified?

Also ask yourself these important questions about the title and the first sentence of your paper:

_____   ■ Is your title made up of several words that tell what the paper is about? (The title should be just several words, *not* a complete sentence.)

_____   ■ Does the first sentence of your paper stand independent of the title? (The reader should *not* have to use the words in the title to make sense of the opening sentence.)

Activity

Use the checklist to locate the seven mistakes in format in the following lines from a student paper. Explain the mistakes in the spaces provided. One mistake is described for you as an example.

	"Being alone"
	This is something that I simply cannot tolera-
	te, and I will go to great lengths to
	prevent it. For example, if I know that I need

1. Hyphenate only between syllables (toler-ate, not tolera-te).

2. _____

3. _____

4. _____

5. _____

6. _____

7. _____

SUBJECTS AND VERBS

The basic building blocks of English sentences are subjects and verbs. Understanding them is an important first step towards mastering a number of sentence skills.

Every sentence has a subject and a verb. Who or what the sentence speaks about is called the *subject;* what the sentence says about the subject is called the *verb*. In the following sentences, the subject is underlined once and the verb twice:

The boy cried.
That fish smells.
Many people applied for the job.
The show is a documentary.

A SIMPLE WAY TO FIND A SUBJECT

To find a subject, ask *who* or *what* the sentence is about. As shown below, your answer is the subject.

Who is the first sentence about? The boy
What is the second sentence about? That fish
Who is the third sentence about? Many people
What is the fourth sentence about? The show

A SIMPLE WAY TO FIND A VERB

To find a verb, ask what the sentence *says about* the subject. As shown below, your answer is the verb.

What does the first sentence *say* about the boy?   He <u><u>cried</u></u>.
What does the second sentence *say* about the fish?   It <u><u>smells</u></u>.
What does the third sentence *say* about the people?   They <u><u>applied</u></u>.
What does the fourth sentence *say* about the show?   It <u><u>is</u></u> a documentary.

A second way to find the verb is to put *I*, *you*, *he*, *she*, *it*, or *they* in front of the word you think is a verb. If the result makes sense, you have a verb. For example, you could put *he* in front of *cried* in the first sentence above, with the result, *he cried*, making sense. Therefore you know that *cried* is a verb. You could use the same test with the other three verbs as well.

Finally, it helps to remember that most verbs show action. In the sentences already considered, the three action verbs are *cried*, *smells*, and *applied*. Certain other verbs, known as *linking verbs*, do not show action. They do, however, give information about the subject. In "The show is a documentary," the linking verb *is* tells us that the show is a documentary. Other common linking verbs include *am*, *are*, *was*, *were*, *feel*, *appear*, *look*, *become*, and *seem*.

Activity

In each of the following sentences, draw one line under the subject and two lines under the verb.

1. The ripening tomatoes glistened on the sunny windowsill.
2. Biofeedback reduces the pain of my headaches.
3. Elena nervously twisted a strand of hair around her fingers.
4. My brother made our stereo cabinet from inexpensive particleboard.
5. A jack-rabbit bounds up to fifteen feet in one leap.
6. The blind woman knits woollen caps for Christmas presents.
7. The amateur astronomer set his alarm for 3 a.m. to view the lunar eclipse.
8. On St. Patrick's Day, our neighbourhood bar serves green beer.
9. Children sometimes eat the dangerous lead-based paint found in old houses.
10. During my parents' divorce, I felt like a rag doll being torn between two people.

MORE ABOUT SUBJECTS AND VERBS

1   A sentence may have more than one verb, more than one subject, or several subjects and verbs.

The <u>engine</u> <u>coughed</u> and <u>sputtered</u>.

Broken <u>glass</u> and empty <u>cans</u> <u>littered</u> the parking lot.

<u>Joyce</u>, <u>Brenda</u>, and <u>Robert</u> <u>met</u> after class and <u>headed</u> downtown.

2   The subject of a sentence never appears within a *prepositional phrase*. A prepositional phrase is simply a group of words that begins with a preposition. Following is a list of common prepositions:

about	before	by	inside	over
above	behind	during	into	through
across	below	except	of	to
among	beneath	for	off	towards
around	beside	from	on	under
at	between	in	onto	with

Cross out prepositional phrases when looking for the subject of a sentence.

The weathered old <u>house</u> <u>perched</u> unsteadily ~~on its rotted foundation~~.

The <u>label</u> ~~on that mayonnaise jar~~ can be easily <u>removed</u> ~~with hot water~~.

The colour <u>picture</u> ~~on our TV set~~ turns black and white ~~during a storm~~.

The murky <u>waters</u> ~~of the polluted lake~~ <u>spilled</u> ~~over the dam~~.

The amber <u>lights</u> ~~on its sides~~ <u>outlined</u> the tractor-trailer ~~in the hazy dusk~~.

3   Many verbs consist of more than one word. Here, for example, are some of the many forms of the verb *work:*

work	worked	should work
works	were working	will be working
does work	have worked	can work
is working	had worked	could be working
are working	had been working	must have worked

Notes

a   Words like *not*, *just*, *never*, *only*, and *always* are not part of the verb although they may appear within the verb.

Rebecca has just finished filling out her tax form.
The intersection has not always been this dangerous.

b   No verb preceded by *to* is ever the verb of a sentence.

At night, my son likes to read under the covers.
Evelyn decided to separate from her husband.

c   No *-ing* word by itself is ever the verb of a sentence. (It may be part of the verb, but it must have a helping verb in front of it.)

They going on a trip this weekend.   (not a sentence, because the verb is not complete)
They are going on a trip this weekend.   (a sentence)

Activity

Draw a single line under subjects and a double line under verbs. Crossing out prepositional phrases may help you to find the subjects.

1.   The top of our refrigerator is covered with dusty pots and pans.
2.   A new muffler and tail pipe were just installed in my car.
3.   The people in the all-night coffee shop seemed weary and lost.
4.   Every plant in the dim room bent towards the small window.
5.   A glaring headline about the conviction of a local city councillor attracted my attention.
6.   Two of the biggest stores on our main shopping street are going out of business.
7.   The glow of the stereo's tiny red light always reminds me to turn off the amplifier.
8.   Both private wells and public reservoirs in our area are contaminated with deadly chemicals.
9.   The jar of peppercorns tumbled from the spice shelf and shattered on the floor.
10.   The scar in the hollow of Brian's throat is the result of an emergency operation to clear his windpipe.

■ **Review Test**

Draw a single line under subjects and a double line under verbs. Crossing out prepositional phrases may help you to find the subjects.

1. With one graceful motion, the shortstop fielded the grounder and threw to first base.
2. Forty-seven czars are buried within the walls of Moscow's Kremlin.
3. Before class, Barbara and Aaron rushed to the coffee machine in the hall.
4. I punched and prodded my feather pillow before settling down to sleep.
5. Waiting in the long ticket line, Matt shifted his weight from one foot to the other.
6. Cattle branding was practised by ancient Egyptians more than four thousand years ago.
7. Lilacs and honeysuckle perfume our yard on summer nights.
8. The mail carrier abruptly halted her Jeep and backed up towards the mailbox.
9. During the War of 1812, some Upper Canadian families of German background sold their land and moved to Pennsylvania, where Amish and Mennonite communities formed.
10. The little girl's frantic family called a psychic to help locate the child.

SENTENCE FRAGMENTS

Every sentence must have a subject and a verb and must express a complete thought. A word group that lacks a subject or a verb and that does not express a complete thought is a *fragment*. Following are the most common types of fragments that people write:

1 Dependent-word fragments
2 *-ing* and *to* fragments
3 Added-detail fragments
4 Missing-subject fragments

Once you understand the specific kind or kinds of fragments that you may write, you should be able to eliminate them from your writing. The following pages explain all four fragment types.

DEPENDENT-WORD FRAGMENTS

Some word groups that begin with a dependent word are fragments. At the top of the next page is a list of common dependent words. Whenever you start a sentence with one of these words, you must be careful that a fragment does not result.

> ### *Dependent Words*
>
> | | | |
> |---|---|---|
> | after | if, even if | when, whenever |
> | although, though | in order that | where, wherever |
> | as | since | whether |
> | because | that, so that | which, whichever |
> | before | unless | while |
> | even though | until | who |
> | how | what, whatever | whose |

The word group beginning with the dependent word *After* in the example below is a fragment.

> After I cashed my paycheque. I treated myself to dinner.

A *dependent statement*—one starting with a dependent word like *After*—cannot stand alone. It depends on another statement to complete the thought. *After I cashed my paycheque* is a dependent statement. It leaves us hanging. We expect in the same sentence to find out *what happened after* the writer cashed the cheque. When a writer does not follow through and complete a thought, a fragment results.

To correct the fragment, simply follow through and complete the thought:

> After I cashed my paycheque, I treated myself to dinner.

Remember, then, that *dependent statements by themselves are fragments*. They must be attached to a statement that makes sense standing alone.

Here are two other examples of dependent-word fragments.

> I won't leave the house. Until I hear from you.
>
> Rick finally picked up the socks. Which he had thrown on the floor days ago.

Until I hear from you is a fragment; it does not make sense standing by itself. We want to know in the same statement *what cannot happen* until I hear from you. The writer must complete the thought. Likewise, *Which he had thrown on the floor days ago* is not in itself a complete thought. We want to know in the same statement what *which* refers to.

How to Correct a Dependent-Word Fragment

In most cases you can correct a dependent-word fragment by attaching it to the sentence that comes after it or the sentence that comes before it:

After I cashed my paycheque, I treated myself to dinner.
(The fragment has been attached to the sentence that comes after it.)

I won't leave the house until I hear from you.
(The fragment has been attached to the sentence that comes before it.)

Rick finally picked up the socks which he had thrown on the floor days ago.
(The fragment has been attached to the sentence that comes before it.)

Another way of correcting a dependent-word fragment is simply to eliminate the dependent word by rewriting the sentence.

I cashed my paycheque and then treated myself to dinner.
I will wait to hear from you.
He had thrown them on the floor days ago.

Notes

a Use a comma if a dependent word group comes at the *beginning* of a sentence (see also page 308):

After I cashed my paycheque, I treated myself to dinner.

However, do not generally use a comma if the dependent word group comes at the *end* of a sentence:

I won't leave the house until I hear from you.
Rick finally picked up the socks which he had thrown on the floor days ago.

b Sometimes the dependent words *who, that, which,* or *where* appear not at the very start but *near* the start of a word group. A fragment often results:

I drove slowly past the old brick house. The place where I grew up.

The place where I grew up is not in itself a complete thought. We want to know in the same statement *where was the place* the writer grew up. The fragment can be corrected by attaching it to the sentence that comes before it:

I drove slowly past the old brick house, the place where I grew up.

Activity 1

Turn each of the dependent word groups into a sentence by adding a complete thought. Put a comma after the dependent word group if a dependent word starts the sentence.

Examples Although I felt miserable

Although I felt miserable, I tried to smile for the photographer.

The man who found my wallet

The man who found my wallet returned it the next day.

1. If I have to work late

    _____

    _____

2. Because it was raining

    _____

    _____

3. When I heard the news

    _____

    _____

4. Because I couldn't find the car keys

    _____

    _____

5. The restaurant that we tried

    _____

    _____

Activity 2

Underline the dependent-word fragment in each selection. Then rewrite the selections, correcting each fragment by attaching it to the sentence that comes before or the sentence that comes after—whichever sounds more natural. Put a comma after the dependent word group if it starts the sentence.

1. Whenever I spray deodorant. My cat arches her back. She thinks she is hearing a hissing enemy.

    _____

    _____

2. My father, a salesman, was on the road all week. We had a great time playing football in the house. Until he came home for the weekend.

_____

_____

3. If Kim takes too long saying good-bye to her boyfriend. Her father will start flicking the porch light. Then he will come out with a flashlight.

_____

_____

4. I bought a calendar watch. Which is running fast. Last week had sixteen days.

_____

_____

5. Before I move, I scrub both my old and new apartments. After all the apartments I've left spick-and-span. I think it's my turn to move into a clean one.

_____

_____

-ING AND *TO* FRAGMENTS

When an *-ing* word appears at or near the start of a word group, a fragment may result. Such fragments often lack a subject and part of the verb. Underline the word groups in the selections below that contain *-ing* words. Each is a fragment.

1. Ellen walked all over the neighbourhood yesterday. Trying to find her dog Bo. Several people claimed they had seen him only hours before.
2. We sat back to watch the movie. Not expecting anything special. To our surprise, we clapped, cheered, and cried for the next two hours.
3. I telephoned the balloon store. It being the day before our wedding anniversary. I knew my wife would be surprised to receive a dozen heart-shaped balloons.

People sometimes write *-ing* fragments because they think the subject in one sentence will work for the next word group as well. Thus, in the first selection, they think the subject *Ellen* in the opening sentence will also serve as the subject for *Trying to find her dog Bo*. But the subject must actually be *in* the sentence.

How to Correct *-ing* Fragments

1   Attach the fragment to the sentence that comes before or the sentence that comes after it, whichever makes sense. Selection 1 could read: "Ellen walked all over the neighbourhood yesterday trying to find her dog Bo."

2   Add a subject and change the *-ing* verb part to the correct form of the verb. Selection 2 could read: "We didn't expect anything special."

3   Change *being* to the correct form of the verb *be* (*am, are, is, was, were*). Selection 3 could read: "It was the day before our wedding anniversary."

How to Correct *to* Fragments

When *to* appears at or near the start of a word group, a fragment sometimes results:

At the Chinese restaurant, Tim used chopsticks. To impress his date. He spent one hour eating a small bowl of rice.

The second word group is a fragment and can be corrected by adding it to the preceding sentence:

At the Chinese restaurant, Tim used chopsticks to impress his date.

Activity 1

Underline the *-ing* fragment in each of the selections that follow. Then make it a sentence by rewriting it, using the method described in parentheses.

Example   Stepping hard on the accelerator. Stan tried to beat the truck to the intersection. He lost by a hood.
(Add the fragment to the sentence that comes after it.)

Stepping hard on the accelerator, Stan tried to beat the truck

to the intersection.

1.   Marble-sized hailstones fell from the sky. Flattening the young plants in the cornfield. A year's work was lost in an hour.
(Add the fragment to the preceding sentence.)

_____

_____

2. My grandmother, who is seventy, delivers papers by car every morning. Then returning home to make breakfast for my grandfather. She has more energy than I do.
   (Correct the fragment by adding the subject *she* and changing *returning* to the proper form of the verb, *returns*.)

   _____

   _____

3. My phone doesn't ring. Instead, a light on it blinks. The reason for this being that I am partially deaf.
   (Correct the fragment by changing *being* to the proper form of the verb, *is*.)

   _____

   _____

Activity 2

Underline the *-ing* or *to* fragment in each selection. Then rewrite each selection, correcting the fragments by using one of the three methods described above.

1. Flora scratched her mosquito bites. Trying to stop the itching. Instead, they began to bleed.

   _____

   _____

2. I put a box of baking soda in the freezer. To get rid of the musty smell. However, my ice cubes still taste like old socks.

   _____

   _____

3. Staring at the clock on the far wall. I nervously began my speech. I was afraid to look at any of the people in the room.

   _____

   _____

4. Larry sat quietly at his desk. Fantasizing about the upcoming weekend. He might meet the girl of his dreams at Saturday night's party.

   _____

   _____

5. To get to the bus station from here. You have to walk two blocks out of your way. The sidewalk is torn up because of construction work.

_____

_____

ADDED-DETAIL FRAGMENTS

Added-detail fragments lack a subject and a verb. They often begin with one of the following words:

| also | especially | except | for example | including | such as |

Underline the one added-detail fragment in each of the selections that follow:

1. Before a race, I eat starchy food. Such as bread and spaghetti. The carbohydrates provide quick energy.
2. Bob is taking a night course in auto mechanics. Also, one in plumbing. He wants to save money on household repairs.
3. My son keeps several pets in his room. Among them, hamsters, mice, and gerbils.

People often write added-detail fragments for much the same reason they write *-ing* fragments. They think the subject and verb in one sentence will serve for the next word group. But the subject and verb must be in *each* word group.

How to Correct Added-Detail Fragments

1 Attach the fragment to the complete thought that precedes it. Selection 1 could read: "Before a race, I eat starchy foods such as bread and spaghetti."

2 Add a subject and a verb to the fragment to make it a complete sentence. Selection 2 could read: "Bob is taking a night course in auto mechanics. Also, he is taking one in plumbing."

3 Change words as necessary to make the fragment part of the preceding sentence. Selection 3 could read: "My son keeps several pets, including hamsters, mice, and gerbils, in his room."

Underline the fragment in each of the selections on the following page. Then make it a sentence by rewriting it, using the method described in parentheses.

Example   My mother likes watching daytime television shows. Especially old movies and soap operas. She says that daytime television is less violent.
(Add the fragment to the preceding sentence.)

My mother likes watching daytime television shows,

especially old movies and soap operas.

1. Luis works evenings in a video store. He enjoys the fringe benefits. For example, seeing the new movies first.
    (Correct the fragment by adding the subject and verb *he sees*.)

    _____

    _____

2. Bob's fingernails are ragged from years of working as a mechanic. And his fingertips are always black. Like ink pads.
    (Add the fragment to the preceding sentence.)

    _____

    _____

3. Schools are beginning to use advanced technology. For instance, computers and word processors. Tomorrow's students will be "computer literate."
    (Correct the fragment by adding the subject and verb *they are using*.)

    _____

    _____

Activity 2

Underline the added-detail fragment in each selection. Then rewrite to correct the fragment. Use one of the three methods described above.

1. Left-handed students face problems. For example, right-handed desks. Spiral notebooks can also be uncomfortable to use.

    _____

    _____

2. Mrs. Daly always wears her lucky clothes to bingo. Such as a blouse printed with four-leaf clovers. She also carries a rhinestone horseshoe.

    _____

    _____

3. With all the moths swarming around the stadium lights. I almost thought it was snowing. The eighty-degree weather, though, made this unlikely.

_____

_____

4. Jack buys and sells paper collectors' items. For instance, baseball cards and movie posters. He sets up a display at local flea markets and fall fairs.

_____

_____

5. I wonder now why I had to learn certain subjects. Such as geometry. No one has ever asked me about the hypotenuse of a triangle.

_____

_____

MISSING-SUBJECT FRAGMENTS

Underline the word group in which the subject is missing in each selection below.

1. Alice loved getting wedding presents. But hated writing thank-you notes.
2. Mickey has orange pop and potato chips for breakfast. Then eats more junk food, like root beer and cookies, for lunch.

How to Correct Missing-Subject Fragments

1 Attach the fragment to the preceding sentence. Selection 1 could read: "Alice loved getting her wedding presents but hated writing the thank-you notes."

2 Add a subject (which can often be a pronoun standing for the subject in the preceding sentence). Selection 2 could read: "Then he eats more junk food, like root beer and cookies, for lunch."

Activity

Underline the missing-subject fragment in each selection. Then rewrite that part of the selection needed to correct the fragment. Use one of the two methods of correction described above.

1. Every other day, Karen runs two miles. Then does fifty sit-ups. She hasn't lost weight, but what she had has been redistributed.

_____

_____

2. I like all kinds of fresh pizza. But refuse to eat frozen pies. The sauce on them is always dried out, and the crust tastes like leather.

3. Scientists have invented a computerized doctor. It takes every Wednesday off. And plays video golf.

4. To be a defensive driver, you must assume the worst. Every other driver on the road is incompetent. And is out there trying to kill you.

5. Last semester, I took six courses. And worked part-time in a discount drug store. Now that the term is all over, I don't know how I did it.

A Review: How to Check for Sentence Fragments

1 Read your paper aloud from the *last* sentence to the *first*. You will be better able to see and hear whether each word group you read is a complete thought.

2 Ask yourself of any word group you think is a fragment: Does this contain a subject and a verb and express a complete thought?

3 More specifically, be on the lookout for the most common fragments:

- Dependent-word fragments (starting with words like *after*, *because*, *since*, *when*, and *before*)
- *-ing* and *to* fragments (*-ing* or *to* at or near the start of a word group)
- Added-detail fragments (starting with words like *for example*, *such as*, *also*, and *especially*)
- Missing-subject fragments (a verb is present but not the subject)

■ Review Test 1

Each word group in the following student paragraph is numbered. In the space provided, write *C* if a word group is a complete sentence; write *F* if it is a fragment. You will find eight fragments in the paragraph.

1. _____
2. _____
3. _____
4. _____
5. _____
6. _____
7. _____
8. _____
9. _____
10. _____
11. _____
12. _____
13. _____
14. _____
15. _____
16. _____
17. _____
18. _____
19. _____
20. _____

1. ¹I'm starting to think that there is no safe place left. ²To ride a bicycle. ³When I try to ride on the highway, in order to go to school. ⁴I feel like a rabbit being pursued by predators. ⁵Drivers whip past me at high speeds. ⁶And try to see how close they can get to my bike without actually killing me. ⁷When they pull onto the shoulder of the road or make a right turn. ⁸Drivers completely ignore my vehicle. ⁹On city streets, I feel more like a cockroach than a rabbit. ¹⁰Drivers in the city despise bicycles. ¹¹Regardless of an approaching bike rider. ¹²Doors of parked cars will unexpectedly open into the street. ¹³Frustrated drivers who are stuck in traffic will make nasty comments. ¹⁴Or shout out obscene propositions. ¹⁵Even pedestrians in the city show their disregard for me. ¹⁶While jaywalking across the street. ¹⁷The pedestrian will treat me, a law-abiding bicyclist, to a withering look of disdain. ¹⁸Pedestrians may even cross my path deliberately. ¹⁹As if to prove their higher position in the pecking order of the city streets. ²⁰Today, bicycling can be hazardous to the rider's health.

Now (on separate paper) correct the fragments you have found. Attach the fragments to sentences that come before or after them or make whatever other change is needed to turn each fragment into a sentence.

■ Review Test 2

Underline the two fragments in each selection below. Then make whatever changes are needed to turn the fragments into sentences

Example   Sharon was going to charge her new suit. ~~But then decided to pay cash instead.~~ She remembered her New Year's resolution. ~~To cut down on her use of credit cards.~~

1. We both began to tire. As we passed the halfway mark in the race. But whenever I'd hear Reggie's footsteps behind me. I pumped my legs faster.

2. I have a few phobias. Such as fear of heights and fear of dogs. My nightmare is to be trapped in a hot-air balloon. With three German shepherds.

3. My children joke that we celebrate "Hanumas." With our Jewish neighbours. We share Hanukkah and Christmas activities. Including making potato pancakes at their house and decorating our tree.

4. Punching all the buttons on his radio in sequence. Phil kept looking for a good song. He was in the mood to cruise down the highway. And sing at the top of his voice.

5. I noticed two cartons of cigarettes. Sticking up out of my neighbour's trash bag. I realized he had made up his mind. To give up smoking for the fifth time this year.

6. I've decided to leave home. And rent an apartment. By being away from home and on my own. I will get along better with my parents.

7. The alley behind our house was flat. Except for a wide groove in the centre. We used to sail paper boats down the groove. Whenever it rained hard enough to create a "river" there.

8. Don passed the computer school's aptitude test. Which qualifies him for nine months of training. Don kidded that anyone could be accepted. If he or she had four thousand dollars.

■ Review Test 3

Turn each of the following word groups into a complete sentence.

Examples With trembling hands

With trembling hands, I headed for the front of the class-room.

As the race wore on

Some runners dropped out as the race wore on.

1. After the storm passed

_____

2. Such as fresh fruits and vegetables

_____

3. During the mystery movie

_____

4. But soon grew frustrated

_____

5. Norma, who hates housework

_____

6. To get to class on time

_____

7. The ants swarming over the lollipop

_____

8. Hurrying to get dressed

_____

9. Up in the attic

_____

10. Losing my temper

_____

RUN-ONS

WHAT ARE RUN-ONS?

A *run-on* is two complete thoughts that are run together with no adequate sign given to mark the break between them.*

Some run-ons have no punctuation at all to mark the break between the thoughts. Such run-ons are known as *fused sentences:* they are fused or joined together as if they were only one thought.

Fused Sentence
Tim told everyone in the room to be quiet his favourite show was on.

Fused Sentence
My blow-dryer shorted out I showed up for work with Harpo Marx hair.

In other run-ons, known as *comma splices*, a comma is used to connect or "splice" together the two complete thoughts. However, a comma alone is *not enough* to connect two complete thoughts. Some stronger connection than a comma alone is needed.

Comma Splice
Tim told everyone in the room to be quiet, his favourite show was on.

Comma Splice
My blow-dryer shorted out, I showed up for work with Harpo Marx hair.

Comma splices are the most common kind of run-on mistake. Students sense that some kind of connection is needed between two thoughts, and so they often put a comma at the dividing point. But the comma alone is *not sufficient*. A stronger, clearer mark between the two thoughts is needed.

Note: Some instructors refer to each complete thought in a run-on as an *independent clause.* A *clause* is simply a group of words having a subject and a verb. A clause may be *independent* (expressing a complete thought and able to stand alone) or *dependent* (not expressing a complete thought and not able to stand alone). Using this terminology, we'd say that a run-on is two independent clauses run together with no adequate sign given to mark the break between them.

HOW TO CORRECT RUN-ONS

Here are three common methods of correcting a run-on:

1 Use a period and a capital letter to break the two complete thoughts into separate sentences.

Tim told everyone in the room to be quiet. His favourite show was on.

My blow-dryer shorted out. I showed up for work with Harpo Marx hair.

2 Use a comma plus a joining word (*and*, *but*, *for*, *or*, *nor*, *so*, *yet*) to connect the two complete thoughts:

Tim told everyone in the room to be quiet, for his favourite show was on.

My blow-dryer shorted out, and I showed up for work with Harpo Marx hair.

3 Use a semi-colon to connect the two complete thoughts:

Tim told everyone in the room to be quiet; his favourite show was on.

My blow-dryer shorted out; I showed up for work with Harpo Marx hair.

A fourth method of correcting a run-on is to use *subordination*. The following activities will give you practice in the first three methods. Subordination will be described fully on page 462, in a section of the book that deals with sentence variety.

Method 1: Period and a Capital Letter

One way of correcting a run-on is to use a period and a capital letter at the break between the two complete thoughts. Use this method especially if the thoughts are not closely related or if another method would make the sentence too long.

Activity

Locate the split in each of the run-ons on the following page. Each is a *fused sentence*—that is, each consists of two sentences that are fused or joined together with no punctuation at all between them. Reading each sentence aloud will help you "hear" where a major break or split in the thought occurs. At such a point, your voice will probably drop and pause.

Correct the run-on sentence by putting a period at the end of the first thought and a capital letter at the start of the next thought.

Example   Bev's clock radio doesn't work anymore. $\overset{S}{\cancel{s}}$he spilled a glass of pop on it.

1. The telephone salesperson offered a deal on vinyl siding he wanted to drop by and give us a free estimate.

2. Joyce, a paralegal, helps some people to write wills she assists others in divorce and child custody proceedings.

3. Vicky has her own unique style of dressing she wore a man's tuxedo with a red bow tie to her cousin's wedding.

4. Ants are attracted to water in the summer they will often enter a house through the dishwasher.

5. Humans have managed to adapt to any environment they can survive in Arctic wastes, tropical jungles, and barren deserts.

6. A five-year-old child knows more than six thousand words he or she has also learned more than one thousand rules of grammar.

7. I rummaged around the crowded drawer looking for a pair of scissors then it suddenly stabbed me in the finger.

8. Squirrels like to jump from trees onto our roof their footsteps sound like ghosts running around our attic.

9. Today I didn't make good time driving to work every traffic light along the way was red.

10. As a result of a cable hook-up, we now receive over forty stations on our television I sometimes waste an entire evening just clicking from one channel to the next.

A Warning—Words That Can Lead to Run-Ons: People often write run-on sentences when the second complete thought begins with one of the following words:

I	we	there	now
you	they	this	then
he, she, it	that	next	

Remember to be on the alert for run-on sentences whenever you use one of these words in writing a paper.

Method 2: Comma and a Joining Word

Another way of correcting a run-on sentence is to use a comma plus a joining word to connect the two complete thoughts. Joining words (also called *conjunctions*) include *and*, *but*, *for*, *or*, *nor*, *so*, and *yet*. Here is what the four most common joining words mean:

and   in addition to, along with

> Teresa works full-time for an accounting firm, and she takes evening classes.

(*And* means *in addition*: Teresa works full time for an accounting firm; *in addition*, she takes evening classes.)

but   however, except, on the other hand, just the opposite

> I turned to the want ads, but I knew my dream job wouldn't be listed.

(*But* means *however*: I turned to the want ads; *however*, I knew my dream job wouldn't be listed.)

for   because, the reason, the cause for something

> Lizards become sluggish at night, for they need the sun's warmth to maintain an active body temperature.

(*For* means *because* or *the reason*: Lizards become sluggish at night; *the reason* is that they need the sun's warmth to maintain an active body temperature.)

so   as a result, therefore

> The canoe touched bottom, so Dave pushed it towards deeper water.

(*So* means *as a result*: The canoe touched bottom; *as a result*, Dave pushed it towards deeper water.)

Activity 1

Insert the joining word (*and*, *but*, *for*, *so*) that logically connects the two thoughts in each sentence.

1. Napoleon may have been a brave general, _____ he was afraid of cats.

2. The large dog was growling at me, _____ there were white bubbles of foam around his mouth.

3. The library had just closed, _____ I couldn't get any of the reserved books.

4. He checked on the new baby every five minutes, _____ he was afraid something would happen to her.

5. Kate thought the milk was fresh, _____ it broke up into little sour flakes in her coffee.

6. An infant elephant has no thumbs, _____ it sucks its trunk.

7. Lew heard a noise and looked out the window, _____ the only thing there was his reflection.

8. Have you noticed that one of our English teacher's eyes is green, _____ the other is brown?

9. My sister saves all her empty wine bottles, _____ she likes to make lamps out of them.

10. A young woman in our neighbourhood recently tried to kill herself, _____ her friends are afraid that she will try it again.

Activity 2

Add a complete and closely related thought to go with each of the following statements. Use a comma plus the italicized joining word when you write the second thought.

Example   *for*   I decided to leave school an hour early, _for I had a_
pounding headache.

but   1. The corner store is convenient _____

_____

for   2. Leo attended night class _____

_____

and   3. Brenda studied for an hour before dinner _____

_____

so   4. Our field trip had been cancelled _____

_____

but   5. I needed a haircut _____

_____

Activity 3

Correct each run-on with either (1) a period and a capital letter or (2) a comma and a logical joining word. Do not use the same method of correction for every sentence.

You will notice that some of the run-ons are fused sentences (there is no punctuation between the two complete thoughts) and some are comma splices (there is only a comma between the two complete thoughts). One sentence is correct.

Example   There was a strange odour in the house, ^SO^ Burt called the gas company immediately.

1. Jackie smeared cream cheese on the bagel half, then she popped it into her mouth.

2. Cockroaches adapt to any environment they have even been found living inside nuclear reactors.

3. My dog was panting from the heat I decided to wet him down with the garden hose.

4. The college installed a dish antenna outside the science building it picks up satellite broadcasting from all over the world.

5. The best-selling items in the zoo gift shop are the stuffed pandas and the polar bear T-shirts the profits from these items help support the real animals in the zoo.

6. The bristles of the paintbrushes were very stiff, soaking them in turpentine made them soft again.

7. Tran bought cassettes to listen to on the way to work, some of them were recordings of best-selling books.

8. Last week, Rita's two boys chased the baby-sitter out of the house, now the girl won't come back.

9. We knew there had been a power failure, for all the clocks in the building were forty-seven minutes slow.

10. I volunteered to run the "Meals on Wheels" service in our city we deliver hot meals to sick or housebound people.

Method 3: Semi-Colon

A third method of correcting a run-on sentence is to use a semi-colon to mark the break between two thoughts. A *semi-colon* (;) looks like a period above a comma and is sometimes called a *strong comma*. A semi-colon signals more of a pause than a comma alone but not quite the full pause of a period. When it is used to correct run-on sentences, the semi-colon can be used alone or with a transitional word.

Semi-Colon Alone: Here are some earlier sentences that were connected with a comma plus a joining word. Now they are connected by a semi-colon alone. Notice that the semi-colon alone—unlike the comma alone—can be used to connect the two complete thoughts in each sentence:

> There had been a huge power failure; every house on the street was dark.
>
> Lew heard a noise and looked out the window; the only thing there was his reflection.
>
> He checked on the new baby every five minutes; he was afraid something would happen to her.
>
> Lizards become sluggish at night; they need the sun's warmth to maintain an active body temperature.
>
> The large dog was growling at me; there were white bubbles of foam around its mouth.

Using the semi-colon can add to sentence variety. For some people, however, the semi-colon is a confusing mark of punctuation. Keep in mind that if you are not comfortable using it, you can and should use one of the first two methods of correcting a run-on sentence.

Activity

Insert a semi-colon where the break occurs between the two complete thoughts in each of the following sentences.

Example   The plumber gave me an estimate of sixty dollars; I decided to repair the faucet myself.

1. The children stared at the artichokes on their plates they didn't know how to eat the strange vegetable.

2. I changed that light bulb just last week now it's blown again.

3. The "no-frills" supermarket doesn't sell perishables like milk or meat customers must bring their own bags or boxes to pack their bargains.

4. Elaine woke up at 3 a.m. to the smell of sizzling bacon her husband was having another insomnia attack.

5. Jamie curled up under the covers she tried to get warm by grasping her icy feet with her chilly hands.

6. Three single mothers rent one house they share bills and help each other out.

7. Ice had formed on the inside edge of our window Joey scratched a *J* in it with his finger.

8. Charles peered into the microscope he saw only his own eyelashes.

9. Guests were laughing and drinking at the party my uncle was doing his John Wayne imitation.

10. I angrily punched a hole in the wall with my fist later I covered the hole with a picture.

Semi-Colon with a Transitional Word   A semi-colon is sometimes used with a transitional word and a comma to join two complete thoughts. Here are some examples:

Larry believes in being prepared for emergencies; therefore, he stockpiles canned goods in his basement.

I tried to cash my paycheque; however, I had forgotten to bring identification.

Athletic shoes must fit perfectly; otherwise, the wearer may injure the feet or ankles.

A short nap at the end of the day relaxes me; in addition, it gives me the energy to spend the evening on my homework.

Some zoo animals have not learned how to be good parents; as a result, baby animals are sometimes brought up in zoo nurseries and even in private homes.

People use seventeen muscles when they smile; on the other hand, they use forty-three muscles when they frown.

On the following page is a list of common transitional words (also known as *adverbial conjunctions*), with brief meanings.

Transitional Word	*Meaning*
however	but
nevertheless	however
on the other hand	however
instead	as a substitute
meanwhile	in the intervening time
otherwise	under other conditions
indeed	in fact
in addition	also, and
also	in addition
moreover	in addition
furthermore	in addition
as a result	thus, therefore
thus	as a result
consequently	as a result
therefore	as a result

Activity

For each sentence, choose a logical transitional word from the group in the box above and write it in the space provided. Put a semi-colon *before* the connector and a comma *after* it.

I dread going to parties; <u>however</u> , my husband loves meeting new people.

1. Jackie suffers from migraine headaches _____ her doctor has advised her to avoid caffeine and alcohol.

2. Ray's apartment is always neat and clean _____ the interior of his car looks like the aftermath of a tornado.

3. I try to attend all my math classes _____ I'll get too far behind to pass the weekly quizzes.

4. Dan was singing Celine Dion tunes in the shower _____ his toast was burning in the kitchen.

5. The reporter was tough and experienced _____ even he was stunned by the tragic events.

A Note on Subordination

A fourth method of joining related thoughts together is to use subordination. *Subordination* is a way of showing that one thought in a sentence is not as important as another thought. (Subordination is explained in full on page 462.) Here are three earlier sentences, recast so that one idea is subordinated to (made less important than) the other idea:

Because the library had just closed, I couldn't get any of the reserved books.

When the canoe touched bottom, Dave pushed the craft towards deeper water.

I didn't make good time driving to work today, because every traffic light was red.

A Review: How to Check for Run-On Sentences

1 To see if a sentence is a run-on, read it aloud and listen for a break marking two complete thoughts. Your voice will probably drop and pause at the break.

2 To check an entire paper, read it aloud from the *last* sentence to the *first*. Doing so will help you hear and see each complete thought.

3 Be on the lookout for words that can lead to run-on sentences:

| I | he, she, it | they | this | then |
| you | we | there | that | next |

4 Correct run-on sentences by using one of the following methods:

- A period and a capital letter
- A comma and a joining word (*and*, *but*, *for*, *or*, *nor*, *so*, *yet*)
- A semi-colon
- Subordination (as explained on page 462)

■ Review Test 1

Correct each run-on with either (1) a period and a capital letter or (2) a comma (if needed) and the joining word *and*, *but*, *for*, or *so*. Do not use the same method of correction for every sentence.

Some of the run-ons are fused sentences (there is no punctuation between the two complete thoughts) and some are comma splices (there is only a comma between the two complete thoughts). One sentence is correct.

1. Our boss expects us to work four hours without a break, he wanders off to a vending machine at least once an hour.
2. By late afternoon the bank had closed its front doors for the day I moved my car into a long line waiting to use the bank's drive-in window.
3. Chuck bent over and lifted the heavy tray then he heard an ominous crack in his back.
4. The branches of the tree were bare they made a dark feathery pattern against the orange-pink sunset.
5. In the grimy bakery window, cobwebs were in every corner, a rat was crawling over a birthday cake.
6. Our class wanted to do something for the earthquake victims, we sent a donation to the Red Cross.
7. My ex-husband hit me just once in our marriage five minutes later I was packed and walking out the door.
8. The boys dared each other to enter the abandoned building then they heard a strange rustling noise coming from the murky interior.
9. The average Canadian teenager spends thirty-eight hours a week on schoolwork the average Japanese teenager spends about sixty.
10. We stocked our backpacks with high-calorie candy bars, and we also brought bags of dried apricots and peaches.

■ Review Test 2

Correct each run-on by using either (1) a period and a capital letter, (2) a comma and a joining word, or (3) a semi-colon. Do not use one method exclusively.

1. The magazine had lain in the damp mailbox for two days its pages were blurry and swollen.
2. With a groan, Margo pried off her high heels, then she plunged her swollen feet into a bucket of baking soda and hot water.
3. At 2 a.m. the last customer left the coffee shop, a busser began stacking chairs on the tables for the night.

4. Hypnosis has nothing to do with the occult it is merely a state of deep relaxation.

5. Many young adults today live at home with their parents this allows them to save money for the future.

6. I waited for the clanking train to clear the intersection rusty boxcars just kept rolling slowly along the rails.

7. Science will soon produce tomatoes that are more nutritious, they will also be square-shaped for easier packing.

8. Originally, horses were too small to carry riders very far larger horses had to be bred for use in warfare.

9. Suitcases circled on the conveyor belt at the airline baggage claim loose oranges from a broken carton tumbled along with them.

10. The broken pop machine dispensed either a cup or pop, it would not provide both at the same time.

■ Review Test 3

Locate and correct the five run-ons in the passage that follows.

My worst experience of the week was going home for lunch, rather than eating at work. My children didn't know I was coming, they had used most of the bread on hand. All I had to make a sandwich with were two thin, crumpled pieces of crust. I sat there eating my tattered sandwich and trying to relax, then the telephone rang. It was for my daughter, who was in the bathroom, she called down to me that I should get the person's name and number. As soon as I sat down again, someone knocked on the door, it was a neatly dressed couple with bright eyes who wanted to talk with me about a higher power in life. I politely got rid of them and went back to finish lunch. I thought I would relax over my coffee I had to break up a fight between my two young sons about which television channel to watch. As a last bit of frustration, my daughter came downstairs and asked me to drive her over to a friend's house before I went back to work.

■ Review Test 4

Write quickly for five minutes about what you did this past weekend. Don't worry about spelling, punctuation, finding exact words, or organizing your thoughts. Just focus on writing as many words as you can without stopping.

After you have finished, go back and correct any run-ons in your writing.

REGULAR AND IRREGULAR VERBS

REGULAR VERBS

A Brief Review of Regular Verbs

Every verb has four principal parts: *present*, *past*, *past participle*, and *present participle*. These parts can be used to build all the verb tenses (the times shown by a verb).

Most verbs in English are regular. The past and past participles of a regular verb are formed by adding *-d* or *-ed* to the present. The *past participle* is the form of the verb used with the helping verbs *have*, *has*, or *had* (or some form of *be* with passive verbs). The *present participle* is formed by adding *-ing* to the present.

Here are the principal parts of some regular verbs:

Present	Past	Past Participle	Present Participle
shout	shouted	shouted	shouting
prepare	prepared	prepared	preparing
surprise	surprised	surprised	surprising
tease	teased	teased	teasing
frighten	frightened	frightened	frightening

Nonstandard Forms of Regular Verbs

Many people have grown up in communities where nonstandard forms of regular verbs are used in everyday speech. Instead of saying, for example, "That girl *looks* tired," a person using a community dialect might say, "That girl *look* tired." Instead of saying, "Yesterday I *fixed* the car," a person using a community dialect might say, "Yesterday I *fix* the car." Community dialects have richness and power but are a drawback in college and in the world of work, where regular English verb forms must be used.

The chart below compares the nonstandard and the regular verb forms of the verb *work*.

Nonstandard Verb Form (Do not use in your writing)		*Regular Verb Form* (Use for clear communication)	
Present tense			
I works	we works	I work	we work
you works	you works	you work	you work
he, she, it work	they work	he, she, it works	they work
Past tense			
I work	we work	I worked	we worked
you work	you work	you worked	you worked
he, she, it work	they work	he, she, it worked	they worked

To avoid nonstandard usage, memorize the forms shown above for the regular verb *work*. Then use the activities that follow to help make the inclusion of verb endings a writing habit.

Present Tense Endings: The verb ending *-s* or *-es* is needed with a regular verb in the present tense when the subject is *he, she, it*, or any *one person or thing*.

He reads every night.

She watches television every night.

It appears they have little in common.

Activity

Some verbs in the sentences that follow need -*s* or -*es* endings. Cross out each nonstandard verb form and write the standard form in the space provided.

_____ 1. My radio wake me up every morning with soft music.

_____ 2. Lyle always clown around at the start of the class.

_____ 3. My wife watch our baby in the morning, and I take over afternoons.

_____ 4. Mark want to go to nursing school next year.

_____ 5. My brain work much better at night than it does in early morning.

Past Tense Endings: The verb ending -*d* or -*ed* is needed with a regular verb in the past tense.

> This morning I completed my research paper.
> The recovering hospital patient walked slowly down the corridor.
> Some students hissed when the new assignment was given out.

Activity

Some verbs in the sentences that follow need -*d* or -*ed* endings. Cross out each nonstandard verb form and write the standard form in the space provided.

_____ 1. One of my teeth cave in when I bit on the hard pretzel.

_____ 2. The accident victim complain of dizziness right before passing out.

_____ 3. We realize a package was missing when we got back from shopping.

_____ 4. I burn a hole in my shirt while ironing it.

_____ 5. The impatient driver edge her car into the intersection while the light was still red.

IRREGULAR VERBS

Irregular verbs have irregular forms in the past tense and past participle. For example, the past tense of the irregular verb *choose* is *chose;* its past participle is *chosen.*

Almost everyone has some degree of trouble with irregular verbs. When you are unsure about the form of a verb, you can check the list of irregular verbs on the following pages. (The present participle is not shown on this list because it is formed simply by adding -*ing* to the base form of the verb.) Or you can check a dictionary, which gives the principal parts of irregular verbs.

A List of Irregular Verbs

Present	Past	Past Participle
arise	arose	arisen
awake	awoke *or* awaked	awoken *or* awaked
be (am, are, is)	was (were)	been
become	became	become
begin	began	begun
bend	bent	bent
bite	bit	bitten
blow	blew	blown
break	broke	broken
bring	brought	brought
build	built	built
burst	burst	burst
buy	bought	bought
catch	caught	caught
choose	chose	chosen
come	came	come
cost	cost	cost
cut	cut	cut
do (does)	did	done
draw	drew	drawn
drink	drank	drunk
drive	drove	driven
eat	ate	eaten
fall	fell	fallen
feed	fed	fed
feel	felt	felt
fight	fought	fought
find	found	found
fly	flew	flown
freeze	froze	frozen
get	got	got *or* gotten
give	gave	given
go (goes)	went	gone
grow	grew	grown
have (has)	had	had
hear	heard	heard
hide	hid	hidden
hold	held	held
hurt	hurt	hurt

Present	*Past*	*Past Participle*
keep	kept	kept
know	knew	known
lay	laid	laid
lead	led	led
leave	left	left
lend	lent	lent
let	let	let
lie	lay	lain
light	lit	lit
lose	lost	lost
make	made	made
meet	met	met
pay	paid	paid
ride	rode	ridden
ring	rang	rung
run	ran	run
say	said	said
see	saw	seen
sell	sold	sold
send	sent	sent
shake	shook	shaken
shrink	shrank	shrunk
shut	shut	shut
sing	sang	sung
sit	sat	sat
sleep	slept	slept
speak	spoke	spoken
spend	spent	spent
stand	stood	stood
steal	stole	stolen
stick	stuck	stuck
sting	stung	stung
swear	swore	sworn
swim	swam	swum
take	took	taken
teach	taught	taught
tear	tore	torn
tell	told	told
think	thought	thought
wake	woke *or* waked	woken *or* waked

Present	Past	Past Participle
wear	wore	worn
win	won	won
write	wrote	written

Activity

Cross out the incorrect verb form in each of the following sentences. Then write the correct form of the verb in the space provided.

flown

Example   After it had ~~flew~~ into the picture window, the dazed bird huddled on the ground.

1. As graduation neared, Michelle worried about the practicality of the major she'd chose.

2. Before we could find seats, the theatre darkened and the opening credits begun to roll.

3. To be polite, I drunk the slightly sour wine that my grandfather poured from his carefully hoarded supply.

4. With a thunderous crack, the telephone pole breaked in half from the impact of the speeding car.

5. The inexperienced nurse shrunk from touching the patient's raw, burned skin.

6. After a day on the noisy construction site, Sam's ears rung for hours with a steady hum.

7. Sheila had forgot to write her Social Insurance Number on the test form, so the computer rejected her answer sheet.

8. If I had went to work ten minutes earlier, I would have avoided being caught in the gigantic traffic snarl.

9. After the bicycle hit a patch of soft sand, the rider was throwed into the thorny bushes by the roadside.

10. Prehistoric people blowed paint over their outstretched hands to stencil their handprints on cave walls.

Nonstandard Forms of Three Common Irregular Verbs

People who use nonstandard forms of regular verbs also tend to use nonstandard forms of three common irregular verbs: _be_, _have_, and _do_. Instead of saying, for example, "My neighbours _are_ nice people," a person using a nonstandard form might say, "Our neighbours _be_ nice people." Instead of saying, "She doesn't agree," they might say, "She *don't* agree." Instead of saying, "We have tickets," they might say, "We *has* tickets."

The following charts compare the nonstandard and the standard forms of *be*, *have*, and *do*.

Be

Dialect Form (Do not use in your writing)		Standard English (Use for clear communication)	
Present tense			
I be (*or* is)	we be	I am	we are
you be	you be	you are	you are
he, she, it be	they be	he, she, it is	they are
Past tense			
I were	we was	I was	we were
you was	you was	you were	you were
he, she, it were	they was	he, she, it was	they were

Have

Dialect Form (Do not use in your writing)		Standard English (Use for clear communication)	
Present tense			
I has	we has	I have	we have
you has	you has	you have	you have
he, she, it have	they has	he, she, it has	they have
Past tense			
I has	we has	I had	we had
you has	you has	you had	you had
he, she, it have	they has	he, she, it had	they had

Do

Dialect Form		Standard English	
(Do not use in your writing)		(Use for clear communication)	
Present tense			
I does	we do	I do	we do
you does	you does	you do	you do
he, she, it do	they does	he, she, it does	they do
Past tense			
I done	we done	I did	we did
you done	you done	you did	you did
he, she, it done	they done	he, she, it did	they did

Note: Many people have trouble with one negative form of *do*. They will say, for example, "She don't agree" instead of "She doesn't agree," or they will say "The door don't work" instead of "The door doesn't work." Be careful to avoid the common mistake of using *don't* instead of *doesn't*.

Activity

Cross out the nonstandard verb form in each sentence. Then write the standard form of *be*, *have*, or *do* in the space provided.

_____ 1. My cat, Tugger, be the toughest animal I know.

_____ 2. He have survived many close calls.

_____ 3. Three years ago, he were caught inside a car's engine.

_____ 4. He have one ear torn off and lost the sight in one eye.

_____ 5. We was surprised that he lived through the accident.

_____ 6. Within weeks, though, he were back to normal.

_____ 7. Then, last year, we was worried that we would lose Tugger.

_____ 8. Lumps that was growing on his back turned out to be cancer.

_____ 9. But the vet done an operation that saved Tugger's life.

_____ 10. By now, we know that Tugger really do have nine lives.

■ **Review Test 1**

Cross out the incorrect verb form in each sentence. Then write the correct form in the space provided.

_____ 1. The health inspectors walk into the kitchen as the cook was picking up a hamburger off the floor.

_____ 2. The thieves would have stole my stereo, but I had had it engraved with a special identification number.

_____ 3. At the Chinese restaurant, Dave choose his food by the number.

_____ 4. He had tore his girl-friend's picture into little pieces and tossed them out the window.

_____ 5. Because I has asthma, I carry an inhaler to use when I lose my breath.

_____ 6. Baked potatoes doesn't have as many calories as I thought.

_____ 7. The grizzly bear, with the dart dangling from its side, begun to feel the effects of the powerful tranquillizer.

_____ 8. Yesterday I check my bank balance and saw my money was getting low.

_____ 9. Many childhood diseases has almost vanished in Canada.

_____ 10. Nancy sticked notes on the refrigerator with fruit-shaped magnets.

■ **Review Test 2**

Write short sentences that use the form requested for the following verbs.

Example Past of grow _I grew my own tomatoes last year._

1. Past of *know* _____

2. Present of *take* _____

3. Past participle of *give* _____

4. Past participle of *write* _____

5. Past of *do* _____

6. Past of *talk* _____

7. Present of *begin* _____

8. Past of *go* _____

9. Past participle of *see* _____

10. Present of *drive* _____

SUBJECT-VERB AGREEMENT

A verb must agree with its subject in number. A *singular subject* (one person or thing) takes a singular verb. A *plural subject* (more than one person or thing) takes a plural verb. Mistakes in subject-verb agreement are sometimes made in the following situations:

1 When words come between the subject and the verb
2 When a verb comes before the subject
3 With compound subjects
4 With indefinite pronouns

Each of these situations is explained on the following pages.

WORDS BETWEEN SUBJECT AND VERB

Words that come between the subject and the verb do not change subject-verb agreement. In the sentence

The crinkly <u>lines</u> *around Joan's eyes* <u>give</u> her a friendly look.

the subject (*lines*) is plural and so the verb (*give*) is plural. The words *around Joan's eyes* that come between the subject and the verb do not affect subject-verb agreement.

To help find the subject of certain sentences, you should cross out prepositional phrases.

The lumpy <u>salt</u> ~~in the shakers~~ <u>needs</u> to be changed.

An old <u>television</u> ~~with a round screen~~ <u>has sat</u> in our basement for years.

Activity

Underline the subject and lightly cross out any words that come between the subject and the verb. Then double-underline the verb choice in parentheses that you believe is correct.

1. Some members of the parents' association (want, wants) to ban certain books from the school library.

2. The rising costs of necessities like food and shelter (force, forces) many elderly people to live in poverty.

3. Misconceptions about apes like the gorilla (has, have) turned a relatively peaceful animal into a terrifying monster.

4. Chuck's trench coat, with its big lapels and shoulder flaps, (make, makes) him feel like a tough private eye.

5. The high-pressure salesclerks in the designer dresses department (make, makes) me feel intimidated.

VERB BEFORE SUBJECT

A verb agrees with its subject even when the verb comes *before* the subject. Words that may precede the subject include *there*, *here*, and, in questions, *who*, *which*, *what*, and *where*.

Here are some examples of verb before subject:

There <u>are</u> wild <u>dogs</u> in our neighbourhood.
In the distance <u>was</u> a <u>billow</u> of black smoke.
Here <u>is</u> the <u>newspaper</u>.
Where <u>are</u> the children's <u>coats</u>?

If you are unsure about the subject, ask *who* or *what* of the verb. With the first example above, you might ask, "*What are* in our neighbourhood?" The answer, *wild dogs*, is the subject.

Activity

Write the correct form of the verb in the space provided.

(is, are) 1. There _____ dozens of frenzied shoppers waiting for the store to open.

(is, are) 2. Here _____ the notes from yesterday's anthropology lecture.

(do, does) 3. When _____ we take our break?

(was, were) 4. There _____ scraps of yellowing paper stuck between the pages of the book.

(was, were) 5. At the very bottom of the grocery list _____ an item that meant a trip all the way back to aisle 1.

COMPOUND SUBJECTS

Subjects joined by *and* generally take a plural verb.

A patchwork <u>quilt</u> and a sleeping <u>bag</u> <u>cover</u> my bed in the winter.
<u>Clark</u> and <u>Lois</u> <u>are</u> a contented couple.

When subjects are joined by *either ... or, neither ... nor, not only ... but also*, the verb agrees with the subject closer to the verb.

Neither the government negotiator nor the union <u>leaders</u> <u>want</u> the strike to continue.

The nearer subject, *leaders*, is plural, and so the verb is plural.

Activity

Write the correct form of the verb in the space provided.

(sit, sits)   1. A crusty baking pan and a greasy plate _____ on the countertop.

(cover, covers)   2. Spidery cracks and a layer of dust _____ the ivory keys on the old piano.

(know, knows)   3. Not only the assistant manager but also the secretaries _____ that the company is folding.

(was, were)   4. In eighteenth-century France, makeup and high heels _____ worn by men.

(make, makes)   5. For women, a dark suit or dress and a pair of plain, closed shoes _____ the best impression at a job interview.

INDEFINITE PRONOUNS

The following words, known as *indefinite pronouns*, always take singular verbs:

(*-one* words)	(*-body* words)	(*-thing* words)	
one	nobody	nothing	each
anyone	anybody	anything	either
everyone	everybody	everything	neither
someone	somebody	something	

Note: *Both* always takes a plural verb.

Activity

Write the correct form of the verb in the space provided.

(suit, suits)   1. Neither of those hairstyles _____ the shape of your face.

(mention, mentions)   2. Somebody without much sensitivity always _____ my birthmark.

(give, gives)   3. Something in certain kinds of aged cheese _____ me a headache.

(enter, enters) 4. Everyone _____ the college kite-flying contest in the spring.

(fall, falls) 5. One of these earrings constantly _____ off my ear.

■ Review Test 1

In the space provided, write the correct form of the verb shown in the margin.

(is, are) 1. Some wheelchair-bound patients, as a result of a successful experiment,
_____ using trained monkeys as helpers.

(was, were) 2. Each of their children _____ given a name picked at random from a page of the Bible.

(seem, seems) 3. Many of the headlines in the tabloids _____ hard to believe.

(is, are) 4. Envelopes, file folders, and a telephone book _____ jammed into Karen's kitchen drawers.

(contains, contain) 5. Neither of the textbooks _____ the answer to question 5 of the "open-book" exam.

(damage, damages) 6. The use of metal chains and studded tires _____ roadways by chipping away at the paved surface.

(was, were) 7. Next to the cash register _____ a can for donations to the animal protection society.

(makes, make) 8. A metal grab bar bolted onto the tiles _____ it easier for elderly people to get in and out of the bathtub.

(cleans, clean) 9. In exchange for a reduced rent, Karla and James _____ the dentist's office beneath their second-floor apartment.

(is, are) 10. One of the hospital's delivery rooms _____ furnished with bright carpets and curtains to resemble a room at home.

■ Review Test 2

Cross out the incorrect verb form in each sentence. In addition, underline the subject or subjects that go with the verb. Then write the correct form of the verb in the space provided.

_____ 1. Why is Martha and her mother digging a hole in their garden so late at night?

_____ 2. Neither of my children look like me.

_____   3. Several packages and a supermarket flyer was lying on the porch mat.

_____   4. The little balls all over my pink sweater looks like woollen goose bumps.

_____   5. Here is the low-calorie cola and the double-chocolate cake you ordered.

_____   6. The odour of those perfumed ads interfere with my enjoyment of a magazine

_____   7. One of my room-mates are always leaving wet towels on the bathroom floor.

_____   8. A tiny piece of gum and some tape is holding my old glasses together.

_____   9. People in their forties often begins to think about making a contribution to the world and not just about their own well-being.

_____ 10. Each of the players on the school's teams plan to give a uniform shirt to the charity auction.

■ Review Test 3

Complete each of the following sentences using *is*, *are*, *was*, *were*, *have*, or *has*. Then underline the subject.

Example   For me, <u>popcorn</u> at the movies   _is like coffee at breakfast._

1. Under my room-mate's bed _____

2. The car with the purple fenders _____

3. My boss and her secretary _____

4. Neither of the football players _____

5. Here are _____

CONSISTENT VERB TENSE

Do not shift verb tenses unnecessarily. If you begin writing a paper in the present tense, do not shift suddenly to the past. If you begin in the past, do not shift without reason to the present. Notice the inconsistent verb tenses in the following selection:

> Jean *punched* down the risen yeast dough in the bowl. Then she *dumps* it onto the floured worktable and *kneaded* it into a smooth, shiny ball.

The verbs must be consistently in the present tense:

> Jean *punches* down the risen yeast dough in the bowl. Then she *dumps* it onto the floured worktable and *kneads* it into a smooth, shiny ball.

Or the verbs must be consistently in the past tense:

> Jean *punched* down the risen yeast dough in the bowl. Then she *dumped* it onto the floured worktable and *kneaded* it into a smooth, shiny ball.

Activity

Make the verbs in each sentence consistent with the *first* verb used. Cross out the incorrect verb and write the correct form in the space at the left.

ran   **Example**   Aunt Helen tried to kiss her little nephew, but he ~~runs~~ out of the room.

_____ 1. An aggressive news photographer knocked a reporter to the ground as the stars arrive for the Genie awards.

_____ 2. As we leafed through the old high school yearbook, we laugh at our outdated clothes and hairstyles.

_____ 3. "My husband is so dumb," said Martha, "that when he went to Monte Carlo he tries to play the stamp machines."

_____ 4. In a zero-gravity atmosphere, water breaks up into droplets and floated around in space.

_____ 5. Elliot lights the oven pilot and then stands back as the blue gas flames flared up.

■ Review Test 1

Make the verbs in each selection consistent with the *first* verb used. Cross out each incorrect verb and write the correct form in the space at the left.

recharge   **Example**   Several times a year, I like to take a day off, go away by myself, and ~~recharged~~ my mental batteries.

_____ 1. Shampooing the plaid sofa upholstery, he was shocked as the colours fade before his eyes.

_____ 2. The jeep swerved around the corner, went up on two wheels, and tips over on its side.

_____ 3. On the TV commercial for mail-order kitchen knives, an actor cuts a tree branch in half and sliced an aluminum can into ribbons.

_____ 4. Ralph ripped open the bag of cheese puffs with his teeth and stuffs handfuls of the salty orange squiggles into his mouth.

_____ 5. The winning wheelchair racer in the marathon slumped back in exhaustion and asks for some ice to soothe his blistered hands.

_____ 6. From his perch high up on the rocky cliff, the eagle spots a white-tailed rabbit and swooped down towards his victim.

_____ 7. Earl wets his fingers and skimmed the rim of his water glass, producing an eerie whistling noise.

_____ 8. When the great earthquake struck Lisbon in 1755, thirty thousand people perish in less than twenty-four hours.

_____ 9. Exploring the cloudy pond, the students collected a jar of tadpoles and gather some aquatic plants to grow in the school aquarium.

_____ 10. After the first Russian satellite was launched in 1957, North American schools gear up their science programs to compete in the space race.

■ **Review Test 2**

Change verbs where needed in the following selection so that they are consistently in the past tense. Cross out each incorrect verb and write the correct form above it, as shown in the example. You will need to make ten corrections.

My uncle's shopping trip last Thursday was discouraging to him. First of all, he had to drive around for fifteen minutes until he ~~finds~~ _found_ a parking space. There was a half-price special on paper products in the supermarket, and every spot is taken. Then, when he finally got inside, many of the items on his list were not where he expected. For example, the pickles he wanted are not on the same shelf as all the other pickles. Instead, they were in a refrigerated case next to the bacon. And the granola was not on the cereal shelves, but in the health food section. Shopping thus proceeds slowly. About halfway through his list, he knew there would not be time to cook dinner and decides to pick up a barbecued chicken. The chicken, he learned, was available at the end of the store he had already passed. So he parks his shopping cart in an aisle, gets the chicken, and came back. After adding half a dozen more items to his cart, he suddenly realizes it contained someone else's food. So he retraced his steps, found his own cart, transfers the groceries, and continued to shop. Later, when he began loading items onto the check-out counter, he notices that the barbecued chicken was missing. He must have left it in the other cart, certainly gone by now. Feeling totally defeated, he returned to the deli counter and says to the clerk, "Give me another chicken. I lost the first one." My uncle told me that when he saw the look on the clerk's face, he felt as if he'd flunked Shop-O-Rama.

ADDITIONAL INFORMATION ABOUT VERBS

The purpose of this special section is to provide additional information about verbs. Some people will find the grammar terms here a helpful reminder of earlier school learning about verbs. For them, the terms will increase their understanding of how verbs function in English. Other people may welcome more detailed information about terms used elsewhere in the text. In either case, remember that the most common mistakes that people make when writing verbs have been treated in earlier sections of the book.

VERB TENSE

Verbs tell us the time of an action. The time that a verb shows is usually called *tense*. The most common tenses are the simple present, past, and future. In addition, there are nine other tenses that enable us to express more specific ideas about time than we could with the simple tenses alone. Shown on the next page are the twelve verb tenses and examples of each tense. Read them over to increase your sense of the many different ways of expressing time in English.

Tenses	*Examples*
Present	I *work*.
	Tony *works*.
Past	Ellen *worked* on her car.
Future	You *will work* on a new project next week.
Present perfect	He *has worked* on his term paper for a month.
	They *have worked* out a compromise.
Past perfect	The nurse *had worked* two straight shifts.
Future perfect	Next Monday, I *will have worked* here exactly two years.
Present progressive	I *am working* on my speech for the debate.
	You *are working* too hard.
	The tape recorder *is* not *working* properly.
Past progressive	He *was working* in the basement.
	The contestants *were working* on their talent routines.
Future progressive	My son *will be working* in our store this summer.
Present perfect progressive	Sarah *has been working* late this week.
Past perfect progressive	Until recently, I *had been working* nights.
Future perfect progressive	My mother *will have been working* as a nurse for forty-five years by the time she retires.

Activity

On separate paper, write twelve sentences using the twelve verb tenses.

HELPING VERBS

There are three common verbs that can either stand alone or combine with (and "help") other verbs. Here are the verbs and their forms:

be (am, are, is, was, were, being, been)
have (has, having, had)
do (does, did)

Here are examples of the verbs:

Used Alone
I *was* angry.
Sue *has* the key.
He *did* well in the test.

Used as Helping Verbs
I *was growing* angry.
Sue *has forgotten* the key.
He *did fail* the previous test.

There are nine helping verbs (traditionally known as *modals*, or *modal auxiliaries*) that are always used in combination with other verbs. Here are the nine verbs and sentence examples of each:

can	I *can see* the rainbow.
could	I *could* not *find* a seat.
may	The game *may be postponed.*
might	Cindy *might resent* your advice.
shall	I *shall see* you tomorrow.
should	He *should get* his car serviced.
will	Tony *will want* to see you.
would	They *would* not *understand.*
must	You *must visit* us again.

Note from the examples that these verbs have only one form. They do not, for instance, add an *-s* when used with *he, she, it*, or any one person or thing.

Activity

On separate paper, write nine sentences using the nine helping verbs.

VERBALS

Verbals are words formed from verbs. Verbals, like verbs, often express action. They can add variety to your sentences and vigour to your writing style. The three kinds of verbals are *infinitives, participles*, and *gerunds*.

Infinitive

An infinitive is *to* plus the base form of the verb.

I love *to dance.*

Lina hopes *to write* for a newspaper.

I asked the children *to clean* the kitchen.

Participle

A participle is a verb form used as an adjective (a descriptive word). The present participle ends in *-ing*. The past participle ends in *-ed* or has an irregular ending.

Peering into the cracked mirror, the *crying* woman wiped her eyes.
The *astounded* man stared at his *winning* lottery ticket.
Swinging a sharp axe, Bob split the *rotted* beam.

Gerund

A gerund is the *-ing* form of a verb used as a noun.

Swimming is the perfect exercise.
Eating junk food is my diet downfall.
Through *doodling*, people express their inner feelings.

Activity

On separate paper, write three sentences using infinitives, three sentences using participles, and three sentences using gerunds.

ACTIVE AND PASSIVE VERBS

When the subject of a sentence performs the action of a verb, the verb is in the *active voice*. When the subject of a sentence receives the action of a verb, the verb is in the *passive voice*.

The passive form of a verb consists of a form of the verb *be* plus the past participle of the main verb. Look at the active and passive forms of the verbs below and on the next page:

Active	*Passive*
Jan *sewed* the curtains. (The subject, *Jan*, is the doer of the action.)	The curtains *were sewn* by Jan. (The subject, *curtains*, does not act. Instead, something happens to them.)
The technician *fixed* the air conditioner. (The subject, *technician*, is the doer of the action.)	The air conditioner *was fixed* by the technician. (The subject, *air conditioner*, does not act. Instead, something happens to it.)

In general, active verbs are more effective than passive ones. Active verbs give your writing a simpler and more vigorous style. At times, however, the passive form of verbs is appropriate when the performer of the action is unknown or is less important than the receiver of the action. For example:

The tests were graded yesterday.
(The performer of the action is unknown.)

Alan was very hurt by your thoughtless remark.
(The receiver of the action, Alan, is being emphasized.)

Activity

Change the following sentences from the passive to the active voice. Note that you may have to add a subject in some cases.

Examples   The dog was found by a police officer.

A police officer found the dog.

The baseball game was called off.

The officials called off the baseball game.

(Here a subject had to be added.)

1. Most of our furniture was damaged by the fire.

_____

2. Marsha's new dress was singed by a careless smoker.

_____

3. The problem was solved by the quiet student in the back of the room.

_____

4. The supermarket shelves were restocked after the truckers' strike.

_____

5. The children were mesmerized by the magician's sleight of hand.

_____

MISPLACED MODIFIERS

Misplaced modifiers are words that, because of awkward placement, do not describe the words the writer intended them to describe. Misplaced modifiers often confuse the meaning of a sentence. To avoid them, place words as close as possible to what they describe.

Misplaced Words	**Correctly Placed Words**
George couldn't drive to work in his small sports car *with a broken leg*. (The sports car had a broken leg?)	With a broken leg, George couldn't drive to work in his small sports car. (The words describing George are now placed next to "George.")
The toaster was sold to us by a charming salesperson *with a money-back guarantee*. (The salesperson had a money-back guarantee?)	The toaster with a money-back guarantee was sold to us by a charming salesperson. (The words describing the toaster are now placed next to it.)
He *nearly* brushed his teeth for twenty minutes every night. (He came close to brushing his teeth, but in fact did not brush them at all?)	He brushed his teeth for nearly twenty minutes every night. (The meaning—that he brushed his teeth for a long time—is now clear.)

Activity

Underline the misplaced word or words in each sentence. Then rewrite the sentence, placing related words together and thereby making the meaning clear.

Examples   Frozen shrimp lay in the steel pans <u>that were melting rapidly</u>.

Frozen shrimp that were melting rapidly lay in the steel pans.

The speaker discussed the problem of crowded prisons <u>at the college</u>.

At the college, the speaker discussed the problem of crowded prisons.

1. The patient talked about his childhood on the psychiatrist's couch.

2. The crowd watched the tennis players with swivelling heads.

3. Damian put four hamburger patties on the counter which he was cooking for dinner.

4. Steve carefully hung the new suit that he would wear to his first job interview in the bedroom closet.

5. Luis ripped the shirt on a car door that he made in sewing class.

6. The latest Arnold Schwarzenegger movie has almost opened in 2,200 theatres across the country.

7. The newscaster spoke softly into a microphone wearing a bullet-proof vest.

8. The tenants left town in a dilapidated old car owing two months' rent.

9. The old man picked up a heavy frying pan with arthritis.

10. I discovered an unusual plant in the greenhouse that oozed a milky juice.

■ Review Test 1

Write *MM* for *misplaced modifier* or *C* for *correct* in the space provided for each sentence.

_____ 1. I nearly napped for twenty minutes during the biology lecture.

_____ 2. I napped for nearly twenty minutes during the biology lecture.

_____ 3. Ron paused as the girl he had been following stopped at a shop window.

_____ 4. Ron paused as the girl stopped at a shop window he had been following.

_____ 5. Marta dropped out of school after taking ten courses on Friday.

_____ 6. On Friday, Marta dropped out of school after taking ten courses.

_____ 7. Under his shirt, the player wore a good luck charm which resembled a tiny elephant.

_____ 8. The player wore a good luck charm under his shirt which resembled a tiny elephant.

_____ 9. I ordered a new telephone from the mail-order catalogue shaped like a cartoon character.

_____ 10. I ordered from the mail-order catalogue a new telephone shaped like a cartoon character.

■ Review Test 2

Make the changes needed to correct the misplaced modifier in each sentence.

1. Margaret Atwood wrote that someone was as innocent as a bathtub full of bullets in a poem.

   _____

2. I almost filled an entire notebook with biology lab drawings.

   _____

3. The apprentice watched the master carpenter expertly fit the door with envious eyes.

   _____

4. The photographer pointed the camera at the shy deer equipped with a special night-vision scope.

   _____

5. The passengers on the bus stared at the ceiling or read newspapers with tired faces.

   _____

DANGLING MODIFIERS

A modifier that opens a sentence must be followed immediately by the word it is meant to describe. Otherwise, the modifier is said to be dangling, and the sentence takes on an unintended meaning. For example, in the sentence

> While reading the newspaper, my dog sat with me on the front steps.

the unintended meaning is that the *dog* was reading the paper. What the writer meant, of course, was that *he* (or *she*), the writer, was reading the paper. The writer should have said,

> While reading the newspaper, *I* sat with my dog on the front steps.

The dangling modifier could also be corrected by placing the subject within the opening word group:

> While *I* was reading the newspaper, my dog sat with me on the front steps.

Here are other sentences with dangling modifiers. Read the explanations of why they are dangling and look carefully at the ways they are corrected.

Dangling	*Correct*
Shaving in front of the steamy mirror, the razor nicked Ed's chin. (*Who* was shaving in front of the mirror? The answer is not *razor* but *Ed*. The subject *Ed* must be added.)	Shaving in front of the steamy mirror, *Ed* nicked his chin with the razor. *Or:* When *Ed* was shaving in front of the steamy mirror, he nicked his chin with the razor.
While turning over the bacon, hot grease splashed my arm. (*Who* is turning over the bacon? The answer is not *hot grease*, as it unintentionally seems to be, but *I*. The subject *I* must be added.)	While *I* was turning over the bacon, hot grease splashed my arm. *Or:* While turning over the bacon, *I* was splashed by hot grease.
Taking the exam, the room was so stuffy that Paula almost fainted. (*Who* took the exam? The answer is not the *room* but *Paula*. The subject *Paula* must be added.)	Taking the exam, *Paula* found the room so stuffy that she almost fainted. *Or:* When *Paula* took the exam, the room was so stuffy that she almost fainted.
To impress the interviewer, punctuality is essential. (*Who* is to impress the interviewer? The answer is not *punctuality* but *you*. The subject *you* must be added.)	To impress the interviewer, *you* must be punctual. *Or:* For *you* to impress the interviewer, punctuality is essential.

The preceding examples make clear two ways of correcting a dangling modifier. Decide on a logical subject and do one of the following:

1 Place the subject *within* the opening word group:

   When *Ed* was shaving in front of the steamy mirror, he nicked his chin.

Note: In some cases an appropriate subordinating word such as *when* must be added, and the verb may have to be changed slightly as well.

2 Place the subject right *after* the opening word group:

   Shaving in front of the steamy mirror, *Ed* nicked his chin.

Activity

Ask *Who?* of the opening words in each sentence. The subject that answers the question should be nearby in the sentence. If it is not, provide the logical subject by using either method of correction described above.

Example   While pitching his tent, a snake bit Tony on the ankle.

While Tony was pitching his tent, a snake bit him on the ankle.

Or: *While pitching his tent, Tony was bitten on the ankle by a snake.*

1. Dancing on their hind legs, the audience cheered wildly as the elephants paraded by.

   _____

   _____

2. Last seen wearing dark glasses and a blond wig, the police spokesperson said the suspect was still being sought.

   _____

   _____

3. Pouring out the cereal, a coupon fell into my bowl of milk.

   _____

   _____

4. Escorted by dozens of police motorcycles, I knew the limousine carried someone important.

   _____

   _____

5. Tired and exasperated, the fight we had was inevitable.

   _____

   _____

6. Packed tightly in a tiny can, Fran had difficulty removing the anchovies.

   _____

   _____

7. Kicked carelessly under the bed, Marion finally found her sneakers.

   _____

   _____

8. Working at the photocopy machine, the morning dragged on.

    _____

    _____

9. Sitting at a sidewalk café, all sorts of interesting people passed by.

    _____

    _____

10. Though somewhat warped, Uncle Zeke played his records from the forties.

    _____

    _____

■ Review Test 1

Write *DM* for *dangling modifier* or *C* for *correct* in the space provided for each sentence.

_____ 1. While riding the bicycle, a vicious-looking German shepherd snapped at Tim's ankles.

_____ 2. While Tim was riding the bicycle, a vicious-looking German shepherd snapped at his ankles.

_____ 3. Afraid to look his father in the eye, Howard kept his head bowed.

_____ 4. Afraid to look his father in the eye, Howard's head remained bowed.

_____ 5. Boring and silly, I turned the TV show off.

_____ 6. I turned off the boring and silly TV show.

_____ 7. Munching leaves from a tall tree, the giraffe fascinated the children.

_____ 8. Munching leaves from a tall tree, the children were fascinated by the giraffe.

_____ 9. At the age of twelve, several colleges had already accepted the child genius.

_____ 10. At the age of twelve, the child genius had already been accepted by several colleges.

■ Review Test 2

Make the changes needed to correct the dangling modifier in each sentence.

1. Not having had much sleep, my concentration during class was weak.

    _____

2. Joined at the hip, a team of surgeons successfully separated the Siamese twins.

    _____

3. Wading in the shallow surf, a baby shark brushed past my leg.

    _____

4. While being restrained by court officials, the judge sentenced the kidnapper.

    _____

5. In a sentimental frame of mind, the music brought tears to Beth's eyes.

    _____

■ Review Test 3

Complete the following sentences. In each case, a logical subject should follow the opening words.

Example   Looking through the door's peephole, _I couldn't see who rang_
the doorbell.

1. Noticing the light turn yellow, _____

2. Being fragile, _____

3. While washing the car, _____

4. Although very expensive, _____

5. Driving by the cemetery, _____

FAULTY PARALLELISM

Words in a pair or a series should have a parallel structure. By balancing the items in a pair or a series so that they have the same kind of structure, you will make the sentence clearer and easier to read. Notice how the parallel sentences that follow read more smoothly than the nonparallel ones.

Nonparallel (Not Balanced)	Parallel (Balanced)
My job includes checking the inventory, initialling the orders, and to call the suppliers.	My job includes checking the inventory, initialling the orders, and calling the suppliers. (A balanced series of *-ing* words: *checking, initialling, calling*)
The game-show contestant was told to be cheerful, charming, and *with enthusiasm.*	The game-show contestant was told to be cheerful, charming, and enthusiastic. (A balanced series of descriptive words: *cheerful, charming, enthusiastic*)
Lola likes to ride her moped, to do needlepoint, and *playing* games on her personal computer.	Lola likes to ride her moped, to do needlepoint, and to play games on her personal computer. (A balanced series of *to* verbs: *to ride, to do, to play*)
We painted the trim in the living room; *the wallpaper was put up by a professional.*	We painted the trim in the living room; a professional put up the wallpaper. (Balanced verbs and word order: *We painted …; a professional put up …*)

Balanced sentences are not a skill you need worry about when writing first drafts. But when you rewrite, you should try to put matching words and ideas into matching structures. Such parallelism will improve your writing style.

Activity 1

The unbalanced part of each of the following sentences is italicized. Rewrite the unbalanced part so that it matches the rest of the sentence. The first one is done for you as an example.

1. Chocolate makes me gain weight, lose my appetite, and *breaking out in hives.* ___break out in hives___

2. Adam convinced most of the audience because he argued logically, calmly, and *was reasonable.* _____

3. If I didn't have to clean the garage and *an English paper that needed finishing,* I could really enjoy my weekend. _____

4. Ed's last job offered security; *a better chance for advancement is offered by his new job.* _____

5. A sale on electrical appliances, *furniture for the patio,* and stereo systems begins this Friday. _____

6. Steven prefers books that are short, scary, and *filled with suspense.*

    _____

7. The novelty shop sells hand buzzers, plastic fangs, and *insects that are fake.* _____

8. Because the dying woman was dignified and *with courage,* she won everyone's respect. _____

9. The politician trusted no one, rewarded loyalty, and *was dependent only on his own instincts.* _____

10. The chickens travel on a conveyor belt, where they are plucked, washed, rinsed, and *bags are put on them.* _____

Activity 2

Following are "plan of development" sentences that have been taken from student essays. Rewrite the sentences as needed so that the three points in each plan of development appear in parallel form.

1. To escape the stresses of everyday life, I rely upon watching television, reading books, and my kitchen.

    _____

    _____

2. If we're not careful, we'll leave the next generation polluted air, contaminated water, and forests that are dying.

_____

_____

3. Qualities that I look for in friends are a sense of humour, being kind, and dependability.

_____

_____

4. My three favourite jobs were veterinary assistant, gardener, and selling toys.

_____

_____

5. Many people have the same three great fears: being in high places, working with numbers, and speeches.

_____

_____

6. Housekeeping shortcuts will help you do a fast job of doing laundry, cleaning rooms, and food on the table.

_____

_____

7. The keys to improving grades are to take effective notes in class, to plan study time, and preparing carefully for exams.

_____

_____

8. To decide on a career, people should think closely about their interests, hobbies, and what they are skilled at.

_____

_____

9. The best programming on television includes news programmes, shows on science, and children's series.

_____

_____

10. People in today's world often try to avoid silence, whether on the job, in school, or when relaxing at home.

_____

_____

■ **Review Test 1**

Draw a line under the unbalanced part of each sentence. Then rewrite the unbalanced part so that it matches the other item or items in the sentence. The first one is done for you as an example.

1. Curling overgrown vines, <u>porch furniture that was rotted</u>, and sagging steps were my first impressions of the neglected house.

    rotting porch furniture

2. In many ways, starting college at forty is harder than to start at eighteen.

    _____

3. The child came home from school with a tear-streaked face, a black eye, and his shirt was torn.

    _____

4. Studying a little every day is more effective than to cram.

    _____

5. At the body shop, the car was sanded down to the bare metal, painted with primer, and red enamel was sprayed on.

    _____

6. There are two ways to the top floor: climb the stairs or taking the elevator.

    _____

7. While waiting for the exam to start, small groups of nervous students glanced over their notes, drank coffee, and were whispering to each other.

    _____

8. In order to become a dancer, she is taking lessons, working in amateur shows, and auditioned for professional companies.

    _____

9. The "street person" shuffled along the street, bent over to pick something up, and was putting it in his shopping bag.

    _____

10. A truckers' strike now would mean interruptions in food deliveries, a slowdown in the economy, and losing wages for workers.

    _____

■ **Review Test 2**

On separate paper, write five sentences of your own that use parallel structure.

PRONOUN AGREEMENT, REFERENCE, AND POINT OF VIEW

Pronouns are words that take the place of *nouns* (persons, places, or things). In fact, the word *pronoun* means "for a noun." Pronouns are shortcuts that keep you from unnecessarily repeating words in writing. Here are some examples of pronouns:

> Eddie left *his* camera on the bus. (*His* is a pronoun that takes the place of *Eddie's*.)
>
> Elena drank the coffee even though *it* was cold. (*It* replaces *coffee*.)
>
> As I turned the newspaper's damp pages, *they* disintegrated in my hands. (*They* is a pronoun that takes the place of *pages*.)

This section presents rules that will help you avoid three common mistakes people make with pronouns. The rules are:

1 A pronoun must agree in number with the word or words it replaces.
2 A pronoun must refer clearly to the word it replaces.
3 Pronouns should not shift unnecessarily in point of view.

PRONOUN AGREEMENT

A pronoun must agree in number with the word or words it replaces. If the word a pronoun refers to is singular, the pronoun must be singular; if that word is plural, the pronoun must be plural. (Note that the word a pronoun refers to is known as the *antecedent*.)

Marie showed me (her) antique wedding band.

Students enrolled in the art class must provide (their) own supplies.

In the first example, the pronoun *her* refers to the singular word *Marie;* in the second example, the pronoun *their* refers to the plural word *Students*.

Activity

Write the appropriate pronoun (*their, they, them, it*) in the blank space in each of the following sentences.

Example   I opened the wet umbrella and put _____it_____ in the bathtub to dry.

1. Kate and Bruce left for the movies earlier than usual, because _____ knew the theatre would be packed.

2. The clothes were still damp, but I decided to fold _____ anyway.

3. Young adults often face a difficult transition period when _____ leave home for the first time.

4. Paul's grandparents renewed _____ marriage vows at a huge fiftieth wedding anniversary celebration.

5. The car's steering wheel began to pull to one side, and then _____ started to shimmy.

Indefinite Pronouns

The following words are always singular.

(*-one* words)	(*-body* words)	
one	nobody	each
anyone	anybody	either
everyone	everybody	neither
someone	somebody	

If a pronoun in a sentence refers to one of these singular words (also known as *indefinite pronouns*), the pronoun should be singular.

Somebody left (her) shoulder bag on the back of a chair.

One of the servers just called and said (he) would be an hour late.

Everyone in the club must pay (his) dues next week.

Each circled pronoun is singular because it refers to an indefinite pronoun.

Note: There are two important points to remember about indefinite pronouns:

1 In the last example, if everyone in the club was a woman, the pronoun would be *her*. If the club had women and men, the pronoun would be *his or her:*

Everyone in the club must pay his or her dues next week.

Some writers follow the traditional practice of using *his* to refer to both women and men. Most writers now use *his or her* to avoid an implied sexual bias. To avoid using *his* or the somewhat awkward *his or her*, a sentence can often be rewritten in the plural:

Club members must pay their dues next week.

2 In informal spoken English, *plural* pronouns are often used with the indefinite pronouns. We would probably not say:

Everybody has his or her own opinion about the election.

Instead, we are likely to say:

Everybody has their own opinion about the election.

Here are other examples:

Everyone in the choir must buy their robes.
Everybody in the line has their ticket ready.
No one in the class remembered to bring their books.

In such cases, the indefinite pronouns are clearly plural in meaning. Also, the use of such plurals helps people to avoid the awkward *his or her*. In time, the plural pronoun may be accepted in formal speech or writing. Until that happens, however, you should use the grammatically correct singular form in your writing.

Activity

Underline the correct pronoun.

1. Neither of the potential buyers had really made up (her, their) mind.
2. Not one of the new cashiers knows what (he, they) should be doing.
3. Each of these computers has (its, their) drawbacks.
4. Anyone trying to reduce (his or her, their) salt intake should avoid canned and processed foods.
5. If anybody calls when I'm out, tell (him, them) I'll return in an hour.

PRONOUN REFERENCE

A sentence may be confusing and unclear if a pronoun appears to refer to more than one word or does not refer to any specific word. Look at this sentence:

> Miriam was annoyed when they failed her car for a faulty turn signal.

Who failed her car? There is no specific word that *they* refers to. Be clear:

> Miriam was annoyed when the inspectors failed her car for a faulty turn signal.

Here are sentences with other faulty pronoun references. Read the explanations of why they are faulty and look carefully at how they are corrected.

Faulty	*Clear*
Wanda told Jennifer that her husband was unhappy. (Whose husband is unhappy: Wanda's or Jennifer's? Be clear.)	Wanda told Jennifer, "My husband is unhappy."
Ming is really a shy person, but she keeps it hidden. (There is no specific word that *it* refers to. It would not make sense to say, "Ming keeps shy hidden.")	Ming is really a shy person, but she keeps her shyness hidden.
Ken attributed his success to his wife's support, which was generous. (Does *which* mean that Ken's action was generous or that his wife's support was generous?)	Generously, Ken attributed his success to his wife's support. *Or:* Ken attributed his success to his wife's generous support.

Activity

Rewrite each of the following sentences to make clear the vague pronoun reference. Add, change, or omit words as necessary.

Example   Susan and her mother wondered if she were tall enough to be a model.

Susan's mother wondered if Susan were tall enough to be a model.

1.   Dad spent all morning bird-watching but didn't see a single one.

   _____

2.   At that fast-food restaurant, they give you free glasses with your soft drinks.

   _____

3.   Ruth told Annette that her bouts of depression were becoming serious.

   _____

4.   Dipping his spoon into the pot of simmering spaghetti sauce, Kyle felt it slip out of his hand.

   _____

5.   Pete visited the tutoring centre because they can help him with his economics course.

   _____

PRONOUN POINT OF VIEW

Pronouns should not shift their point of view unnecessarily. When writing a paper, be consistent in your use of first-, second-, or third-person pronouns.

	Singular	*Plural*
First-person pronouns	I (my, mine, me)	we (our, us)
Second-person pronouns	you (your)	you (your)
Third-person pronouns	he (his, him)	they (their, them)
	she (her)	
	it (its)	

Note: Any person, place, or thing, as well as any indefinite pronoun like *one*, *anyone*, *someone*, and so on (page 368), is a third-person word.

For instance, if you start writing in the first person, *I*, do not jump suddenly to the second person, *you*. Or if you are writing in the third person, *they*, do not shift unexpectedly to *you*. Look at the examples.

Inconsistent	*Consistent*
One of the fringe benefits of my job is that *you* can use a company credit card for gasoline. (The most common mistake people make is to let a *you* slip into their writing after they start with another pronoun.)	One of the fringe benefits of my job is that *I* can use a company credit card for gasoline.
In this course, a person can be in class for weeks before the professor calls on *you*. (Again, the *you* is a shift in point of view.)	In this course, a person can be in class for weeks before the professor calls on *him or her*. (See also the note on *his or her* references on page 369.)

Activity

Cross out inconsistent pronouns in the following sentences and write the correct form of the pronoun above each crossed-out word.

Example   When I examined the used car, ~~you~~ could see where a dent in the door panel had been repaired.

1. Ron refuses to eat pepperoni pizza because he says it gives you indigestion.
2. When I buy lipstick or nail polish, you never know how the colour will actually look.
3. All you could hear was the maddening rattle of the heating registers, even though I buried my face in the pillow.
4. Hank searched the roadside mailboxes for the right name, but you couldn't see much in the pouring rain.
5. As we pulled on the heavy door, you could tell it wasn't going to budge.

■ Review Test

Cross out the pronoun error in each sentence on the opposite page and write the correction in the space provided at the left. Then circle the letter that correctly describes the type of error that was made.

Examples

Anyone without a ticket will lose their place in the line.
his or her *Mistake in:* a. pronoun reference (b.) pronoun agreement

Ellen When Ellen takes her daughter Cara to the park, she enjoys herself.
(or Cara) *Mistake in:* (a.) pronoun reference b. pronoun point of view

From where we stood on the mountain, could see three counties.
we *Mistake in:* a. pronoun agreement (b.) pronoun point of view

1. Many people are ignorant of side effects that diets can have on your health.
   Mistake in: a. pronoun reference b. pronoun point of view

2. Could someone volunteer their services to clean up after the party?
   Mistake in: a. pronoun reference b. pronoun agreement

3. At the city council meeting, we asked them to provide better police protection for our neighbourhood.
   Mistake in: a. pronoun reference b. pronoun agreement

4. During the border crisis, each country refused to change their aggressive stand.
   Mistake in: a. pronoun reference b. pronoun agreement

5. Darlene tried to take notes during class, but she didn't really understand it.
   Mistake in: a. pronoun reference b. pronoun agreement

6. If people don't like what the government is doing, you should let Parliament know.
   Mistake in: a. pronoun reference b. pronoun point of view

7. Neither of those girls appreciates their parents' sacrifices.
   Mistake in: a. pronoun reference b. pronoun agreement

8. There wasn't much to do on Friday nights after they closed the only movie theatre in town.
   Mistake in: a. pronoun reference b. pronoun agreement

9. Rick never buys a shirt with horizontal stripes because he knows they make you look fat.
   Mistake in: a. pronoun reference b. pronoun point of view

10. Any student who is working full-time and going to school knows that you need at least a twenty-five-hour day.
    Mistake in: a. pronoun agreement b. pronoun point of view

PRONOUN TYPES

This section describes some common types of pronouns: subject and object pronouns, possessive pronouns, and demonstrative pronouns.

SUBJECT AND OBJECT PRONOUNS

Pronouns change their form depending upon the place that they occupy in a sentence. In the box that follows is a list of subject and object pronouns.

Subject Pronouns	Object Pronouns
I	me
you	you (no change)
he	him
she	her
it	it (no change)
we	us
they	them

Subject Pronouns

The subject pronouns are subjects of verbs.

> *He* is wearing an artificial arm. (*He* is the subject of the verb *is wearing*.)
>
> *They* are moving into our old apartment. (*They* is the subject of the verb *are moving*.)
>
> *We* students should have a say in the decision. (*We* is the subject of the verb *should have*.)

Several kinds of mistakes that people sometimes make with subject pronouns are explained starting below.

1 Use a subject pronoun in spots where you have a compound (more than one) subject.

Incorrect	*Correct*
My brother and *me* are Leonard Cohen fanatics.	My brother and *I* are Leonard Cohen fanatics.
Him and *me* know the lyrics to all of Cohen's songs.	*He* and *I* know the lyrics to all of Cohen's songs.

Hint: If you are not sure what pronoun to use, try each pronoun by itself in the sentence. The correct pronoun will be the one that sounds right. For example, "Him knows the lyrics to all of Cohen's songs" does not sound right; "He knows the lyrics to all of Cohen's songs" does.

2 Use a subject pronoun after forms of the verb *be*. Forms of *be* include *am*, *are*, *is*, *was*, *were*, *has been*, *have been*, and others.

> It was *I* who left the light on.
> It may be *they* in that car.
> It is *he*.

The sentences above may sound strange and stilted to you because they are seldom used in conversation. When we speak with one another, forms such as "It was me," "It may be them," and "It is him" are widely accepted. In formal writing, however, the grammatically correct forms are still preferred.

Hint: Avoid having to use the pronoun form after *be* by simply rewording a sentence. Here is how the preceding examples could be reworded:

I was the one who left the light on.
They may be in that car.
He is here.

3   Use subject pronouns after *than* or *as*. The subject pronoun is used because a verb is understood after the pronoun.

You play better than I (play). (The verb *play* is understood after *I*.)

Jenny is as bored as I (am). (The verb *am* is understood after *I*.)

We don't need the money as much as they (do). (The verb *do* is understood after *they*.)

Hint: Avoid mistakes by mentally adding the "missing" verb at the end of the sentence.

Object Pronouns

The object pronouns (*me, him, her, us, them*) are the objects of verbs or prepositions. (*Prepositions* are connecting words like *for, at, about, to, before, by, with,* and *of*. See also page 303.)

Tony helped me.   (*Me* is the object of the verb *helped*.)

We took *them* to the college.   (*Them* is the object of the verb *took*.)

Leave the children with *us*.   (*Us* is the object of the preposition *with*.)

I got in line behind *him*.   (*Him* is the object of the preposition *behind*.)

People are sometimes uncertain about what pronoun to use when two objects follow the verb.

Incorrect	*Correct*
I gave a gift to Ray and *she*.	I gave a gift to Ray and *her*.
She came to the movie with Bobbie and *I*.	She came to the movie with Bobbie and *me*.

Hint: If you are not sure what pronoun to use, try each pronoun by itself in the sentence. The correct pronoun will be the one that sounds right. For example, "I gave a gift to she" does not sound right; "I gave a gift to her" does.

Activity

Underline the correct subject or object pronoun in each of the following sentences. Then show whether your answer is a subject or object pronoun by circling the *S* or *O* in the margin. The first one is done for you as an example.

S (*O*)   1. The sweaters Mom knitted for Victor and (I, <u>me</u>) are too small.

S *O*   2. The umpire and (he, him) started to argue.

S *O*   3. No one has a quicker temper than (she, her).

S *O*   4. Your grades prove that you worked harder than (they, them).

S *O*   5. (We, Us) runners train indoors when the weather turns cold.

S *O*   6. (She, Her) and Betty never put the cap back on the toothpaste.

S *O*   7. Chris and (he, him) are the most energetic kids in the first grade,

S *O*   8. Arguing over clothes is a favourite pastime for my sister and (I, me).

S *O*   9. The rest of (they, them) will be arriving in about ten minutes.

S *O*   10. The head of the ticket committee asked Sam and (I, me) to help with sales.

POSSESSIVE PRONOUNS

Here is a list of possessive pronouns:

my, mine	our, ours
your, yours	your, yours
his	their, theirs
her, hers	
its	

Possessive pronouns show ownership or possession.

> Clyde revved up *his* motorcycle and blasted off.
> The keys are *mine.*

Note: A possessive pronoun *never* uses an apostrophe. (See also page 397.)

Incorrect	*Correct*
That coat is *hers'*.	That coat is *hers.*
The card table is *theirs'*.	The card table is *theirs.*

Activity

Cross out the incorrect pronoun form in each of the sentences below. Write the correct form in the space at the left.

Example   ___hers___   Those gloves are ~~hers'~~.

_____   1. I discovered that my car had somehow lost its' rear licence plate.

_____   2. Are those seats theirs'?

_____   3. I knew the sweater was hers' when I saw the monogram.

_____   4. The dog in that cage is our's.

_____   5. These books are yours' if you want them.

DEMONSTRATIVE PRONOUNS

Demonstrative pronouns point to or single out a person or thing. There are four demonstrative pronouns:

this	these
that	those

Generally speaking, *this* and *these* refer to things close at hand; *that* and *those* refer to things farther away. The four pronouns are commonly used in the role of demonstrative adjectives as well.

> Is anyone using *this* spoon?
> I am going to throw away *these* magazines.
> I just bought *that* white Volvo at the curb.
> Pick up *those* toys in the corner.

Note: Do not use *them*, *this here*, *that there*, *these here*, or *those there* to point out. Use only *this*, *that*, *these*, or *those*.

Activity

Cross out the incorrect form of the demonstrative pronoun and write the correct form in the space provided.

Example _Those_ ~~Them~~ tires look worn.

_____ 1. This here map is out of date.

_____ 2. Leave them keys out on the coffee table.

_____ 3. I've seen them girls somewhere before.

_____ 4. Jack entered that there dog in an obedience contest.

_____ 5. Where are them new knives?

■ Review Test

Underline the correct word in the parentheses.

1. If the contract negotiations are left up to (they, them), we'll have to accept the results.

2. (Them, Those) student crafts projects have won several awards.

3. Our grandmother told David and (I, me) to leave our muddy shoes outside on the porch.

4. The judge decided that the fault was (theirs', theirs) and ordered them to pay the damages.

5. I gave the money to (she, her) and asked her to put it in the bank's night deposit slot.

6. The black-masked raccoon stared at Rudy and (I, me) for an instant and then ran quickly away.

7. When we saw the smashed window, Lynn and (I, me) didn't know whether to enter the house.

8. (This here, This) is my cousin Manuel.

9. This coat can't be (hers, her's); it's too small.

10. Because we weren't wearing shoes, Tara and (I, me) had a hard time walking on the sharp gravel.

ADJECTIVES
AND ADVERBS

ADJECTIVES

What Are Adjectives?

Adjectives describe nouns (names of persons, places, or things) or pronouns.

> Polly is a *wise* woman. (The adjective *wise* describes the noun *woman*.)
>
> She is also *funny*. (The adjective *funny* describes the pronoun *she*.)
>
> I'll carry the *heavy* bag of groceries. (The adjective *heavy* describes the noun *bag*.)
>
> It is *torn*. (The adjective *torn* describes the pronoun *it*.)

Adjectives usually come before the word they describe (as in *wise* woman and *heavy* bag). But they also come after forms of the verb *be* (*is, are, was, were*, and so on). They also follow verbs such as *look, appear, seem, become, sound, taste*, and *smell*.

> That road is *slippery*. (The adjective *slippery* describes the road.)
>
> The dogs are *noisy*. (The adjective *noisy* describes the dogs.)
>
> Those customers were *impatient*. (The adjective *impatient* describes the customers.)
>
> Your room looks *neat*. (The adjective *neat* describes the room.)

Using Adjectives to Compare

For all one-syllable adjectives and some two-syllable adjectives, add *-er* when comparing two things and *-est* when comparing three or more things.

> Phil's beard is *longer* than mine, but Lee's is the *longest*.
>
> Meg may be the *quieter* of the two sisters; but that's not saying much, since they're the *loudest* girls in school.

For some two-syllable adjectives and all longer adjectives, add *more* when comparing two things and *most* when comparing three or more things.

> Daniel Richler is *more* famous than his brother; but their father, Mordecai Richler, is still the *most* famous member of the family.
>
> The red letters on the sign are *more noticeable* than the black ones, but the Day-Glo letters are the *most noticeable*.

You can usually tell when to use *more* and *most* by the sound of a word. For example, you can probably tell by its sound that "carefuller" would be too awkward to say and that *more careful* is thus correct. In addition, there are many words for which both *-er* or *-est* and *more* or *most* are equally correct. For instance, either "a more fair rule" or "a fairer rule" is correct.

To form negative comparisons, use *less* and *least*.

> During my first dance class, I felt *less graceful* than an injured elephant.
>
> When the teacher came to our house to complain to my parents, I offered her the *least* comfortable chair in the house.

Points to Remember about Comparing

Point 1: Use only one form of comparison at a time. In other words, do not use both an *-er* ending and *more* or both an *-est* ending and *most:*

Incorrect	*Correct*
My suitcase is always *more heavier* than my father's.	My suitcase is always *heavier* than my father's.
Scanners is still the *most frighteningest* movie I've ever seen.	*Scanners* is still the *most frightening* movie I've ever seen.

Point 2: Learn the irregular forms of the words shown below.

	Comparative (for comparing two things)	Superlative (for comparing three or more things)
bad	worse	worst
good, well	better	best
little (in amount)	less	least
much, many	more	most

Do not use both *more* and an irregular comparative or *most* and an irregular superlative.

Incorrect	Correct
It is *more better* to give than to receive.	It is *better* to give than to receive.
Last night I got the *most worst* snack attack I ever had.	Last night I got the *worst* snack attack I ever had.

Activity

Add to each sentence the correct form of the word in the margin.

bad

Examples The _____worst_____ job I ever had was baby-sitting for spoiled four-year-old twins.

wonderful

The ___most wonderful___ day of my life was when my child was born.

good

1. The _____ chocolate cake I ever ate had bananas in it.

young

2. Aunt Sonja is the _____ of the three sisters.

bad

3. A rain that freezes is _____ than a snowstorm.

unusual

4. That's the _____ home I've ever seen—it's shaped like a teapot.

little

5. Being painfully shy has made Leon the _____ friendly person I know.

ADVERBS

What Are Adverbs?

Adverbs describe verbs, adjectives, or other adverbs. They usually end in *-ly*.

> The father *gently* hugged the sick child. (The adverb *gently* describes the verb *hugged*.)
>
> Newborns are *totally* innocent. (The adverb *totally* describes the adjective *innocent*.)
>
> The lecturer spoke so *terribly* fast that I had trouble taking notes. (The adverb *terribly* describes the adverb *fast*.)

A Common Mistake with Adverbs and Adjectives

People often mistakenly use an adjective instead of an adverb after a verb.

Incorrect	*Correct*
Sam needs a haircut *bad*.	Sam needs a haircut *badly*.
I laugh too *loud* when I'm embarrassed.	I laugh too *loudly* when I'm embarrassed.
You might have won the race if you hadn't run so *slow* at the beginning.	You might have won the race if you hadn't run so *slowly* at the beginning.

Activity

Underline the adjective or adverb needed. (Remember that adjectives describe nouns, and adverbs describe verbs, or other adverbs.)

1. As Mac danced, his ear-ring bounced (rapid, rapidly).

2. A drop of (thick, thickly) pea soup dripped down his chin.

3. I hiccupped (continuous, continuously) for fifteen minutes.

4. The detective opened the door (careful, carefully).

5. All she heard when she answered the phone was (heavy, heavily) breathing.

Well and Good

Two words that are often confused are *well* and *good*. *Good* is an adjective; it describes nouns. *Well* is usually an adverb; it describes verbs. *Well* (rather than *good*) is also used when referring to a person's health.

Activity

Write *well* or *good* in each of the sentences that follow.

1. If you girls do a _____ job of cleaning the garage, I'll take you for some ice cream.

2. If I organize the office records too _____, my bosses may not need me any more.

3. After eating a pound of peanuts, I didn't feel too _____.

4. When Ernie got AIDS, he discovered who his _____ friends really were.

5. Just because brothers and sisters fight when they're young doesn't mean they won't get along _____ as adults.

■ Review Test 1

Underline the correct word in the parentheses.

1. The waitress poured (littler, less) coffee in my cup than in yours.

2. Humid air seems to make Sid's asthma (more worse, worse).

3. The movie is so interesting that the three hours pass (quick, quickly).

4. The talented boy sang as (confident, confidently) as a seasoned performer.

5. Our band played so (good, well) that a local firm hired us for its annual dinner.

6. Tri Lee is always (truthful, truthfully), even when it might be better to tell a white lie.

7. The driver stopped the bus (sudden, suddenly) and yelled, "Everybody out!"

8. Shirt and pants in one colour make you look (more thin, thinner) than ones in contrasting colours.

9. Your intentions may have been (good, well), but I'd prefer that you ask before arranging a blind date for me.

10. Our cat likes to sit in the (warmest, most warm) spot in any room—by a fireplace, on a windowsill in the sunshine, or on my lap.

■ **Review Test 2**

Write a sentence that uses each of the following adjectives and adverbs correctly.

1. careless _____

2. angrily _____

3. well _____

4. most relaxing _____

5. best _____

CAPITAL LETTERS

MAIN USES OF CAPITAL LETTERS

Capital letters are used with:

1 The first word in a sentence or direct quotation
2 Names of persons and the word *I*
3 Names of particular places
4 Names of days of the week, months, and holidays
5 Names of commercial products
6 Titles of books, magazines, newspapers, articles, stories, poems, films, television shows, songs, papers that you write, and the like
7 Names of companies, institutions, associations, unions, clubs, religious and political groups, and other organizations

Each use is illustrated on the pages that follow.

First Word in a Sentence or Direct Quotation

The corner store was robbed last night.

The alien said, "Take me to your leader."

"If you feel lonely," said Carla, "call me. I'll be over in no time."

Note: In the third example, *If* and *I'll* are capitalized because they start new sentences. But *call* is not capitalized, because it is part of the first sentence.

Names of Persons and the Word *I*

Last night, I saw a hilarious movie starring John Candy and Dan Aykroyd.

Names of Particular Places and Institutions

Although Bill dropped out of Port Charles High School, he eventually earned his degree and got a job with Atlas Realty Company.

But: Use small letters if the specific name of a place is not given.

Although Bill dropped out of high school, he eventually earned his degree and got a job with a real estate company.

Names of Days of the Week, Months, and Holidays

On the last Friday afternoon in June, the day before Canada Day, my boss is having a barbecue for all the employees.

But: Use small letters for the seasons—summer, fall, winter, spring.

Most people feel more energetic in the spring and fall.

Names of Commercial Products

My little sister knows all the words to the jingles for Maple Leaf hot dogs, Diet Pepsi, Meow Mix cat food, and McDonald's hamburgers.

But: Use small letters for the *type* of product (hot dogs, cat food, hamburgers, and so on.)

Titles of Books, Magazines, Newspapers, Articles, Stories, Poems, Films, Television Shows, Songs, Papers That You Write, and the Like

We read the book *The Handmaid's Tale*, by Margaret Atwood, for our English class.

In the doctor's waiting room, I watched *All My Children*, read an article in *Saturday Night*, and leafed through *The Toronto Star*.

Names of Companies, Associations, Unions, Clubs, Religious and Political Groups, and Other Organizations

Joe Naples is a Roman Catholic, but his wife is a Presbyterian.

The Hilldale Square Dancers' Club has won many competitions.

Brian, a member of Bricklayers Local 431 and the Knights of Columbus, works for Ace Construction.

Activity

Underline the words that need capitals in the following sentences. Then write the capitalized form of the words in the spaces provided. The number of spaces tells you how many corrections to make in each case.

Example   In our sociology class, each student must do a report on an article in the magazine *chatelaine*.   ___Chatelaine___

1. Leon's collection of beatles souvenirs includes a pair of tickets from their last concert at massey hall, in Toronto.

   _____   _____   _____

2. Yumi read in *canadian geographic* magazine that henry hudson was abandoned by the crew of his ship.

   _____   _____   _____   _____

3. When i have a cold, I use vick's ointment and chew listerine lozenges.

   _____   _____   _____

4. This spring, the boy scouts and the girl guides will clean up laurier Park.

   _____   _____   _____   _____

5. A nature trail for the blind in point pelee, ontario, has signs written in braille which encourage visitors to smell and touch the plants.

   _____   _____   _____

6. At a restaurant on Broad street called Joe's italian palace, the chefs use pasta machines to make fresh noodles right in the dining room.

    _____   _____   _____

7. My father is a confirmed Edmonton oilers fan, though he lives in winnipeg.

    _____   _____

8. Martha bought a sugar-free tab to wash down her vachon jos. louis.

    _____   _____   _____   _____

9. Vince listened to a Celine Dion album called *The Colour of My Love* while Donna read an article in *harrowsmith* entitled "How To grow Great tomatoes."

    _____   _____   _____

10. After having her baby, joan received a card from one of her friends that read, "congratulations, we all knew you had it in you."

    _____   _____

OTHER USES OF CAPITAL LETTERS

Capital letters are also used with:

1 Names that show family relationships
2 Titles of persons when used with their names
3 Specific school courses
4 Languages
5 Geographic locations
6 Historical periods and events
7 Races, nations, and nationalities
8 Opening and closing of a letter

Each use is illustrated on the pages that follow.

Names That Show Family Relationships

All his life, Father has been addicted to gadgets.
I browsed through Grandmother's collection of old photographs.
Aunt Florence and Uncle Bill bought a mobile home.

But: Do not capitalize words like *mother, father, grandmother, grandfather, uncle, aunt,* and so on when they are preceded by a possessive word (*my, your, his, her, our, their*).

All his life, my father has been addicted to gadgets.
I browsed through my grandmother's collection of old photographs.
My aunt and uncle bought a mobile home.

Titles of Persons When Used with Their Names

I contributed to Mayor Hall's campaign fund.
Is Dr. Gregory on vacation?
Professor Adams announced that there would be no tests in his course.

But: Use small letters when titles appear by themselves, without specific names.

I contributed to my mayor's campaign fund.
Is the doctor on vacation?
The professor announced that there would be no tests in his course.

Specific School Courses

The college offers evening sections of Introductory Psychology I, Abnormal Psychology, Psychology and Statistics, and Educational Psychology.

But: Use small letters for general subject areas.

The college offers evening sections of many psychology courses.

Languages

My grandfather's Polish accent makes his English difficult to understand.

Geographic Locations

He grew up in the Maritimes but moved to the West to look for a better job.

But: Use small letters in directions.

Head west for five blocks and then turn south on Queen Street.

Historical Periods and Events

During the Middle Ages, the Black Death killed more than one-quarter of Europe's population.

Races, Nations, Nationalities

The census questionnaire asked if the head of our household were Caucasian, Negro, Oriental, or Native Canadian.

Linda has lived on army bases in Germany, Italy, and Spain.

Denise's beautiful features are the result of her Chinese and Mexican parentage.

Opening and Closing of a Letter

Dear Sir: Sincerely yours,
Dear Ms. Henderson: Truly yours,

Note: Capitalize only the first word in a closing.

Activity

Underline the words that need capitals in the following sentences. Then write the capitalized forms of the words in the spaces provided. The number of spaces tells you how many corrections to make in each case.

1. During world war II, some canadians were afraid that the japanese would invade British Columbia.

   _____   _____   _____   _____

2. Many college students are studying spanish and french to help them in their business careers.

   _____   _____

3. When uncle harvey got the bill from his doctor, he called the Ontario Medical Association to complain.

   _____   _____

4. Dr. Freeling of the business department is offering a new course called introduction to computers.

   _____   _____

5. A new restaurant featuring vietnamese cuisine has just opened on the south side of the city.

   _____

UNNECESSARY USE OF CAPITALS

Activity

Many errors in capitalization are caused by using capitals where they are not needed. Underline the incorrectly capitalized letters in the following sentences and write the correct forms in the spaces provided. The number of spaces tells you how many corrections to make in each sentence.

1. Kim Campbell—the first woman Prime Minister—also had the shortest tenure in Office.

   _____ _____ _____

2. While she cleans and cooks, my Mother wears a pair of Sony Stereo Headphones.

   _____ _____ _____

3. Canadians were delighted when the Toronto Blue Jays were the first Canadian Baseball Team to win the World Series.

   _____ _____

4. The Voyager spacecraft sent back pictures of Saturn's Rings which prove that they are made up of Millions of Small, icy Particles.

   _____ _____ _____ _____

5. Einstein's theory of relativity, which he developed when he was only twenty-six, led to the invention of the Electron Microscope, Television, and the Atomic bomb.

   _____ _____ _____ _____

■ Review Test 1

Add capitals where needed in the following sentences.

Example   In an injured tone, Mary demanded, "$\overset{W}{\cancel{w}}$hy wasn't $\overset{U}{\cancel{u}}$ncle Lou invited to the party?"

1. To keep warm, a homeless old man sits on a steam vent near the sears building on tenth street.

2. Silent movie stars of the twenties, like charlie chaplin and gloria swanson, earned more than a million tax-free dollars a year.

3. Unique in Canada to the carolinian zone of south-western ontario are such plants as the green dragon Lily and sassafras trees.

4. Fidel Castro, the cuban leader, once tried out for the Washington senators, a professional baseball team.

5. In the marx brothers movie, an attractive young lady invited groucho to join her.

6. "why?" asked groucho. "are you coming apart?"

7. I was halfway to the wash & dry laundromat on elm street when i realized that my box of sunlight detergent was still home on the kitchen counter.

8. Every october, I make another vow that I will not gain weight between thanksgiving and new year's day.

9. *Flare* magazine features an article about the latest alfred sung collection and a review of a new film *ready to wear*.

10. Celebrities earn big money for endorsing items like bauer skates, trident gum, and jell-O pudding.

■ Review Test 2

On separate paper, write:

1. Seven sentences demonstrating the seven main uses of capital letters

2. Eight sentences demonstrating the eight other uses of capital letters

APOSTROPHE

The two main uses of the apostrophe are:

1 To show the omission of one or more letters in a contraction
2 To show ownership or possession

Each use is explained on the pages that follow.

APOSTROPHE IN CONTRACTIONS

A contraction is formed when two words are combined to make one word. An apostrophe is used to show where letters are omitted in forming the contraction. Here are two contractions:

have + not = haven't (the *o* in *not* has been omitted)
I + will = I'll (the *wi* in *will* has been omitted)

Following are some other common contractions:

I + am = I'm	it + is = it's
I + have = I've	it + has = it's
I + had = I'd	is + not = isn't
who + is = who's	could + not = couldn't
do + not = don't	I + would = I'd
did + not = didn't	they + are = they're

Note: Will + not has an unusual contraction: won't.

Activity

Write the contractions for the words in parentheses. One is done for you.

1. (Are not) _____*Aren't*_____ the reserve books in the library kept at the circulation desk?

2. If (they are) _____ coming over, (I had) _____
   better cook more hot dogs.

3. (I am) _____ the kind of student (who is) _____
   extremely nervous before tests.

4. (We are) _____ hoping to find out (who is) _____

   responsible for this error; (it is) _____ important to us to
   keep our customers happy.

5. I (can not) _____ remember if (there is) _____
   gas in the car or not.

Note: Even though contractions are common in everyday speech and in written dialogue, usually it is best to avoid them in formal writing.

APOSTROPHE TO SHOW OWNERSHIP OR POSSESSION

To show ownership or possession, we can use such words as *belongs to*, *possessed by*, *owned by*, or (most commonly) *of*.

> the umbrella that *belongs to* Mark
> the tape recorder *owned by* the school
> the gentleness *of* my father

But the apostrophe plus *s* (if the word does not end in *s*) is often the quickest and easiest way to show possession. Thus we can say:

> Mark's umbrella
> the school's tape recorder
> my father's gentleness

Points to Remember

1 The *'s* goes with the owner or possessor (in the examples given, *Mark*, *the school*, *my father*). What follows is the person or thing possessed (in the examples given, *the umbrella*, *the tape recorder*, *gentleness*).

2 In handwritten work, there should always be a break between the word and the *'s*.

Mark's   not   Marks

Yes   No

Activity 1

Rewrite the *italicized* part of each of the sentences below, using the *'s* to show possession. Remember that the *'s* goes with the owner or possessor.

Example   The wing of the bluejay was broken.
        The bluejay's wing was broken.

1. *The baton owned by the twirler* bounced on the ground.

   _____

2. *The performance of the quarterback* is inconsistent.

   _____

3. *The thin hand belonging to the old lady* felt as dry as parchment.

   _____

4. In *the window of the truck stop* is a sign: "Five Hundred Mile Coffee."

   _____

5. A fly flew into *the mouth of the TV weatherperson.*

   _____

6. *The new denim shirt belonging to Lamont* was as scratchy as sandpaper.

   _____

7. *The granite steps of the post office* were covered with green plastic turf.

   _____

8. *The bowl of cereal belonging to Dan* refused to snap, crackle, or pop.

   _____

9. *The Honda owned by Donna* was crammed with boxes and furniture.

   _____

10. *The previous tenant of the apartment* had painted all the walls bright green.

   _____

Activity 2

Add *'s* to each of the following words to make them the possessors or owners of something. Then write sentences using the words. The first one is done for you.

1. rock star _rock star's_____
   The rock star's limousine pulled up to the curb._____

2. Arnold _____
   _____

3. pilot _____
   _____

4. neighbour _____
   _____

5. school _____
   _____

6. gunslinger _____
   _____

Apostrophe versus Possessive Pronouns

Do not use an apostrophe with possessive pronouns. They already show ownership. Possessive pronouns include *his*, *hers*, *its*, *yours*, *ours*, and *theirs*.

The sun warped his albums.	***not***	The sun warped his' albums.
The restored Meteor is theirs.	***not***	The restored Meteor is theirs'.
The decision is yours.	***not***	The decision is yours'.
The plaid suitcase is ours.	***not***	The plaid suitcase is ours'.
The lion charged its prey.	***not***	The lion charged its' prey.

Apostrophe versus Simple Plurals

When you want to make a word plural, just add an *s* at the end of the word. Do *not* add an apostrophe. For example, the plural of the word *movie* is *movies*, not *movie's* or *movies'*. Look at this sentence:

Tim coveted his room-mate's collection of cassette tapes and compact discs.

The words *tapes* and *discs* are simple plurals, meaning more than one tape, more than one disc. The plural is shown by adding *s* only. On the other hand, the *'s* after *room-mate* shows possession—that the room-mate owns the tapes and discs.

Activity

Insert an apostrophe where needed to show possession in the following sentences. Write *plural* above words where the *s* ending simply means more than one thing.

Example   Arlene's tinted contact lenses protect her eyes from glare.

plural above *lenses* and *eyes*

1. Harry grasped his wifes arm as she stood up on skates for the first time.

2. Vonettes decision to study computer science is based on predictions of good opportunities for women in that field.

3. The fires extreme heat had melted the telephones in the office and welded its metal chairs into a twisted heap.

4. Maria tried her sisters fad diet, which forbids eating any food that is white.

5. At the doctors request, Jim pulled up his shirt and revealed the zipperlike scars from his operation.

6. At the end of the day, Cals shirt and pants smelled like gasoline, and his fingernails were rimmed with grease.

7. Most peoples fear of flying is based on their fear of giving control over their destinies to someone else—in this case, the pilot.

8. Tinas camping handbook suggests that we bring water purification tablets and nylon ropes.

9. Carmens leaky pen had stained her fingers a deep blue.

10. The rattlesnakes head has a sensitive pit below the eyes, capable of detecting the body heat of warm-blooded prey.

Apostrophe with Words Ending in *-s*

If a word ends in *-s*, show possession by adding only an apostrophe. Most plurals end in *-s*, and so show possession simply by adding the apostrophe.

the Thompsons' porch
James' cowboy boots
the players' victory
her parents' motor home
the Rolling Stones' last album
the soldiers' hats

Activity

Add an apostrophe where needed.

1. Dennis sudden appearance startled his wife.
2. The Murrays phone bill is more than $200 a month.
3. Many buildings steep steps make it difficult for wheelchair-bound people to negotiate them.
4. The twins habit of dressing alike was started by their mother when they were children.
5. All the neighbours lawns are as parched as straw.

■ Review Test

In each sentence underline the two words that need apostrophes. Then write the words correctly in the spaces provided.

_____ 1. Although I hadnt met him before, Donalds voice sounded familiar to me.
_____

_____ 2. A shaky rope ladder led from the barns wooden floor to the haylofts dusty
_____   shadows.

_____ 3. The paperback books glaring purple and orange cover was designed to
_____   attract the hurrying customers eye.

_____ 4. Phils essay was due in a matter of hours, but he suffered a writers block that
_____   emptied his brain.

_____ 5. While he waited in his boss office, Charlies nervous fingers shredded a
_____   Styrofoam coffee cup into a pile of jagged white flakes.

_____ 6. Jacks son stepped cautiously along the top of the farmyards splintery
_____   wooden fence.

_____ 7. Members of the parents association constructed a maze made of old tires for
_____   the childrens playground.

_____ 8. Barrys greatest accomplishment was conquering his addiction to his mothers
_____   chocolate pecan pie.

_____ 9. The suns rays beat down until the streets tarred surface softened with the
_____   heat.

_____ 10. The rivers swirling floodwaters lapped against the Thompsons porch.
_____

QUOTATION MARKS

The two main uses of quotation marks are:

1 To set off the exact words of a speaker or writer
2 To set off the titles of short works

Each use is explained on the pages that follow.

QUOTATION MARKS TO SET OFF THE WORDS OF A SPEAKER OR WRITER

Use quotation marks to show the exact words of a speaker or writer.

"I feel as though I've been here before," Angie murmured to her husband.
(Quotation marks set off the exact words that Angie spoke to her husband.)

Cyril Connolly once wrote, "The one way to get thin is to re-establish a purpose in life."
(Quotation marks set off the exact words that Cyril Connolly wrote.)

"Did you know," said the nutrition expert, "that it's healthier to be ten pounds overweight?"
(Two pairs of quotation marks are used to enclose the nutrition expert's exact words.)

The biology professor said, "Ants are a lot like human beings. They farm their own food and raise smaller insects as livestock. And, like humans, ants send armies to war."
(Note that the end quotation marks do not come until the end of the biology professor's speech. Place quotation marks before the first quoted word and after the last quoted word. As long as no interruption occurs in the speech, do not use quotation marks for each new sentence.)

Punctuation Hint: In the four examples on the preceding page, notice that a comma sets off the quoted part from the rest of the sentence. Also observe that commas and periods at the end of a quotation always go *inside* quotation marks.

Complete the following statements that explain how capital letters, commas, and periods are used in quotations. Refer to the four examples as guides.

1. Every quotation begins with a _____ letter.

2. When a quotation is split (as in the sentence of the nutrition expert), the second part does not begin with a capital letter unless it is a _____ sentence.

3. _____ are used to separate the quoted part of a sentence from the rest of the sentence.

4. Commas and periods that come at the end of a quotation go _____ quotation marks.

The answers are *capital*, *new*, *Commas*, and *inside*.

Activity 1

Place quotation marks around the exact words of a speaker or writer in the sentences that follow.

1. I'll worry about that tomorrow, Scarlett said to Rhett.

2. Beatrice asked, Do you give a discount to senior citizens?

3. This hamburger is raw! cried Leon.

4. The bumper sticker on the rear of the battered old car read, Don't laugh—it's paid for.

5. I know why Robin Hood robbed only the rich, said the comedian. The poor don't have any money.

6. These records, proclaimed the television announcer, are not sold in any store.

7. When chefs go to great lengths, the man at the reducing centre said, I go to great widths.

8. Did you know, the counsellor said to my husband and me, that it now costs $85,000 to raise a child to the age of eighteen?

9. On a tombstone in a Manitoba cemetery are the words, Here lies an atheist, all dressed up and no place to go.

10. The advice columnist advised, Be nice to people on your way up because you'll meet them on your way down.

Activity 2

1. Write a sentence in which you quote a favourite expression of someone you know. Identify the relationship of the person to you.

   Example My grandfather's favourite expression is, "It can't be as bad as all that."

   _____

   _____

2. Write a quotation that contains the words *Nick asked Fran*. Write a second quotation that includes the words *Fran replied*.

   _____

   _____

   _____

   _____

   _____

   _____

   _____

3. Write down a sentence or two that interests you from a book or magazine. Identify the title and author of the work.

   Example In "The Purpose of Pornography" by Robertson Davies, the author writes, "Erotic books feed a part of the fantasy life without which man cannot exist."

   _____

   _____

   _____

   _____

   _____

   _____

Indirect Quotations

An indirect quotation is a rewording of someone else's comments rather than a word-for-word direct quotation. The word *that* often signals an indirect quotation.

Direct Quotation	*Indirect Quotation*
The nurse said, "Some babies cannot tolerate cows' milk." (The nurse's exact spoken words are given, so quotation marks are used.)	The nurse said that some babies cannot tolerate cows' milk. (We learn the nurse's words indirectly, so no quotation marks are used.)
Vicky's note to Dan read, "I'll be home by 7:30." (The exact words that Vicky wrote in the note are given, so quotation marks are used.)	Vicky left a note for Dan that said she would be home by 7:30. (We learn Vicky's words indirectly, so no quotation marks are used.)

Activity

Rewrite the following sentences, changing words as necessary to convert the sentences into direct quotations. The first one has been done for you as an example.

1. Teddy asked Margie if she wanted to see his spider collection.

   Teddy asked, "Margie, do you want to see my spider collection?"

2. Andy said that his uncle looks just like a large basset hound.

   _____

   _____

3. Nathan said that he wanted a box of the extra-crispy chicken.

   _____

   _____

4. My boss told me that I could make mistakes as long as I didn't repeat them.

   _____

   _____

5. The announcer said that tonight's regular TV programmes have been cancelled.

   _____

   _____

QUOTATION MARKS TO SET OFF THE TITLES OF SHORT WORKS

Titles of short works are usually set off by quotation marks, while titles of long works are underlined. Use quotation marks to set off the titles of such short works as articles in books, newspapers, or magazines; chapters in a book; short stories; poems; and songs. But you should underline the titles of books, newspapers, magazines, plays, movies, record albums, and television shows. Following are some examples.

Quotation Marks	*Underlines*
the essay "Bicycles"	in the book Urban Scrawl
the article "The Problem of Acid Rain"	in the newspaper The Vancouver Sun
the article "Living with Inflation"	in the magazine Maclean's
the chapter "Chinese Religion"	in the book Paths of Faith
the story "The Sin Eater"	in the book Bluebeard's Egg
the poem "When I Have Fears"	in the book Complete Poems of John Keats
the song "Ziggy Stardust"	in the album Changes
	the television show The Nature of Things
	the movie High Noon

Note: In printed works, italic type—slanted type that looks *like this*—is used instead of underlining.

Activity

Use quotation marks or underlines as needed.

1. In his short story entitled A Girl's Story, David Arnason describes a male writer's experience with creating the thoughts and feelings of a female character.

2. I bought the National Enquirer to read an article entitled How Video Games Are Hazardous to Your Mental Health.

3. We read the chapter The Motive for Metaphor in Northrop Frye's book The Educated Imagination.

4. Jane used an article titled Ten Ways to Unplug Your Kid's TV Habit in her research paper for developmental psychology.

5. The movie Casablanca, which starred Humphrey Bogart, was originally cast with Ronald Reagan in the leading role.

6. My favourite old TV show was Thriller, a horror series hosted by Boris Karloff, the man who starred in the 1931 movie Frankenstein.

7. When the Beatles' movie A Hard Day's Night was first shown, fans screamed so much that no one could hear the songs or the dialogue.

8. On my father's wall is a framed front page of The Edmonton Journal of February 25, 1911—the day he was born.

9. The sociology test will cover the first two chapters: Culture and Diversity and Social Stratification.

10. An article in Family Health called Which Cereal for Breakfast? claims that children can learn to like low-sugar cereals like Harvest Crunch and Weetabix.

OTHER USES OF QUOTATION MARKS

Quotation marks are also used as follows:

1 To set off special words or phrases from the rest of a sentence:

In elementary school, we were taught a little jingle about the "i before e" spelling rule.

What is the difference between "it's" and "its"?

(In this book, *italics* are often used instead of quotation marks to set off words.)

2 To mark off a quotation within a quotation:

The physics professor said, "Do the problems at the end of Chapter Five, 'Work and Energy,' for class on Friday."

Elliot remarked, "Did you know that Humphrey Bogart never actually said, 'Play it again, Sam' in the movie *Casablanca*?"

Note: A quotation within a quotation is indicated by *single* quotation marks, as shown above.

■ Review Test 1

Insert quotation marks where needed in the sentences that follow.

1. The psychology class read a short story called Silent Snow, Secret Snow about a young boy who creates his own fantasy world.

2. When asked for advice on how to live a long life, the old man said, Don't look back; something may be gaining on you.

3. I'm against elementary school students using pocket calculators, said Fred. I spent three years learning long division, and so should they.

4. One updated version of an old saying goes, Absence makes the heart grow fonder—of somebody else.

5. When I gagged while taking a foul-tasting medicine, my wife said, Put an ice cube on your tongue first, and then you won't taste it.

6. I looked twice at the newspaper headline that read, Man in River Had Drinking Problem.

7. Gene reported to his business class on an article in *Canadian Business* magazine entitled Cashing In on the Energy Boom.

8. When a guest at the wedding was asked what he was giving the couple, he replied, About six months.

9. Pierre Elliott Trudeau, an occasionally controversial prime minister, once said, Power only tires those who don't exercise it.

10. If you're ever in trouble, said the police officer, you'll have a better chance of attracting aid if you shout Fire instead of Help.

■ Review Test 2

Go through the comics section of a newspaper to find a comic strip that amuses you. Be sure to choose a strip where two or more characters are speaking to each other. Write a full description that will enable people who have not read the comic strip to visualize it clearly and appreciate its humour. Describe the setting and action in each panel and enclose the words of the speakers in quotation marks.

COMMA

SIX MAIN USES OF THE COMMA

Commas are used mainly as follows:

1 To separate items in a series
2 To set off introductory material
3 On both sides of words that interrupt the flow of thought in a sentence
4 Between two complete thoughts connected by *and, but, for, or, nor, so, yet*
5 To set off a direct quotation from the rest of a sentence
6 For certain everyday material

You may find it helpful to remember that the comma often marks a slight pause or break in a sentence. Read aloud the sentence examples given for each rule, and listen for the minor pauses or breaks that are signalled by commas.

1 Comma between Items in a Series

Use commas to separate items in a series.

> The street vendor sold watches, necklaces, and earrings.
> The pitcher adjusted his cap, pawed the ground, and peered over his shoulder.
> The exercise instructor told us to inhale, exhale, and relax.
> Joe peered into the hot, still-smoking engine.

Notes

a The final comma in a series is optional, but it is often used.

b A comma is used between two descriptive words in a series only if *and* inserted between the words sounds natural. You could say:

Joe peered into the hot *and* still-smoking engine.

But notice in the following sentence that the descriptive words do not sound natural when *and* is inserted between them. In such cases, no comma is used.

Tony wore a pale green tuxedo. (A pale *and* green tuxedo does not sound right, so no comma is used.)

Activity

Place commas between items in a series.

1. The old kitchen cabinets were littered with dead insects crumbs and dust balls.

2. Rudy stretched out on the swaying hammock popped open a frosty can of pop and balanced it carefully on his stomach.

3. The children splashed through the warm deep swirling rainwater that flooded the street.

4. The freezer was crammed with mysterious foil-wrapped lumps boxes of frozen french fries and empty ice cube trays.

5. The musty shadowy cellar with the crumbling cement floor was our favourite playground.

2 Comma after Introductory Material

Use a comma to set off introductory material.

Just in time, Sherry slid a plastic tray under the overwatered philodendron.

Muttering under his breath, Ken reviewed the terms he had memorized.

In a wolf pack, the dominant male holds his tail higher than the other pack members.

Although he had been first in the check-out line, Dave let an elderly woman go ahead of him.

After the fire, we slogged through the ashes of the burned-out house.

Note: If the introductory material is brief, the comma is sometimes omitted. In the activities here, you should include the comma.

Activity

Place commas after introductory material.

1. As Chen struggled with the stuck window gusts of cold rain blew in his face.

2. Before taking a blood sample the nurse taped Jake's arm to make a large vein stand out.

3. Along the once-pretty river people had dumped old tires and loads of household trash.

4. When the movie still hadn't come on well after dusk the occupants of the cars parked at the drive-in began beeping their horns.

5. Setting down a smudged glass of murky water the waitress tossed Dennis a greasy menu and asked if he'd care to order.

3   Comma around Words Interrupting the Flow of Thought

Use a comma on both sides of words or phrases that interrupt the flow of thought in a sentence.

> The vinyl car seat, sticky from the heat, clung to my skin.
>
> Marty's personal computer, which his wife got him as a birthday gift, occupies all of his spare time.
>
> The hallway, dingy and dark, was illuminated by a bare bulb hanging from a wire.

Usually you can "hear" words that interrupt the flow of thought in a sentence by reading it aloud. In cases where you are not sure if certain words are interrupters, remove them from the sentence. If it still makes sense without the words, you know that the words are interrupters and that the information they give is nonessential. *Such nonessential or extra information is set off with commas.*

In the following sentence,

> Sue Dodd, who goes to aerobics class with me, was in a serious car accident.

the words *who goes to aerobics class with me* are extra information not needed to identify the subject of the sentence, *Sue Dodd.* Commas go around such nonessential information. On the other hand, in the sentence

The woman who goes to aerobics class with me was in a serious accident.

the words *who goes to aerobics class with me* supply essential information—information needed for us to identify the woman being spoken of. If the words were removed from the sentence, we would no longer know who was in the accident. Here is another example:

Watership Down, a novel by Richard Adams, is the most thrilling adventure story I've ever read.

Here the words *a novel by Richard Adams* could be left out, and we would still know the basic meaning of the sentence. Commas are placed around such nonessential material. But in the sentence

Richard Adams' novel *Watership Down* is the most thrilling adventure story I've ever read.

the title of the novel is essential. Without it the sentence would read, "Richard Adams' novel is the most thrilling adventure story I've ever read." We would not know which of Richard Adams' novels was so thrilling. Commas are not used around the title, because it provides essential information.

Most of the time you will be able to "hear" words that interrupt the flow of thought in a sentence and will not have to think about whether the words are essential or nonessential.

Activity

Use commas to set off interrupting words.

1. A slight breeze muggy with heat ruffled the bedroom curtains.

2. The defrosting chickens loosely wrapped in plastic left a pool on the counter.

3. Lenny's wallet which he kept in his front pants pocket was linked to his belt with a metal chain.

4. Mr. LeBlanc who is an avid Canadiens fan remembers the great days of Jacques Plante and Bernie Geoffrion.

5. The fleet of tall ships a majestic sight made its way into the harbour.

4 Comma between Complete Thoughts

Use a comma between two complete thoughts connected by *and, but, for, or, nor, so, yet.*

Sam closed all the windows, but the predicted thunderstorms never arrived.
I like wearing comfortable clothing, so I buy oversized shirts and sweaters.
Peggy doesn't envy the skinny models in magazines, for she is happy with her own well-rounded body.

Notes

a The comma is optional when the complete thoughts are short ones.

The ferris wheel started and Wilson closed his eyes.
Irene left the lecture hall for her head was pounding.
I made a wrong turn so I doubled back.

b Be careful not to use a comma in sentences having one subject and a double verb. The comma is used only in sentences made up of two complete thoughts (two subjects and two verbs). In this sentence,

The doctor stared over his bifocals and lectured me about smoking.

there is only one subject (*doctor*) and a double verb (*stared* and *lectured*). No comma is needed. Likewise, the following sentence

Frank switched the lamp on and off and then tapped it with his fingers.

has only one subject (*Frank*) and a double verb (*switched and tapped*); therefore, no comma is needed.

Activity

Place a comma before a joining word that connects two complete thoughts (two subjects and two verbs). Remember, do *not* place a comma within sentences that have only one subject and a double verb.

1. The television sitcom was interrupted for a special news bulletin and I poked my head out of the kitchen to listen to the announcement.

2. The puppy was beaten by its former owner and cringes at the sound of a loud voice.

3. The eccentric woman brought all her own clips and rollers to the hairdresser's for she was afraid to use the ones in the shop.

4. The tuna sandwich in my lunch is crushed and the cream-filled cupcake is plastered to the bottom of the bag.

5. Lynn unscrewed the front panel of the air conditioner and removed the plastic foam filter in order to clean it.

6. Ruth was tired of summer reruns so she visited the town library to pick up some interesting books.

7. Debbie tried to trap the jumbo bumblebee bumping along the ceiling but the angry insect stayed just out of reach.

8. Carl strolled among the exhibits at the comic book collectors' convention and stopped to look at a rare first edition of *Superman*.

9. Our neighbourhood crime patrol escorts elderly people to the local bank and installs free dead-bolt locks on their apartment doors.

10. Brendan tapped the small geraniums out of their pots and carefully planted them on his grandfather's grave.

5   Comma with Direct Quotations

Use a comma to set off a direct quotation from the rest of a sentence.

The carnival barker cried, "Step right up and win a prize!"

"Now is the time to yield to temptation," my horoscope read.

"I'm sorry," said the restaurant hostess. "You'll have to wait."

"For my first writing assignment," said Scott, "I have to turn in a five-hundred-word description of a stone."

Note: Commas and periods at the end of a quotation go inside quotation marks. See also page 401.

Activity

Use commas to set off direct quotations from the rest of the sentence.

1. The coach announced "In order to measure your lung capacity, you're going to attempt to blow up a plastic bag with one breath."

2. "A grapefruit" said the comedian "is a lemon that had a chance and took advantage of it."

3. The psychology professor said "Dreams about feeling paralyzed in emergencies can represent a real-life inability to cope with stressful situations."

4. "Speak louder" a man in the back row said to the guest speaker. "I paid five dollars to hear you talk, not whisper."

5. The zookeeper explained to the visitors "We can't tell the sex of a giant tortoise for almost ten years after its birth."

6   Comma with Everyday Material

Use a comma with certain everyday material.

Persons Spoken to

If you're the last to leave, Paul, please switch off the lights.
Fred, I think we're on the wrong road.
Did you see the play-off game, Lisa?

Dates

June 30, 1996, is the day I make the last payment on my car.

Addresses

I buy discount children's clothing from Isaacs Baby Wear Factory, Box 900, Vancouver, British Columbia V6H 4Z1.

Note: No comma is used to mark off the postal code.

Openings and Closings of Letters

| Dear Santa, | Sincerely yours, |
| Dear Larry, | Truly yours, |

Note: In formal letters, a colon is used after the opening: Dear Sir: *or* Dear Madam: *or* Dear Allan: *or* Dear Ms. Mohr:.

Numbers

The insurance agent sold me a $50,000 term life insurance policy.

Activity

Place commas where needed.

1. Would you mind George if we borrowed your picnic cooler this weekend?

2. The souvlaki served at Odysseus 468 Danforth Avenue are the best in town.

3. On December 29 1989 Vaclav Havel the dissident Czech playwright became President of Czechoslovakia.

4. The mileage chart shows Elaine that we'll have to drive 1231 kilometres to get to Red Deer Alberta.

5. The coupon refund address is 2120 Maritime Highway Halifax Nova Scotia B3J 1V2.

■ Review Test 1

Insert commas where needed. In the space provided below each sentence, summarize briefly the rule that explains the comma or commas used.

1. "Kleenex tissues" said the history professor "were first used as gas mask filters in World War I."

_____

2. Dee ordered a sundae with three scoops of rocky road ice cream miniature marshmallows and raspberry sauce.

_____

3. While waiting to enter the movie theatre we studied the faces of the people just leaving to see if they had liked the show.

_____

4. I had left my wallet on the store counter but the clerk called me at home to say that it was safe.

_____

5. The demonstrators protesting nuclear arms carried signs reading "Humans have never invented a weapon that they haven't used."

_____

6. Large cactus plants which now sell for very high prices are being stolen from national parks and protected desert areas.

_____

7. On June 11 1995 Rondell White set a Montreal Expos scoring record in a game against the Giants.

    _____

8. Tom watched nervously as the dentist assembled drills mirrors clamps picks and cylinders of cotton on a tray next to the reclining chair.

    _____

9. The talk show guest a former child star said that one director threatened to take away his dog if he didn't cry on cue.

    _____

10. Cats and dogs like most animals love the taste of salt and will lick humans' hands to get it.

    _____

■ Review Test 2

Insert commas where needed. Mark the one sentence that is correct with a *C*.

1. Before leaving for the gym Ellen added extra socks and a tube of shampoo to the gear in her duffel bag.
2. My father said "Golf isn't for me. I can't afford to buy lots of expensive sticks so that I can lose lots of expensive white balls."
3. Clogged with soggy birds' nests the chimney had allowed dangerous gases to accumulate in our house.
4. Bill took a time-exposure photo of the busy highway and the cars' taillights appeared in the developed print as winding red ribbons.
5. The graduating students sweltering in their hot black gowns fanned their faces with commencement programs.
6. Puffing a cigarette twitching his lips and adjusting his hat Bogie sized up the dangerous situation.
7. On July 1 1867 Upper and Lower Canada united to form the Dominion of Canada.
8. "When I was little" said Ernie "my brother told me it was illegal to kill praying mantises. I still don't know if that's true or not."
9. A huge side of beef its red flesh marbled with streaks of creamy fat hung from a razor-sharp steel hook.
10. A line of dancing bookworms on *Bookmice* kicked across the screen like a chorus line.

■ Review Test 3

In the following passage, there are ten missing commas. Add the commas where needed. The types of mistakes to look for are shown in the box below.

> 2 commas missing between items in a series
> 1 comma missing after introductory material
> 4 commas missing around interrupting words
> 2 commas missing between complete thoughts
> 1 comma missing with a direct quotation

When I was about ten years old I developed several schemes to avoid eating liver, a food I despise. My first scheme involved my little brother. Timmy too young to realize what a horrible food liver is always ate every bit of his portion. On liver nights, I used to sit next to Tim and slide my slab of meat onto his plate when my parents weren't paying attention. This strategy worked until older and wiser Tim decided to reject his liver along with the rest of us. Another liver-disposal method I used was hiding the meat right on the plate. I'd cut the liver into tiny squares half the size of postage stamps and then I would carefully hide the pieces. I'd put them inside the skin of my baked potato beneath some mashed peas, or under a crumpled paper napkin. This strategy worked perfectly only if my mother didn't look too closely as she scraped the dishes. Once she said to me "Do you know you left a lot of liver on your plate?" My best liver trick was to hide the disgusting stuff on a three-inch-wide wooden ledge that ran under our dining-room table. I'd put little pieces of liver on the ledge when Mom wasn't looking; I would sneak the dried-up scraps into the garbage early the next day. Our dog would sometimes smell the liver try to get at it, and bang his head noisily against the bottom of the table. These strategies seemed like a lot of work but I never hesitated to take whatever steps I could. Anything was better than eating a piece of meat that tasted like old socks soaked in mud.

■ Review Test 4

On separate paper, write six sentences, one illustrating each of the six main comma rules.

OTHER PUNCTUATION MARKS

COLON (:)

Use the colon at the end of a complete statement to introduce a list, a long quotation, or an explanation.

1   A list:

The store will close at noon on the following dates: October 5, December 24, and December 31.

2   A long quotation:

The humorist Stephen Leacock wrote: "Writing is no trouble: you just jot down ideas as they occur to you. The jotting is simplicity itself—it is the occurring which is difficult."

3   An explanation:

Here's a temporary solution to a dripping faucet: tie a string to it and let the drops slide down the string to the sink.

Activity

Place colons where needed in the sentences below:

1. Bring these items to registration a ballpoint pen, your student ID card, and a cheque made out to the college.
2. In our veterinarian's office is a grisly item a real dog's heart removed from an animal infested with heartworms.
3. Gabrielle Roy, the French Canadian author, wrote "The life of a writer is tragic: the more we advance, the farther there is to go, and the more there is to say, the less time there is to say it."

SEMI-COLON (;)

The main use of the semi-colon is to mark the break between two complete thoughts, as explained on pages 326–327. Another use is to mark off items in a series when the items themselves contain commas. Here are some examples:

Sharon's children are named Melantha, which means "black flower"; Yonina, which means "dove"; and Cynthia, which means "moon goddess."

My favourite albums are *Ingenue*, by k.d. lang; *Reckless* by Bryan Adams; and *God Shuffled His Feet* by Crash Test Dummies.

Activity

Place semi-colons where needed in the sentences below.

1. Strange things happen at very low temperatures a rose will shatter like glass.
2. My sister had a profitable summer: by mowing lawns, she earned $125 by washing cars, $85 and by walking the neighbours' dogs, $110.
3. The salad bar was well stocked it included fresh spinach and sliced almonds.

DASH (—)

A dash signals a degree of pause longer than a comma but not as complete as a period. Use a dash to set off words for dramatic effect:

I was so exhausted that I fell asleep within seconds—standing up.

He had many good qualities—sincerity, honesty, and thoughtfulness—yet he had few friends.

The letter from my father finally arrived—too late.

Notes

a The dash is formed on the keyboard by striking the hyphen twice (—). In handwriting, the dash is as long as two letters would be.

b Be careful not to overuse dashes.

Activity

Place dashes where needed in the following sentences.

1. The victim's leg broken in three places lay twisted at an odd angle on the pavement.
2. With a shriek, Jeannette dropped the hot iron pan on her toe.
3. After I had seen every exhibit and ride at Canada's Wonderland, there was only one other thing I wanted to see my motel room.

PARENTHESES ( )

Parentheses are used to set off extra or incidental information from the rest of a sentence:

> In 1913, the tax on an annual income of four thousand dollars (a comfortable wage at that time) was one penny.

> A small mirror (a double-faced one) is useful to a camper for flashing signals or starting fires.

Note: Do not use parentheses too often in your writing.

Activity

Add parentheses where needed.

1. Though the original *Star Trek* series originally ran for only three seasons 1965–1968, it can still be seen on many stations around the world.
2. Whenever Jack has too much to drink even one drink is sometimes too much, he gets loud and abusive.
3. When I opened the textbook, I discovered that many pages mostly those in the first chapter were completely blank.

HYPHEN (-)

1 Use a hyphen with two or more words that act as a single unit describing a noun.

The light-footed burglar silently slipped open the sliding glass door.

While being interviewed on the late-night talk show, the quarterback announced his intention to retire.

With a needle, Rich punctured the fluid-filled blister on his toe.

2 Use a hyphen to divide a word at the end of a line of writing or typing. When you need to divide a word at the end of a line, divide it between syllables. Use your dictionary to be sure of correct syllable divisions (see also page 423).

Mark's first year at college was a time filled with numerous new pressures and responsibilities.

3 Word processing has eliminated the need to divide words at the end of lines. When you are selecting your page format, check whether your instructor prefers full justification of lines or "ragged right" margins. In either format, the software programme will not split your final word; the word will be fitted into the line you are typing or moved to the beginning of the next line.

Notes

a Do not divide words of one syllable.

b Do not divide a word if you can avoid it.

Activity

Place hyphens where needed.

1. The record breaking summer temperatures coincided with an upsurge of assaults and murders in the city.
2. My father, who grew up in a poverty stricken household, remembers putting cardboard in his shoes when the soles wore out.
3. The well written article in *Maclean's* described the nerve wracking experiences of peacekeeping forces in Bosnia.

■ **Review Test**

At the appropriate spot, place the punctuation mark shown in the margin.

—
1. A bad case of flu, a burglary, the death of an uncle it was not what you would call a pleasant week.

( )
2. My grandfather who will be ninety in May says that hard work and a glass of wine every day are the secrets of a long life.

:
3. Robertson Davies wrote "The most original thing a writer can do is write like himself. It is also his most difficult task."

-
4. The passengers in the glass bottomed boat stared at the colourful fish in the water below.

( )
5. Ellen's birthday December 27 falls so close to Christmas that she gets only one set of presents.

;
6. The police officer had spotted our broken headlight consequently, he stopped us at the next corner.

—
7. I feel I have two chances of winning the lottery slim and none.

-
8. Well stocked shelves and friendly service are what Mrs. Dale demands of her staff.

;
9. Some people need absolute quiet in order to study they can't concentrate with the soft sounds of a radio, air conditioner, or television in the background.

:
10. There are three work habits my boss hates taking long coffee breaks, making personal phone calls, and missing staff meetings.

USING THE DICTIONARY

The dictionary is a valuable tool. To take advantage of it, you need to understand the main kinds of information that a dictionary gives about a word. Look at the information provided for the word *tattoo* in the following entry from *The Concise Oxford Dictionary,* seventh edition.*

Spelling, syllabication and pronunciation

Number in meanings listed

Part(s) of speech

tattoo'² *v.t.* & *n.* **1.** *v.t.* mark (skin etc.) with indelible patterns by inserting pigments in punctures; make (pattern) thus; hence ~**ER**¹, ~**IST**⁽³⁾, *ns.* **2.** *n.* such mark. [v.f.n.f. Polynesian]

Meanings

Other forms of the word

Derivation of the word [Etymology]

The Concise Oxford Dictionary. Copyright © Oxford University Press 1964, 1976, 1982.

SPELLING

The first bit of information, in the boldface (heavy type) entry itself, is the spelling of *tattoo*. Get into the habit of using the dictionary for spelling. When you revise your paper, allow yourself time to look up the spelling of words you are unsure about. After typing your final draft, *always* use your processor's spell-checker to go over each page of your essay. *Double-check* in the dictionary words with which you have had problems in the past and simple but tricky "same sound" words like *it's* and *its* and *there, they're,* and *their.*

Use your dictionary to correct the spelling of the following words:

accomodate _____   intermit _____

crediter _____   privlege _____

decimel _____   recesion _____

unanamous _____   propasition _____

barbeque _____   jepardy _____

equivilent _____   transmitt _____

embarass _____   adolesent _____

SYLLABICATION

The second bit of information that the dictionary gives, also in the boldface entry, is the syllabication of *tattoo*. Dictionaries vary in their demarcation of syllables; either a raised dot (bullet) or apostrophe may separate syllables.

Use your dictionary to mark the syllable divisions in the following words. Also indicate how many syllables are in each word.

f r u g a l   (_____ syllables)

t r a n s l u c e n t   (_____ syllables)

a n t i p a t h y   (_____ syllables)

s e m i a n n u a l   (_____ syllables)

i n f e r i o r i t y   (_____ syllables)

Noting syllable divisions will enable you to *hyphenate* a word, that is, divide it at the end of one line of writing and complete it at the beginning of the next line. You can correctly hyphenate a word only at a syllable division, and you may have to check your dictionary to make sure of a particular word's syllable divisions.

PRONUNCIATION

The third bit of information in the dictionary entry is the pronunciation of *tattoo* (**tattōō′**). You already know how to pronounce *tattoo*, but if you did not, the information within the parentheses would serve as your guide. Use your dictionary to complete the following exercises that relate to pronunciation.

Vowel Sounds

You will probably use the pronunciation key in your dictionary mainly as a guide to pronouncing different vowel sounds (vowels are the letters *a*, *e*, *i*, *o*, and *u*). Here is part of the pronunciation key in *The Concise Oxford Dictionary*:

ă as in (făt)   ī as in (bīt) = bite
ā as in (fāt) = fate   ĭ as in (bĭt)
                              i as in (bā′s*i*n)
ě as in (mět)
ē as in (mēt) = meet

The key tells you, for example, that the sound of the short *a* is pronounced like the *a* in *fat*, the sound of the long *a* is like the *a* in *fate*, and the sound of the short *e* is like the *e* in *met*, and so on.

Look at the pronunciation key in your dictionary. It is probably located in the front of the dictionary or at the bottom of every page. What common word in the key tells you how to pronounce each of the following sounds?

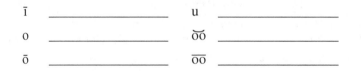

ī _____   u _____

o _____   o͞o _____

ō _____   o̅o̅ _____

Note: The long vowel always has the sound of its own name.

The Schwa (ə)

The symbol ə looks like an upside-down *e*. The International Phonetic Alphabet calls this sound a *schwa*, and it stands for the unaccented sound in such words as *ago*, *item*, *easily*, *gallop*, and *circus*. More approximately, it stands for the sound *uh*—like the *uh* that speakers sometimes make when they hesitate in their speech. Perhaps it would help to remember that *a* or *uh*, as well as ə, could be used to represent the schwa sound.

Your dictionary may use the International Phonetic Alphabet to facilitate pronunciation. If so, in your dictionary, you should be able to find three words that make use of the schwa in the pronunciation in parentheses after the main entry. Write three such words and their pronunciations in the spaces below.

1. _____   (_____)

2. _____   (_____)

3. _____   (_____)

Stress Marks

A primary accent or emphasis in pronunciation is shown by a heavy stroke ($'$). For example, in the word *individual* (ĭndĭvĭ′dūal) the stress, or accent, falls chiefly on the third syllable. Some dictionaries show a secondary accent or stress with a lighter stroke ($'$).

Use your dictionary to add stress marks to the following words:

prologue   (prō log)

tacit   (tăc ĭt)

corroborate   (cor rŏb o rāte)

animosity   (ăn ĭ mŏs ĭ tў)

magnanimous   (măg năn ĭ mous)

Note: Your dictionary may show pronunciation in the International Phonetic Alphabet; in which case, "corroborate" will be shown thus: (kō rob ə rāt).

Full Pronunciation

Use your dictionary to write out the full pronunciation (the information given either in boldface or in parentheses) for each of the following words.

binary _____

facsimile _____

vestige _____

antebellum _____

covert _____

euphemism _____

capitulate _____

derisive _____

tenacious _____

vociferous _____

satiate _____

aesthetic _____

anachronism _____

posthumous _____

millennium _____

Now practise pronouncing each word. Use the pronunciation key in your dictionary as an aid to sounding out each syllable. Do *not* try to pronounce a word all at once; instead, work on mastering *one syllable at a time*. When you can pronounce each of the syllables in a word successfully, then say them in sequence, add the accent, and pronounce the entire word.

PARTS OF SPEECH

The next bits of information that the dictionary gives about *tattoo* are the letters *v.t.* and *n.* These abbreviations mean that the meanings of *tattoo* as a verb and as a noun will follow.

Use your dictionary if necessary to fill in the meanings of the following abbreviations:

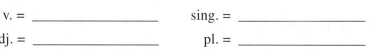

v. = _____   sing. = _____

adj. = _____   pl. = _____

PRINCIPAL PARTS OF IRREGULAR VERBS

Tattoo is a regular verb and forms its principal parts by adding *-ed*, *-ed*, and *-ing* to the stem of the verb. When a verb is irregular, the dictionary lists its principal parts. For example, with *give* the present tense comes first (the entry itself, *give*). Next comes the past tense (*gave*), and then the past participle, identified as *p.p.*, (*given*)—the form of the verb used with such helping words as *have*, *had*, and *was*. Then comes the present participle, identified as *part.*, (*giving*)—the *-ing* form of the verb.

Look up the parts of the following irregular verbs and write them in the spaces provided. The first one is done for you.

Present	*Past*	*Past Participle*	*Present Participle*
swim	swam	swum	swimming
lie			
drink			
freeze			

PLURAL FORMS OF IRREGULAR NOUNS

The dictionary supplies the plural forms of all irregular nouns (regular nouns like *tattoo* form the plural by adding *-s* or *-es*). Give the plurals of the following nouns. If two forms are shown, write down both.

crisis _____

phenomenon _____

library _____

cactus _____

shelf _____

MEANINGS

When there is more than one meaning to a word, the meanings are numbered in the dictionary, as with the word *tattoo*. In many dictionaries, the most common meanings of a word are presented first. The introductory pages of your dictionary will explain the order in which meanings are presented.

Use the sentence context to try to explain the meaning of the italicized word in each of the following sentences. Write your definition in the space provided. Then look up and record the dictionary meaning of the word. Be sure you pick out the meaning that fits the word as it is used in the sentence.

1. During the hiking trip, we had to *navigate* some difficult trails.

    Your definition _____

    Dictionary definition _____

2. I had a *yen* for ice cream, but I knew I should stick to my diet.

   Your definition _____

   Dictionary definition _____

3. I faced a *gauntlet* of questions from my parents after arriving home at 4 a.m.

   Your definition _____

   Dictionary definition _____

4. Mel tried to *cajole* me into going to the party, but I wasn't in the mood.

   Your definition _____

   Dictionary definition _____

ETYMOLOGY

Etymology refers to the origin and historical development of a word. *Tattoo* is originally a Polynesian word. Such information is usually enclosed in brackets and may more likely be present in a hardbound dictionary than in a paperback one. Good dictionaries include:

The Gage Canadian Dictionary
Funk & Wagnalls Canadian College Dictionary
The Oxford Advanced Learner's Dictionary
The Concise Oxford Dictionary

See if your dictionary gives the origins of each of the following words:

guillotine _____

cereal _____

derrick _____

Note: The *Oxford Advanced Learner's Dictionary* is an especially good choice for college students, and it is available in paperback format.

USAGE LABELS

As a general rule, use only standard English words in your writing. If a word is not standard English, your dictionary will probably give it a usage label like one of the following: *informal, colloquial, nonstandard, slang, vulgar, obsolete, archaic, rare.*

Look up the following words and record how your dictionary labels them. Remember that a recent hardbound dictionary may be the best source of information about usage.

brass (meaning "rudeness") _____

dope (meaning "very stupid person") _____

beat (meaning "exhausted") _____

croak (meaning "die") _____

flab (meaning "fatty flesh") _____

SYNONYMS

A *synonym* is a word that is close in meaning to another word. Using synonyms helps you avoid unnecessary repetition of the same word in a paper. A paperback dictionary is not likely to give you synonyms for words, but a good desk dictionary will.

Consult a dictionary that gives you synonyms for the following words and write the synonyms in the space provided.

leave _____

difficult _____

important _____

You might also want to own a *thesaurus*, a book that lists synonyms and *antonyms*—words approximately opposite in meaning to another word. A thesaurus can improve your writing, helping you find the precise word needed to express your thoughts. A thesaurus works much like a dictionary. You look up a word, and instead of definitions provided by a dictionary, you get a list of synonyms for the word. Here are three good thesauruses:

The New Roget's Thesaurus, Paperback Edition
The Random House Thesaurus
Webster's Collegiate Thesaurus

■ Your word-processing programme may also contain a thesaurus. The thesaurus is useful for offering a variety of synonyms for a particular word, but differences between various words' meanings are not explained. Always check your dictionary for the meaning of a new word you intend to use.

IMPROVING
SPELLING

Poor spelling often results from bad habits developed in early school years. With work, such habits can be corrected. If you can write your name without misspelling it, there is no reason why you cannot do the same with almost any word in the English language. Following are steps you can take to improve your spelling.

STEP 1: USE THE DICTIONARY AND THE SPELL-CHECKER ON YOUR PROCESSOR

Get into the habit of using the dictionary. When you write a paper, allow yourself time to look up the spelling of all those words you are unsure about. Do not overlook the value of this step just because it is such a simple one. By using the dictionary, you can probably make yourself a 95 percent better speller. *Always* use the spell-checker when you have completed the typing of the final draft on your word-processor.*

STEP 2: KEEP A PERSONAL SPELLING LIST

Keep a list of words you misspell and study the words regularly. Put the words on the back page of a frequently used notebook or on a separate sheet of paper titled "Personal Spelling List."

*__*Note:__ Your word-processing programme may show the options "US Lex" or "UK Lex." "US Lex" refers to the American spelling and hyphenation patterns for words; "UK Lex," which this textbook uses, refers to the British (and predominantly Canadian) spelling and uses of hyphenation. Most Canadian colleges and universities will prefer British/Canadian spelling.

To master the words on your personal spelling list, do the following:

1   Write down any hint that will help you remember the spelling of a word. For example, you might want to note that *occasion* is spelled with two *c*'s, or that *all right* is two words, not one word.

2   Study a word by looking at it, saying it, and spelling it. You may also want to write out the word one or more times, or "air write" it with your finger in large, exaggerated motions.

3   When you have trouble spelling a long word, try to break the word into syllables and see whether you can spell the syllables. For example, *inadvertent* can be spelled easily if you can hear and spell in turn its four syllables: *in ad ver tent*. Or the word *consternation* can be spelled easily if you hear and spell in turn its four syllables: *con ster na tion*. Remember, then: Try to see, hear, and spell long words in terms of their syllable parts.

4   Keep in mind that review and repeated self-testing are the keys to effective learning. When you are learning a series of words, go back after studying each new word and review all the preceding ones.

STEP 3: MASTER COMMONLY CONFUSED WORDS

Master the meanings and spellings of the commonly confused words on pages 439–447. Your instructor may assign twenty words for you to study at a time and give you a series of quizzes until you have mastered the words.

STEP 4: LEARN KEY WORDS IN MAJOR SUBJECTS

Make up and master lists of words central to the vocabulary of your major subjects. For example, a list of key words in business might include: *economics, management, resources, scarcity, capitalism, decentralization, productivity, enterprise*, and so on; in psychology: *behaviour, investigation, experimentation, frustration, cognition, stimulus, response, organism*, and so on. Set aside a specific portion of your various course notebooks to be used only for such lists, and study them using the methods for learning words that are described above.

STEP 5: STUDY A BASIC WORD LIST

Study the spellings of the words in the following list. They are 250 often misspelled words in English. Your instructor may assign twenty-five or fifty words for you to study at a time and give you a series of quizzes until you have mastered the list.

250 Basic Words

absence	column	hammer
ache	comfortable	handkerchief
achieve	committed	harass
acknowledge	completely	height
advice	conceit	hospital
aisle	conscience	hundred
all right	conscious	husband
already	conversation	imitation
amateur	cruelty	incredible
answer	50 daughter	independent
anxious	deceit	instant
appearance	definite	instead
appetite	deposit	intelligence
attempt	dictionary	interest
attendance	disastrous	interfere
autumn	disease	interrupt
awful	distance	irresistible
bachelor	doctor	January
balance	doubt	kindergarten
bargain	efficient	100 leisure
basically	eighth	library
beautiful	either	lightning
believe	emphasize*	likely
beneficial	entrance	livelihood
25 bottom	environment	loneliness
breathe	exaggerate	loose
brilliant	examine	magazine
bureau	existence	making
business	familiar	maintain
cafeteria	fascinate	marriage
calendar	February	material
candidate	financial	mathematics
category	foreign	medicine
ceiling	forty	minute
cemetery	75 friend	mortgage
chief	furniture	muscle
choose	government	naturally
cigarette	grammar	necessary
citizen	grieve	neither
college	guidance	nickel

*Note: Please see the section of the Introduction on variations in spellings for Canadian usage and consistency of spelling patterns in this text.

niece
ninety
noise
obedience
125 obstacle
occasion
occur
occurrence
omission
opinion
opportunity
optimist
ounce
outrageous
pageant
pamphlet
people
perform
persistent
physically
picnic
plausible
pleasant
policeman
possible
precede
prefer
preference
prejudice
150 prescription
probably
psychology
pursue
quantity
quarter
quiet
quiz
raise
really
recede
receive
recognize
recommend

reference
region
reign
relieve
religion
representative
resistance
restaurant
rhythm
ridiculous
right
175 safety
said
salary
scarcely
scholastic
science
scissors
secretary
seize
separate
sergeant
several
severely
shriek
siege
similar
sincerely
sophisticated
succeed
suppress
straight
telephone
temperature
tenant
tendency
200 tenth
than
theatre
though
thousand
through
tomorrow

tongue
tonight
tournament
towards
transferred
trousers
truly
twelfth
unanimous
until
unusual
usage
used
usual
usually
vacuum
valuable
225 variety
vegetable
vengeance
view
villain
visitor
voice
wear
weather
Wednesday
weigh
weird
welcome
wherever
whether
which
woman
women
won't
writing
written
wrong
yesterday
yolk
your
250 you're

Please note that *a lot* is two words, never one.

STEP 6: USE ELECTRONIC AIDS

There are three electronic aids that may help your spelling. First, the word-processing programme you use with either your computer or the computers at your college undoubtedly has a *spell-checker* as part of its capabilities. Making use of the spell-checker for every document you prepare will enable you to identify incorrectly spelled words and to select from suggested correct spellings. Spell-checking systems cannot differentiate between unintentional mistakes in word usage, though. "Same sound" words, homonyms like *its* and *it's* or *there*, *their*, and *they're*, spelled correctly but used incorrectly, cannot be corrected by a spell-checker. You may want to highlight these words on your processor screen and double-check your intended meaning and spelling with the dictionary.

Second, *electronic spell-checkers* are pocket-size devices that look much like pocket calculators. They are among the latest examples of how technology can help the learning process. Electronic spellers can be found in the computer and electronics sections of most department, office supplies, or electronics stores. The checker includes a tiny keyboard. You type out the word the way you think it is spelled, and the checker supplies the correct spelling of related words. Some checkers even *pronounce* the word aloud for you. Canadian students will want to ask whether British/Canadian or American spelling systems are programmed into the spell-checker they select, and should find out whether or not instructors permit the use of these devices in classes and exams.

Third, many *electronic typewriters* on the market today will beep automatically when you misspell or mistype a word. They include built-in dictionaries that will then give you the correct spelling.

VOCABULARY DEVELOPMENT

A good vocabulary is a vital part of effective communication. A command of many words will make you a better writer, speaker, listener, and reader. Studies have shown that students with strong vocabularies, or students who work to improve a limited vocabulary, are more successful in school. And one research study found that a *good vocabulary, more than any other factor, was common to people enjoying successful careers in life*. This section will describe three ways of developing your word power: (1) regular reading, (2) vocabulary wordsheets, and (3) vocabulary study books. You should keep in mind from the start, however, that none of the approaches will help unless you truly decide to make vocabulary development an important goal. Only when you have this attitude can you begin doing the sustained work needed to improve your word power.

REGULAR READING

Through reading a good deal, you will learn words by experiencing them a number of times in a variety of sentences. Repeated exposures to a word in context will eventually make it a part of your working language.

You should develop the habit of reading a daily newspaper and one or more magazines like *Maclean's*, *Saturday Night*, or even *People*, as well as magazines suited to your interests. In addition, you should try to do some book reading for pleasure. This may be especially difficult at times when you also have textbook reading to do. Try, however, to redirect a regular one-half to one hour of your recreational time to book reading, rather than watching television, listening to music, or the like. By doing so, you may eventually reap the rewards of an improved vocabulary *and* the discovery that reading can be truly enjoyable.

WORDSHEETS

Another means of vocabulary development is to use vocabulary wordsheets. You should first mark off words in your reading that you want to learn. After you have accumulated a number of words, sit down with a dictionary and look up basic information about each of them. Put this information on a wordsheet like the one shown on the next page. Be sure also to write down a sentence in which each word appears. A word is always best learned not in a vacuum but in the context of surrounding words.

Study each word as follows. First, make sure you can correctly pronounce the word and its derivations. (Page 424 explains the dictionary pronunciation key that will help you properly pronounce each word.) Second, study the main meanings of the word until you can say them without looking at them. Finally, spend a moment looking at the example of the word in context. You should then go on to follow the same process with the second word. Then, after testing yourself on the first and the second words, go on to the third word. Remember to continue going back and testing yourself on all the words you have studied after you learn each new word. Such repeated self-testing is the key to effective learning.

Activity

Locate four words in your reading that you would like to master. Enter them in the spaces on the vocabulary wordsheet that starts below and fill in all the needed information. Your instructor may then check your wordsheet and perhaps give you a quick oral quiz on selected words.

You may receive a standing assignment to add five words a week to a wordsheet and to study the words. Note that you can create your own wordsheets using loose-leaf paper, or your instructor may give you copies of the wordsheet that appears below.

Vocabulary Wordsheet

1. Word: _tenacious_   Pronunciation: _tenā′cious (-shus)_

   Meanings: _1. Keeping a firm hold_

   2. Persistent; stubborn

   Other forms of the word: _tenaciously   tenacity_

   Use of the word in context: _I tried to loosen the tick's tenacious grip_

   on my skin.

2. Word: _____   Pronunciation: _____

    Meanings: _____

    _____

    _____

    Other forms of the word: _____

    Use of the word in context: _____

    _____

3. Word: _____   Pronunciation: _____

    Meanings: _____

    _____

    _____

    Other forms of the word: _____

    Use of the word in context: _____

    _____

4. Word: _____   Pronunciation: _____

    Meanings: _____

    _____

    _____

    Other forms of the word: _____

    Use of the word in context: _____

    _____

5. Word: _____   Pronunciation: _____

    Meanings: _____

    _____

    _____

    Other forms of the word: _____

    Use of the word in context: _____

    _____

VOCABULARY STUDY BOOKS

A third means of increasing your word power is the use of vocabulary study books. Various books on vocabulary development may be available in the learning skills centre at your school. The best of these books help you learn a word by asking you to look at the context, or the words around the unfamiliar word, to unlock its meaning. This method is called *using context clues*, or *using word clues*.

Here are some individual vocabulary study books you can find at some bookstores or through your college bookstore:

1100 Words You Need to Know (Barron's)—Bromberg and Gordon
Improving Vocabulary Skills (Townsend Press)—Nist and Mohr
Instant Word Power (Signet Books)—Lewis
The Least You Should Know About Vocabulary Building (Holt Rinehart and Winston)—Glazier

Many other vocabulary books and programs are available. The best are those which present words in one or more contexts and then provide several reinforcement activities for each word. The books will help you increase your vocabulary *if* you have the determination required to work with them on a regular basis.

COMMONLY CONFUSED WORDS

HOMONYMS

The commonly confused words (also known as *homonyms*) on the following pages have the same sounds but different meanings and spellings. Complete the activity for each set of words, and check off and study the words that give you trouble.

all ready   completely prepared
already   previously; before

It was *already* four o'clock by the time I thought about lunch.
My report was *all ready*, but the class was cancelled.

Fill in the blanks: David was _____ to sign up for the course

when he discovered that it had _____ closed.

brake   stop
break   come apart

The mechanic advised me to add *brake* fluid to my car.
During a commercial *break*, Marie lay on the floor and did fifty sit-ups.

Fill in the blanks: Tim, a poor driver, _____s at the last minute

and usually _____s the speed limit as well.

course   part of a meal; a school subject; direction
coarse   rough

> At the movies, I tried to decide on a *course* of action that would put an end to the *coarse* language of the man behind me.

Fill in the blanks: Over the _____ of time, jagged, _____ rocks will be polished to smoothness by the pounding waves.

hear   perceive with the ear
here   in this place

> I can *hear* the performers so well from *here* that I don't want to change my seat.

Fill in the blanks: The chairperson explained that the meeting was held _____ in the auditorium to enable everyone to _____ the debate.

hole   an empty spot
whole   entire

> A *hole* in the crumbling brick mortar made a convenient home for the small bird and its *whole* family.

Fill in the blanks: The _____ in Dave's arguments wouldn't exist if he put his _____ concentration into his thinking.

its   belonging to it
it's   the shortened form for "it is" or "it has"

> The tall giraffe lowered *its* head (the head belonging to the giraffe) to the level of the car window and peered in at us.
> *It's* (it is) too late to sign up for the theatre trip to Toronto.

Fill in the blanks: I decided not to take the course because _____ too easy; _____ content offers no challenge whatever.

knew past form of *know*
new not old

No one *knew* our *new* phone number, but the obscene calls continued.

Fill in the blanks: Even people who _____ Charlie well didn't recognize him with his _____ beard.

know to understand
no a negative

By the time students complete that course, they *know* two computer languages and have *no* trouble writing their own programmes.

Fill in the blanks: Dogs and cats usually _____ by the tone of the speaker's voice when they are being told "_____."

passed went by; succeeded in; handed to
past a time before the present; by, as in "I drove past the house"

As Yvonne *passed* exit six on the highway, she knew she had gone *past* the correct turn-off.

Fill in the blanks: Lewis asked for a meeting with his boss to learn why he had been _____ over for promotion twice in the _____ year.

peace calm
piece a part

The best *piece* of advice she ever received was to maintain her own inner *peace*.

Fill in the blanks: Upon hearing that _____ of music, my angry mood was gradually replaced by one of _____.

plain   simple
plane   aircraft

The *plain* box contained a very expensive model *plane* kit.

Fill in the blanks: After unsuccessfully trying to overcome her fear, Sally finally admitted the _____ truth: she was terrified of flying in _____ ˢ .

principal   main; a person in charge of a school
principle   a law or standard

If the *principal* ingredient in this stew is octopus, I'll abandon my *principle* of trying everything at least once.

Fill in the blanks: Our _____ insists that all students adhere to the school's _____ ˢ regarding dress, tardiness, and smoking.

right   correct; opposite of "left"
write   what you do in English

Without the *right* amount of advance planning, it is difficult to *write* a good research paper.

Fill in the blanks: Connie wanted to send for the CDs offered on TV, but she could not _____ fast enough to get all the _____ information down before the commercial ended.

than (thăn)   used in comparisons
then (thĕn)   at that time

I made more money *then*, but I've never been happier *than* I am now.

Fill in the blanks: When I was in high school, I wanted a racy two-seater convertible more _____ anything else; but _____ my friends pointed out that only one person would be able to ride with me.

their   belonging to them

there   at that place; a neutral word used with verbs like *is*, *are*, *was*, *were*, *have*, and *had*

they're   the shortened form of "they are"

> The tenants *there* are complaining because *they're* being cheated by *their* landlord.

Fill in the blanks: The tomatoes I planted _____ in the back of

the garden are finally ripening, but _____ bright red colour will

attract hungry raccoons, and I fear _____ going to be eaten.

threw   past form of *throw*

through   from one side to the other; finished

> As the inexperienced pizza maker *threw* the pie into the air, he punched a hole *through* its thin crust.

Fill in the blanks: As the Prime Minister moved slowly _____

the cheering crowd, the RCMP officer suddenly _____ himself at a man waving a small, metal object.

to   a verb part, as in to *smile;* towards, as in "I'm going *to* heaven"

too   overly, as in "The pizza was *too* hot"; also, as in "The coffee was hot, *too*."

two   the number 2

> I ran *to* the car *to* roll up the windows. (The first *to* means "towards"; the second *to* is a verb part that goes with *roll*.)
>
> That amusement park is *too* far away; I hear that it's expensive, *too*. (The first *too* means "overly"; the second *too* means "also.")
>
> The *two* players (2 players) jumped up to tap the basketball away.

Fill in the blanks: The _____ of them have been dating for a year,

but lately they seem _____ be arguing _____ often to pretend nothing is wrong.

wear   to have on
where   in what place

Where I will *wear* a purple feather boa is not the point; I just want to buy it.

Fill in the blanks: _____ were we going the night I refused to _____ a tie?

weather   atmospheric conditions
whether   if it happens that; in case; if

Although meteorologists are *weather* specialists, even they can't predict *whether* a hurricane will change course.

Fill in the blanks: The gloomy _____ report in the paper this morning ended all discussion of _____ to pack a picnic lunch for later.

whose   belonging to whom
who's   the shortened form for "who is" and "who has"

"*Who's* the patient *whose* filling fell out?" the dentist's assistant asked.

Fill in the blanks: _____ the salesperson _____ customers are always complaining about his high-pressure tactics?

your   belonging to you
you're the shortened form of "you are"

You're making a fool of yourself; *your* Elvis imitation isn't funny.

Fill in the blanks: If _____ having trouble filling out _____ tax return, why don't you call Revenue Canada's local line?

OTHER WORDS FREQUENTLY CONFUSED

Here is a list of other words that people frequently confuse. Complete the activities for each set of words, and check off and study the words that give you trouble.

a   Both *a* and *an* are used before other words to mean, approximately, "one."
an

Generally you should use *an* before words starting with a vowel (*a, e, i, o, u*):

   an orange   an umbrella   an indication   an ape   an effort

Generally you should use *a* before words starting with a consonant (all other letters):

   a genius   a movie   a speech   a study   a typewriter

Fill in the blanks: The morning after the party, I had _____ pounding headache and _____ upset stomach.

accept (ăk sĕpt′)   receive; agree to
except (ĕk sĕpt′)   exclude; but

   It was easy to *accept* the book's plot, *except* for one unlikely coincidence at the very end.

Fill in the blanks: Nan would have _____ *ed* the position, _____ that it would add twenty minutes to her daily commute.

advice (ăd vīs′)   a noun meaning "an opinion"
advise (ăd vīz′)   a verb meaning "to counsel, to give advice"

   I have learned not to take my sister's *advice* on straightening out my life.
   A counsellor can *advise* you about the courses you'll need next year.

Fill in the blanks: Ayesha seems so troubled about losing her job that I _____ *ed* her to seek the _____ of a professional counsellor.

affect (uh fĕkt′)   a verb meaning "to influence"
effect (ĭ fĕkt′)   a verb meaning "to bring about something"; a noun meaning "result"

The bad weather will definitely *affect* the outcome of the election.
If we can *effect* a change in George's attitude, he may do better in his courses.
One *effect* of the strike will be dwindling supplies in the supermarkets.

Fill in the blanks: Scientists have studied the _____ of large quantities of saccharine on lab animals but have yet to learn how similar amounts _____ human beings.

among   implies three or more
between   implies only two

After the team of surgeons consulted *among* themselves, they decided that the bullet was lodged *between* two of the patient's ribs.

Fill in the blanks: _____ halves, one enthusiastic fan stood up _____ his equally fanatic friends and took off his coat and shirt.

beside   along the side of
besides   in addition to

Besides doing daily inventories, I have to stand *beside* the cashier whenever the store gets crowded.

Fill in the blanks: _____ those books on the table, I plan to use these magazines stacked _____ me while doing my research paper.

fewer   used with things that can be counted
less   refers to amount, value, or degree

I've taken *fewer* classes this semester, so I hope to have *less* trouble finding time to study.

Fill in the blanks: This beer advertises that it has _____ calories and is _____ filling.

former   refers to the first of two items named
latter   refers to the second of two items named

Sue yelled at her sons, Greg and John, when she got home; the *former* had left the refrigerator open and the *latter* had left wet towels all over the bathroom.

Fill in the blanks: Marco collects coupons and parking tickets: the _____ save him money and the _____ are going to cost him a great deal of money some day.

learn   to gain knowledge
teach   to give knowledge

I can't *learn* a new skill unless someone with lots of patience *teaches* me.

Fill in the blanks: Because she is quick to _____ new things, Mandy has offered to _____ me how to play the latest video games.

loose (lo͞os)   not fastened; not tight-fitting
lose (lo͞oz)   misplace; fail to win

In this strong wind, the house may *lose* some of its *loose* roof shingles.

Fill in the blanks: A _____ wire in the television set was causing us to _____ the picture.

quiet (kwi'ĭt)   peaceful
quite (kwīt)   entirely; really; rather

Jennifer seems *quiet* and demure, but she has *quite* a temper at times.

Fill in the blanks: Most people think the library is _____ a good place to study, but I find the extreme _____ distracting.

Activity

These sentences check your understanding of *its, it's; there, their, they're; to, too, two;* and *your, you're.* Underline the two incorrect spellings in each sentence. Then spell the words correctly in the spaces provided.

_____

_____

1. "Its not a very good idea," yelled Alexandra's boss, "to tell you're customer that the striped dress she plans to buy makes her look like a pregnant tiger."

_____

_____

2. You're long skirt got stuck in the car door, and now its sweeping the highway.

_____

_____

3. When your young, their is a tendency to confuse a crush with true love.

_____

_____

4. After too hours of typing, Lin was to tired to type any longer.

_____

_____

5. It is unusual for a restaurant to lose it's licence, but this one had more mice in its' kitchen than cooks.

_____

_____

6. The vampires bought a knife sharpener in order too sharpen there teeth.

_____

_____

7. Your sometimes surprised by who you're friends turn out to be in difficult times.

_____

_____

8. When the children get to quiet, Clare knows their getting into trouble.

_____

_____

9. There friendship developed into love as the years passed, and now, in midlife, their newlyweds.

_____

_____

10. There is no reason to panic if you get a bad grade or too. Its well known that many successful people were not great students.

■ Review Test 1

Underline the correct word in the parentheses. Rather than guessing, look back at the explanations of the words when necessary.

1. I (know, no) that several of the tenants have decided (to, too, two) take (their, there, they're) case to court.

2. (Whose, Who's) the author of that book about the (affects, effects) of eating (to, too, two) much protein?

3. In our supermarket is a counter (where, wear) (your, you're) welcome to sit down and have free coffee and doughnuts.

4. (Its, It's) possible to (loose, lose) friends by constantly giving out unwanted (advice, advise).

5. For a long time, I couldn't (accept, except) the fact that my husband wanted a divorce; (then, than) I decided to stop being angry and get on with life.

6. I spent the (hole, whole) day browsing (threw, through) the chapters in my business textbook, but I didn't really study them.

7. The newly appointed (principal, principle) is (quite, quiet) familiar with the problems (hear, here) at our school.

8. I found that our cat had (all ready, already) had her kittens (among, between) the weeds (beside, besides) the porch.

9. I (advice, advise) you not to take children to that movie; the special (affects, effects) are (to, too, two) frightening.

10. It seems that nobody will ever be able to (learn, teach) Mario to take (fewer, less) chances in his car.

■ Review Test 2

On separate paper, write short sentences using the ten words shown below.

1. accept
2. its
3. you're
4. too
5. then
6. principal
7. their
8. passed
9. fewer
10. who's

EFFECTIVE WORD CHOICE

Choose your words carefully when you write. Always take the time to think about your word choices rather than simply use the first word that comes to mind. You want to develop the habit of selecting words that are appropriate and exact for your purposes. One way you can show your sensitivity to language is by avoiding slang, clichés, pretentious words, and wordiness.

SLANG

We often use slang expressions when we talk because they are so vivid and colourful. However, slang is usually out of place in formal writing. Here are some examples of slang expressions:

Someone *ripped off* Ken's new Adidas running shoes from his locker.
After the game, we *stuffed our faces* at the restaurant.
I finally told my parents to *get off my case*.
The movie really *grossed me out*.

Slang expressions have a number of drawbacks. They go out of date quickly, they become tiresome if used excessively in writing, and they may communicate clearly to some readers but not to others. Also, the use of slang can be an evasion of the specific details that are often needed to make one's meaning clear in writing. For example, in "The movie really grossed me out," the writer has not provided the specific details about the movie necessary for us to clearly understand the statement. Was it the acting, the special effects, or the violent scenes in the movie that the writer found so disgusting? In general, then, you should avoid the use of slang in your writing. If you are in doubt about whether an expression is slang, it may help to check a recently published dictionary.

Activity

Rewrite the following sentences, replacing the italicized slang words with more formal ones.

Example   When we told the neighbours to can the noise, they *freaked out*.

When we told the neighbours to be quiet, they got upset.

1. I didn't realize how *messed up* Joey was until he stole some money from his parents and *split* for a month.

   _____

   _____

   _____

2. After a hard day, I like to *veg* out in front of the *idiot box*.

   _____

   _____

   _____

3. Paul was so *wiped out* after his workout at the gym that he couldn't *get it together* to defrost a frozen dinner.

   _____

   _____

   _____

4. When Rick tried to *put the move on* Lola at the school party, she told him to *shove off*.

   _____

   _____

   _____

5. My father claims that most *grease monkeys* are *rip-off artists*.

   _____

   _____

   _____

CLICHÉS

A *cliché* is an expression that has been worn out through constant use. Some typical clichés are:

short but sweet	last but not least
drop in the bucket	work like a dog
had a hard time of it	all work and no play
word to the wise	it goes without saying
it dawned on me	at a loss for words
sigh of relief	taking a big chance
too little, too late	took a turn for the worse
singing the blues	easier said than done
in the nick of time	on top of the world
too close for comfort	time and time again
saw the light	make ends meet

Clichés are common in speech but make your writing seem tired and stale. Also, they are often an evasion of the specific details that you must work to provide in your writing. You should, then, avoid clichés and try to express your meaning in fresh, original ways.

Activity 1

Underline the cliché in each of the following sentences. Then substitute specific, fresh words for the trite expression.

Example   My boyfriend has stuck with me <u>through thick and thin</u>.
    <u>through good times and bad</u>

1. As the only girl in an otherwise all-boy family, I got away with murder.

    _____

2. When I realized I'd lost my textbook, I knew I was up the creek without a paddle.

   _____

3. My suggestion is just a shot in the dark, but it's better than nothing.

   _____

4. Janice got more than she bargained for when she offered to help Larry with his math homework.

   _____

5. Bob is pushing his luck by driving a car with bald tires.

   _____

6. On a hot, sticky, midsummer day, iced tea or any frosty drink really hits the spot.

   _____

7. Melissa thanks her lucky stars that she was born with brains, beauty, and humility.

   _____

8. Anything that involves mathematical ability has always been right up my alley.

   _____

9. Your chances of buying a good used car from that dealer are one in a million.

   _____

10. Even when we are up to our eyeballs in work, our boss wonders if we have enough to do.

    _____

Activity 2

Write a short paragraph describing the kind of day you had. Try to put as many clichés as possible into your writing. For example, "I got up at the crack of dawn, ready to take on the world. I grabbed a bite to eat. . . ." By making yourself aware of clichés in this way, you should lessen the chance that they will appear in your writing.

PRETENTIOUS WORDS

Some people feel that they can improve their writing by using fancy and elevated words rather than more simple and natural words. They use artificial and stilted language that more often obscures their meaning than communicates it clearly. Here are some unnatural-sounding sentences:

> It was a splendid opportunity to get some slumber.
> We relished the delicious repast.
> The officer apprehended the intoxicated operator of the vehicle.
> This establishment sells women's apparel and children's garments.

The same thoughts can be expressed more clearly and effectively by using plain, natural language, as below:

> It was a good chance to get some sleep.
> We enjoyed the delicious meal.
> The officer arrested the car's drunken driver.
> This store sells women's and children's clothes.

Here is a list of some other inflated words and the simpler words that could replace them.

Inflated Words	Simpler Words
subsequent to	after
finalize	finish
transmit	send
facilitate	help
component	part
initiate	begin
delineate	describe
manifested	shown
to endeavour	to try

Activity

Cross out the artificial words in each sentence. Then substitute clear, simple language for the artificial words.

Example   The ~~conflagration~~ was ~~initiated~~ by an arsonist.

<u>The fire was started by an arsonist.</u>

1. Mark and his brother do not interrelate in a harmonious manner.

2. The meaning of the movie's conclusion eluded my comprehension.

3. The departmental conference will commence promptly at two o'clock.

4. A man dressed in odd attire accosted me on the street.

5. When my writing implement malfunctioned, I asked the professor for another.

WORDINESS

Wordiness—using more words than necessary to express a meaning—is often a sign of lazy or careless writing. Your readers may resent the extra time and energy they must spend when you have not done the work needed to make your writing direct and concise.

Here are examples of wordy sentences:

In this paper, I am planning to describe the hobby that I enjoy of collecting old comic books.

In Dan's opinion, he thinks that cable television will change and alter our lives in the future.

Omitting needless words improves the sentences:

I enjoy collecting old comic books.
Dan thinks that cable television will change our lives.

At the top of the next page is a list of some wordy expressions that could be reduced to single words.

Wordy Form	*Short Form*
at the present time	now
in the event that	if
in the near future	soon
due to the fact that	because
for the reason that	because
is able to	can
in every instance	always
in this day and age	today
during the time that	while
a large number of	many
big in size	big
red in colour	red
five in number	five
return back	return
good benefit	benefit
commute back and forth	commute
postponed until later	postponed

Activity

Rewrite the following sentences, omitting needless words.

1. In conclusion, I would like to end my paper by summarizing each of the major points covered within my report.

   _____

   _____

2. Controlling the quality and level of the television shows that children watch is a continuing challenge to parents that they must meet on a daily basis.

   _____

   _____

3. In general, I am the sort of person who tends to be shy, especially in large crowds or with strangers I don't know well.

   _____

   _____

4. Someone who is analyzing magazine advertising can find hidden messages that, once uncovered, are seen to be clever and persuasive.

_____

_____

5. My greatest mistake that I made last week was to hurt my brother's feelings and then not to have the nerve to apologize and say how sorry I was.

_____

_____

■ Review Test 1

Certain words are italicized in the following sentences. In the space provided, identify the words as slang (*S*), a cliché (*C*), or pretentious words (*PW*). Then replace the words with more effective diction.

_____ 1. Losing weight is *easier said than done* for someone with a sweet tooth.

_____

_____ 2. After dinner, we washed the *culinary utensils* and wrapped the *excess* food.

_____

_____ 3. Bruce is so stubborn that talking to him is like *talking to a brick wall.*

_____

_____ 4. Michelle spent the summer *watching the tube* and *catching rays.*

_____

_____ 5. The fans, *all fired up* after the game, *peeled out* of the parking lot and honked their horns.

_____

_____ 6. The stew I made *contained everything but the kitchen sink.*

_____

_____ 7. That *guy* isn't really a criminal; he's just gotten a *bum rap.*

_____

_____ 8. My new *photographic equipment* is so complex that it *hinders my enjoyment* of taking pictures.

_____

_____   9. I failed the test, and to *add insult to injury*, I got a low grade on my paper.

_____   10. I *perused* several *periodicals* while I waited for the doctor.

■ Review Test 2

Rewrite the following sentences, omitting needless words.

1. In today's uncertain economic climate, it is clear that people, namely, average middle-class working people, have great difficulty saving much money or putting anything aside for emergencies.

2. He is of the opinion that children should be required by law to attend school until they reach the age of sixteen years old.

3. I reached the decision that I did not have quite enough native talent to try out to be one of the players on the basketball team.

4. We thought the television programme that was on last night was enjoyable, whereas our parents reacted with dislike to the content of the show.

5. Because of the bad weather, the school district felt it would be safer to cancel classes and let everyone stay home than risk people having accidents on the way to school.

6. It seems to me that all the *Rocky* movies have been over-rated, and that many people thought they were much better movies than they actually were.

7. I have a strong preference for candy over fruit, which, in my opinion, doesn't taste as good as candy does.

    _____

    _____

8. Lynn is one of those people who rarely admit to being wrong, and it is very unusual to hear her acknowledge that she made a mistake.

    _____

    _____

9. It seems obvious to me, and it should be to everyone else too, that people can be harmed as much by emotional abuse as by physical abuse, even if you don't lay a hand on them.

    _____

    _____

10. Out of all the regrets in my life so far, one of my greatest ones to the present time is that I did not take word-processing lessons when I was still in high school and had a chance to do so.

    _____

    _____

SENTENCE
VARIETY

One part of effective writing is to vary the kinds of sentences that you write. If every sentence follows the same pattern, writing may become monotonous to read. This section of the book explains four ways you can create variety and interest in your writing style. It will also describe co-ordination and subordination— two important techniques for achieving different kinds of emphasis in writing.

The following are four methods you can use to make simple sentences more complex and sophisticated:

1 Add a second complete thought (co-ordination).
2 Add a dependent thought (subordination).
3 Begin with a special opening word or phrase.
4 Place adjectives or verbs in a series.

Each method will be discussed in turn.

ADD A SECOND COMPLETE THOUGHT

When you add a second complete thought to a simple sentence, the result is a compound (or double) sentence. The two complete statements in a compound sentence are usually connected by a comma plus a joining or co-ordinating word (*and*, *but*, *for*, *or*, *nor*, *so*, *yet*).

A compound sentence is used when you want to give equal weight to two closely related ideas. The technique of showing that ideas have equal importance is called *co-ordination*. Following are some compound sentences. In each case, the sentence contains two ideas that the writer regards as equal in importance.

Frank worked on the engine for three hours, but the car still wouldn't start.

Bananas were on sale this week, so I bought a bunch for the children's lunches.

We laced up our roller skates, and then we moved cautiously onto the rink.

Activity

Combine the following pairs of simple sentences into compound sentences. Use a comma and a logical joining word (*and*, *but*, *for*, *so*) to connect each pair of statements.

Note: if you are not sure what *and*, *but*, *for*, and *so* mean, review page 323.

Example
- The weather was cold and windy.
- Al brought a thick blanket to the football game.

The weather was cold and windy, so Al brought a thick

blanket to the football game.

1.
   - Stanley was starving.
   - He hadn't eaten a thing since breakfast.

2.
   - I tried to sleep.
   - The thought of tomorrow's math exam kept me awake.

3.
   - This coffee shop has its own bakery.
   - It has take-out service as well.

4.
   - The cardboard storage boxes were soggy.
   - Rainwater had seeped into the basement during the storm.

5.
   - I didn't have enough money to buy my parents an anniversary present.
   - I offered to mow their lawn for the whole summer.

ADD A DEPENDENT THOUGHT

When you add a dependent thought to a simple sentence, the result is a complex sentence.* A dependent thought begins with one of the following subordinating words:

after	if, even if	when, whenever
although, though	in order that	where, wherever
as	since	whether
because	that, so that	which, whichever
before	unless	while
even though	until	who
how	what, whatever	whose

A complex sentence is used when you want to emphasize one idea over another in a sentence. Look at the following complex sentence:

Although the exam room was very quiet, I still couldn't concentrate.

The idea that the writer wishes to emphasize here—*I still couldn't concentrate*—is expressed as a complete thought. The less important idea—*Although the exam room was very quiet*—is subordinated to the complete thought. The technique of giving one idea less emphasis than another is called *subordination*.

Following are other examples of complex sentences. In each case, the part starting with the dependent word is the less emphasized part of the sentence.

Even though I was tired, I stayed up to watch the horror movie.
Before I take a bath, I check for spiders in the tub.
When Ivy feels nervous, she pulls on her earlobe.

---

*The two parts of a complex sentence are sometimes called an *independent clause* and a *dependent clause*. A *clause* is simply a word group that contains a subject and a verb. An independent clause expresses a complete thought and can stand alone. A dependent clause does not express a complete thought in itself and "depends on" the independent clause to complete its meaning. Dependent clauses always begin with a dependent or subordinating word.

Activity

Use logical subordinating words to combine the following pairs of simple sentences into sentences that contain a dependent thought. Place a comma after a dependent statement when it starts the sentence.

Example ■ Rita bit into the hard caramel.
  ■ She broke a filling.

When Rita bit into the hard caramel, she broke a filling.

1. ■ I had forgotten to lock the front door.
    ■ I had to drive back to the house.

    _____

    _____

    _____

2. ■ The bear turned over the rotten log.
    ■ Fat white grubs crawled in every direction.

    _____

    _____

    _____

3. ■ Kevin had mailed away for a set of tools.
    ■ He changed his mind about spending the money.

    _____

    _____

    _____

4. ■ Lew is allergic to wool.
    ■ He buys only sweaters made from acrylic.

    _____

    _____

    _____

5. ■ Sara types one hundred words a minute.
    ■ She is having trouble landing a secretarial job.

    _____

    _____

    _____

BEGIN WITH A SPECIAL OPENING WORD OR PHRASE

Among the special openers that can be used to start sentences are -*ed* words, -*ing* words, -*ly* words, *to* word groups, and prepositional phrases. Here are examples of all five kinds of openers:

-ed *word*	Concerned about his son's fever, Paul called a doctor.
-ing *word*	Humming softly, the woman browsed through the rack of dresses.
-ly *word*	Hesitantly, Sue approached the instructor's desk.
to *word group*	To protect his hair, Binh uses the lowest setting on his blow dryer.
prepositional phrase	During the exam, drops of water fell from the ceiling.

Activity

Combine each of the following pairs of simple sentences into one sentence by using the opener shown at the left and omitting repeated words. Use a comma to set off the opener from the rest of the sentence.

Example   -ing *word*   ■ The pelican scooped small fish into its baggy bill.
■ It dipped into the waves.

Dipping into the waves, the pelican scooped small fish into its baggy bill.

-ed *word*   1. ■ The night sky glittered.
■ It was studded with thousands of stars.

_____

_____

-ing *word*   2. ■ She wondered how to break the news to the children.
■ She sat in the cold living room.

_____

_____

-ly *word* 3. ■ Shirley signed the repair contract.
            ■ She was reluctant.

_____

_____

to *word* 4. ■ Alan volunteered to work overtime.
group   ■ He wanted to improve his chances of promotion.

_____

_____

prepositional 5. ■ The accused murderer grinned at the witnesses.
phrase   ■ He did this during the trial.

_____

_____

-ed *word* 6. ■ The vet's office was noisy and confusing.
            ■ It was crowded with nervous pets.

_____

_____

-ing *word* 7. ■ Barry tried to find something worth watching.
             ■ He flipped from channel to channel.

_____

_____

-ly *word* 8. ■ My father asked me where I had been until 5 a.m.
            ■ He was casual.

_____

_____

to *word* 9. ■ Stan stood on the table with a carrot behind each ear.
group   ■ He did this to attract everyone's attention.

_____

_____

prepositional 10. ■ Doctors used leeches to draw blood from sick patients.
phrase   ■ They did this at one time.

_____

_____

PLACE ADJECTIVES OR VERBS IN A SERIES

Various parts of a sentence may be placed in a series. Among these parts are adjectives (descriptive words) and verbs. Here are examples of both in a series:

Adjectives   I gently applied a *sticky new bandage to the deep, ragged* cut on my finger.

Verbs   The truck *bounced* off a guard-rail, *side-swiped* a tree, and *plunged* down the embankment.

Activity

Combine the simple sentences into one sentence by using adjectives or verbs in a series and by omitting repeated words. In most cases, use a comma between the adjectives or verbs in a series.

Example
- Jesse spun the basketball on one finger.
- He rolled it along his arms.
- He dribbled it between his legs.

Jesse spun the basketball on one finger, rolled it along his arms, and dribbled it between his legs.

1.
- The baby toddled across the rug.
- He picked up a button.
- He put the button in his mouth.

_____

_____

2.
- Water dribbled out of the tap.
- The water was brown.
- The water was foul-tasting.
- The tap was rusty.
- The tap was metal.

_____

_____

3.
- In the dressing room, Pat tried on the swimsuit.
- She looked in the full-length mirror.
- She screamed.

_____

_____

4. ■ Art approached the wasps' nests hanging under the eaves.
   ■ The nests were large.
   ■ The nests were papery.
   ■ The eaves were old.
   ■ The eaves were wooden.

   _____

   _____

5. ■ Reeds bordered the pond.
   ■ The reeds were slim.
   ■ The reeds were brown.
   ■ The pond was green.
   ■ The pond was stagnant.

   _____

   _____

■ Review Test 1

On separate paper, use co-ordination or subordination to combine the groups of simple sentences on the opposite page into one or more longer sentences. Omit repeated words. Since various combinations are possible, you might want to jot down several combinations in each case. Then read them aloud to find the combination that sounds best.

Keep in mind that, very often, the relationship among ideas in a sentence will be clearer when subordinating rather than co-ordinating words are used.

Example ■ Brent arrived at the supermarket.
 ■ Brent had a painful thought.
 ■ He had clipped all the coupons from the paper.
 ■ He had forgotten to bring them.

 When Brent arrived at the supermarket, he had a painful

 thought. He had clipped all the coupons from the paper, but

 he had forgotten to bring them.

Comma Hints

a Use a comma at the end of a word group that starts with a subordinating word (as in "When Brent arrived at the supermarket, …").

b Use a comma between independent word groups connected by *and*, *but*, *for*, *or*, *nor*, *so*, *yet* (as in "He had clipped all the coupons from the paper, but ...").

1. ■ Dan had repaired his broken watch-band with a paper clip.
   ■ The clip snapped.
   ■ The watch slid off his wrist.

2. ■ The therapist watched.
   ■ Julie tried to stand on her weakened legs.
   ■ They crumpled under her.

3. ■ There were spaces on the street.
   ■ Richie pulled into an expensive parking garage.
   ■ He had just bought a new car.
   ■ He was afraid it would get dented.

4. ■ A sudden cold front hit the area.
   ■ Temperatures dropped ten degrees in less than an hour.
   ■ My teeth began to chatter.
   ■ I was not wearing a warm jacket.

5. ■ The verdict was announced.
   ■ The spectators broke into applause.
   ■ The defendant looked stunned.
   ■ Then he let out a whoop of joy.

6. ■ The teacher watched closely.
   ■ The second-graders made candles.
   ■ Suddenly, one boy began to cry.
   ■ He had spilled hot wax on his arm.

7. ■ Vern works as a model.
   ■ He has to look his best.
   ■ He gained ten pounds recently.
   ■ He had to take off the extra weight.
   ■ He would have lost his job.

8. ■ The ball game was about to begin.
   ■ A dog ran onto the field.
   ■ The dog began nipping the infielders' ankles.
   ■ The game had to be delayed.
   ■ The dog was chased away.

9. ■ The lion was hungry.
   ■ It watched the herd of gazelle closely.
   ■ A young or sick animal wandered away from the group.
   ■ The lion would move in for the kill.

10. ■ I am a good mechanic.
   ■ My boyfriend is a fast typist.
   ■ We decided to advertise our skills on the college bulletin board.
   ■ Unfortunately, we didn't get any calls at first.
   ■ We had forgotten to include our phone numbers on the notices.

■ Review Test 2

On separate paper, write:

1. Two sentences of your own that begin with -*ed* words
2. Two sentences that begin with -*ing* words
3. Two sentences that begin with -*ly* words
4. Two sentences that begin with *to* word groups
5. Two sentences that begin with prepositional phrases

Also write:

6. Two sentences of your own that contain a series of adjectives
7. Two sentences that contain a series of verbs

EDITING TESTS

PROOFREADING FOR SENTENCE-SKILLS MISTAKES

The ten editing tests in this section will give you practice in proofreading for sentence-skills mistakes. People often find it hard to proofread a paper carefully. They have put so much work into their writing, or so little, that it's almost painful for them to look at the paper one more time. You may simply have to *force* yourself to proofread. Remember that eliminating sentence-skills mistakes will improve an average paper and help ensure a strong grade on a good paper. Further, as you get into the habit of "proofing" your papers, you will get into the habit of using the sentence skills consistently. They are a basic part of clear and effective writing.

In the first five tests, the spots where errors occur have been underlined; your job is to identify each error. In the last five tests, you must locate as well as identify the errors.

■ Editing Test 1

Identify the sentence-skills mistakes at the underlined spots in the selection that follows. From the box below, choose the letter that describes each mistake and write it in the space provided. The same mistake may appear more than once. In one case, there is no mistake.

a. sentence fragment	d. dangling modifier
b. run-on	e. missing comma
c. inconsistent verb tense	f. no mistake

   I had a strange experience last <u>winter, I</u> was shopping for Christmas presents when
1
I came to a small clothing shop. I was going to pass it by. <u>Until I saw a beautiful purple</u>
                                                                                     2
<u>robe on a mannequin in the window.</u> <u>Stopping to look at it,</u> the mannequin seemed to
                                                                          3
wink at me. I was really <u>startled, I</u> looked around to see if anyone else was watching.
                                      4
Shaking my <u>head I</u> stepped closer to the window. Then I really began to question my
                     5
<u>sanity, it</u> looked like the mannequin moved <u>its</u> legs. My face must have shown alarm
      6   7
because the mannequin then <u>smiles.</u> <u>And even waved her arm.</u> I sighed with <u>relief, it</u>
                                           8   9   10
was a human model after all.

1. _____   3. _____   5. _____   7. _____   9. _____

2. _____   4. _____   6. _____   8. _____   10. _____

■ Editing Test 2

Identify the sentence-skills mistakes at the underlined spots in the selection that follows. From the box below, choose the letter that describes each mistake and write it in the space provided. The same mistake may appear more than once.

a. run-on	d. missing quotation marks
b. mistake in subject- verb agreement	e. wordiness
	f. slang
c. faulty parallelism	g. missing comma

It is this writer's opinion that smokers should quit smoking for the sake of those

     1

who are around them. Perhaps the most helpless creatures that suffer from being near

a smoker is unborn babies, one study suggests that the risk of having an undersized baby

     2   3

is doubled if pregnant women are exposed to cigarette smoke for about two hours a day.

Pregnant women both should refrain from smoking and to avoid smoke-filled rooms.

                                                              4

Spouses of smokers are also in big trouble. They are more likely than spouses of non-

                                   5

smokers to die of heart disease and the development of fatal cancers. Office workers are a

                                           6

final group that can be harmed by a smoke-filled environment. The Minister of Health

and Welfare has said "Workers who smoke are a health risk to their co-workers. While it is

                      7   8

undoubtedly true that one can argue that smokers have the right to hurt themselves they

     9   10

do not have the right to hurt others. Smokers should abandon their deadly habits for

the health of others at home and at work.

1. _____ 3. _____ 5. _____ 7. _____ 9. _____

2. _____ 4. _____ 6. _____ 8. _____ 10. _____

■ Editing Test 3

Identify the sentence-skills mistakes at the underlined spots in the selection that follows. From the box below, choose the letter that describes each mistake and write it in the space provided. The same mistake may appear more than once.

a.	sentence fragment	e.	dangling modifier
b.	run-on	f.	missing comma
c.	mistake in subject-verb agreement	g.	wordiness
d.	misplaced modifier	h.	slang

North America will never be a drug-free <u>society but</u> we could eliminate many of our drug-
1
related problems by legalizing drugs. Drugs would be sold by companies and not criminals

<u>if they were legal</u>. The drug trade would then take place like any other <u>business freeing</u>
2   3
the police and courts to devote their time to other problems. Lawful drugs would be sold

at a fair <u>price, no</u> one would need to steal in order to buy them. <u>By legalizing drugs,</u>
4   5
organized crime would lose one of its major sources of revenue. <u>It goes without saying</u>
6
<u>that</u> we would, instead, create important tax revenues for the government. Finally, if

drugs <u>was</u> sold through legal outlets, we could reduce the drug problem among our young
7
people. It would be illegal to sell drugs to people under a certain age. <u>Just as is the case</u>

<u>now with alcohol</u>. And because the profits on drugs would no longer <u>be out of sight,</u>
8   9
there would be little incentive for drug pushers to sell to young people. Decriminalizing

drugs, in short, could be a solution. <u>To many of the problems that result from the illegal</u>
10
<u>drug trade</u>.

1. _____   3. _____   5. _____   7. _____   9. _____

2. _____   4. _____   6. _____   8. _____   10. _____

■ Editing Test 4

Identify the sentence-skills mistakes at the underlined spots in the selection that follows. From the box below, choose the letter that describes each mistake and write it in the space provided. The same mistake may appear more than once. In one case, there is no mistake.

a. sentence fragment	e. mistake with quotation marks
b. run-on	f. mistake in pronoun point of view
c. mistake in subject-verb agreement	
d. mistake in verb tense	g. spelling error
	h. no mistake

One reason that I enjoy the commute to school is that the drive gives me <u>uninterupted</u>

₁

time to myself. The classes and socializing at college <u>is</u> great, and so is the time I spend

₂

with my family, but sometimes all this togetherness keeps <u>you</u> from being able to think.

₃

In fact, I look forward to the time I have <u>alone,</u> it gives me a chance to plan what I'll

₄

accomplish in the day ahead. For example, one Tuesday afternoon my history professor

<u>announces</u> that a rough outline for our semester report was due that Friday. <u>Fortunatly,</u>

₅ ₆

I had already done some <u>reading, and</u> I had checked my proposed topic with her the

₇

week before. <u>Therefore, on the way home in the car that evening.</u> I planned the entire

₈

history report in my mind. Then all I had to do when I got home was quickly jot it down

before I forgot it. <u>When I handed the professor the outline at 8:30 Wednesday morning.</u>

₉

She asked me <u>"if I had stayed up all night working on it."</u> She was amazed when I told

₁₀

her that I owed it all to commuting.

1. _____   3. _____   5. _____   7. _____   9. _____

2. _____   4. _____   6. _____   8. _____   10. _____

■ Editing Test 5

Identify the sentence-skills mistakes at the underlined spots in the selection that follows. From the box below, choose the letter that describes each mistake and write it in the space provided. The same mistake may appear more than once. In one case, there is no mistake.

a. sentence fragment	f. dangling modifier
b. run-on	g. homonym mistake
c. mistake in subject-verb agreement	h. missing apostrophe
	i. cliché
d. missing comma	j. no mistake
e. missing capital letter	

Cars can destroy your ego. First of <u>all the</u> kind of car you drive can make you feel
1
like a second-class citizen. <u>If you can't afford a new, expensive car, and are forced to</u>
2
<u>drive an old clunker.</u> You'll be the object of pitying stares and nasty sneers. Drivers of
newer-model cars just <u>doesn't</u> appreciate it when a '68 <u>buick</u> with terminal body rust
3   4
lurches into the next parking space. You may even find that drivers go out of <u>their</u> way
5
not to park near you. Breakdowns, too, can damage your self-respect. You may be an
assistant bank manager or a job <u>foreman, you'll</u> still feel <u>like two cents</u> when <u>your</u> sitting
6   7   8
on the side of the road. As the other cars whiz past, you'll stare helplessly at your <u>cars</u>
9
open hood or steaming radiator. In cases like this, you may even be turned into that
lowest of creatures, the pedestrian. <u>Shuffling humbly along the highway to the nearest</u>
10
<u>pay phone,</u> your car has delivered another staggering blow to your self-esteem.

1. _____ 3. _____ 5. _____ 7. _____ 9. _____

2. _____ 4. _____ 6. _____ 8. _____ 10. _____

■ **Editing Test 6**

See if you can locate and correct the ten sentence-skills mistakes in the following passage. The mistakes are listed in the box below. As you locate mistakes, put the sentence numbers in the spaces provided.

---

1 sentence fragment _____   1 missing comma after
1 run-on _____   introductory material _____
1 mistake in verb tense _____   2 missing quotation marks
1 nonparallel structure _____
1 dangling modifier _____   _____ _____
1 mistake in pronoun point of   1 missing apostrophe _____
  view _____

---

¹The greatest of my everyday fears is technology. ²Beginning when I couldn't master bike riding and extending to the present day. ³Fear kept me from learning to operate a jigsaw, start an outboard motor, or even using a simple tape recorder. ⁴I almost didn't learn to drive a car. ⁵At age sixteen, Dad lifted the hood of our Chevy and said, All right, you're going to start learning to drive. ⁶Now, this is the distributor . . . When my eyes glazed over he shouted, "Well, I'm not going to bother if youre not interested!" ⁷Fortunately, the friend who later taught me to drive skipped what goes on under the hood. ⁸My most recent frustration is the 35 mm camera, I would love to take professional-quality pictures. ⁹But all the numbers and dials and metres confuse me. ¹⁰As a result, my unused camera is hidden away on a shelf in my closet. ¹¹Just last week, my sister gives me a beautiful digital watch for my birthday. ¹²I may have to put it on the shelf with the camera—the alarm keeps going off, and you can't figure out how to stop it.

■ Editing Test 7

See if you can locate and correct the ten sentence-skills mistakes in the following passage. The mistakes are listed in the box below. As you locate mistakes, put the sentence numbers in the spaces provided.

1 sentence fragment _____	1 mistake in subject-verb
1 run-on _____	agreement _____
1 missing comma around an	2 missing quotation marks _____
interrupter _____	_____
2 apostrophe mistakes _____	1 misplaced modifier _____
_____	1 nonparallel structure _____

¹I was six years old when, one day, my dog was struck by a car while getting ready for school. ²My mother and I heard the terrifying sound of squealing brake's. ³In a low voice, she said, Oh, my God—Blackie. ⁴I remember trailing her out the door and seeing a car filled with teenagers and a spreading pool of bright blood on our cobblestoned street. ⁵To me, it seemed only a matter of seconds until a police car pulled up. ⁶The officer glanced at the crumpled dog under the car. ⁷And drew his gun. ⁸My mother shouted, "No!" ⁹She crawled halfway under the car and took the dog, like a sack of flour, out from under the wheels. ¹⁰Her housedress was splashed with blood, she cradled the limp dog in her arms and ordered the officers to drive her to the vets office. ¹¹It was only then that she remembered me, I think. ¹²She patted my head, was telling me to walk up to school, and reassured me that Blackie would be all right. ¹³The rest of the story including Blackie's slow recovery and few more years of life, are fuzzy and vague now. ¹⁴But the sights and sounds of those few moments are as vivid to me now as they were twenty-five years ago.

■ Editing Test 8

See if you can locate and correct the ten sentence-skills mistakes in the following passage. The mistakes are listed in the box below. As you locate mistakes, put the sentence numbers in the spaces provided.

2 sentence fragments _____
_____
1 run-on _____
1 mistake in subject-verb
agreement _____

1 nonparallel structure _____
2 apostrophe mistakes _____
_____
3 missing commas _____
_____ _____

¹Most products have little or nothing to do with sex a person would never know that by looking at ads'. ²A television ad for a headache remedy, for example shows the product being useful because it ends a womans throbbing head pain just in time for sex. ³Now she will not say "Not tonight, Honey." ⁴Another ad features a detergent that helps a single woman meet a man in a laundry room. ⁵When it comes to products that do relate to sex appeal advertisers often present more obvious sexuality. ⁶A recent magazine ad for women's clothing, for instance, make no reference to the quality of or how comfortable are the company's clothes. ⁷Instead, the ad features a picture of a woman wearing a low-cut sleeveless T shirt and a very short skirt. ⁸Her eyes are partially covered by semi-wild hair. ⁹And stare seductively at the reader. ¹⁰A recent television ad for perfume goes even further. ¹¹In this ad, a boy not older than twelve reaches out to a beautiful woman. ¹²Sexily dressed in a dark room filled with sensuous music. ¹³With such ads, it is no wonder that young people seem preoccupied with sex.

■ Editing Test 9

See if you can locate and correct the ten sentence-skills mistakes in the following passage. The mistakes are listed in the box below. As you locate mistakes, put the sentence numbers in the spaces provided.

---

1 sentence fragment _____   2 missing apostrophes _____

1 run-on _____   _____

1 mistake in subject-verb   1 nonparallel structure _____

  agreement _____   1 dangling modifier _____

2 missing commas after   1 mistake in pronoun point

  introductory material   of view _____

  _____ _____

---

¹Being a waitress is an often under-rated job. ²A waitress needs the tact of a diplomat, she must be as organized as a business executive, and the ability of an acrobat. ³Serving as the link between customers and kitchen, the most demanding diners must be satisfied and the often-temperamental kitchen help must be kept tamed. ⁴Both groups tend to blame the waitress whenever anything goes wrong. ⁵Somehow, she is held responsible by the customer for any delay (even if it's the kitchens fault), for an overcooked steak, or for an unavailable dessert. ⁶While the kitchen automatically blames her for the diners who change their orders or return those burned steaks. ⁷In addition she must simultaneously keep straight who ordered what at each table, who is yelling for the bill, and whether the new arrivals want cocktails or not. ⁸She must be sure empty tables are cleared, everyone has refills of coffee, and no one is scowling because a request for more rolls are going unheard. ⁹Finally the waitress must travel a hazardous route between the busy kitchen and the crowded dining room, she has to dodge a diners leg in the aisle or a swinging kitchen door. ¹⁰And you must do this while balancing a tray heaped with steaming platters. ¹¹The hardest task of the waitress, though, is trying to maintain a decent imitation of a smile on her face—most of the time.

■ **Editing Test 10**

See if you can locate and correct the ten sentence-skills mistakes in the following passage. The mistakes are listed in the box below. As you locate mistakes, put the sentence numbers in the spaces provided.

2 sentence fragments _____   2 missing capital letters

_____   _____ _____

1 run-on _____   1 mistake in pronoun point
2 irregular verbs _____   of view _____

_____   1 subject pronoun mistake _____

1 misplaced modifier _____

¹The thirtieth anniversary party of my uncle and aunt was the worst family gathering I've ever attended. ²On a hot saturday morning in july, Mom and I drove out into the country to Uncle Ted's house. ³It had already rained heavily, and the only place left to park was in a muddy field. ⁴Then, you would not believe the crowd. ⁵There must have been two hundred people in Uncle Ted's small yard, including his five daughters with their husbands and children, all the other relatives, all the neighbours, and the entire congregation of their church. ⁶Since the ground was soaked and light rain was falling. ⁷Mom and me went under the big rented canopy with everybody else. ⁸We couldn't move between the tables, and the humidity fogged my glasses. ⁹After wiping my glasses, I seen that there was a lot of food. ¹⁰It was mainly cold chicken and potato and macaroni salads, I ate a lot just because there was nothing else to do. ¹¹We were surprised that Uncle Ted and his wife were doing all the work themselves. ¹²They ran back and forth with trays of food and gathered trash into plastic bags staggering with exhaustion. ¹³It didn't seem like much of a way to celebrate. ¹⁴Mom was upset that she didn't get to speak with them. ¹⁵When we left, I was hot, sticky, and sick to my stomach from overeating. ¹⁶But quickly pushed our car out of the mud and got us on the road. ¹⁷I have never been happier to leave a party.

PART FIVE

READINGS
FOR
WRITING

INTRODUCTION
TO THE
READINGS

The reading selections in Part Five will help you find topics for writing. Each selection deals in some way with interesting, often thought-provoking concerns or experiences of contemporary life. One selection, for example, describes new kinds of stress that students face in college; another reminds us of neighbourhoods where we may have grown up; a third discusses the issue of "respectable" sado-masochism. The varied subjects should inspire lively class discussions as well as serious individual thought. The selections should also provide a continuing source of high-interest material for a wide range of writing assignments.

The selections serve another purpose as well. They will help develop reading skills with direct benefits to you as a writer. Through close reading, you will learn how to recognize the thesis in a selection and to identify and evaluate the supporting material that develops the thesis. In your own writing, you will aim to achieve the same essential structure: an overall thesis followed by detailed and valid support for that thesis. Close reading will also help you explore a selection and its possibilities thoroughly. The more you understand about what is said in a piece, the more ideas and feelings you may have about writing on an assigned topic or a related topic of your own. A third benefit of close reading is becoming more aware of authors' stylistic devices—for example, their introductions and conclusions, their ways of presenting and developing a point, their use of transitions, their choice of language to achieve a particular tone. Recognizing these devices in other people's writing will help you enlarge your own range of ideas and writing techniques.

THE FORMAT OF EACH SELECTION

Each selection begins with a short overview that gives helpful background information and stimulates interest in the piece. The selection is followed by two sets of questions.

■ First, there are ten reading comprehension questions to help you measure your understanding of the material. These questions involve several important reading skills: understanding vocabulary in context, recognizing a subject or topic, determining the thesis or main idea, identifying key supporting points, and making inferences. Answering the questions will enable you and your instructor to check your basic understanding of a selection quickly. More significantly, as you move from one selection to the next, you will sharpen your reading skills as well as strengthen your thinking skills—two key factors in making you a better writer.

■ Following the comprehension questions are seven discussion questions. In addition to dealing with issues of content, these questions focus on matters of structure, style, and tone.

Finally, several writing assignments accompany each selection. The assignments range from personal narratives to expository and persuasive essays about issues in the world at large. Many assignments provide detailed guidelines on how to proceed, including suggestions for prewriting and appropriate methods of development. When writing your essay responses to the readings, you will have opportunities to apply all the methods of development presented in Part Three of this book.

HOW TO READ WELL: FOUR GENERAL STEPS

Skilful reading is an important part of becoming a skilful writer. Following is a series of four steps that will make you a better reader—both of the selections here and in your reading at large.

1   Concentrate As You Read

To improve your concentration, follow these tips:

■ First, read in a place where you can be quiet and alone. Don't choose a spot where there is a TV or stereo on or where friends or family are talking nearby.

- Next, sit in an upright position when you read. If your body is in a completely relaxed position, sprawled across a bed or nestled in an easy chair, your mind is also going to be completely relaxed. The light muscular tension that comes from sitting in an upright chair promotes concentration and keeps your mind ready to work.

- Third, consider using your index finger (or a pen) as a pacer while you read. Lightly underline each line of print with your index finger as you read down a page. Hold your hand slightly above the page and move your finger at a speed that is a little too fast for comfort. This pacing with your index finger, like sitting upright on a chair, creates a slight physical tension that will keep your body and mind focused and alert.

2 Skim Material before You Read It

In skimming, you spend about two minutes rapidly surveying a selection, looking for important points and skipping secondary material. Follow this sequence when skimming:

- Begin by reading the overview that precedes the selection.

- Then study the title of the selection for a few moments. A good title is the shortest possible summary of a selection; it often tells you in several words— or even a single word—just what a selection is about. For example, the title "Shame" suggests that you're going to read about a deeply embarrassing condition or incident in a person's life.

- Next, form a basic question (or questions) out of the title. For instance, for the selection titled "Shame," you might ask, "What exactly is the shame?" "What caused the shame?" "What is the result of the shame?" Forming questions out of a title is often a key to locating a writer's thesis, your next concern in skimming.

- Read the first and last couple of paragraphs in the selection. Very often a writer's thesis, *if* it is directly stated, will appear in one of these places and will relate to the title. For instance, in "The Advertiser's Man" the author says in her final paragraph that advertisers target exactly those men "who feel removed" from the pull of ads.

- Finally, look quickly at the rest of the selection for other clues to important points. Are there any subheadings you can relate in some way to the title? Are there any words the author has decided to emphasize by setting them off in *italic* or **boldface** type? Are there any major lists of items signalled by words such as *first*, *second*, *also*, *another*, and so on?

3 Read the Selection Straight Through with a Pen in Hand

Read the selection without slowing down or turning back; just aim to understand as much as you can the first time through. Place a check or star beside answers to basic questions you formed from the title, and beside other ideas that seem important. Number as *1, 2, 3* . . . lists of important points. Circle words you don't understand. Put question marks in the margin next to passages that are unclear and that you will want to reread.

4 Work with the Material

Go back and reread passages that were not clear the first time through. Look up words that block your understanding of ideas and write their meanings in the margin. Also, reread carefully the areas you identified as most important; doing so will enlarge your understanding of the material. Now that you have a sense of the whole, prepare a short written outline of the selection by answering the following questions:

- What is the thesis?
- What key points support the thesis?
- What seem to be other important ideas in the selection?

By working with the material in this way, you will significantly increase your understanding of a selection. Effective reading, just like effective writing, does not happen all at once. Rather, it must be worked on. Often you begin with a general impression of what something means, and then, by working at it, you move to a deeper level of understanding of the material.

HOW TO ANSWER THE COMPREHENSION QUESTIONS: SPECIFIC HINTS

Several important reading skills are involved in the ten reading comprehension questions that follow each selection. The skills are:

- Understanding vocabulary in context
- Summarizing the selection in a title
- Determining the main idea
- Recognizing key supporting details
- Making inferences

The following hints will help you apply each of these reading skills:

- **Vocabulary in context.** To decide on the meaning of an unfamiliar word, consider its context. Ask yourself, "Are there any clues in the sentence that suggest what this word means?"

- **Subject or title.** Remember that the title should accurately describe the *entire* selection. It should be neither too broad nor too narrow for the material in the selection. It should answer the question "What is this about?" as specifically as possible. Note that you may at times find it easier to do the title question *after* the main-idea question.

- **Main idea.** Choose the statement that you think best expresses the main idea—also known as the *central point* or *thesis*—of the entire selection. Remember that the title will often help you focus on the main idea. Then ask yourself the question, "Does most of the material in the selection support this statement?" If you can answer *Yes* to this question, you have found the thesis.

- **Key details.** If you were asked to give a two-minute summary of a selection, the key, or major, details are the ones you would include in that summary. To determine the key details, ask yourself the question, "What are the major supporting points for the thesis?"

- **Inferences.** Answer these questions by drawing upon the evidence presented in the selection and your own common sense. Ask yourself, "What reasonable judgments can I make on the basis of the information in the selection?"

On pages 656–657 is a chart on which you can keep track of your performance as you answer the ten questions for each selection. The chart will help you identify reading skills you may need to strengthen.

LOOKING INWARD

Shame

Dick Gregory

In this selection, Dick Gregory—the comedian and social critic—narrates two painful experiences from his boyhood. Although the incidents show graphically what it can be like to grow up black and poor, the essay also deals with universal emotions: shame, embarrassment, and the burning desire to hold onto one's self-respect.

I never learned hate at home, or shame. I had to go to school for that. I was about seven   1
years old when I got my first big lesson. I was in love with a little girl named Helene
Tucker, a light-complected little girl with pigtails and nice manners. She was always clean
and she was smart in school. I think I went to school then mostly to look at her. I brushed
my hair and even got me a little old handkerchief. It was a lady's handkerchief, but I
didn't want Helene to see me wipe my nose on my hand. The pipes were frozen again,
there was no water in the house, but I washed my socks and shirt every night. I'd get a
pot, and go over to Mister Ben's grocery store, and stick my pot down into his soda
machine. Scoop out some chopped ice. By evening the ice melted to water for washing.
I got sick a lot that winter because the fire would go out at night before the clothes were
dry. In the morning I'd put them on, wet or dry, because they were the only clothes I had.

Everybody's got a Helene Tucker, a symbol of everything you want. I loved her for   2
her goodness, her cleanness, her popularity. She'd walk down my street and my brothers and sisters would yell, "Here comes Helene," and I'd rub my tennis sneakers on the

back of my pants and wish my hair wasn't so nappy and the white folks' shirt fit me better. I'd run out on the street. If I knew my place and didn't come too close, she'd wink at me and say hello. That was a good feeling. Sometimes I'd follow her all the way home, and shovel the snow off her walk and try to make friends with her Momma and her aunts. I'd drop money on her stoop late at night on my way back from shining shoes in the taverns. And she had a Daddy, and he had a good job. He was a paper hanger.

I guess I would have gotten over Helene by summertime, but something happened   3
in that classroom that made her face hang in front of me for the next twenty-two years. When I played the drums in high school it was for Helene and when I broke track records in college it was for Helene and when I started standing behind microphones and heard applause I wished Helene could hear it, too. It wasn't until I was twenty-nine years old and married and making money that I finally got her out of my system. Helene was sitting in that classroom when I learned to be ashamed of myself.

It was on a Thursday. I was sitting in the back of the room, in a seat with a chalk   4
circle drawn around it. The idiot's seat, the troublemaker's seat.

The teacher thought I was stupid. Couldn't spell, couldn't read, couldn't do arith-   5
metic. Just stupid. Teachers were never interested in finding out that you couldn't concentrate because you were so hungry, because you hadn't had any breakfast. All you could think about was noontime, would it ever come? Maybe you could sneak into the cloakroom and steal a bite of some kid's lunch out of a coat pocket. A bite of something. Paste. You can't really make a meal of paste, or put it on bread for a sandwich, but sometimes I'd scoop a few spoonfuls out of the big paste jar in the back of the room. Pregnant people get strange tastes. I was pregnant with poverty. Pregnant with dirt and pregnant with smells that made people turn away, pregnant with cold and pregnant with shoes that were never bought for me, pregnant with five other people in my bed and no Daddy in the next room, and pregnant with hunger. Paste doesn't taste too bad when you're hungry.

The teacher thought I was a troublemaker. All she saw from the front of the room   6
was a little black boy who squirmed in his idiot's seat and made noises and poked the kids around him. I guess she couldn't see a kid who made noises because he wanted someone to know he was there.

It was on a Thursday, the day before the Negro payday. The eagle always flew on   7
Friday. The teacher was asking each student how much his father would give to the Community Chest. On Friday night, each kid would get the money from his father, and on Monday he would bring it to the school. I decided I was going to buy a Daddy right then. I had money in my pocket from shining shoes and selling papers, and whatever Helene Tucker pledged for her Daddy I was going to top it. And I'd hand the money right in. I wasn't going to wait until Monday to buy me a Daddy.

I was shaking, scared to death. The teacher opened her book and started calling out   8
names alphabetically.

"Helene Tucker?"   9

"My Daddy said he'd give two dollars and fifty cents."   10

"That's very nice, Helene. Very, very nice indeed."   11

That made me feel pretty good. It wouldn't take too much to top that. I had almost   12
three dollars in dimes and quarters in my pocket. I stuck my hand in my pocket and held

onto the money, waiting for her to call my name. But the teacher closed her book after she called everybody else in the class.

I stood up and raised my hand.

"What is it now?"

"You forgot me?"

She turned toward the blackboard. "I don't have time to be playing with you, Richard."

"My Daddy said he'd . . ."

"Sit down, Richard, you're disturbing the class."

"My Daddy said he'd give . . . fifteen dollars."

She turned around and looked mad. "We are collecting this money for you and your kind, Richard Gregory. If your Daddy can give fifteen dollars you have no business being on relief."

"I got it right now, I got it right now, my Daddy gave it to me to turn in today, my Daddy said . . ."

"And furthermore," she said, looking right at me, her nostrils getting big and her lips getting thin and her eyes opening wide, "we know you don't have a Daddy."

Helene Tucker turned around, her eyes full of tears. She felt sorry for me. Then I couldn't see her too well because I was crying, too.

"Sit down, Richard."

And I always thought the teacher kind of liked me. She always picked me to wash the blackboard on Friday, after school. That was a big thrill, it made me feel important. If I didn't wash it, come Monday the school might not function right.

"Where are you going, Richard!"

I walked out of school that day, and for a long time I didn't go back very often. There was shame there.

Now there was shame everywhere. It seemed like the whole world had been inside that classroom, everyone had heard what the teacher had said, everyone had turned around and felt sorry for me. There was shame in going to the Worthy Boys Annual Christmas Dinner for you and your kind, because everybody knew what a worthy boy was. Why couldn't they just call it the Boys Annual Dinner, why'd they have to give it a name? There was shame in wearing the brown and orange and white plaid mackinaw the welfare gave to three thousand boys. Why'd it have to be the same for everybody so when you walked down the street the people could see you were on relief? It was a nice warm mackinaw and it had a hood, and my Momma beat me and called me a little rat when she found out I stuffed it in the bottom of a pail full of garbage way over on Cottage Street. There was shame in running over to Mister Ben's at the end of the day and asking for his rotten peaches, there was shame in asking Mrs. Simmons for a spoonful of sugar, there was shame in running out to meet the relief truck. I hated that truck, full of food for you and your kind. I ran into the house and hid when it came. And then I started to sneak through alleys, to take the long way home so the people going into White's Eat Shop wouldn't see me. Yeah, the whole world heard the teacher that day, we all know you don't have a Daddy.

It lasted for a while, this kind of numbness. I spent a lot of time feeling sorry for myself. And then one day I met this wino in a restaurant. I'd been out hustling all day, shining shoes, selling newspapers, and I had googobs of money in my pocket. Bought me a bowl of chili for fifteen cents, and a cheeseburger for fifteen cents, and a Pepsi for five cents, and a piece of chocolate cake for ten cents. That was a good meal. I was eating when this old wino came in. I love winos because they never hurt anyone but themselves.

The old wino sat down at the counter and ordered twenty-six cents worth of food. 30 He ate it like he really enjoyed it. When the owner, Mister Williams, asked him to pay the check, the old wino didn't lie or go through his pocket like he suddenly found a hole.

He just said: "Don't have no money." 31

The owner yelled: "Why in hell you come in here and eat my food if you don't have 32 no money? That food cost me money."

Mister Williams jumped over the counter and knocked the wino off his stool and beat 33 him over the head with a pop bottle. Then he stepped back and watched the wino bleed. Then he kicked him. And he kicked him again.

I looked at the wino with blood all over his face and I went over. "Leave him alone, 34 Mister Williams. I'll pay the twenty-six cents."

The wino got up, slowly, pulling himself up to the stool, then up to the counter, hold- 35 ing on for a minute until his legs stopped shaking so bad. He looked at me with pure hate. "Keep your twenty-six cents. You don't have to pay, not now. I just finished paying for it."

He started to walk out, and as he passed me, he reached down and touched my shoul- 36 der. "Thanks, sonny, but it's too late now. Why didn't you pay it before?"

I was pretty sick about that. I waited too long to help another man. 37

■ Reading Comprehension Questions

1. The word *pregnant* in "pregnant with poverty" (paragraph 5) means
   a. full of.
   b. empty of.
   c. sick.
   d. satisfied.

2. The word *hustling* in "I'd been out hustling all day" (paragraph 29) means
   a. learning.
   b. stealing.
   c. making friends.
   d. working hard.

3. Which of the following would be a good alternative title for this selection?
   a. Helene Tucker
   b. The Pain of Being Poor
   c. Losing a Father
   d. Mr. Williams and the Wino

4. Which sentence best expresses the main idea of the selection?
   a. Richard felt that being poor was humiliating.
   b. Richard liked Helene Tucker very much.
   c. Richard had to work hard as a child.
   d. The wino refused Richard's money.

5. The teacher disliked Richard because he
   a. was dirty.
   b. liked Helene.
   c. was a troublemaker.
   d. ate paste.

6. *True or false?* _____ Helene Tucker felt sorry for Richard when the teacher embarrassed him.

7. Richard's problems in school were due to his being
   a. hungry.
   b. distracted by Helene.
   c. lonely.
   d. unable to read.

8. The author implies that Richard
   a. was not intelligent.
   b. was proud.
   c. had many friends.
   d. and Helene became friends.

9. The author implies that
   a. Mr. Williams felt sorry for the wino.
   b. Richard's teacher was insensitive.
   c. Richard liked people to feel sorry for him.
   d. Richard's father was dead.

10. The author implies that
    a. the mackinaws were poorly made.
    b. Helene was a sensitive girl.
    c. Helene disliked Richard.
    d. the wino was ashamed of his poverty.

■ **Discussion Questions**

About Content

1. How might Dick Gregory's teacher have handled the Community Chest incident without making him feel ashamed?

2. What are some of the lessons Gregory learns from the incident involving the wino at the restaurant?

3. Where in "Shame" do we find evidence that Dick Gregory finally does escape from poverty?

About Structure

4. Since Dick Gregory is actually writing about an embarrassing incident in school, why does he devote his first three paragraphs to his feelings about Helene Tucker?

5. What is the connection between the incident involving the wino at the restaurant and the rest of the essay?

About Style and Tone

6. In the paragraph beginning, "Now there was shame everywhere," Gregory uses a device called *repetition* when he begins several sentences with the words "There was shame . . ." What is the effect of this repetition?

7. Why does Gregory use dialogue when he narrates the incidents in the classroom and in the restaurant?

■ Writing Assignments

Assignment 1

Dick Gregory tells us in "Shame" that he was ashamed of his poverty and of being on welfare—to the point that he threw away the warm hooded mackinaw he had been given simply because it was obvious proof that he and his family were on welfare. Do you think Gregory was justified in feeling so ashamed of his situation? How about other people who are on welfare? Are they justified if they feel ashamed? Choose either of the following thesis statements and develop it in an essay of several paragraphs:

■ People on welfare are justified in feeling ashamed.

■ People on welfare should not feel ashamed.

Then develop your thesis by thinking of several reasons to support the statement you have chosen.

You might think along the following lines:

Availability of jobs

Education or lack of education

Number of young children at home requiring care

Illness, physical disability

Psychological factors—depression, work habits, expectations, mental illness

Society's attitude towards people on welfare

Assignment 2

At some time in your life, you probably had an experience like Dick Gregory's in "Shame"—something that happened in a classroom, a group of friends or peers, or a family situation that proved to be both embarrassing and educational. At the time, the experience hurt you very much, but you learned from it. Write a narrative essay in which you retell this experience. Try to include vivid details and plenty of conversation so that the incident will come to life.

Assignment 3

Write an essay about three basic things that people must have in order to feel self-respect. In your thesis statement, name these three necessities and state that a person must possess them in order to feel self-respect. On the following page are some ideas to consider:

A certain number of material possessions

A job

A loving family or a special person

A clear conscience

A feeling of belonging

Freedom from addictions

In your supporting paragraphs, discuss the factors you have chosen, showing specifically why each is so important. In order to avoid falling into the trap of writing generalities, you may want to give examples of people who lack these necessities and show how such people lose self-respect. Your examples may be drawn from personal experience, or they may be hypothetical examples.

Outharbor Menu

Ray Guy

Ray Guy is a unique and distinctly different Canadian voice; the award-winning humourist from Newfoundland reminds readers from other parts of Canada that "The Rock" has its own culture, language patterns, and history unlike those of the rest of the country. Guy writes conversationally to readers about aspects of life in a province which has yet to become part of the "mass North American culture" of the late 20th century.

What feeds we used to have. Not way back in the pod auger days,[1] mind you. That was 1 before my time. I mean not long ago, just before the tinned stuff and the packages and the baker's bread started to trickle into the outports.

Out where I come from the trickle started when I was about six or seven years old. 2 One day I went next door to Aunt Winnie's (that's Uncle John's Aunt Winnie) and she had a package of puffed rice someone sent down from Canada.[2]

She gave us youngsters a small handful each. We spent a long time admiring this new 3 exotic stuff and remarking on how much it looked like emmets' eggs. We ate it one grain at a time as if it were candy, and because of the novelty didn't notice the remarkable lack of taste.

"Now here's a five cent piece and don't spend it all in sweets, mind." You never got 4 a nickel without this caution attached.

Peppermint knobs. White capsules ringed around with flannelette pink stripes. 5 Strong! You'd think you were breathing icewater. They're not near as strong today.

Chocolate mice shaped like a crouching rat, chocolate on the outside and tough pink 6 sponge inside. Goodbye teeth. Bullseyes made from molasses. And union squares—pastel blocks of marshmallow.

Those mysterious black balls that were harder than forged steel, had about 2,537 dif- 7 ferent layers of color and a funny tasting seed at the centre of the mini-universe.

Soft drinks came packed in barrels of straw in bottles of different sizes and shapes 8 and no labels. Birch beer, root beer, chocolate, lemonade, and orange.

Spruce beer, which I could never stomach, but the twigs boiling on the stove 9 smelled good. Home brew made from "Blue Ribbon" malt and which always exploded like hand grenades in the bottles behind the stove.

---

[1]the pod auger days: a common Newfoundland expression meaning "the old days." A pod auger is an auger with a lengthwise groove.

[2]from Canada: Newfoundland did not join Confederation until 1949, after the time Ray Guy describes.

Rum puncheons. Empty barrels purchased from the liquor control in St. John's. You poured in a few gallons of water, rolled the barrel around, and the result was a stronger product than you put down $7.50 a bottle for today.

Ice cream made in a hand-cranked freezer, the milk and sugar and vanilla in the can in the middle surrounded by ice and coarse salt. I won't say it was better than the store-bought stuff today but it tasted different and I like the difference.

Rounders (dried tom cods) for Sunday breakfast without fail. Cods heads, boiled sometimes, but mostly stewed with onions and bits of salt pork.

Fried cod tongues with pork scruncheons.[3] Outport soul food. Salt codfish, fish cakes, boiled codfish and drawn butter, baked cod with savoury stuffing, stewed cod, fried cod.

Lobsters. We always got the bodies and the thumbs from the canning factories. When eating lobster bodies you must be careful to stay away from the "old woman," a lump of bitter black stuff up near the head which is said to be poisonous.

I was always partial to that bit of red stuff in lobster bodies but never went much on the pea green stuff although some did.

We ate turrs[4] (impaled on a sharpened broomstick and held over the damper hole to singe off the fuzz), some people ate tickleaces[5] and gulls but I never saw it done.

We ate "a meal of trouts," seal, rabbits that were skinned out like a sock, puffin' pig (a sort of porpoise that had black meat), mussels and cocks and hens, otherwise known as clams, that squirt at you through air holes in the mud flats.

Potatoes and turnips were the most commonly grown vegetables although there was some cabbage and carrot. The potatoes were kept in cellars made of mounds of earth lined with sawdust or goosegrass. With the hay growing on them they looked like hairy green igloos.

A lot was got from a cow. Milk, certainly, and cream and butter made into pats and stamped with a wooden print of a cow or a clover leaf, and buttermilk, cream cheese. And I seem to remember a sort of jellied sour milk. I forget the name but perhaps the stuff was equivalent to yogurt.

There was no fresh meat in summer because it wouldn't keep. If you asked for a piece of meat at the store you got salt beef. If you wanted fresh beef you had to ask for "fresh meat."

Biscuits came packed in three-foot long wooden boxes and were weighed out by the pound in paper bags. Sultanas, Dad's cookies, jam jams, lemon creams with caraway seeds, and soda biscuits.

Molasses was a big thing. It was used to sweeten tea, in gingerbread, on rolled oats porridge, with sulphur in the spring to clean the blood (eeeccchhhh), in bread, in baked beans, in 'lassie bread.

It came in barrels and when the molasses was gone, there was a layer of molasses sugar at the bottom.

---

[3]pork scruncheons: crisp slices of fried pork fat.
[4]turr: the murre, an edible seabird.
[5]tickleace: the kittiwake, a kind of gull.

Glasses of lemon crystals or strawberry syrup or limejuice. Rolled oats, farina, Indian 24
meal. Home-made bread, pork buns, figgy duff,[6] partridgeberry tarts, blanc mange, gin-
ger wine, damper cakes.[7]

Cold mutton, salt beef, peas pudding, boiled cabbage, tinned bully beef for lunch on 25
Sunday, tinned peaches, brown eggs, corned caplin.[8]

And thank God I was twelve years old before ever a slice of baker's bread passed 26
my lips.

■ Reading Comprehension Questions

1. The word *impaled* in "impaled on a sharpened broomstick" (paragraph 16)
   means
   a. glued.
   b. wrapped.
   c. stuck, pierced through.
   d. wound.

2. The word *equivalent* in "perhaps the stuff was equivalent to yogurt" (paragraph 19) means
   a. similar
   b. a substitute for
   c. related
   d. equal

3. Which of the following would be a good alternative title for this selection?
   a. Familiar Foods
   b. Nostalgia and Necessity
   c. Sweets and Sentiments
   d. Homemade Memories

4. Which sentence best expresses the main idea of the selection?
   a. Ray Guy's family were good cooks and lots of food was available.
   b. Newfoundlanders ate a great variety of excellent food.
   c. Because of careful home cooking, Ray Guy's mother managed to make
      local food into an interesting menu.
   d. Food in Newfoundland in the 1940s was like food in the rest of Canada
      at that time.

5. *True or false?* _____ Ray Guy didn't enjoy everything his mother put
   on the family table.

[6]figgy duff: boiled raisin pudding.
[7]damper cakes: a kind of bannock made on the damper (upper surface) of a cookstove.
[8]caplin: a small and edible ocean fish often used by cod fishermen as bait.

6. *True or false?* _____ There was no money left for "store-bought" treats during the author's childhood.

7. According to the author, there was such a variety of dishes made from fish because
   a. cod, seal, mussels, and clams were what Newfoundlanders could catch.
   b. Newfoundlanders knew fish was a healthier choice than meat.
   c. his mother was such an inventive cook.
   d. cod in any form was the family's favourite meal.

8. The main nonfish items on the family menu were
   a. boiled salt beef and buns.
   b. sweets and biscuits shipped in from the mainland of Canada.
   c. seabirds, rabbit, seal, porpoise, potatoes, and turnips.
   d. cabbage, eggs, and canned corned beef.

9. We can assume that Ray Guy remembers candy and pop so clearly because
   a. they were such rare and exotic treats.
   b. like today, he enjoyed the variety and peculiar character of candies available.
   c. he loved homemade spruce beer and ice cream so much.
   d. there were no sweets allowed in the family's daily diet.

10. The author implies that
   a. food was so important to him because there wasn't much of it.
   b. in spite of limited dietary resources, his family ate well and memorably.
   c. food, pop, and even rum were better fifty years ago.
   d. he preferred the "store-bought" cookies and candy to homemade food.

■ Discussion Questions

About Content

1. What does the children's reaction to the puffed rice cereal tell readers about their knowledge of packaged foods?

2. Were there really "2,537 layers of color" in a blackball? How could anyone enjoy a candy "harder than forged steel"?

3. Why was molasses "the big thing"?

About Structure

4. How much of Guy's essay consists of examples? Is there any order to the writer's long presentation of his examples? Does he have any purpose in his essay other than to amuse readers with a long food catalogue?

5. The author's opening sentence may be a very concisely worded thesis statement; how does it indicate the subject-matter and Guy's point of view about his subject?

About Style and Tone

6. Ray Guy's essay is full of expressions peculiar to Newfoundland. Do these make the essay more interesting, or simply more difficult for other Canadian readers? Why?

7. Guy uses colourful and "homey" figures of speech. He describes with one analogy or simile the root cellars, saying "With the hay growing on them they looked like hairy green igloos." (18) What other similes and metaphors can you find in the essay?

8. Guy's style is chatty and informal. Moreover, the essay is full of unique points of style, among which your English instructor would find "sentence fragments": "Chocolate mice shaped like a crouching rat, chocolate on the outside and tough pink sponge inside. Goodbye teeth." The author also switches "pronoun point of view"; he begins speaking as "we," switches to "I" in paragraph 2, then to "you" in paragraph 4. Would Ray Guy fail Introductory College English, or is his style justified by his content and intent as a writer?

■ Writing Assignments

Assignment 1

Food and culture in Canada have become increasingly standardized and "internationalized." Does our identity as a country diminish as we consume more "fast food" tacos, pizzas, burgers, falafels, and so on? Food and the rituals of the preparation of meals are important parts of any country's or social group's traditions. But food as a major consumer commodity is most prone to the powers of advertising and promotion.

Ray Guy writes about the 1940s, when Newfoundland was already experiencing some imported food changes, like packaged cereals. Today, our eating habits are changing as quickly as our TV viewing habits. Family meals, like those Guy describes or those most of us know from holidays and family celebrations, are changing as well. Do we want to lose all our traditions, all the patterns of our families' cultures, to modern life?

Write an article for your college paper about a particular meal in which your family is involved. Discuss the meaning of this meal, its preparation, any rituals which are important, and the foods you eat.

Assignment 2

Everyone's childhood favourite foods have special meanings for them. Compare or contrast some personal memories and foods or meals from your own past with those of Ray Guy's. Did you grow up in an urban setting or in the country? Did this affect what you ate? Did you like candy as much as Ray Guy and his friends did? What foods were memorable to you? Who did the cooking at home? Which meals did you like or dislike especially? Why?

In your conclusion, consider whose memories of food seem more powerful, and why.

Assignment 3

Newfoundland is still very different in many ways from the rest of Canada. As you have read, it did not join Confederation until 1949. Its economy makes news today because of the difficulties of earning a living in a Maritime fishing culture. Cod wars, seal fishing, and fur trapping are survival issues in Newfoundland, irrespective of the pressures of ecological groups and government interference. The humour of "Newfie" speech, Screech, and jokes about backwardness are undercut by the harshness of living in Newfoundland. With outside pressure for change, traditions may be lost in other parts of Canada as well.

Write an essay which argues for or against some externally administered change to your part of the country: what effects could such change have on people's living patterns, on your local economy, and on the special identity of your part of the country?

Stones and the Mountain

Jean Mallinson

How affected are we by the geography, the exterior landscape of where we live? West Coast essayist and poet Jean Mallinson writes movingly of her deep connection with the Rocky Mountains, amid whose grandeur she grew up. Those of us who live in the more mundane settings of cities may marvel at, if not envy, the writer's discovery of herself within the craggy splendour of towering mountains.

I keep my stone collection in the living room: stones from Roberts Creek, the Charlottes, 1
Nantucket, the Bow River. I picked them up from tidal pools and from the sand where
the glacial deposits of the island meet the Atlantic. My daughter brought the stones from
the Charlottes and the Bow.

Recently my sister sent me some snapshots of the mountains that form the valley in 2
the Interior where we lived as children. I looked again at the irregular line of mountains
against the sky, and at the rock slides—fan-shaped swathes of stones. On the mountain
on the far side of the river the letter *K*, formed by rock slides. Thus I grew up under a
sign of the alphabet inscribed by stones. The remarkable fact that the name of the town
built in the shadow of the mountain began with a *K* suggested a mute correspondence
between nature and human naming, but to a child it seemed no more extraordinary than
the liquid sound of "flume" and "Similkameen," or the fit between mountains and sky.

We grew up with the vocabulary of mountains as household words: K Mountain, the 3
Richter Pass, the Columns, the Cascades, the Rockies. Descriptively, it was a lexicon of
verticals: peak, summit, snow line, tree line, canyon, chasm. In terms of narrative, it was
a lexicon of some peril: rock slides, switch-backs, grades, tunnels, hairpin turns and
horseshoe curves. The small stretches between mountains were called flats.

Stories of settlement we heard as children were tales of brave souls who came on 4
horseback through the Richter Pass with their things on pack-horses and their babies in
saddle bags. Since the valley was surrounded by mountains, it seemed a miracle that they
found the pass at all. But the enclosure of mountains, far from being confining, was a
comfort, especially after I was told that I lived, not, as I had thought, inside a round world,
but on the outside of one, with my head pointed toward infinite space.

When I was four, my mother took us to a small town on the plains of Saskatchewan 5
where there was a lightning storm at night. Waking up, I thought the sky was on fire and
begged my mother to take me home where the mountains would protect me. I loved to listen in church to the first words of the 121st Psalm, "I will lift up mine eyes unto the hills,
from whence cometh my help." It seemed natural to me that help would come from the hills.

But I was from the Coast and always knew that unlike the families who ranched or kept 6
orchards, who owned land, my mother, my sister and I would one day leave the Interior.
And leave we did, my mother fearing that her daughters—like some of the teachers who
came to the valley and married local men—might get stuck in the Interior forever. Though
I could scarcely imagine living outside the blue bowl of mountains, we moved to the
Coast, and in a few years I moved to Toronto to go to graduate school.

I lived in Toronto for ten years, but never, in all that time, felt located in the strict 7
sense of being geographically situated. There were no vistas to tell me where I was. On
a map of Canada, I could see the Great Lakes—blue ink blots joined by ink lines of
rivers—but I did not feel them in day-to-day life. I knew Lake Ontario was there and
occasionally I saw it; a few times I took the ferry to Toronto Island. There was no line
of blue beyond its flat horizon.

I was never aware of missing the Coast and the mountains, though everyone I met 8
from B.C. in Toronto dreamed of going back. But finally, on the train moving west from
Calgary, when I saw the irregular line of blue against the sky, like a paper cutout, I real-

ized that it matched some pattern inside me, that the landscape had rearranged itself into a shape that corresponded to my inner sense of what ought to be there. As the train moved into the mountains, I stood at one of the half-doors between coaches and sobbed. I felt properly located again, oriented toward earth and sky. After the train pulled into Vancouver I kept looking at the ragged skyline, where rock and trees meet air. I loved and still love that line, in its variety as one moves east or west in the city. I love the moving shadows of clouds on mountains, and their unaccountable blueness. I love knowing that north of us is hinterland, almost empty of human beings: there is a limit to settlement. I know where I am. I do not have to imagine it, to check it in an atlas: I can see it every day—look up at the mountains, walk down to the ocean. And when I look west I do not see the horizon line of an expanse of ocean reaching all the way to Asia, but the blue line of mountainous islands. I am at home on this edge, with the uneven line of blue against the sky, where to locate myself all I have to do is open my eyes and look around.

I confess I no longer want to live in the mountains; I have fallen in love with the mountainous coast—the best of worlds—but I still hanker now and then after that enclosure, that grandeur, those shadows and the shapes of rock slides. So I bought a two-hour video from the Kettle Valley Heritage Association, of which I am a member, because when we left the Coast when I was three to live in the Interior, it was the Kettle Valley Train that jostled us in mid-winter through the gorges and canyons of the Coquihalla and Tulameen Rivers to Princeton. The video consists of 120 minutes of moving-pictures taken from a train on the old tracks between Okanagan Falls and Merritt. The vistas of mountains and canyons are punctuated at rare intervals by the laconic comments of train men, who know that mountains speak for themselves. There is mercifully no music, no syrupy voice-over gratuitously praising the spectacular scenery, and the images jiggle enough to make me imagine I am on the train. Then when I close my eyes I can see the shapes of mountains, and open them in the morning to find I am where I want to be: on the Coast, with the mountains behind me, and a collection of stones in my living room.

■ Reading Comprehension Questions

1. The word *lexicon* in "a lexicon of verticals" or "a lexicon of some peril" (paragraph 3) means
   a. assortment.
   b. dictionary.
   c. collection.
   d. map.

2. The word *gratuitously* in "no syrupy voice-over gratuitously praising the spectacular scenery" (paragraph 9) means
   a. stupidly.
   b. blandly.
   c. unnecessarily.
   d. boringly.

3. Which of the following would be a good alternative title for this selection?
   a. Rocky Mountain High
   b. East and West
   c. Waves and the Peaks
   d. Landscapes of the Heart

4. Which sentence best expresses the main idea of the selection?
   a. Surroundings can feel like "homing devices" and answers to inner needs.
   b. Mountains, like those of her childhood, make the writer feel safe and secure.
   c. Mountains are important features in our environment.
   d. The most fulfilling places to live are where the mountains meet the water.

5. As a child, the author believed
   a. she lived in a country full of mysterious names.
   b. she would catch fire from prairie lightning.
   c. she lived within a round world.
   d. she would never leave the interior of B.C.

6. *True or false?* _____ The writer found the mysterious relationship between nature and words remarkable in her childhood.

7. While living in Toronto, the author found
   a. she missed the mountains and the West Coast every day.
   b. she had no longing for the Coast.
   c. she strongly felt the presence of Lake Ontario.
   d. she felt geographically comfortable.

8. The author implies that
   a. there is a deep, necessary relationship between elements of where she lives and her inner self.
   b. the stones from the rivers and oceans remind her of the mountains.
   c. her past is often forgotten as she moves from place to place.
   d. her dream was settling down to married life in the Interior.

9. From the essay, we may conclude that
   a. all travels lead back to our beginnings.
   b. everyone could be equally sensitive to their geographical surroundings.
   c. living in a location satisfying to one's memories and needs is a fortunate thing.
   d. seeing all of Canada promotes personal growth.

10. *True or false?* _____ The dreams and fantasies of Mallinson's earlier years dominate every aspect of her present life.

■ Discussion Questions

About Content

1. Several things bring to Jean Mallinson's mind pieces of her past. What are they? Do they all seem equally important, and why or why not?
2. Mallinson shares a perception of the mountains with the early settlers: what is this feeling? Is it contradictory to the usual way people regard such terrain, and how?
3. The author states in her final paragraph, "I am where I want to be." What helps her to achieve this state of satisfaction? What are the meanings of those things to her?

About Structure

4. What change of direction signal is used in paragraph 6? _____
5. The author uses a number of strongly emotional verbs with "I" to begin sentences in paragraphs 8 and 9; how many examples of these simple opening phrases are there, and what do they tell you about Mallinson?

About Style and Tone

6. Why do you think the writer uses such long lists of words for the mountains in paragraph 3?
7. What impression does the figure of speech "blue ink blots joined by ink lines of rivers," used to describe the Great Lakes in paragraph 7, convey of the author's feelings about these geographical features?

■ Writing Assignments

Assignment 1

Jean Mallinson's narrative tracing of her return to her coastal home is like a series of snapshots. Indeed, snapshots are among the evocative objects Mallinson uses to conjure up points of connection to place and memory in her life. All good description, in fact, all good writing, *shows* rather than *tells*—it tries to do with words what graphic images do with line and shape. Mallinson uses phrases and metaphors (word-pictures) such as "fan-shaped swathes of stones" to create a picture of rockslides. She finds words so magical that she includes lists of them, "lexicons," to evoke the world of the mountains.

Draw your own set of "snapshots"; choose from your memory-bank *three* meaningful moments connected to three specific places in your life. How was each event connected to a place? What effect did the location have on your feelings about what happened there? What meaning do the place and the event together have for you?

When you have made an outline of the three "sketches" for your essay, try to think how these memory-pictures themselves may be connected: is there a single emotion which links them, a sense of discovery at each point? This connection, drawn from your personal experience, will help you to compose a clear thesis statement and will make your essay cohesive, unified, and smooth-flowing for your reader.

Your essay may certainly be written in the first person, since you are drawing word-sketches from personal memories of your own sense of how our location may mirror, or perhaps occasionally contrast with, our internal landscape.

Assignment 2

Symbols are powerful conveyors of meaning. Mallinson's title consists of two physical things which are symbolic of many meanings and emotions for her. Actually, symbols are not as difficult to understand as many well-meaning English teachers have led students to believe. A symbol, in writing, is simply a word which has other meanings as well as its simple definition. The stones in Mallinson's living room are souvenirs of other places, other experiences: any souvenir we buy or bring home acts in this symbolic sense for us. In the same way, "the Mountain" in her title is the subject of an essay's worth of meanings. A symbol of any kind is just something which stands for something else.

In a five-paragraph essay, define the meanings of three symbolic objects in "Of Stones and the Mountain," and discuss what each says about the writer herself and tells readers about her life and her experiences.

Assignment 3

There are many discussions about how much people are influenced by their environment, and whether or not certain types of surroundings are beneficial or harmful to those who live in them.

Here are two statements which could form the basis for two different thesis statements and accompanying essays:

- People are products of, and shaped by, their geographical and social environments.
- People are only as affected by their surroundings as they let themselves be. External influences are limited by our awareness of them, and by the importance we choose to attach to them.

Choose one of these positions, and write a persuasive essay which defends your position logically, with well-chosen supporting details and examples drawn from your own experience and reading.

Smash Thy Neighbor

John McMurtry

We think of football as one of those great North American sports, like hockey or basketball. Children play football from grade school through university. Hours of network TV are devoted to football coverage of Grey Cup games and *Monday Night Football*. In this selection, however, a former Canadian football player says that football games are cruel contests that injure players and bring out the worst in fans.

A few months ago my neck got a hard crick in it. I couldn't turn my head; to look left or right I had to turn my whole body. But I'd had cricks in my neck since I started playing grade-school football and hockey, so I just ignored it. Then I began to notice that when I reached for any sort of large book (which I do pretty often as a philosophy teacher at the University of Guelph), I had trouble lifting it with one hand. I was losing the strength in my left arm, and I had such a steady pain in my back that I often had to stretch out on the floor to relieve the pressure.

Several weeks after my problems with book-lifting, I mentioned to my brother, an orthopedic surgeon, that I'd lost the power in my arm since my neck began to hurt. Twenty-four hours later I was in a Toronto hospital, not sure whether I might end up with a wasted upper limb. Apparently the steady pounding I had received playing college and professional football in the late fifties and early sixties had driven my head into my backbone so that the disks had crumpled together at the neck—"acute herniation"—and had cut the nerves to my left arm like a pinched telephone wire (without nerve stimulation, of course, the muscles atrophy, leaving the arm crippled). So I spent my Christmas holidays in the hospital in heavy traction, and much of the next three months with my neck in a brace. Today most of the pain has gone, and I've recovered most of the strength in my arm. But from time to time I still have to don the brace, and surgery remains a possibility.

Not much of this will surprise anyone who knows football. It is a sport in which body wreckage is one of the leading conventions. A few days after I went into the hospital for that crick in my neck, another brother, an outstanding football player in college, was undergoing spinal surgery in the same hospital two floors above me. In his case it was a lower, more massive herniation, which every now and again buckled him so that he was unable to lift himself off his back for days. By the time he entered the hospital for surgery he had already spent several months in bed. The operation was successful, but, as in all such cases, it will take him a year to recover fully.

These aren't isolated experiences. Just about anybody who has ever played football 4 for any length of time, in high school, college, or one of the professional leagues, has suffered for it later.

Indeed, it is arguable that body shattering is the very *point* of football, as killing and 5 maiming are of war. (In the United States, for example, the game results in fifteen to twenty deaths a year and about fifty thousand major operations on knees alone.) To grasp some of the more conspicuous similarities between football and war, it is instructive to listen to the imperatives most frequently issued to the players by their coaches, teammates, and fans. "Hurt 'em!" "Level 'em!" "Kill 'em!" "Take 'em apart!" Or watch for the plays that are most enthusiastically applauded by the fans, where someone is "smeared," "knocked silly," "creamed," "nailed," "broken in two," or even "crucified." (One of my coaches when I played corner linebacker with the Calgary Stampeders in 1961 elaborated, often very inventively, on this language of destruction: admonishing us to "unjoin" the opponent, "make 'im remember you," and "stomp 'im like a bug.") Just as in hockey, where a fight will bring fans to their feet more often than a skillful play, so in football the mouth waters most of all for the really crippling block or tackle. For the kill. Thus the good teams are "hungry," the best players are "mean," and "casualties" are as much a part of the game as they are of a war.

The family resemblance between football and war is, indeed, striking. Their lan- 6 guages are similar: "field general," "long bomb," "blitz," "take a shot," "front line," "pursuit," "good hit," "the draft," and so on. Their principles and practices are alike: mass hysteria, the art of intimidation, absolute command and total obedience, territorial aggression, censorship, inflated insignia and propaganda, blackboard maneuvers and strategies, drills, uniforms, formations, marching bands, and training camps. And the virtues they celebrate are almost identical: hyperaggressiveness, coolness under fire, and suicidal bravery.

One difference between war and football, though, is that there is little or no protest 7 against football. Perhaps the most extraordinary thing about the game is that the systematic infliction of injuries excites in people not concern, as would be the case if they were sustained at, say, a rock festival, but a collective rejoicing and euphoria. Players and fans alike revel in the spectacle of a combatant felled into semiconsciousness, "blindsided," "clotheslined," or "decapitated." I can remember, in fact, being chided by a coach in pro ball for not "getting my hat" injuriously into a player who was lying helpless on the ground.

After every game, of course, the papers are full of reports on the day's injuries, a 8 sort of post-battle "body count," and the respective teams go to work with doctors and trainers, tape, whirlpool baths, cortisone, and morphine to patch and deaden the wounds before the next game. Then the whole drama is reenacted—athletes held together by adhesive, braces, and drugs—and the days following it are filled with even more feverish activity to put on the show yet again at the end of the week. (I remember being so taped up in college that I earned the nickname "Mummy.") The team that survives this merry-go-round spectacle of skilled masochism with the fewest incapacitating injuries usually wins. It is a sort of victory by ordeal: "We hurt them more than they hurt us."

My own initiation into this brutal circus was typical. I loved the game from the moment I could run with a ball. Played shoeless on a green, open field with no one keeping score and in a spirit of reckless abandon and laughter, it's a very different sport. Almost no one gets hurt, and it's rugged, open, and exciting (it still is for me). But, like everything else, it starts to be regulated and institutionalized by adult authorities. And the fun is over.

So it was as I began the long march through organized football. Now there were a coach and elders to make it clear by their behavior that beating other people was the only thing to celebrate and that trying to shake someone up every play was the only thing to be really proud of. Now there were severe rule enforcers, audiences, formally recorded victors and losers, and heavy equipment to permit crippling bodily moves and collisions (according to one survey, more than 80 percent of all football injuries occur to fully equipped players). And now there was the official "given" that the only way to keep playing was to wear suffocating armor, to play to defeat, to follow orders silently, and to renounce spontaneity in favor of joyless drill. The game has been, in short, ruined. But because I loved to play, and play skillfully, I stayed. And progressively and inexorably, as I moved through high school, college, and pro leagues, my body was dismantled. Piece by piece.

I started off with torn ligaments in my knee at thirteen. Then, as the organization and the competition increased, the injuries came faster and harder. Broken nose (three times), broken jaw (fractured in the first half and dismissed as a "bad wisdom tooth," so I played with it for the rest of the game), ripped knee ligaments again. Torn ligaments in one ankle and a fracture in the other (which I remember feeling relieved about because it meant I could honorably stop drill-blocking a 270-pound defensive end). Repeated rib fractures and cartilage tears (usually carried, again, through the remainder of the game). More dislocations of the left shoulder than I can remember (the last one I played with because, as the Calgary Stampeders' doctor said, it "couldn't be damaged any more"). Occasional broken or dislocated fingers and toes. Chronically hurt lower back (I still can't lift with it or change a tire without worrying about folding). Separated right shoulder (as with many other injuries, like badly bruised hips and legs, needled with morphine for the games). And so on. The last pro game I played—against the Winnipeg Blue Bombers in the Western finals in 1961—I had a recently dislocated left shoulder, a more recently wrenched right shoulder, and a chronic pain center in one leg. I was so tied up with soreness that I couldn't drive to the airport. But it never occurred to me that I should miss a play as a corner linebacker.

By the end of my football career, I had learned that physical injury—giving it and taking it—is the real currency of the sport. And that in the final analysis, the "winner" is the man who can hit to kill even if only half his limbs are working. In brief, a warrior game with a warrior ethos into which (like almost everyone I played with) my original boyish enthusiasm had been relentlessly conditioned.

In thinking back on how all this happened, though, I can pick out no villains. As with 13
the social system as a whole, the game has a life of its own. Everyone grows up inside
it, accepts it, and fulfills its dictates as obediently as Helots. Far from questioning the
principles of the activity, most men simply concentrate on executing these principles
more aggressively than anybody else. The result is a group of people who, as the leagues
become of a higher and higher class, are progressively insensitive to the possibility that
things could be otherwise. Thus, in football, anyone who might question the wisdom or
enjoyment of putting on heavy equipment on a hot day and running full speed at someone else with the intention of knocking him senseless would be regarded as not really a
devoted athlete and probably "chicken." The choice is made straightforward. Either you,
too, do your very utmost to smash efficiently and be smashed, or you admit incompetence or cowardice and quit. Since neither of these admissions is very pleasant, people
generally keep any doubts they have to themselves, and carry on.

Of course, it would be a mistake to suppose that there is more blind acceptance of 14
brutal practices in organized football than elsewhere. On the contrary, a recent Harvard
study argues that football's characteristics of "impersonal acceptance of inflicted injury,"
an overriding "organization goal," the "ability to turn oneself on and off," and being,
above all, "out to win" are prized by ambitious executives in many large corporations.
Clearly, football is no sicker than the rest of our society. Even its organized destruction
of physical well-being is not anomalous. A very large part of our wealth, work, and time
is, after all, spent in systematically destroying and harming human life; manufacturing,
selling, and using weapons that tear opponents to pieces; making ever bigger and faster
predator-named cars with which to kill and injure one another by the million every
year; and devoting our very lives to outgunning one another for power in an ever-more-
destructive rat race. Yet all these practices are accepted without question by most
people, even zealously defended and honored. Competitive, organized injuring is inte-
gral to our way of life, and football is one of the more intelligible mirrors of the whole
process: a sort of colorful morality play showing us how exciting and rewarding it is to
Smash Thy Neighbor.

Now, it is fashionable to rationalize our collaboration in all this by arguing that, well, 15
men *like* to fight and injure their fellows, and such games as football should be encouraged to discharge this original-sin urge into less harmful channels than, say, war. Public-
show football, this line goes, plays the same sort of cathartic role as Aristotle said stage
tragedy does: without real blood (or not much), it releases players and audience from
unhealthy feelings stored up inside them.

As an ex-player in this seasonal coast-to-coast drama, I see little to recommend such 16
a view. What organized football did to me was make me *suppress* my natural urges and
reexpress them in alienating, vicious form. Spontaneous desires for free bodily exuber-
ance and fraternization with competitors were shamed and forced under ("If it ain't
hurtin', it ain't helpin'"), and in their place were demanded armored, mechanical moves,
and cool hatred of all opposition. Endless authoritarian drill and dressing-room harangues
(ever wonder why competing teams can't prepare for a game in the same dressing room?)
were the kinds of mechanisms employed to reconstruct joyful energies into mean and
alien shapes. I am quite certain that everyone else around me was being similarly forced

into this heavily equipped military precision and angry antagonism, because there was always a mutinous attitude about full-dress practices, and everybody (the pros included) had to concentrate incredibly hard for days to whip himself into just one hour's hostility a week against another club. The players never speak of these things, of course, because everyone is anxious to appear tough.

The claim that men like seriously to battle one another to some sort of finish is a myth. It endures only because it wears one of the oldest and most propagandized of masks—the romantic combatant. I sometimes wonder whether the violence all around us doesn't depend for its survival on the existence and preservation of this tough-guy disguise.

As for the effect of organized football on the spectator, the fans are not so much released from supposed feelings of violent aggression by watching their athletic heroes perform it as they are encouraged in the view that people-smashing is an admirable mode of self-expression. The most savage attackers, after all, are, by general agreement, the most efficient and worthy players of all (the biggest applause I ever received as a football player occurred when I ran over people or slammed them so hard that they couldn't get up). . . . Watching well-advertised strong men knock other people around, make them hurt, is in the end like other tastes. It does not weaken with feeding and variation in form. It grows.

I got out of football in 1962. In a preseason intersquad game, I ripped the cartilage in my ribs on the hardest block I'd ever thrown. I had trouble breathing, and I had to shuffle-walk with my torso on a tilt. The doctor in the local hospital said three weeks rest; the coach said scrimmage in two days. Three days later I was back home reading philosophy.

■ Reading Comprehension Questions

1. The word *atrophy* in "without nerve stimulation, of course, the muscles atrophy, leaving the arm crippled" (paragraph 2) means
   a. get stronger.
   b. flex.
   c. weaken.
   d. are unaffected.

2. The word *imperatives* in "It is instructive to listen to the imperatives most frequently issued to the players. . . . 'Hurt 'em!' 'Level 'em!' 'Kill 'em!'" (paragraph 5) means
   a. insults.
   b. commands.
   c. compliments.
   d. questions.

3. Which of the following would be a good alternative title for this selection?
   a. The Violence of Football

  b. Football in North America
  c. A Man Who Played Football
  d. Football and Corporate Competition

4. Which sentence best expresses the main idea of the selection?
  a. Playing football has caused the author much physical pain.
  b. Most football coaches try to make the game less violent.
  c. Football's popularity is a reflection of some negative aspects of society.
  d. Violence is a central part of organized football both for the teams and for the fans.

5. The author says that organized football is like
  a. all other sports.
  b. philosophy.
  c. war.
  d. football played without coaches and rules.

6. For the author, football was ruined by
  a. people who play without equipment.
  b. the regulation of adult authorities.
  c. people who dislike its violence.
  d. ambitious executives.

7. According to the author, watching football makes people
  a. believe that "smashing thy neighbor" is good.
  b. realize that football is too violent.
  c. feel a great release from their own violent feelings.
  d. escape from the anxieties of their jobs.

8. The author implies that
  a. society is much less brutally competitive than football.
  b. football players never have doubts about the brutality of the game.
  c. the brutal values of football exist in other parts of society.
  d. many people question the violence in football.

9. The author implies that fans
  a. get rid of unhealthy feelings when watching football.
  b. encourage the violence in football.
  c. are unaware of the violence in football.
  d. discourage the really savage attacks in football.

10. In the last paragraph of the selection, the author implies that
  a. his injuries were mild.
  b. the doctor exaggerated the extent of his injuries.
  c. the coach thought that his injuries were mild.
  d. the coach cared more about winning than about his players' injuries.

■ Discussion Questions

About Content

1. According to McMurtry, what qualities of our society are reflected in football?
2. The author makes an analogy between war and football. In what ways are the two activities alike?
3. Do you agree with McMurtry that the violence of football encourages people's taste for "people-smashing [as] an admirable mode of self-expression" (paragraph 18)?

About Structure

4. What method of introduction does the author use?
   a. Anecdote
   b. An opposite
   c. Quotation
5. What method of development is used in paragraphs 5 and 6?
   a. Reasons
   b. Comparison
   c. Examples

About Style and Tone

6. Why does the author call his essay "Smash Thy Neighbor"? To answer, think about how the title may be a play on the words in a familiar biblical command.
7. McMurtry uses terms such as *body wreckage*, *body shattering*, and *skilled masochism* to describe organized football. What effect does he hope this language will have on the reader? Find three other phrases the author uses to describe football (beginning with paragraph 9), and write them in the spaces below:

_____

_____

_____

■ Writing Assignments

Assignment 1

Imagine that you are a professional football coach (or, if you prefer, the head coach of your school's football team). You have just read "Smash Thy Neighbor" in a national magazine, and you feel angered and hurt by McMurtry's opinion of football. How would you answer his accusations about the sport? Write a letter to the editor of the magazine in which you give three reasons why John McMurtry is wrong about football and its effects on people. You might want to get started with this thesis statement:

I feel John McMurtry is wrong about football for several reasons.

Then continue your letter, describing each reason in detail. Write a separate paragraph for each detail.

Alternatively, imagine that, as a coach, you agree with McMurtry, and write a letter in which you detail three reasons for agreeing.

Assignment 2

Write a narrative essay about a bad experience you had with sports. Among the topics you might write about are:

An injury

Not being chosen for a team

Missing an important point or goal

Being pressured by a parent or coach

Being the clumsiest person in gym class

Being embarrassed while trying to learn a sport

You could begin the essay with a sentence or two about your experience with sports in general—whether sports have been an area of pain or pleasure for you. Your thesis should name the particular experience you will write about and tell your readers that this experience was bad (or embarrassing, or humiliating, or disillusioning, or any other word that seems appropriate).

Then organize your supporting paragraphs by dividing your experience into two or three time phases. You may want to review first the chapter on the narrative essay (pages 206–215).

Assignment 3

Write an essay about a sport you feel is a good one. In each of your supporting paragraphs, give one reason why this sport is good for either players or spectators.

My Body Is My Own Business

Naheed Mustafa

On many streets in Canada today, women and girls from African and Near or Far Eastern nations wear the traditional long robes of Muslim female dress and the *hijab*, or head covering, as well. Those accustomed to feminist thought of the last thirty years see such dress as symbolic of male oppression in Islamic cultures, but Naheed Mustafa presents an opposing argument. Mustafa, educated at the University of Toronto and Ryerson, is a journalist in her native Pakistan, who *chooses* to wear the *hijab* for reasons which are at odds with commonly held stereotypes of Muslim belief and behaviour.

I often wonder whether people see me as a radical, fundamentalist Muslim terrorist packing an AK-47 assault rifle inside my jean jacket. Or maybe they see me as the poster girl for oppressed womanhood everywhere. I'm not sure which it is.

I get the whole gamut of strange looks, stares and covert glances. You see, I wear the *hijab*, a scarf that covers my head, neck and throat. I do this because I am a Muslim woman who believes her body is her own private concern.

Young Muslim women are reclaiming the *hijab*, reinterpreting it in light of its original purpose—to give back to women ultimate control of their own bodies.

The Koran teaches us that men and women are equal, that individuals should not be judged according to gender, beauty, wealth or privilege. The only thing that makes one person better than another is her or his character.

Nonetheless, people have a difficult time relating to me. After all, I'm young, Canadian born and raised, university-educated—why would I do this to myself, they ask.

Strangers speak to me in loud, slow English and often appear to be playing charades. They politely inquire how I like living in Canada and whether or not the cold bothers me. If I'm in the right mood, it can be very amusing.

But why would I, a woman with all the advantages of a North American upbringing, suddenly, at 21, want to cover myself so that with the *hijab* and the other clothes I choose to wear, only my face and hands show?

Because it gives me freedom.

Women are taught from early childhood that their worth is proportional to their attractiveness. We feel compelled to pursue abstract notions of beauty, half realizing that such a pursuit is futile.

When women reject this form of oppression, they face ridicule and contempt. Whether it's women who refuse to wear makeup or to shave their legs or to expose their bodies, society, both men and women, have trouble dealing with them.

In the Western world, the *hijab* has come to symbolize either forced silence or rad- 11
ical, unconscionable militancy. Actually, it's neither. It is simply a woman's assertion that
judgment of her physical person is to play no role whatsoever in social interaction.

Wearing the *hijab* has given me freedom from constant attention to my physical self. 12
Because my appearance is not subjected to public scrutiny, my beauty, or perhaps lack
of it, has been removed from the realm of what can legitimately be discussed.

No one knows whether my hair looks as if I just stepped out of a salon, whether or 13
not I can pinch an inch, or even if I have unsightly stretch marks. And because no one
knows, no one cares.

Feeling that one has to meet the impossible male standards of beauty is tiring and 14
often humiliating. I should know, I spent my entire teenage years trying to do it. I was a
borderline bulimic and spent a lot of money I didn't have on potions and lotions in hopes
of becoming the next Cindy Crawford.

The definition of beauty is ever-changing; waifish is good, waifish is bad, athletic 15
is good—sorry, athletic is bad. Narrow hips? Great. Narrow hips? Too bad.

Women are not going to achieve equality with the right to bare breasts in public, as 16
some people would like to have you believe. That would only make us party to our own
objectification. True equality will be had only when women don't need to display themselves to get attention and won't need to defend their decision to keep their bodies to
themselves.

■ Reading Comprehension Questions

1. The word *unconscionable* in "radical, unconscionable militancy" (paragraph
   11) means
   a. unbelievable.
   b. unsuitable.
   c. inappropriate.
   d. unthinkable.

2. The word *waifish* in "waifish is good, waifish is bad, athletic is good" (paragraph 15) means
   a. womanly, robust in appearance.
   b. curvaceous, shapely.
   c. sickly.
   d. skinny, neglected-looking.

3. Which of the following would be a good alternative title for this selection?
   a. The Mysterious Eastern Woman
   b. Eastern Privacy and Western Prejudice
   c. Harems and Headgear
   d. My Culture and My Choice of Clothing

4. Which sentence best expresses the main idea of the selection?
   a. Muslim women have the right to dress as they wish.
   b. Women should wear clothing which disguises their bodies to avoid harassment.
   c. Women will be truly free when their appearance is no longer of primary importance.
   d. Every woman has the right to privacy of her person.

5. People don't know what to make of Naheed Mustafa because
   a. she chooses to dress in an outlandish Eastern way.
   b. the *hijab* symbolizes stereotypes of women as victims or Islamic terrorists.
   c. her clothing disguises her true identity.
   d. she is hiding her identity as an educated Canadian under an ethnic costume.

6. *True or false?* _____ Only men have trouble dealing with women who no longer pursue media-dictated ideals of grooming and beauty.

7. The Koran's teaching about the sexes states
   a. that women unintentionally represent temptation to men.
   b. that men and women are judged by their actions.
   c. that no one should be judged by external factors.
   d. that both sexes have the right to privacy.

8. The author implies that
   a. people see her as a militant feminist.
   b. people find stereotyping easier than looking beyond appearances.
   c. people don't want to know her.
   d. her Canadian upbringing and education are disadvantages.

9. The author implies that
   a. women can achieve a degree of personal freedom by clothing choices.
   b. Western women are slow to catch up with Muslim wisdom about dress.
   c. women will never understand what beauty is all about.
   d. women everywhere are totally obsessed by impossible ideas of beauty.

10. Wearing the *hijab* has given the author
   a. a decent anti-fashion statement appropriate to her religion.
   b. a sense of being able to be whoever she truly is by her own standards.
   c. a place to hide from men's expectations of her.
   d. an exotic refuge from the everyday world of Canadian society.

■ Discussion Questions

About Content

1. How does the author feel that people on the street see her? Why?
2. What are the practical advantages of wearing the *hijab?* What are the ideological reasons for Mustafa's adoption of the garments?
3. What does the author suggest is the basic problem with beauty?

About Structure

4. The clearest statement of the author's thesis is in the last one-third of the essay. Find it and write it in the spaces below:

   _____

   _____

5. What is the "change of direction" word in paragraph 11?

About Style and Tone

6. What is the effect on your perception of Naheed Mustafa when you read such statements as "I was a borderline bulimic . . ." who "spent a lot of money I didn't have . . . in hopes of becoming the next Cindy Crawford," and "waifish is good, waifish is bad . . ."?
7. We describe subjects by saying what they are not, as well as by saying what they are. In what terms does the author set up her reasons for believing the *hijab* is an ideal form of clothing for her?
8. The author begins her essay with an exaggerated description of one stereotyped image and confesses her defeat at trying to become another stereotyped ideal. Do the essay's examples give you a clear picture of the "real" person?

■ Writing Assignments

Assignment 1

Naheed Mustafa writes about a personal decision to wear certain clothing, which defines her in one way to observers, but which means something very different to her as wearer. Our clothing choices *do,* in some ways, define us, and communicate information about us to others. The message sent out may not always be the one we intend to communicate. Think about the clothes and accessories you wear to classes every day. What is the result of your choice(s) on those who observe you? What do certain garments and jewellery "say" about you, to yourself, and to others? Do these messages occasionally conflict?

Write an article for your college newspaper in which you defend some choice of personal attire or decoration which may be misinterpreted by others. You could discuss something ordinary like a baseball cap, a pierced nostril, a garment belonging to your ethnic background, or even a certain type of makeup.

In your argument, use the cause and effect method of organizing your points of defence. Notice how Mustafa has repeatedly used the word *because*, and various transition words, like *actually*, before setting out her points of explanation. Set out your own details about your clothing or accessories in this pattern of causes, effects, and explanations.

Assignment 2

The image of beauty in any society is constantly changing, and subject to the whims of advertising. Should any of us, men or women, model ourselves on TV and magazine concepts of what is attractive? Nearly our entire consumer economy is based on selling various products to us which will make us more like someone else's ideal of what is a beautiful, strong, healthy, or even "good person."

Write an essay in which you choose one of the following sentences as the basis for your thesis statement, and argue for its validity from your own experience and knowledge.

■ We are losing our ability to decide what we should look like because of ads which promote famished supermodels and Schwarzenegger/Stallone lookalikes.

■ We choose ideals of male and female beauty *knowingly and willingly* because they appeal to our desire to be the best we can be. Fitness and beauty aren't sins.

Assignment 3

What stereotypes do we carry around with us of various national and cultural groups, based on aspects of their appearance or behaviour? Are there any points of truth in these stereotypes? Do such preconceived notions blind us to the characters of people inside the clothing or behind the counter at the store? Think about one such stereotype based on appearance or on behaviour patterns. In an essay which makes your point by logical and clear examples, discuss your own reaction to this stereotype, and how it has or has not been altered by knowledge of persons belonging to a particular group.

A Hanging

George Orwell

*You are about to attend an execution. In this essay, George Orwell (author of
1984) recalls a hanging he witnessed when he was an English police officer
stationed in Burma. Orwell's sensitivity and vividly descriptive writing will
make you see and feel what it is like to take the seemingly endless walk from
cell to gallows. You will share the guards' uneasiness and the prisoner's terror.
And, after you finish the selection, you may also share Orwell's views on capital
punishment.*

It was in Burma, a sodden morning of the rains. A sickly light, like yellow tinfoil, was   1
slanting over the high walls into the jail yard. We were waiting outside the condemned
cells, a row of sheds fronted with double bars, like small animal cages. Each cell measured about ten feet by ten and was quite bare within except for a plank bed and a pot of
drinking water. In some of them brown silent men were squatting at the inner bars, with
their blankets draped round them. These were the condemned men, due to be hanged
within the next week or two.

One prisoner had been brought out of his cell. He was a Hindu, a puny wisp of a   2
man, with a shaven head and vague liquid eyes. He had a thick, sprouting moustache,
absurdly too big for his body, rather like the moustache of a comic man on the films.
Six tall Indian warders were guarding him and getting him ready for the gallows. Two
of them stood by with rifles with fixed bayonets, while the others handcuffed him, passed
a chain through his handcuffs and fixed it to their belts, and lashed his arms tight to his
sides. They crowded very close about him, with their hands always on him in a careful,
caressing grip, as though all the while feeling him to make sure he was there. It was like
men handling a fish which is still alive and may jump back into the water. But he stood
quite unresisting, yielding his arms limply to the ropes, as though he hardly noticed what
was happening.

Eight o'clock struck and a bugle call, desolately thin in the wet air, floated from the   3
distant barracks. The superintendent of the jail, who was standing apart from the rest of
us, moodily prodding the gravel with his stick, raised his head at the sound. He was an
army doctor, with a grey toothbrush moustache and a gruff voice. "For God's sake hurry
up, Francis," he said irritably. "The man ought to have been dead by this time. Aren't you
ready yet?"

Francis, the head jailer, a fat Dravidian in a white drill suit and gold spectacles,   4
waved his black hand. "Yes sir, yes sir," he bubbled. "All iss satisfactorily prepared. The
hangman iss waiting. We shall proceed."

"Well, quick march, then. The prisoners can't get their breakfast till this job's over."   5

We set out for the gallows. Two warders marched on either side of the prisoner, with their rifles at the slope; two others marched close against him, gripping him by arm and shoulder, as though at once pushing and supporting him. The rest of us, magistrates and the like, followed behind. Suddenly, when we had gone ten yards, the procession stopped short without any order or warning. A dreadful thing had happened—a dog, come goodness knows whence, had appeared in the yard. It came bounding among us with a loud volley of barks, and leapt round us wagging its whole body, wild with glee at finding so many human beings together. It was a large woolly dog, half Airedale, half pariah. For a moment it pranced round us, and then, before anyone could stop it, it had made a dash for the prisoner, and jumping up tried to lick his face. Everyone stood aghast, too taken aback even to grab at the dog.

"Who let that bloody brute in here?" said the superintendent angrily. "Catch it, someone!"

A warder, detached from the escort, charged clumsily after the dog, but it danced and gambolled just out of his reach, taking everything as part of the game. A young Eurasian jailer picked up a handful of gravel and tried to stone the dog away, but it dodged the stones and came after us again. Its yaps echoed from the jail walls. The prisoner, in the grasp of the two warders, looked on incuriously, as though this was another formality of the hanging. It was several minutes before someone managed to catch the dog. Then we put my handkerchief through its collar and moved off once more, with the dog still straining and whimpering.

It was about forty yards to the gallows. I watched the bare brown back of the prisoner marching in front of me. He walked clumsily with his bound arms, but quite steadily, with that bobbing gait of the Indian who never straightens his knees. At each step his muscles slid neatly into place, the lock of hair on his scalp danced up and down, his feet printed themselves on the wet gravel. And once, in spite of the men who gripped him by each shoulder, he stepped slightly aside to avoid a puddle on the path.

It is curious, but till that moment I had never realised what it means to destroy a healthy, conscious man. When I saw the prisoner step aside to avoid the puddle, I saw the mystery, the unspeakable wrongness, of cutting a life short when it is in full tide. This man was not dying; he was alive just as we were alive. All the organs of his body were working—bowels digesting food, skin renewing itself, nails growing, tissues forming—all toiling away in solemn foolery. His nails would still be growing when he stood on the drop, when he was falling through the air with a tenth of a second to live. His eyes saw the yellow gravel and the grey walls, and his brain still remembered, foresaw, reasoned—reasoned even about puddles. He and we were a party of men walking together, seeing, hearing, feeling, understanding the same world; and in two minutes, with a sudden snap, one of us would be gone—one mind less, one world less.

The gallows stood in a small yard, separate from the main grounds of the prison, and overgrown with tall prickly weeds. It was a brick erection like three sides of a shed, with planking on top, and above that two beams and a crossbar with the rope dangling. The hangman, a grey-haired convict in the white uniform of the prison, was waiting beside his machine. He greeted us with a servile crouch as we entered. At a word from Francis the two warders, gripping the prisoner more closely than ever, half led, half pushed him to the gallows and helped him clumsily up the ladder. Then the hangman climbed up and fixed the rope round the prisoner's neck.

We stood waiting, five yards away. The warders had formed in a rough circle round 12 the gallows. And then, when the noose was fixed, the prisoner began crying out to his god. It was a high, reiterated cry of "Ram! Ram! Ram! Ram!" not urgent and fearful like a prayer or a cry for help, but steady, rhythmical, almost like the tolling of a bell. The dog answered the sound with a whine. The hangman, still standing on the gallows, produced a small cotton bag like a flour bag and drew it down over the prisoner's face. But the sound, muffled by the cloth, still persisted, over and over again: "Ram! Ram! Ram! Ram! Ram!"

The hangman climbed down and stood ready, holding the lever. Minutes seemed to 13 pass. The steady, muffled crying from the prisoner went on and on, "Ram! Ram! Ram!" never faltering for an instant. The superintendent, his head on his chest, was slowly poking the ground with his stick; perhaps he was counting the cries, allowing the prisoner a fixed number—fifty, perhaps, or a hundred. Everyone had changed colour. The Indians had gone grey like bad coffee, and one or two of the bayonets were wavering. We looked at the lashed, hooded man on the drop, and listened to his cries—each cry another second of life; the same thought was in all our minds: oh, kill him quickly, get it over, stop that abominable noise!

Suddenly the superintendent made up his mind. Throwing up his head he made a 14 swift motion with his stick. "Chalo!" he shouted almost fiercely.

There was a clanking noise, and then dead silence. The prisoner had vanished, and 15 the rope was twisting on itself. I let go of the dog, and it galloped immediately to the back of the gallows; but when it got there it stopped short, barked, and then retreated into a corner of the yard, where it stood among the weeds, looking timorously out at us. We went round the gallows to inspect the prisoner's body. He was dangling with his toes pointed straight downwards, very slowly revolving, as dead as a stone.

The superintendent reached out with his stick and poked the bare body; it oscillated, 16 slightly. "*He's* all right," said the superintendent. He backed out from under the gallows, and blew out a deep breath. The moody look had gone out of his face quite suddenly. He glanced at his wristwatch. "Eight minutes past eight. Well, that's all for this morning, thank God."

The warders unfixed bayonets and marched away. The dog, sobered and conscious 17 of having misbehaved itself, slipped after them. We walked out of the gallows yard, past the condemned cells with their waiting prisoners, into the big central yard of the prison. The convicts, under the command of warders armed with lathis, were already receiving their breakfast. They squatted in long rows, each man holding a tin pannikin, while two warders with buckets marched round ladling out rice; it seemed quite a homely, jolly scene, after the hanging. An enormous relief had come upon us now that the job was done. One felt an impulse to sing, to break into a run, to snigger. All at once everyone began chattering gaily.

The Eurasian boy walking beside me nodded towards the way we had come, with a 18 knowing smile: "Do you know, sir, our friend (he meant the dead man), when he heard his appeal had been dismissed, he pissed on the floor of his cell. From fright.—Kindly take one of my cigarettes, sir. Do you not admire my new silver case, sir? From the boxwallah, two rupees eight annas. Classy European style."

Several people laughed—at what, nobody seemed certain. 19

Francis was walking by the superintendent, talking garrulously: "Well, sir, all hass 20 passed off with the utmost satisfactoriness. It wass all finished—flick! like that. It iss not always so—oah, no! I have known cases where the doctor wass obliged to go beneath the gallows and pull the prisoner's legs to ensure decease. Most disagreeable!"

"Wriggling about, eh? That's bad," said the superintendent. 21

"Ach, sir, it iss worse when they become refractory! One man, I recall, clung to the 22 bars of hiss cage when we went to take him out. You will scarcely credit, sir, that it took six warders to dislodge him, three pulling at each leg. We reasoned with him. 'My dear fellow,' we said, 'think of all the pain and trouble you are causing to us!' But no, he would not listen! Ach, he wass very troublesome!"

I found that I was laughing quite loudly. Everyone was laughing. Even the superin- 23 tendent grinned in a tolerant way. "You'd better all come out and have a drink," he said quite genially. "I've got a bottle of whisky in the car. We could do with it."

We went through the big double gates of the prison, into the road. "Pulling at his 24 legs!" exclaimed a Burmese magistrate suddenly, and burst into a loud chuckling. We all began laughing again. At that moment Francis's anecdote seemed extraordinarily funny. We all had a drink together, native and European alike, quite amicably. The dead man was a hundred yards away.

■ Reading Comprehension Questions

1. The word *reiterated* in "the high, reiterated cry of 'Ram! Ram!'" (paragraph 12) means
   a. reluctant.
   b. lonely.
   c. repeated.
   d. useless.

2. The word *amicably* in "we all had a drink together, . . . quite amicably" (paragraph 24) means
   a. with hostility.
   b. unnecessarily.
   c. quietly.
   d. in a friendly way.

3. Which of the following would be a good alternative title for this selection?
   a. A Burmese Prisoner
   b. Capital Punishment
   c. Eyewitness to an Execution
   d. What It Means to Take a Life

4. Which sentence best expresses the main idea of the selection?
   a. Capital punishment is unpleasant to carry out, but it is necessary in some cases.
   b. Executions in Burma were done in an inefficient and amateurish way.
   c. Taking another person's life, no matter why, is morally wrong.
   d. No one cared about the Burmese prisoner who was hanged.

5. Just before he was executed, the prisoner
   a. protested his innocence.
   b. cried out to his god.
   c. tried to escape from the gallows.
   d. said a quiet prayer.

6. *True or false?* _____ The prisoner had been convicted of murder.

7. After the execution, the author and the other authorities
   a. felt relief.
   b. became very depressed.
   c. realized they had done something wrong.
   d. couldn't speak for a long while.

8. The author implies that
   a. the dog that interrupted the march to the gallows belonged to the prisoner.
   b. no one has the right to take another person's life.
   c. the authorities knew the prisoner was innocent.
   d. other methods of execution are more humane than hanging.

9. The author implies that
   a. the prisoner would have escaped if he had not been so heavily guarded.
   b. the prisoner did not die immediately.
   c. the hangman had volunteered for the job.
   d. the superintendent of the jail was nervous and upset about the hanging.

10. The author implies that
    a. the people who witnessed the hanging later laughed and joked to cover up the uneasiness they felt.
    b. the native people and the Europeans felt differently about the hanging.
    c. he had become friends with the prisoner before the execution.
    d. Burmese officials were corrupt.

■ Discussion Questions

About Content

1. How does the prisoner act as he is led out to be hanged? On the basis of his actions, what state of mind do you feel he is in?

2. Why does everyone stand "aghast" when the stray dog licks the prisoner's face? Why is this incident important? (To answer, you might consider what qualities the dog represents or symbolizes.)

3. The author has a moment of understanding when the prisoner steps "slightly aside to avoid a puddle on the path." What realization does the author come to? How is this realization related to the small incident of avoiding a puddle?

About Structure

4. The best statement of the author's thesis is in paragraph 10. Find it and write it in the spaces below:

_____

_____

About Style and Tone

5. Why do you think Orwell ends the narrative with the statement, "The dead man was a hundred yards away"?

6. Orwell uses several *similes* (comparisons using the words *like* or *as*) to add vividness to the narrative. He says, for example, that the guards handled the prisoner "like men handling a fish which is still alive and may jump back into the water." Find two more similes and write them here:

_____

_____

7. In part, Orwell uses dialogue to tell his story; we hear the actual voices of the superintendent, Francis, the prisoners, and others. Find and underline all the lines spoken by the superintendent. Discuss how the words the superintendent speaks (and the tone of voice he speaks them in) reflect the emotional changes the superintendent goes through.

■ Writing Assignments

Assignment 1

Use examples and details from "A Hanging" to support the following thesis statement:

In "A Hanging," George Orwell constantly contrasts death with life in order to show us how wrong it is to kill another human being.

You might organize your supporting paragraphs by showing how death is contrasted with life (1) on the way to the gallows; (2) at the gallows; (3) after the hanging.

To get started, reread the selection closely, noting words and incidents that seem to be closely related to either death or life. For example, in paragraph 2, Orwell describes the prisoner as "quite unresisting, yielding his arms limply to the ropes." It is as if the prisoner is already dead. In contrast, the guards are filled with life and action: they handcuff the prisoner, lash his arms, and keep a "careful, caressing grip" on him. At many other points in the story, this strong contrast between death and life is described.

Use a point-by-point method of contrast in developing your essay. You may want to look first at the example of this method on page 163.

Assignment 2

Capital punishment is no longer legal in Canada. The sensational nature of some highly publicized trials sometimes brings this issue back to public awareness. Imagine that a national referendum by each province will soon be undertaken, in which you are eligible to give your opinion on the return of capital punishment. Would you decide for or against changing the current law? Give reasons for your decision. For example, if you believe your province should re-instate capital punishment, and you would wish to change the law, you might give the reasons in the following essay outline:

Thesis: Manitoba should allow a jury to vote for "death by lethal injection" as a method of capital punishment for convicted criminals, and I would vote to introduce such a law.

Topic sentences

a. First of all, the death penalty saves thousands of tax dollars that would be spent to keep criminals in prison for life.

b. In addition, the punishment acts as a deterrent to other criminals.

c. Most important, death is an appropriate punishment for someone who commits a terrible crime.

In order to avoid writing in vague, general terms, you may want to use specific examples of cases or crimes currently being discussed in the news. You may also need facts and statistics you can find by consulting the card or computerized catalogue in your college library under the subject heading *Capital Punishment* and by skimming the appropriate books.

Assignment 3

On the basis of the knowledge you have gained by reading this selection and by observation of news items on the subject, write an essay with *either* of the thesis statements below:

- Executions today are as brutal as the one described in "A Hanging."
- Executions today are humane compared with the one described in "A Hanging."

You may want to write about each of the following areas in your supporting paragraphs:

Methods of execution and atmosphere in which executions are conducted
Kinds of people who are executed
Fairness of the trials and judges

The Image of Beauty

Catherine Pigott

Is everyone, particularly women, always dissatisfied with themselves in terms of their weight or size? Are women more prone to mistaken images of themselves than are men? Are only the well-fed inhabitants of the West subject to the obsessive pursuit of thinness? Catherine Pigott, an Ontario writer and radio producer, writes in direct and clear terms about learning to re-appraise her views of female beauty and weight-consciousness in a Third World country. She lived with a Gambian family while teaching English in Africa, and observed more than superficial differences in North American and African cultural perceptions about food and physical appearance.

The women of the household clucked disapprovingly when they saw me. It was the first 1 time I had worn African clothes since my arrival in tiny, dusty Gambia, and evidently they were not impressed. They adjusted my head-tie and pulled my *lappa*, the ankle-length fabric I had wrapped around myself, even tighter. "You're too thin," one of them pronounced. "It's no good." They nicknamed me "Chicken-hips."

I marvelled at this accolade, for I had never been called thin in my life. It was some- 2
thing I longed for. I would have been flattered if those ample-bosomed women hadn't
looked so distressed. It was obvious I fell far short of their ideal of beauty.

I had dressed up for a very special occasion—the baptism of a son. The women heaped 3
rice into tin basins the size of laundry tubs, shaping it into mounds with their hands. Five
of us sat around one basin, thrusting our fingers into the scalding food. These women ate
with such relish, such joy. They pressed the rice into balls in their fists, squeezing until
the bright-red palm oil ran down their forearms and dripped off their elbows.

I tried desperately, but I could not eat enough to please them. It was hard for me to 4
explain that I come from a culture in which it is almost unseemly for a woman to eat too
heartily. It's considered unattractive. It was even harder to explain that to me thin is beautiful, and in my country we deny ourselves food in our pursuit of perfect slenderness.

That night, everyone danced to welcome the baby. Women swivelled their broad hips 5
and used their hands to emphasize the roundness of their bodies. One needed to be round
and wide to make the dance beautiful. There was no place for thinness here. It made people sad. It reminded them of things they wanted to forget, such as poverty, drought and
starvation. You never knew when the rice was going to run out.

I began to believe that Africa's image of the perfect female body was far more real- 6
istic than the long-legged leanness I had been conditioned to admire. There, it is beautiful—not shameful—to carry weight on the hips and thighs, to have a round stomach
and heavy, swinging breasts. Women do not battle the bulge, they celebrate it. A body is
not something to be tamed and moulded.

The friends who had christened me Chicken-hips made it their mission to fatten me up. 7
It wasn't long before a diet of rice and rich, oily stew twice a day began to change me. Every
month, the women would take a stick and measure my backside, noting with pleasure its
gradual expansion. "Oh Catherine, your buttocks are getting nice now!" they would say.

What was extraordinary was that I, too, believed I was becoming more beautiful. 8
There was no sense of panic, no shame, no guilt-ridden resolves to go on the miracle
grape-and-water diet. One day, I tied my *lappa* tight across my hips and went to the market to buy beer for a wedding. I carried the crate of bottles home on my head, swinging
my hips slowly as I walked. I felt transformed.

In Gambia, people don't use words such as "cheating," "naughty," or "guilty" when 9
they talk about eating. The language of sin is not applied to food. Fat is desirable. It holds
beneficial meanings of abundance, fertility and health.

My perception of beauty altered as my body did. The European tourists on the beach 10
began to look strange and skeletal rather than "slim." They had no hips. They seemed
devoid of shape and substance. Women I once would have envied appeared fragile and
even ugly. The ideal they represented no longer made sense.

After a year, I came home. I preached my new way of seeing to anyone who would 11
listen. I wanted to cling to the liberating belief that losing weight had nothing to do with
self-love.

Family members kindly suggested that I might look and feel better if I slimmed down a 12
little. They encouraged me to join an exercise club. I wandered around the malls in a

dislocated daze. I felt uncomfortable trying on clothes that hung so elegantly on the mannequins. I began hearing old voices inside my head: "Plaid makes you look fat. . . . You're too short for that style. . . . Vertical stripes are more slimming. . . . Wear black."

I joined the club. Just a few weeks after I had worn a *lappa* and scooped up rice with my hands, I was climbing into pink leotards and aerobics shoes. The instructor told me that I had to set fitness goals and "weigh in" after my workouts. There were mirrors on the walls and I could see women watching themselves. I sensed that even the loveliest among them felt they were somehow flawed. As the aerobics instructor barked out commands for arm lifts and leg lifts, I pictured Gambian women pounding millet and dancing in a circle with their arms raised high. I do not mean to romanticize their rock-hard lives, but we were hardly to be envied as we ran like fools between two walls to the tiresome beat of synthesized music.

We were a roomful of women striving to reshape ourselves into some kind of pubertal ideal. I reverted to my natural state: one of yearning to be slimmer and more fit than I was. My freedom had been temporary. I was home, where fat is feared and despised. It was time to exert control over my body and my life. I dreaded the thought of people saying, "She's let herself go."

If I return to Africa, I am sure the women will shake their heads in bewildered dismay. Even now, I sometimes catch my reflection in a window and their voices come back to me. "Yo! Chicken-hips!"

■ Reading Comprehension Questions

1. The word *accolade* in "I marvelled at this accolade . . ."(paragraph 2) means
    a. insult.
    b. praise.
    c. phrase.
    d. nickname.

2. The word *pubertal* in "a roomful of women striving to reshape ourselves into some kind of pubertal ideal" (paragraph 14) means
    a. adolescent.
    b. skeletal.
    c. unreal.
    d. unhealthy.

3. Which of the following would be a good alternative title for this selection?
    a. Skinny Like Me
    b. Chicken-Hips
    c. Canadian Discontent
    d. Women and Weight

4. Which sentence best expresses the main idea of the selection?
    a. Western concepts of female beauty are health-related.
    b. African women are healthier, happier, and more fertile than Canadian women.

    c. Cultural forces can shape women's bodies and ideas in unnatural ways.

    d. The pursuit of external beauty is a worthy struggle.

5. The women's dance at the christening conveyed the harmony of beauty and happiness because

    a. the dancers had enough money to afford food.

    b. the contours of the women's bodies fit the motions of the dance.

    c. there were no unhappy memories of drought or starvation.

    d. there was a surplus of stored rice.

6. *True or false?* _____ The author had felt at ease with her body-image in Canada before leaving for Africa.

7. The women eating with the writer at the christening party

    a. ate so much because they were afraid of the food running out.

    b. ate with great relish because it was a celebration, and eating caused no guilt.

    c. ate generously because sharing food was important to demonstrate hospitality.

    d. ate heartily because they wanted to gain weight and be more beautiful.

8. The author implies that

    a. African notions of beauty are inappropriate to the 20th century.

    b. overweight women are so because of fears of famine-caused starvation.

    c. African women are not obsessed by fashion because of their clothing styles.

    d. African women's concepts of health, beauty, and eating are preferable to ours.

9. The concept of beauty, according to the selection, is

    a. variable because of cultural and environmental factors.

    b. a constant throughout all ages and times.

    c. dependent on an individual's sense of themselves.

    d. determined by unhealthy and unrealistic external pressures everywhere.

10. The author implies that her natural, or intrinsic sense of herself

    a. is now more balanced after her experiences in Africa.

    b. is just as uncertain and as dependent on outside influences as ever.

    c. is only a temporary sense of freedom at best.

    d. is now firmly rooted in a strong base of self-knowledge.

■ Discussion Questions

About Content

1. The author says she "fell far short of their [the African women's] ideal of beauty." Why? Is her response to their evaluation totally negative?

2. Why do you think the writer stated that, as she gained weight, she felt "transformed"? Is it simply because of the positive reactions of the Gambian women?

3. In the end, do you think the author is pleased by her sense of her physical self? How do the responses of her Canadian friends and family to her on her return home compare to, or contrast with, those of the Gambian women?

About Structure

4. Catherine Pigott's essay is a good example of the comparison/contrast format. In the portraits of the African women in paragraph 5 and of the European tourists in paragraph 10, which details serve as points of contrast? Which two other paragraphs show such contrasting details?

5. Does this selection make use of the "point-by-point" or of the "one side at a time" method of comparison/contrast? Give evidence to support your answer.

About Style and Tone

6. In paragraph 5, the author uses verbs metaphorically; she borrows words from warfare, animal training, and sculpture to describe Western attitudes towards the female body. What does the use of such verbs imply about our treatment of our bodies? What verb shows the contrasting African attitude towards the robust female body?

7. Which three nouns in paragraph 9 parallel and contrast with the three words "cheating," "naughty," and "guilty," as used in the first sentence of the paragraph to describe attitudes about eating? What do the three positive nouns say about the differences between African and North American life?

8. The author includes pieces of dialogue in her essay. What is the effect on you as a reader of these lines of direct speech? How is the fundamental basis of contrast in the selection expressed through such quotations from others?

■ Writing Assignments

Assignment 1

Open your favourite magazine and you see advertisements using male and female models. Are these models in any way "realistic" in appearance, or do they represent ideals created by dieting, exercise, heredity, and photographic skills? Do images of your own gender leave you feeling envious and dissatisfied with yourself? What would be the effect on you of seeing models who were more "life-like," perhaps not super-slender or incredibly muscular? Would you feel more attracted by the advertisement? Would you still want to buy the product?

Write a letter to the advertising department of a company whose ads use models to whom you are unable to relate, models who represent unrealistic and unattainable ideals for readers. Your letter should outline and support your point of view on the type of models you feel would better represent a "realistic" consumer of the company's product, and why.

Assignment 2

Why is North America and the rest of the "First World" so obsessed by thinness? To other centuries and societies, and to the Gambian women in Pigott's essay, being thin meant sadness, and "things they wanted to forget, such as poverty, drought, and starvation" (paragraph 5). What is your own attitude towards weight and self-image? Write an essay in which you compare or contrast specific aspects of your own point of view with that expressed in "The Image of Beauty."

Assignment 3

Women are still, even in an era of "equality," far more prone to be dissatisfied with themselves physically, and to suffer from eating disorders. Both sexes may crowd gyms and fitness centres, but would a North American man have written a parallel essay to this selection? Would a man have written an essay like Naheed Mustafa's "My Body Is My Own Business"? Is there a fundamental, *not* culture-driven, difference between the sexes, in terms of the importance each attaches to physical attractiveness? Would a man change his view of himself because of spending time with an imaginary group who valued baldness and beer-bellies as symbols of virility?

Write an essay which either argues with, or persuades the reader of the validity of, the following position:

■ Men are as insecure and as vulnerable to popular ideas about their appearance and attractiveness as are women.

Of Lemons and Lemonade

Sherwin Tija

Like many people today, Sherwin Tija grew up in the suburbs, in the "familiar gridiron of Scarborough, Ontario." Vividly contrasting the reality of childhood surroundings with the "dreamscape" of a holiday in Algonquin Park, the writer wonders what changes a knowledge of natural beauty might have made to character and thinking. Tija, still a university student, describes with equal intensity the alien familiarity of a home neighbourhood and the unfamiliar, exquisite sheen of lake water at night.

When I came across the word "cornflowers" in Margaret Laurence's The Diviners, *I didn't know what it meant. I couldn't tell you whether cornflowers were proud and glowing or taciturn and sweet; I just didn't know. The same thing occurred when I stumbled over "couchgrass" and "peonies." I had heard of them before, the names were familiar, yet, I couldn't put the names to a face, to a fragrance, or a touch.*

I can however, tell you about concrete, steel, tar and glass, and go on endlessly about the myriad uses of bricks. Of these, their structures and lines remain rigid in my visual vocabulary; of these I can envision with clarity. Though disgracefully ignorant about the natural world, this is my world, this world of malls and lawns and faceless houses, generic streets and measured sidewalks and parks where one can see the other side by standing at one end. And while sometimes one grows strangely nostalgic for a world one's never really seen, except through a movie lens or the inscribed word, for what experience would I leave my familiar gridiron of Scarborough, Ontario? Would I leave it for a world of limitless lands, unscarred sunsets and fields? In a second. What kind of fields? I don't care; fields of wheat, grain, weeping willow leaves—fields of anything but shorn green grass and playgrounds. But I've never been to those places, so let me tell you about what I can see.

I can tell you about skinning bare knees on the coarse schoolyard lot, and getting up bleeding and crying with pebbles still embedded like shrapnel around one's wicked-looking wound. I can tell you about the tremendous impetus the fixed playground was for our imaginations. When every recess game had to be new, the jungle gym becomes an island, a base, a prison, a fortress. The angular teeter-totters become skyward-gazing missile silos; the swings jet planes, or catapults; the sand pit the Middle East, the baseball cage an enemy wall to be climbed—everything was something. The playground was a proving ground.

When I do come across flora in the books though, I can't just dismiss it. To keep the illusion of the story intact I have to pull them in somehow; they must still exist somewhere. In such cases, I contrive a scattershot barrage of green, like in a Seurat paint-

ing, and let that pass. Or maybe I see pretty pink and red and yellow flowers and dot them among the green, but all to the purpose of setting the atmosphere that I want to feel as I'm sinking into the narrative. A flower's a flower, I tell myself, so it doesn't feel as if I'm missing much.

Suburban nights are quiet, if you're in among the houses deep. I can tell you about 5 the reflected glow of lamplight in rain-wet streets, dark like soil, but solid like glass, and how each car that passes glares with eyes of opulence and self-proclaimed righteousness. I can tell you about the perversion of grass that we cultivate; not long and billowy, but short and flat and uniform. Conform, they seem to say, even as I mow them angrily down and fret at the uselessness of the task. But we all do this because there is a law against not doing it, passed by those who can afford to pay others to do it for them. And so we conform, and grow affectionate for our lawns rather than standing up for what we believe. I can tell you about dull, repetitive genetic housing, as if they're all spawned from the same master plan—a monotonous mother brick. There's the fear of getting lost in one's own neighborhood, or even on one's own street if we're just not good with numbers. When all the streets for blocks all look the same at night, and when all the people stay safe with the face of the same expression, and we allow ourselves to grow detached, and we look warily at our neighbours for lack of knowing—this would make me leave. This is the essence of freshly mowed grass.

Once I went up north to Algonquin Park, and though I didn't know the name of any- 6 *thing, I picked up a water flower, fragrant and wet, and I knew that that was what I would see first the next time I thought about canoeing on a lake. It was a water lily, I later learned, and I smiled because it should have been obvious.*

Let me tell you about the beauty of hydrofields, the great open spaces of our land, 7 with their gigantic metal men, striding into the distance, clutching their living lines. Sometimes these lines hum and join the crickets in a chorus in the blazing summer's heat. Sometimes they are downed in storms and children are electrocuted, and these children's dogs, and then scavengers which come to feed . . . in the late summer, when the grass is yellow in the sunset, I like to pretend that it's Africa, on the Serengeti Plain. The animals are there, if only in my mind. Though sometimes the hazing of the heat causes them to appear in earnest and I wonder if it's sunstroke or an altered state of consciousness. Most often there are lone figures like me with their dogs before them, and once when I was very young, a couple making love. I remember the shadow on her upturned face as a very intense blue.

Sometimes I wish I had that natural vocabulary, and that I had grown up close to water, 8 *and that some old woman had taken me by the hand, and showed me the woods and pointed with gnarled stick at nature's ornaments, revealing their nature and their name.*

Let me tell you about the curious relationship between a sidewalk's crack and your 9 mother's back.

Sometimes I wish I could take my experiences in the wilderness for granted, like 1
those who have had cabins up north all their lives. For while I would lose the aching
awe of the wild world that I carry today, a childhood growing up among such won-
ders might have shaped me into a different person; possibly one more comfortable
in situations requiring relinquishing thought and reason in favor of intuition and
instinct. I don't know, maybe I would be less constrained, repressed. It is this pos-
sibility I regret, even if I had no choice at the time.

Let me tell you about the brilliance of the clouds at night over the car dealerships 1
on the next street. Let me tell you about the ubiquitous red stop signs, complementing
green grass and vivid against a blue sky. Let me tell you about the stream of cars that
flows continuously, under formidable bridges that span neighborhood to neighborhood,
district to district. Let me tell you about the crescents and the lanes, the circles and cir-
cuits, groves and gates, courts and squares, all connected like a madman's maze, in some
secular sequence. And even in the rurality of Suburbia, the churches are not the tallest
structures as they once used to be. Today it's the apartment buildings. Are we losing or
finding ourselves? Or do we have to do both?

The next time I think about entering the gates of heaven, what I'll remember is coast- 1
ing in a canoe across glassy water at night, shining a flashlight though the rising
mists off the lake; the paddles not making a sound.

Let me tell you about the all-night donut shops, immaculate, unchanging and over- 1
charging; the perpetual light even at night; the charisma and cheap intensity of malls; the
lack of open-ended gathering places; the solace of libraries; the elephantine dumpsters;
daily road kill to greet school kids walking home; the reined imagination in knowing
what's over the next horizon—more of the same; and parking lot wastelands and furtive
gropings.

Sometimes I am glad of the mystery of nature. That I cannot name with a glance every 1
plant or leaf that comes into view, is important. That I can look at a landscape and
wonder at its being, instead of understanding it by clarifying it, defining it, is a free-
dom. Despite this, when I first swam in an Algonquin lake at sunset, when the col-
ors imbued the waters, my first thought was that of swimming in a postcard.

Let me tell you a tale of lemons and lemonade. A boy and a girl are selling lemon- 1
ade by the side of the road. From a card table with a plastic tablecloth hangs a sign alert-
ing passersby that a cup of their brew costs only 50 cents. I buy a cup and when I ask
them if it's made out of real lemons, they tell me no, it's from a can of concentrate, the
same can wherein they have deposited my two quarters with a self-satisfied clink.

"But why didn't you use real lemons?" I say, finishing my cup.   1
"Because this is all we had," the girl said.   1
The cups are styrofoam, and I drop mine into their plastic garbage bag.   1

■ Reading Comprehension Questions

1. The word *impetus* in "the tremendous impetus [of] the fixed playground" (paragraph 3) means
    a. toy.
    b. arena.
    c. drive.
    d. space.

2. The word *ubiquitous* in "the ubiquitous red stop signs, complementing green grass" (paragraph 11) means
    a. hideous.
    b. bright-coloured.
    c. found everywhere.
    d. beautiful.

3. Which phrase of the following might be a good alternative title for this essay?
    a. Of Loneliness and Landscapes
    b. Neighbourhood Nostalgia
    c. Paradise Lost
    d. Playgrounds and Plastic Cups

4. Which sentence best expresses the main idea of the selection?
    a. The suburbs are a hideous place in which to grow up.
    b. Knowing both nature and urban life helps people to know themselves.
    c. The suburbs have their own beauty and mystery.
    d. Nature is beautiful, but beyond our knowledge.

5. The writer remembers the school playground
    a. as harsh and dangerous.
    b. as causing the children's aggressive and warlike behaviour.
    c. as barren and empty.
    d. as an inspiration to flights of fancy.

6. *True or false?* _____ The author finds nature more "real" than a suburban neighbourhood.

7. The author's main problem with the streets in her area is
    a. that the neighbours drive expensive cars and employ lawn-care services.
    b. having to trim the lawn to legal standards.
    c. a fear of getting lost near home.
    d. the sense of imposed order and distance from neighbours.

8. The writer implies that
    a. because of a suburban upbringing, a person will never understand nature.
    b. environments may, but need not, limit our imaginations.

c. children will never experience the truth of natural things.

d. the beauty of nature can be understood only by relating it to pictures.

9. The writer implies that

a. there is a reality beyond one's defining abilities.

b. the suburbanite cannot really understand his or her "world."

c. suburban childhood was dreary and boring.

d. such a childhood leaves people alienated and alone.

10. *True or false?* _____ The author implies that the children selling concentrated lemonade are pathetic because they haven't experienced the "real thing."

■ Discussion Questions

About Content

1. Sherwin Tija tells readers about knowing certain flowers and plants only by name. What were her only sources of information about these aspects of nature? What features of daily surroundings does the writer know instead?

2. Which elements of the suburban landscape are appealing, and which are described as unattractive?

3. What do you think are the writer's feelings towards the children who are selling lemonade at the end of the essay? Which experiences described in "Of Lemons and Lemonade" would lead to these feelings?

About Structure

4. Why does the author alternate between paragraphs in italics and paragraphs in normal print? Do the two types of paragraphs change in length as the essay progresses? Why?

5. What is the connection between the final episode, the "tale" with dialogue about two children selling lemonade, and the rest of the essay?

About Style and Tone

6. Why do you think the writer "personifies," or gives human qualities to, various nonhuman things in paragraphs 5 and 7?

7. Tija consciously repeats certain words and phrases like "I can tell you," "Let me tell you," and "sometimes." What is the effect of this repetition?

8. Compare Tija's use of a "catalogue" or pile-up of details with Ray Guy's food lists in "Outharbor Menu." How do you respond to each of these lists?

■ Writing Assignments

Assignment 1

Everyone has memories of the areas where they grew up. Many people in Canadian cities spent their childhoods in suburbs similar to Scarborough, and experienced natural settings only occasionally. But not everyone's reactions to either their childhood environments or to nature are similar to those of Sherwin Tija.

Write a letter to a friend in which you describe the streets, neighbourhood, or area where you grew up. Try to capture clearly the sights, sounds, and sense details of the place, and to recreate in words the emotions those details awakened in you. Limit the dimensions of the area you describe as much as possible, so that your description is intense and clearly focused. Choose a path or route you will follow as you describe your chosen place, and try to take your reader with you.

Remember that a letter follows the same structural patterns as an essay, with an introductory paragraph like a thesis statement to give your reader clear ideas of both your dominant impression and the three strongest memories of places or objects which support that impression. Be sure your conclusion follows naturally from your supporting details, and end with a final thought to sum up your feelings and reconnect yourself with the reader of your letter.

Assignment 2

Sherwin Tija effectively contrasts personal reflections awakened by nature with those caused by everyday surroundings. Choose some environment you do *not* particularly enjoy, but must frequent for some purpose (perhaps a work-place or a relative's home), and a place where you are very happy. Try to ensure that the two locations are of relatively equal time- or detail-value, so that your contrast is not lop-sided. Contrast the two environments in terms of what pleases or displeases you about them. Use order of importance to lead up to your strongest point of contrast, and use point-by-point format for your essay, as Tija has, to bring out specific elements of contrast. Your conclusion may point to a "moral" about why your feelings may be divided or it may point to the absolute superiority of one place over the other.

Assignment 3

You are an environmental columnist for your local community newspaper. Two possible assignments are offered to you: one a puff-piece selling your community's building restoration and quality of life to build investor interest in your community, the other a slam at recent and older social, lighting, and drainage problems which have been causing trouble for residents and visitors. While trying to decide which job to take, you make a list of words under the simple headings of "good" and "bad," and try to group your words under some headings.

Since you're trying to find out which side would make the more forceful article, you are looking for where your strongest feelings lie. You tend to write a better argument for your own side.

Here is your rough unfinished list of "goods" and "bads," and the tentative headings.

Good	Bad
1. Streets	**1. Streets**
– new fronts/stores, restaurants	– dirty/ominous alleyways/threats
–	– forbidding, frightening unlit areas
– clean, crisp architectural details	– rickety doorways & shattered glass
2. People	**2. People**
– entrepreneurs/exciting retail	– panhandlers/pathetic, annoying
– young families/fresh money	–
–	– teen gangs, loitering/lingering
3. Enviro/Atmosphere	**3. Enviro/Atmosphere**
– revived, reawakened	– streetcars/clean, but racket of grinding
– air quality/?	– sewers/stench, fetid
– trees/natural, verdant, leafy	–

Make your own list of words based on three distinct aspects of your area. Write either the positive or the negative article about your own part of the town or city where you live. Structure your argument to be most convincing, and begin with a solid thesis statement containing your major ideas, with your strongest point in the final position.

OBSERVING OTHERS

Safety First, Fun a Distant Second

Amy Willard Cross

Is being a parent hazardous to your capacity for fun? Will you develop "Dangervision" when you have children? Toronto-based writer and broadcaster Amy Willard Cross believes that North Americans have become obsessively overcautious in the '90s. If parenting is as difficult as Mary Ann Lamanna and Agnes Reidmann indicate in another essay in the text, perhaps we now substitute overprotective consumerism for common sense in raising our children. Is a long and nitpickingly regulated life worth living? Cross suspects that our children may end up "like domesticated animals . . . unable to fend off normal predators," and that as adults we are substituting simulated dangers for the ordinary excitements of existence. Maybe it's only a short hop from the seatbelted Jolly Jumper to the bungy-jump, but is it worth the ride any more?

My sister used to be fearless. She lived by herself in neighbourhoods where people held 1 riots on their days off. She hitch-hiked. Snorkled in shark-infested waters. Dared.

Then she had a child. Her first Christmas as a mother, she met me at the airport in 2 a new car: a big, silver car of European extraction with heavy metal exterior, buttery leather interior.

"Nice car, eh?" she said. "We got it for the baby. It's got great crash stats. If I 3 collide with a small import, my hood might crunch, but I could probably hop out and play tennis."

"Would you really feel like tennis after trash-compacting somebody—even if he did 4 drive a Japanese car?"

"Buckle your seat belt," she said. Despite the one-in-a-something chance of having an accident within a five-mile radius from her house, we arrived unscathed.

Once home, it was clear she had redecorated: the look was late 20th-Century Safety. Knee-high plastic gates closed off areas unsupervised by adults. Smoke alarms stood guard in every room, shrieking warnings at exuberant smokers or burnt toast. What really stood out was the TV. It had been moved some 15 feet away from the sofa, so you would need binoculars to see the weather map. I moved closer, turned it on.

"Get back," my sister cried, "you're in the electromagnetic field." Apparently, those friendly watts and volts that had once powered our nightlight when we were kids and chilled our Jell-O had mutated into agents of danger that threatened cancer and other bad luck. To contain this malevolent force, plastic covers blocked each plug—staving off electrocution and keeping electromagnetic fields where they belonged.

Like others who have managed to reproduce themselves genetically, my sister sees potential danger in any situation—call it Dangervision. As the gift of prophecy yields glimpses of the future, Dangervision reveals a parallel reality of worst-case scenarios: freak accidents, falls, fires, or drowning in bath water.

Dangervision probably has an evolutionary role. But even those without this second sight get help protecting themselves against themselves. Well-meaning safety campaigns warn against things most of us avoid instinctively, slowly undoing the undemocratic notion that only the fittest survive. Nowadays, anybody can survive—just follow the safety tips inside every package. In fact, during the past decade accidental deaths have plummeted. Fewer and fewer people go with a bang, splat or gurgle; most of us die slowly, remaining eligible for an open casket. The Heimlich manoeuvre, pool covers, home fire extinguishers, childproof caps, guard rails, seat belts, smoke-free dining rooms and life vests certainly played a part. Finally, we know that plastic dry-cleaning bags are *not* toys. And lots of guardian angels are out of work.

Sure we're living longer, but it seems longer, too. It's hard to have fun when you're being careful. You can't drink champagne on afternoon canoe rides any more—it's the law. Heaven knows, you could pass out, fall into the lake and drown. You can't feel crispness of wind in your hair while galloping through the meadows, or racing country roads on a 10-speed, because helmets trap a steamy, sweaty halo of dead air around your head. God forbid, the horse could shy, your tire could blow, and your brains could split open.

Children suffer from safety even more. The fearlessness is very quickly beaten out of them by adoring parents. Following the advice of kid safety handbooks, new moms and dads crawl around the floor to experience coffee-table-level perils as their toddler would. They bug their kid's room with baby intercoms. Parents won't let kids play in the park without a grown-up around to stop them from climbing trees or swinging upside down. Like Irish crystal, kids get dusted off on important occasions and handled ever so carefully—after all, there's usually only one to the set. You wonder, will children raised in padded environments languish like domesticated animals released into the wild, unable to fend off normal predators?

Besides editing all risk from our lives, Dangervision has robbed us of the pleasure of surviving. Those few sweet moments after a close call felt great: nearly fell off the observation deck, nearly drowned, nearly went over the median!

Now people take safe, accident-free lives for granted. If the average life span is 73 13
years, they figure they've got it coming to them. Fate or God's will or bad luck better
not get in the way. And if it does, watch out. Accidents don't just happen, they're someone else's fault. And faults get sued. For a lot of money. Disclaimers are posted everywhere in a vain effort to prevent product liability suits: not responsible for accidental
dismemberment with the Brush 'Em automatic tooth-cleaning system.

Europeans don't share this need to protect their fellow citizens from themselves. 14
They don't ruin architecture with unsightly metal guard rails, but let any stupid tourist
climb up fortifications or Roman amphitheatres. The attitude is probably a form of population control for a very crowded continent.

Now that cleaners hide behind childproof cabinets, now that railings protect balconies, 15
now that no one smokes in bed after tousling the sheets, we're finally safe. Strangely, people flirt with danger recreationally. The same people with air bags, life vests and smoke
alarms spend their weekends heli-skiing, hang-gliding, parachuting and racing cars. So bri-
dled in normal life, people travel miles to dare the latest craze: bungy-jumping. They pay
piles of money to jump off bridges attached to nothing but a giant rubber band from which
they bounce—narrowly escaping the water's surface. Apparently, it's an exhilarating nearly.

By the time the nephew makes it to adulthood accident-free, he'll probably fly 16
straight to Australia and jump some bungies.

■ Reading Comprehension Questions

1. The word *exuberant* in "shrieking warnings at exuberant smokers or burnt
   toast" (paragraph 6) means
   a. errant.
   b. obnoxious.
   c. excited.
   d. smelly.

2. The word *malevolent* in "To contain this malevolent force, plastic covers
   blocked each plug" (paragraph 7) means
   a. evil.
   b. significant.
   c. powerful.
   d. amazing.

3. Which of the following would be a good alternative title for this selection?
   a. Household Horrors
   b. Safe is Never Sorry
   c. Fear, Fun, and Foolishness
   d. Warning: Children at Play

4. Which sentence best expresses the main idea of this selection?
   a. Survival is still risky today, and children must be protected from accidents.
   b. Taking chances has all but been eliminated from our lives.

    c. Taking precautions in everyday life is wise, if sometimes time-consuming.

    d. Taking the risk from life takes some of the pleasure and challenge from life.

5. The author finds safety-obsessed Canadians
    a. leading dull, physically inactive lives.
    b. becoming obsessive consumers.
    c. suffering from overprotected lives, and missing some joys in life.
    d. unwilling to have large families.

6. *True or false?* _____ Deaths from most types of accident continue to rise, despite increasing consumer awareness and product safety features.

7. *True or false?* _____ Increased interest in safety and protection is a world-wide phenomenon of the 1990s.

8. The author implies that
    a. no one knew that electricity was dangerous when she was a child.
    b. her sister's response to electrical plugs and the TV is unrealistic.
    c. her sister doesn't understand electromagnetism.
    d. television and electrical appliances are not really dangerous.

9. The author implies that
    a. human instincts will protect people from most dangers.
    b. following safety rules is undemocratic and unnecessary.
    c. people do not live longer now because they are careful.
    d. drinking outdoors and riding bikes and horses are not risky.

10. The author implies that
    a. enjoying "close calls" with death is perverse.
    b. "Dangervision" results in timid children and bored adults.
    c. people are no longer responsible for most mishaps.
    d. "Dangervision" is a necessary component of contemporary life.

■ Discussion Questions

About Content

1. Are any of the author's sister's modifications to her life based on concern for her child realistic? Which changes make sense? Why?

2. Amy Willard Cross says "Nowadays, anybody can survive. . . ." (9) Why does she say this? Why does the author take issue with this idea?

3. The author feels that we take our very safe lives for granted today. What has this led to, and what have we lost? Have we discovered new forms of irresponsibility?

About Structure

4. What method of introduction is used in paragraph 1?
   a. Quotation
   b. Anecdote
   c. Explaining the importance of the topic
5. How is unity of structure reinforced by the opening and closing paragraphs of the essay?
6. Which paragraph contains the author's thesis statement?

About Style and Tone

7. How would you describe the tone of "Safety First"? Are there serious points in some of Cross' examples? Which examples show use of the comic technique of exaggeration? Which examples show seriousness of intention? How does the mixture of two tones affect your acceptance of the author's message?
8. There are several examples of what your English instructor and this textbook call *sentence fragments* in this essay. Examples include the two final sentences of paragraph 1. Find another fragment. What distinguishes such stylistic usages from mere sentence errors? What is the effect of these phrases on the tone of the piece?
9. Irony and comic writing often utilize the technique of understatement, where undercutting an idea's usual strength minimizes its seriousness. Examples of this technique appear in paragraph 9.

    List some of the examples in this paragraph.

    _____

    _____

    List another example of understatement found in this essay.

    _____

    Why would Cross wish to limit the strength of the ideas you have listed?

■ Writing Assignments

Assignment 1

Cross offers bungy-jumping, hang-gliding, and parachuting as examples of dangerous amusements in which we now participate, perhaps as substitutes for "real-life" terrors. How about nonactive thrill-seeking, like horror movies, tabloids, and amusement arcades? Do you agree that we are now looking for substitute stimulation because of the lack of peril in our lives? Have Canadians become a nation of "consumer thrill-seekers," buying our fun? Or does life still offer enough genuine challenges? What about negotiating a blizzard on the highway?

Write an essay in which you choose either to support Cross' thesis that we have lost our "edge" or to argue that life now offers new challenges. Be sure to choose sufficient and convincing examples to make your argument convincing, and to choose the strongest order in which to place your examples.

Assignment 2

Each summer local and national newspapers print articles about drowning and home and playground accidents which have happened to children across Canada. Write a letter to the editor of your local newspaper which *contrasts* the dangers to which children are still exposed with the advantages of taking various precautions to prevent such accidents. Limit your points of contrast to three of the strongest cases for providing adequate and basic protection to children in *specific* situations.

Assignment 3

Do you enjoy a sport or activity which involves an element of risk? Write an instructive process essay so that a reader can learn to play your sport or perform your activity *safely*.

If you find humour in your daily commute or some other routine, you may choose to write in a comic tone, as Cross has done.

Why My Mother Can't Speak English

Garry Engkent

Adjustment to Canadian culture and to the English language are difficult and long-term processes for anyone new to this country. Many aspects of becoming comfortable and productive within any culture are tied to the ability to use its dominant language. English is a difficult and complex tongue, incredibly rich in vocabulary and shades of meaning, but also incredibly confusing in its usage, grammar, and spelling, even to native English speakers. Engkent's mother suffered with a dilemma common among first-generation immigrants to Canada: the fear of losing one's original identity and past history along with one's original language. The author, who still speaks Cantonese, successfully accustomed himself to Canada to the extent of becoming a writer and a teacher of English language and literature at universities and colleges. Nonetheless, he felt his mother's frustration and misery most acutely, while experiencing the annoyance and frustration of one aware of the demands, rules, and expectations of his new country.

My mother is seventy years old. Widowed for five years now, she lives alone in her own house except for the occasions when I come home to tidy her household affairs. She has been in *gum san*, the golden mountain, for the past thirty years. She clings to the old-country ways so much so that today she astonishes me with this announcement: 1

"I want to get my citizenship," she says as she slaps down the *Dai Pao*, "before they come and take away my house." 2

"Nobody's going to do that. This is Canada." 3

"So everyone says," she retorts, "but did you read what the *Dai Pao* said? Ah, you can't read Chinese. The government is cutting back on old-age pensions. Anybody who hasn't got citizenship will lose everything. Or worse." 4

"The *Dai Pao* can't even typeset accurately," I tell her. Sometimes I worry about the information Mother receives from the biweekly community newspaper. "Don't worry—the Ministry of Immigration won't send you back to China." 5

"Little you know," she snaps back. "I am old, helpless, and without citizenship. Reasons enough. Now, get me citizenship. Hurry!" 6

"Mother, getting citizenship papers is not like going to the bank to cash in your pension cheque. First, you have to—" 7

"Excuses, my son, excuses. When your father was alive—" 8

"Oh, Mother, not again! You throw that at me every—" 9

"—made excuses, too." Her jaw tightens. "If you can't do this little thing for your own mother, well, I will just have to go and beg your cousin to . . ." 10

Every time I try to explain about the ways of the *fan gwei*, she thinks I do not want to help her. 11

"I'll do it, I'll do it, okay? Just give me some time." 12

"That's easy for you," Mother snorts. "You're not seventy years old. You're not going to lose your pension. You're not going to lose your house. Now, how much *lai-shi* will this take?" 13

After all these years in *gum san* she cannot understand that you don't give government officials *lai-shi*, the traditional Chinese money gift to persons who do things for you. 14

"That won't be necessary," I tell her. "And you needn't go to my cousin." 15

Mother picks up the *Dai Pao* again and says: "Why should I beg at the door of a village cousin when I have a son who is a university graduate?" 16

I wish my father were alive. Then he would be doing this. But he is not here, and as a dutiful son, I am responsible for the welfare of my widowed mother. So I take her to Citizenship Court. 17

There are several people from the Chinese community waiting there. Mother knows a few of the Chinese women and she chats with them. My cousin is there, too. 18

"I thought your mother already got her citizenship," he says to me. "Didn't your father—" 19

"No, he didn't." 20

He shakes his head sadly. "Still, better now than never. That's why I'm getting these people through." 21

"So they've been reading the *Dai Pao*." 22

He gives me a quizzical look, so I explain to him, and he laughs.

"You are the new generation," he says. "You didn't live long enough in *hon san*, the sweet land, to understand the fears of the old. You can't expect the elderly to renounce all attachments to China for the ways of the *fan gwei*. How old is she, seventy now? Much harder."

"She woke me up this morning at six, and Citizenship Court doesn't open until ten."

The doors of the court finally open, and Mother motions me to hurry. We wait in line for a while.

The clerk distributes applications and tells me the requirements. Mother wants to know what the clerk is saying, so half the time I translate for her.

The clerk suggests that we see one of the liaison officers.

"Your mother has been living in Canada for the past thirty years and she still can't speak English?"

"It happens," I tell the liaison officer.

"I find it hard to believe that—not one word?"

"Well, she understands some restaurant English," I tell her. "You know, French fries, pork chops, soup, and so on. And she can say a few words."

"But will she be able to understand the judge's questions? The interview with the judge, as you know, is an important part of the citizenship procedure. Can she read the booklet? What does she know about Canada?"

"So you don't think my mother has a chance?"

"The requirements are that the candidate must be able to speak either French or English, the two official languages of Canada. The candidate must be able to pass an oral interview with the citizenship judge, and then he or she must be able to recite the oath of allegiance—"

"My mother needs to speak English," I conclude for her.

"Look, I don't mean to be rude, but why didn't your mother learn English when she first came over?"

I have not been translating this conversation, and Mother, annoyed and agitated, asks me what is going on. I tell her there is a slight problem.

"What problem?" Mother opens her purse, and I see her taking a small red envelope—*lai-shi*—I quickly cover her hand.

"What's going on?" the liaison officer demands.

"Nothing," I say hurriedly. "Just a cultural misunderstanding, I assure you."

My mother rattles off some indignant words, and I snap back in Chinese: "Put that away! The woman won't understand, and we'll be in a lot of trouble."

The officer looks confused, and I realize that an explanation is needed.

"My mother was about to give you a money gift as a token of appreciation for what you are doing for us. I was afraid you might misconstrue it as a bribe. We have no intention of doing that."

"I'm relieved to hear it."

We conclude the interview, and I take Mother home. Still clutching the application, Mother scowls at me.

"I didn't get my citizenship papers. Now I will lose my old-age pension. The gov- 47
ernment will ship me back to China. My old bones will lie there while your father's will
be here. What will happen to me?"

How can I teach her to speak the language when she is too old to learn, too old to 48
want to learn? She resists anything that is *fan gwei*. She does everything the Chinese way.
Mother spends much time staring blankly at the four walls of her house. She does not
cry. She sighs and shakes her head. Sometimes she goes about the house touching her
favourite things.

"This is all your dead father's fault," she says quietly. She turns to the photograph 49
of my father on the mantel. Daily, she burns incense, pours fresh cups of fragrant tea,
and spreads dishes of his favourite fruits in front of the framed picture as is the custom.
In memory of his passing, she treks two miles to the cemetery to place flowers by his
headstone, to burn ceremonial paper money, and to talk to him. Regularly, rain or shine,
or even snow, she does these things. Such love, such devotion, now such vehemence.
Mother curses my father, her husband, in his grave.

When my mother and I emigrated from China, she was forty years old, and I, five. 50
My father was already a well-established restaurant owner. He put me in school and
Mother in the restaurant kitchen, washing dishes and cooking strange foods like hot dogs,
hamburgers, and French fries. She worked seven days a week from six in the morning until
eleven at night. This lasted for twenty-five years, almost to the day of my father's death.

The years were hard on her. The black-and-white photographs show a robust woman; 51
now I see a withered, frail, white-haired old woman, angry, frustrated with the years, and
scared of losing what little material wealth she has to show for the toil in *gum san*.

"I begged him," Mother says. "But he would either ignore my pleas or say: 'What 52
do you need to know English for? You're better off here in the kitchen. Here you can talk
to the others in our own tongue. English is far too complicated for you. How old are you
now? Too old to learn a new language. Let the young speak *fan gwei*. All you need is to
understand the orders from the waitresses. Anyway, if you need to know something, the
men will translate for you. I am here; I can do your talking for you.'"

As a conscientious boss of the young male immigrants, my father would force them 53
out of the kitchen and into the dining room. "The kitchen is no place for you to learn
English. All you do is speak Chinese in here. To survive in *gum san*, you have to speak
English, and the only way you can do that is to wait on tables and force yourselves to
speak English with the customers. How can you get your families over here if you can't
talk to the immigration officers in English?"

A few of the husbands who had the good fortune to bring their wives over to Canada 54
hired a retired school teacher to teach a bit of English to their wives. Father discouraged
Mother from going to those once-a-week sessions.

"That old woman will get rich doing nothing. What have these women learned? *Fan* 55
gwei ways—make-up, lipstick, smelly perfumes, fancy clothes. Once she gets through with
them, they won't be Chinese women any more—and they certainly won't be white either."

Some of the husbands heeded the words of the boss, for he was older than they, and 56
he had been in the *fan gwei*'s land longer. These wives stayed home and tended the children, or they worked in the restaurant kitchen, washing dishes and cooking *fan gwei*

foods, and talking in Chinese about the land and the life they had been forced to leave behind.

"He was afraid that I would leave him. I depended on him for everything. I could not go anywhere by myself. He drove me to work and he drove me home. He only taught me how to print my name so that I could sign anything he wanted me to, bank cheques, legal documents . . ."

Perhaps I am not Chinese enough any more to understand why my mother would want to take in the sorrow, the pain, and the anguish, and then to recount them every so often.

Once, I was presumptuous enough to ask her why she would want to remember in such detail. She said that the memories didn't hurt any more. I did not tell her that her reminiscences cut me to the quick. Her only solace now is to be listened to.

When my father died five years ago, she cried and cried. "Don't leave me in this world. Let me die with you."

Grief-stricken, she would not eat for days. She was so weak from hunger that I feared she wouldn't be able to attend the funeral. At his grave side, she chanted over and over a dirge, commending his spirit to the next world and begging the goddess of mercy to be kind to him. By custom, she set his picture on the mantel and burned incense in front of it daily. And we would go to the cemetery often. There she would arrange fresh flowers and talk to him in the gentlest way.

Often she would warn me: "The world of the golden mountain is so strong, *fan gwei* improprieties, and customs. They will have you abandon your own aged mother to some old-age home to rot away and die unmourned. If you are here long enough, they will turn your head until you don't know who you are—Chinese."

My mother would convert the months and the days into the Chinese lunar calendar. She would tell me about the seasons and the harvests and festivals in China. We did not celebrate any *fan gwei* holidays.

My mother sits here at the table, fingering the booklet from the Citizenship Court. For thirty-some years, my mother did not learn the English language, not because she was not smart enough, not because she was too old to learn, and not because my father forbade her, but because she feared that learning English would change her Chinese soul. She only learned enough English to survive in the restaurant kitchen.

Now, Mother wants *gum san* citizenship.

"Is there no hope that I will be given it?" she asks.

"There's always a chance," I tell her. "I'll hand in the application."

"I should have given that person the *lai shi*," Mother says obstinately.

"Maybe I should teach you some English," I retort. "You have about six months before the oral interview."

"I am seventy years old," she says. "*Lai-shi* is definitely much easier."

My brief glimpse into Mother's heart is over, and it has taken so long to come about. I do not know whether I understand my aged mother any better now. Despite my mother's constant instruction, there is too much *fan gwei* in me.

The booklet from the Citizenship Court lies, unmoved, on the table, gathering dust for weeks. She has not mentioned citizenship again with the urgency of that particular time. Once in a while, she would say: "They have forgotten me. I told you they don't want old Chinese women as citizens."

Finally, her interview date is set. I try to teach her some ready-made phrases, but she forgets them. 73

"You should not sigh so much. It is bad for your health," Mother observes. 74

On the day of her examination, I accompany her into the judge's chamber. I am more nervous than my mother. 75

Staring at the judge, my mother remarks: *Noi yren*." The judge shows interest in what my mother says, and I translate it: "She says you're a woman." 76

The judge smiles, "Yes. Is that strange?" 77

"If she is going to examine me," Mother tells me, "I might as well start packing for China. Sell my house. Dig up your father's bones, and I'll take them back with me." 78

Without knowing what my mother said, the judge reassures her. "This is just a formality. Really. We know that you obviously want to be part of our Canadian society. Why else would you go through all this trouble? We want to welcome you as a new citizen, no matter what race, nationality, religion, or age. And we want you to be proud—as a new Canadian." 79

Six weeks have passed since the interview with the judge. Mother receives a registered letter telling her to come in three weeks' time to take part in the oath of allegiance ceremony. 80

With patient help from the same judge, my mother recites the oath and becomes a Canadian citizen after thirty years in *gum san.* 81

"How does it feel to be a Canadian?" I ask. 82

"In China, this is the eighth month, the season of harvest." Then she adds: "The *Dai Pao* says that the old-age pension cheques will be increased by nine dollars next month." 83

As we walk home on this bright autumn morning, my mother clutches her piece of paper. Citizenship. She says she will go up to the cemetery and talk to my father this afternoon. She has something to tell him. 84

■ Reading Comprehension Questions

1. The word *quizzical* in "He gives me a quizzical look, so I explain to him, and he laughs" (paragraph 23) means
   a. ridiculous.
   b. questioning.
   c. angry.
   d. confused.

2. The word *dirge* in "At his grave side, she chanted over and over a dirge" (paragraph 61) means
   a. prayer.
   b. name.
   c. sad song.
   d. request.

3. Which of the following would be a good alternative title for this selection?
   a. Mother and the Judge
   b. A Woman's Struggle
   c. The Red Envelope
   d. A Long Life and a New Language

4. Which sentence best expresses the main idea of the selection?
   a. Immigrants find it easier to stick to the patterns and languages of their native countries.
   b. Engkent's mother can't speak English because of her late husband's attitude towards his fellow immigrants learning the language.
   c. Engkent's mother learned only a few words of English to avoid losing her pension.
   d. Engkent's mother's greatest problem in learning English was her fear of losing her Chinese identity.

5. The author's explanations of Canadian ways are taken by his mother as
   a. excuses for his own unwillingness to do as she wishes.
   b. evidence that he doesn't want to help her.
   c. evidence of his feeling of superiority as a university graduate.
   d. ignorance of the information printed in the *Dai Pao*.

6. *True or false?* _____ Engkent's mother's greatest fear at her first citizenship interview is that she will be sent back to China.

7. The author's father did not teach his wife English because
   a. he wished her to remain dependent on him so that she would not leave him.
   b. he felt she was not intelligent enough to learn such a complex language.
   c. he wanted her to maintain her Chinese heritage.
   d. he did not want her to become more successful than he was.

8. The author's cousin, whom he meets at the Citizenship Court,
   a. is kinder to the author's mother than is the author.
   b. has more importance in the Chinese community than the author does.
   c. offers an insight into the dilemma faced by the author's mother.
   d. feels superior because of living longer in China than the author.

9. The author implies that
   a. his mother's feelings for her husband are based mainly on Chinese traditions.
   b. his mother's feelings for her husband remain intense and strongly mixed.
   c. his mother remembers only the best about her deceased husband.
   d. his mother despises the memory of his late father.

10. The author implies that
    a. his mother is intimidated by the citizenship hearing.
    b. his mother is unaware of the importance of becoming a Canadian citizen.
    c. his mother has already decided her own fate.
    d. his mother has a down-to-earth view of citizenship, but also realizes its import.

■ Discussion Questions

About Content

1. Why does Engkent's mother so suddenly decide she must become a Canadian citizen? What are the problems with her ideas about obtaining citizenship?

2. What three qualifications are required to obtain Canadian citizenship, according to the liaison officer at the Citizenship Court? How many of these are actually relevant or necessary when Engkent's mother finally sees the citizenship judge? Why does the judge alter the requirements?

3. What is the difference between the author's mother's feelings about recalling the details of her life with her husband and the author's own feelings about hearing her recollections? Why are their feelings different?

About Structure

4. In which paragraphs in the essay do you find three of the main *causes* for Engkent's mother's inability to speak English after thirty years in Canada? What is the final *effect* that comes out at the end of the essay?

5. Where in the essay do you find the author's thesis statement, the answer to the question posed by the title? What relationship exists between the facts of the thesis and the concluding statements of the essay?

6. Why has the author chosen to use so many brief paragraphs, rather than longer sections of indirect reporting of the actions and ideas of the essay? What effect do all these short sections have on your sense of his feelings about his subject?

About Style and Tone

7. There are many Chinese phrases in this essay. Are their meanings clearly explained? List three such phrases and their meanings.

_____   _____   _____

How does their inclusion affect your sense of the people and situations involved?

8. "Why My Mother Can't Speak English" is written mainly in the present tense and is mainly told through dialogue. Do these two stylistic choices by the author make the narrative more or less lively? How? Do they bring you closer to the characters and their problems? How?

■ Writing Assignments

Assignment 1

Many of us have relatives who have emigrated to Canada from another country. For each person, there are different adjustments to be made, different cultural problems to be faced. But some dilemmas, some problems, have common elements for all who arrive in a new country.

Write an essay which is a descriptive character sketch about either you or a relative facing some learning experience in a new country or location. Ideally, your essay should tell a story involving adjustment to, and/or resistance to, new circumstances in a new environment. What were the *causes* of the problems experienced? What were the *effects* of the effort to try to resolve the problems? Did you or your relative change as a result of the challenge? How? Try to isolate and clearly define the nature and personal ramifications of the problem. When you are making your essay outline, list what you see as the major causes of this problem and the results of trying to overcome aspects of this difficulty.

Assignment 2

Canada is a nation which has called itself a "mosaic," where those from other countries are encouraged, and often funded, to maintain their native languages and cultures. Communities across the country celebrate various multicultural holidays and festivals. Many cities have TV, radio, and printed material available in a number of languages. Does this always result in a country with a distinct and unique personality or unified identity? Are we enriched by having many sides to our national character, or merely confused? Do newcomers maintain isolated groupings within our country, or do we have a genuinely exciting and diverse character as a country?

State and defend one side or another of this issue with clear examples drawn either from your personal experience or from outside reading.

Assignment 3

At some time in our lives, most of us have struggled with someone else's stubbornness, as Engkent did with his mother's. We are frustrated by such a struggle, but we learn from it. Write a narrative essay about your own experience. As you explain what you felt and learned, use vivid details and dialogue to bring your essay to life.

The New Media-Friendly S & M

Rachel Giese

Sado-masochism, or S & M, used to be a subject outside the bounds of polite conversation, and one frequently confined to the back pages of "questionable magazines." The regalia of S & M, studded black leather gear, handcuffs, boots, and chains: these items are worn by performers and audiences at many rock concerts, are standard features of music videos, and are the subjects of humour in movies and TV shows these days. Does this mean that an aspect of human sexuality once considered odd at the very least has now become normal and accepted?

Rachel Giese explores this question in her article about "Living in Leather IV," an S & M convention held in Toronto in 1994. As we near the end of the 20th century, will every human habit and oddity become "just another New Age commodity" to publicize and sell?

I'm late for the S&M convention press conference and, to make matters worse, when I arrive at the hotel, no one has heard of any press conference. A butch young woman dressed in an LAPD uniform leads me around the Howard Johnson's hotel where the weekend conference is taking place, barking orders. "Find me the damn press conference," she says into her walkie-talkie. Finally, a cherubic young guy with a pierced septum and a dog collar directs us to the Westminister Room. 1

I needn't have worried about missing the show. As a free-lancer for a local gay paper, I'm the only journalist who has come to question the six delegates from "Living in Leather IV." But that's not because the press isn't interested in people who beat each other up for fun—the other journalists just prefer to conduct their interviews one-on-one. *The Globe and Mail* has already been by. So have *The Toronto Star, The Toronto Sun* and the CBC. The mainstream media have had their interest in S&M piqued ever since Madonna's book *Sex* was released. And in Toronto, the convention, which has brought together S&M players from across the U.S. and Canada, couldn't have happened at a better time. An S&M bawdy-house in an expensive suburb of Toronto has just been raided and *Exit to Eden*, an S&M film starring Dan Aykroyd, has just been banned in Saskatchewan. Sado-masochism is the word on the mouths of CBC panels and op/ed columnists across the country. And, surprisingly, most people seem to think that whips and chains are just fine. But I can't help wondering, standing around at this very upstanding hotel press conference, how all of this mainstream acceptance is affecting a subculture which lives off its dangerous and subversive mystique. I was expecting serious attitude from the conference organizers about the mainstreaming of S&M—maybe calls for the public flogging of Dan Aykroyd and Madonna. Instead, I find them delighted 2 by the attention. In fact, this conference is about gaining *more* institutional recognition for their "culture."

"We've got big plans," says a delegate from Ohio. "We have plans in the works for a 3 leather archives in order to preserve our history. We're also asking our members to donate pro-S&M and pro-kink books, and how-to manuals, to the libraries at their alma maters."

The woman who speaks so excitedly about S&M pedagogy is plump, forty-ish and 4 dressed in a blouse and skirt. Like most of the people in the room, she's wearing her regular clothes in honour of this very earnest event. Come to think of it, my cop escort and the dog-collar man are the most obviously S&M types I've seen so far. One woman walks past the door in a leather corset—a glimpse of the underworld. Unfortunately, she's chosen to wear the corset over a Cotton Ginny-esque jumper, knee-high flat-soled boots, and her mousy hair is growing out an indifferent perm. So much for a sexy story.

The press material I'm handed matches the delegates' outfits. It is very professional 5 and the language is straight out of a Feminism 101 primer. *Working groups* have been struck. *Caucuses* have been formed. S&M players are to be considered a *marginalized community* with a distinct *culture*. As at every convention, from Star Trek to Mary Kay, the delegates are happily exhausted and they keep cracking the same joke about some guy who had acted crazy at last night's party. Here one man plays absentmindedly, with a brand new paddle, slapping it against his knee.

But despite the parties and trade shows, it's clear that the real purpose of the con- 6 ference is networking and politicking towards S&M's new quest for social acceptance. A recent cover story in *New York* magazine declared "S&M Culture Goes Mainstream." And it has. Very willingly.

Mary is still wearing the leather sash with "Ms. Leather" written across it in metal studs. 7 She was awarded the title at last night's Living in Leather competition—the Miss Universe pageant of the S&M world. During her reign, she tells me, she hopes to "help other heterosexual women heal their shame around S&M." Somewhat uncharacteristic plans for a woman who takes a submissive role with men during S&M scenes and who earned her title by groveling and begging to be dominated. Isn't shame what it's all about? If Mary fulfils her plans and the shame is healed, won't the desire to grovel also disappear? Won't there be no more S&M?

These questions are not a concern for the Living in Leather crowd. There has been 8 a lot of celebrating at the conference over the recent announcement that the latest edition of the *Diagnostic and Statistical Manual*, the bible of mental disorders, will stop labeling S&M behaviours and fantasies as pathological—a first in this type of publication. As the jargon goes: it is the shame that must be healed, not the behaviours.

There is something distinctly self-help and new-age about the whole conference. A 9 lot of people claim S&M has helped them heal their pain over childhood incest. Women, especially, like to justify their participation by claiming that all forms of sexuality are about power—dominance and submission—and S&M, with its clearly defined roles, is at least honest and explicit about it. Others insist that S&M is safe sex with thrills. Someone else tells a story about a 41-year-old man who lives in New York. He has cystic fibrosis and shouldn't have lived beyond the age of 10. He attributes his longevity to

S&M because, when he's not in his hospital bed hooked up to a respirator, he's being whipped, tortured and degraded. S&M, the delegates claim, saved his life.

And, in an absurd example of the politics of oppression, this convention has even 10 resolved to approach Amnesty International to ask the human rights group to include S&M players on its list of groups that are persecuted for their beliefs and practices. In other words, people shouldn't be tortured or degraded for using torture and degradation in their sex play.

Conferences like these don't seem to attract the hard-core players but rather are ini- 11 tiations for the newly converted. Unsure themselves, the delegates want to prove their normalcy and their legitimacy to the world at large. "Safe, sane and consensual" are the S&M buzz words. And with this mantra, they maintain that S&M is healing and non-pathological. The participants seem attracted to this new S&M community the way people were drawn to the verbally and emotionally aggressive EST seminars of the 1970s. Admit you're an asshole and you'll release all your baggage. With S&M, engage in the shameful and humiliating and you'll overcome your shame and humiliation.

To drive the normalcy point home, the mainstream media and the new S&M com- 12 munity love to point out that the majority of S&M players are heterosexual, the folks next door. In the *New York* article, professions of people are juxtaposed beside pictures of them in S&M costumes. THE EDITOR, it says, beside a picture of Michelle, who has "a monthly assignation with a born-again Christian from the Midwest." THE ACCOUNTANT, it says, above a young woman in a red corset and a dog chain, caressing the boot of Master D, THE LAWYER.

The idea that regular folks are tying each other up, spanking each other and dress- 13 ing up in leather and rubber is, of course, the kinkiness of it all. S&M exists because it is dirty, nasty and secret. It is the allure of the forbidden that turns people on. Healing the shame of it defeats the allure.

My hairdresser is "in the scene," as he puts it, and the thought of an organized hotel con- 14 vention leaves him cold. "It's great that it brought some new guys to the bars but leather isn't a lifestyle, it's just fun. It's just a fetish. It's not something you should organize." As San Francisco writer Alvin Orloff puts it: "when I was a kid, leather queens were sexy, raunchy, perverse, and sexy. Now we have the 'Leather Community' which is very rich, very dull, very prissy, and not very sexy at all. Nobody's got that grungy outlaw look that made Marion Brando so hot in *The Wild Ones*. Leather men ought to live in ramshackle clubhouses on the outskirts of town. They're supposed to be ravishingly handsome but woefully inarticulate hooligans."

In the gay community, S&M people have had a special place. Like drag queens, 15 they've been vilified as immoral and asked by more conservative gays and lesbians to tone it down. Serious questions have also been raised about the ethics of using the iconography of slavery and the Holocaust as erotic statements. The debate continues to rage, but not as fiercely as it once did, and most gay people have grown used to the presence of leather people at Pride Day marches and at other community events. Last year's request by New York's Pride Day committee that the press not focus solely on drag queens and leather people seemed ridiculous and self-hating. Leather people, whether you approve or not, represent rebellion and defiance; their presence in the gay community reaffirms the sexual nature of sexual orientation and it plays with traditional notions of gender and power.

Unfortunately, this new leather movement has lost its sense of humour. And believe me, a 300-pound man in chaps without a sense of irony is not a pretty sight. Leather people could take a lesson from drag queens. Drag—the antithesis of leather—is about the hyper-exaggeration of femininity, while leather is hyper-exaggeration of masculinity and *machismo*. At opposite ends of the spectrum, drag and leather represent the same thing—fantasy. Knowing what a dominatrix does nine-to-five destroys the fantasy and ruins the façade. The Marquis de Sade would turn over in his grave if he knew his name was being used by a group of New Age accountants searching for emotional fulfillment.

Last year, a leather group booked a hotel in New York for a conference. The hotel staff assumed a leather conference meant a gathering of textile merchants and when the actual conventioneers showed up in harnesses and chains, the staff were confused and shocked. This year in Toronto, the Howard Johnson's staff don't seem fazed a bit. It's the delegates who have some issues to work out. During a demonstration of male genital torture techniques, a maid accidentally stuck her head in the door, assuming the room was empty. The participants shrieked and squealed that their "space" had been "violated." They were going to lodge a complaint. The maid looked at the group, shrugged, and moved on to clean the next room.

■ Reading Comprehension Questions

1. The word *septum* in "a cherubic young guy with a pierced septum and a dog collar" (paragraph 1) means
   a. earlobe.
   b. nose.
   c. navel.
   d. lower lip.

2. The words *alma maters* in "to donate pro-S & M and pro-kink books . . . to the libraries at their alma maters" (paragraph 3) means
   a. local research institutes.
   b. favourite nightspots.
   c. colleges and universities people attended.
   d. psychiatric institutions.

3. Which of the following would be a good alternative title for this selection?
   a. The Nasty and the Normal
   b. Conventional Immorality
   c. The Media Meet the Masochists
   d. Publicity, Perversity, and Forbidden Fruit

4. Which sentence best expresses the main idea of the selection?
    a. Openness about, and acceptance of, S & M may end its fascination.
    b. S & M is a set of normal behaviour patterns for ordinary people.
    c. Persecution of participants in S & M amounts to violation of human rights.
    d. S & M is simply another excuse to promote safe sex.

5. The general public's attitude towards S & M, according to Rachel Giese, is
    a. one of curiosity and furtive fascination.
    b. seemingly complete acceptance.
    c. disgust and contempt.
    d. one of supportiveness.

6. *True or False?* _____ Publicity material and delegates' costumes seemed strange and exotic to the writer.

7. Conferences like "Living in Leather IV" attract
    a. every sort of person.
    b. long-time participants in dominance and submission games.
    c. people newly involved in sadomasochism.
    d. fetishists and journalists.

8. The author implies that
    a. sadomasochism has become dull, normal, and boring.
    b. S & M is just another trendy issue and money-maker.
    c. sadomasochism is perfectly normal human behaviour.
    d. S & M might lose its allure if overexposed.

9. *True or false?* _____ The author implies that sadomasochism is connected to deviance from the acceptable, and to sexuality and power.

10. The author implies that
    a. leather or S & M adherents looking for acceptance are wasting their time.
    b. drag queens are into sadomasochism and have no sense of humour.
    c. knowledge and understanding of its participants' everyday lives enhances S & M's fascination.
    d. S & M usually offends those who accidentally witness its activities.

■ Discussion Questions

About Content

1. Which recent mainstream media releases suggest to the author that S & M has become "just fine" to the general public?

2. What specific details of this convention make it seem so much like any other convention to Ms. Giese? What is the effect on you as a reader of discovering such facts?

3. Which three contradictions in logic does the author note in current pro–S & M arguments heard at the convention?

About Structure

4. The essay is divided into three sections. Where do you find the "breaks" in the essay? What aspect(s) of content does each section cover? How does the progression of ideas in the essay lead through the sections to the author's main ideas?

5. The best statement of the author's thesis is in paragraph 13. Find it and write it in the space provided below.

_____

_____

About Style and Tone

6. There are at least ten descriptive details about the author's activities and the people she meets in the opening paragraph of this essay. What are these details and what do they suggest to you about the general tone of the essay and the author's attitude towards her subject?

7. The writer uses nongrammatical English in the final sentence of paragraph 7. What is the error in this sentence and how does it affect your sense of the author's tone?

8. The concluding paragraph of the essay uses which technique, usually associated with introductions?
   a. summary
   b. anecdote
   c. prediction
   d. broad to narrow

   Does the use of an unusual closing add to your understanding of the meaning of the essay? How?

■ Writing Assignments

Assignment 1

S & M, or sadomasochistic sexual behaviour, may seem more generally acceptable today. Because we see clothing and paraphernalia associated with S & M around us in various "fashion looks," and because rock videos and films exploit the imagery of sadomasochism, do we really understand what black leather, whips, and chains mean, in terms of human behaviour? Anne Rice's novel *Exit to Eden*, in which S & M was a healthy outlet for power dynamics implicit in male–female relationships, was turned into a comedy film that made dominance-and-submission patterns look as normal as a trip to Club Med. Is such thinking a product of New Age ideas, or lack of ethical consideration? Is S & M "safe, sane" *and normal?*

After arriving at what you think is a good explanation, in your own words, of "sadomasochism," decide on your own view of this area of behaviour. Write an essay of definition and explanation, which details clearly and logically your defence of your opinion.

Assignment 2

In the last thirty years, cultural changes have made acceptable and permissible in public aspects of behaviour, speech, and dress which would been shocking or frowned on previously.

Consider these facts of everyday life in the 1990s:

- swearing and profanity in films and daily speech
- revealing, scanty, and/or see-through clothing
- open and direct sexual statements in lyrics, magazines, and television scripts
- nudity in movies and magazine ads

Has the fact that "bad language," people's bodies, and sexuality are no longer considered private matters lessened their fascination? Is secrecy part of the power to intrigue? Write a letter to the editor of your local paper in which you defend your views for or against current openness as it affects some single issue in contemporary life.

Assignment 3

Imagine that you have been asked to make a speech justifying your worst "bad habit." What would you write about? Procrastination? Smoking? Overeating? Gambling? Lying? Shopping compulsively? In your speech, you are addressing others with this habit, whom you wish would stop feeling guilty and accept themselves as "normal." Choose a habit, and write a speech which has the message "it is the shame that must be healed, not the behaviour."

Top Dogs

Sondra Gotlieb

Everyone who has ever owned a pet has feelings about the intelligence, or lack thereof, of their pet. But is anyone willing to accept a seemingly rigid classification of animal intelligence by breed? Are we so desperate to classify and categorize our surroundings that we now rate our household pets by their IQs? What about classifying humanity in terms of intelligence by race? Sondra Gotlieb is a journalist and wife of the former Canadian ambassador to the United States; her wry sense of humour and personal experiences tend to confirm our intuitive sense that our pets probably vary in cleverness as individuals, rather than as specimens of a particular breed.

I was at a bookshop flipping through *The Bell Curve* by Richard Herrnstein and Charles Murray and *The Intelligence of Dogs* by Stanley Coren. Both books discuss something called the "g" factor, which means cognitive ability, or general intelligence. Whatever. The scientific data in *The Bell Curve* were too difficult for my cognitive abilities so I bought *The Intelligence of Dogs* instead. The single "fact" I gleaned from *The Bell Curve* was that the smartest people in the world, smarter even than East Asians, were Ashkenazi Jews, like me. So if I am so smart why do I pick such stupid dogs? *The Intelligence of Dogs* ranks my Tibetan terriers Sweet Pea (deceased) and Archie (still in this vale of tears) a humiliating sixty-second out of seventy-nine breeds. 1

According to *The Intelligence of Dogs*, Border collies rank first in working intelligence. So one might conclude that Border collies are the Ashkenazi Jews of the canine world. This is where I take issue with Coren. I know Border collies—Tofu, for example, who belongs to a gentleman farmer (a euphemism for a man who gives cocktail parties in a farmhouse designed by an interior decorator). As the guests drink, Tofu circles round their heels, nudging and herding them so close that the guests in the centre of the fulcrum find themselves standing on Victorian settees without knowing why. 2

Poodles rank number two on the dog bell curve, but they come expensive what with their neurotic beauty needs. Rottweilers—the brutes—rank high, ninth out of seventy-nine. Princess Di's nickname for her rival, Camilla Parker-Bowles, was "The Rottweiler." Believe me, if there's one thing Englishwomen know, it's dogs. 3

Borrowing from the controversial *Bell Curve*'s terminology, the "underclass" of the canine world includes: a) the Afghan hound, seventy-ninth out of seventy-nine: tendency to run amuck if too many humans are about; b) basenji, seventy-eighth out of seventy-nine: bites without giving notice; c) bulldogs, seventy-seventh out of seventy-nine: short-term memory loss because of squashed-in brains; d) chow-chows, seventy-sixth out of seventy-nine: lazy and stupid; culinary delicacy for Chinese (black-coated variety believed to have better fat for frying). 4

St Bernards, mastiffs, basset hounds, and Chihuahuas are on the margins of the 5
underclass. Chihuahuas tend to get stuck in cooked turkey carcasses. St Bernards and
Pekingese are considered white trash by Coren.

The Bell Curve has enraged liberal and fair-minded people by using data to argue 6
that some races are supposed to be smarter than others—e.g. the Chinese are smarter than
Caucasians. As far as I know there have been no aghast and appalled responses to *The
Intelligence of Dogs. Aux armes* Afghan, basenji, chow-chow, and bulldog lovers.
Protest. Or are you as illiterate and lazy as your dogs?

I bought our first family dog in Ottawa. Hector was an Airedale terrier, a breed that ranks 7
on the top third of the dog bell curve. Not a bad choice for a woman who knew nothing of
the intelligence of dogs. However, terriers, according to Coren, do not belong in obedience
competitions. I didn't need to buy his book to find that out. Hector hated the leash and wandered through urban Ottawa as if he was Heathcliff roaming the moors. Because of his
devotion to the family, we called him Hector the Protector, but others called him the Beast
of Parliament Hill. Hector's bite was worse than his bark. Hector attacked MPs crossing
the Hill from the East Block to the West on their way for a snack in the subsidized cafeteria. And he killed any animal smaller than himself except babies. What did it matter that
Hector was high on the bell curve when cat lovers and politicians forced us to put him down?

Call it fear, call it irrationality—I bought my first Tibetan terrier because I thought 8
my husband was going to be fired. One evening in Washington, at a private party, Allan,
then ambassador to the United States, picked a fight with George Shultz, then secretary
of state in the Reagan cabinet. No, it wasn't about shingles and shakes or pork or canola
seed, the contentious but mego (mine eyes glaze over) trade issues between our great countries. They argued about the *Weltanschauung* of America. Arguing with George Shultz,
who used to be a marine, is like arguing with an Easter Island statue. Shultz's expression
never changes, but he is much better at combat warfare than my husband. We got home
late that night and I couldn't sleep because I was sure that Shultz would demand Allan's
recall. I needed a friend. So, heeding local lore—"if you need a friend in Washington, buy
a dog"—I scoured the pet ads in *The Washington Post* and bought Sweet Pea at 7 a.m.,
while my husband slept. I thought a Tibetan terrier would be a smaller, more hospitable
Hector. But Sweet Pea didn't resemble an Airedale; his hair was long and silky, and he
had long moustache wisps like a Chinese court eunuch. The breeder told me that Sweet
Pea was highly bred and would have been her show dog if it "wasn't for his overbite."

One thing I'll say for Tibetan terriers, they love luxury. Born to leap from sofa to 9
sofa, born to dine in embassies. In fact, Tibetans were used as palace dogs by the Grand
Lamas. Early on, Sweet Pea, and then later Archie, followed waiters carrying canapés,
on the ready for the inevitable spill. Sweet Pea's greatest defect was indecisiveness, like
Bill Clinton. Sweet Pea would stand by the door to be let out. But when the door was
opened he straddled the ledge, hating to make up his mind.

Archie, Sweet Pea's nephew, was not so highly bred, one of his parents coming from 10
low-caste Tibetan-terrier stock. More macho than Sweet Pea, he tried to impregnate the
Soviet ambassador's wife and once vomited on Shultz's lap, who took it like a marine.

Archie's brain is basically made up of two wires, stamped "eat" and "walk." Since his 11
castration at the age of fifty-six, the wires have crossed. When I say "Archie walk," he runs

to the kibble bowl, which he's left untouched for hours, and proceeds to crunch his way to the bottom. I have to shake the leash in his face to remind him of his other pleasure in life.

Archie is a foodie. I have no reason to buy a Dustbuster because Archie's there to 12 hoover up the crumbs. Even on my sweater. In fact I can't leave a roasted chicken lower than six feet off the ground because Archie, being a mountain dog, leaps like Michael Jordan to reach what he really wants for dinner.

A vet told me that the beverage of choice for Border collies, poodles, and German 13 shepherds (the top three on the canine bell curve) is toilet water. Toilet water is Archie's beverage of choice as well. Perhaps he's higher on the bell curve than I thought.

■ Reading Comprehension Questions

1. The word *fulcrum* in "herding them so close that the guests in the centre of the fulcrum find themselves standing on Victorian settees without knowing why" (paragraph 2) means
   a. crowd.
   b. floorspace.
   c. periphery.
   d. lever support point.

2. The word *lore* in "So, heeding local lore—'if you need a friend in Washington, buy a dog'" (paragraph 8) means
   a. advice.
   b. traditional stories.
   c. nonsense.
   d. authority.

3. Which of the following would be a good alternative title for this selection?
   a. The Unpredictable Intelligence of Dogs
   b. Biters and Bowl-Drinkers
   c. Bad Dog Behaviour
   d. Smart Dogs, Stupid Categories

4. Which sentence best expresses the main idea of the selection?
   a. Canine and human intelligence can be grouped by racial origin.
   b. Rating dogs by breed for their intelligent behaviour is useful to owners.
   c. Systems which classify humans or animals in rigid categories are prone to error.
   d. The author's dogs have all been bad examples of their breeds' capabilities.

5. The author found the top dog, as rated for intelligence by Stanley Coren,
   a. to be driven by compulsive habit patterns.
   b. to have a sense of social behaviour.
   c. to be unable to perform its tasks on any occasion.
   d. to have aggressive tendencies towards people.

6. Both *The Bell Curve* and *The Intelligence of Dogs*, according to the author,
   a. demonstrate unarguable findings about intelligence groups in humans and dogs.
   b. carefully back up their conclusions with many examples of each category.
   c. use data about their intelligence classifications in a potentially misleading way.
   d. make logical distinctions between various races' and breeds' intelligence.

7. *True or false?* _____ The author's findings about her three dogs all contradict their ratings in *The Intelligence of Dogs*.

8. The author implies that
   a. breed-stereotyping in dogs is less controversial than similar classifications for humans.
   b. dogs and humans can be easily rated for intelligence by simple criteria.
   c. most dogs' behaviour defies the intelligence ratings of breeds in Coren's book.
   d. people choose their pets for their intelligence rather than for other qualities.

9. The author implies that
   a. her dogs have been responsible for international diplomatic problems.
   b. her pets have been all been wise and rational choices on her part.
   c. her dogs have frustrated her with their annoying behaviour.
   d. most dogs have inexplicable but occasionally amusing habits.

10. The author implies that
    a. qualities used for canine IQ ratings may not make all such dogs unsuitable pets.
    b. all the dogs rated as low in intelligence make poor pets.
    c. a less intelligent dog is always a more loveable creature.
    d. she always picks stupid dogs because she isn't very bright herself.

■ Discussion Questions

About Content

1. Why does Gotlieb purchase *The Intelligence of Dogs*, rather than *The Bell Curve*? Do you believe she is entirely serious about her reason for doing so? What facts in the essay support your conclusion?

2. Which breeds of dogs constitute the "underclass of the canine world"? What aspects of their behaviour place them there?

3. What circumstances prompted the author to purchase her first Tibetan terrier?

About Structure

4. What type of introductory paragraph does the author use for this essay?
    a. Stating the importance of the topic
    b. Broad to narrow
    c. Starting with an opposite
5. The author uses three anecdotes drawn from her own experiences with family pets. How do the facts in these stories bear out her conclusions about dogs and their intelligence? How do her findings compare with the data in *The Intelligence of Dogs*?

About Style and Tone

6. For what kind of audience do you think this selection was written?
    a. Special-interest groups like dogbreeders
    b. General public
    c. Sociologists and students of behaviourism

    Give reasons for your answer.
7. Gotlieb is generally known as a humorous writer and acute social observer. Some of the devices common to humorous writers are self-deprecation, sarcasm, and unexpected shifts in tone in word-use.

    In paragraph 1, an example of self-deprecation by the narrator is _____

    _____

    _____ .

    In paragraph 3, an example of sarcasm is _____

    _____

    _____ .

    In paragraph 4, an example of shift in tone in usage is _____

    _____

    _____ .

    Find at least one other example of each of these humorous devices in the essay. How do they affect your sense of the author's seriousness about her subject?

■ Writing Assignments

Assignment 1

Most of us have had pets, or have known other people's pets with distinctive personalities and habits. You have been assigned to write an article about a noteworthy pet for *Pet Monthly* magazine. Your column is to analyze the differences and points of similarity found in the animal you know and love or loathe, compared to the most commonly held preconceptions about this breed of animal. In your article, set up or classify three aspects of the breed's behaviour which your subject does or does not display, and justify your conclusions about such classifications based on how well the pet in question fits the criteria.

Assignment 2

Beneath the comic surface of the author's essay lurks a very serious subject: that of *eugenics*, or the racial classification of human beings according to a given criterion, such as intelligence or physical attractiveness. What is your own view of such attempts at classification or stereotyping? World War II and Nazism provided a hideous example of such classification carried to extremes. Unfortunately, current Canadian society is prone to such stereotyping as well. "All Jamaicans give great parties. All Chinese are brilliant at computers." So go the apparently harmless clichés. How harmless are such statements? Is there any truth in such generalizations?

Write an essay which discusses three aspects of one such racial or national stereotype with which you are familiar. Your essay should examine (a) the reasons for such a stereotype, (b) any possible truth behind such a classification, and (c) the results of such beliefs as you have observed them in specific situations.

Assignment 3

Dogs help the blind to function in a sighted world, and stroking a pet can lower blood pressure. Today, many hospitals and homes for the elderly allow patients pets for their therapeutic value. Only *part* of what we value about animals is relevant to their intelligence.

Write an essay which defends "pet therapy" and describes three benefits a pet could provide for a hospitalized or elderly person.

Five Parenting Styles

Mary Ann Lamanna and Agnes Reidmann

Parenting has been called "the biggest on-the-job training programme ever." Parents have to raise children without much guidance or advance instruction, and sometimes this results in a "parenting style" that causes problems. In the following textbook selection, the authors discuss five parenting styles. See if you can identify your parents—or yourself—in one of the classifications.

Considering the lack of consensus about how to raise children today, it may seem diffi- 1
cult to single out styles of parenting. From one point of view there are as many parenting styles as there are parents. . . . Yet certain elements in relating to children can be
broadly classified. One helpful grouping is provided in E. E. LeMasters' listing of five
parenting styles: the martyr, the pal, the police officer, the teacher-counselor, and the athletic coach. . . . We will discuss each of these.

The Parent as Martyr. Martyring parents believe "I would do anything for my 2
child." . . . Some common examples of martyring are parents who habitually wait on their
children or pick up after them; parents who nag children rather than letting them remember things for themselves; parents who buy virtually anything the child asks for; and parents who always do what the children want to do.

This parenting style presents some problems. First, the goals the martyring parent 3
sets are impossible to carry out, and so the parent must always feel guilty. Also, . . . martyring tends to be reciprocated by manipulating. In addition, it is useful to ask if persons
who consistently deny their own needs can enjoy the role of parenting and if closeness
between parent and child is possible under these conditions.

The Parent as Pal. Some modern parents, mainly those of older children and ado- 4
lescents, feel that they should be pals to their children. They adopt a **laissez-faire** policy, *letting their children set their own goals, rules, and limits*, with little or no guidance
from parents. . . . According to LeMasters, "pal" parents apparently believe that they can
avoid the conflict caused by the generation gap in this way.

Pal parenting is unrealistic. For one thing, parents in our society *are* responsible for 5
guiding their children's development. Children deserve to benefit from the greater
knowledge and experience of their parents, and at all ages they need some rules and limits, although these change as children grow older. Much research points to the conclusion that laissez-faire parenting is related to juvenile delinquency, heavy drug use, and
runaway behavior in children. . . .

LeMasters points out that there are also relationship risks in the pal-parent model. 6
If things don't go well, parents may want to retreat to a more formal, authoritarian style
of parenting. But once they've established a buddy relationship, it is difficult to regain
authority. . . .

The Parent as Police Officer. The police officer (or drill sergeant) model is just 7
the opposite of the pal. These parents make sure the child obeys all the rules at all
times, and they punish their children for even minor offenses. Being a police officer
doesn't work very well today, however, and **autocratic discipline**, *which places the
entire power of determining rules and limits in the parents' hands*—like laissez-faire
parenting—has been associated with juvenile delinquency, drug use, and runaway
teenagers. . . .

There are several reasons for this. First, Americans have tended to resist anything 8
that smacks of tyranny ever since the days of the Boston Tea Party. Hence, children are
socialized to demand a share of independence at an early age.

A second reason why policing children doesn't work well today is that rapid social 9
change gives the old and the young different values and points of view and even different knowledge. In our complex culture, youth learn attitudes from specialized professionals, such as teachers and school counselors, who often "widen the intellectual gap between parent and child." . . . For example, many young people today may advocate Judy Blume's novel for teens, *Forever* (1975), which is explicit about and accepting of premarital sex. Many parents, however, disapprove of the book.

A third reason why the police officer role doesn't work is that children, who find sup- 10
port from their adolescent peers, will eventually confront and challenge their parents. LeMasters points out that the adolescent peer group is "a formidable opponent" to any cop who insists on strict allegiance to autocratic authority. . . .

A fourth reason is that autocratic policing just isn't very effective in molding chil- 11
dren's values. One study of 451 college freshmen and sophomores at a large western university found that adolescents were far more likely to be influenced by their parents' referent or expert power . . . than by coercive or legitimate power. The key was respect and a close relationship; habitual punishment or the "policing" of adolescents were far less effective modes of socialization. . . .

The Parent as Teacher-Counselor. The parent as teacher-counselor acts in accord 12
with the **developmental model of child rearing**, *in which the child is viewed as an extremely plastic organism with virtually unlimited potential for growth and development.* The limits to this rich potential are seen as encompassed in the limits of the parent to tap and encourage it. . . . This model conceptualizes the parent(s) as almost omnipotent in guiding children's development. . . . If they do the right things at the right time, their children will more than likely be happy, intelligent, and successful.

Particularly during the 1960s and 1970s, authorities have stressed the ability of par- 13
ents to influence their children's intellectual growth. Psychologist J. McVicker Hunt, for example, stated that he believes "you could raise a middle-class child's I.Q. by twenty points with what we know about child-rearing." . . .

The teacher-counselor approach has many fine features, and children do benefit from 14
environmental stimulation. Yet this parenting style also poses problems. First, it puts the needs of the child above the parents' needs. It may be unrealistic for most parents to always be there, ready to stimulate the child's intellect or to act as a sounding board. Also, parents who respond as if each of their child's discoveries is wonderful may give the child the mistaken impression that he or she is the center of everyone's universe. . . .

A second difficulty is that this approach expects parents to be experts—an expecta- 15
tion that can easily produce guilt. Parents can never learn all that psychologists, sociologists, and specialized educators know. Yet if anything goes wrong, teacher-counselor parents are likely to feel they have only themselves to blame. . . .

Finally, contemporary research suggests more and more that this view greatly exag- 16
gerates the power of the parent and the passivity of children. Children also have inherited intellectual capacities and needs. Recent observers point instead to an **interactive perspective**, *which regards the influence between parent and child as mutual and reciprocal*, not just a "one-way street." . . .

The "athletic coach" model proceeds from this perspective.   1

The Parent as Athletic Coach. Athletic-coach parenting incorporates aspects of the   1
developmental point of view. The coach (parent) is expected to have sufficient ability and
knowledge of the game (life) and to be prepared and confident to lead players (children)
to do their best and, it is hoped, to succeed.

This parenting style recognizes that parents, like coaches, have their own personal-   1
ities and needs. They establish team rules, or *house rules* (and this can be done somewhat democratically with help from the players), and teach these rules to their children.
They enforce the appropriate penalties when rules are broken, but policing is not their
primary concern. Children, like team members, must be willing to accept discipline and,
at least sometimes, to subordinate their own interests to the needs of the family team.

Coaching parents encourage their children to practice and to work hard to develop   2
their own talents. But they realize that they can not play the game for their players.
LeMasters says:

> The coach's position here is quite analogous to that of parents; once the game has begun it
> is up to the players to win or lose it. . . . [He] faces the same prospect as parents of sitting
> on the sidelines and watching players make mistakes that may prove disastrous.

LeMasters also points out that coaches can put uncooperative players off the team   2
or even quit, but no such option is available to parents.

■ Reading Comprehension Questions

1. The word *plastic* in "an extremely plastic organism" (paragraph 12) means
   a. sickly.
   b. stiff.
   c. transparent.
   d. pliable.

2. The word *autocratic* in "autocratic discipline, which places the entire power
   . . . in the parents' hands" (paragraph 7) means
   a. unfocused.
   b. independent.
   c. dictatorial.
   d. generous.

3. Which of the following would be a good alternative title for this selection?
   a. Mistakes Parents Make
   b. How to Be a Good Parent
   c. Kinds of Parents
   d. Parents as Coaches

4. Which sentence best expresses the main idea of the selection?
   a. There are as many parenting styles as there are parents.
   b. Styles of parenting can be broadly classified into five groups.
   c. The "police officer" parenting approach can lead to delinquency.
   d. The influence between parent and child must be mutual.

5. Martyr parents
   a. act as buddies to their children.
   b. buy anything the child asks for.
   c. insist on strict obedience.
   d. establish house rules.

6. *True or false?* _____ The athletic-coach approach regards the parent–child relationship as a one-way street.

7. Teacher-counsellor parents
   a. often blame themselves if something goes wrong.
   b. use autocratic discipline.
   c. adopt a laissez-faire policy.
   d. let their children set their own limits.

8. The authors imply that
   a. the teacher-counsellor style of parenting is most effective.
   b. the athletic-coach style of parenting is most effective.
   c. "pal" parents have solved the problem of the generation gap.
   d. parents should set all the rules for the household.

9. *True or false?* _____ Sometimes children learn different values at school.

10. We might conclude from this selection that
    a. parenting is a complex and difficult role.
    b. the best parents are unsophisticated ones.
    c. different parenting styles are appropriate at different stages of growth.
    d. the authors favour the parent as teacher-counsellor.

■ Discussion Questions

About Content

1. What reasons do the authors give for saying that parents cannot be pals to their children? Do you agree?

2. Which parenting style do you think the authors prefer? How can you tell?

3. Why is it difficult for parents to act as teacher-counsellors? Give examples from your own experience.

About Structure

4. What method of development is used in the section "The Parent as Police Officer"?
   a. Reasons
   b. Contrast
   c. Narrative

5. Analyze the third paragraph of "The Parent as Teacher-Counselor." Where is the topic sentence? What kind of support is given for this topic sentence?

6. What are three transition words used in paragraph 3?

   _____   _____   _____

7. Find at least four terms that are defined in the selection. Write the terms in the spaces below:

   _____   _____

About Style and Tone

8. Below are aids to understanding often used in textbooks. Which three appear in this selection?
   a. Preview and summary
   b. Charts
   c. Headings and subheadings
   d. Definitions and examples
   e. Boldface and italic type
   f. Graphs

■ Writing Assignments

Assignment 1

Write a description of "Three Childing Styles." In other words, write an essay similar to "Five Parenting Styles" in which you discuss three different behaviour patterns of being a child in a family. Choose from the following behaviour patterns listed on the next page, or others that may occur to you.

The child as:

Prima donna or spoiled brat
Miniature adult
Helpless baby
"Daddy's girl" or "Mama's boy"

> Tough kid
> Rebel
> Show-off
> Carbon copy of parent
> Little angel

In separate supporting paragraphs, describe in detail how each of your three types behaves.

Assignment 2

Write an essay that uses the following thesis statement:

> My parents were (tried to be) _____.

Fill in the blank with one of the five parenting styles described in the article (or with another one that you think up). Then present three different incidents that show your parents acting according to that style. (You may, of course, choose to write about only one parent.)

Assignment 3

Write an essay in which you argue that "a _____ (name a particular parenting style described in the selection) is the ideal parent." Develop the essay by giving three reasons why such parents are best.

Feel free to use any of the styles the authors describe; you could, for example, come up with a convincing argument that "police officer" parents are best, based on your own experience or reasoning.

The Firewood Gatherers

Thierry Mallet

Thierry Mallet was a fur trader and inspector of trading posts in the Canadian Arctic in the early part of this century, when the far north was much less well-known or travelled than it is at present. Despite a busy and physically demanding outdoor life, he found time to write two books of his experiences and observations among the natives of the Arctic region. "The Firewood Gatherers" is a fine example of his clean and strong descriptive abilities, as well as of his compassionate and unsparing eye for the details of the lives of the native Canadians he encountered.

Our camp had been pitched at the foot of a great, bleak, ragged hill, a few feet from the swirling waters of the Kazan River. The two small green tents, pegged down tight with heavy rocks, shivered and rippled under the faint touch of the northern breeze. A thin wisp of smoke rose from the embers of the fire. 1

Eleven o'clock, and the sun had just set under a threatening bank of clouds far away to the northwest. It was the last day of June and daylight still. But the whole country seemed bathed in gray, boulders, moss, and, even the few willow shrubs scattered far apart in the hollows of the hills. Half a mile away, upstream, the caribou-skin topeks of an Eskimo settlement, fading away amid the background, were hardly visible to the eye. 2

Three small gray specks could be seen moving slowly above our camp. Human shapes, but so puny, so insignificant-looking against the wild rocky side of that immense hill! Bending down, then straightening up, they seemed to totter aimlessly through the chaos of stone, searching for some hidden treasure. 3

Curiosity, or perhaps a touch of loneliness, suddenly moved me to leave camp and join those three forlorn figures so far away above me near the sky line. 4

Slowly I made my way along the steep incline, following at first the bed of a dried-up stream. Little by little the river sank beneath me, while the breeze, increasing in strength, whistled past, lashing and stinging my face and hands. I had lost sight momentarily of the three diminutive figures which had lured me on to these heights. After a while a reindeer trail enabled me to leave the coulee and led me again in the right direction, through a gigantic mass of granite which the frost of thousands of years had plucked from the summit of the hill and hurled hundreds of feet below. 5

At last I was able to reach the other side of the avalanche of rocks and suddenly emerged comparatively in the open, on the brim of a slight depression at the bottom of which a few dead willow bushes showed their bleached branches above the stones and the gray moss. There I found the three silent figures huddled close together, gathering, one by one, the twigs of the precious wood. Two little girls, nine or ten years old, so small, so helpless, and an aged woman, so old, so frail, that my first thought was to marvel at the idea of their being able to climb so far from their camp to that lonely spot. 6

An Eskimo great-grandmother and her two great-granddaughters, all three contributing their share to the support of the tribe. Intent on their work, or most probably too shy to look up at the strange white man whom, until then, they had only seen at a distance, they gave me full opportunity to watch them. 7

All were dressed alike, in boots, trousers, and coats of caribou skin. The children wore little round leather caps reaching far over their ears, the crown decorated with bead-work designs. One of them carried on the wrist, as a bracelet, a narrow strip of bright 8 red flannel. Their faces were round and healthy, the skin sunburned to a dark copper color, but their cheeks showed a tinge of blood which gave them, under the tan, a peculiar complexion like the color of a ripe plum. Their little hands were bare and black, the scratches caused by the dead twigs showing plainly in white, while their fingers seemed cramped with the cold.

The old woman was bareheaded, quite bald at the top of the head, with long wisps 9 of gray hair waving in the wind. The skin of her neck and face had turned black, dried up like an old piece of parchment. Her cheeks were sunken and her cheek bones protruded horribly. Her open mouth showed bare gums, for her teeth were all gone, and her throat, thin and bare as a vulture's neck, showed the muscles like cords. Her hands were as thin as the hands of a skeleton, the tip of each finger carved in like a claw. Her eyes, once black, now light gray, remained half closed, deep down in their sockets.

She was stone blind. 10

Squatting on her heels, she held, spread in front of her, a small reindeer skin. As soon 11 as the children dropped a branch beside her, she felt for it gropingly; then, her hands closing on it greedily, like talons, she would break it into small pieces, a few inches long, which she carefully placed on the mat at her feet.

Both little girls, while searching diligently through the clumps of dead willows for 12 what they could break off and carry away, kept absolutely silent. Not only did they never call to one another when one of them needed help, but they seemed to watch each other intently whenever they could. Now and then, one of them would hit the ground two or three times with the flat of her hand. If the other had her head turned away at the time, she appeared to be startled and always wheeled round to look. Then both children would make funny little motions with their hands at one another.

The little girls were deaf and dumb. 13

After a while they had gathered all the wood the reindeer skin could contain. Then 14 the children went up to the old woman and conveyed to her the idea that it was time to go home. One of them took her hands in hers and guided them to two corners of the mat, while the other tapped her gently on the shoulder.

The old, old woman understood. Slowly and carefully she tied up the four corners 15 of the caribou skin over the twigs, silently watched by the little girls. Groaning, she rose to her feet, tottering with weakness and old age, and with a great effort swung the small bundle over her back. Then one little girl took her by the hand, while the other, standing behind, grasped the tail of her caribou coat. Slowly, very slowly, step by step they went their way, following a reindeer trail around rocks, over stones, down, down the hill, straight toward their camp, the old woman carrying painfully for the young, the deaf and dumb leading and steering safely the blind.

■ Reading Comprehension Questions

1. The word *diminutive* in "I had lost sight momentarily of the three diminutive figures which had lured me on to these heights" (paragraph 5) means
   a. shadowy.
   b. tiny.

    c. disappearing.

    d. fascinating.

2. The word *parchment* in "The skin of her neck and face had turned black, dried up like an old piece of parchment" (paragraph 9) means

    a. tanned-leather paper.

    b. charred board.

    c. seal hide.

    d. dried peel.

3. Which of the following would be a good alternative title for this selection?

    a. Life in the Barrens

    b. Northern Poverty

    c. Helping Hands

    d. Age, Youth, and Agony

4. Which sentence best expresses the main idea of the selection?

    a. The Inuit great-grandmother and the children scraped out an existence as castoffs from their society.

    b. Both the old woman and the children are disabled by our standards, but they helped each other and their tribe to maintain a life.

    c. The harshness of life in the Arctic ruined the health of both the aged woman and the young girls.

    d. Although the aged woman could no longer perform useful tasks, the young girls accompanied her on what seemed to be a daily ritual.

5. The author concluded that the three isolated figures didn't look up at him

    a. because they were unaware of him.

    b. because they were too shy to look back at him.

    c. because they couldn't see him.

    d. because the distance between them was too great.

6. *True or false?* _____ The writer is travelling in late June, so the weather, even in the Arctic, is warm.

7. The author sees the great-grandmother as

    a. helpless, and no help in the wood gathering.

    b. only with the girls as a baby-sitter.

    c. still strong enough to break branches and carry the bundle.

    d. fragile, blind, and barely alive.

8. The author implies that

    a. he is content and self-contained in the barren countryside.

    b. he is intimidated by the surroundings.

    c. he wants to visit the Eskimo village.

    d. he feels isolated enough to wonder about the figures he sees on the horizon.

9. The author implies that
   a. an efficient system of communication exists among the three figures.
   b. the old woman and the girls can barely perform their simple task.
   c. the girls were so busy watching each other that nothing was accomplished.
   d. even working together, the three did not manage to gather much wood.

10. The author implies that
    a. less-developed societies cannot care for the elderly and the young.
    b. although disadvantaged, the old woman and the girls still did necessary work.
    c. the Arctic environment is too harsh for the survival of healthy humans.
    d. the old woman has become too hideous and feeble to remain with the tribe.

■ Discussion Questions

About Content

1. The author first describes the three figures he sees as "searching for some hidden treasure." In what sense is this true of the object of the firewood gatherers' efforts?

2. Why does Mallet say, in paragraph 6, that his "first thought was to marvel at the idea of their being able to climb so far from their camp to that lonely spot"? What makes their achievement more amazing?

3. How well do the three know their way home? What do they use to guide their steps? What does this tell us of their knowledge of their environment?

About Structure

4. Mallet uses chronological, or time-sequence, order to tell his story. Beginning with paragraph 2, he gives the reader "signals," or "time-markers" (some of which are used repeatedly), which give his narrative a clear sense of the pace of the actions described. Find at least eight "time-signal" words in the essay. How do these, and the repetition of some words, contribute to the flow and feel of the narrative?

5. What elements make the final sentence of the essay so powerful? How do the author's words stir our emotions?

About Style and Tone

6. Compare and contrast the two word-portraits found in paragraphs 8 and 9. Which details most effectively show the differences between the girls and the

old woman? What are the three *similes* or comparisons with the word "like" Mallet uses in describing the great-grandmother? What effect do these three comparisons have on you as a reader?

7.   Thierry Mallet spent years in the Arctic and absorbed a keen sense of his surroundings. He uses the device of personification to describe physical elements of his environment: i.e., the tents "shivered and rippled" in the breeze (1). Where else do you find an example of the writer giving human attributes to a part of nature?

8.   Mallet's style seems plain and straightforward. Does this economy in his use of words suit his subject? Does it make the message of the narrative stronger or weaker? Why?

■ Writing Assignments

Assignment 1

The three characters in "The Firewood Gatherers" are strongly shaped by their environment, as in different ways are the narrators of "Stones and the Mountain," "Of Lemons and Lemonade," and "Outharbor Menu." To what extent have you been shaped by the area in which you grew up? Write an essay about three aspects of the physical environment of your early life which have contributed to the way you are now. How do you as you are now reflect the influence of your early surroundings?

Assignment 2

Traditional Native Canadian society and our current society have different ways of dealing with the elderly and the disadvantaged. We often find it preferable to shut such people out of the "mainstream," to render them useless to society, and thus to deprive them of feeling useful. Rarely do we live with, or take advantage of, our extended families. Which seems preferable to you at this stage in your life, the life of the northern great-grandmother or the relative comfort of existence in a nursing or retirement home? Defend your point of view in an essay based on your experience with relatives or family friends.

Assignment 3

The great-grandmother in Mallet's story comes to life because of the author's use of precise physical details. In an earlier essay, Garry Engkent described his mother using almost no physical details. Could you "see" one woman more clearly than the other? Write a portrait of someone older who has been important to you, describing three distinct aspects of this person which have influenced you.

The Advertiser's Man

Jennifer Nicholson

In the following selection, Victoria, B.C., writer Jennifer Nicholson analyzes and neatly classifies those glossy, well-groomed male figures who look back at us from the pages of popular magazines. New men's publications appear on the store shelves every month: do they, or their ads, say anything new about men? Have men changed because of changes in women's lives? Do new advertisements reflect "new men," or do they try to create new targets? Are men on the way to becoming "victimized" by the same consumer pressures women have felt for years?

John opens a GQ. Within seconds, cologne reeks from the advertising flaps. Clashing 1
odors waft in my direction. What are the stakes in these perfume wars? I wonder. Can
Chanel's Egoïste outstench Obsession?

GQ, Esquire, Men's Fitness, Details, Men's Health. . . . At first glance, or whiff, 2
these magazines seem only the masculine versions of *Cosmopolitan*. It's a hunt to find
that rare glimmer of editorial poking through the pages of these pseudo-catalogues. An
issue's fashion spreads become indistinguishable from the reams of advertisements, the
male models as uniformly Ken as the Barbies of female fashion—thoroughbreds, ideal
"speci-men" photographed to cast perfect shadows on perfectly sculpted jawlines.

John frowns as he thumbs through the chiseled features and blank stares. 3

"Do you ever compare yourself with those guys?" I ask him, sensing a familiar 4
insecurity.

"I'm smarter than that." John laughs. 5

Still, I wonder. After all, even the most discerning of men are swayed by the media 6
pull.

With the aftermath of the sexual revolution, new voices are scrambling for attention 7
in developing a new men's social conscience. The once concrete male ideal of the '50s
is being transformed by the complex socio-cultural climate of the '90s. The influences
are many: feminist charges, politically correct force (and its equally radical backlash)
and, increasingly, the drumming rituals of the thriving men's movement. These have all
conspired to create an image of man so multi-faceted, it rivals the collapsing demands
of the '80s superwoman.

The result? One confused, if not schizophrenic, target male. 8

By creating a variety of new male identities, advertisers gain access to a wider col- 9
lection of pocketbooks. Whether the '90s man is actually changing is irrelevant—the
point is to convince him that he's part of a market-driven trend.

"What about this?" I ask, pointing to an advertisement of an upwardly mobile busi- 10
nessman in Wall Street suspenders off to close a deal. But the picture includes one progressive '90s addition—a squeaky-clean baby strapped to his back. Both of them are
beaming above the caption: "Success is knowing which appointments to keep." Men
should do it all, this ad proclaims: have a lucrative career, be a great husband/father, and
never fail to give your kid the very best. The baby is waving a sterling silver rattle.

"What are they trying to do, make me feel guilty?" John smirks.   11

Perhaps. By developing new stereotypes and anxieties, the media has created a new, 12
lucrative market. The product, of course, is secondary. After all, advertising isn't so much
about proving a product as it is about marketing insecurity. And nothing can compare with
threatening media images to plant the seeds of inadequacy. It's been a marketing ploy
used on women since the days of dishwater hands, and (horrors) feminine odor.

Advertisers are opportunists, and now is the time to seize the shifting male ego and 13
create profitable new stereotypes.

Liz Claiborne's "Claiborne—the fragrance for men" recent advertising campaign 14
proclaims that "Man is not so simple, after all." It is characteristic of the bait dangling
before the new male market. No longer will the modern multi-faceted man be forced into
a one-dimensional strait-jacket. Instead, he will be led to one of many equally restrain-
ing stereotypes. Here are just a few to choose from.

He's a Sex Object

The '80s marked the beginning of a revolution in advertising, as designers realized that 15
the sexist techniques perfected on women could easily be transferred to men.

The objectification of specific men's body parts, pioneered by the yuppie-targeted 16
Soloflex campaign of the mid '80s, continues to thrive in Calvin Klein's Obsession
cologne and underwear ads. These men are faceless, their heads turned away, the photograph cropped to decapitate. It's a dehumanization technique custom-made for a society more at ease with the external than the internal. The body reigns supreme—a well
chiseled icon of success.

Feminists have long battled the use of Playboy bunny-looking women to sell unre- 17
lated products (i.e. cars, liquor, watches, etc). But what about Playgirl's pets? Take the
headless hunk in an ad for Bugatti ties. He could well be employed by the Chippendales'
stripper revue.

Ten years ago, a Paco Rabanne advertisement created a stir by presenting an image 18
of a cavalier male the morning after a tryst with a career woman. She's off on a business
trip, and he's languishing in bed. She's left him a note assuring him that she can't wait
to get back to his sexy scent. This ad trumpets a new male sex object who isn't afraid of
an aggressive woman and isn't a slave to a conventional job.

Today, such modern role reversals abound. Remarkably, though, they continue to rely 19
on images of sexy women. One of the recent Virginia Slims ads features a sultry blonde
in an outfit the off-putting shade of a "Men Working" sign, perched above her enlightened feminist slogan: "There's nothing wrong with letting a man go first as long as you
enjoy the view."

This ad talks change, but there are no visuals to prove it. There are no cute male butts 20 waddling away—and even if there were, the only twist would be this: "We've come such a long way, baby, now we can ogle men too."

These are little different than typecast sexist guy ads like the Johnnie Walker ad fea- 21 turing two jocks ogling on the beach: "She looks even better walking toward you. And she drinks Johnnie Walker Red." Only the victim has changed. The game itself remains the same.

Where change can clearly be seen is in the breadth of sexual imagery. Robert 22 Mapplethorpe's shocking images may not have swept the masses, but subtle homo-erotic and androgynous images have been popping up in Calvin Klein ads for years. They are a safe commercial bet; appealing to image-conscious men of all sexual preferences and to women as well.

Increasingly, sexually aggressive images of violent homo-erotica are also penetrat- 23 ing mainstream publications. In an ad for Nanni Italian belts, a perfect male body waits, submissive and abandoned in a parched desert. He's leaning forward, crouched on his elbows, his head covered by a leather Nanni belt which tightly binds his wrists. At first glance, this is an artistic photograph of a beautiful body. But it is unmistakably eerie, a photograph selling belts with a body in bondage. Why not? For years, Georges Marciano has been profiting from near-rape images to sell Guess jeans, so why not Nanni and belts?

He's the New Victim

Almost as progressive as making man a piece of meat, is making him the bad guy. 24

After analyzing 1,000 commercials in 1987, researcher Fred Hayward reported in 25 *Family Therapy Networker* (Nov./Dec. 1988) that "when an ad called for a negative portrayal in a male-female interaction, an astonishing 100 per cent of the time the 'bad guy' was a man."

Likewise, Kathryn Robinson observed in her "Are Men the New Victims" (*Seattle* 26 *Weekly*): "Insidiously, male bashing seems to have found its way onto the list of enlightened endeavors—right alongside recycling and writing Amnesty International letters . . ."

Last year, Geoff Pevere's Canadian Broadcasting Corporation *Prime Time* radio pro- 27 gram devoted a segment to the current trend of male bashing in television advertising. In one of the featured ads—a business lunch—a savvy, health-conscious modern woman busily educated her dunce-like male lunch companion about the caloric content of salad dressing.

Do advertisers really think they are equalizing gender inequities by making a man 28 stupid about detergent and salad dressings? Certainly, diminishing men rather than women is a shallow feminist victory. Shallow or not, it is a safe demographic bet in an advertising campaign, reinforcing female insecurities while hiding behind a flimsy mask of political correctness. If these ads qualify as sexually appropriate, it's merely because they are stabbing at the correct gender.

Nor is this trend limited to the advertising industry. It has filtered into the pop psy- 29 chology book market as well. Not convinced? Pick up a copy of *No Good Men* or the classic *Men Who Hate Women and The Women Who Love Them*, somewhere in the sea of the Harlequins.

He's the Sensitive Converted Feminist, Politically Correct Dude

Career-aged yuppies, the prime target of glossy men's advertising, are stuck in a bind. 30 Old enough to have been raised with traditional attitude but young enough to have felt the impact of feminist changes, these modern males are scrambling for a sense of themselves amidst the misguided barrage of "politically correct" hostility.

"The feminist perspective on relationships has become like fluoride in water," 31 claims Warren Farrell in *Family Therapy Networker* (Nov./Dec. 1988). ". . . We drink it without being aware of its presence. The idea that men are jerks has become integrated into our unconscious."

This "Sensitive, Converted Feminist Politically Correct Dude" is willing to take on 32 this burden—he views it as penance. "After all," says an old friend and recently converted SNAG (Sensitive New Age Guy), "after thousands of years of oppressing women, it only makes sense that we should now be put in the wrong."

So it should come as little surprise how quick marketers are to tap into this newfound 33 conscience, not to mention its bittersweet guilt. Maidenform lingerie, after decades of shocking the masses with public images of women posing in their underwear, has finally thrown in the skivvy and turned to new models: men. With images of lady-killers like Omar Sharif and Corbin Bernsen (who discloses, in the ad, that he finds shopping for lingerie "intimidating"), advertisers are targeting a "new woman" in search of this curious and sensitive "new man". A virile 30-something is photographed in deep sexy shadows. His caption teases: "A friend of mine says she has better luck choosing her lingerie than she does her dinner companions . . . perhaps there's just a better selection of lingerie out there." But underneath those puppy dog eyes is more a look of seduction than a statement of male humility. He may talk sweet, but he's still a lady killer.

Other advertising images deliver similarly mixed messages of this new misunder- 34 standing. An ad for Fathom cologne with a photo-montage of macho men promises a scent "For Men Whose Emotions Run Deep". Allowing men to have traditionally female qualities opens up a whole new world for advertisers. Thus the age of . . .

He's the New Domestic Man

He does his own cooking, buys his own clothes, and makes his own purchasing decisions. 35 But before we assume that this new and improved male reflects a role-change in household chores, we'd best remember that these ads cater not to women, but to a single man who is affluent enough to be independent of any woman for domestic support.

The hyper-yuppie Johnnie Walker ad campaign is a prime example. In one ad, a man 36 running with a buddy on the beach makes mention of his latest squeeze, "She loves my cooking. And she drinks Johnnie Walker." He's the pinnacle of achievement in our society: financially successful, cooks for himself and, doubtless, has all the women running his way. He's the "New Domestic Man", the man who does it all; which leads us to the inevitable . . .

He's Super Man

Money maker, super cook, great pectorals, sensitive, a wonderful parent, in touch with 37 his masculinity, and he's good in bed!

Having finally realized the demands on the '80s career woman were unreasonable, 38 we're being offered an alternative . . . He's the man who can do it all.

To avoid being phased out by feminine selection, ads tell us, a man must be a per- 39 fect balance of gentle and macho virtue. Revlon's That Man cologne urges users to "Sense the confidence. The warmth. The power. Sense the man."

Revlon is promising one hell of a man. He's successful, and he's got an equally suc- 40 cessful woman at his side. According to Farrell, "Even successful women have not relaxed the pressure for men to succeed."

Another purveyor of gainful gender myths is the ubiquitous Johnnie Walker cam- 41 paign. One ad highlights two upwardly mobile men at a business lunch, both with the unseen woman: "She was law review", and of course, "she drinks Johnnie Walker." Here is an affirmation of the male ego. This "Super Man" is smart enough to choose an ambi- tious woman, a woman that is man enough to drink scotch. Unfortunately, she's little more than his commodity.

To balance this high-powered Johnnie Walker "Super Man", other ads in the campaign 42 feature (and thus implicitly recognize) the non-competitive masculine hero. A woman, seemingly successful only because of her beauty, confides to a colleague in a modeling dressing room: "He doesn't mind if I make more than he does. And he drinks . . ."

The next stage for this multi-faceted man is to become a Super Dad. Men with their 43 cherubic tots are advertising everything from GAP sportswear to Giorgio Armani suits. Does it matter that these men are never doing anything with these babies, that they are simply on display? Apparently not. It's the romantic fathering image, not the act of true diapery, slobbery, messy parenting, that sells. Adolescent girls' bedroom walls from sea to shining sea boast arty posters of shirtless, sinewy hunks in faded jeans; all of them pictured with naked babies. After all, what could be sexier than a man holding a baby?

The only advertisement I could find that offered men any solace from these demand- 44 ing media images was a campaign for Tag-Heuer watches. It shows the furrowed brows of a driven man, and offers the advice: "Don't crack under pressure." Given the prevail- ing strains of modern manhood, that warning may be in vain.

He's Iron John's Man (The New Masculinists)

It comes as no surprise that within an environment of old and new male stereotypes, there 45 are an increasing number of men gravitating to the forest; challenging male-accepted roles of workhorse provider, dispensable cannon fodder in time of war, or helpless vic- tim of the sexual revolution. It's no coincidence that Robert Bly's *Iron John* has attracted more male attention than the '80s *Real Men Don't Eat Quiche*. In a time when men don't know who to believe, the book offers a perfect solution. As Kathryn Robertson sees it, Bly is operating on the theory that "Men carry around a profound sense of inadequacy where their sense of maleness used to be."

To compensate for this lost maleness, advertisers are filling the void with empty 46 images, twisting the movement's valid concerns into profitable marketing directions.

Many of the ads which reflect this trend appeal to the primal male who has oppressed 47 his manliness in the modern city. A recent Ralph Lauren Polo ad shows a long-haired stallion-looking male elegantly dressed in a three-piece suit. He's the image of Iron John, the wild man trapped within the confines of urban life—aching to break out of his gray flannel suit and discover his masculinity in the rituals of his roots.

Likewise, a new campaign for Cuervo Gold tequila displays a stampede of tribal men 48 charging from the page. They're wearing masks, wielding bows, armor, arrows, and the new symbol of the men's movement: drums. The caption reads: "No other ritual comes close." Marketers realize that if they can link the idea of drinking buddies with their regained primal rituals, they might be able to sell by association.

He's a Rugged Individualist Evolving into the Existential Man

The Marlboro man has long symbolized man's freedom and rugged individuality. The 49 appeal of this old selling tactic has evolved into a slightly more sophisticated neo-individualist ad ploy in the '90s.

Still the sexy modern loner, this existential fellow is no longer simply a hanger for 50 stylish clothing. Now he's contemplating Kafka or solving the crisis in the Middle East. These ads exalt solitude—and, by association, spending—to the most honorable male pastime. A recent *American Photographer* essay describes them: ". . . Sitting alone, they burrow darkly into their superb sense of style, meditating in their Armanis."

Doug Coupland's *Generation X* labels our generation's exclusionary trend as the 51 "Cult of Aloneness": "The need for autonomy at all costs, usually at the expense of long-term relationships. Often brought about by overly high expectations of others."

Whether these ads pretend to reflect society's high expectations of man, or simply 52 his high expectations of others, they offer this evolving existential man a way out of the chaos of modern relationships.

To avoid the inevitable disappointment with mere mortals, this stylish man is better 53 off alone. He's searching for direction, and these ads guide him to the insular world of consumerism. The irony is that while these ads exalt the solitary fashion mission, the first step is a trip to the long line-ups of crowded, chaotic shopping malls.

He's Self-Obsessed

Every movement has a backlash, and the advertising trend towards male sensibility is no 54 exception. That's why some marketers have given up on the new sensitivity, and are returning to the tried and true method of marketing men as the power elite.

This wave of self-obsession is even more frightening than gratuitous images of sex- 55 ual role-reversals. It is downright vanity. Here is a man who deserves to be proud, a man who deserves to be in love with himself.

The latest Obsession ad is true to its name. Here is a WASP unmired by guilt over 56 years of oppression, a man who can't get enough of himself. Staring at himself in the mirror, he's a perfect statue, fixated by his own image. He's the modern version of the myth of Narcissus, in love with his own reflection in the pool (swimming pool, that is). This is safe, solitary sex. And in the '90s, it sells.

Other ads echo the cry of this politically correct backlash. A slogan from a Lagerfeld 57 cologne campaign proclaims "Power begets power". The Franklin Mint Golden Falcon Watch puts it best: "Some men have it. Most never will."

But the most alarming model of this new, prideful man is Chanel's new men's 58 cologne, Egoïste. "To assume he is aloof or uncaring is to misread him. He walks on that fine line separating arrogance from an awareness of self-worth." This cologne is going to be snapped right up by any man who needs an elaborate justification for an inflated ego.

Despair not. Marketers have not even begun to exhaust their plans to mold the mod- 59 ern man. There's always . . .

The Self-Actualized Male

Market researchers promise a new breed of man who isn't worried about his thinning hair- 60 line, flabby physique and failing eyesight. He's at ease with himself and his place in the world. Not that this signals the collapse of an insecurity-driven industry. Ads will simply appeal to men's new, self-actualized ways. For example, Lee Jeans' new ad featuring an easy going guy: "We don't think wearing jeans should raise your voice an octave."

Despite any newfound self-awareness, this "Self-Actualized Male" won't be shopping 61 any less. "As sensitivity has spread, it has lost its moorings in the therapeutic experience," reports *Working Woman* (April 1990), "and come to signify the heightened receptivity associated with consumerism: a vague appreciation that lends itself to aimless shopping."

Claiborne's "Man is not so simple any more" campaign reveals four panels of a 62 man's internal questioning, finalizing in his self-acceptance: 1. "Am I really at the height of my powers?" 2. "Is my masculinity on the wane?" 3. "Is it all downhill from here?" and then . . . 4. (*the revelation*) "Nah." Let's just hope he proves to be right.

And He's Oblivious

I showed these ads to a dozen or so males ranging in age from 25 to 45, and was surprised 63 by their homogenous response.

"That isn't me," they said. "Other men might react to that ad, but not me . . ." 64

These men may read high-end glossy men's magazines, but they feel removed from 65 their advertising pull. Of course, it is precisely these men, these "others", that the advertisers are targeting. And like it or not, they don't have to realize it.

■ Reading Comprehension Questions

1. The word *discerning* in "even the most discerning of men are swayed by the media pull" (paragraph 6) means
    a. distinguished.
    b. discriminating.

    c. disconnected.

    d. disapproving.

2. The word *androgynous* in "subtle homo-erotic and androgynous images have been popping up in Calvin Klein ads for years" (paragraph 22) means
    a. elegant and sophisticated.
    b. strange and exotic.
    c. both male and female.
    d. neither ugly nor beautiful.

3. Which of the following would be a good alternative title for this selection?
    a. Men and Marketing
    b. Oblivion or Obsession?
    c. New Images: New Identities?
    d. Sales and Stereotypes: Old Problem, New Victim

4. Which sentence best expresses the main idea of the selection?
    a. The "new men" in '90s ads are more realistic than female ad stereotypes.
    b. Stereotyped concepts like "new men" fail to find their targets.
    c. Advertising creates new ways to victimize a new market.
    d. Men are less likely than women to succumb to simplified images of themselves.

5. Recent influences on marketing trends for men include
    a. decreasing fashion-consciousness in male consumers.
    b. more disposable income in yuppie households.
    c. political correctness, incorrectness, and the men's movement.
    d. increased affluence among the gay market.

6. *True or false?* _____ Advertisers show us successful and beautiful people to motivate us to be like them.

7. Advertising executives realized that
    a. current attitudes facilitated promoting men as sex objects and bumbling fools.
    b. men currently popular in the media could promote household products and lingerie.
    c. men deserved oppression after centuries of oppressing women.
    d. men had come a long way, too.

8. *True or false?* _____ The author concludes that the men she interviewed did not need to be aware that they were the intended audience for ad campaigns.

9. The author implies that
   a. because being a father is messy, it is no longer a saleable image.
   b. because men have lost their traditional roles, they are risky target markets.
   c. shopping is acceptable for the "New Man."
   d. because men are now in competition with successful women, they will buy the same products that women buy.

10. The author implies that men will become even more prone to consumerism
    a. because they have become more like women.
    b. because "sensitive," "fully actualized" men are still insecure and even more receptive to marketing ploys.
    c. because their egos demand products to reinforce their self-images.
    d. because men with more roles to play need more clothes and accessories.

■ Discussion Questions

About Content

1. Who are the "profitable new stereotypes" (13) that the author says advertising has created for the 1990s? Do these exist among your friends and family, or only in the media?
2. Who are the targets for such promotions as those of Calvin Klein's products? Which marketing image does the writer find "unmistakably eerie," and why?
3. What are advertisers offering to make up for the apparent "inadequacy" felt by men in this decade?

About Structure

4. In the opening paragraph of this selection, Nicholson writes "John opens a *GQ*. Within seconds, cologne reeks from the advertising flaps. Clashing odors waft in my direction." What method of introduction is the author using?
   a. Broad to narrow
   b. Anecdote
   c. Beginning with an opposite
5. Quotations from friends of the author and from authorities on the subjects of psychology and the media punctuate and reinforce Nicholson's own views on men and advertising. How does the presence of these quotations affect the reader's perception of the writer as an informed, fair, and credible source of information?

About Style and Tone

6. "[M]ale models *as uniformly Ken as the Barbies* of female fashion," "the *headless hunk* in an ad": Nicholson uses lively and arresting descriptive phrases to capture her subject. Find at least *two* other examples of such phrases.

■ Writing Assignments

Assignment 1

"After all, advertising isn't so much about proving a product as it is about marketing insecurity. And nothing can compare with threatening media images to plant the seeds of inadequacy" (paragraph 12).

The results of media techniques causing insecurity and inadequacy appear in other selections in this text, including Naheed Mustafa's "My Body Is My Own Business" and Catherine Pigott's "The Image of Beauty," which discuss women's feelings of physical insecurity. Jennifer Nicholson states that advertising techniques used on women are now being used successfully on male audiences.

Choose one ad aimed at men from a current magazine. Using your advertisement as a reference, compare or contrast your own views with those of Nicholson on insecurity as motivation in men's advertisements, using three of her specific points from this selection. Attach your ad to your essay when you submit it.

Assignment 2

You work for an advertising agency, and you must create a report on possible categories of the "youth/young male segment" of your area's demographic (population). Choose three of your male friends or acquaintances who represent three different categories or types of male consumers. Give each classification a name that describes that consumer's main characteristic, so that your report contains headings like those in Jennifer Nicholson's essay. Your introduction should explain why you chose your three classifications, and what they represent, in a general statement.

After dividing up your market segment (your three types), write a brief analysis of each. Possible areas for consideration in your analysis could include spending habits, personal interests, possible motivating factors, disposable income, and product preferences: these amount to "character sketches" of each type.

In your conclusion, you could point to any similarities existing between the three categories, or to any trends you see emerging from your group as young male consumers.

Assignment 3

Who would be appropriate male images to promote various consumer products? If yuppie executives and "too-perfect" models are sexist, and make male readers feel inadequate, then what types of male figures should be used in the marketing of three of the following products?

- Running shoes
- Stereo equipment
- Jeans
- Bottled water
- Fashion watches
- Credit cards
- Dress shirts
- Leather jackets
- Underwear
- Men's cologne
- Motorcycles
- Beer

Persuade your reader of your reasons for each of your three choices, using good and/or bad examples from your own examination of ads, and from your own experience.

What Makes Teenagers Tick?

Lynn Turner

Your teenage years could be just behind you, or they could be half a lifetime away, as you read this selection. You may be still trying to understand your own adolescence, or you may be struggling with a teen-aged son or daughter at home. Since the end of World War II in North America, when teenagers became a distinct and recognizable social group, parents, educators, and psychologists have been trying to understand and deal with these emotional and turbulent years. Maritime writer Lynn Turner examines some of the results of research by Dr. Dianne Looker, and some of the reactions of Nova Scotia teenagers and educators to questions which probably plagued both you and your parents.

Remember the year you were seventeen? Most adults do. it was a year of momentous decisions, raging hormones, fervent beliefs, and paralysing Saturday-morning lethargy. If you were a teenager in the 60s, you heard Abbie Hoffman warn, "Never trust anyone over thirty." Chances are there was a time when you believed that Love could conquer all—war, disease, poverty. You remember the first time you . . . well . . . you know. Now you're probably yelling at your own kids to turn that blasted head-banging music down. (How loudly did you play Purple Haze?) 1

Seventeen is not an easy age. The same year that awesome idealism wells within, cold, hard reality knocks without. 2

Sociologist Dr. E. Dianne Looker has studied 17-year-olds since her doctorate year at McMaster University in 1975. She is a likeable woman who inhabits a tiny cement cell of an office at Acadia University in Wolfville that is plastered with bright pictures her children have drawn on computer paper. When she wants to stress a point, as she often does, her voice raises in pitch at the end of the sentence. It is obvious Dr. Looker cares deeply about her work. 3

I suspect her highly approachable manner accounts for much of her success working with teenagers. I'd talk to her if I were 17. I'd even fill out her 60-page questionnaire. That's right. Sixty pages. She has interviewed hundreds of students and their parents in each of her surveys: in Hamilton, Halifax, and rural Nova Scotia. 4

Dr. Looker has specific areas of study in her surveys, but basically she wants to know what teenagers have on their minds. Her results are tabulated and analysed under broad headings such as future plans, rural-urban differences, gender differences and parental influence. 5

Dianne Looker knows 17-year-olds. She says they don't fit the stereotype. If you visualize dyed hair full of mousse, mono-syllable conversation and an abiding interest in Charles and Di, not so. 6

Melanie Lenihan works weekends selling hamburgers at Harvey's. She borrows her parents' car when her boyfriend is without wheels, says she is concerned about world hunger, hates people who are snobs and is a popular 17-year-old. Remarkably serious about her future, she says she plans to go to university and then embark on a challenging, interesting and secure career. At the same time, she expects to get married (when she's 30) and have children. She's not one of Dr.Looker's subjects, but Melanie personifies most of her findings. 7

One of the most interesting findings is that two thirds of teenagers have a fairly clear idea of what they plan to do in the future. "I think education is more important to 17-year-olds than most people think," Dr. Looker says. "They are very concerned with what they are going to do after high school." Students in Nova Scotia are more attuned to 8 tougher economic times than those in Ontario. "In Ontario they talk about getting a *better* job. In Nova Scotia they are more likely to ask 'How am I going to get *a* job'."

As might be expected, students who enjoy school and who have parents with post- 9 secondary education are likely to go on to university. But a comparison of urban and rural students with these same characteristics indicates that rural students, especially men, are not as likely to continue their education. "For young people in rural areas, the decision to go on in terms of schooling means leaving your home. In the cities, you don't have to link these two decisions." Young people in rural areas usually have a closer tie to their community so they have a harder time deciding to leave.

Dr. Looker says, "Students who have already decided that they can't afford to go to 10 university have long ago said that they don't want to go. The really bright students have gotten enough feedback from teachers and counsellors that they assume they will go to university and assume that they will be eligible for scholarships. Outstanding students are not going to be held back by financial constraints. It's the ones in the middle that are affected."

The research confirms that ending up with a steady job is a top priority for males 11 and females. But, uh oh, some old stereotypes are alive and well. The majority of 17-year-old boys say that as soon as they get married they have to work. Girls say that as soon as they have children, they'll have to stay at home. "Whereas the family responsibilities push the boys into the labour force, the family responsibilities pull the girls out of the labour force." If you ask girls what they want to do, they will answer with the same list of job requirements: challenging, interesting, and secure. They are just as committed to careers as boys, but many also say they are going to stay home with their preschool age children. "Sixty-three percent of the young women interviewed strongly agree that mothers and fathers should share equal responsibility for child care but only 34 percent of the men strongly agree with this statement. Putting these together, somebody's in for a shock."

Dr. Looker says most boys wear blinders when they imagine the kinds of jobs they 12 want as adults. The girls say they expect to have careers in what are considered traditionally women's jobs. However, many of them also aspire to the professions which have traditionally been men's jobs. The boys, on the other hand, often disregard careers saying, "I won't do that because it's women's work. Boys would rather take a lousy, insecure, low-paying man's job than be a clerk, or a typist, or a secretary which is clean, which is secure, which is often better paying, because that's women's work."

Dr. Looker says parents have a great deal of influence on the decisions of their chil- 13 dren. That's why she also interviews them. Although 80 percent of kids say that at least one parent is the most important influence on their plans—more important than friends, teachers, or guidance counsellors—problems do exist. "Young people frequently have no idea what parents want for them." Not only do parents expect their children to perform according to society's rules, children expect their parents to conform as well. If neither parent has talked about exactly what they think, the teen will assume things.

Dr. Looker says 17-year-olds really *want* to be influenced by their parents. She says 14 it is difficult to "put that together with the notion that teenagers are always fighting with their parents. They do have conflicts, but they don't influence how much impact the parent has on the teen's decision making."

Asked for advice she says, "Don't expect that just because you've been sending a 15
message that they've been receiving that message. And remember, it only takes one parent to say 'Yes'. It is important for the kid to be autonomous. Or to say: 'Yes, you should
go to university.' That one parent will have a dramatic impact on the teen."

Donnie Clarke, a guidance counsellor at Central Kings High School in the Annapolis 16
Valley, listened with interest when Dr. Looker spoke at a recent teacher inservice. He also
has advice for parents: "When you are talking to your teenager, ask yourself how you
would respond if this person was an adult friend, not your child. Would you say the same
thing to a friend? How would you feel if a friend spoke to you using those words?"

Melanie Lenihan says, "We're right in between. We're not adults, but we're not kids 17
either. Next year we'll be off to college. We're getting our lives on track. We're making
important decisions. We should be treated as adults and, instead of having things
imposed upon us, we should have discussions about things like curfews."

Clarke agrees but says kids shouldn't be given free rein. "They need some space, but 18
they also need direction." He cites course selection as a good example. In the old system
of high school curriculum, every student took the same classes. Today students as early as
grade nine are asked course decisions that stream them into different career choices.
Dropping math in grade nine, for instance, is going to greatly limit the number of higher
education programs that will accept them. Teens need and want their parents' guidance in
these matters. If they make a wrong, uninformed choice, they could affect future options.

Clarke says he has seen the consequences. "A lot of 17-year-olds are disappointed. 19
They know now that they're in grade 12 that they should have taken this course or that
course and now it's too late." He doesn't suggest that schools should revert to the old system because he isn't convinced that even at 17 all students are mature enough to make
the choices that affect the rest of their lives. He wants to see a system in place in which
young people could go out and get a taste of the real world before they have to make up
their minds, and he says many dropouts have returned to school after having tried it.

Why do people return to school? Dianne Looker says "they come time and time again 20
looking to get back into the system because when they get out of school they realize that
there are no possibilities for them. A lot of doors are closed to them, doors that they
thought were open when they left. In the majority of cases they weren't told what the
implications of leaving school would be."

Dianne Looker says, "The things that seem to get them back in school are parental 21
encouragement and the difficulty in finding a job. The experience in the big, bad world."
Her studies show an increase in the number of former dropouts who left school at some
point but returned.

"More and more kids are coming back to school and doing a great job," says Donnie 22
Clarke. "They tell me that they're enjoying learning. They are getting good marks but
what is important to them is that they're really enjoying school." Clarke works with teens
every day and says he has a solid respect for them. "On the surface they seem more interested in music and friends and what's happening at home, on the street, and around. But
in the back of their minds there are always the serious concerns."

He's right of course. Seventeen-year-olds do not lead quiet, carefree, sheltered lives. 23
As adults we often look back at the teen years with affection, remembering only the good

times. We remember dancing with that special person, not the hours cowering on the sidelines hoping someone would notice us. We remember listening to our favourite song over and over again, but we forget that it took hour after hour of dishing out hamburgers or punching cash registers in order to earn the money to buy that song. And those are the innocent relatively insignificant concerns.

According to Statistics Canada, of Nova Scotia residents 17 years or younger, 409   24 gave birth and 42 girls were married in 1990. There were 3,500 cases from that age group heard by youth court. Seventeen is not an easy age. The highs soar alpine clear, but the lows . . .

"Seventeen-year-olds are dealing with a lot of emotional needs. They are becoming   25 an adult but they aren't there yet. They need support, but they also need independence. They have to deal with the freedom to indulge in access to drugs, sexual activity, and so on. They need a lot of social support to deal with these pressures because they don't have all the answers yet."

Dr. Looker says it's important for kids to fit in somewhere, and that's sometimes dif-   26 ficult for the shy or timid students at smaller or rural schools. She says parents influence the big picture question but peer pressure affects the kids' social behaviour. Kids can find a group, or clique, easily enough in larger schools, but when it's important to feel that they belong somewhere, it's not always easy in smaller ones.

I spoke with a lot of people about 17-year-olds—teachers, administrators, sociolo-   27 gists, counsellors, and kids themselves. They all say today's teens are much more concerned, reasonable, and serious than most people think. It's a tightly packed, overstressed, highly charged time. Perhaps, instead of ordering teens to tone it down, they should be encouraged to turn it up, to listen to some of that head-banging music before they hit the books. They're going to need some release before the reality of what comes after 17 really sets in.

■ Reading Comprehension Questions

1. The word *autonomous* in "It is important for the kid to be autonomous" (paragraph 15) means
   a. confident.
   b. independent.
   c. approachable.
   d. informed.

2. The word *cowering* in "not the hours cowering on the sidelines hoping someone would notice us" (paragraph 23) means
   a. suffering patiently
   b. shivering.
   c. hovering nervously.
   d. hiding.

3. Which of the following would be a good alternative title for this selection?
   a. Adolescence and Agony
   b. Difficult Years, Difficult Decisions
   c. Employment or Education: Which Is Best?
   d. What Have We Forgotten about Teenage Years?

4. Which sentence best expresses the main idea of the selection?
   a. Seventeen-year-olds are concerned about jobs, but in many ways are the same as they always were.
   b. As teenagers, young people are often quite mature, yet they face decisions and pressures which some guidance might make easier.
   c. At seventeen, young people are usually in conflict with all forms of authority.
   d. Maritime teenagers face tougher economic problems than do teens in the rest of Canada.

5. Dr. Looker's surveys showed
   a. many teenagers don't want to go to university.
   b. teens from country areas frequently don't go away to university.
   c. getting a good job is less important for young women than it is for young men.
   d. both sexes believe childcare should be equally shared by both parents.

6. *True or false?* _____ Male bias against jobs once considered "women's work" is still alive and well.

7. Research showed that, although at least one parent is most influential,
   a. teens are uncertain about what a parent may want for them.
   b. teens think parents' ideas are ridiculous and old-hat.
   c. teens expect parents to have all the answers for them.
   d. parents' behaviour is often not up to teens' expectations.

8. Parent–teen conflicts
   a. destroy all hope of inter-generation communication.
   b. are typical, but the parent retains the power to be important in decisions.
   c. are so frequent that they diminish parental influence.
   d. have no effect on the messages parents are sending.

9. The author implies that
   a. teenage crime is not a significant problem in Nova Scotia.
   b. nostalgic adults have forgotten what it is to be a teenager.
   c. teenage years are full of complex needs and stressful decisions.
   d. teens who return to school rarely get into trouble.

10. In concluding, the author implies that
    a. teenagers need diversions from the pressures ahead of them.
    b. teenagers should settle down and work more conscientiously.

c. teenagers need more discipline from parents.

d. teenagers should have more fun and study less.

■ Discussion Questions

About Content

1. What support do Melanie Lenihan's actions and ideas give to the author's statement that seventeen is "The same year that awesome idealism wells within, [and] cold, hard reality knocks without" (2)?

2. What three categories of students approaching university does Dr. Looker identify in her research?

3. What specific details in the essay, from which sources, support the author's final description of teenage years as a "tightly packed, over-stressed, highly charged time" (27)?

About Structure

4. What method of introduction does Lynn Turner use for this selection?
   a. Quotation
   b. Incident or brief story
   c. Series of questions

5. What are the major ideas of the essay, and how are they presented to the reader?

6. Find, in this selection, at least four causes for various aspects of teenage behaviour.

_____   _____

_____   _____

What are the corresponding effects?

_____   _____

_____   _____

About Style and Tone

7. The author appears in the first person only three times: early in the fourth paragraph, and again near the end of the essay in paragraphs 23 and 27. How does her use of other voices and other sources of information affect your view of the credibility of her content?

8. How does the author "balance" her presentation of each of her major ideas?

■ Writing Assignments

Assignment 1

"Remember the year when *you* were seventeen?"
  Brainstorm for either of the following:

- The three most significant events of that year of your life; what lasting effects did these events have on you?
- The three most important people in your life when you were seventeen; how have these people affected you specifically, in terms of personal choices, ideas, and actions?

Write an essay based on one of these choices, which shows how either certain events or certain people caused changes in your life.

Assignment 2

You are a psychologist or sociologist specializing in teenage behaviour and problems. In a report to a concerned parents' group, give your findings concerning, three major problems or concerns of teenagers in the mid-nineties. You may use "case study" examples from your own life (with suitably disguised names) and perhaps some of the ideas from Lynn Turner's article. You could also use a question and answer format: your three problems will be set up in the form of headings/questions, with your supporting information set up as the answers.

  Be sure to open your report with a clear and strong statement of your thesis (your findings), and to frame your report in a clear and convincing way.

Assignment 3

Based on your own experience, write an essay which defines "adolescence." Your thesis statement should specify what the word means, or meant, to *you*. Look for three ideas of equal significance which best characterize adolescence for you.

CONSIDERING CONCEPTS

Mind Over Myth

Beppi Crosariol

Despite the facts that we live in the "Information Age," which is ruled by computers, and that most of us own or at least use these machines, we are still baffled by what goes on inside their cases. Because most people are not technicians, we tend to believe whatever we hear or read about whatever can go wrong with our beloved PC or Mac. Some of these legends from current computer "mythology" are no longer true, and Crosariol, a technological journalist, offers some simple and knowledgeable explanations for popular misconceptions.

Computers are insanely logical. Which is probably why we feel the need to attribute so 1 many irrational myths to them.

A classic is the one about laptop PCs getting fried by airport X-ray machines. Many 2 business travellers still insist on having their portable PCs visually inspected at the departure gate to avoid damaging their hard drives. It's a nuisance to fellow travellers because the passenger has to unzip the case, lug out the computer and turn it on in front of an inspector to prove it's not a fancy cocaine urn.

It's also unnecessary. The hard drive, which stores data and software, is encased in 3 a solid metal cabinet that low-level rays emitted by the security scanner can't penetrate, so the disk can't suffer radiation damage.

Ted Procher, an inspector with Transport Canada at Toronto's Pearson International   4
Airport, says he's not aware of any instance of laptop damage due to an X-ray machine.
But he adds that most airports continue to indulge travellers' paranoia. So don't look for
the bottlenecks to let up soon.

FLOPPY FEARS Much the same goes for floppy diskettes. Although they're encased   5
in thin plastic shells, rugged floppies are transparent to low-level X-rays. As for those
lead-lined cases you order through the mail, don't bother. They were probably dreamed
up by the same person who persuaded airlines that seat belts are useful in plane crashes.

Another misconception about floppies is that they can get nuked if they're too close   6
to a telephone when it rings. Okay, this *is* true, but only if you still have one of those near-
extinct black collector's items owned by the phone company. The gigantic magnet that
gives those clunkers their heft also generates a strong electromagnetic field. But for most
phones in use today, this is not an issue.

For an industry in which technology is the definition of change, it's ironic that com-   7
mon wisdom evolves so slowly. Another example is the dreaded phenomenon of phosphor burn-in. Time was when, if you left your computer on for days without altering the
image on the screen, an impression would gradually etch itself onto the glass. This is
because computer screens produce light by firing electrons at the glass, which is coated
in fluorescent phosphor. Especially vulnerable are those old mainframe terminals kicking around at the office that display the same command line at the top of the screen at
all times and that rarely get turned off.

Today's screens are essentially immune to this problem. "It would take an extended   8
period of time, definitely years," says Kirt Yanke, a product engineer with computer-screen
maker NEC Technologies Inc. in Chicago. PC users today tend to shift back and forth
among different programs, helping eradicate the problem. As well, a colour screen distributes its electron beam over three colour dots—red, green and blue—to compose each
point of light, while each dot on a monochrome screen gets the full force of the beam.

Oddly enough, burn-in scare became a publicity issue just as it was declining as a   9
technological problem. For this we can thank enterprising companies such as Toronto's
Delrina Corp. and California's Berkeley Systems Inc., which sell so-called screen-saver
programs. These programs give alternating portions of the screen a rest by replacing sta-
tic images with moving ones, usually cartoons, when the keyboard goes untouched for
a specified period.

While a screen saver will run you a mere $30 to $50, a potentially more costly myth   10
is the one that maintains you can get a better deal on a used PC from a friend than you
can from a dealer. This may hold for cars, but consumers so far seem unable to face the
stark realities of the PC marketplace. Consider an ad that went up recently on an office
bulletin board. It listed a Toshiba monochrome laptop with an Intel 386 microprocessor
running at 25 megahertz, a 120 megabyte hard disk, 10 megabytes of RAM memory and
a modem. The bottom line: $1,150 (U.S.).

A term that comes to mind here is museum piece. The 386 processor is about as cur-   11
rent as a turntable, lacking the guts to run much of today's popular software. Gary
Guhman, sales manager at the Boston Computer Exchange, one of North America's

largest used-PC dealerships, says the Toshiba described above would go for "no more than \$850" at his store. Computer owners, he says, are patently out of touch. "Even though they paid \$4,000 for a machine, they think they can get \$3,000 for it three years later, when in reality they're lucky if they can get \$1,000."

MISSING IN ACTION And the most regrettable computer myth of all time? The lie 12 of the deleted file. In the analog world, we think of deleting in literal terms. In the computer world, words often stray from the dictionary. Instruct a computer to "delete" a file and what you're really doing is wiping out index information, such as the address of the file on the hard disk. The effect is to enable the computer to write over the file when new storage space is needed—say, the next time you save a file or install new software.

Fortunately, it's possible to recover the file with a utility program (prices range from 13 \$90 Canadian to \$150). Among the best are *The Norton Utilities* from Symantec Corp. for IBM-compatibles or Macintoshes and *PC Tools* or *MacTools* from Central Point Software of Beaverton, Ore. These programs have the ability to root around your hard disk, display the contents of non-addressed files and recatalogue them. Just remember, the moment you realize you've accidentally deleted a file, try to avoid using the save function until you've found and restored the lost file. And maybe cross your fingers for good luck. That's a myth, too, but old habits are hard to break.

■ Reading Comprehension Questions

1. The word *paranoia* in "most airports continue to indulge travellers' paranoia" (paragraph 4) means
   a. crazy hysterical fears.
   b. irrational suspicions of others.
   c. wild behaviour.
   d. careful precautions.

2. The word *eradicate* in "PC users today tend to shift back and forth among different programs, helping eradicate the problem" (paragraph 8) means
   a. worsen.
   b. improve.
   c. eliminate.
   d. complicate.

3. Which of the following would be a good alternative title for this selection?
   a. PC Made Easy
   b. Protect Your Processor; Save Your Screen
   c. A Little Knowledge Is a Dangerous Thing
   d. Speedy Technology and Slow Learners

4. Which sentence best expresses the main idea of the selection?
   a. Computers are too logical for people to completely understand them, so we invent myths to explain problems.

b. Computer technology evolves so quickly that earlier information is often obsolete before we know it.

c. None of the current computer myths has any basis in reality for computer users today.

d. Using a screen saver, buying a utility program, and buying a good used processor privately can protect you from most problems.

5. A prevailing misconception about airport computer inspections is

a. that the X-rays are at a high enough level to damage a laptop's hard drive.

b. that X-rays can erase the contents of floppy diskettes and hard drives.

c. that inspectors believe that computer cases can conceal illicit drugs.

d. lead-lined cases cannot protect your floppy diskettes from damage.

6. *True or false?* _____ Burnt-in phosphor patterns on computer screens don't occur today.

7. *True or false?* _____ Deleting information from your computer means removing the index information which the processor uses to retrieve that information.

8. We can conclude that

a. screen savers emerged only when new monitors had lessened the need for them.

b. screen savers eliminate the danger of screen burn-in.

c. colour monitors completely eliminate the need for screen savers.

d. only older monochrome mainframe monitors require screen savers.

9. The author implies that

a. newer technology is not always better for, or required by, the consumer.

b. new software means increasingly powerful hardware is needed to make it usable.

c. computer purchases still represent a good resale return on the consumer's initial investment.

d. new high-powered computers are about as meaningful in functional terms as new high-powered cars.

10. *True or false?* _____ With a utilities programme installed on your processor, you are completely safe from ever totally losing a deleted file.

■ Discussion Questions

About Content

1. According to Crosariol, as well as the Transport Canada inspector, laptop hard drives can't be damaged by airport X-rays. Why, then, does the average portable computer owner not trust airport baggage inspectors?

2. What component of older telephones can damage floppy diskettes left near the phone set? How?

3. Why does a colour monitor result in lower chances of monitor screen phosphor damage?

About Structure

4. What method does Crosariol use to introduce his essay?
   a. Anecdote
   b. Beginning with an opposite
   c. Broad to narrow

5. The author discusses five current myths about computers in this essay. How does he connect, or create transitions between, each of his five ideas? List the addition transitions and repeated words and phrases in the first sentences of paragraphs where you find transitions linking subject matter to be discussed with what has preceded it.

6. There are two headers used in this essay, but five topics examined. Should there be five distinct headings, or would this make the article more or less clear? Why, or why not?

About Style and Tone

7. "Not a fancy cocaine urn" (2), "old mainframe terminals kicking around at the office" (7): the author purposely makes some casual, sometimes humorous word-choices. Find at least two other examples of this stylistic and tonal choice. Why would Crosariol use such phrases, given the subject matter? Where would you likely find an article written in this style?

8. The title and the opening and closing sentences of any piece of writing are traditional points of emphasis. Readers respond especially to the information and tone in these sections. How are these areas of Crosariol's essay linked? What device unifies them? What is the effect of such linkage?

■ Writing Assignments

Assignment 1

Admit it. You too believe in "computer myths." You too probably endure some daily difficulties wrestling with the "insanely logical" Mr. Spock/Data of the technology world. Write an article for your college newspaper in which you classify under separate headings and discuss three of your most significant difficulties in dealing with computers. Within each section, write about the steps you took to overcome each problem. Remember that you are writing a column for a student paper; your title should be suitably eye-catching, and your tone, technical terms, and language geared to your audience.

Assignment 2

Computers are omnipresent in our lives today. We can't make the simplest purchase of gas or groceries without the information being entered on a terminal. Our books and newspapers are computer typeset. News reaches us at light-speed. We are able to type essays without seven hundred spelling errors. Computerized visual effects in films are dazzling. No one disputes the convenience and speed of information retrieval that computers have brought to our lives.

But what about the "down side" of computers? The possible loss of privacy in terms of personal information because of number-based access to our credit, employment, and parking-offence histories seems endless. The Internet gobbles up users' time and disseminates more unshaped and uncensored information than any human can possibly use. As Crosariol's article points out, there are simple problems with the rate of human absorption of information compared to the rate of technological growth.

Can we control computers, or do they already control us?

Write an essay in which you answer this question, based on your own experience and any possible outside reading. Confine your arguments to specific ideas and evidence so that your essay will be most persuasive.

Assignment 3

Write an essay which describes and corrects, with clear explanations, three "myths" or mistaken beliefs connected to some subject about which *you* are knowledgeable.

Here's to Your Health

Joan Dunayer

Dunayer contrasts the glamorous "myth" about alcohol, as presented in advertising and popular culture, with the reality—which is often far less appealing. After reading her essay, you will be more aware of how we are encouraged to think of alcohol as being tied to happiness and success. You may also become a more critical observer of images presented by advertisers.

As the only freshman on his high school's varsity wrestling team, Tod was anxious to fit 1
in with his older teammates. One night after a match, he was offered a tequila bottle on
the ride home. Tod felt he had to accept, or he would seem like a sissy. He took a swallow, and every time the bottle was passed back to him, he took another swallow. After
seven swallows, he passed out. His terrified teammates carried him into his home, and his
mother then rushed him to the hospital. After his stomach was pumped, Tod learned that
his blood alcohol level had been so high that he was lucky not to be in a coma or dead.

Although alcohol sometimes causes rapid poisoning, frequently leads to long-term 2
addiction, and always threatens self-control, our society encourages drinking. Many parents, by their example, give children the impression that alcohol is an essential ingredient of social gatherings. Peer pressure turns bachelor parties, fraternity initiations, and
spring-semester beach vacations into competitions in "getting trashed." In soap operas,
glamorous characters pour Scotch whiskey from crystal decanters as readily as most people turn on the faucet for tap water. In films and rock videos, trend-setters party in night-
clubs and bars. And who can recall a televised baseball or basketball game without a beer
commercial? By the age of 21, the average American has seen drinking on TV about
75,000 times. Alcohol ads appear with pounding frequency—in magazines, on billboards,
in college newspapers—contributing to a harmful myth about drinking.

Part of the myth is that liquor signals professional success. In a slick men's maga- 3
zine, one full-page ad for Scotch whiskey shows two men seated in an elegant restaurant. Both are in their thirties, perfectly groomed, and wearing expensive-looking gray
suits. The windows are draped with velvet, the table with spotless white linen. Each place-
setting consists of a long-stemmed water goblet, silver utensils, and thick silver plates.
On each plate is a half-empty cocktail glass. The two men are grinning and shaking hands,
as if they've just concluded a business deal. The caption reads, "The taste of success."

Contrary to what the liquor company would have us believe, drinking is more closely 4
related to lack of success than to achievement. Among students, the heaviest drinkers
have the lowest grades. In the work force, alcoholics are frequently late or absent, tend
to perform poorly, and often get fired. Although alcohol abuse occurs in all economic
classes, it remains most severe among the poor.

Another part of the alcohol myth is that drinking makes you more attractive to the 5
opposite sex. "Hot, hot, hot," one commercial's soundtrack begins, as the camera scans
a crowd of college-age beachgoers. Next it follows the curve of a woman's leg up to her
bare hip and lingers there. She is young, beautiful, wearing a bikini. A young guy, carrying an ice chest, positions himself near to where she sits. He is tan, muscular. She does-
n't show much interest—until he opens the chest and takes out a beer. Now she smiles
over at him. He raises his eyebrows and, invitingly, holds up another can. She joins him.
This beer, the song concludes, "attracts like no other."

Beer doesn't make anyone sexier. Like all alcohol, it lowers the levels of male hor- 6
mones in men and of female hormones in women—even when taken in small amounts.
In substantial amounts, alcohol can cause infertility in women and impotence in men.
Some alcoholic men even develop enlarged breasts, from their increased female hormones.

The alcohol myth also creates the illusion that beer and athletics are a perfect com- 7
bination. One billboard features three high-action images: a baseball player running at
top speed, a surfer riding a wave, and a basketball player leaping to make a dunk shot.
A particular light beer, the billboard promises, "won't slow you down."

"Slow you down" is exactly what alcohol does. Drinking plays a role in over six mil-   8
lion injuries each year—not counting automobile accidents. Even in small amounts, alcohol dulls the brain, reducing muscle coordination and slowing reaction time. It also
interferes with the ability to focus the eyes and adjust to a sudden change in brightness—
such as the flash of a car's headlights. Drinking and driving, responsible for over half of
all automobile deaths, is the leading cause of death among teenagers. Continued alcohol abuse can physically alter the brain, permanently impairing learning and memory.
Long-term drinking is related to malnutrition, weakening of the bones, and ulcers. It
increases the risk of liver failure, heart disease, and stomach cancer.

Finally, according to the myth fostered by the media in our culture, alcohol gener-   9
ates a warm glow of happiness that unifies the family. In one popular film, the only food
visible at a wedding reception is an untouched wedding cake, but beer, whiskey, and
vodka flow freely. Most of the guests are drunk. After shouting into the microphone to
get everyone's attention, the band leader asks the bride and groom to come forward. They
are presented with two wine-filled silver drinking cups branching out from a single stem.
"If you can drink your cups without spilling any wine," the band leader tells them, "you
will have good luck for the rest of your lives." The couple drain their cups without taking a breath, and the crowd cheers.

A marriage, however, is unlikely to be "lucky" if alcohol plays a major role in it.   10
Nearly two-thirds of domestic violence involves drinking. Alcohol abuse by parents is
strongly tied to child neglect and juvenile delinquency. Drinking during pregnancy can
lead to miscarriage and is a major cause of such birth defects as deformed limbs and mental retardation. Those who depend on alcohol are far from happy: over a fourth of the
patients in state and county mental institutions have alcohol problems; more than half of
all violent crimes are alcohol-related; the rate of suicide among alcoholics is fifteen times
higher than among the general population.

Alcohol, some would have us believe, is part of being successful, sexy, healthy, and   11
happy. But those who have suffered from it—directly or indirectly—know otherwise. For
alcohol's victims, "Here's to your health" rings with a terrible irony when it is accompanied by the clink of liquor glasses.

■ Reading Comprehension Questions

1. The word *caption* in "In a slick men's magazine, one full-page ad for Scotch
   whiskey shows two men seated in an elegant restaurant. . . . The caption
   reads 'the taste of success'" (paragraph 3) means
   a. menu.
   b. man.
   c. words accompanying the picture.
   d. contract that seals the business deal.

2. The word *impairing* in "Continued alcohol abuse can physically alter the
   brain, permanently impairing learning and memory" (paragraph 8) means
   a. postponing.

      b. doubling.

      c. damaging.

      d. teaching.

3. Which one of the following would be a good alternative title for this selection?
      a. The Taste of Success
      b. Alcohol and Your Social Life
      c. Too Much Tequila
      d. Alcohol: Image and Reality

4. Which sentence best expresses the main idea of the selection?
      a. Sports and alcohol don't mix.
      b. The media and our culture promote false images about success and happiness.
      c. The media and our culture promote false beliefs about alcohol.
      d. Liquor companies should not be allowed to use misleading ads about alcohol.

5. According to the selection, drinking can
      a. actually unify a family.
      b. lower hormone levels.
      c. temporarily improve performance in sports.
      d. increase the likelihood of pregnancy.

6. *True or false?* _____ Alcohol abuse is most severe among the middle class.

7. *True or false?* _____ The leading cause of death among teenagers is drinking and driving.

8. From the first paragraph of the essay, we can conclude that
      a. even one encounter with alcohol can actually lead to death.
      b. tequila is the worst type of alcohol to drink.
      c. wrestlers tend to drink more than other athletes.
      d. by the time students reach high school, peer pressure doesn't influence them.

9. *True or false?* _____ The author implies that one or two drinks a day are probably harmless.

10. The author implies that heavy drinking can lead to
      a. poor grades.
      b. getting fired.
      c. heart disease.
      d. all of the above.

■ Discussion Questions

About Content

1. According to Dunayer, how many parts are there to the myth about alcohol? Which part do you consider the most dangerous?
2. Drawing on your own experience, provide examples of ways in which our culture encourages drinking.

About Structure

3. What method does Dunayer use to begin her essay?
   a. Broad to narrow
   b. Idea that is contrary to what will be developed
   c. Incident
4. The body of Dunayer's essay is made up of four pairs of paragraphs (paragraphs 3 and 4; 5 and 6; 7 and 8; 9 and 10) that serve to introduce and develop each of her four main supporting points. What is the pattern by which she divides each point into two paragraphs?
5. Dunayer introduces the first part of the myth about alcohol with the words "Part of the myth is . . ." (See the first sentence of paragraph 3.) Then she goes on to use an addition transition to introduce each of the three other parts of the myth—in the first sentences of paragraphs 5, 7, and 9. Write those addition transitions here:

   _____   _____   _____

6. What method does Dunayer use to conclude her essay?
   a. Prediction or recommendation
   b. Summary and a final thought
   c. Thought-provoking question

About Style and Tone

7. Why is the title of the essay appropriate?

■ Writing Assignments

Assignment 1

Describe and analyze several recent advertisements for wine, beer, or liquor on television or radio, in newspapers or magazines, or on billboards. Argue whether the ads are socially and humanly responsible or irresponsible in the way that they portray drinking. Your thesis might be something like one of the following examples:

> In three recent ads, ad agencies and liquor companies have acted irresponsibly in their portrayal of alcohol.
>
> In three recent ads, ad agencies and liquor companies have acted with a measure of responsibility in their portrayal of alcohol.

Alternatively, write about what you consider responsible or irresponsible advertising for some other product or service: cigarettes, weight loss, and cosmetics are possibilities to consider.

Assignment 2

If you have a friend, relative, or classmate who drinks a lot, write a letter warning him or her about the dangers of alcohol. If appropriate, use information from Dunayer's essay. Remember that since your purpose is to get someone you care about to control or break a dangerous habit, you should make your writing very personal. Don't bother explaining how alcoholism affects people in general. Instead, focus directly on what you see it doing to your reader.

Divide your argument into at least three supporting paragraphs. You might, for instance, talk about how your reader is jeopardizing his or her relationship with three of the following: family, friends, boss and co-workers, teachers and classmates.

Assignment 3

Dunayer describes how alcohol advertisements promote false beliefs, such as the idea that alcohol will make you successful. Imagine that you work for a public service ad agency given the job of presenting the negative side of alcohol. What images would you choose to include in your ads?

Write a report to your boss in which you propose in detail three anti-alcohol ads. Choose from among the following:

> An ad counteracting the idea that alcohol leads to success
> An ad counteracting the idea that alcohol is sexy
> An ad counteracting the idea that alcohol goes well with athletics
> An ad counteracting the idea that alcohol makes for happy families

Coffee

Alan Durning

Is there a mug of coffee in your hand as you read this page? Have you ever stopped to think about what went into that mug before it reached your hands? You may have gone as far as to grind the beans, measure the coffee, pour the water into the tank of the coffee maker, place a filter in the machine's basket, and then turn on the power, but where did the ingredients themselves come from? How did they reach you? In his essay, Alan Durning "deconstructs" a simple cup of coffee into its basic elements and traces them back to their origins. In this "reverse process essay," we see the complex nature of an everyday substance.

Beans

I brewed a cup of coffee. It took 100 beans—about one fortieth of the beans that grew 1 on the coffee tree that year. The tree was on a small mountain farm in the region of Colombia called Antioquia. The region was cleared of its native forests in the first coffee boom three generations ago. These "cloud forests" are among the world's most endangered ecosystems.

The beans ripened in the shade of taller trees. Growing them did not require plow- 2 ing the soil, but it did take several doses of insecticides, which were synthesized in factories in the Rhine River Valley of Europe. Some of the chemicals entered the respiratory systems of farm workers. Others washed downstream and were absorbed by plants and animals.

The beans were picked by hand. In a diesel powered crusher they were removed from 3 the fruit that encased them. They were dried under the sun and shipped to New Orleans in a 132 pound bag. The freighter was fueled by Venezuelan oil and made in Japan. The shipyard built the freighter out of Korean steel. The Korean steel mill used iron mined on tribal lands in Papua New Guinea.

At New Orleans the beans were roasted for 13 minutes at temperatures above 400 4 degrees F. The roaster burned natural gas pumped from the ground in Oklahoma. The beans were packaged in four-layer bags constructed of polyethylene, nylon, aluminum foil and polyester. They were trucked to a Seattle warehouse and later to a retail store.

Bag

I carried the beans out of the grocery in a brown paper bag made at an unbleached kraft 5 paper mill in Oregon. I transported them home in an automobile that burned one sixth of a gallon of gasoline during the five mile round-trip to the market.

Grinder

In the kitchen, I measured the beans in a disposable plastic scoop molded in New Jersey   6
and spooned them into the grinder. The grinder was assembled in China from imported
steel, aluminum, copper, and plastic parts. It was powered by electricity generated at the
Ross Dam on the Skagit River.

I dumped the coffee into a gold-plated mesh filter made in Switzerland of Russian   7
ore. I put the filter into a plastic-and-steel drip coffee maker.

I poured eight ounces of tap water into the appliance. The water came by pipe from   8
the Cedar River on the west slope of the Cascade Mountains. An element heated the water
to more than 200 degrees F. The hot water seeped through the ground coffee and dissolved
some of its oils and solids. The brew trickled into a glass carafe.

Paper Cup

The coffee mugs were all dirty so I poured the coffee into a paper cup. The cup was made   9
from bleached wood pulp in Arkansas. A fraction of the chlorine in the bleach was discharged
from the pulp mill into the Arkansas River. In the river, the chlorine ended up as TCDD,
which is often simply called dioxin. It is the most carcinogenic substance known.

Cream

I stirred in one ounce of cream. The cream came from a grain-fed dairy cow in the low-   10
lands north of Seattle. The cow liked to graze on a stream bank and walk in the stream.
This muddied the water and made life difficult for native trout.

The cow's manure was rich in nitrogen and phosphorus. The soils of the pasture   11
where the cow grazed were unable to absorb these quickly enough, so they washed into
the stream when it rained. The infusion of nutrients fertilized algae, which absorbed a
larger share of the oxygen dissolved in the water. The shortage of oxygen made life more
difficult for native trout.

Sugar

I measured out two tablespoons of sugar. It came from the canefields south of Lake   12
Okeechobee in Florida. These plantations have deprived the Everglades of water, endan-
gering waterfowl and reptile populations.

■ Reading Comprehension Questions

1. The word *synthesized* in "several doses of insecticides, which were synthe-
    sized in factories in the Rhine River Valley of Europe" (paragraph 2) means
    a. processed.
    b. manufactured.
    c. combined.
    d. packaged.

2. The word *infusion* in "The infusion of nutrients fertilized algae, which absorbed a larger share of the oxygen dissolved in the water" (paragraph 11) means
   a. pollution.
   b. instilling.
   c. formula.
   d. combination.

3. Which one of the following would make a good alternative title for this selection?
   a. Eco-Disaster in the A.M.
   b. Juan Valdez or the Exxon Valdez?
   c. The Whole World in Your Pot
   d. Your Daily Cup of Toxins

4. Which statement best expresses the main idea of the selection?
   a. No single item in our world is detachable from other aspects of existence.
   b. The production of coffee entails many polluting and harmful processes.
   c. Everything is more complex than it first seems.
   d. All foods are ecologically disastrous to manufacture.

5. According to the selection,
   a. destruction of Colombian rainforests is the most disastrous effect of coffee-growing and production.
   b. coffee production is a totally automated process.
   c. producing coffee is a combination of agriculture, human labour, and technical expertise.
   d. world resources are being depleted to produce coffee.

6. *True or false?* _____ All the paper products mentioned by the author create toxic substances in their manufacture.

7. *True or false?* _____ The normal habits of a dairy cow affect the balance of the ecology.

8. From the first three paragraphs of the article, we can conclude that the author
   a. feels nothing but environmentally based guilt about making his cup of coffee.
   b. worries too much about problems caused by coffee production.
   c. feels sorry for the farm labourers involved in coffee growing.
   d. understands both the industrial problems and the global trade inter-connections in coffee production.

9. *True or false?* _____ All instances of water pollution in the essay arise from industrial waste.

10. We might infer that the author
    a. believes we often don't know when we are harming the environment.
    b. believes we don't care about pollution or Third World industrial oppression.
    c. is careful to use only "ecologically safe," "nonexploitive" products.
    d. puts all the blame for ecological imbalances on human beings.

■ Discussion Questions

About Content

1. In the opening paragraphs of his essay, the author points out two major industrially caused ecological problems. What are they? Which would seem the more harmful to you, and why?

2. How many countries does it take to produce Alan Durning's cup of coffee? How many American states are needed to assist in the process? What do these numbers tell you about products we use every day?

About Structure

3. This essay "deconstructs" a cup of coffee. If this is a "process essay in reverse," which method of introduction has the author used "in reverse"?
   a. Stating the importance of the topic
   b. Starting with an opposite
   c. Going from broad to narrow

4. Durning divides his essay into sections with sparse headings. Does each section cover only the subject named by its title? If not, which sections cover more than one subject? Why?

5. This is a rare example of a process essay almost devoid of simple or obvious transitions. If there are no ordinary "connecting word" transitions, what rhetorical device has the author used in their place? What method of ordering ideas common to all process writing has the author used? Does this method help you to follow the sequence of ideas? How?

About Style and Tone

6. Durning's style in "Coffee" is as plain and severe as his title. How many sentences are simple statements starting with "I"? What is the effect of this style on you as a reader? Is the information conveyed by the essay as uncomplicated as the style?

7. Writers with strong biases or social concerns are often accused of being unfair or overbearing because of the vehement tone of their work. Alan Durning is

a prominent environmentalist. Does his tone "suffocate" or badger the reader? Are there "objective" concepts in the essay? Is the article calm enough to allow the reader room to consider their own point of view? If so, how is this achieved?

■ Writing Assignments

Assignment 1

Coffee is an ordinary product with a fascinating story behind it. How much do any of us know about everyday foods and beverages? Choose one fairly simple item, preferably one whose package does not have thousands of untraceable chemicals, and do some research into the origins of its ingredients. Phone the manufacturer or consult your library to find out where its ingredients originate.

Write a descriptive or explanatory process essay about the history and the geographical origins of the raw materials in your chosen product. Place the ingredients in three groups for ease of paragraphing. You should organize your essay as Durning has done, starting "from the end" and taking your product apart piece by piece. You may choose to start with either the largest or the smallest of its ingredients, depending on the order you feel your reader will find most interesting.

Assignment 2

If our world is shrinking and we are all interdependent, why do we still drink coffee and drive fossil fuel powered cars? Many manufacturers and retailers would like the public to believe that they are doing their best to preserve the world's ecological balance. Are their claims sincere or just more sophisticated marketing tactics? Will concern for the world's biological condition ever change business? Will damage to the world's ecosystems force business to change its methods?

Write an essay in which you either defend the efforts of one "world-conscious" company or argue that such efforts are merely a way of "jumping on the bandwagon." Justify your argument logically, and make use of some objective information from your own knowledge or from outside reading.

Assignment 3

Your have chosen to write an article for the "World Watch" column in your college newspaper. Your article describes three specific ways in which college students could be active in improving their college and local environment. Your column may extend each example to a relevant global concern.

The Motive for Metaphor

Northrop Frye

Nearly every college student wants to know why they have to "take English."
Nearly every college instructor has several answers to this question. Beyond
responses based on practical matters like learning to assemble a resume or
write business and technical formats, the question "why take English?" splits
into two separate questions: why study the language, and why study literature?
The eminent and world-famous Canadian scholar Northrop Frye has several
answers for these questions in the essay which follows. The answers are
surprisingly practical, and interestingly tied to the business of survival.

For the past twenty-five years I have been teaching and studying English literature in a   1
university. As in any other job, certain questions stick in one's mind, not because people keep asking them, but because they're the questions inspired by the very fact of being
in such a place. What good is the study of literature? Does it help us to think more clearly,
or feel more sensitively, or live a better life than we could without it? What is the function of the teacher and scholar, or of the person who calls himself, as I do, a literary critic?
What difference does the study of literature make in our social or political or religious
attitude? In my early days I thought very little about such questions, not because I had
any of the answers, but because I assumed that anybody who asked them was naïve. I
think now that the simplest questions are not only the hardest to answer, but the most
important to ask, so I'm going to raise them and try to suggest what my present answers
are. I say try to suggest, because there are only more or less adequate answers to such
questions—there aren't any right answers. The kind of problem that literature raises is
not the kind that you ever 'solve'. Whether my answers are any good or not, they represent a fair amount of thinking about the questions. As I can't see my audience, I have to
choose my rhetorical style in the dark, and I'm taking the classroom style, because an
audience of students is the one I feel easiest with.

There are two things in particular that I want to discuss with you. In school, and in   2
university, there's a subject called 'English' in English-speaking countries. English
means, in the first place, the mother tongue. As that, it's the most practical subject in the
world: you can't understand anything, or take part in your society without it. Wherever
illiteracy is a problem, it's as fundamental a problem as getting enough to eat or a place
to sleep. The native language takes precedence over every other subject of study: nothing else can compare with it in usefulness. But then you find that every mother tongue,
in any developed or civilized society, turns into something called literature. If you keep
on studying 'English', you find yourself trying to read Shakespeare and Milton.
Literature, we're told, is one of the arts, along with painting and music, and, after you've

looked up all the hard words and the Classical allusions and learned what words like imagery and diction are supposed to mean, what you use in understanding it, or so you're told, is your imagination. Here you don't seem to be in quite the same practical, and useful area: Shakespeare and Milton, whatever their merits, are not the kind of thing you must know to hold any place in society at all. A person who knows nothing about literature may be an ignoramus, but many people don't mind being that. Every child realizes that literature is taking him in a different direction from the immediately useful, and a good many children complain loudly about this. Two questions I want to deal with, then, are, first: what is the relation of English as the mother tongue to English as a literature? Second: what is the social value of the study of literature, and what is the place of the imagination that literature addresses itself to, in the learning process?

Let's start with the different ways there are of dealing with the world we're living in. Suppose you're shipwrecked on an uninhabited island in the South Seas. The first thing you do is to take a long look at the world around you, a world of sky and sea and earth and stars and trees and hills. You see this world as objective, as something set over against you and not yourself or related to you in any way. And you notice two things about this objective world. In the first place, it doesn't have any conversation. It's full of animals and plants and insects going on with their own business, but there's nothing that responds to you: it has no morals and no intelligence, or at least none that you can grasp. It may have a shape and a meaning, but it doesn't seem to be a human shape or a human meaning. Even if there's enough to eat and no dangerous animals, you feel lonely and frightened and unwanted in such a world.

In the second place, you find that looking at the world, as something set over against you, splits your mind in two. You have an intellect that feels curious about it and wants to study it, and you have feelings or emotions that see it as beautiful or austere or terrible. You know that both these attitudes have some reality, at least for you. If the ship you were wrecked in was a Western ship, you'd probably feel that your intellect tells you more about what's really there in the outer world, and that your emotions you more about what's going on inside you. If your background were Oriental, you'd be more likely to reverse this and say that the beauty or terror was what was really there, and that your instinct to count and classify and measure and pull to pieces was what was inside your mind. But whether your point of view is Western or Eastern, intellect and emotion never get together in your mind as long as you're simply looking at the world. They alternate, and keep you divided between them.

The language you use on this level of the mind is the language of consciousness or awareness. It's largely a language of nouns and adjectives. You have to have names for things, and you need qualities like 'wet' or 'green' or 'beautiful' to describe how things seem to you. This is the speculative or contemplative position of the mind, the position in which the arts and sciences begin, although they don't stay there very long. The sciences begin by accepting the facts and the evidence about an outside world without trying to alter them. Science proceeds by accurate measurement and description, and follows the demands of the reason rather than the emotions. What it deals with is there, whether we like it or not. The emotions are unreasonable: for them it's what they like and don't like that comes first. We'd be naturally inclined to think that the arts follow the path of emotion, in contrast to the sciences. Up to a point they do, but there's a complicating factor.

That complicating factor is the contrast between 'I like this' and 'I don't like this'. 6
In this Robinson Crusoe life I've assigned you, you may have moods of complete peacefulness and joy, moods when you accept your island and everything around you. You wouldn't have such moods very often, and when you had them, they'd be moods of identification, when you felt that the island was a part of you and you a part of it. That is not the feeling of consciousness or awareness, where you feel split off from everything that's not your perceiving self. Your habitual state of mind is the feeling of separation which goes with being conscious, and the feeling 'this is not a part of me' soon becomes 'this is not what I want'. Notice the word 'want': we'll be coming back to it.

So you soon realize that there's a difference between the world you're living in and 7
world you want to live in. The world you want to live in is a human world, not an objective one: it's not an environment but a home; it's not the world you see but the world you build out of what you see. You go to work to build a shelter or plant a garden, and as soon as you start to work you've moved into a different level of human life. You're not separating only yourself from nature now, but constructing a human world and separating it from the rest of the world. Your intellect and emotions are now both engaged in the same activity, so there's no longer any real distinction between them. As soon as you plant a garden or a crop, you develop the conception of a 'weed', the plant you don't want in there. But you can't say that 'weed' is either an intellectual or an emotional conception, because it's both at once. Further, you go to work because you feel you have to, and because you want something at the end of the work. That means that the important categories of your life are no longer the subject and the object, the watcher and the things being watched: the important categories are what you have to do and what you want to do—in other words, necessity and freedom.

One person by himself is not a complete human being, so I'll provide you with 8
another shipwrecked refugee of the opposite sex and an eventual family. Now you're a member of a human society. This human society after a while will transform the island into something with a human shape. What that human shape is, is revealed in the shape of the work you do: the buildings, such as they are, the paths through the woods, the planted crops fenced off against whatever animals want to eat them. These things, these rudiments of city, highway, garden and farm, are the human form of nature, or the form of human nature, whichever you like. This is the area of the applied arts and sciences, and it appears in our society as engineering and agriculture and medicine and architecture. In this area we can never say clearly where the art stops and the science begins, or vice versa.

The language you use on this level is the language of practical sense, a language of 9
verbs or words of action and movement. The practical world, however, is a world where actions speak louder than words. In some ways it's a higher level of existence than the speculative level, because it's doing something about the world instead of just looking at it, but in itself it's a much more primitive level. It's the process of adapting to the environment, or rather of transforming the environment in the interests of one species, that goes on among animals and plants as well as human beings. The animals have a good

many of our practical skills: some insects make pretty fair architects, and beavers know quite a lot about engineering. In this island, probably, and certainly if you were alone, you'd have about the ranking of a second-rate animal. What makes our practical life really human is a third level of the mind, a level where consciousness and practical skill come together.

This third level is a vision or model in your mind of what you want to construct. 1C There's that word 'want' again. The actions of man are prompted by desire, and some of these desires are needs, like food and warmth and shelter. One of these needs is sexual, the desire to reproduce and bring more human beings into existence. But there's also a desire to bring a social human form into existence: the form of cities and gardens and farms that we call civilization. Many animals and insects have this social form too, but man knows that he has it: he can compare what he does with what he can imagine being done. So we begin to see where the imagination belongs in the scheme of human affairs. It's the power of constructing possible models of human experience. In the world of the imagination, anything goes that's imaginatively possible, but nothing really happens. If it did happen, it would move out of the world of imagination into the world of action.

We have three levels of the mind now, and a language for each of them, which in 1 English-speaking societies means an English for each of them. There's the level of consciousness and awareness, where the most important thing is the difference between me and everything else. The English of this level is the English of ordinary conversation, which is mostly monologue, as you'll soon realize if you do a bit of eavesdropping, or listening to yourself. We can call it the language of self-expression. Then there's the level of social participation, the working or technological language of teachers and preachers and politicians and advertisers and lawyers and journalists and scientists. We've already called this the language of practical sense. Then there's the level of imagination, which produces the literary language of poems and plays and novels. They're not really different languages, of course, but three different reasons for using words.

On this basis, perhaps, we can distinguish the arts from the sciences. Science begins 1. with the world we have to live in, accepting its data and trying to explain its laws. From there, it moves towards the imagination: it becomes a mental construct, a model of a possible way of interpreting experience. The further it goes in this direction, the more it tends to speak the language of mathematics, which is really one of the languages of the imagination, along with literature and music. Art, on the other hand, begins with the world we construct, not with the world we see. It starts with the imagination, and then works towards ordinary experience: that is, it tries to make itself as convincing and recognizable as it can. You can see why we tend to think of the sciences as intellectual and the arts as emotional: one starts with the world as it is, the other with the world we want to have. Up to a point it is true that science gives all intellectual view of reality, and that the arts try to make the emotions as precise and disciplined as sciences do the intellect. But of course it's nonsense to think of the scientist as a cold unemotional reasoner and the artist as somebody who's in a perpetual emotional tizzy. You can't distinguish the arts from the sciences by the mental processes the people in them use: they both operate on a mixture of hunch and common sense. A highly developed science and a highly developed art are very close together, psychologically and otherwise.

Still, the fact that they start from opposite ends, even if they do meet in the middle, 13
makes for one important difference between them. Science learns more and more about
the world as it goes on: it evolves and improves. A physicist today knows more physics
than Newton did, even if he's not as great a scientist. But literature begins with the possible model of experience, and what it produces is the literary model we call the classic.
Literature doesn't evolve or improve or progress. We may have dramatists in the future
who will write plays as good as *King Lear*, though they'll be very different ones, but
drama as a whole will never get better than *King Lear*. *King Lear* is it, as far as drama
is concerned; so is *Oedipus Rex*, written two thousand years earlier than that, and both
will be models of dramatic writing as long as the human race endures. Social conditions
may improve: most of us would rather live in nineteenth-century United States than in
thirteenth-century Italy, and for most of us Whitman's celebration of democracy makes
a lot more sense than Dante's Inferno. But it doesn't follow that Whitman is a better poet
than Dante: literature won't line up with that kind of improvement.

So we find that everything that does improve, including science, leaves the literary 14
artist out in the cold. Writers don't seem to benefit much by the advance of science,
although they thrive on superstitions of all kinds. And you certainly wouldn't turn to contemporary poets for guidance or leadership in the twentieth-century world. You'd hardly
go to Ezra Pound, with his fascism and social credit and Confucianism and anti-
semitism. Or to Yeats, with his spiritualism and fairies and astrology. Or to D. H.
Lawrence, who'll tell you that it's a good thing for servants to be flogged because that
restores the precious current of blood-reciprocity between servant and master. Or to
T. S. Eliot, who'll tell you that to have a flourishing culture we should educate an élite,
keep most people living in the same spot, and never disestablish the Church of England.
The novelists seem to be a little closer to the world they're living in, but not much. When
Communists talk about the decadence of bourgeois culture, this is the kind of thing they
always bring up. Their own writers don't seem to be any better, though; just duller. So
the real question is a bigger one. Is it possible that literature, especially poetry, is something that a scientific civilization like ours will eventually outgrow? Man has always
wanted to fly, and thousands of years ago he was making sculptures of winged bulls and
telling stories about people who flew so high on artificial wings that the sun melted them
off. In an Indian play fifteen hundred years old, *Sakuntala*, there's a god who flies around
in a chariot that to a modern reader sounds very much like a private aeroplane. Interesting
that the writer had so much imagination, but do we need such stories now that we have
private aeroplanes?

This is not a new question: it was raised a hundred and fifty years ago by Thomas 15
Love Peacock, who was a poet and novelist himself, and a very brilliant one. He wrote
an essay called *Four Ages of Poetry*, with his tongue of course in his cheek, in which he
said that poetry was the mental rattle that awakened the imagination of mankind in its
infancy, but that now, in an age of science and technology, the poet has outlived his social
function. 'A poet in our times,' said Peacock 'is a semi-barbarian in a civilized community. He lives in the days that are past. His ideas, thoughts, feelings, associations, are all
with barbarous manners, obsolete customs, and exploded superstitions. The march of his
intellect is like that of a crab, backwards.' Peacock's essay annoyed his friend Shelley,

who wrote another essay called *A Defence of Poetry* to refute it. Shelley's essay is a wonderful piece of writing, but it's not likely to convince anyone who needs convincing. I shall be spending a good deal of my time on this question of the relevance of literature in the world of today, and I can only indicate the general lines my answer will take. There are two points I can make now, one simple, the other more difficult.

The simple point is that literature belongs to the world man constructs, not to the 16
world he sees; to his home, not his environment. Literature's world is a concrete human world of immediate experience. The poet uses images and objects and sensations much more than he uses abstract ideas; the novelist is concerned with telling stories, not with working out arguments. The world of literature is human in shape, a world where the sun rises in the east and sets in the west over the edge of a flat earth in three dimensions, where the primary realities are not atoms or electrons but bodies, and the primary forces not energy or gravitation but love and death and passion and joy. It's not surprising if writers are often rather simple people, not always what we think of as intellectuals, and certainly not always any freer of silliness or perversity than anyone else. What concerns us is what they produce, not what they are, and poetry, according to Milton, who ought to have known, is 'more simple, sensuous and passionate' than philosophy or science.

The more difficult point takes us back to what we said when we were on that South 17
Sea island. Our emotional reaction to the world varies from 'I like this' to 'I don't like this'. The first, we said, was a state of identity, a feeling that everything around us was part of us, and the second is the ordinary state of consciousness, or separation, where art and science begin. Art begins as soon as 'I don't like this' turns·into 'this is not the way I could imagine it'. We notice in passing that the creative and the neurotic minds have a lot in common. They're both dissatisfied with what they see; they both believe that something else ought to be there, and they try to pretend it is there or to make it be there. The differences are more important, but we're not ready for them yet.

At the level of ordinary consciousness the individual man is the centre of everything, 18
surrounded on all sides by what he isn't. At the level of practical sense, or civilization, there's a human circumference, a little cultivated world with a human shape, fenced off from the jungle and inside the sea and the sky. But in the imagination anything goes that can be imagined, and the limit of the imagination is a totally human world. Here we recapture, in full consciousness, that original lost sense of identity with our surroundings, where there is nothing outside the mind of man, or something identical with the mind of man. Religions present us with visions of eternal and infinite heavens or paradises which have the form of the cities and gardens of human civilization, like the Jerusalem and Eden of the Bible, completely separated from the state of frustration and misery that bulks so large in ordinary life. We're not concerned with these visions as religion, but they indicate what the limits of the imagination are. They indicate too that in the human world the imagination has no limits, if you follow me. We said that the desire to fly produced the aeroplane. But people don't get into planes because they want to fly; they get into planes because they want to get somewhere else faster. What's produced the aeroplane is not so much a desire to fly as a rebellion against the tyranny of time and space. And that's a process that can never stop, no matter how high our Titovs and Glenns may go.

For each of these six talks I've taken a title from some work of literature, and my title   19
for this one is 'The Motive for Metaphor', from a poem of Wallace Stevens. Here's the poem:

> You like it under the trees in autumn,
> Because everything is half dead.
> The wind moves like a cripple among the leaves
> And repeats words without meaning.
>
> In the same way, you were happy in spring,
> With the half colors of quarter-things,
> The slightly brighter sky, the melting clouds,
> The single bird, the obscure moon—
>
> The obscure moon lighting an obscure world
> Of things that would never be quite expressed,
> Where you yourself were never quite yourself
> And did not want nor have to be,
>
> Desiring the exhilarations of changes:
> The motive for metaphor, shrinking from
> The weight of primary noon,
> The A B C of being
>
> The ruddy temper, the hammer
> Of red and blue, the hard sound—
> Steel against intimation—the sharp flash,
> The vital, arrogant, fatal, dominant X.

What Stevens calls the weight of primary noon, the A B C of being, and the dominant X
is the objective world, the world set over against us. Outside literature, the main motive
for writing is to describe this world. But literature itself uses language in a way which
associates our minds with it. As soon as you use associative language, you begin using
figures of speech. If you say this talk is dry and dull, you're using figures associating it
with bread and breadknives. There are two main kinds of association, analogy and identity, two things that are like each other and two things that are each other. You can say
with Burns, 'My love's like a red, red rose', or you can say with Shakespeare:

> Thou that art now the world's fresh ornament
> And only herald to the gaudy spring.

One produces the figure of speech called the simile; the other produces the figure called
metaphor.

In descriptive writing you have to be careful of associative language. You'll find that   20
analogy, or likeness to something else, is very tricky to handle in description, because
the differences are as important as the resemblances. As for metaphor, where you're really
saying 'this is that', you're turning your back on logic and reason completely, because

logically two things can never be the same thing and still remain two things. The poet, however, uses these two crude, primitive, archaic forms of thought in the most uninhibited way, because his job is not to describe nature, but to show you a world completely absorbed and possessed by the human mind. So he produces what Baudelaire called a 'suggestive magic including at the same time object and subject, the world outside the artist and the artist himself'. The motive for metaphor, according to Wallace Stevens, is a desire to associate, and finally to identify, the human mind with what goes on outside it, because the only genuine joy you can have is in those rare moments when you feel that although we may know in part, as Paul says, we are also a part of what we know.

■ Reading Comprehension Questions

1. The word *speculative* in "This is the speculative or contemplative position of the mind, the position in which the arts and sciences begin" (paragraph 5) means
   a. studious.
   b. guessing.
   c. thinking.
   d. decisive.

2. The word *archaic* in "The poet, however, uses these two crude, primitive, archaic forms of thought in the most uninhibited way" (paragraph 20) means
   a. useless.
   b. pointless.
   c. outmoded.
   d. unrelated.

3. Which of the following would be a good alternative title for this selection?
   a. Language and Living
   b. The Logic of Literature
   c. Words to Shape Worlds
   d. The Uses of Poetry

4. Which sentence best expresses the main idea of the selection?
   a. Literature is a practical and imaginative attempt to recreate our "home" world.
   b. Literature cannot evolve because it is limited by mortal artists' opinions.
   c. Literature is based on emotion and imagination, and science on logic.
   d. Literature and neurosis both begin with dissatisfaction with their surroundings.

5. The simplest questions asked by Frye's students
   a. are asked by naive students.
   b. have too many possible answers.
   c. are most difficult to answer because they are the most important.
   d. are those for which he has no answers.

6. *True or false?* _____ The study of the English language is important, but not necessary for daily life.

7. The Western mind
   a. uses its feelings and intellect equally to understand the world.
   b. tends to value analysis of the external world over internal emotional response.
   c. realizes that feelings describe the world more accurately than intellect.
   d. believes that rational approaches to external reality are the only valid ones.

8. The author implies that
   a. work is a natural result of human desires and evolution.
   b. work involves only the physical and intellectual sides of humanity.
   c. work is an externally imposed method of limiting human freedom.
   d. work is done only because we feel we have to do it.

9. The author implies that the world of practical creation
   a. is better left to other animals.
   b. involves distinctly human activity, based on action and conscious awareness.
   c. has little use for the passive powers of the imagination.
   d. is based on satisfying our basic needs for food, shelter, and companionship.

10. The author implies that art and literature
    a. begin in neurotic displeasure with reality.
    b. belong only to the world within our imaginations.
    c. place humans at the centre of creation.
    d. are attempts to re-unite ourselves with the immediacy of reality.

■ **Discussion Questions**

About Content

1. Why does Frye say that literature is difficult to approach? Why do people sometimes find it annoying? What are your own thoughts about literature?

2. What are the three levels of language Frye describes? What is the origin of each level? Who uses which "language," and for what purposes?

3. What is the motivation behind types of writing other than literature? What is the problem with using figures of speech?

About Structure

4. "The Motive for Metaphor" was originally part of a radio broadcast series. Given this fact, does the first paragraph adequately introduce the author's sub-

ject matter and prepare the audience for what follows? Which methods of introduction are present in the first paragraph?

5. Where do you find the essay's thesis statement? _____ What is Frye's thesis? Which of the four questions asked in the opening paragraph does the thesis statement most nearly answer?

6. Choose four paragraphs from the essay and find their topic sentences. Do they always occur at the beginning of Frye's paragraphs? Would changing the order of the sentences make some paragraphs easier to understand? How?

About Style and Tone

7. The author states that, because he is addressing an unseen audience, he chooses "the classroom style" because it's the most comfortable for him. Which rhetorical elements of teaching do you find in this essay?
   a. enumeration
   b. question and answer patterns
   c. definition and explanation
   d. repetition for emphasis

   Do these stylistic choices make the essay's subject clearer? Easier to grasp? How?

8. Although Frye, as an English professor, may refer to poets with whom you may not be familiar, is his vocabulary suitable for a wider audience? Is his tone academic and dry, or direct and fairly casual? Give examples which support your opinions.

9. Does the author's placing you on an imaginary "desert island" enable you to see his ideas more clearly? How?

■ Writing Assignments

Assignment 1

Why study English as language? Northrop Frye makes a very direct claim for its importance: "it's the most practical subject in the world: you can't understand anything, or take part in your society without it. Wherever illiteracy is a problem, it's as fundamental a problem as getting enough to eat or a place to sleep . . . nothing else can compare with it in usefulness." (2)

Consider the plight of Garry Engkent's mother in "Why My Mother Can't Speak English" as it relates to Frye's statement. If this statement is valid, then the better we are able to use English, the better we should be able to manage our lives.

Write an essay which explains your own views about the importance of learning to use the English language well. What aspects of your life are affected by your command of English, by your ability to express yourself clearly in speech, and in writing? Be sure to use specific examples to back up your point of view.

Assignment 2

If literature doesn't improve or progress, what use is it? Why should we read at all? Think of your most honest answers to this question.

Try two brainstorming lists based on the following example:

Reading pro's	**Reading con's**
– learning about other people's lives	– a waste of time I could spend
– relaxation, distraction	on hobbies, or with friends
– favourite authors always please me	– too difficult; prefer TV or movies
– see other places and other sides	– too isolated when reading; I
of life	like people

Many students will find they have both positive and negative responses to the idea of reading. Look at your list and decide where your strongest feelings and reasons lie. Write a thesis statement based on the three strongest ideas: either pro or con, or a mixture of both. Now construct an essay which defends and explains your feelings about the usefulness of reading to you.

Assignment 3

If, as Frye states, artists are limited to commenting on life and scientists improve human existence, whose ideal world or utopia would you prefer, and why? Write an essay in which you create and explain a "utopia" run *either* by artists *or* by scientists.

In Praise of the Humble Comma

Pico Iyer

Punctuation is usually a subject of considerable annoyance to students. Its rules, which have bedevilled generations of students, are not even hallowed by the passage of time. Most contemporary punctuation is a product of the age of mechanized print and, as Iyer notes, has been used consistently for only one hundred years. Shakespeare barely bothered to punctuate, and contemporary writers toy with abandoning punctuation altogether. To the consternation of those learning English, punctuation is not even consistent among different languages. Only English teachers and Internet addresses require correct punctuation. Despite its relative unpopularity, Pico Iyer finds much to celebrate and value in punctuation; he likens it to musical notation and its careful use to "a labor of love" which adds finesse and meaning to human communication.

The gods, they say, give breath, and they take it away. But the same could be said— 1 could it not?—of the humble comma. Add it to the present clause, and, of a sudden, the mind is, quite literally, given pause to think; take it out if you wish or forget it and the mind is deprived of a resting place. Yet still the comma gets no respect. It seems just a slip of a thing, a pedant's tick, a blip on the edge of our consciousness, a kind of printer's smudge almost. Small, we claim, is beautiful (especially in the age of the micro-chip). Yet what is so often used, and so rarely recalled, as the comma—unless it be breath itself?

Punctuation, one is taught, has a point: to keep up law and order. Punctuation marks 2 are the road signs placed along the highway of our communication—to control speeds, provide directions and prevent head-on collisions. A period has the unblinking finality of a red light; the comma is a flashing yellow light that asks us only to slow down; and the semicolon is a stop sign that tells us to ease gradually to a halt, before gradually starting up again. By establishing the relations between words, punctuation establishes the relations between the people using words. That may be one reason why schoolteachers exalt it and lovers defy it ("We love each other and belong to each other let's don't ever hurt each other Nicole let's don't ever hurt each other," wrote Gary Gilmore to his girl-friend). A comma, he must have known, "separates inseparables," in the clinching words of H. W. Fowler, King of English Usage.

Punctuation, then, is a civic prop, a pillar that holds society upright. (A run-on sen- 3 tence, its phrases piling up without division, is as unsightly as a sink piled high with dirty dishes.) Small wonder, then, that punctuation was one of the first proprieties of the Victorian age, the age of the corset, that the modernists threw off: the sexual revolution might be said to have begun when Joyce's Molly Bloom spilled out all her private thoughts in 36 pages of unbridled, almost unperioded and officially censored prose; and another rebellion was surely marked when e. e. cummings first felt free to commit "God" to the lower case.

Punctuation thus becomes the signature of cultures. The hot-blooded Spaniard 4 seems to be revealed in the passion and urgency of his doubled exclamation points and question marks (*"¡Caramba! ¿Quien sabe?"*), while the impassive Chinese traditionally added to his so-called inscrutability by omitting directions from his ideograms. The anarchy and commotion of the '60s were given voice in the exploding exclamation marks, riotous capital letters and Day-Glo italics of Tom Wolfe's spray-paint prose; and in

Communist societies, where the State is absolute, the dignity—and divinity—of capital letters is reserved for Ministries, Sub-Committees and Secretariats.

Yet punctuation is something more than a culture's birthmark: it scores the music in our minds, gets our thoughts moving to the rhythm of our hearts. Punctuation is the notation in the sheet music of our words, telling us when to rest, or when to raise our voices; it acknowledges that the meaning of our discourse, as of any symphonic composition, lies not in the units but in the pauses, the pacing and the phrasing. Punctuation is the way one bats one's eyes, lowers one's voice or blushes demurely. Punctuation adjusts the tone and color and volume till the feeling comes into perfect focus: not disgust exactly, but distaste; not lust, or like, but love. 5

Punctuation, in short, gives us the human voice, and all the meanings that lie between the words. "You aren't young, are you?" loses its innocence when it loses the question mark. Every child knows the menace of a dropped apostrophe (the parent's "Don't do that" shifting into the more slowly enunciated "Do not do that"), and every believer, the ignominy of having his faith reduced to "faith." Add an exclamation point to "To be or not to be . . ." and the gloomy Dane has all the resolve he needs; add a comma, and the noble sobriety of "God save the Queen" becomes a cry of desperation bordering on double sacrilege. 6

Sometimes, of course, our markings may be simply a matter of aesthetics. Popping in a comma can be like slipping on the necklace that gives an outfit quiet elegance, or like catching the sound of running water that complements, as it completes, the silence of a Japanese landscape. When V. S. Naipaul, in his latest novel, writes, "He was a middle-aged man, with glasses," the first comma can seem a little precious. Yet it gives the description a spin, as well as a subtlety, that it otherwise lacks, and it shows that the glasses are not part of the middle-agedness, but something else. 7

Thus all these tiny scratches give us breadth and heft and depth. A world that has only periods is a world without inflections. It is a world without shade. It has a music without sharps and flats. It is a martial music. It has a jackboot rhythm. Words cannot bend and curve. A comma, by comparison, catches the gentle drift of the mind in thought, turning in on itself and back on itself, reversing, redoubling and returning along the course of its own sweet river music; while the semicolon brings clauses and thoughts together with all the silent discretion of a hostess arranging guests around her dinner table. 8

Punctuation, then, is a matter of care. Care for words, yes, but also, and more important, for what the words imply. Only a lover notices the small things: the way the afternoon light catches the nape of a neck, or how a strand of hair slips out from behind an ear, or the way a finger curls around a cup. And no one scans a letter so closely as a lover, searching for its small print, straining to hear its nuances, its gasps, its sighs and hesitations, poring over the secret messages that lie in every cadence. The difference between "Jane (whom I adore)" and "Jane, whom I adore," and the difference between them both and "Jane—whom I adore—" marks all the distance between ecstasy and heartache. "No iron can pierce the heart with such force as a period put at just the right place," in Isaac Babel's lovely words: a comma can let us hear a voice break, or a heart. Punctuation, in fact, is a labor of love. Which brings us back, in a way, to gods. 9

■ Reading Comprehension Questions

1. The word *pedant* in "It seems just a slip of a thing, a pedant's tick, a blip on the edge of our consciousness, a kind of printer's smudge almost" (paragraph 1) means
   a. conscientious teacher.
   b. careful typesetter.
   c. fussy academic.
   d. messy writer.

2. The word *sacrilege* in "the noble sobriety of 'God Save the Queen' becomes a cry of desperation bordering on double sacrilege" (paragraph 6) means
   a. overwhelming agony.
   b. extreme disrespect.
   c. sheer misery.
   d. utter exasperation.

3. Which of the following would be a good alternative title for this selection?
   a. The Complex Comma
   b. Punctuation and Propriety
   c. Punctuation: Points of Fine Tuning and Finesse
   d. Mysterious and Melodious Markings

4. Which sentence best expresses the main idea of the selection?
   a. Careful punctuation clarifies and adds rhythm and subtlety to writing.
   b. Punctuation is always important, but often only decorative.
   c. All points of punctuation are needed, but the comma is most useful.
   d. Punctuation cannot alter the meaning of words within a sentence.

5. Chinese printed text is even more mysterious to us because
   a. the Chinese use a different system of marks.
   b. the Chinese do not punctuate their script.
   c. the punctuation marks are unrecognizable.
   d. punctuation is included within the ideograms.

6. Punctuation adds meaning and colour to written words
   a. because it follows a consistent set of rules.
   b. because it creates space between words.
   c. because various marks precisely indicate pauses and changes in phrases.
   d. because it adds elegance to the printed sentence.

7. *True or false?* _____ Sentences using only periods can sound as abrupt as a military march.

8. The author implies that
   a. punctuation is a product of the culture of a particular time and place.
   b. punctuation can reflect the flavour or social climate of a culture.

    c. punctuation is used similarly by most cultures to indicate similar ideas.

    d. punctuation is the signature of a literate culture.

9. The author implies that

    a. use of punctuation is a sign of a highly developed culture.

    b. care in punctuation indicates a writer's concern for exactness of meaning.

    c. careful punctuation is the result of superhuman effort.

    d. good punctuation requires a sense of rhythm and a musical ear.

10. *True or false?* _____ Love, unlike written communication, reflects intense concern with fine details and shades of meaning.

■ Discussion Questions

About Content

1. According to Iyer, punctuation signs act like traffic signals. Which punctuation mark corresponds with which traffic sign? Explain the meaning of each section of this metaphor in terms of the punctuation of words in a sentence.

2. What are the four examples given by the author of culturally determined changes in punctuation? What does each say about the culture mentioned? Can you think of any other variations from English punctuation? Consider the French use of the comma rather than a period in writing sums of money.

3. What does Iyer mean when he writes "Punctuation is a matter of care. Care for words, yes, but also, and more important, for what the words imply"? Does what he says apply only to lovers, as in his example?

About Structure

4. Examine the opening sentences of each of the author's nine paragraphs. Is each an adequate topic sentence? Choose three paragraphs and explain the relationship of the idea(s) in the topic sentences to the contents of the paragraphs which follow.

5. Are there evident transition words to facilitate the reader's passage from paragraph to paragraph? What other rhetorical methods has the writer used to maintain unity in this essay?

6. What elements in the opening and closing sentences of this essay create a sense of unity in the essay?

About Style and Tone

7. The author uses his favourite punctuation mark very deliberately at several points in the essay to demonstrate the virtues and powers of the comma. What three examples are obvious in paragraph 1? What is the effect of their use in

these sentences? What other such direct demonstration of another punctuation mark does Iyer provide? Does it clarify and strengthen his point? How?

8. To how many other things is a comma compared throughout the essay? How many of these figures of speech are *similes* or *analogies*, using "like" or "as"? How many are *metaphors*, where the comma is directly described as something else? What is the effect of so many ideas associated with one small punctuation mark? Are the subjects of the comparison apt for describing written communication? Why? Does the reader ultimately have a clearer picture of why Iyer is so fond of the comma?

■ Writing Assignments

Assignment 1

The possibility of finding a college student who would, like Pico Iyer, call punctuation "a labor of love" is indeed slim. "A labour of confusion and loathing" is probably closer to the truth. Instead of writing in praise of a particular item of punctuation, write an essay which describes the piece of punctuation which has generally given you the most problems. Why has this mark caused you such misery? How long have you suffered from punctuation anxiety? Which particular functions of your troublesome punctuation mark have defeated you time and time again? Have you conquered it yet, or do some of its uses still baffle you? What does this mark remind you of? Have there ever been instructors who offered sensible advice for managing your point of distress? How do you intend to meet the challenge of this punctuation mark?

Assignment 2

Iyer's essay discusses the importance of one symbol in the grand scheme of human communication. Small misunderstandings and errors in daily communication often have large consequences. Using the cause and effect format, describe an example of "miscommunication" in your life and its consequences.

Assignment 3

Our lives are often full of small things which have great meaning and significance for each of us. While the comma may not have particular importance to you, there is undoubtedly some object which does. Little, often trivial, objects can symbolize something of great importance to people. Consider dashboard ornaments and car decals: what do they all mean? What about cellular phones?

Write an essay about some ordinary object and its symbolic meanings to you. Speculate on other possible meanings to people in other situations, and the reasons for their different interpretation of this object as a symbol.

On Euthanasia and Dying Well

E.J. McCullough

Your own direct experience with death may be limited and painful to contemplate. While death is the subject of much literature and artistic expression, and a commonplace in films and TV, it always has the power to awaken strong emotion when it comes close to us. Death seems to be the opposite of life and happiness, and, as such, we fear contact with it. But what about euthanasia, or willingly chosen death? When does life become so intolerable that assisted suicide and the unknown are preferable? Is it possible to "make a good death," and to "die with dignity," and even joy?

E.J. McCullough's essay is a highly personal and carefully constructed examination of the meanings of happiness, and of death, and an argument for death as a final "gift of love" to others.

We have all experienced the death of family members, close friends, or acquaintances. 1
Few of those deaths could be described as happy. We might use words like painful, lingering, lonely, or courageous, but rarely would we characterize death as a happy event. Is the term "happy death," then, an oxymoron? Are happiness and death irreconcilable? If so, we have a problem with the term "euthanasia," which in its root meaning signifies dying well or happily.

Euthanasia is the practice of actively terminating life in the name of compassion. If 2
it is voluntary, it is a species of suicide. If it is involuntary, it is murder. The case I should like to make is that death can be a truly happy event, but that the notion of dying well or happily in assisted self-destruction is unacceptable.

The Roman philosopher Lucretius saw no problem with suicide if one's pleasures 3
diminished and pain became intolerable. His emphasis was on feelings and personal interests. In contemporary terms we would call this consequentialism, utilitarianism, or pragmatism. The Stoic school of philosophy had a more developed ethical doctrine. Many Stoics were quite explicit about the desirability of death under difficult circumstances. "Amid the miseries of life on earth," declared Pliny the Elder, "suicide is God's best gift to man." The Roman emperor Marcus Aurelius said, "The house is smoking, and I quit it. Why do you think that this is any trouble?" The emphasis in the Stoics is on rationality: if the price of continued life is continual suffering, then it is eminently reasonable to "quit the house."

The Platonic and Aristotelian attitude toward death is quite different, since neither 4
Plato nor Aristotle was prepared to deny the possibility of the continuance of life in eternity. The finest exemplar of this view is Plotinus, a disciple of both Plato and Aristotle, who said:

When a man contrives the dissolution of the body, it is he that has used violence. . . . Suicide is an act of violence. If there be a period allotted to all by fate, to anticipate the hour could not be a happy act. . . . If everyone is to hold in another world a standing determined by the state in which he quitted this, then there must be no withdrawal as long as there is any hope of progress.

But the practice of euthanasia received its most severe criticism from the Roman philosopher Boethius, who wrote from the perspective of personal tragedy. Boethius argued that the circumstance he faced—his own death and the ruin of his family—necessitated a more complete response to the problem of suffering in human life. When all personal worth is destroyed, when relationships with family and friends are demolished, the only relationship left is with the divine, and in this relationship lies goodness and hope. Boethius began where Aristotle and Plotinus had left off, with the conclusion that happiness is not a feeling but, to quote Aristotle, "a life lived in accordance with virtue." He went on to the view that continuity in this life is extended to relationship with God in a future life.

There are four notions of happiness implicit in this brief historical account: happiness as pleasure without pain, happiness as the satisfaction of desire but including pain, happiness as a life lived in accordance with virtue, and happiness as a life lived in accordance with virtue and fulfilled in relationship with the divine.

Happiness as pleasure and the absence of pain is probably the dominant view, based as it is in bodily sensations and feelings. John Stuart Mill wrote that happiness is an existence exempt as far as possible from pain and as rich as possible in enjoyment. By this he did not mean physical pleasures only, but pleasures of the mind and spirit as well. In this perception, suicide is intuitively accepted as a release from pain. The notion that happiness must include both pleasure and pain, on the other hand, is one the Stoics could have embraced quite easily. In the case of a serious imbalance of pain over pleasure, suicide is justified, but reason must provide the justification.

Happiness as the permanent state of a life lived in accordance with virtue would resist the most severe temptations to suicide, for happiness of this kind disposes one to accept misfortune courageously. The fourth type of happiness—that of a life lived in accordance with virtue, supported by a sense of community and one's relationship with the divine—likewise precludes the possibility of suicide. These two notions of happiness put events in our control, whereas the first two place us at the mercy of events.

What of death? Two notions of death—as the termination of physical function, or as the termination of physical and psychological function—represent the nihilist's view of death as the end of life; there is no extension beyond the moment. Two other views present themselves: the fundamentalist view that death is a beginning, and the view that death is a transition. In these two notions, again, continuity of existence precludes the possibility of suicide. The nihilist holds for radical discontinuity, the fundamentalist for a modified continuity, and the non-fundamentalist for a real continuity in community and with the divine.

Given the four notions of happiness and the four notions of death, can we find a place for euthanasia as a legitimate practice? According to the first two definitions of happiness and death, euthanasia is entirely acceptable. On the basis of the second two, it is not. But only the fourth definition of both happiness and death fully corresponds to our lived experience.

There is a joke about René Descartes, the seventeenth-century French thinker who 11 arrived at one of the most famous conclusions in the history of philosophy: "I think, therefore I am." When his sister offered him a cup of tea, he said, "I think not," and promptly disappeared. It is the philosophy of Descartes and his successors which has given rise to a picture of human life as episodic, discrete, and discontinuous. But history, conceptual analysis, and unacceptable alternatives lead us to the conclusion that continuity in human life is not only plausible but demonstrable. This continuity makes it possible to conceive of a happy death, and to characterize many deaths as happy. Euthanasia is not the way to a happy death or to dying well.

Consider my own case. In July 1990 I went for a routine checkup in order to pur- 12 chase an insurance policy. I felt wonderful. I'd been working out regularly, running anywhere from three to ten miles a day. My pulse was fifty, my blood pressure was a hundred over sixty. I played tennis regularly. The doctor wanted to have a look at a spot on my arm. He also wanted to examine my prostate. The spot turned out to be a malignant melanoma. The prostate was also cancerous. CAT scans and bone scans indicated that there was probably further involvement with the lymphatic system, and possible bone cancer as well.

My entire plan of life was shattered, and my notions of death and dying became mat- 13 ters for urgent reflection. My personal ideas were radically altered. I suddenly saw death as a gift. My relationships changed: some for the worse, most for the better. In the end, I was both cured and healed.

There were many reasons for this: family, faith, friends, science. The common view 14 of dying as a physical process which one undergoes passively is being radically reshaped. The pro-euthanasia movement states that we should take an active role in the process, terminating life if it is of inferior quality or involves great suffering. At the same time, modern medicine has identified the role of the dying person as an active one, one which can result in a reduction of suffering, or even a cure; having experienced the positive role one can play in pain management, I know that physical suffering can be almost totally controlled. Philosophers and theologians, too, recognize that active participation in healing—as distinct from curing—is a central feature of the intellectual and spiritual life.

These factors have brought us to see that dying is not a process to which we submit 15 with resignation, but an action which we can shape in a variety of ways. Do we want to shape it by simply bringing it to an abrupt and violent end? The financial burdens imposed by the dying, and the conviction that suffering is a personal tragedy, have led the people of Holland to a national policy of assisted suicide. Perhaps twenty-five percent of people dying in Holland today die an assisted death. Is that the way we want to go? The report of the Law Reform Commission of Canada tabled in 1983 says no, but there is a steady erosion of that position in the public mind. If we are to credit the polls, more and more people accept assisted dying as an option.

As with abortion in its early stages of acceptance, we are now being besieged with 16 propaganda concerning death and dying. There are three basic arguments, corresponding to three principles of moral life: the nature of action, the social nature of death and dying, and the nature of the good. The first argument in favour of euthanasia is that we have the right to choice and autonomy in the major issues of our life, and that all rights are based on this right. This seems plausible until one notes that the decision is forced by pain. A truly free decision would be to resist those physical forces which threaten life and relationships.

The second argument is that a compassionate society should accept the rights of oth- 17 ers to self-determination, and its laws should tolerate the ethical views of others even if our own views differ. This argument centres on the right to privacy. It is the common view of politicians and many others who would neither seek euthanasia themselves nor force their opinions on others. What these people fail to understand is that laws against euthanasia play a primary teaching role in society and in the support for a life ethic. A virtuous society enshrines its virtues in laws against murder, rape, child abuse, and a variety of other vicious practices.

The third argument in favour of euthanasia is simply that it is in our best interests 18 to avoid pain and seek pleasure. But each person's sense of interest differs, and society's interests are often in conflict with the individual's.

The greatest difficulty faced by those who would make a case against euthanasia 19 comes from the steady erosion of the law. It will begin in Canada, as it began elsewhere, with the inability of the courts to prosecute people for performing an action which seems so compassionate. For that reason, the basis for the law must be made clear. There must also be a legal distinction between homicide and euthanasia, between intention and motivation, and the punishment for breach of the law must be vastly different from the punishment imposed for homicide; perhaps some form of community service would be appropriate. Finally, social circumstances must be provided to make old age a joyful experience of passage.

Our attitude to dying is a proclamation of our stance toward life. If we actively par- 20 ticipate in the process, we proclaim something of inestimable value to those we love. It becomes the most beautiful gift we can offer. "The critical difference," wrote Henri Nouwen, "has to do with how I die."

> If I die with much anger and bitterness, I will leave my family and friends behind in confusion, guilt, shame, or a sense of impotence. When I felt my death approaching, I suddenly realized how much I could influence the hearts of those whom I would leave behind. If I could truly say that I was grateful for what I had lived, eager to forgive and be forgiven, full of hope that those who loved me would continue their lives in joy and peace, and confident that Jesus would guide all who had belonged to my life—if I could do that, I would, in the hour of my death, create more spiritual freedom than I had been able to create in all the years of my life.
>
> I realized with new intensity that dying is the most important act of living. It involves a choice to bind with guilt or to set free with gratitude. The choice is between a death that gives life and a death that kills.

Euthanasia is an act of violence. It kills not only the person who dies but the spirit 21 of those left behind. My own experience has been one of unbounded love. My students wrote poems for me; my colleagues held a healing service; my family prayed fervently; my friends—religious and atheist alike—held my hands and embraced me in a manner

I can only understand as a divine gift. It would not have comforted me in my worst moments if someone had offered to assist me by a violent act in my passage.

Healing is the action of making whole. It is paradoxical that this divine gift may 22 come at a time when our bodies cannot be made whole except in the sense of witnessing to the sacred and mysterious moment when we give the best of ourselves to others. Dying is an active gift, a healing gift, and a proclamation to the world. Contrast that with the violence of killing, even in the name of compassion, and there is no doubt where wisdom lies.

> An aged man is but a paltry thing,
> A tattered coat upon a stick, unless
> Soul clap its hands and sing, and louder sing
> For every tatter in its mortal dress. . . .
> —W. B. Yeats, "Sailing to Byzantium"

Take the hands of the sick and the dying, the aged amongst you, the "paltry things." 23 Take their hands and tell them that you love them, and euthanasia as an issue will disappear. The dying will stay for your sake. They will see dying as the last and most beautiful act of a soul yearning for ecstasy, full of hope, leaving a legacy of love.

■ Reading Comprehension Questions

1. The word *oxymoron* in "Is the term 'happy death,' then, an oxymoron?" (paragraph 1) means
   a. definition.
   b. pun.
   c. contradiction.
   d. joke.

2. The word *nihilist* in "represent the nihilist's view of death as the end of life; there is no extension beyond the moment" (paragraph 9) means
   a. agnostic.
   b. pessimist.
   c. optimist.
   d. believer in nothing.

3. Which of the following would be a good alternative title for this selection?
   a. Suicide and Suffering
   b. Four Views of Death
   c. The Final Gift of Love
   d. Death and Free Will

4. Which sentence best expresses the main idea of the selection?
   a. Society's views of old age, death, and dying are in the process of changing.

     b.   The right to live ensured by law should be extended to guarantee the right to die in humane circumstances.

     c.   Compassionate, humane treatment of dying people can lessen pain and prolong their lives.

     d.   A happy death offers two gifts of love: that of the living for the dying and that of the dying for the living.

5. Stoic philosophers viewed suicide
     a.   as a desirable way of dying.
     b.   as a rational choice in unendurable circumstances.
     c.   as way of evading suffering.
     d.   as a way of causing the least trouble to others.

6. A definition of happiness which denies the legitimacy of euthanasia is
     a.   a pleasurable lack of pain.
     b.   life as a mixture of pleasure and pain.
     c.   the pursuit of virtue and of relationships with society and with the divine.
     d.   the acceptance of life's joy and misery, and a conscious attempt to be good.

7. *True or false?* _____ A natural death is the ultimate offering of one's self to others and to a higher good.

8. The author implies that
     a.   all Christian views of death are similar.
     b.   fundamentalists do not value life.
     c.   Christian views of death vary, but do commit to an afterlife.
     d.   atheists believe that only physical life ends at death.

9. The author implies that
     a.   his own experience taught him to enjoy each moment of life.
     b.   the acceptance of death is still important to the terminally ill.
     c.   the patient's positive attitude often results in a total recovery.
     d.   the mind and spirit may experience growth, although the body is ill.

10. The reader may conclude that, for the author,
     a.   if painful and violent, death has little value as part of the life process.
     b.   death is painful, if one is surrounded by loving friends.
     c.   compassionate help in assisting death is beneficial to friends and family.
     d.   the mystery of death lies in the gifts of the spirit as the body ceases to be.

■ Discussion Questions

About Content

1. McCullough cites Lucretius on the subject of suicide. Which three words does the author use to describe Lucretius' views? Define these words, and describe how they could be applied to the issue of suicide.
2. What are the differences between
   a. the views of the Stoics towards suicide, and Lucretius' attitude?
   b. the views of the Platonists, Aristotelians, and Boethius as opposed to Lucretius and the Stoics?

   What trend in belief is evident in the author's choice of philosophers?
3. What three areas of human thought does McCullough say have led to rejection of Descartes' views of life and death? Have these areas of thought changed our view of life's continuity? How?

About Structure

4. What method(s) of introduction does the author use for this essay?
   a. Anecdote
   b. Questions
   c. Broad to narrow
   d. Stating the importance of the subject
5. This essay could be analyzed or broken down into distinct sections. Identify the paragraphs described by the following descriptive headings.
   a. Definition of terms
   b. Historical or personal background
   c. Direct personal (subjective) argument
   d. Objectively based argument

   What does the author achieve by allotting various amounts of his essay to different methods of exposition?

About Style and Tone

6. Where is the essay's argument most developed by logical means? Where does the author use emotion to persuade? In your view, when is the essay's argument most effective? Why?
7. In which paragraphs do you find the author's tone to be direct and straightforward? Why? Where do you find the tone to be harsh? Why? Which words does McCullough use to achieve bluntness? Where is the essay's tone softer? What subjects are described in this tone?

■ Writing Assignments

Assignment 1

Write an essay about your experience of the death of someone important to you in some way. Such an essay has a classical name: a eulogy. Look up the term prior to writing your essay, and define the word for yourself and your readers in terms of what it means to you and your relationship with the person about whom you are writing. Reconsider McCullough's essay and what it says about the gifts of those who have died to the living. What legacies have you received from this person who died? How do they continue to affect your life?

Assignment 2

Euthanasia is a subject which brings out strong, often vehement opinions in those concerned with it. You have read one author's argument against the concept, and examined the way he structures his argument. Consider either euthanasia or some other contentious issue such as animal rights, "no-fail" educational systems, or the legalization of drugs. Write a persuasive essay which sets out your views on the subject chosen, using both objective and anecdotal evidence in the most convincing proportions.

Assignment 3

How many kinds of happiness exist? Philosophers and self-help books have many definitions and categories for this emotion. Write an essay which illustrates and clearly describes three types of happiness.

How to Make It in College, Now That You're Here

Brian O'Keeney

The author of this selection presents a compact guide to being a successful student. He will show you how to pass tests, how to avoid becoming a student zombie, how to find time to fit in everything you want to do, and how to deal with personal problems while keeping up with your studies. These and other helpful tips have been culled from the author's own experience and his candid interviews with fellow students.

Today is your first day on campus. You were a high school senior three months ago. Or 1
maybe you've been at home with your children for the last ten years. Or maybe you work
full time and you're coming to school to start the process that leads to a better job.
Whatever your background is, you're probably not too concerned today with staying in
college. After all, you just got over the hurdle (and the paperwork) of applying to this
place and organizing your life so that you could attend. And today, you're confused and
tired. Everything is a hassle, from finding the classrooms to standing in line at the bookstore. But read my advice anyway. And if you don't read it today, clip and save this article. You might want to look at it a little further down the road.

By the way, if this isn't your very first day, don't skip this article. Maybe you haven't 2
been doing as well in your studies as you'd hoped. Or perhaps you've had problems juggling your work schedule, your class schedule, and your social life. If so, read on. You're
about to get the inside story on making it in college. On the basis of my own experience
as a final-year student, and on dozens of interviews with successful students, I've
worked out a no-fail system for coping with college. These are the inside tips every student needs to do well in school. I've put myself in your place, and I'm going to answer
the questions that will cross (or have already crossed) your mind during your stay here.

What's the Secret of Getting Good Grades?

It all comes down to getting those grades, doesn't it? After all, you came here for 3
some reason, and you're going to need passing grades to get the credits or degree you
want. Many of us never did much studying in high school; most of the learning we did
took place in the classroom. College, however, is a lot different. You're really on your
own when it comes to passing courses. In fact, sometimes you'll feel as if nobody cares
if you make it or not. Therefore, you've got to figure out a study system that gets results.
Sooner or later, you'll be alone with those books. After that, you'll be sitting in a classroom with an exam sheet on your desk. Whether you stare at that exam with a queasy
stomach or whip through it fairly confidently depends on your study techniques. Most
of the successful students I talked to agreed that the following eight study tips deliver
solid results.

1   Set Up a Study Place. Those students you see "studying" in the cafeteria or 4
game room aren't learning much. You just can't learn when you're distracted by people
and noise. Even the library can be a bad place to study if you constantly find yourself
watching the clouds outside or the students walking through the stacks. It takes guts to
sit, alone, in a quiet place in order to study. But you have to do it. Find a room at home
or a spot in the library that's relatively quiet—and boring. When you sit there, you won't
have much to do except study.

2   Get into a Study Frame of Mind. When you sit down, do it with the attitude 5
that you're going to get this studying done. You're not going to doodle in your notebook
or make a list for the supermarket. Decide that you're going to study and learn *now*, so
that you can move on to more interesting things as soon as possible.

3   **Give Yourself Rewards.** If you sweat out a block of study time, and do a good job on it, treat yourself. You deserve it. You can "psych" yourself up for studying by promising to reward yourself afterwards. A present for yourself can be anything from a favorite TV show to a relaxing bath to a dish of double chocolate ice cream.

4   **Skim the Textbook First.** Lots of students sit down with an assignment like "read chapter five, pages 125–150" and do just that. They turn to page 125 and start to read. After a while, they find that they have no idea what they just read. For the last ten minutes, they've been thinking about their five-year-old or what they're going to eat for dinner. Eventually, they plod through all the pages but don't remember much afterwards.

In order to prevent this problem, skim the textbook chapter first. This means: look at the title, the subtitles, the headings, the pictures, the first and last paragraphs. Try to find out what the person who wrote the book had in mind when he or she organized the chapter. What was important enough to set off as a title or in bold type? After skimming, you should be able to explain to yourself what the main points of the chapter are. Unless you're the kind of person who would step into an empty elevator shaft without looking first, you'll soon discover the value of skimming.

5   **Take Notes on What You're Studying.** This sounds like a hassle, but it works. Go back over the material after you've read it, and jot down key words and phrases in the margins. When you review the chapter for a test, you'll have handy little things like "definition of rationalization" or "example of assimilation" in the margins. If the material is especially tough, organize a separate sheet of notes. Write down definitions, examples, lists, and main ideas. The idea is to have a single sheet that boils the entire chapter down to a digestible lump.

6   **Review after You've Read and Taken Notes.** Some people swear that talking to yourself works. Tell yourself about the most important points in the chapter. Once you've said them out loud, they seem to stick better in your mind. If you can't talk to yourself about the material after reading it, that's a sure sign you don't really know it.

7   **Give Up.** This may sound contradictory, but give up when you've had enough. You should try to make it through at least an hour, though. Ten minutes here and there are useless. When your head starts to pound and your eyes develop spidery red lines, quit. You won't do much learning when you're exhausted.

8   **Take a College Skills Course If You Need It.** Don't hesitate or feel embarrassed about enrolling in a study skills course. Many students say they wouldn't have made it without one.

How Can I Keep Up with All My Responsibilities without Going Crazy?

You've got a class schedule. You're supposed to study. You've got a family. You've got a husband, wife, boyfriend, girlfriend, child. You've got a job. How are you possibly going to cover all the bases in your life and maintain your sanity? This is one of the toughest problems students face. Even if they start the semester with the best of intentions, they eventually find themselves tearing their hair out trying to do everything they're supposed to do. Believe it or not, though, it is possible to meet all your responsibilities. And you don't have to turn into a hermit or give up your loved ones to do it.

The secret here is to organize your time. But don't just sit around half the semester 14 planning to get everything together soon. Before you know it, you'll be confronted with midterms, papers, family, and work all at once. Don't let yourself reach that breaking point. Instead, try these three tactics.

1 Monthly Calendar. Get one of those calendars with big blocks around the 15 dates. Give yourself an overview of the whole term by marking down the due dates for papers and projects. Circle test and exam days. This way those days don't sneak up on you unexpectedly.

2 Study Schedule. Sit down during the first few days of this semester and make 16 up a sheet listing the days and hours of the week. Fill in your work and class hours first. Then try to block out some study hours. It's better to study a little every day than to create a huge once-or-twice-a-week marathon session. Schedule study hours for your hardest classes for the times when you feel most energetic. For example, I battled my tax law textbook in the mornings; when I looked at it after 7:00 P.M., I may as well have been reading Chinese. The usual proportion, by the way, is one hour of study time for every class hour.

In case you're one of those people who get carried away, remember to leave blocks 17 of free time, too. You won't be any good to yourself or anyone else if you don't relax and pack in the studying once in a while.

3 A "To-Do" List. This is the secret that single-handedly got me through college. 18 Once a week (or every day if you want to), write a list of what you have to do. Write down everything from "write English paper" to "buy cold cuts for lunches." The best thing about a "to do" list is that it seems to tame all those stray "I have to" thoughts that nag at your mind. Just making the list seems to make the tasks "doable." After you finish something on the list, cross it off. Don't be compulsive about finishing everything; you're not Superman or Wonder Woman. Get the important things done first. The secondary things you don't finish can simply be moved to your next "to do" list.

What Can I Do If Personal Problems Get in the Way of My Studies?

One student, Roger, told me this story:

19

> Everything was going OK for me until the middle of the spring semester. I went through a terrible time when I broke up with my girlfriend and started seeing her best friend. I was trying to deal with my ex-girlfriend's hurt and anger, my new girlfriend's guilt, and my own worries and anxieties at the same time. In addition to this, my mother was sick and on

a medication that made her really irritable. I hated to go home because the atmosphere was so uncomfortable. Soon, I started missing classes because I couldn't deal with the academic pressures as well as my own personal problems. It seemed easier to hang around my girlfriend's apartment than to face all my problems at home and at school.

Another student, Marian, told me: 20

I'd been married for eight years and the relationship wasn't going too well. I saw the handwriting on the wall, and I decided to prepare for the future. I enrolled in college, because I knew I'd need a decent job to support myself. Well, my husband had a fit because I was going to school. We were arguing a lot anyway, and he made it almost impossible for me to study at home. I think he was angry and almost jealous because I was drawing away from him. It got so bad that I thought about quitting college for a while. I wasn't getting any support at home and it was just too hard to go on.

Personal troubles like these are overwhelming when you're going through them.   21
School seems like the least important thing in your life. The two students above are perfect examples of this. But if you think about it, quitting or failing school would be the worst thing for these two students. Roger's problems, at least with his girlfriends, would simmer down eventually, and then he'd regret having left school. Marian had to finish college if she wanted to be able to live independently. Sometimes, you've just got to hang tough.

But what do you do while you're trying to live through a lousy time? First of all,   22
do something difficult. Ask yourself, honestly, if you're exaggerating small problems as an excuse to avoid classes and studying. It takes strength to admit this, but there's no sense in kidding yourself. If your problems are serious, and real, try to make some human contacts at school. Lots of students hide inside a miserable shell made of their own troubles and feel isolated and lonely. Believe me, there are plenty of students with problems. Not everyone is getting A's and having a fabulous social and home life at the same time. As you go through the term, you'll pick up some vibrations about the students in your classes. Perhaps someone strikes you as a compatible person. Why not speak to that person after class? Share a cup of coffee in the cafeteria or walk to the parking lot together. You're not looking for a best friend or the love of your life. You just want to build a little network of support for yourself. Sharing your difficulties, questions, and complaints with a friendly person on campus can make a world of difference in how you feel.

Finally, if your problems are overwhelming, get some professional help. Why do you   23
think colleges spend countless dollars on counseling departments and campus psychiatric services? More than ever, students all over the country are taking advantage of the help offered by support groups and therapy sessions. There's no shame attached to asking for help, either; in fact, almost 40 percent of college students (according to one survey) will use counseling services during their time in school. Just walk into a student center or counseling office and ask for an appointment. You wouldn't think twice about asking a dentist to help you get rid of your toothache. Counselors are paid—and want—to help you with your problems.

Why Do Some People Make It and Some Drop Out?

Anyone who spends at least one semester in college notices that some students give up 24
on their classes, The person who sits behind you in accounting, for example, begins to
miss a lot of class meetings and eventually vanishes. Or another student comes to class
without the assignment, doodles in his notebook during the lecture, and leaves during the
break. What's the difference between students like this and the ones who succeed in
school? My survey may be nonscientific, but everyone I asked said the same thing: attitude. A positive attitude is the key to everything else—good study habits, smart time
scheduling, and coping with personal difficulties.

What does "a positive attitude" mean? Well, for one thing, it means avoiding the 25
zombie syndrome. It means not only showing up for your classes, but also doing something while you're there. Really listen. Take notes. Ask a question if you want to. Don't
just walk into a class, put your mind in neutral, and drift away to never-never land.

Having a positive attitude goes deeper than this, though. It means being mature about 26
college as an institution. Too many students approach college classes like six-year-olds
who expect first grade to be as much fun as *Sesame Street*. First grade, as we all know,
isn't as much fun as *Sesame Street*. And college classes can sometimes be downright dull
and boring. If you let a boring class discourage you so much that you want to leave
school, you'll lose in the long run. Look at your priorities. You want a degree, or a certificate, or a career. If you have to, you can make it through a less-than-interesting class
in order to achieve what you want. Get whatever you can out of every class. But if you
simply can't stand a certain class, be determined to fulfill its requirements and be done
with it once and for all.

After the initial high of starting school, you have to settle in for the long haul. If you 27
follow the advice here, you'll be prepared to face the academic crunch. You'll also live
through the semester without giving up your family, your job, or *Monday Night Football*.
Finally, going to college can be an exciting time. You do learn. And when you learn
things, the world becomes a more interesting place.

■ Reading Comprehension Questions

1. The word *queasy* in "with a queasy stomach" (paragraph 3) means
   a. intelligent.
   b. healthy.
   c. full.
   d. nervous.

2. The word *tactics* in "try these three tactics" (paragraph 14) means
   a. proofs.
   b. problems.
   c. methods.
   d. questions.

3. Which of the following would be a good alternative title for this selection?
   a. Your First Day on Campus
   b. Coping with College
   c. How to Budget Your Time
   d. The Benefits of College Skills Courses

4. Which sentence expresses the main idea of the selection?
   a. In high school, most of us did little homework.
   b. You should give yourself rewards for studying well.
   c. Sometimes personal problems interfere with studying.
   d. You can succeed in college by following certain guidelines.

5. According to the author, "making it" in college means
   a. studying whenever you have any free time.
   b. getting a degree by barely passing your courses.
   c. quitting school until you solve your personal problems.
   d. getting good grades without making your life miserable.

6. If your personal problems seem overwhelming, you should
   a. drop out for a while.
   b. try to ignore them.
   c. tell another student.
   d. seek professional help.

7. Which of the following is *not* described by the author as a means of time control?
   a. Monthly calendar
   b. To-do list
   c. Study schedule
   d. Flexible job hours

8. We might infer that the author
   a. is a writer for the school newspaper.
   b. is president of his or her class.
   c. has taken a study skills course.
   d. was not a successful student in his or her first year of college.

9. From the selection we can conclude that
   a. college textbooks are very expensive.
   b. it is a good practice to write notes in your textbook.
   c. taking notes on your reading takes too much time.
   d. a student should never mark up an expensive textbook.

10. The author implies that
    a. fewer people than before are attending college.
    b. most students think that college is easy.
    c. most students dislike college.
    d. coping with college is difficult.

■ Discussion Questions

About Content

1. What pitfalls does O'Keeney think are waiting for students just starting college? Are there other pitfalls not mentioned in the article?

2. What is the secret that the author says got him through college? What do you think is the most helpful or important suggestion the author makes in the selection?

3. Do you agree with the author that Roger and Marian should stay in school? Are there any situations where it would be better for students to quit school or leave temporarily?

About Structure

4. What is the thesis of the selection? Write here the number of the paragraph in which it is stated: _____

5. Why does the article begin with the first day on campus?

6. What method of introduction does the author use in the section on personal problems (starting on page 637)? What is the value of using this method?

About Style and Tone

7. This essay is obviously written for college students. Can you guess where an essay like this one would appear? (*Hint:* Reread the first paragraph.)

■ Writing Assignments

Assignment 1

Write a process essay similar to the one you've just read that explains how to succeed in some other field—for example, a job, a sport, marriage, child rearing. First, brainstorm the three or four problem areas a newcomer to this experience might encounter. Then, under each area you have listed, jot down some helpful hints and techniques for overcoming these problems. For example, a process paper on "How to Succeed as a Waitress" might describe the following problem areas in this kind of job:

Developing a good memory

Learning to do tasks quickly

Coping with troublesome customers

Each supporting paragraph in this paper would discuss specific techniques for dealing with these problems. Be sure that the advice you give is detailed and specific enough to really help a person in such a situation.

You may find it helpful to look over the process essays on pages 138–140.

Assignment 2

Write a letter to Roger or Marian, giving advice on how to deal with the personal problem mentioned in the article. You could recommend any or all of the following:

Face the problem realistically. (By doing what?)

Make other contacts at school. (How? Where?)

See a counsellor. (Where? What should this person be told?)

Realize that the problem is not so serious. (Why not?)

Ignore the problem. (How? By doing what instead?)

In your introductory paragraph, explain why you are writing the letter. Include a thesis statement that says what plan of action you are recommending. Then, in the rest of the paper, explain the plan of action (or plans of action) in detail.

Assignment 3

Write an essay contrasting college *as you thought it would be* with college *as it is*. You can organize the essay by focusing on three specific things that are different from what you expected. Or you can cover three areas of difference. For instance, you may decide to contrast your expectations of (1) a college residence room, (2) your room-mate, and (3) dining hall food with reality. Or, you could contrast your expectations of (1) fellow students, (2) college professors, and (3) college courses with reality.

Refer to the section on comparison and contrast essays in this book (pages 157–173) to review point-by-point and one-side-at-a-time methods of development. Be sure to make an outline of your essay before you begin to write.

In Praise of the F Word

Mary Sherry

What does it take to get by in high school? Too little, according to the author, a teacher in an "educational-repair shop." In this article, which originally appeared in *Newsweek*, Mary Sherry describes the ways she sees students being cheated by their schools and proposes a remedy you may find surprising.

Tens of thousands of 18-year-olds will graduate this year and be handed meaningless 1 diplomas. These diplomas won't look any different from those awarded their luckier classmates. Their validity will be questioned only when their employers discover that these graduates are semiliterate.

Eventually a fortunate few will find their way into educational-repair shops—adult- 2 literacy programs, such as the one where I teach basic grammar and writing. There, high school graduates and high school dropouts pursuing graduate-equivalency certificates will learn the skills they should have learned in school. They will also discover they have been cheated by our educational system.

As I teach, I learn a lot about our schools. Early in each session I ask my students 3 to write about an unpleasant experience they had in school. No writers' block here! "I wish someone would have had made me stop doing drugs and made me study." "I liked to party and no one seemed to care." "I was a good kid and didn't cause any trouble, so they just passed me along even though I didn't read well and couldn't write." And so on.

I am your basic do-gooder, and prior to teaching this class I blamed the poor acad- 4 emic skills our kids have today on drugs, divorce and other impediments to concentration necessary for doing well in school. But, as I rediscover each time I walk into the classroom, before a teacher can expect students to concentrate, he has to get their attention, no matter what distractions may be at hand. There are many ways to do this, and they have much to do with teaching style. However, if style alone won't do it, there is another way to show who holds the winning hand in the classroom. That is to reveal the trump card of failure.

I will never forget a teacher who played that card to get the attention of one of my 5 children. Our youngest, a world-class charmer, did little to develop his intellectual talents but always got by. Until Mrs. Stifter.

Our son was a high school senior when he had her for English. "He sits in the back 6 of the room talking to his friends," she told me. "Why don't you move him to the front row?" I urged, believing the embarrassment would get him to settle down. Mrs. Stifter looked at me steely-eyed over her glasses. "I don't move seniors," she said. "I flunk them." I was flustered. Our son's academic life flashed before my eyes. No teacher had ever threatened him with that before. I regained my composure and managed to say that

I thought she was right. By the time I got home I was feeling pretty good about this. It was a radical approach for these times, but, well, why not? "She's going to flunk you," I told my son. I did not discuss it any further. Suddenly English became a priority in his life. He finished out the semester with an A.

I know one example doesn't make a case, but at night I see a parade of students who are angry and resentful for having been passed along until they could no longer even pretend to keep up. Of average intelligence or better, they eventually quit school, concluding they were too dumb to finish. "I should have been held back," is a comment I hear frequently. Even sadder are those students who are high school graduates who say to me after a few weeks of class, "I don't know how I ever got a high school diploma."

Passing students who have not mastered the work cheats them and the employers who expect graduates to have basic skills. We excuse this dishonest behavior by saying kids can't learn if they come from terrible environments. No one seems to stop to think that—no matter what environments they come from—most kids don't put school first on their list unless they perceive something is at stake. They'd rather be sailing.

Many students I see at night could give expert testimony on unemployment, chemical dependency, abusive relationships. In spite of these difficulties, they have decided to make education a priority. They are motivated by the desire for a better job or the need to hang on to the one they've got. They have a healthy fear of failure.

People of all ages can rise above their problems, but they need to have a reason to do so. Young people generally don't have the maturity to value education in the same way my adult students value it. But fear of failure, whether economic or academic, can motivate both.

Flunking as a regular policy has just as much merit today as it did two generations ago. We must review the threat of flunking and see it as it really is—a positive teaching tool. It is an expression of confidence by both teachers and parents that the students have the ability to learn the material presented to them. However, making it work again would take a dedicated, caring conspiracy between teachers and parents. It would mean facing the tough reality that passing kids who haven't learned the material—while it might save them grief for the short term—dooms them to long-term illiteracy. It would mean that teachers would have to follow through on their threats, and parents would have to stand behind them, knowing their children's best interests are indeed at stake. This means no more doing Scott's assignments for him because he might fail. No more passing Jodi because she's such a nice kid.

This is a policy that worked in the past and can work today. A wise teacher, with the support of his parents, gave our son the opportunity to succeed—or fail. It's time we return this choice to all students.

■ Reading Comprehension Questions

1. The word *validity* in "[the diplomas'] validity will be questioned . . . when . . . employers discover that these graduates are semiliterate" (paragraph 1) means
   a. soundness.
   b. dates.

    c. age.

    d. supply.

2. The word *impediments* in "I blamed the poor academic skills our kids have today on drugs, divorce and other impediments to concentration" (paragraph 4) means

    a. questions.

    b. paths.

    c. skills.

    d. obstacles.

3. Which one of the following would be a good alternative title for this selection?

    a. Learning to Concentrate in School

    b. Teaching English Skills

    c. A Useful Tool for Motivating Students

    d. Adult Literacy Programs

4. Which sentence best expresses the main idea of the selection?

    a. Many adults cannot read or write well.

    b. English skills can be learned through adult literacy programs.

    c. Schools should include flunking students as part of their regular policy.

    d. Before students will concentrate, the teacher must get their attention.

5. Sherry's night students are

    a. usually unemployed.

    b. poor students.

    c. motivated to learn.

    d. doing drugs.

6. According to the author, many students who get "passed along"

    a. are lucky.

    b. never find a job.

    c. don't get into trouble.

    d. eventually feel angry and resentful.

7. Sherry feels that to succeed, flunking students as a regular policy requires

    a. adult-literacy programs.

    b. graduate-equivalency certificates.

    c. the total co-operation of teachers and parents.

    d. a strong teaching style.

8. The author implies that the present educational system is

    a. the best in the world.

    b. doing the best that it can.

    c. very short of teachers.

    d. not demanding enough of students.

9. *True or false?* _____ Sherry implies that high school students often don't realize the value of academic skills.

10. From the selection, we may conclude that the author based her opinion on
    a. statistics.
    b. educational research.
    c. her personal and professional experiences.
    d. expert professional testimony.

■ **Discussion Questions**

About Content

1. Sherry writes that "before a teacher can expect students to concentrate, he has to get their attention, no matter what distractions may be at hand." What distractions does she mention in the article? Can you think of any others?

2. Do you feel your high school made an honest effort to give you the skills you need—and to make you aware of the importance of those skills? If not, what should your school have done that it did not do?

About Structure

3. The main method of development of this selection is
    a. narration.
    b. description.
    c. argumentation and persuasion.

4. In which paragraph does the author first state her main idea? Paragraph

    _____. What are the other paragraphs in which she states her main idea?

    _____ _____

5. What contrast transitions are used in the first sentences of paragraphs 7 and 10? What ideas are being contrasted in those sentences?

About Style and Tone

6. Why do you think Sherry titles her essay "In Praise of the F Word"? Why doesn't she simply use the word *fail?*

7. What stylistic method does Sherry use in paragraph 11 to add rhythm and force to her points about flunking as a regular policy?

■ Writing Assignments

Assignment 1

Write an essay which has as its thesis one of the following points:

- In my opinion, students have no one to blame but themselves if they leave school without having learned basic skills.
- When students graduate or quit school lacking basic skills, they are the victims of an inadequate educational system.
- Flunking students has more disadvantages than advantages.

Support your thesis with several points, each developed in its own paragraph.

Assignment 2

Sherry proposes using "flunking as a regular policy" as a way to encourage students to work harder. What else might school systems do to help students? Write an essay in which you suggest a few policies for our public schools and give the reasons you think those changes will be beneficial. On the next page are some possible policies you may wish to consider:

More writing in all classes

Shorter summer vacations

Less emphasis on memorization and more on thinking skills

A language requirement

A daily quiet reading session in elementary grades

Assignment 3

Here are two letters sent to *Newsweek* by teachers in response to Sherry's article:

Letter 1

Mary Sherry's essay advocating the use of flunking as a teaching tool was well intentioned but naive. In the first place, my local school district--and I doubt it's unique--discourages the practice by compiling teachers' failure rates for comparison (would you want to rank first?). More important though, F's don't even register on many kids' Richter scales. When your spirit has been numbed--as some of my students' spirits have--by physical, sexual, and psychological abuse, it's hard to notice an F. Walk a mile in one of my kids' shoes. Real fear has little to do with school.

Kay Keglovits
Arlington, Texas

Letter 2

Sherry is right: flunking poor students makes sense. But, as she notes, "making it work again would take a dedicated, caring conspiracy between teachers and parents." I once failed a high school junior for the year. I received a furious call from the student's mother. I was called to a meeting with the school superintendent, the principal, the mother, and the student. There it was decided that I would tutor the student for four months so that the F could be replaced with a passing grade. This was a total sham; the student did nothing during this remedial work, but she was given a passing grade. No wonder education is in the condition that we find it today.

Arthur J. Hochhalter
Minot, North Dakota

These letters suggest that schools that want to try using flunking as a regular policy will have to plan their policy carefully. Write an essay in which you discuss ways to make the failing of poor students as a regular policy work. Your thesis statement can be something like this: "In order for a policy of flunking to work, certain policies and attitudes would need to be changed in many schools." As support in your essay, use the ideas in these letters, Sherry's ideas, and any other ideas you have heard or thought of. Describe your supporting ideas in detail and explain why each is necessary or useful.

The Pain of Animals

David Suzuki

David Suzuki is a noted geneticist, and well known to most Canadians from his television series, *Suzuki on Science* and *The Nature of Things*. In the essay that follows, he offers some insights into the development of his own attitudes towards animal life. E.J. McCullough's views of suffering and death in the human community appear in "On Euthanasia and Dying Well." In "The Pain of Animals," Suzuki reveals his views of the universality of pain and of human rights within "the great chain of being." How is our view of ourselves as "supreme among beasts" now being affected by the suffering and death we inflict upon animals?

Medical technology has taken us beyond the normal barriers of life and death and thereby 1
created unprecedented choices in *human* lives. Until recently, we have taken for granted
our right to use other species in any way we see fit. Food, clothing, muscle power have
been a few of the benefits we've derived from this exploitation. This tradition has continued into scientific research where animals are studied and "sacrificed" for human benefit. Now serious questions are being asked about our right to do this.

Modern biological research is based on a shared evolutionary history of organisms 2
that enables us to extrapolate from one organism to another. Thus, most fundamental concepts in heredity were first shown in fruit flies, molecular genetics began using bacteria
and viruses and much of physiology and psychology has been based on studies in mice
and rats. But today, as extinction rates have multiplied as a result of human activity, we
have begun to ask what right we have to use all other animate forms simply to increase
human knowledge or for profit or entertainment. Underlying the "animal rights" movement is the troubling question of where we fit in the rest of the natural world.

When I was young, one of my prized possessions was a BB gun. Dad taught me how 3
to use it safely and I spent many hours wandering through the woods in search of prey.
It's not easy to get close enough to a wild animal to kill it with a BB gun, but I did hit a
few pigeons and starlings. I ate everything I shot. Then as a teenager, I graduated to a
.22 rifle and with it, I killed rabbits and even shot a pheasant once.

One year I saw an ad for a metal slingshot in a comic book. I ordered it, and when 4
it arrived, I practised for weeks shooting marbles at a target. I got to be a pretty good
shot and decided to go after something live. Off I went to the woods and soon spotted a
squirrel minding its own business doing whatever squirrels do. I gave chase and began
peppering marbles at it until finally it jumped onto a tree, ran to the top and found itself
trapped. I kept blasting away and grazed it a couple of times so it was only a matter of
time before I would knock it down. Suddenly, the squirrel began to cry—a piercing shriek
of terror and anguish. That animal's wail shook me to the core and I was overwhelmed
with horror and shame at what I was doing—for no other reason than conceit with my
prowess with a slingshot, I was going to *kill* another being. I threw away the slingshot
and my guns and have never hunted again.

All my life, I have been an avid fisherman. Fish have always been the main source 5
of meat protein in my family, and I have never considered fishing a sport. But there is
no denying that it is exciting to reel in a struggling fish. We call it "playing" the fish, as
if the wild animal's desperate struggle for survival is some kind of game.

I did "pleasure-fish" once while filming for a television report on the science of fly 6
fishing. We fished a famous trout stream in the Catskill Mountains of New York state
where all fish had to be caught and released. The fish I caught had mouths gouged and
pocked by previous encounters with hooks. I found no pleasure in it because to me fish
are to be caught for consumption. Today, I continue to fish for food, but I do so with a
profound awareness that I am a predator of animals possessing well-developed nervous
systems that detect pain. Fishing and hunting have forced me to confront the way we
exploit other animals.

I studied the genetics of fruit flies for twenty-five years and during that time prob- 7
ably raised and killed tens of millions of them without a thought. In the early seventies,

my lab discovered a series of mutations affecting behaviour of flies, and this find led us into an investigation of nerves and muscles. I applied for and received research funds to study behaviour in flies on the basis of the *similarity* of their neuromuscular systems to ours. In fact, psychologists and neurobiologists analyse behaviour, physiology and neuroanatomy of guinea pigs, rats, mice and other animals as *models* for human behaviour. So our nervous systems must closely resemble those of other mammals.

These personal anecdotes raise uncomfortable questions. What gives us the right to exploit other living organisms as we see fit? How do we know that these other creatures don't feel pain or anguish just as we do? Perhaps there's no problem with fruit flies, but where do we draw the line? I used to rationalize angling because fish are cold blooded, as if warm-bloodedness indicates some kind of demarcation of brain development or greater sensitivity to pain. But anyone who has watched a fish's frantic fight to escape knows that it exhibits all the manifestations of pain and fear. 8

I've been thinking about these questions again after spending a weekend in the Queen Charlotte Islands watching grey whales close up. The majesty and freedom of these magnificent mammals contrasted strikingly with the appearance of whales imprisoned in aquariums. Currently, the Vancouver Public Aquarium is building a bigger pool for some of its whales. In a radio interview, an aquarium representative was asked whether even the biggest pool can be adequate for animals that normally have the entire ocean to rove. Part of her answer was that if we watched porpoises in the pool, we'd see that "they are quite happy." 9

That woman was projecting human perceptions and emotions on the porpoises. Our ability to empathize with other people and living things is one of our endearing qualities. Just watch someone with a beloved pet, an avid gardener with plants or, for that matter, even an owner of a new car and you will see how readily we can personalize and identify with another living organism or an object. But are we justified in our inferences about captive animals in their cages? 10

Most wild animals have evolved with a built-in need to move freely over vast distances, fly in the air or swim through the ocean. Can a wild animal imprisoned in a small cage or pool, removed from its habitat and forced to conform to the impositions of our demands, ever be considered "happy"? 11

Animal rights activists are questioning our right to exploit animals, especially in scientific research. Scientists are understandably defensive, especially after labs have been broken into, experiments ruined and animals "liberated." But just as I have had to question my hunting and fishing, scientists cannot avoid confronting the issues raised, especially in relation to our closest relatives, the primates. 12

People love to watch monkeys in a circus or zoo and a great deal of the amusement comes from the recognition of ourselves in them. But our relationship with them is closer than just superficial similarities. When doctors at Loma Linda hospital in California implanted the heart of a baboon into the chest of Baby Fae, they were exploiting our close *biological* relationship. 13

Any reports on experimentation with familiar mammals like cats and dogs are sure to raise alarm among the lay public. But the use of primates is most controversial. In September 1987, at the Wildlife Film Festival in Bath, England, I watched a film shot 14 on December 7, 1986, by a group of animal liberationists who had broken into SEMA, a biomedical research facility in Maryland. It was such a horrifying document that many in the audience rushed out after a few minutes. There were many scenes that I could not watch. As the intruders entered the facility, the camera followed to peer past cage doors, opened to reveal the animals inside. I am not ashamed to admit that I wept as baby monkeys deprived of any contact with other animals seized the fingers of their liberators and clung to them as our babies would to us. Older animals cowered in their tiny prisons, shaking from fear at the sudden appearance of people.

The famous chimpanzee expert, Jane Goodall, also screened the same film and as a 15 result asked for permission to visit the SEMA facility. This is what she saw (*American Scientist*, November-December 1987):

> Room after room was lined with small, bare cages, stacked one above the other, in which monkeys circled round and round and chimpanzees sat huddled, far gone in depression and despair.
>
> Young chimpanzees, three or four years old, were crammed, two together into tiny cages measuring 57 cm by 57 cm and only 61 cm high. They could hardly turn around. Not yet part of any experiment, they had been confined in these cages for more than three months.
>
> The chimps had each other for comfort, but they would not remain together for long. Once they are infected, probably with hepatitis, they will be separated and placed in another cage. And there they will remain, living in conditions of severe sensory deprivation, for the next several years. During that time they will become insane.

Goodall's horror sprang from an intimate knowledge of chimpanzees in their native 16 habitat. There, she has learned, chimps are nothing like the captive animals that we know. In the wild, they are highly social, requiring constant interaction and physical contact. They travel long distances, and they rest in soft beds they make in the trees. Laboratory cages do not provide the conditions needed to fulfill the needs of these social, emotional and highly intelligent animals.

Ian Redmond (*BBC Wildlife*, April 1988) gives us a way to understand the horror of 17 what lab conditions do to chimps:

> Imagine locking a two- or three-year-old child in a metal box the size of an isolette—solid walls, floor and ceiling, and a glass door that clamps shut, blotting out most external sounds—and then leaving him or her for months, the only contact, apart from feeding, being when the door swings open and masked figures reach in and take samples of blood or tissue before shoving him back and clamping the door shut again. Over the past 10 years, 94 young chimps at SEMA have endured this procedure.

Chimpanzees, along with the gorilla, are our closest relatives, sharing ninety-nine 18 per cent of our genes. And it's that biological proximity that makes them so useful for research—we can try out experiments, study infections and test vaccines on them as models for people. And although there are only about 40,000 chimps left in the wild, compared to millions a few decades ago, the scientific demand for more has increased with the discovery of AIDS.

No chimpanzee has ever contracted AIDS, but the virus grows in them, so scientists 19 argue that chimps will be invaluable for testing vaccines. On February 19, 1988, the National Institute of Health in the U.S. co-sponsored a meeting to discuss the use of chimpanzees in research. Dr. Maurice Hilleman, Director of the Merck Institute for Therapeutic Research, reported:

> We need more chimps. . . . The chimpanzee is certainly a threatened species and there have been bans on importing the animal into the United States and into other countries, even though . . . the chimpanzee is considered to be an agricultural pest in many parts of the world where it exists. And secondly, it's being destroyed by virtue of environmental encroachment—that is, destroying the natural habitat. So these chimpanzees are being eliminated by virtue of their being an agricultural pest and by the fact that their habitat is being destroyed. So why not rescue them? The number of chimpanzees for AIDS research in the United States [is] somewhere in the hundreds and certainly, we need thousands.

Our capacity to rationalize our behaviour and needs is remarkable. Chimpanzees 20 have occupied their niche over tens of millennia of biological evolution. *We* are newcomers who have encroached on *their* territory, yet by defining them as *pests* we render them expendable. As Redmond says, "The fact that the chimpanzee is our nearest zoological relative makes it perhaps the unluckiest animal on earth, because what the kinship has come to mean is that we feel free to do most of the things to a chimp that we mercifully refrain from doing to each other."

And so the impending epidemic of AIDS confronts us not only with our inhuman- 21 ity to each other but to other species.

■ Reading Comprehension Questions

1. The word *extrapolate* in "Modern biological research is based on a shared evolutionary history . . . that enables us to extrapolate from one species to another" (paragraph 2) means
   a. stretch.
   b. move.
   c. estimate.
   d. evolve.

2. The word *expendable* in "*We* are newcomers who have encroached on *their* territory, yet by defining them as *pests* we render them expendable" (paragraph 20) means
   a. disposable.
   b. useless.
   c. pathetic.
   d. hostile.

3. Which one of the following would be a good alternative title for this selection?
   a. The Inhumane Society
   b. Global Cruelty
   c. Our Innate Right to Inflict Misery
   d. Science, Recreation, and Sadism

4. Which sentence best expresses the main idea of the selection?
   a. Because all animate life exists on a continuum, we have no right to kill any creature.
   b. Because of the threats of disease and our nutritional needs, we must sacrifice some animals.
   c. All creatures have similar nervous systems; therefore, any damage to an animal causes the same pain we would feel.
   d. Alternative testing procedures and alterations in our attitudes towards animal intelligence and emotion must come about.

5. According to the selection
   a. the author is a vegetarian who finds all killing of animals hateful.
   b. fish are a necessary source of protein, but fishing makes him uncomfortable.
   c. insects are unsuitable as scientific research subjects.
   d. our emotions and reactions are mirrored in most animals.

6. *True or false?* _____ Caged primates show similar behaviour patterns to those they demonstrate in their native habitat.

7. The AIDS researcher Dr. Hilleman states that chimpanzees
   a. harm farming land and will be destroyed anyway in some areas.
   b. should not be imported into the United States.
   c. should be rescued from their shrinking environments and used for experiments.
   d. are an endangered species and the U.S. has a duty to save them.

8. The author implies that
   a. he was always idealistic.
   b. despite his work and recreational practices, his attitudes towards animals are changing.
   c. he was not a "typical boy."
   d. he finds hunting, fishing, and all forms of animal captivity and testing repulsive.

9. After reading the essay, we can conclude that the author regards humans as
   a. selfish enough to justify our needs and to ignore our place in the ecosystem.
   b. unwilling to face the tragic proportions of the AIDS epidemic.

    c.   aware of threats to other life-forms, but unwilling to do anything about it.

    d.   ready to make any sacrifice to prolong human life.

10. *True or false?* _____ The author implies that the human capacity for self-delusion or "double think" is generally supported by the scientific community.

■ Discussion Questions

About Content

1. What benefits have we derived from the use of animals in the past? What new "benefit" have we acquired from such use? In which areas of 20-century life are animals now most useful, according to the second paragraph? With which of these uses does the author take issue? Which does he not dispute? Why?

2. Does anything distinguish the responses of mammals from those of cold-blooded animals? Are the reactions we see in animals always understandable, based on human experience?

3. What examples does Suzuki use to point out the irony of our relationship with chimpanzees? Why are the examples ironic?

About Structure

4. What method of introduction does the author use?

    a.   Anecdote

    b.   Broad to narrow

    c.   Explaining the importance of the subject

    d.   Starting with an opposite

    Does the second paragraph imitate or reverse the technique used in the first? How?

5. How many personal anecdotes does Suzuki use to clarify his ideas in the first half of the essay? How are they ordered? Which phrases in these paragraphs indicate the ordering method used? What is the significance of the order used to the subject discussed?

6. Several paragraphs contain objective examples, based on impartial scientific data or statistics. Are these more or less convincing than his personal experiences? Why?

About Style and Tone

7. How many of the essay's paragraphs take the first-person approach to point of view? How many use a "third-person" approach, with a sort of inclusive, impersonal "we"? How do the subjects of these two groups of paragraphs

relate to the two types of point of view? What is the effect on you as a reader of this mixture of two viewpoints? Is it more or less convincing as a form of argument than one consistent point of view?

8. The second half of the essay includes three citations from other sources. Are these sources unbiased? Why or why not? How strongly does each speaker make their case? Does each quotation add equally to Suzuki's argument? Why or why not?

■ Writing Assignments

Assignment 1

David Suzuki quotes Ian Redmond's statement in this essay: "The fact that the chimpanzee is our nearest zoological relative makes it perhaps the unluckiest animal on earth, because . . . we feel free to do most of the things to a chimp that we mercifully refrain from doing to each other." (20) We may well be most inhumane to those who cannot fight back against our treatment of them. We may well be ignoring, as Durning also claims in his article "Coffee," the global nature and inter-connection of many of our actions. Using the model of Suzuki's essay argument, write a persuasive essay of your own about your feelings and thoughts on some aspect of animal treatment. Consider circuses and zoos, trapping, hunting, food production, fashion, or cosmetic and scientific testing. Choose your subject based on two criteria: personal experience or knowledge, and the strength of your opinion or conviction.

Assignment 2

Are the porpoises in the Vancouver Public Aquarium really "quite happy"? How do you think zoo inmates feel? What might a cow feel during the truck ride to a packing plant? Try an exercise in writing from a different point of view. Become another species for a while, perhaps a salmon unknowingly swimming upstream towards fishing nets. Write an essay which describes what another creature might feel from their perspective, in their native environment, as they progress through "a day in the life." You may not wish to reveal your adopted identity until the end of your essay. Whether or not you write a horror story is up to you.

Assignment 3

Transplanted baboon hearts, animal bone marrow transplants for AIDS patients . . . Big Macs and leather backpacks: can we justify any of these uses of animals? Write an essay which contrasts three "acceptable" uses of animals with three unnecessary/unjustifiable examples of such use. A statement of your point of view of what is "acceptable and necessary" in the use of animals should appear in your thesis statement.

READING COMPREHENSION CHART

Write an X through the numbers of any questions you missed while answering the comprehension questions for each selection in Part Five, "Readings for Writing." Then write in your comprehension score. The chart will make clear any skill question you get wrong repeatedly, so that you can pay special attention to that skill in the future.

Selection	Vocabulary in Context	Subject or Title	Thesis or Main Idea	Key Details			Inferences			Comprehension Score
Gregory	1 2	3	4	5	6	7	8	9	10	%
Guy	1 2	3	4	5	6	7	8	9	10	%
Mallinson	1 2	3	4	5	6	7	8	9	10	%
McMurtry	1 2	3	4	5	6	7	8	9	10	%
Mustafa	1 2	3	4	5	6	7	8	9	10	%
Orwell	1 2	3	4	5	6	7	8	9	10	%
Pigott	1 2	3	4	5	6	7	8	9	10	%
Tija	1 2	3	4	5	6	7	8	9	10	%
Willard Cross	1 2	3	4	5	6	7	8	9	10	%
Engkent	1 2	3	4	5	6	7	8	9	10	%

Selection	Vocabulary in Context	Subject or Title	Thesis or Main Idea	Key Details			Inferences			Comprehension Score
Giese	1 2	3	4	5	6	7	8	9	10	%
Gotlieb	1 2	3	4	5	6	7	8	9	10	%
Lamanna and Reidmann	1 2	3	4	5	6	7	8	9	10	%
Mallet	1 2	3	4	5	6	7	8	9	10	%
Nicholson	1 2	3	4	5	6	7	8	9	10	%
Turner	1 2	3	4	5	6	7	8	9	10	%
Crosariol	1 2	3	4	5	6	7	8	9	10	%
Dunayer	1 2	3	4	5	6	7	8	9	10	%
Durning	1 2	3	4	5	6	7	8	9	10	%
Frye	1 2	3	4	5	6	7	8	9	10	%
Iyer	1 2	3	4	5	6	7	8	9	10	%
McCullough	1 2	3	4	5	6	7	8	9	10	%
O'Keeney	1 2	3	4	5	6	7	8	9	10	%
Sherry	1 2	3	4	5	6	7	8	9	10	%
Suzuki	1 2	3	4	5	6	7	8	9	10	%

PERMISSIONS

INDEX

STUDENT REPLY CARD

In order to improve future editions, we are seeking your comments on
College Writing Skills with Readings, First Canadian Edition
by John Langan and Sharon Winstanley. After you have read this text, please
answer the following questions and return this form via Business Reply Mail.
Your opinions matter! Thank you in advance for your feedback!

Name of your college or university: ——————————————

Major program of study: ——————————————————

Course title: ———————————————————————

Were you required to buy this book?   ——— yes ——— no

Did you buy this book new or used?   ——— new ——— used ($ ———)

Do you plan to keep or sell this book? ——— keep——— sell

Is the order of topic coverage consistent with what was taught in your course?

Are there chapters or sections of this text that were not assigned for your course?
Please specify:

Were there topics covered in your course that are not included in this text?
Please specify:

What did you like most about this text?

What did you like least?

If you would like to say more, we'd love to hear from you. Please write to us at the
address shown on the reverse of this card.

CORRECTION SYMBOLS

Here is a list of symbols your instructor may use when marking essays. The numbers in parentheses refer to the pages that explain the skill involved.

Agr	Correct the mistake in agreement of subject and verb (341–346) or pronoun and the word the pronoun refers to (368–370).
Apos	Correct the apostrophe mistake (394–398).
Bal	Balance the parts of the sentence so they have the same (parallel) form (363–366).
Cap	Correct the mistake in capital letters (386–393).
Coh	Revise to improve coherence (63–72; 96–98).
Comma	Add a comma (407–416).
CS	Correct the comma splice (320–331).
DM	Correct the dangling modifier (358–362).
Det	Support or develop the topic more fully by adding details (41–45; 93–95).
Frag	Attach the fragment to a sentence or make it a sentence (306–319).
lc	Use a lower case (small) letter rather than a capital (392).
MM	Correct the misplaced modifier (355–357).
¶	Indent for a new paragraph.
No ¶	Do not indent for a new paragraph.
Pro	Correct the pronoun mistake (367–379).
Quot	Correct the mistake in quotation marks (400–406).
R-O	Correct the run-on (320–331).
Sp	Correct the spelling error (430–449).
Trans	Supply or improve a transition (67–70).
Und	Underline (404).
Verb	Correct the verb or verb form (332–340; 347–354).
Wordy	Omit needless words (455–459).
WW	Replace the marked word with a more accurate one.
?	Write clearly the illegible word.
/	Eliminate the word, letter, or punctuation mark so slashed.
∧	Add the omitted word or words.
;/:/-/—/	Add the semi-colon (418) or colon (417) or hyphen (420) or dash (418).
✓	You have something fine or good here: an expression, a detail, an idea.